A student-centered text...

Prepare your students to enter *today's* workforce by focusing on practical career planning, money management and independent living skills. Up-to-the-minute content includes: the latest statistics from the *Occupational Outlook Handbook*, current tax schedules, new credit card and check cashing regulations... and more!

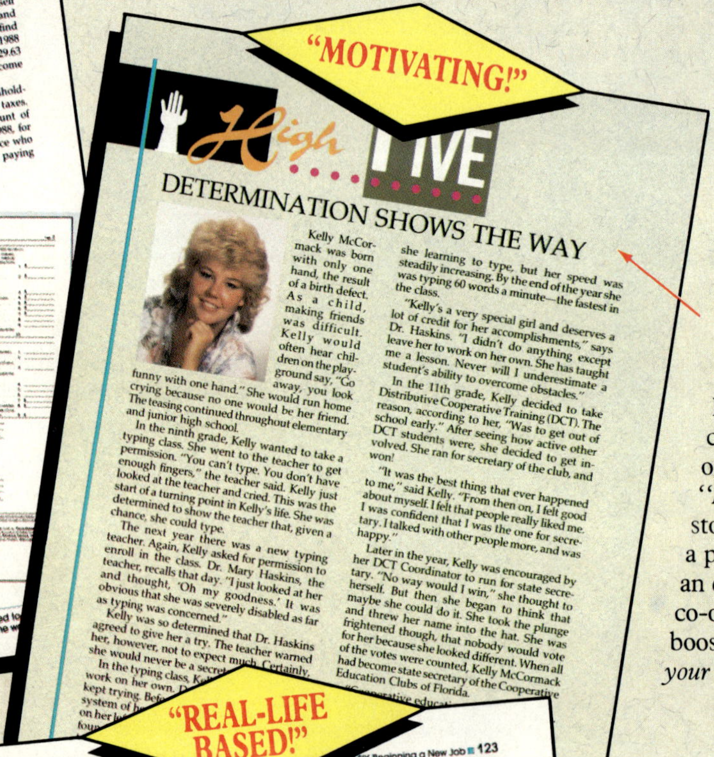

"PRACTICAL!"

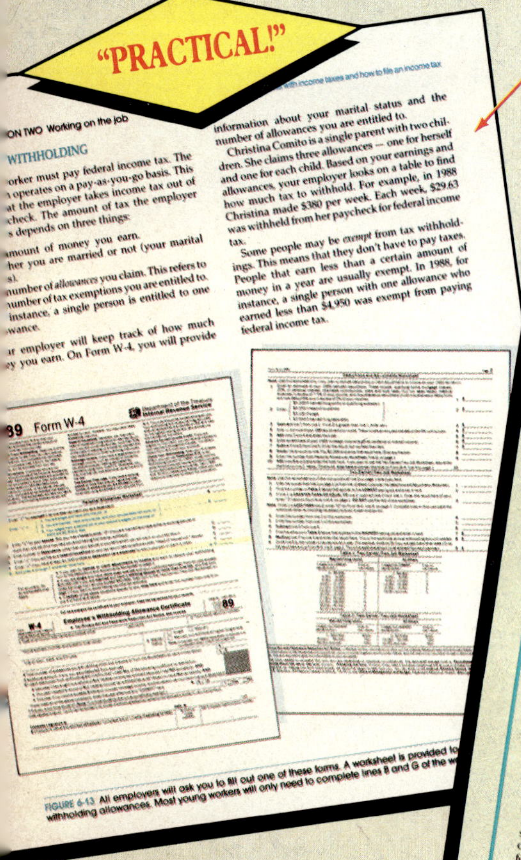

"MOTIVATING!"

Only in Working: Skills for a New Age!

Promote a "Yes, I can" attitude by opening to the *"High-Five"* success stories. Each provides a positive account of an everyday student's co-op experience to boost expectations in *your* classroom.

"REAL-LIFE BASED!"

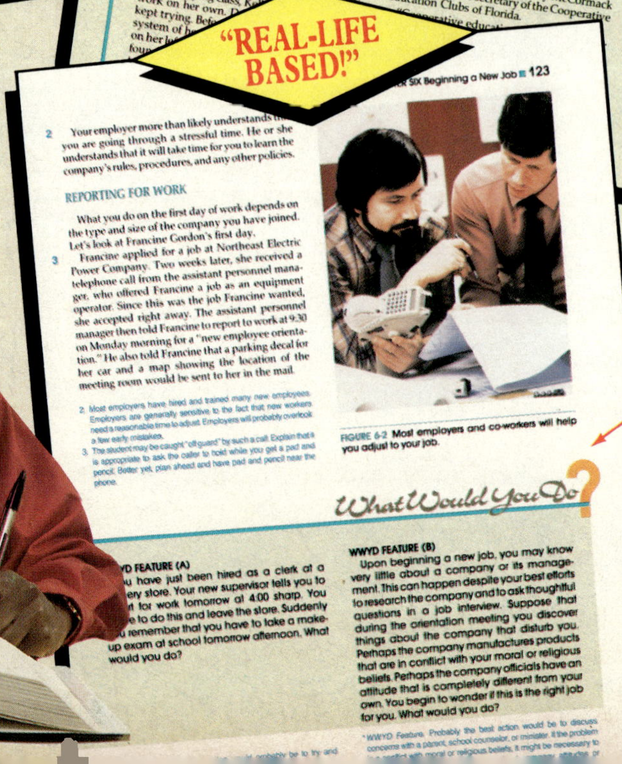

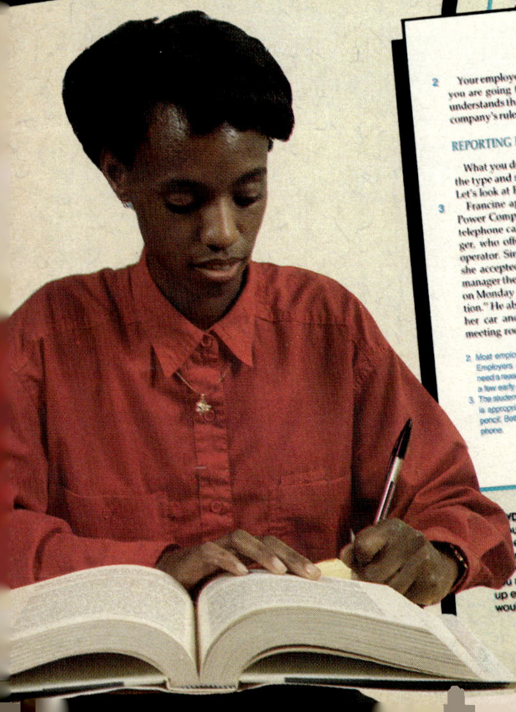

Ask your students, *"'What Would You Do?'* if faced with the circumstances in these realistic case studies?" Debate the "best" solutions to conflicts between family, school and work responsibilities. And help students develop critical decision-making skills along the way!

with outstanding teacher-based support!

"RELEVANT!"

At Delmar, we invite you to put this text and its outstanding support materials "to work" in your classroom! We're certain they'll pass every test with flying colors.

"THE WORKS!"

★ Student Text and Teacher's Annotated Edition
★ Teacher's Resource Package
★ Teacher's Guide
★ Student Activity Workbook
★ Career Planning and Success Skills Transparencies
★ Microtest (Computerized Test Bank)
★ Coming Alive with Co-op (Orientation Video)
★ Career and Life Skills Video Series

Tackle the very issues your students are likely to encounter on the job using the special *"Features"* articles as your starting point. Employee drug testing is just one of the topical concerns you'll explore.

About the Author

There's no doubt Dr. Larry Bailey has been **Working**, developing **Skills for a New Age!** Former farm hand, factory worker, carpenter — and now educator — he has put his Ed.D. in Vocational Education to work by serving as a member of both the National Advisory Council for the ERIC Clearinghouse on Career Education and the Advisory Council on Adult, Vocational and Technical Education (State of Illinois).

Currently teaching at Southern Illinois University, Dr. Bailey is the author of a highly respected professional career text, *plus* over 100 related articles.

Comprehensive, fun and easy-to-use...

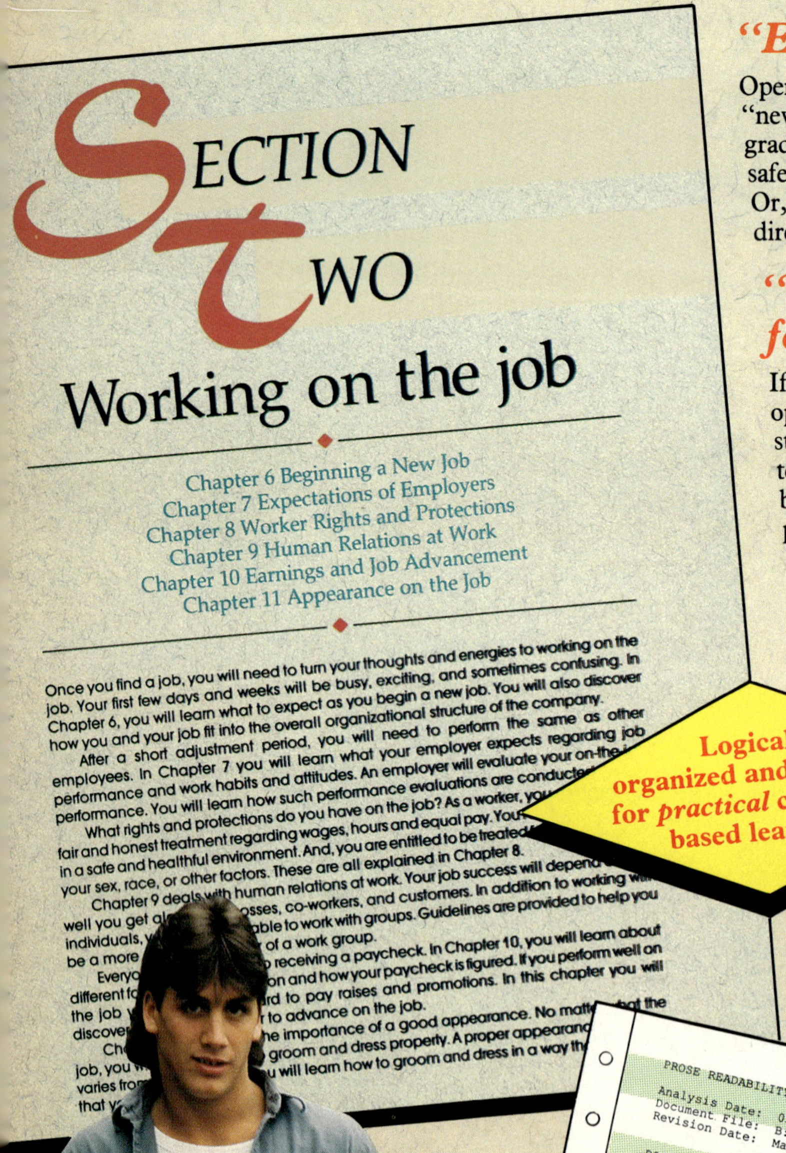

SECTION TWO
Working on the job

Chapter 6 Beginning a New Job
Chapter 7 Expectations of Employers
Chapter 8 Worker Rights and Protections
Chapter 9 Human Relations at Work
Chapter 10 Earnings and Job Advancement
Chapter 11 Appearance on the Job

Once you find a job, you will need to turn your thoughts and energies to working on the job. Your first few days and weeks will be busy, exciting, and sometimes confusing. In Chapter 6, you will learn what to expect as you begin a new job. You will also discover how you and your job fit into the overall organizational structure of the company.

After a short adjustment period, you will need to perform the same as other employees. In Chapter 7 you will learn what your employer expects regarding job performance and work habits and attitudes. An employer will evaluate your on-the-[job] performance. You will learn how such performance evaluations are conducted.

What rights and protections do you have on the job? As a worker, you [are entitled to] fair and honest treatment regarding wages, hours and equal pay. You [are entitled to be treated] in a safe and healthful environment. And, you are entitled to be treated [fairly regardless of] your sex, race, or other factors. These are all explained in Chapter 8.

Chapter 9 deals with human relations at work. Your job success will depend [on how] well you get along [with your] bosses, co-workers, and customers. In addition to working with individuals, you [must be] able to work with groups. Guidelines are provided to help you be a more [effective member] of a work group.

Everyone [looks forward to] receiving a paycheck. In Chapter 10, you will learn about different forms [of compensation] and how your paycheck is figured. If you perform well on the job you [will work hard] to pay raises and promotions. In this chapter you will discover [how] to advance on the job.

Chapter [11 deals with] the importance of a good appearance. No matter what the job, you [must] groom and dress properly. A proper appearance varies from [job to job. You] will learn how to groom and dress in a way that [is appropriate for the job] that you [have].

"Emphasizes skill development"

Open **Working** and prepare your students to greet the "new age" with vitally important life skills. Choose gradual development of essential communication, math, safety, leadership, computer, and entrepreneurial skills. Or, jump right to *Section #4 ("Success Skills")* to draw direct attention to the task at hand.

"Written at a level appropriate for your students"

If your students don't enjoy reading a text, they won't open it. It's that simple. That's why we've taken extra steps to ensure that the writing style in the **Working** text is lively, engaging, and easy-to-read. (But don't be surprised if you still find them looking at the 500+ pictures!)

"Meets requirements of all work experience programs"

32 stand-alone chapters provide maximum flexibility to pick and choose from a comprehensive array of topics based on available classroom time, or to tailor instruction to suit student needs. So start planning your own customized curriculum today! We promise that you'll find this text as fun to use on the first day of class as on the last.

Logically organized and designed for *practical* classroom-based learning!

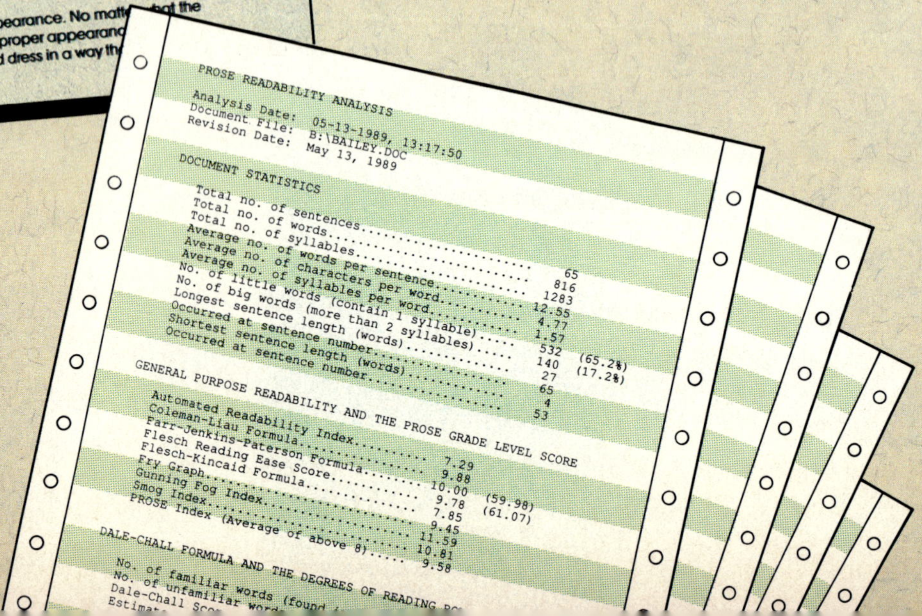

```
PROSE READABILITY ANALYSIS
Analysis Date:    05-13-1989, 13:17:50
Document File:    B:\BAILEY.DOC
Revision Date:    May 13, 1989

DOCUMENT STATISTICS

Total no. of sentences................      65
Total no. of words....................     816
Total no. of syllables................    1283
Average no. of words per sentence.....   12.55
Average no. of characters per word....    4.77
Average no. of syllables per word.....    1.57
No. of little words (contain 1 syllable)  532  (65.2%)
No. of big words (more than 2 syllables)  140  (17.2%)
Longest sentence length (words).......      27
Occurred at sentence number...........      65
Shortest sentence length (words)......       4
Occurred at sentence number...........      53

GENERAL PURPOSE READABILITY AND THE PROSE GRADE LEVEL SCORE

Automated Readability Index...........    7.29
Coleman-Liau Formula..................    9.88
Farr-Jenkins-Paterson Formula.........   10.00  (59.98)
Flesch Reading Ease Score.............    9.78  (61.07)
Flesch-Kincaid Formula................    7.85
Fry Graph.............................    9.59
Gunning Fog Index.....................   11.51
Smog Index............................   10.81
PROSE Index (Average of above 8)......    9.58

DALE-CHALL FORMULA AND THE DEGREES OF READING PO[WER]
No. of familiar words (found i[n list])
No. of unfamiliar words
Dale-Chall sc[ore]
Estimat[ed]
```

The *new* Co-op Text *for the 90's!*

For you...
Teacher's Annotated Edition

Simply opening the *Teacher's Annotated Edition of Working: Skills for a New Age* will put everything you need for practical classroom-based learning at your fingertips! Everything except the students, that is.

No more flipping back and forth between text(s) and lesson plan(s). No more breaks in instructional continuity as you struggle to recall ideas for guiding discussions and emphasizing salient points.

And perhaps best of all, the *Teacher's Guide* is conveniently bound in the back as a handy reference! It's all there, ready and waiting for you to put it to work!

And your students...
Student Text

Your students will be "front and center," ready to use this practical text! That's because *Working* contains exactly what they want to know: how to step out into the world with the skills needed to achieve their goals. They'll also find abundant pedagogical aids, student-oriented issues, and a fresh look — all carefully designed to heighten their enthusiasm.

Unleash student energy into activities thoughtfully designed to underscore important life skills presented in the text!

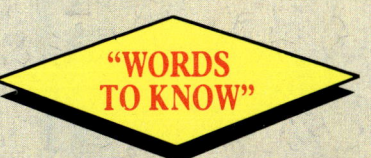
Identify key words from the start... ...and master every term in the comprehensive glossary at the finish!

Direct your students to the review questions at the end of each chapter. They'll be open to learning; you'll be able to measure their performance!

Working Support Materials let you open each new chapter with ease and flexibility!

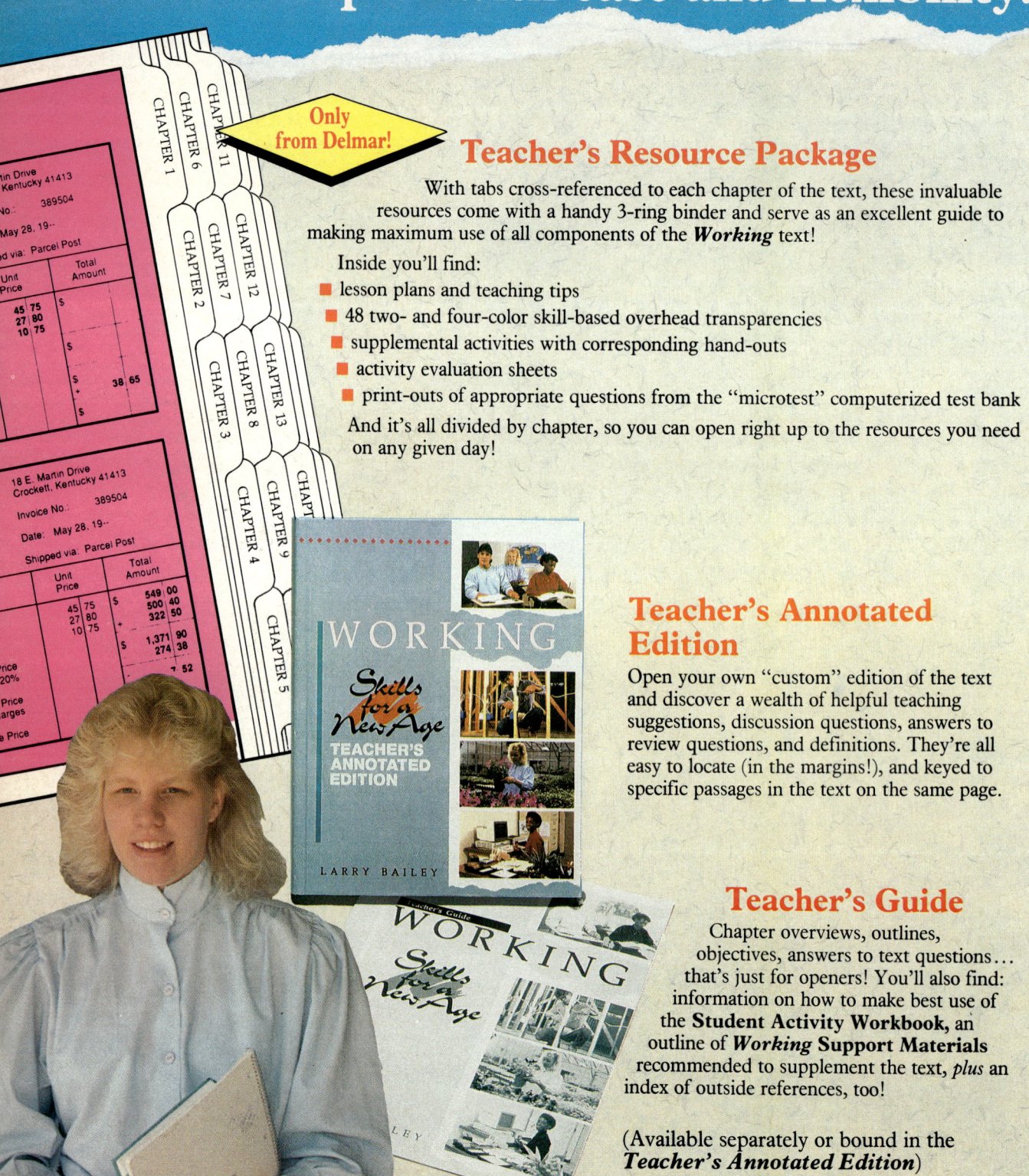

Only from Delmar!

Teacher's Resource Package

With tabs cross-referenced to each chapter of the text, these invaluable resources come with a handy 3-ring binder and serve as an excellent guide to making maximum use of all components of the *Working* text!

Inside you'll find:
- lesson plans and teaching tips
- 48 two- and four-color skill-based overhead transparencies
- supplemental activities with corresponding hand-outs
- activity evaluation sheets
- print-outs of appropriate questions from the "microtest" computerized test bank

And it's all divided by chapter, so you can open right up to the resources you need on any given day!

Teacher's Annotated Edition

Open your own "custom" edition of the text and discover a wealth of helpful teaching suggestions, discussion questions, answers to review questions, and definitions. They're all easy to locate (in the margins!), and keyed to specific passages in the text on the same page.

Teacher's Guide

Chapter overviews, outlines, objectives, answers to text questions... that's just for openers! You'll also find: information on how to make best use of the **Student Activity Workbook,** an outline of *Working* Support Materials recommended to supplement the text, *plus* an index of outside references, too!

(Available separately or bound in the ***Teacher's Annotated Edition***)

Let *Delmar* bring *Co-op to life!*

From the first day...
Coming Alive with Co-op (Video)

Only from Delmar!

Lights, camera, action! With this 8½ minute, full-color video you're ready for an exciting opening day which begins with an up-beat introduction to the co-op experience. You and your students will focus on the 3 students featured on the **Working** cover. You'll observe each student's day in a co-op program. You'll see them open new chapters in their lives, and you'll begin to form your own "great expectations." Guaranteed to generate excitement, this video serves as an ideal orientation for new teachers and parents, too! And the enthusiasm will be recaptured every time you and your students glance at the **Working** text!

To the last day...
Microtest (Computerized Test Bank)

We've chosen a wide assortment of multiple-choice, true/false, and matching questions for you to use to generate an unlimited number of "custom" exams and quizzes. With special features like on-screen editing, scrolling, and automatic cross-references to sections in the **Working** text, there's no option that isn't open to you!

(Available for use with Apple or IBM personal computers, **Microtest** arrives complete with a *free* 64-page, user-friendly documentation manual.)

And every day in between!

Student Activity Workbook

More than 100 individual- and group-based activities reinforce important chapter objectives. Most are easily completed in a single class period. And there's a special section to help students match unique skills/interests with employment goals, too!

Video Series

A full-color video series is available to help you maintain the excitement of opening day. Each video is 3-5 minutes in length, and is certain to provide your students with an entertaining, thought-provoking look at modern "on-the-job" situations.

Transparencies

Only from Delmar!

Make classroom presentations more colorful with 48 two- and four-color skill-based transparencies! The set features key graphs and charts from the **Working** text, plus many illustrations targeted specifically toward improving students' math skills.

(Available separately or as part of the **Teacher's Resource Package**.)

WORKING

WORKING

Skills for a New Age

LARRY J. BAILEY

Professor
Vocational Education Studies
Southern Illinois University
Carbondale, Illinois

DELMAR PUBLISHERS INC.

NOTICE TO READER

Publisher does not warrant or guarantee any of the products described herein or perform any independent analysis in connection with any of the product information contained herein. Publisher does not assume, and expressly disclaims, any obligation to obtain and include information other than that provided to it by the manufacturer.

The reader is expressly warned to consider and adopt all safety precautions that might be indicated by the activities described herein and to avoid all potential hazards. By following the instructions contained herein, the reader willingly assumes all risks in connection with such instructions.

The publisher makes no representations or warranties of any kind, including but not limited to, the warranties of fitness for particular purpose or merchantability, nor are any such representations implied with respect to the material set forth herein, and the publisher takes no responsibility with respect to such material. The publisher shall not be liable for any special consequential or exemplary damages resulting, in whole or in part, from the readers' use of, or reliance upon, this material.

Cover Photos
Joseph Schuyler Photography

Delmar Staff

Associate Editor: Jay Whitney
Project Editor: Eleanor Isenhart
Production Supervisor: Karen Seebaldt

Art Manager: John Lent
Design Coordinator: Susan C. Mathews

For information, address Delmar Publishers Inc.,
2 Computer Drive West, Box 15-015,
Albany, New York 12212

COPYRIGHT © 1990
BY DELMAR PUBLISHERS INC.

All rights reserved. No part of this work covered by the copyright hereon may be reproduced or used in any form or by any means — graphic, electronic, or mechanical, including photocopying, recording, taping, or information storage and retrieval systems — without written permission of the publisher.

Printed in the United States of America
Published simultaneously in Canada
by Nelson Canada
A Division of The Thomson Corporation

10 9 8 7 6 5 4 3 2 1

Library of Congress Cataloging-in-Publication Data
Bailey, Larry J.
    Working : Skills for a New Age / Larry J. Bailey.
      p.   cm.
    Includes index.
    Summary: Discusses survival in the working world, covering such aspects as applying for a job, starting a new job, planning a career, managing money, and being a responsible citizen.
    ISBN: 0-8273-3344-7 Student Edition   ISBN: 0-8273-3349-8 Teacher's Annotated Edition
    1. Vocational education — United States. 2. Vocational guidance — United States.
3. High school students — United States — Life skills guides. [1. Vocational guidance.
2. Work. 3. Life skills.]
I. Title.
[LC1045.B24   1990]   89-11994
370.11'3'0973—dc20   CIP
                                                                               AC

CONTENTS

Preface xiii

PREPARING FOR WORK 1

Chapter 1 Learning About Work 2
    Why People Work 2
    Work, Occupation, and Job 5
    Work Experience Education 6
    Chapter Review 13

Chapter 2 The Job Ahead 16
    Sample Work Histories 16
    Moving Toward a Stable Job 18
    The Future Begins Now 22
    Chapter Review 23

v

Chapter 3 Looking for a Job 25
Thinking About Your Job Goals 25
Getting Ready 26
Finding Job Leads 27
Keeping Track of Job Leads 31
Chapter Review 33

Chapter 4 Applying for a Job 35
Personal Data Sheet 36
Job Application Form 37
Writing a Resume 39
Contacting Employers 40
Pre-employment Tests 44
Chapter Review 46

Chapter 5 Interviewing for a Job 48
Before the Interview 48
During the Interview 53
After the Interview 57
Accepting or Rejecting a Job 59
Chapter Review 60

SECTION 2

WORKING ON THE JOB 63

Chapter 6 Beginning a New Job 64
Pre-employment Anxiety 64
Reporting for Work 65
Orientation to the Workplace 68
Organizational Structure 68
Working Under Supervision 73
Payroll Withholding 74
Chapter Review 75

Chapter 7 Expectations of Employers 78
Job Performance 78
Work Habits and Attitudes 82
Rating Work Behavior 86
Chapter Review 89

Chapter 8 Worker Rights and Protections 92
Honesty and Respect 93
Fair Employment Practices 93
Protection from Discrimination 96
Worker Safety and Health 97

CONTENTS ■ vii

    Agencies Providing Services to Workers 99
    Chapter Review 102

Chapter 9 Human Relations at Work 104
    Bosses, Co-workers, and Customers 104
    Group Participation 111
    Chapter Review 114

Chapter 10 Earnings and Job Advancement 116
    Your Job Earnings 116
    Your Paycheck 120
    Pay Raises 122
    Job Advancement 124
    Chapter Review 127

Chapter 11 Appearance on the Job 129
    Grooming and Appearance 129
    Dressing for the Job 132
    Chapter Review 136

SECTION 3

CAREER PLANNING 139

Chapter 12 Career Decision-making 140
    The Decision-making Process 140
    Individuals and Decision-making 145
    Other Influences on Decision-making 148
    Chapter Review 150

Chapter 13 Information About Your Self 152
Types of Self-information 152
Relationships Among Self-information Factors 159
Self and Other Life Roles 161
Chapter Review 162

Chapter 14 Career Information 164
The World of Work 164
Tomorrow's Jobs 168
Exploring Occupations 173
Chapter Review 177

SECTION 4

SUCCESS SKILLS 181

Chapter 15 Communication Skills 182
Listening 183
Speaking 185
Reading 188
Writing 189
Chapter Review 194

Chapter 16 Math and Measurement Skills 196
Basic Math 196
Basic Measurement 200
Systems of Measure 205
Chapter Review 208

Chapter 17 Safety Skills 211
Accidents 212
Personal Safety 212
Public Safety 218
Chapter Review 220

Chapter 18 Leadership Skills 223
Organizational Leadership 223
Vocational Student Organizations 225
Parliamentary Procedure 228
Chapter Review 233

Chapter 19 Computer Skills 236
Keyboarding Skills 236
How Computers Work 238
Computers in the Workplace 241
The Future of Computers 245
Chapter Review 248

Chapter 20 Entrepreneurial Skills 250
Nature of Small Business 252
Advantages and Disadvantages of Self-employment 254
Ingredients for Success 258
Are You the Type? 260
Choosing a Business 260
Chapter Review 263

SECTION 5

MANAGING YOUR MONEY 267

Chapter 21 Our Economic World 268
- Principles of Economics 269
- Economic Systems 272
- The American Free Enterprise System 273
- Economic Growth 275
- Economic Freedom 278
- Chapter Review 279

Chapter 22 The Consumer in the Marketplace 282
- You as a Consumer 283
- What is Consuming? 283
- Advertising and the Consumer 285
- Consumer Rights 292
- Consumer Responsibilities 293
- Consumer Complaints 293
- Chapter Review 296

Chapter 23 Banking and Credit 299
- Financial Institutions and Services 299
- Checking Accounts 301
- Managing a Checking Account 304
- Credit and Its Use 310
- Chapter Review 314

Chapter 24 Budgeting, Saving, and Investing Money 318
- Income and Spending Patterns 318
- Developing and Using a Budget 320
- Saving Money 327
- Types of Savings Accounts 329

CONTENTS ■ xi

    Figuring Interest Rates 331
    Investing Money 332
    Chapter Review 335

Chapter 25 Insuring Against Loss 339
    Nature of Insurance 339
    Health Insurance 340
    Life Insurance 342
    Home Insurance 346
    Auto Insurance 347
    Chapter Review 350

Chapter 26 Taxes and Taxation 353
    Taxation 353
    Types of Taxes 354
    The Federal Income Tax 355
    Filing an Income Tax Return 358
    Chapter Review 362

Chapter 27 Social Security 364
    Social Security 364
    Major Social Insurance Programs 365
    Eligibility and Financing 370
    Individual Retirement Accounts 371
    Chapter Review 375

SECTION 6

INDEPENDENT LIVING 379

Chapter 28 The Legal System 380
    The Nature of Law 380
    The Court System 384
    Legal Services 385
    Chapter Review 387

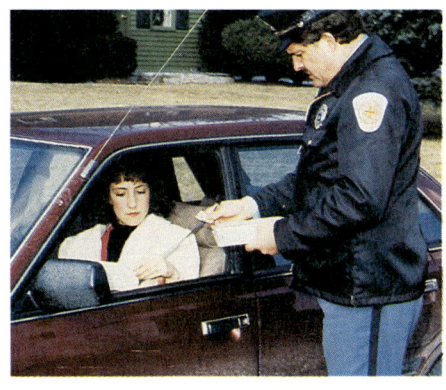

Chapter 29 Where to Live 390
    Choosing a Type of Housing 390
    Rent or Buy? 392
    Apartment Hunting 393
    The Rental Agreement 397
    Landlord-Tenant Relationships 398
    Chapter Review 399

Chapter 30 Healthful Living 401
    Nutrition and Diet 401
    Stress and Its Control 403
    Physical Fitness 405
    Chapter Review 408

Chapter 31 Responsible Citizenship 411
    Responsibilities of Citizenship 411
    Voting and Self-government 412
    Thinking Clearly 415
    Chapter Review 417

Chapter 32 Education Beyond High School 419
    Education and Training 420
    Types of Education and Training 421
    Educational Information 425
    Chapter Review 428

Glossary 431

Index 438

PREFACE

Change is taking place in the United States and throughout the industrialized world. The world has become a global village with countries competing for international standing and economic markets. Knowledge, information, and skills have become the raw materials of international commerce. Learning is the essential investment required for success in this new era. We have entered a new age.

In response to these needs and challenges, American education is also undergoing change. Secondary schools across the country are revising curricula to meet the demands for increased academic requirements and higher standards. There is a clear recognition that yesterday's skills are insufficient for the world of tomorrow.

The attention being given education is not just confined to the so-called *basic skills*. Some are proposing that *readiness for work* become education's fourth "R." There is also an emphasis on integrating academic and vocational education. Partnerships between education and employers are being expanded to help young people bridge the gap between school and work. Many educational authorities and respected organizations have called for more emphasis on learning about and preparing for work.

> ...emphasizing the dignity and the significance of work should be an important goal of a high school education.[1]

> What is called for...is a collaboration of school and elements of the workplace in assuring a broad career perspective for every student.[2]

> ...we urge greater use of cooperative education programs which combine basic education with part-time work experiences, and we recommend that business participate in these programs.[3]

> ...cooperative education's full potential has yet to be explored. We believe it to be appropriate and useful for many more high school students than are now exposed to it.[4]

This book was written with an awareness of the changes that are taking place in both the workplace and in the Nation's schools. The title, *Working: Skills for a New Age*, was chosen to convey the idea that this is a *new* book, with *new* objectives and content, for a *new* generation, and a *new* age.

Purpose and Use

This book was developed for use as a high school level text in several types of existing and emerging work experience education programs. Descriptions of specific applications follow.

- ***Cooperative Vocational Education.*** In cooperative education, students learn occupational skills while working part-time at a training station in their community. Students also attend classes at their local high school, in which they participate in a "related" co-op class. This book is intended for use in such a class. Most related classes are one-year; a few are conducted for two years. This

[1] Boyer, E. L., *High School: A Report on Secondary Education in America.* New York, NY: Harper & Row, 1983, p. 114.
[2] Goodlad, J. I., *A Place Called School: Prospects for the Future.* New York, NY: McGraw-Hill, 1984, p. 345.
[3] *Investing in our Children: Business and the Public Schools.* A Statement by the Research and Policy Committee, New York, NY: Committee For Economic Development, 1985, p. 8.
[4] *The Forgotten Half: Non-College Youth in America.* Washington, DC: Youth and America's Future: The William T. Grant Commission on Work, Family and Citizenship, 1988, p. 42.

xiii

book can be conveniently covered in one year. Sufficient topics and activities are included, however, to allow the book to be profitably used for two-year programs.
- *Work-study.* In work-study, part-time school is also combined with a part-time job. Unlike co-op education, however, this program seeks to develop general work habits and attitudes rather than specific occupational skills. Otherwise, the program is operated very similar to co-op. Work study students enroll in a related class, for which this text is ideally suited.
- *Pre-employment Training.* Many cities and states have developed a variety of youth employment programs to enhance student retention and academic achievement of potential drop-outs. For those who have already dropped out, programs are available to encourage high school completion and provide job training. Some are privately supported and involve close collaboration between schools and employers. Others are funded under the federal Job Training Partnership Act. This book can be used as a primary text in such programs.
- *Related Courses.* Because each of the six sections can stand alone, this book is appropriate for one-semester and shorter-term courses in career education, consumer education, introduction to occupations, and related courses.

Features

Working: Skills for a New Age consists of 32 chapters organized in six sections. The content and objectives meet requirements for vocational cooperative education and work-study programs. The manuscript was reviewed and validated by a sample of secondary school teacher/coordinators prior to publication. Each chapter is organized, written, and produced in ways that foster successful teaching and learning.

- Each chapter begins with an outline of main headings and a listing of specific objectives to be achieved. These give students a good overview of the nature of the chapter.
- Carefully chosen headings are arranged to aid the teacher in presenting the material and the student in understanding it.
- Numerous examples, illustrations, and case studies are blended with the text narrative to make the material more relevant and to promote greater understanding.
- High quality, color photographs and figures are used throughout to generate interest and to illustrate and demonstrate application of concepts.
- Key words and phrases are italicized for emphasis. A complete *Glossary* is provided at the end of the book.
- Topical features are inserted in each chapter to enrich content and provide interesting, related material.
- At least two *What Would You Do?* features are included in each chapter to stimulate thinking and discussion. Many pose ethical questions that can be used to help students ponder and clarify their values.
- A *Chapter Review* section summarizes important concepts and principles, lists words to define, and provides study questions to answer about the chapter. Supplemental *Activities to Do* and *Topics to Discuss* provide opportunities for advanced learning through a variety of individualized, team, and group activities.
- Communication, math and measurement, leadership, and human relation skills are applied and reinforced throughout the book.

Related Materials

The student textbook and teacher's annotated edition are the primary components of a comprehensive set of work experience education materials. An optional Student Activity Workbook is correlated with each chapter to provide dozens of additional activities, exercises, puzzles, games, problems, and case studies. A Teacher's Resource Package, a set of Transparencies, videos, a separate Teacher's Guide and Microtest software are also available.

Acknowledgments

The author wishes to thank Southern Illinois University at Carbondale for granting a sabattical leave and for providing additional assigned time each semester to write portions of this book. I am pleased to have had the opportunity to work with a number of competent, innovative, and courageous staff at Delmar Publishers Inc. I am grateful to Jay Whitney and Lynn Brenn for much more than I am undoubtedly aware. The work experience teachers/coordinators, listed, provided thorough evaluations and many helpful suggestions during the preparation of the manuscript.

Tim Bandy
Springfield Public Schools
Springfield, IL

Dorothy L. Beaubien
Westlake High School
Thousand Oaks, CA

Jim Black
Plant City High School
Plant City, FL

Marguerite Bolejack
Joliet Central High School
Joliet, IL

William Craig Fee
Springfield Southeast High School
Springfield, IL

Ted E. Coakley
Cincinnati Public Schools
Cincinnati, OH

Peggy Courtwright
Springfield High School
Springfield, IL

Gennie C. Dickens
Cocoa Beach High School
Cocoa Beach, FL

Betty Fletcher
Lonoke High School
Lonoke, AR

Mary Lynn Fracaroli
New Jersey State Department of Education
Trenton, NJ

Patricia Jansen
Queen City Vocational Center
Cincinnati, OH

Margaret Lindsey
Austin Independent School District
Austin, TX

Martha Marshall
Cabot High School
Cabot, AR

Juanita Motley
Fairfax High School
Fairfax, VA

David Patzarian
Mt. Pleasant High School
Schenectady, NY

Karen Purvis
Mena High School
Mena, AR

Charles W. Severens
Springfield Public Schools
Springfield, IL

Vivian Smith
Fort Worth Independent School District
Fort Worth, TX

Robert M. Taber
Whitesboro High School
Whitesboro, TX

Marcia L. Tokarz
Walter M. Williams High School
Burlington, NC

Bill Tunstall
Salisbury High School
Salisbury, NC

About the Author

Larry J. Bailey was born and raised in rural Indiana where he first worked as a farm laborer, carpenter, painter, factory worker, and janitor. He then attended Ball State University on a full academic scholarship where he graduated with honors. He taught high school industrial arts for two years before going to the University of Illinois to complete the Doctor of Education degree in Vocational Education. He conducted research as a faculty member at the University of Illinois and the University of Iowa before moving to Southern Illinois University in 1969, where he is currently. He is author of a professional text on career education and nearly 100 other books, book chapters, articles, research reports and related writings. In 1975, he was appointed to the National Advisory Council on Career Education. He has also served as a member of the National Advisory Council for the ERIC Clearinghouse on Career Education and the Advisory Council on Adult, Vocational and Technical Education, State of Illinois.

High Five

EXPOSURE TO THE WORKING WORLD

Courtney Vales vividly recalls the first time she heard about WECEP (Work Experience Career Exploration Program). The program coordinator, Helen Fabbri, had come to her school to explain the program. "This was the first time I remember anyone coming into our school to provide students with something we actually needed—exposure to the working world. She explained the difference between having a job and a career. She stressed the importance of setting goals, of directing one's own future path, and taking on responsibility. It was hard for a young person growing up in East St. Louis to listen when someone said, 'You can be whatever you want to be.' But when Mrs. Fabbri said it, I somehow believed her."

In addition to living in an economically-depressed region, Courtney had to overcome personal tragedy. Her mother was killed in an auto accident when she was 18-months old. At seven, her father died of a heart attack. Fortunately, she had loving grandparents who raised her and her three brothers and sisters.

As a participant in WECEP, Courtney worked for the Aldermanic Council of the City of East St. Louis for two hours in the afternoon, three days a week. When the school year ended, she was hired during the summer months. She so impressed her employer, that she worked each summer until she graduated from high school.

"I gained valuable experience there," she states. "I also had the opportunity to meet some very influential city officials and to establish contacts that I still maintain." Courtney notes that she was able to use such contacts as references for two later jobs, a work-study job in college and a summer job at Union Electric Company in St. Louis.

Courtney Vales graduated from Northwestern University and began permanent employment at Union Electric. She has progressed from the Personnel Department, to Public Relations, to Information Services, where she is a Training Supervisor. Courtney says that, "Cooperative education provided me with many of the tools I needed to succeed in the real world. It also gave me the opportunity to interact with people. Learning how to communicate with others is a lesson that no book can truly illustrate; no instructor can ever teach. The knowledge, ideas, and experiences gained from cooperative education continue to play a vital role in my life. I think, perhaps, they always will."

Section One
Preparing for Work

Chapter 1 Learning About Work
Chapter 2 The Job Ahead
Chapter 3 Looking for a Job
Chapter 4 Applying for a Job
Chapter 5 Interviewing for a Job

Most adults in our society work. You need to learn about work and prepare for it. Having a paid job will enable you to establish your independence. In Chapter 1, you will learn about the role work plays in people's lives. You will discover how work experience education can benefit you as you begin your career.

The jobs you hold during your working life form your work history. In Chapter 2, you will examine different types of work histories. You will discover that there are many routes to a permanent, satisfying job. There are common characteristics of stable jobs. Knowing them can help you in thinking about and planning your career. A career does not just happen. It is shaped and influenced by your own actions.

Chapter 3 encourages you to clarify your job goals. What you want out of a job will influence how and where you look for it. Six different sources of job leads are explained. A method is suggested for keeping track of information about job leads. Since most employers are eager to fill vacant jobs, the need to take quick action on job leads is emphasized.

How do you go about applying for a job? This is discussed in Chapter 4. You will learn how to develop a personal data sheet, a job resume, and how to fill out a job application form. The three methods of contacting an employer about a job are explained. You may have to take some type of pre-employment test as part of the job application process. Guidelines in preparing for and taking a test are provided.

The job interview is generally the last and most important step in the job-search process. This is the focus of Chapter 5. You will discover what to do before, during and after the interview. If a job offer is made, you will learn how to respond to it. But, not all interviews will result in a job offer. There are recommended ways of dealing with that also.

1. Ask students with jobs if they have discovered that people respond differently to them. Also discuss if and how the students' lives may have changed as a result of getting a job.

2. Research studies conducted over a number of years consistently reveal these findings.

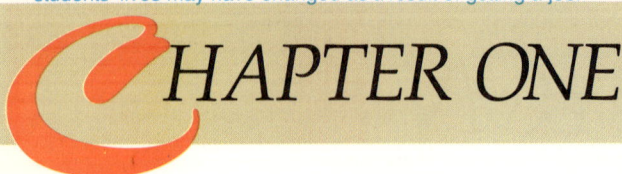

CHAPTER ONE

Learning About Work

FIGURE 1-1 A job carries with it the expectation of mature behavior. *Photo by Paul E. Meyers*

OUTLINE
Why People Work
Work, Occupation, and Job
Work Experience Education
Chapter Review

OBJECTIVES

After reading this chapter, you should be able to:
- Discuss reasons why people work.
- Define what is meant by the terms *work, occupation,* and *job.*
- Name three types of work experience education.
- Explain the role of a related class as part of a cooperative vocational education or work-study program.
- Identify the benefits of work experience education.

---

1 The years of adolescence are a time of change from youth to young adult. An important step in this change is getting a job. Working at a paid job will enable you to establish your independence and define your own life. As a working person, other people will see and respond to you in new ways. You will become more accepted as an adult and be granted greater rights and responsibilities of adulthood. This can be an exciting and enjoyable time of your life.

WHY PEOPLE WORK

People's views about work vary greatly. It would be untrue to say that all people value and enjoy their work. For most Americans, though, work is an important part of a well-rounded life. They generally like what they do. Many studies have shown that 2 most people would work even if they didn't have to. This view of work is not limited to adults. The interest of young people in learning about and preparing for work has never been greater.

People work for many different reasons. The reasons vary from person to person. The most common reasons for working follow.

Earn Money

The major reason why people work is to earn money. Earnings are needed to buy food, shelter, clothing, and other necessities. Beyond meeting basic needs, money is used to purchase goods and services that provide comfort, enjoyment, and security.

Social Satisfaction

People are social creatures. Working gives people a chance to be with others and to make friends. In the work environment, people can give and receive understanding and acceptance.

F•E•A•T•U•R•E

The Changing Workplace

♦ ♦ ♦

When this country was founded in 1776, most people lived and worked on small, family-owned farms. The farm family raised livestock, poultry, and grain. Surplus food was traded for other products.

As trading increased, small villages grew along rivers and other transportation routes. The growth of towns provided new jobs for shop owners, bankers, blacksmiths, and others. Employment in nonagricultural occupations grew steadily. Agriculture, however, still remained the base of the economy.

In 1876, the share of the labor force working in agriculture stood at about fifty percent. Gradually, the number of farmers decreased as more and more people moved to cities. Meanwhile, agricultural production increased due to better equipment, improved plant and animal strains, and new farming methods. By 1990, the number of workers employed in agriculture had shrunk to less than three percent of the labor force.

In the second half of the 1800s, U.S. industry expanded rapidly. Growing towns and cities

FIGURE 1-FEATURE Work is an important part of our culture. *Photos (A, B) by David W. Tuttle, (C) by Paul E. Meyers, (D) Niagara Mohawk Power Corporation*

needed more and more goods. Typical workers in the early 1900s had factory jobs. They produced steel, machinery, and other manufactured goods. By 1920, over sixty percent of all workers were employed in goods-producing industries.

Growing industry and a growing population needed many kinds of business, transportation, communication, personal, and government services. In response to these demands, service industries began to expand. About 1955, the number of workers providing services passed the number of workers producing goods. Typical service occupations included secretary, clerk, salesperson, and manager.

The shift to service industries and occupations has continued. In 1990, over seventy percent of all workers were employed in services. This service economy, however, is also undergoing change. A new economy is evolving based on knowledge and information.

New ways of dealing with information are changing many types of industries. Here are some examples. Not long ago, communications meant sending information through cable or between ground-to-ground stations. Now, orbiting satellites beam communications around the world.

The use of robots in auto manufacturing is another example. Before robots, skilled workers used hand-held spray guns to apply paint finishes. Now robots do this, receiving their instructions from computers.

Computers haven't just changed the communications and auto industries. Computers are influencing almost all industries and occupations. In many offices, for example, computers are replacing typewriters. Computers are the backbone of the information society.

With the computer have come many new occupations. These include laser nurse, computer animator, fiber optics technician, and robotics repairer. The Bureau of Labor Statistics forecasts that "high-tech" industries will generate about 1.7 million new jobs by 1995. Many of you now in high school will probably work at some of these new occupations.

*The Changing Workplace. Summarize the four changes that have occurred in the U.S. economy: (a) the decline of agriculture, (b) the rise of goods-producing industries, (c) the shift from goods to services, and (d) the new information society. Explain what is meant by the new "information society" (one based on knowledge and information). An excellent resource for this concept is Naisbitt, J., *Megatrends: Ten New Directions Transforming Our Lives.* New York, Warner Books, 1982.

Positive Feelings

People get satisfaction from their work. For instance, your work may give you a sense of accomplishment. Think of how you feel when you finish a school project or a difficult job task.

Working also gives people a feeling of self-worth. The feeling comes from knowing that other people will pay you for your skills.

Prestige

Some people work because of the prestige or status they enjoy. Prestige is an admiration that society has for an occupation. Prestige is separate from how well the job is performed. What occupations do you consider to have prestige?

FIGURE 1-2 The pride of accomplishment can be one of the greatest rewards of working. *Courtesy of Simpson Industries, Inc.*

3. Ask students to give examples of work tasks from which they have derived a sense of accomplishment.
4. Discuss occupations that have status or prestige.
5. People who enjoy their work live longer.
6. *Interests* refer to likes and preferences. *Abilities* and *talents* refer to things we do well.

7. The terms *work*, *occupation*, and *job* are used in ways that are consistent with how they are generally used in the fields of career psychology and career guidance.

CHAPTER 1 Learning About Work ■ 5

Personal Development

Many people have a drive to improve themselves. Work can provide an opportunity to learn and grow. Work can often be a great teacher.

Contributions to Health

Work can be very important for mental and physical health. This results from the work itself as well as the physical activity and exercise involved. People who are active and happy in their work tend to feel better.

What Would You Do?

You have been working for about a year at a small nursery and garden center. You enjoy the informality, the variety of work, caring for plants, and being out-of-doors. You have learned about a job opening in the garden department of a large discount store. Your primary duties would be waiting on customers and operating the cash register. The job pays quite a bit more than you presently earn. But you don't think you would enjoy the new job as much as your present one. You can't decide whether to give up a satisfying job for the opportunity to make more money. What would you do?

FIGURE 1-3 Through work, people can learn, develop interests, and contribute to the community. *Photo by Ruby Gold*

to oneself and/or to society. For instance, work can provide you with money and a sense of accomplishment. Work by a teacher or nurse provides benefits to society. Another characteristic of work is that it may be paid or unpaid.

Occupation

All occupations carry out work. An *occupation* is the name given to a group of similar tasks that a person performs for pay. For example: typing, filing,

Self-expression

We all have interests, abilities, and talents. Work can be a way in which we express ourselves. It doesn't matter what kind of work it is as long as it suits the worker.

WORK, OCCUPATION, AND JOB

People often use the terms *work*, *occupation*, and *job* interchangeably. They do have a number of similarities. In this book, however, the terms will be used in different ways.

Work

Work can be defined as activity directed toward a purpose or goal that produces something of value

8. Ask students to name as many different types of work as possible (employment, schoolwork, homework, household work, volunteer work, and so on).

FIGURE 1-4 Some work is unpaid. *Courtesy of General Dynamics*

* *WWYD Feature A.* The issue here involves competing work values, i.e., feelings about what is important. Values are very personal.

6 ■ SECTION 1 Preparing for Work

maintaining records, placing phone calls, and scheduling meetings are tasks performed by the occupation of secretary. Carpenter, salesclerk, attorney, truck driver, and chef are examples of common occupations that involve groups of similar tasks.

Most occupations require specific knowledge and skills to perform them. Occupations are learned on the job or in various kinds of education and training programs. A person having an occupation can work at a number of different jobs.

Job

A *job* is a paid position at a specific place or setting. A job can be in an office, store, factory, farm, or mine. For example, a nurse (an occupation) can work at jobs in a doctor's office, clinic, hospital, home, school, factory, or nursing home. The relationship between work, occupation, and job is illustrated in Figure 1-5.

> 9. Do not use the term *career* as a synonym for *occupation*. A chemical engineer and an accountant are both occupations—not careers. It is correct, however, to say that a person has a "career in the field of" engineering or business. These are important distinctions that you should try to become comfortable with.

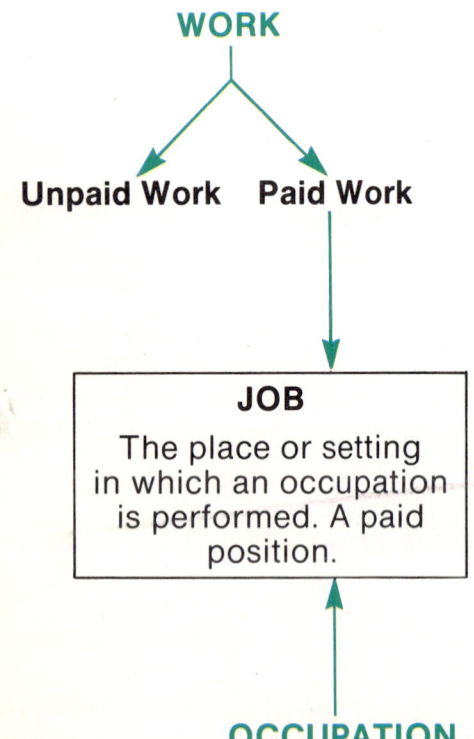

FIGURE 1-5 The relationship between work, occupation, and job

> 10. The term *employment* may be used synonymously with the term *job*.

> 11. The concept that "a person having an occupation can work at a number of different jobs" is important. Show several different examples on the board.

WORK EXPERIENCE EDUCATION

During the last twenty-five years many kinds of education programs have been developed to help young people learn about and prepare for work. Programs of this type are called *work experience education*. Their purpose is to provide opportunities for students to explore or participate in work as an extension of the regular school environment.

Types of Work Experience Programs

Unlike many countries, the United States does not have a national system of education. As a result, state and local programs like work experience education are called by many different names. Whatever it is called, a work experience program is probably one of the following.

Cooperative (co-op) vocational education. Vocational education is a program in which students learn specific *occupational skills* for employment. One kind of vocational education is taught in school-based classrooms, shops, and laboratories. Instruction may be provided in such occupational areas as agriculture, business, marketing, industrial-technical, home economics, and health occupations.

FIGURE 1-6 Students learn their skills in classrooms and laboratories. *Courtesy of Siena College, Loudonville, NY*

> 12. This is simply a broad, generic term useful to categorize and explain a number of related types of educational programs and concepts.

13. The autonomy of state and local education agencies results in many different names.
14. Usually called "cooperative education" or "co-op."

CHAPTER 1 Learning About Work ■ 7

Another kind of vocational education is cooperative (co-op) vocational education. This is a cooperative program between a secondary school (or community college) and a local employer. Most cooperative education students attend classes at their school campus for part of the day. Students then spend the rest of the day working at a training site in a local business or industry. Students receive both pay and school credit for their co-op jobs.

In cooperative vocational education, the student learns and applies occupational skills on the job rather than only in a school shop or laboratory. Another part of cooperative vocational education is a related class. This is taught at the school to reinforce skills used at a job site. Students study such topics as job-seeking, consumer skills, independent living, and career planning. This textbook is probably being used as part of a related class.

Cooperative vocational education follows certain guidelines and procedures. A cooperative education teacher/coordinator employed by the school system usually manages the program. The coordinator reviews and approves student applications for the program. The coordinator also approves each student's place of employment, called the *training station*.

The training station may be any type of job that relates to the student's career objectives. Common training stations include stores, offices, hospitals, restaurants, and auto repair shops. At the training station, the student is under the direction of a supervisor.

15. Emphasize and give examples of the difference between learning occupational skills in a school shop or lab and learning occupational skills on the job.

17. This is a place where you may wish to explain in detail the nature and operation of your school's work experience program. Show and discuss a training agreement and a training plan as appropriate.

FIGURE 1-7 These cooperative vocational education students are learning how to write a job resume as part of a related class. *Photo by David W. Tuttle*

16. This text was written primarily to be used as part of a related class.

If you are coordinating a work-study instead of a co-op program, you will probably discuss co-op only briefly and then elaborate on your work-study program.

SECTION 1 Preparing for Work

SAMPLE TRAINING AGREEMENT

Student's Name _____ School _____ Date _____
Age _____ Social Security No. _____ Job Title _____
Co. Name _____ Co. Address _____
Co. Phone _____ Employer Identification No. _____
Co. Supervisor _____ Student Hours _____
Wages _____ Date Covered by Agreement _____

Responsibilities of the Student-Learner:

1. The student-learner will keep regular attendance, both in school and on the job, and cannot work on any school day that he/she fails to attend school; he/she will notify the school and employer if unable to report.
2. The student's employment will be terminated if he/she does not remain in school.
3. The student will show honesty, punctuality, courtesy, a cooperative attitude, proper health and grooming habits, good dress and a willingness to learn.
4. The student will consult the teacher-coordinator about any difficulties arising at the training station.
5. The student will conform to the rules and regulations of the training station.
6. The student will furnish the teacher-coordinator with all necessary information and complete all necessary reports.

Responsibilities of the Training Sponsor:

1. The training sponsor will endeavor to employ the student for at least the minimum number of hours each day and each week for the entire agreed training period.
2. The training sponsor will adhere to all Federal and State regulations regarding employment, child labor laws, minimum wages and other applicable regulations.
3. The training sponsor will see that the study is not allowed to remain in any one operation, job, or phase of the occupation beyond the period of time where such experience is of educational value.
4. The training sponsor will consult the teacher-coordinator about any difficulties arising at the training station.
5. The training sponsor will provide experiences that will contribute to the attainment of the students career objective.
6. The training sponsor will assist in evaluating the student.
7. The training sponsor will provide time for consultation with the teacher-coordinator concerning the student.
8. The training sponsor will provide instructional material and occupational guidance for the student as needed and available.

Responsibilities of the Teacher-Coordinator:

1. The teacher-coordinator will coordinate related classroom instruction and on-the-job training to improve job performance and to better prepare the student for his/her occupational career objective.
2. The teacher-coordinator will see that the necessary related classroom instruction is provided.
3. The teacher-coordinator will make periodic visits as necessary to the training station to observe the student and consult with the employer and training sponsor.
4. The teacher-coordinator will assist in the evaluation of the student.

This agreement may be terminated by mutual consent of the training sponsor and the teacher-coordinator.

It is understood the parties participating in this agreement will not discriminate in employment opportunities on the basis of race, religion, color, sex, or national origin.

Student	(Date)	Training Sponsor	(Date)
Parent	(Date)	Teacher Coordinator	(Date)

Source: Gooch, B.G. *Cooperative Vocational Education Handbook, Second Edition.* Carbondale, IL: Southern Illinois University, June 1988.

FIGURE 1-8 Sample training agreement

The cooperative education program is a three-way relationship involving the student, the employer-supervisor, and the cooperative education coordinator. Early on, all three parties sign a *training agreement* and participate in the development of a step-by-step *training plan*.

CHAPTER 1 Learning About Work ■ 9

18. If your school has both co-op and work-study programs, you will probably wish to provide specific illustrations of each type of program.

Work-study. Work-study programs, sometimes called general work experience education, are like cooperative vocational education in several ways. Both allow students to attend school part-time while working part-time. For these jobs, students receive pay and school credit. Each program is supervised by a work experience coordinator.

Unlike cooperative vocational education, work-study is *not* a program of on-the-job training for a specific occupation. Rather, the program deals with the development of what are called *employability skills.* These are required in all jobs. They include such things as punctuality, dependability, and cooperation.

Many students find that the combination of school and work is more interesting than school alone. Also, the opportunity to earn money keeps some students who might otherwise drop out before graduation in school.

Exploratory work experience education. Many schools provide exploratory work experience education for junior-high and early high-school-age students. The purpose of this type of program is to provide students with opportunities to observe work and to try out various work tasks. This is why the program is called "exploratory." Students explore various occupations in order to discover or to confirm occupational interests. Thus, the program is concerned with *career guidance* rather than the development of occupational or employability skills.

FIGURE 1-9 A training plan is used to help guide on-the-job learning experiences. *Photo by Joe Schuyler*

* WWYD Feature B. Lead a discussion regarding the nature of school-based vocational education courses and cooperative education.

What Would You Do?

Your school has both school-based vocational education and cooperative vocational education. You can't decide which one to enroll in. The advantages of the school-based program are that you know the teacher, you are familiar with the equipment, and you would be taking the course with your friends. In the co-op program, you would meet new people, earn some money, and work on more advanced equipment. You have been told by other students that in co-op you will work harder and that more will be expected of you. What would you do?

FIGURE 1-10 "Job shadowing" is often a part of exploratory work experience. Why do you think the term is used? *Photo by Joe Schuyler*

19. Some of the more commonly used names are "career education," "occupational (or career) exploration," "occupational (or career) information," and "occupational (or career)

orientation." In addition, there are specific types of learning activities and methods such as "job shadowing" and "occupational simulation" that can be called exploratory.

FIGURE 1-11 Training sites often have tools and equipment not available in schools. *Reprinted with permission from Westvaco Corporation*

20. These are independent, but overlapping, benefits of work experience.

21. Ask students to identify the primary benefits that Janet derived from co-op (learned occupational skills and discovered career interests and goals).

Exploratory programs may last only a few days or a few weeks. Students receive no pay for the work they do, but they usually receive school credit.

Benefits of Work Experience

Depending on the type of program in which you are enrolled, work experience can benefit you in the following ways. You can:

- *Learn Occupational Skills.* You can acquire marketable skills through on-the-job training in an actual work setting.

- *Develop Employability Skills.* Success on the job requires more than occupational skills. Work experience provides opportunities to develop the types of work habits and attitudes that employers expect.

- *Establish a Work Record.* It is often hard to get a job if you lack previous experience. Completing a work experience program will make it easier for you to get a job later.

- *Earn While You Learn.* Earning your own money will give you a sense of accomplishment. You will be able to save money, buy things that you might not otherwise be able to afford, or both. For some students, the money they earn can be the difference between staying in school and dropping out.

- *Discover Career Interests and Goals.* Work experience can help you find out what type of career you want. You may either confirm your present interests and goals or find new ones.

- *Recognize the Relationship Between Education and Work.* Work experience can provide something that may be missing in your present education. Education can take on new meaning as you come to recognize a greater connection between what you are learning in school and what you are doing on the job.

- *Remain Employed After Graduation.* Many students in work experience jobs are offered permanent jobs after graduation. This benefits both students and employers. If you are pleased with your job, you won't have to look for a new one. Hiring a former work experience student saves the employer both interviewing and training time. Some students continue in co-op jobs while they attend post-high school education.

Let us see in more detail how work experience education has helped two young people.

Janet is enrolled in a business occupations program. This is a type of cooperative vocational education program for students interested in secretarial, accounting, information-processing, and similar occupations. Janet has a part-time job at a firm that distributes packaging equipment. She enters data and keyboards on a computer, files, and performs other office duties.

One day the sales manager asked Janet to sit in on a sales meeting and take notes. After the meeting, she prepared a short summary report. The manager was impressed and complimented Janet on her ability to organize and present the material well. Afterward, the manager began to give Janet more duties of this type.

Janet discovered a skill and an interest of which she wasn't aware. She also learned that there is a demand in the business world for skilled stenographers. After graduation, Janet will enroll in a new Technical Stenography program offered at a local community college. The program provides training in Computer-aided Transcription. This is a system in which a computer directly translates shorthand notes into English.

FIGURE 1-12 Because of a successful cooperative education experience, many students continue their training beyond high school. *Photo by David W. Tuttle*

At the end of his junior year, Wilson had thoughts about not returning to school in the fall. He came from a large family supported only by his mother. There was little income available for extras. Wilson was discouraged about school. He did not have the nice clothes or money to participate in school activities like most other students.

SECTION 1 Preparing for Work

A friend suggested that Wilson talk to the school's work experience coordinator. With the help of the coordinator, Wilson found a work-study job at the city highway garage. He helps clean and take care of the fleet of city-owned vehicles. While he does not want to do this type of work forever, Wilson is happy to have a paying job.

After signing up for work-study, Wilson decided to finish high school. The money he earns allows him to buy some new clothes and do a few things that he could not afford to do before. School has become enjoyable for him, and his grades are improving. Wilson is encouraging his younger brother and sister to enroll in a work experience program.

Which benefits of work experience education would be most important to *you*?

FIGURE 1-13 Participating in a work-study program can motivate students to stay in school. *Photo by David W. Tuttle*

22. Ask students to identify the primary benefits that Wilson derived from work-study (earned while he learned and recognized the relationship between education and work).

23. Discuss the benefits informally here or perhaps assign Activity 3 at this point. In Chapter 3, these benefits will be used as a basis for students to identify their job goals.

CHAPTER REVIEW

Chapter in Brief

- For most people, work is an important part of a well-rounded life. People work for many reasons, including: money, social satisfaction, positive feelings, prestige, personal development, contributions to health, and self-expression. The specific reasons vary from person to person.
- The terms *work, occupation,* and *job* have different meanings. Work is activity directed toward a goal that produces something of value. It may be paid or unpaid. An occupation is the name given to a group of similar tasks that a person performs for pay. A job is a paid position at a specific place or setting.
- Work experience programs may be called different things depending on the state and community in which you live. Generally speaking, there are three common types of work experience education: cooperative vocational education, work-study, and exploratory work experience education.
- Work experience programs can benefit you in a number of ways. You can: learn occupational skills, develop employability skills, establish a work record, earn while you learn, discover career interests and goals, recognize the relationship between education and work, and remain employed after graduation.

Words to Know

career guidance assisting students in career planning and decision-making.

employability skills the general work habits and attitudes required in all jobs.

job a paid position at a specific place or setting.

occupation name given to a group of similar tasks that a person performs for pay.

occupational skills learned abilities to perform tasks or duties of a specific occupation.

training agreement a signed agreement outlining the relationships and responsibilities of the parties involved in a work experience education program.

training plan a listing of knowledges, attitudes, and skills to be developed by the student participating in a work experience education program.

training station a work experience student's place of employment.

work activity directed toward a purpose or goal that produces something of value to oneself and/or to society.

work experience education education programs designed to provide opportunities for students to explore or participate in work as an extension of the regular school environment.

SECTION 1 Preparing for Work

Questions to Answer

1. Name the seven reasons why people work.
2. Name two ways you can get positive feelings from working.
3. Give examples that show the difference between an occupation and a job.
4. Identify and briefly explain the three kinds of work experience education programs.
5. How does cooperative vocational education differ from the other form of vocational education?
6. The term *exploratory* describes well one type of work experience education. Explain why.
7. What is the benefit of establishing a work record? After you answer, give an example.
8. How can work experience make schooling more meaningful?
9. How can work experience education help you discover career interests and goals?
10. Name some ways in which Wilson benefited from work-study.

Activities to Do

1. Interview a student who has taken a cooperative vocational education or work-study program. Ask the person what he or she thinks are the major benefits of the program. Ask also about whether the person found any disadvantages to the program. Discuss your findings in class.
2. Interview an employer who has provided a training site for a co-op or work-study student. List the ways in which the employer has benefited from the program. Prepare an oral report and present it to the class.
3. Write a short statement (a paragraph or so) about what you hope to gain from being in a work experience program. Read your statement to the class. Compare and discuss the statements of different students.
4. Examine a copy of the training agreement used by your school. Discuss the purpose and requirements of the agreement. Make sure that you ask questions about any part that you don't understand.
5. Collect cartoons about work from your daily and weekend newspapers. You may be surprised at the number you find. Display them on a classroom bulletin board.

---

1. Earn money, social satisfaction, positive feelings, prestige, personal development, contributions to health, and self-expression.
2. Accomplishment, the feeling of satisfaction on having completed a task. Self-worth, the feeling that you have something to offer that other people recognize.
3. Any number of examples can be cited. Make sure that the distinction is made between *what* a person does (occupation) and *where* they do it (job).
4. *Cooperative vocational education*—an educational program in which students learn specific occupational skills for employment. *Work-study*—an educational program focusing on the development of employability skills, not specific occupational skills. *Exploratory work experience education*—a career guidance activity that allows students to observe and try out different occupations.
5. "Regular" vocational education is conducted within a school shop or laboratory. Co-op is conducted on the job.
6. Because students get to explore (test, examine, investigate) several different occupations in order to discover or confirm interests.
7. It will make it easier to get a job later. For instance, some employers will require previous work experience as a condition for employment.
8. It can help you see the relationship between what you are learning in school and what you have to do on the job. For example, how writing skills are used on the job.
9. Your job may acquaint you with activities or occupations that you were unaware of.
10. School became more enjoyable, his grades improved, he earned money to buy clothes and do things that were previously unavailable to him.

24. Students enjoy reading the cartoons. Collect and display some yourself to initiate the activity.

Topics to Discuss

1. How would your future plans be changed if you suddenly won or inherited a lot of money? Would you go to college? Would you plan on working? What type of work would you do?
2. In what ways can you influence and shape the direction of your career?
3. Are there any types of work experience programs in your school or community not mentioned in the chapter?
4. How might knowledge and skills learned in the following school subjects be applied on the job: English, mathematics, science, social studies, and foreign language?
5. In what ways might your interests and abilities be expressed in work? Cite examples of both paid and unpaid work.

25. Studies have found that a surprisingly large proportion of lottery winners continue to work at their same jobs. Even for many financially secure people, work plays an important role in their lives.
26. A variety of state- and federally-funded youth employment programs and community partnerships exist throughout the country. Identify and discuss any such programs in your area.

1. Vocational psychologists use the term *career* to refer to a person's work history. A *career* is the sequence of work activities in which a person engages throughout his or her lifetime. The term *career* is not used here because it is an abstract concept that many people confuse with the term *occupation*.

CHAPTER TWO

The Job Ahead

OUTLINE
Sample Work Histories
Moving Toward a Stable Job
The Future Begins Now
Chapter Review

OBJECTIVES
After reading this chapter, you should be able to:
- Explain what is meant by a work history.
- Discuss how different work histories can lead to a stable job.
- List characteristics of stable jobs.
- Identify what you can do to shape your own career.

1   The jobs that you hold during your working life represent your unique *work history*. One person's work history may be a movement from job to job within the same occupation. Another person's work history may include one or more changes to entirely different occupations and jobs. A third person's work history may have no orderly pattern at all. Some people have long periods of unemployment with only an occasional short-term job. They are unable to establish a successful work history.

SAMPLE WORK HISTORIES

3   Knowing about different work histories can help you think about and plan for your own career. Let's examine the work histories of four different people.

Terry got a job in a small electronics sales and repair shop as part of a co-op program. After he graduated from high school, he took a full-time job in the electronics department of a large discount store. He often did small repair jobs for friends and neighbors during evenings and weekends.

2

FIGURE 2-1 People who work in the sales and marketing fields often move from one stable job to another. *Photo by Paul E. Meyers*

2. Illustrate on the board examples of movement from job to job within the same occupation and changes to entirely different occupations and jobs.

FIGURE 2-2 This automotive teacher moonlights by working at a second job. How did this term originate? *Photo by Information/Education Inc.*

3. We want young people to understand about work histories (i.e., careers) in order for them to see the potential for planning and creating their own careers.

4. The term *stable job* will be defined in the next section.

CHAPTER 2 The Job Ahead ■ 17

Next, he got a job repairing TVs and installing antennas. He took this job in order to save enough money to open his own business. Terry now has a stable job as owner-manager of an electronics supply firm.

When Marie graduated from high school, she didn't know what she wanted to do. After being out of work for several months, she found a full-time job. It was working as a salesclerk in a fashionable clothing store. From working in the store, Marie discovered that she enjoyed retail selling and had a talent for it.

After two years, she quit her job and enrolled in college to major in marketing. During college, she had a part-time job in a clothing store in the campus town. After she finished a marketing degree, she took a job as a sales manager for a national department store. She worked at that job for five years before staying at home two years with young children. Marie just started working again at a job that is similar to the one she left earlier.

Cindy was an outstanding athlete who never worked while attending high school or college. After college, her first job turned out to be a stable one. It was as a high school teacher and coach. After six years, however, she had a desire to do something else.

A friend in the sporting goods business offered her a job. She was not sure whether she would like it, but quit her teaching job to give it a try. Somewhat to her surprise, Cindy enjoyed the challenge of the job. After a year in the job, she took another job with a large sporting goods manufacturer. She is now in charge of their school athletic sales. Cindy plans to make this a stable job.

FIGURE 2-4 Some people never find a stable job. *Photo by David W. Tuttle*

Rick never liked school and could not wait to get out. After high school, he got a job stocking shelves in a grocery store. He worked a couple of months before getting into an argument with the store manager. Rick was fired.

His next job was working evenings and weekends as a service station attendant. After working at that job for about a year, Rick decided that he should learn a skill. Rick then moved to another town and got an apartment with a friend. He enrolled in a technical school to learn computer programming. He had heard this was a growing field.

While going to school, Rick took a part-time job at another service station. He quit school after six months because he had to study too hard. Now Rick has another job driving a delivery truck while he decides whether to join the Armed Forces or start his own business!

FIGURE 2-3 An athletic and coaching career is good preparation for the sporting goods business. *Photo by David W. Tuttle*

5. Compare the reasons why Rick changed jobs with those of Terry, Marie, and Cindy. Point out that Rick doesn't seem to know what he wants to do or be able to stick with anything. Ask students if they think Rick will actually "join the Armed Forces or start his own business."

18 ■ SECTION 1 Preparing for Work

The four work histories illustrate that jobs can serve different purposes at different times in one's life. Jobs are often used as a way to achieve something else. One purpose may be to learn occupational skills. Another purpose may be to earn money for college. Some jobs are used to gain experience in order to *qualify* for a better job. For most people, first jobs are only stepping stones to later ones.

MOVING TOWARD A STABLE JOB

Different work histories can lead to a stable job. You read how Terry, Marie, and Cindy followed different paths to a stable job. One route is not necessarily better than another. Some work histories like Rick's, however, only lead to detours and dead ends.

A *stable job* is one that you consider to be permanent and which may last several years. This does not mean, however, that you stay in the job forever. (Remember Cindy.) You may have a stable job at any time in your work life. Following are additional characteristics of stable jobs. Being aware of them can help you gain greater control over your work history.

Self-direction

Gaining a stable job does not usually happen by accident. Most successful careers come from hard work and *self-direction*. This means knowing what you want and taking steps to get there. Part of being self-directed is developing your skills through education or training.

Once you get a job, you want to keep it. This means performing well on the job tasks you are being paid to do. It also means learning and growing on the job. Much of this involves keeping up to date with what is going on in your field. Advancing in a job usually requires doing more than your share. To put yourself in a position for *promotion* or advancement you may also need to get more education or training.

Sometimes, advancing in a career also involves taking risks. For example, Robin was offered a promotion. To accept the new position would mean giving up a secure job, selling a house, and moving the family across the country. Decisions like these are not easy to make. A willingness to take a risk, though, often leads to greater personal and career success.

6. Emphasize that "jobs can serve different purposes at different times in one's life." Getting an entry-level job is a means to an end, rather than a permanent life goal.

7. Academic courses are not the only route to a good job. Many people follow alternate routes to good jobs and successful lives.

What Would You Do?

A fellow employee approaches you at work with some advice. "Listen," he says. "You're working too hard. Slow down a little bit. You're making the rest of us look bad. You don't want us all to be mad at you, do you?" The comments upset you. You are just trying to do the job the best way you know how. You are not trying to show anyone up. But now you wonder if you should slack off a bit. What would you do?

* *WWYD Feature A.* Suggest to students that they should always do their best on the job, notwithstanding the dilemma that this poses. Perhaps the individual could seek advice from a respected co-worker.

FIGURE 2-5 Getting additional education or training often pays off in career advancement. *Courtesy of International Business Machines Corporation*

Effort Pays Off

Not enough jobs are available for everyone who wants one. This is especially true for young people. If you want to work, you may have to accept any job that you can get. It may be low paying, boring, or undesirable in some other way. But a job is a job! Many adults started their careers this way.

It can be argued that there are no "bad jobs" as long as they are not illegal, immoral, or otherwise harmful. A job is a beginning. It is a way to earn money, get experience, learn skills, and prove

8. The term *stable job* (along with *initial jobs* and *trial jobs*) was coined by two occupational sociologists named Form and Miller. It is used here in simplified form.

9. Ask students to provide examples of behaviors and actions that indicate self-direction (setting goals and then working toward them).

CHAPTER 2 The Job Ahead ■ 19

yourself. Things can get better if you are cooperative, follow rules and directions, take an interest in what you are doing, and do your best. Employers tend to recognize and reward good work. Jerry's experience is a good example.

Jerry had finished his junior year in high school and started to look for a summer job. He went to the Job Service office. Little was available for students like him. Most of the job openings were permanent positions for people eighteen and over. Jerry was only seventeen and could not take a permanent job. One job was available. It was offered by someone who wanted a person to mow grass and do yardwork one day a week. He took the job.

When Jerry showed up at the Porter's house, Mrs. Porter showed him what to do. For the rest of the day he mowed, raked, pruned, trimmed, and pulled weeds. The lawn and garden were beautiful and Jerry took pride in making them even more attractive. After he finished, he cleaned the mower, put away the tools, and swept the walk and driveway. Mrs. Porter thanked him and paid him.

He returned a week later and did a really good job. When Mrs. Porter paid him this time, she complimented him and gave him a bonus. She said that it was very difficult to find people willing and able to do good work. Mrs. Porter asked him if he would be interested in doing yardwork for some of her neighbors.

Before long Jerry had all the jobs he was able to do. He learned that quality effort pays off. Because his work was appreciated, Jerry was able to use Mrs. Porter's name as a reference for a later job. Mrs. Porter was a well-respected member of the community. Her recommendations helped Jerry many times in later years.

Change is Certain

The world of work is continually changing. Some industries and occupations become *obsolete* (no longer used) as new ones are created. For example, the number of telephone operators has steadily decreased because of new electronic switching equipment. This *technology*, however, has created a need for new types of workers who can install and maintain such equipment. During your worklife, you will probably have to adjust to great change.

People who are more successful are generally those who anticipate and adapt to change. Marilyn and Bob are good examples. Marilyn and Bob own a typing and printing service. Most of their clients are small business owners and college students.

FIGURE 2-6 Give your job your best effort, even if you would prefer a different kind of job. *Courtesy of Knight-Ridder Inc.*

10. Point out that taking risks is not the same as gambling.
11. Ask students if they can provide personal examples of employers recognizing and rewarding good work.

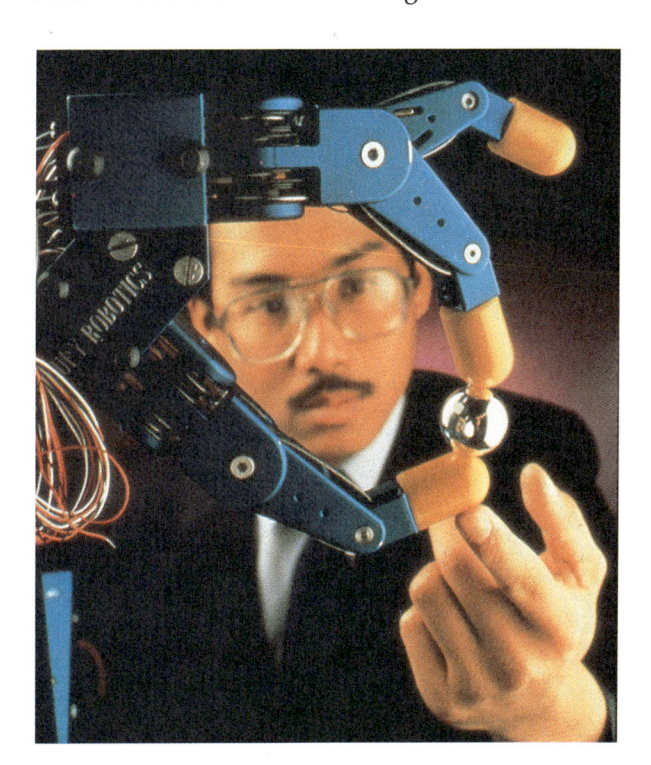

FIGURE 2-7 Industrial robots have launched many new industries and occupations. *Courtesy of Martin Marietta Corporation*

12. This case study illustrates one of the basics of job success.
13. Discuss with students some of the changes they have observed in their short lifetime.

20 ■ SECTION 1 Preparing for Work

What Would You Do?

You have been operating your own small business for several years. You make a good income and are optimistic about the future. One day a salesperson calls on you to demonstrate a new piece of manufacturing equipment. He claims that this new machine will make the current method obsolete in a few years. He also says that most businesses like yours are already planning to install the equipment. You are not so sure. The new machine is very expensive. Since your business is currently doing very well, you question whether you actually need it. What would you do?

* *WWYD Feature B.* This example raises a couple of the considerations involved (expense and actual need) in adapting to change. The owner can probably postpone the purchase until it becomes more apparent that it is definitely needed.

In the mid-1980s, they started to get an increase in the number of requests to do typing on a word processor. They had to decline the business. They explained that their office had only electric typewriters. However, Marilyn and Bob saw the changes that were coming. They remembered years earlier having to switch from manual to electric typewriters.

To meet the needs of the clients, they installed a commercial word processor. Bob, Marilyn, and the office staff took extra time to learn how to use the new equipment. They are glad they did. They now have more business and have been able to pay for the new equipment with the increased earnings.

Part of your preparation for a career should include planning for change. Become familiar with how the workplace is changing. Then try to develop the skills you will need in tomorrow's workplace. Look over the Table of Contents for this book. You will find that much of the later material is concerned with preparing you for the challenge of change.

14

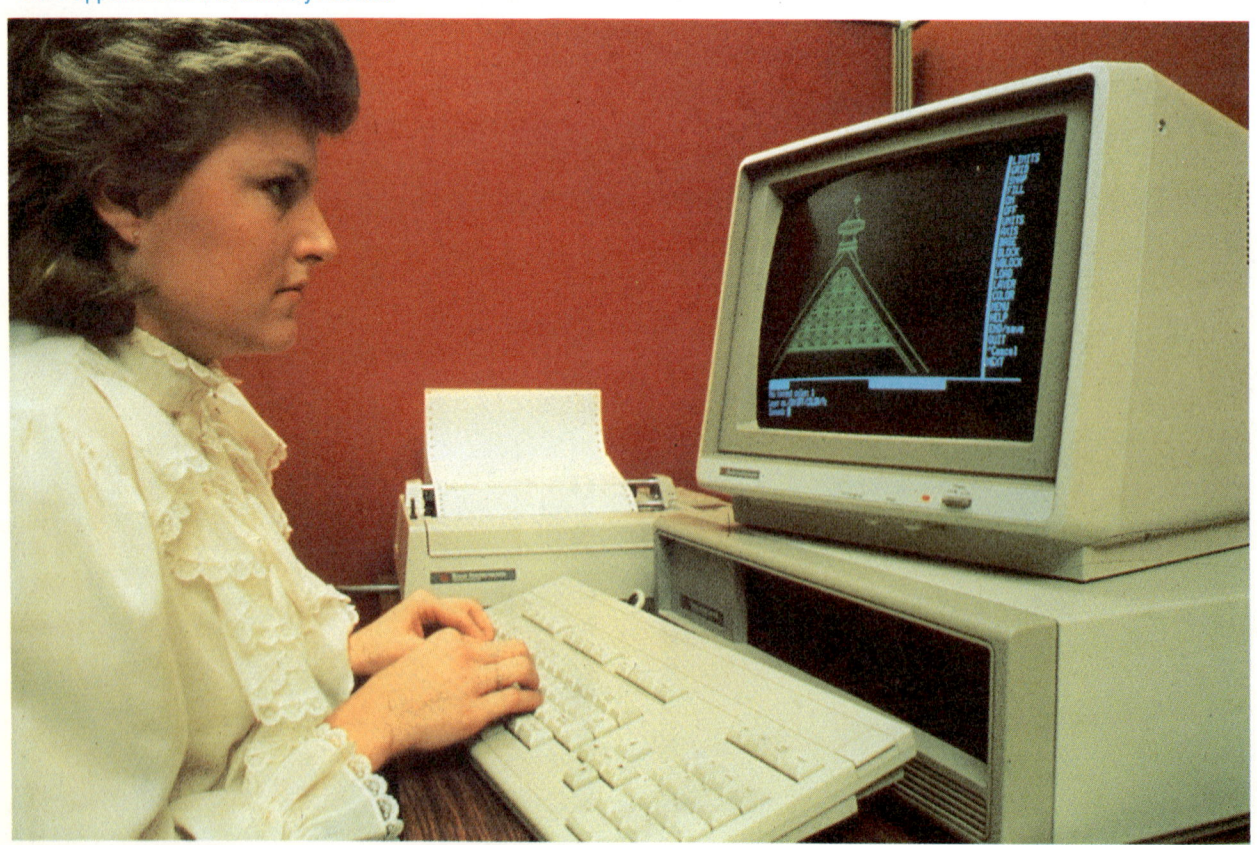

FIGURE 2-8 New technologies often increase productivity. Can you give some examples? *Courtesy of SIUC Photocommunications*

14. The changing workplace will be examined in more detail in Chapter 14.

F·E·A·T·U·R·E

Coping with Shift Work

You may apply for or be offered a job someday that requires you to work different shifts. The demand for round-the-clock shift workers has doubled since 1960. About 25 million Americans now work the night shift (midnight to 8 A.M.). This trend is expected to continue as more businesses stay open 24 hours.

Some employees work the second and third shifts on a permanent basis. Others are rotated frequently from shift to shift. Time shuffling can have its price, however. The health and productivity of shift workers may suffer. An upside-down schedule disturbs the body's "inner clock." This can cause fatigue and digestive problems. Rotating shift workers also make more mistakes. For example, between midnight and dawn nurses dispense wrong medication more often and truckers have more single-vehicle accidents.

A new breed of scientists called *chronobiologists* are beginning to solve some of these problems. Most problems are related to the direction and rate of shift rotation. Rotation can be clockwise (going to work later at each change) or counterclockwise (going to work earlier). Shifts may change every day or two or every several weeks. It has been found that the body adjusts better to a clockwise rotation schedule; that is, rotating from the day shift to the swing shift to the night shift. At least three weeks should elapse between shift changes. Companies trying this pattern have found major improvement in production and less workers' complaints about schedules.

FIGURE 2-FEATURE At some point in your life, you are likely to work nights. *Courtesy of USX Corporation*

*Coping With Shift Work. Make students aware of some of the potential problems, and the need for people to adapt to such a schedule.

THE FUTURE BEGINS NOW

Some young people regard school as something to get through so they can be free to do what they want. What is the problem with this attitude? Well, school is a workplace, too. A prospective employer will look at your school record for clues as to what kind of an employee you might be. A poor school record is hard to defend. Blaming teachers or someone else for your problems won't impress anyone.

Perhaps you have done poorly in school thus far. What can you do now? You can always work harder during what is left of your high school career. A marked improvement in your attitude and performance will be helpful later. It will show teachers and employers that you have become a more mature person.

Now is the time to change habits and attitudes that may hold you back in the workplace. If, for example, you are frequently absent or late to school, make a greater effort to go to school and to be on time. Or, if you often commit careless errors in your schoolwork, take the time to reread or recheck your work before turning it in.

Also consider taking more courses that will strengthen your academic background. Most jobs require basic mathematics and communication skills. You may want to take more math or English. If you haven't done so already, how about trying a beginning computer course? Being familiar with computers is required in many jobs. Your work experience coordinator or school counselor may have other suggestions depending on your background and needs.

In Chapter 3, you will learn how to look for a job. You may discover that a job search can be frustrating. You may end up accepting a job that is less than what you had hoped for. If so, do not get discouraged. Remember what you have learned in this chapter about the different routes to a stable, satisfying job. *How you begin your career is less important than getting it started.* You can then use the beginning job as a stepping stone to something better.

FIGURE 2-9 It is never too late to change an attitude or behavior. *Photo by Liane Enkelis*

15. Ask students to name ways in which the roles of student and employee are similar (both work under supervision, are assigned specific tasks to perform, are expected to demonstrate good work habits, are evaluated, and so on).
16. Using a job as a stepping stone to something better is an example of how a job is a means to an end.

CHAPTER REVIEW

Chapter in Brief

- The jobs that you hold during your working life form a work history. People often have very different work histories. Knowing about work histories can help you think about and plan your own career.
- A job can serve different purposes at different times in your life. Beginning jobs are often used to achieve something else, for example, to learn a skill, save money for college, or qualify for a better job.
- A stable job is one that you consider to be permanent. It may last for several years. Many different routes can lead to a stable job. One route is not necessarily better than another.
- There are other common characteristics of stable jobs. One is that most stable jobs result from hard work and self-direction. Another is that quality effort on a job usually pays off. The world of work is continually changing. A third characteristic is that people with successful, stable jobs are generally ones who anticipate and adapt to change.
- You can take steps now to influence the direction of your career. Work harder during what is left of your high school years. Change habits and attitudes that may hold you back in the workplace. Consider taking additional courses to strengthen your academic background.

Words to Know

obsolete outdated; no longer in use.

promotion advancement to a higher level job or position.

qualify meeting the preliminary requirements for another job or position.

self-direction setting goals and working toward them.

stable job a job considered to be permanent and which may last several years.

technology application of scientific knowledge to practical uses.

work history all of the jobs that one holds during the course of a working lifetime.

Questions to Answer

1. What are some reasons why people are unable to establish a successful work history?
2. Give an example to show how knowledge of work histories can help you think about and plan a career.
3. Name three reasons why a person might voluntarily leave a stable job.
4. Jobs can serve different purposes at different times in our lives. Give three examples.

1. Lack of occupational and employability skills, unwillingness to work hard, lack of self-direction, and unwillingness to take risks.
2. The primary one is to recognize that there are many different routes to a stable job.
3. (a) To take another job or to change occupations. (b) To return to school. (c) Personal reasons—pregnancy, move to another town, and so on.
4. (a) Learn occupational skills. (b) Earn money for college or other education. (c) Gain experience to qualify for a better job.

5. Give an example to show how taking a risk can lead to greater success in a career.
6. How can technological change influence a career? Give one positive and one negative example.
7. Why are employers usually interested in how well you have done in school?
8. Name three things that you might begin to do now to influence your career.

Activities to Do

1. Ask a parent or other adult to list all the jobs he or she has held. Compare the work histories in class. What are the similarities and differences? Which types of work histories are the more common?
2. In doing Activity 1, did you note how work histories may be influenced by such things as illnesses, accidents, economic hard times, wars, and so on? List as many things as you can that are beyond one's control that may influence a career. Discuss your answers in class.
3. Think about your own work habits and attitudes. Write down two or three things that need improving. (We all have a few faults.) Go over the list with your work experience coordinator. Discuss what you can do to improve your performance.

Topics to Discuss

1. Reread the case study about Rick's work history. Discuss why you think he has not progressed toward a stable job. What would you recommend that he do next?
2. If you are currently employed, do you think that your present job might develop into a stable job? Why or why not?
3. Do you think that hard work and quality effort pays off? Or is this just a myth that parents, teachers, and employers want you to believe?
4. Some young people not enrolled in a work experience program leave after school and go to a job. They often work from 3:30 or 4:00 in the afternoon to 10:30 or 11:00 at night. On weekends, they may put in eight to sixteen additional hours. Do you think that some teenagers are trying to work too much while attending high school? Share any relevant personal experiences that you may have.

---

5. A common one is accepting a promotion that requires a geographic move and greater job responsibility.
6. Positive-technology often leads to the creation of new occupations and new opportunities. Negative-technology often makes some occupations obsolete.
7. Because the school is a workplace, one's school record is often an indication of how well one will perform on the job.
8. (a) Work harder during what is left of your high school career. (b) Change bad habits and attitudes. (c) Take additional courses.

17. This is designed to reinforce the notion that there are a number of routes to a stable job. (The activity may also reveal that some people never achieve a stable job. Be sensitive to this.)
18. Even though we want students to recognize that they can plan and create a career, it must be acknowledged that misfortune can temporarily or permanently sidetrack career plans and progress.
19. This activity should be conducted in a positive and sensitive manner. It is desirable for students to be able to recognize and correct shortcomings.

20. It is natural for students to get tired of hearing adults say this. Allow them to explain their feelings. Try to maintain a positive discussion. Summarize by pointing out that more often than not (but not always) quality effort pays off.
21. A 1986 book by Greenberger entitled *When Teenagers Work: The Psychological and Social Cost of Adolescent Employment* suggested that school performance and other things suffer when teenagers work "long hours" during high school. The significant factor seems to be the number of hours worked, not the work itself.

1. Individual programs may vary from state to state and district to district. Explain the operation of your program here if it differs from the general model.

2. At the beginning of the school year, some students may not have a job. This material will help to get students placed in a job as soon as possible.

CHAPTER THREE

Looking for a Job

OUTLINE
Thinking About Your Job Goals
Getting Ready
Finding Job Leads
Keeping Track of Job Leads
Chapter Review

OBJECTIVES
After reading this chapter, you should be able to:
- Describe the importance of clarifying job goals before looking for employment.
- Explain how to get a social security number and work permit.
- Identify different sources of job leads.
- Illustrate how to prepare a job-lead card.
- Summarize the benefits of using job-lead cards.

FIGURE 3-1 The coordinator must approve your work experience job. Why is this a good idea? *Courtesy of Micro Switch, A Honeywell Division*

Students enrolled in work experience education programs get jobs in several ways. In cooperative vocational education, the coordinator plays a major role. The coordinator usually "sets up" training stations in the community and interviews and selects qualified students for admission to the program. The coordinator then takes into account students' interests, aptitudes, and job goals. These are matched with suitable jobs. It is up to the student, however, to interview with the employer and get the job.

In work-study programs, a student may get a job before or after entering the program. Some students will already have a job and ask to continue it for school credit. This may be done as long as the coordinator approves the training station. Students who don't have jobs when they enroll in a work-study program will need to find one.

In this chapter and Chapters 4 and 5, you will learn how to find a job. If you don't have a job, you will be able to use the information right away. If you are working now, the material will help you in your next job search.

THINKING ABOUT YOUR JOB GOALS
Why do you want a job? Be prepared to answer this question. You will be hearing it often. Your work experience coordinator will certainly ask it. The coordinator wants to help you find a job that suits your interests and abilities. By getting to know you better, your coordinator can help you get a job you will enjoy. Counselors, placement officers, and others you approach for job leads will ask you about your job goals. And, of course, an interviewer will probably ask the question during a job interview.

Thinking about your job goals will help you, too. What you want out of a job will influence how and where you look for one. Since you are now enrolled in a work experience program, you have probably already done some thinking about your goals.

SECTION 1 Preparing for Work

Reviewing the benefits of work experience education covered in Chapter 1 can help you clarify your job goals. If you recall, these are:

- Learning occupational skills.
- Developing employability skills.
- Establishing a work record.
- Earning while you learn.
- Discovering career interests and goals.
- Recognizing the relationship between education and work.
- Remaining employed after graduation.

FIGURE 3-2 During your job search, you will be asked many times why you want a job. Be prepared with a good answer. *Photo by David W. Tuttle*

You may want to rank the benefits in order of their importance to you. Doing this can help you focus on your most important goals.

It was not difficult for Rachel to decide what she wanted out of a job. She had been interested in printing for a long time. In the ninth grade, she took a year of industrial education where she learned about basic principles of offset printing.

Next, she took two years of vocational graphics and printing. In those courses, she learned about all aspects of offset printing. She liked the printing courses. What she was most interested in, however, was computer graphics. But the high school didn't offer any courses in that area.

3. Type and duplicate a list of these seven benefits. Spend some class time reviewing the benefits/goals. Have students place their goals in order of importance.

4. Rachel's primary goals are to learn occupational skills (computer graphics) and to remain employed after graduation.

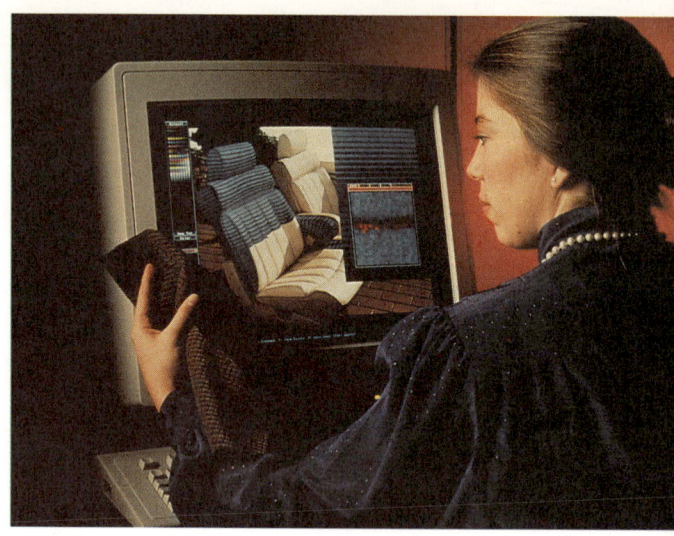

FIGURE 3-3 Learning computer graphics is one possible job goal. *Courtesy of Chrysler Corporation*

Rachel enrolled in a cooperative vocational education program so she could get a job in her area of interest. She now works for the publications department of a large company. Rachel is learning a lot about computer graphics. Rachel likes what she is doing. Her only regret is that she can't work full time. She hopes that the company will hire her full time when she graduates. Can you name Rachel's goals? You will learn more about career planning in Section 3 of this book.

GETTING READY

If you don't have a social security number, you should get one before you start a job search. (A new law took effect in 1988. It requires every person who is five years of age or older to have a social security number in order to be claimed as a dependent on a tax form 1040.) You may also need to get a work permit.

Social Security Number

Social Security is a national program of social insurance. Your employer will withhold money from your paycheck. This money will go to the Social Security system. When you retire, you will receive income payments from Social Security. You will learn more about Social Security in Chapter 27.

In order for the government to keep a record of your earnings, you will need a Social Security number. The number will remain with you for life. No one else has the same number. An employer will

5. In January 1989, thirty-eight states allowed parents to apply for a newborn child's Social Security card before the baby leaves the hospital. The program is called "Enumeration at Birth."

6. Ask students if they are aware of any other uses for Social Security numbers.

CHAPTER 3 Looking for a Job ■ 27

You can apply for a number at any Social Security office. You must fill out the application form shown in Figure 3-4 and provide proof of your date of birth, identity, and U.S. citizenship. You will receive a Social Security card about two to four weeks after you apply.

Work Permit

Various federal and state laws protect the health and safety of *minors.* Such laws regulate working conditions and working hours of students under the age of sixteen or eighteen. For instance, the Fair Labor Standards Act states that a person under the age of sixteen may not be employed *during school hours.* Some states have stricter laws than others regarding child labor.

A *work permit,* however, makes it legal for a "student learner" to work during school hours as part of a work experience education program. School officials issue work permits for students under a certain age. In some states, the age is sixteen. In others, it is eighteen.

Besides a work permit, your state or school district may require other kinds of approval before you can work. Ask your school counselor or work experience coordinator about such rules.

7
8
9

FIGURE 3-4 Application for a Social Security number. *Courtesy of Social Security Administration*

ask for your number when you apply for a job or start work. Your Social Security number may have other uses, too. For example, in some states, your driver's license ID number is the same as your Social Security number.

6

FIGURE 3-5 You will receive your Social Security card after you submit the application. *Courtesy of Social Security Administration*

7. For students who don't have a Social Security number, have applications on hand or require them to obtain one. Provide instruction to complete the form.

FINDING JOB LEADS

It was the first day of the new school year. Sally was on the way to her work experience education class. "I wonder what job they will have for me," thought Sally.

The bell rang and students turned their attention to Mr. Amed, the teacher-coordinator. He took attendance and then began to explain about work experience education.

"A requirement of this program," he explained, "is that each of you must have a job. Some of you already have jobs. For the rest of you, your first 'job' will be to get a job. I don't have any jobs to assign."

Sally was somewhat surprised. She raised her hand to ask a question. "But I don't know where to get a job," she said.

10

"Don't worry," said Mr. Amed. "I'll help you learn about sources of job leads and how to apply for a job."

If you don't have a job yet either, you will need to plan how to get one. At this point in your life, you will probably apply for an entry-level job. An *entry-level job* requires little or no experience. The following sources of job leads are those through which you are most likely to find a job.

8. Explain the child labor law in your state.
9. Explain any other relevant work-approval rules.
10. Ask if any students thought that they would be assigned a job.

28 ■ SECTION 1 Preparing for Work

What Would You Do?

You learn about a job opening for a part-time custodian at the shopping mall. The hours are good and the pay is decent for a beginning job. You can't decide whether to apply. You really don't want to empty wastebaskets and mop floors. You wonder how you will feel if your friends see you working. What would you do?

WWYD Feature A. Discuss openly. Recall earlier material in Chapter 2 about using a beginning job as a stepping stone to something else.

FIGURE 3-6 Many students are surprised to find that they will have to get their own jobs. *Photo by David W. Tuttle*

Family and Friends

Start your job search by making a list of your relatives, neighbors, and friends. Include your working friends. They may know of job leads from their own job searches. Don't forget places where you and your family do business. You may want to have a family member review your final list.

Do not hesitate asking family or friends for help. However, don't expect them to find a job for you. Getting a job lead is the most you should hope for. It will be up to you to pursue the lead.

In-school Sources

Three good sources of job leads may be available within your school. One is your cooperative vocational education or work experience coordinator. He or she is probably already involved in helping you. Do not sit back and wait for the coordinator to find you a job.

Most schools also have a guidance office or guidance counselor. It is common for local employers to contact counselors when looking for workers. The counselor will usually keep a list of job openings or post them on a bulletin board. Tell the counselor that you are looking for a job and ask to see any information available about job openings.

A third source is job placement offices or career centers. Interested students generally register with the office. They may receive job counseling and other services. Job counselors help to match up students with job openings and make *referrals* for interviews. That is, they send students to employers who are hiring.

FIGURE 3-7 Some larger schools now have their own job placement offices. *Courtesy SIUC Photocommunications*

11. Review the types of in-school sources available. Invite the guidance counselor or school placement officer to class as appropriate.

12. The four kinds of ads explained here simply provide a functional way of examining the nature of help-wanted ads. Some ads may be a combination of types. As you discuss the

CHAPTER 3 Looking for a Job ■ 29

Newspaper Classified Ads

When employers have jobs to fill, they often advertise them in the newspaper. Most newspapers have a section that includes help-wanted ads. Four common kinds of ads are shown in Figure 3-8.

```
PART-TIME CLERK TYPIST.
Approximately 20 hours per week,
including some evenings and
Saturdays. Experience with typing,
filing, telephone reception and
work with public desirable. Must
be dependable and able to work
non-regular hours. $4.10 per hour.
Applications accepted until
Tuesday, Jan. 15, 1985 at 5 P.M. to
Mary Campbell, Alton Public
Library, 405 W. Main, Alton, MA
43331, 473-6235.
```
OPEN AD

```
Draftsman
$18,000 & Up
Fee Paid

Male or female, at least 2 years
experience. Call us or bring in
your resume to compare your
experience with our company
requirements
      JOLEN
EMPLOYMENT AGENCY
17 Plaza Offices, P.O Box 531
     Tucker, TX 95313
        635-4792
```
AGENCY SPOT AD

```
      EARN
$100 TO $500

   Write for details
     P.O. Box 113,
  Sunnyvale, CA 75391
```
CATCH-TYPE AD

```
         CLERICAL
Local manufacturer has im-
mediate part-time clerical
position open. Involves heavy
computer entry, 4 hours a
day, 5 days a week, prefer
afternoons. Reply to:
       Write: CLERICAL
P.O. Box 75A Union Station,
   Green Hills, NY 10112
```
BLIND AD

FIGURE 3-8 Four common kinds of help-wanted ads.

The first kind is an *open ad*. It tells about the job requirements, identifies the employer, and tells how to apply. This is the best type of ad.

The second kind is the *blind ad*. The name, address, and phone number of the employer are not shown. Employers do this to keep from being bombarded with phone calls. It also allows them to screen applications carefully. Only qualified applicants are then invited for an interview.

A *catch-type ad* is the third kind. It tends to promise good salary and downplay the qualifications needed for the job. The "catch" is that the job is usually for door-to-door salespeople.

The last kind of ad is the *agency spot ad*. Note that the ad omits the name of the employer. It is used by private employment agencies to advertise jobs available only through the agency.

Job Service

Every state has a system of public employment offices called the *Job Service*. Their services are free. Some offices have a Youth Counselor who works mainly with young people. Job Service counselors often cooperate closely with local work experience programs.

To use the Job Service, you must fill out an application. A counselor will interview you to find out your interests and qualifications. You might be asked to take an interest inventory or aptitude test. If a job is available, the counselor will arrange an interview for you.

FIGURE 3-9 A Job Service is more likely to list entry-level jobs than a private employment agency. *Courtesy of Liane Enkelis*

ads, you may wish to assign Activity 2. An alternative would be for you (or the school librarian) to bring in a collection of newspaper classified ads.

13. You might be able to get a Job Service counselor to come to class to explain the Job Service.

F•E•A•T•U•R•E

Temporary Work

♦ ♦ ♦

One of the fast-growing industries in America is the temporary services industry. These are companies like Kelly Services, Manpower, and others that belong to the National Association of Temporary Services (NATS). They provide listings of available workers to employers who need short-term help. On any given day, more than 800,000 "temps" are on the job.

Temporary workers are hired to fill in when a permanent employee quits, gets sick, or goes on vacation. Some are hired to help out when a special project requires extra people for a short time. The most common temporary jobs involve secretaries, receptionists and bookkeepers. However, a growing number of services place professionals like attorneys and librarians. Ten percent of temp jobs are in health care. Nurses are in particular demand.

About five million Americans work each year as temporaries. Over sixty percent are women. Who are these temporary workers? They fall into five categories:

1. *Rusty Skills.* Some people haven't worked for a while and are uncertain of their abilities. Temping gives them a chance to brush up on old skills before looking for a permanent job.
2. *Uncertain Goals.* Some people aren't sure what type of work they want to do. Temping allows them to sample different jobs before deciding.
3. *Between Jobs.* New high school or college graduates often can't find the right position. Temping is a way to finance a job hunt so they don't have to accept the first offer.
4. *Supporting Another Occupation.* Some people who work as writers, artists, or performers don't have permanent jobs. They do temp work to pay the bills while they pursue their preferred line of work.
5. *Extra Money.* Students working their way through college are a major source of temps. So are retirees looking to pick up additional income.

A temporary job may be as short as a day or as long as a year. The average length is one to two weeks. At some point in your life, a temporary job may meet your needs. Locate a service by looking in the newspaper classified section under "Temporary Services." Look also in the phone book Yellow Pages under "Employment Contractors—Temporary Help."

FIGURE 3-FEATURE Conventions and trade shows often employ a lot of temporary workers.

Temporary Work. Note that this is one particular type of private employment agency. Do students know of anyone who has worked as a temp? Discuss. Have students use the newspaper classified ads and the Yellow Pages to identify possible temporary services employers in your area.

Private Employment Agencies

These are businesses that find people jobs for a *fee.* The fee is paid either by the employer or the employee. If you use a private employment agency, be sure that you understand the financial arrangements *before* signing a contract or accepting an interview.

Private agencies do not generally deal with clients under eighteen and those who are looking for part-time entry-level jobs. So don't be discouraged if you are turned down by a private agency.

Direct Employer Contact

Many people find jobs by talking directly to employers. A help-wanted sign posted in a business is the oldest method of announcing a job opening. If you see such a sign, ask the employer for an application.

FIGURE 3-10 Some employers use this simple method to announce job openings. *Photo by Paul E. Meyers*

Employers often have unadvertised job openings. A list of the twenty-five leading occupations is shown in Figure 3-11. Study this list to get an idea of the types of employers that hire a lot of young workers. You might then use the telephone Yellow Pages to make a list of companies to contact.

Another means of direct employer contact is to visit a company employment office. Go dressed as you would for an interview. Be prepared to fill out an employment application form. Check bulletin boards outside the personnel office, too. Available jobs are often listed there. Some companies also have a separate telephone number that provides prerecorded messages about job openings.

Occupation

- Cashiers
- Retail salesclerks
- Machine operators, assemblers, inspectors, and tenders
- Stock handlers and baggers
- Cooks
- Child-care workers
- Janitors and maids
- Food counter workers
- Misc. food preparation workers
- Laborers, includes construction
- Waiters and waitresses
- Secretaries and typists
- Dining room attendants
- Construction trade workers, includes carpenters, painters, electricians, and so on
- Receptionists and information clerks
- Truck drivers
- File and library clerks
- Farm and nursery workers, gardeners and grounds keepers
- Stock and shipping clerks
- Freight and materials movers
- Garage and service station attendants
- Nurses aides, orderlies, and attendants
- General office clerks
- Bookkeepers and financial record clerks
- Computer operators

FIGURE 3-11 The twenty-five leading occupations of job entrants, aged sixteen to nineteen

KEEPING TRACK OF JOB LEADS

"Hey Steve," said Kevin. "I got my first job lead yesterday. I was eating lunch at the Central Restaurant when I noticed the manager putting up a sign. It was for a part-time kitchen helper. So I wrote the information down."

"Great! What did the sign say?" asked Steve.

"Let me see," answered Kevin. "I've got the information here someplace."

Kevin continued to search his backpack for the scrap of paper on which he took notes. Finally he said, "Darn, I must have lost it. Oh well, I'll go back this weekend and get the information again."

Kevin is off to a shaky start in his search for a job. He was alert to notice the sign and to write down the information. Kevin was careless, though, in misplacing his notes. He also showed poor judgment in not going back or calling right away. When he returned on the weekend, he found the job was filled.

14. This list of the twenty-five leading occupations entered by young people can offer considerable insight into potential types of jobs. One approach is to assign each student an occupation and have them use the Yellow Pages to identify five or more companies to contact. A composite list could then be compiled and duplicated for each student.

32 ■ SECTION 1 Preparing for Work

What Would You Do?

A schoolmate approaches you and says he heard you were looking for a job. He has a buddy who needs some people to deliver "packages" on weekends. The work is easy. You simply ride the bus around town and drop off packages at various places of business. The pay is $10 per hour in cash. You are told not to ask questions or to discuss the job with other people. You are concerned about taking the job because it sounds "fishy." What would you do?

Job-lead Card

Whenever you learn about a job lead, make up a *job-lead card.* An example is shown in Figure 3-12. A five-by-eight-inch card works best because it gives you a lot of room to record information and make notes. the card has two parts.

15. See Activity 3. Have cards on hand. Practice filling out sample cards. Provide all students with a supply for their use.
16. Ask students to name other benefits of the job-lead card.

The "job lead" part is where you record all important information about the job. If you have a newspaper help-wanted ad, tape it onto the card. If the lead comes from a different source, write on the card the company name, address, phone number, and the person to contact about the job.

The "Action Taken" part is where you record what you do to follow up the job lead. Write down the date when you contacted the employer and the person's name with whom you talked. Also write down the results of the contact. If you get an appointment, record the date, time, and place. If you need directions to the interview, be sure to ask. Write the directions on the back of the card. Any follow-up you do after an interview should also be noted.

What are some benefits of using job-lead cards? They keep you from forgetting important information. They save you time, too. By being organized, you can get more results from the time you spend. Can you name other benefits?

Following Through

You read earlier how Kevin failed to act on a job lead. His big mistake was in not talking to the manager when he saw her posting a help-wanted sign. Had he done so, he might have gotten the job. Most employers want to fill job openings as quickly as they can.

You face stiff competition for jobs. Don't hold back. As soon as you learn about a job lead, follow through with quick action. The early applicant gets the job. If you don't get the job immediately, call or go back a few days later. Let the employer know that you are really interested in the job.

FIGURE 3-12 Sample job-lead card

FIGURE 3-13 Act quickly to show your interest in a job vacancy. *Photo by Paul E. Meyers*

* *WWYD Feature B.* The suggestion here is that the job may involve something illegal. Students should avoid any job in which they are told not to ask questions or to discuss the job.

17. Perhaps students can share personal experiences here regarding how quick action may have gotten them a job.

CHAPTER REVIEW

Chapter in Brief

- What you want out of a job will influence how and where you look for it. Therefore, think about your job goals before beginning the job search. Do this by reviewing the seven benefits of work experience education.
- Apply for a Social Security number as soon as possible. An employer will ask for your number when you apply for a job or start work. In some states, you may also need to get a work permit.
- To be enrolled in cooperative vocational education or work-study, you must have a job. If you don't already have one, your first "job" will be to get a job. The most common sources of entry-level jobs are: (a) family and friends, (b) in-school sources, (c) newspaper classified ads, (d) Job Service, (e) private employment agencies, and (f) direct employer contact.
- Whenever you learn about a job lead, make up a job-lead card. It will help you remember important information, save you time, and help you get more positive results. After recording all important information about a job lead, follow through with quick action. Most employers want to fill job openings as soon as possible.

Words to Know

entry-level job a beginning job that does not require any previous knowledge or experience.

fee a sum of money charged by a private employment agency for helping someone to find a job.

job-lead card a card on which to record information and notes about a job lead.

Job Service local branches of the state employment service that help unemployed people find jobs.

minors people who have not reached the full legal age.

referrals directing a student to a potential employer for a job interview.

work permit a form issued by school officials that gives a student permission to work during school hours as part of a work experience education program.

Questions to Answer

1. Sarah has a part-time job. She is starting a work experience program. How can she keep her job and get school credit?
2. Why is it important to clarify your job goals before beginning the job search?
3. Why must you get a Social Security number before you start work?
4. Andrea hesitates about asking friends and family for job leads. She says she would "feel funny" about doing so. Do you agree with her? Why or why not?

1. She can keep the job if the coordinator approves the training station.
2. The work experience coordinator and potential employer will probably ask. Also, what you want out of a job will influence how and where you look for one.
3. It is necessary in order for the government to keep a record of your earnings as a part of the federal Social Security system.
4. No. Andrea should take advantage of every opportunity to identify a job lead.

34 ■ SECTION 1 Preparing for Work

5. Your school may have three sources of job leads. Name them.
6. Name the four kinds of newspaper help-wanted ads.
7. What are the main differences between a public and a private employment agency?
8. Employers use various methods to announce job openings. Name the oldest method.
9. Name the two parts of a job-lead card?
10. Why should you follow through with quick action on a job lead?

Activities to Do

1. Find out your state's requirements on student employment during school hours. If a work permit or other type of approval is required, take the necessary steps to complete the approval process.
2. Get the help-wanted section of a Sunday newspaper that serves your geographic area. Cut out examples of the four types of ads described earlier in the chapter. Tape the examples onto a sheet of paper and label each type of ad. Then give the paper to your instructor. When you get your paper back, discuss your ads with the class.
3. Perhaps your instructor can arrange to make copies of a job-lead card. Or someone in the class might volunteer to make a sample. Duplicate enough so that each person has at least ten. Divide the printing cost among class members.
4. Using the telephone Yellow Pages, list the names and phone numbers of four possible job leads in each of the following categories: (a) employment agencies, (b) temporary agencies, (c) charitable organizations, (d) labor organizations, and (e) trade and professional associations.

Topics to Discuss

1. What role does the teacher/coordinator play in helping students find jobs in work experience education programs?
2. Why have state and federal laws been passed restricting the hours of employment and regulating the working conditions of minors?
3. Six major sources of job leads are discussed in this chapter. Can you think of other sources in your city or community that have not been mentioned?
4. The ease or difficulty of finding a job may be influenced by where you live, for example, whether you live in a city or rural area. What other environmental, economic, or occupational factors influence job availability?

---

5. (a) Work experience coordinators. (b) Guidance counselors. (c) Placement offices or career centers.
6. (a) Open ad. (b) Blind ad. (c) Catch-type ad. (d) Agency spot ad.
7. With a private agency, you will probably have to sign a contract and you may have to pay a fee if they find you a job.
8. A "Help Wanted" sign posted in a place of business.
9. The "Job Lead" part and "Action Taken" part.
10. Most employers try to fill job openings as quickly as possible.

18. There are a wide variety of community-based organizations and local-state-federal government agencies and partnerships that sponsor youth employment programs and projects. Identify and discuss some of these.
19. Possible factors include nature of the economy (prosperity or recession), plant openings or closings, seasonal employment (farm labor, resorts, amusement parks), competition (college town with large numbers of students), and the like.

1. A job lead very often results in the immediate need to make application. Ask if any students have found this to be the case.
2. A *personal data sheet* and a *resume*, while containing some common types of information, do not serve the same purpose. This will become apparent in later sections.

CHAPTER FOUR

Applying for a Job

OUTLINE
Personal Data Sheet
Job Application Form
Writing a Resume
Contacting Employers
Pre-employment Tests
Chapter Review

OBJECTIVES
After reading this chapter, you should be able to:
- Prepare a personal data sheet.
- Complete a job application form.
- Prepare a job resume.
- Explain the three methods of contacting employers about a job.
- Describe the two most common types of pre-employment tests.

FIGURE 4-1 If you find a job lead, act quickly on it. *Photo by Paul E. Meyers*

Finding job leads may seem to take a long time. It does indeed take a lot of time to contact family and friends, search the newspaper help-wanted ads, and identify other leads. Once you find a good job lead, however, things can speed up very quickly.

Richard learned from his Uncle Geraldo about a bowling buddy who was expanding his hardware store. Uncle Geraldo thought his friend might be hiring some new employees and suggested that Richard give him a call.

The next day Richard called Mr. Stevenson at the hardware store. He explained that he was looking for a job and that his uncle had told him to call. Mr. Stevenson said that he had already received several inquiries about a job.

"However," he went on to say, "I'd be happy to have you fill out a job application form. Why don't you stop by and see me after school tomorrow?"

"Thank you very much," said Richard. "I'll be there at four o'clock tomorrow afternoon."

Donna is also on the trail of a hot job lead. She read an ad in the newspaper for a "Hair Stylist/Shampoo Assistant." "Experience helpful but not necessary," the ad said. "Full training available. Send a resume to The Hair Performers, 638 North Walnut St., Muncie, IN, 47396."

"This sounds like what I'm looking for," Donna told her family. "I'd better get a letter of application typed and put my resume in the mail at once."

Richard and Donna were ready to take quick action on job leads. Richard already had a *personal data sheet* prepared to assist him in filling out a *job application form*. Likewise, Donna had a stack of job *resumes* ready and waiting. She also knew how to write a *letter of application*. Richard and Donna have learned some valuable skills needed to apply for a job. In this chapter, you will learn how to do these things, too.

PERSONAL DATA SHEET

Let's say that you are in Richard's shoes and have to fill out a job application form tomorrow. Will you be prepared? Can you, for example, remember the name, address, and telephone number of each employer for whom you have worked? Or do you know your high school class rank and grade point average? How about references? Will you be prepared to list the names of people who could provide an evaluation of you?

Most employers require job seekers to fill out an application form. Some applications ask for very brief information. Others, however, may be very detailed. To be ready, you need to prepare a personal data sheet. You won't give it directly to an employer. You will take it with you and *use it to help you fill out a job application form.* You will also *use it to help prepare a job resume.*

4. A personal data sheet is: (a) used to help fill out a job application form; and (b) used to help prepare a job resume. Note also that it is kept by the student and not given to an employer.

An outline for a personal data sheet is shown in Figure 4-2. Add to it or take out parts to meet your own needs.

FIGURE 4-3 If you want to list someone as a reference, ask for permission to do so. *Courtesy of Liane Enkelis*

PERSONAL DATA SHEET (OUTLINE)

Name _____ Soc. Sec. # _____
Address _____
Birth Date _____ Birth Place _____
Telephone _____ Height _____ Weight _____
Hobbies/Interests _____
Honors/Awards/Offices _____
Sports/Activities _____
Other _____

Educational Background (Add lines as necessary.)

	Name	Address	Dates Attended From:	To:
Grade School				
Junior High				
High School				

Course of Study _____ Rank _____ GPA _____
Favorite Subject(s) _____

Employment History (Start with present or most recent. Add employers as necessary.)

Company _____ Telephone _____
Address _____
Dates of Employment — From: _____ To: _____
Name of Supervisor _____
Job Title and Duties _____

Last Wage _____ Reason for Leaving _____

References (Names of persons who can provide information about your personal, school, or work background.)

	Name	Address	Telephone Home	Work	Relationship
1.					
2.					
3.					

FIGURE 4-2 Follow this general outline in preparing a personal data sheet. Use it to help you fill out a job application form and to help prepare a resume.

3. A personal data sheet is necessary in order to have this information available.

5. You may wish to assign Activity 1 at this time.

6. Point out that an incomplete or sloppy application form is usually rejected immediately.

JOB APPLICATION FORM

When employers have jobs to fill, they usually ask interested people to fill out a job application form. The information provided on the form helps employers to sort out the best qualified persons for the job. After screening the application forms, a small number of people are invited for an interview.

If you have done a personal data sheet, you will have taken a big step toward filling out a job application form. You will be able to copy facts and information from the personal data sheet directly onto the job application form. Take your personal data sheet with you each time you contact an employer or employment office.

CHAPTER 4 Applying for a Job ■ 37

What Would You Do?

You see an ad in the newspaper for a computer operator. The job is exactly what you are looking for. However, the ad states that "prior work experience is required." You have not had any prior employment as a computer operator. But you have been operating your own computer for five years. You are confident that you can do the job. Should you ignore the stated requirement and apply for the job? What would you do?

FIGURE 4-4 All of these people are waiting to fill out job application forms. Only a few will be chosen for an interview. *Photo by Paul E. Meyers*

7. Emphasize that students should take their personal data sheet along on each job search.

* *WWYD Feature A.* People are often qualified to perform a job even though they may not be able to meet stated requirements. Encourage students to apply for such positions.

38 ■ SECTION 1 Preparing for Work

FIGURE 4-5 A typical job application form.

The type of job application form that is used will differ from company to company. A typical form is shown in Figure 4-5. Follow these tips in filling out a job application form.

- Before you begin to fill out the form, read it over carefully. Study the instructions so that you will know what information to provide. Note which parts are "for employer use only."
- You may receive an application form through the mail or have a chance to fill it out on your own and return it later. If your typing is fair to poor, print your answers in black ink. You may want to get an erasable ballpoint pen. This will allow you to correct mistakes easily. Be as neat as possible.
- You will probably be asked to print the information. It is a good idea to print even if it doesn't say to. Be sure to sign your name in those places where it asks for your signature. Use your correct name, not a nickname.
- Answer all questions on the form. If a question doesn't apply to you, put "NA" for "not applicable." Don't leave a blank space because the employer might think you forgot to answer the question.

- Answer all questions honestly. Giving false information can catch up with you later. If you don't have the information or don't know the answer, write in "unknown."
- List the specific position or job for which you are applying. Don't write "anything" in the space. You may be willing to accept any job. However, what you want to convey is that you are interested in and qualified for a certain job.
- Misspelled words give a poor impression of your ability. Take a small pocket dictionary with you (and use it).
- You may be asked to name the "wages or salary expected." It is best to discuss salary in a personal interview with the employer. So write "open" in the space provided.
- In the employment history part, you may be asked to give the reason for leaving a previous job. Don't put down anything that criticizes a past employer or shows that you weren't an acceptable employee. Examples of appropriate reasons for leaving a job are: "returned to school," "left for a better job," and "job terminated."
- After you have filled out the form, check it over carefully before mailing it or handing it over.

8. Assemble a collection of different job application forms for examination by students. Some teachers display them on a bulletin board during the time this chapter is being taught. (Slip the forms into plastic covers to discourage students from writing on them.)
9. You may wish to assign Activity 2 at this time.

CHAPTER 4 Applying for a Job ■ 39

department" is too lengthy. It can be condensed into a shorter phrase that provides the same information: "Analyzed production cost sheets."

An example of a completed resume is shown in Figure 4-7. The resume provides five kinds of information. Personal information is given at the top of the page. Your name, address, and phone number are all that is needed.

FIGURE 4-6 Because of the numerous requests for accurate information on the job application form, experienced job seekers come prepared with personal data sheets and resumes. *Photo by Paul E. Meyers*

What happens after you submit the job application form? Do you wait to hear from the employer? Are you supposed to go for an interview or make contact later with the employer? Make sure you find out what to do next. Write the information down on the job-lead card that you are using to keep track of job leads.

WRITING A RESUME

When applying in person for a job, you may be asked for a resume (pronounced rez'-oo-'-may). You should send a resume when applying for a job by letter.

If you have done a personal data sheet, you already have the basic information you will include in your resume. You will need to choose which of that information to use. Then you will have to arrange the information into a neat, organized format.

Your resume should be detailed enough to give an employer the information needed to judge your qualifications. It should also be brief. A busy employer wants the important facts in as few words as possible. In describing your work experience, for example, the sentence, "I was responsible for analyzing the cost sheets from the production

> RESUME
> Ronald R. Fisher
> 6428 Valley Road
> Cambden, Ohio 67423
> (627) 353-2761
>
> CAREER GOALS
>
> My immediate objective is to obtain a job at a new car dealership as an engine and powertrain mechanic. My long-range goal is to become a shop supervisor or service manager. I am willing to complete additional training as required.
>
> EDUCATIONAL BACKGROUND
>
> 1989 graduate of Hillside Community College in Eastbrook, Ohio. Received Associate of Applied Science Degree in Automotive Technology. Member of first-place team in regional engine troubleshooting competition
>
> Licensed in July 1989 as a state auto and truck inspector (Ohio).
>
> 1987 graduate of Cambden High School. Completed two years of vocational auto and one year of cooperative vocational education. President of local Vocational Industrial Clubs of America (VICA).
>
> WORK EXPERIENCE
>
> June 1989 to present: Goodman's Tire and Auto Center, Cambden, Ohio. Duties include tune-ups, general engine repair, front wheel alignment, and wheel and brake work.
>
> June 1987 to May 1989: Hunter's Auto Repair, Eastbrook, Ohio. Part-time and weekend work while attending college. Performed engine diagnosis, general engine repair, tune-ups, and transmission repair.
>
> August 1986 to May 1987: Texacon Service Station, Cambden, Ohio. Part-time cooperative vocational education student-learner. Performed routine auto maintenance service and minor engine repair.
>
> REFERENCES
>
> Mr. Earl Thompson (Service Mgr.)
> Goodman's Tire & Auto Center
> 219 E. Sycamore
> Cambden, OH 67423
> (314) 472-6415
>
> Mr. Archie Hunter (Owner-Mgr.)
> Hunter's Auto Repair
> 2025 W. Walnut
> Eastbrook, OH 67513
> (314) 682-1924
>
> Mr. Frank Hopkins (Automotive Inst.)
> Vocational Education Department
> Hillside Community College
> Eastbrook, OH 67513
> (314) 684-7367

FIGURE 4-7 Sample resume

In the next section, give a short statement of your career goals. Be specific about the type of job you are seeking. Don't limit yourself to one particular employer, though. (You want to be able to give the resume to many different employers.) Examples of possible goals might be:

- "...to obtain training and acquire experience in retail sales."
- "...to gain practical work experience while saving money for college."
- "...to further develop my skills as a licensed practical nurse."

10. With the exception of career goals, everything needed for the resume should be on the personal data sheet.

11. Prepare an overhead transparency showing the five parts of the resume and a transparency of a completed resume to use in teaching this section.

The third kind of information is about your education. List all high schools, colleges, technical schools, and so on. Begin with the most recent one. List any diplomas, degrees, licenses, and certificates you earned. Also mention any honors or awards you received. Name any job-related activities in which you participated. For example, Ronald Fisher's performance in an engine troubleshooting contest proves he has diagnostic and mechanical skills.

FIGURE 4-8 Mention job-related honors, awards, and special activities on a resume. *Courtesy of Muhlenberg Co. AVEC*

The fourth section is a summary of paid work experience. Begin with your present or most recent job. Identify previous employers, the time period worked, and the type of job duties you performed. Include co-op or work-study jobs here rather than in the section on educational background.

If you have limited paid work experience, it is all right to list such paid or unpaid experience as babysitting, yardwork, newspaper delivery, and so on. You can also mention volunteer work experience such as being a junior volunteer, camp counselor, or campaign worker. If you think about it, you can probably identify many kinds of work experience that can compensate for having limited paid job experience.

The last section of the resume is a listing of *references*. These are individuals who have direct knowledge of your job performance. Two or three references are satisfactory. Present and previous employers and supervisors are best. A prospective employer will probably contact the references listed to inquire about your work habits, attitudes, and skills. If you are a recent graduate, you can list teachers who are familiar with your school work. A personal reference, such as a family friend, who can comment about your character may be listed as one of the references.

The resume should have a neat, error-free, professional appearance. Try to limit the length to one page. Type the resume on the same typewriter that was used for the letter of application. After it is typed, have multiple copies of the resume reproduced on a good quality paper.

FIGURE 4-9 Most quick-print shops can provide professional-looking, inexpensive copies of a resume. *Photo by Paul E. Meyers*

CONTACTING EMPLOYERS

As you have learned, filling out a job application form is one way to apply for a job. Other methods include applying in person, by phone, and by letter.

Applying in Person

A help-wanted ad or sign will often contain the phrase "apply in person." The ad or sign may give the name of a person to contact or it may say to "ask for the manager." In some cases, though, the ad only tells you the name of the company.

When you apply for a job in person, first impressions are very important. Some employers, in fact, judge an applicant's appearance, self-confidence, and social skills this way. You want to be well-groomed and appropriately dressed. Introduce yourself and explain who you are. (For example, you may want to say you are a high school work experience education student.) Then state your interest in the job advertised. If the first meeting goes well, the employer will probably ask you to fill out a job application form or leave a resume. Be prepared. Take along your personal data sheet and a copy of your resume.

FIGURE 4-10 When you apply for a job in person, first impressions are very imporant. *Photo by Paul E. Meyers*

Applying in person for a job is similar to going for a job interview. Most of the material in Chapter 5 on interviewing for a job will apply to this situation.

Applying by Telephone

Skillful use of the telephone is very important to a successful job search. By using the telephone you can make many contacts in the time it takes to make one personal visit. Of course, applying in person will still be necessary and desirable for some job leads.

The purpose of telephoning is to convert a job lead into an appointment for a job interview. In some cases, you may be following a suggestion from a family member or friend. An opening might not exist. For other leads, you know a certain opening is available. Perhaps you are answering a help-wanted ad.

FIGURE 4-11 Get organized and have your purpose in mind *before* you call an employer. *Courtesy of Brodock Press Inc.*

Whatever your reasons for making the call, the following guidelines should help you:

- Get organized before you call. Have your job-lead card, pen, and paper ready. Know the purpose of your call. Plan what you are going to say. Write down information quickly so you don't have to ask the person to repeat what was said.
- Call from a quiet place. You don't want any background noise during the call.
- Speak clearly and directly into the telephone mouthpiece. Don't have anything in your mouth when you talk.
- Give your name when calling and state your business as briefly as you can. Use the employer's name several times during the conversation. (Make sure it is correct.)
- Be courteous, friendly, and interested. Speak with a pleasant, even tone of voice. Put a "smile" in your voice, but talk naturally.
- Ask for a definite appointment, but don't sound pushy. If you get an appointment, write down the time, place, and the interviewer's name.

42 ■ SECTION 1 Preparing for Work

What Would You Do?

One of your job-lead cards is for an opening at a business owned by your best friend's mother. You are not sure how to apply for the job. Should you call her at home or at work? Should you have your friend ask his mother for you? Should you give her a resume even though she already knows you? Should you address her as Betty, which you normally do, or as Mrs. Thompson? What would you do?

Letter of Application

Another way to act on a job lead is to write a letter of application. You might do this when acting on a suggestion from another person or responding to a newspaper help-wanted ad. A letter of application is often known as a *cover letter* when it is mailed along with a resume.

An example of a combination cover letter and letter of application is shown in Figure 4-12. Such a letter should have four parts.

6428 Valley Road
Cambden, OH 67423
April 6, 1989

Mr. Donald Young
Service Manager
Smith Auto Sales, Inc.
274 Oakland Street
Cambden, OH 67423

Dear Mr. Young:

I learned from one of your employees, Mr. Ken Jenkins, that you plan to hire a new mechanic in a few weeks. I would like to apply for the position.

I have the training and experience to do the job. For the last two years, I have worked at Goodman's Tire and Auto Center. I primarily do tune-ups, general engine repair, front wheel alignments, and wheel and brake work. I am satisfied with my present job. However, I would like to work for a new car dealership where I can better use my diagnostic and mechanical abilities. I hold a state inspection license and own my own tools.

I have enclosed a copy of my resume that provides further details about my background. I could be available for employment following a two-week notice to my present employer.

May I have an appointment to discuss the job with you? I can be reached after 4:00 p.m. at (627) 353-2761. I would appreciate being considered for the job.

Sincerely,

Ronald Fisher

FIGURE 4-12 Sample letter of application

16. Prepare an overhead transparency of a sample cover letter to use in teaching this section.

* **WWYD Feature B.** The student should be advised to approach the job lead in the same formal manner as any other potential position.

1. In the first paragraph, you should explain your reason for writing. Name the job for which you are applying. Also, tell how you learned about the job.
2. Use the second paragraph to briefly point out your qualifications. Give the facts, but don't brag. (Employers will look carefully at this paragraph.)
3. The third paragraph calls attention to the resume. It may also be wise to give a date when you are available for employment.
4. In the last paragraph, ask for an appointment. Tell how you can be contacted. Close the letter with a courteous comment or a thank-you.

Notice that the sample letter is short and to the point. The purpose of the letter is to attract and hold the reader's interest. It should not attempt to give facts that are better stated in a resume and job interview. If you are qualified for the job, the letter and resume should make the employer want to invite you for an interview.

The form and appearance of the letter is also very important. Write several drafts of the letter until you feel that it is correct. Then have a teacher or parent check it over for correct spelling and grammar. Type the letter neatly following a standard business-letter format. Use a good typewriter or word processor that will produce clean copy.

FIGURE 4-13 Always type your letter of application and resume. *Photo by Paul E. Meyers*

Proofread the letter carefully to check for errors. Ask a friend or family member to do the same. Make a copy of the letter for your files. You will be able to use it in the future as a guide in writing additional letters.

17. Have students practice writing sample cover letters. Students should orient their letters to an actual job lead found in the classified ads.

F·E·A·T·U·R·E

Lie Detector and Honesty Tests

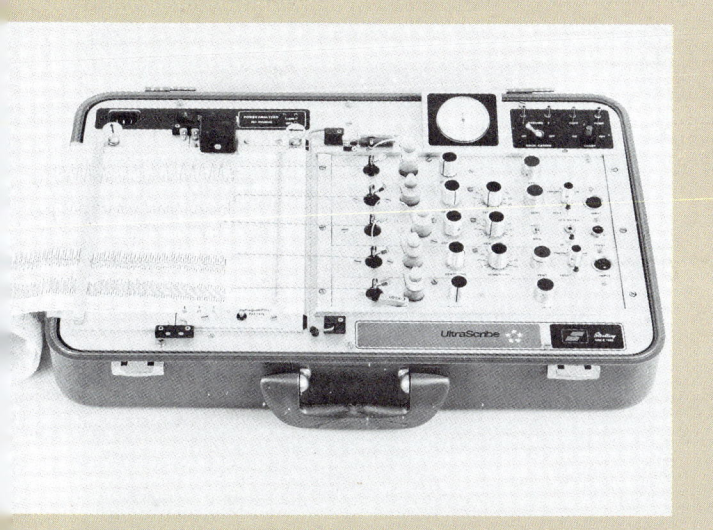

FIGURE 4-FEATURE Some employers claim that polygraph tests discourage employee theft. *Courtesy of Stoelting Company*

If you apply for a job in which money, merchandise, or drugs are handled, you may have to take an "honesty test." One type is a polygraph (lie detector) test. A polygraph is an electronic machine that is connected to the body of a subject. The person is asked a series of questions, while the machine records electronic impulses on a graph. If the person tells a lie, the device supposedly detects slight changes in the body's chemistry.

Many experts in the field question the accuracy of polygraph tests. As a result, Congress passed a law in 1988 to restrict the use of such tests. Before that, about two million polygraph tests were administered each year to employees and job applicants.

The law, which went into effect in December 1988, prohibits the use of polygraph tests for screening job applicants. An exception is for those seeking jobs in government, as security guards, or who will be handling narcotics. The new law also curtails the use of polygraphs for workers already on the job. Managers can't ask employees to take the test unless there is a "reasonable suspicion" that they have committed a crime. Even then the test is voluntary. An employee can't be fired for refusing to take it. The law will probably eliminate the use of most polygraph tests.

To avoid the problems and cost of polygraph tests, some companies use written honesty tests. Even before they were restricted, more written tests were probably administered each year than polygraphs. The tests consist of multiple choice or yes-no items. For example:

- Have you ever stolen anything from an employer?   yes   no
- Have you ever cheated in school?   yes   no
- Have you ever lied to a teacher or boss?   yes   no

The test is interpreted by comparing an applicant's answers to those of persons already judged to be honest. This type of test is as controversial as a polygraph test. Whether they help to screen out the most honest job applicant is open to debate. But unless laws are passed restricting their use, millions of job applicants will probably be required to take them.

---

* *Lie Detector and Honesty Tests.* The feature notes that a new federal law regulating polygraph tests went into effect in December 1988. Some lawyers suggest that part of the statute's vague language may have to be resolved in court.

Restrictions on the use of polygraph tests may lead to expanded use of written tests or other alternative measures. But the new law may encourage court cases testing legal issues regarding written tests. Be alert to information in newspapers and magazines that can be used to update this topic.

PRE-EMPLOYMENT TESTS

Dorothy lives in the city that is her state's capital. A large state university is nearby. The state government and university are two of the city's major employers.

Because they hire many employees, Dorothy applied for work at both the government's and the university's employment offices. She was surprised to learn that she would have to take a test before she would be asked to interview for a job. Dorothy found something that is very common.

To apply for almost all state and federal government jobs, applicants must take one or more *pre-employment tests*. A test that people take before being considered for a government job is called a *civil service test*.

Nongovernment (private) employers may also give pre-employment tests. Large employers often give them as part of the job application process. For entry-level jobs with the government or private employers, the most common types of tests are general ability tests and performance tests.

ability to work with others. There is also a structured interview and a medical test.

General Ability Tests

A general ability test measures basic learning skills such as reading, spelling, vocabulary, and arithmetic. These written tests are similar to the types of tests that you have taken throughout your school years.

Performance Tests

In a performance test you demonstrate skills needed for a specific occupation. Some performance tests are paper-and-pencil tests. An example would be a clerical skills test that requires you to proofread a business letter for possible errors.

Many performance tests are hands-on tests. They require you to use actual tools or machines. Suppose you are applying for a job as a data processing operator. Before being considered, you might be tested on a computer. By testing your skills now, employers avoid possible surprises later.

FIGURE 4-14 A pre-employment test may be either written or hands-on. *Photo by Paul E. Meyers*

18. One of the most detailed screenings takes about fifteen hours of an applicant's time. The applicant is tested in reading, verbal skills, mechanical skills, performance capabilities, and the

19. Emphasize the difference between general ability tests and performance tests and the difference between paper-and-pencil and hands-on performance tests.

Figure 4-15 If you have to take a test the next day, be sure to get enough rest. *Photo by Paul E. Meyers*

Taking a Test

Don't let the thought of taking a pre-employment test scare you away from a possible job. You will do better on the test if you don't spend time worrying about it. Most tests don't require any advance preparation. However, if you haven't used your skills for a while, you may want to do some practicing before you take a performance test.

Many tests have time limits. You will be told how much time you have. Listen carefully to the instructions you receive. If you don't understand what you are expected to do, be sure to ask questions *before* the test begins. After you start the test, work steadily and carefully. Don't spend too much time on any one question. If math is required, double check each answer. If you finish ahead of time, use the remaining time to go back and complete unanswered questions or recheck answers.

Once the test is over, do not worry about it. Employers don't expect perfection. They just want some idea of whether or not you can do the work. Do not leave until you know what the next step will be. Ask when and how you will be told the test results. Some employers will hold an interview immediately after a pre-employment test. The test may even be scored at this time. Other employers will invite applicants back after they have examined the job application and the test results. Regardless of the procedure, if your test scores are good, you probably will get a job interview. (Chapter 5 covers what to do in the interview.)

CHAPTER REVIEW

Chapter in Brief

- To help you in filling out a job application form, you need to prepare a personal data sheet. A personal data sheet contains the types of information most often requested by employers. You will also use the personal data sheet in preparing a job resume.
- Job application forms are used by employers to help sort out qualified people from a pool of applicants. Follow the recommended guidelines in the chapter to increase your chances of being selected for an interview.
- A job resume is often used when applying for a job in person or by letter. It should be limited to one page and contain the five types of information discussed in the chapter. The resume should have a neat, error-free, professional appearance.
- You can contact an employer about a job in person, by phone, or by letter. Applying in person usually also serves as a job interview. The purpose of phone and letter contacts is to gain an interview. In all three approaches, do everything possible to present yourself and your qualifications in the best possible light.
- Many employers administer pre-employment tests to job applicants. These may be either general ability tests or performance tests. After beginning the test, work steadily and carefully.

Words to Know

civil service test a pre-employment test that is administered to a job applicant seeking a government job.

cover letter a letter of application accompanied by a job resume that is sent to a potential employer.

job application form a form used by employers to collect personal, educational, and occupational information from a job applicant.

personal data sheet a summary of personal, educational, and occupational information that is used to help fill out a job application form and to prepare a job resume.

pre-employment test a paper-and-pencil test or performance exercise administered by an employer as part of the job application process.

references names of individuals listed on a job application form or resume that are qualified to provide information about the applicant.

resume a one-page description of a job seeker's history and qualifications for employment.

CHAPTER 4 Applying for a Job ■ 47

Questions to Answer
1. What are the two main uses for a personal data sheet?
2. What kinds of people might you give as job references?
3. Why do employers use job application forms? Give an example.
4. If a question on a job application form doesn't apply to you, how should you answer it?
5. Name the five kinds of information provided in a job resume.
6. You can contact employers about jobs in three ways. Name them.
7. What is the main advantage of using the telephone in a job search?
8. What is the main thing you should do in the last paragraph of a letter of application?
9. What are the two most common types of pre-employment tests? What is the purpose of each?
10. If you finish a pre-employment test before the time limit is up, what should you do?

Activities to Do
1. Develop a personal data sheet following the outline shown in Figure 4-2. Ask your instructor to look it over before it is typed.
2. Using your personal data sheet, practice filling out the sample forms provided by the teacher.
3. Prepare a job resume according to the format shown in Figure 4-7. After the resume is finished, write a sample letter of application. Turn in both of them to your instructor.
4. Practice role-playing in class how you would use a telephone to contact an employer for a job interview. One student can be the applicant and one the employer. Follow the guidelines on telephone use given earlier in this chapter.

Topics to Discuss
1. Young people sometimes make mistakes growing up. This might include getting into trouble at school, getting arrested for a minor infraction, or getting fired from a job. If a question is asked about things like this on a job application, how should you respond? What if it means that your answer will keep you from getting the job?
2. If you had an option to apply for a job in person or by letter, which would you choose? Discuss the advantages of each and why you chose the option you did.
3. What do you think about the practice of requiring a lie detector test as part of the job application process? Discuss both your and the employer's point of view.

---

1. (a) To help in filling out a job application form. (b) To help prepare a job resume.
2. Someone who knows you well enough to tell an employer about your abilities, work habits and attitudes, conduct, and so on. Examples include teachers, counselors, club advisors, former employers, co-workers, clergy, and so on.
3. To sort out the best qualified applicants from a large pool. A company might have dozens or hundreds of applications for only a few jobs.
4. Put "NA" for "not applicable."
5. (a) Personal information. (b) Career goals. (c) Education. (d) Work experience. (e) References.
6. (a) In person. (b) By phone. (c) By letter.
7. You can make many contacts in the time it takes to make one personal visit.
8. Ask for an appointment.
9. *General ability tests*—measure basic academic skills and reasoning. *Performance tests*—measure skills needed to perform a certain occupation.
10. Use the remaining time to go back and complete unanswered questions or re-check answers.

20. Advise students to answer all questions honestly and accurately. A student who has made a mistake in the past should be prepared to admit the mistake and to explain how the misbehavior has been or is being corrected.
21. Such tests raise a number of legitimate issues. However, there are certain jobs for which testing is probably justified. See if students can agree on some of them.

1. Point out how politely and confidently Ron responded to Mr. Young's statement, "It seems as if you would like to get out of your present job." Ask students why they think Mr. Young made the comment. (He could actually have that impression or he might be "fishing" for a hidden motive related to Ron's leaving.)

CHAPTER FIVE

Interviewing for a Job

OUTLINE
Before the Interview
During the Interview
After the Interview
Accepting or Rejecting a Job
Chapter Review

OBJECTIVES
After reading this chapter, you should be able to:
- Name and describe the five things to do in preparation for a job interview.
- List and discuss types of questions asked by interviewers.
- Summarize how one should act during a job interview.
- Name and describe the two things to do after an interview.
- Discuss how to respond to a job offer.

Ron Fisher had just gotten home from work when the telephone rang. He answered it: "Hello, Ron Fisher speaking."

"Hello, Ron, this is Donald Young at Smith Auto Sales. I have your letter of application and resume in front of me. It seems as if you would like to get out of your present job."

"No, sir, 'getting out' is not the main reason that I am looking for a job. I like my job at Goodman's, but most of our work involves doing routine repairs on older cars. I have some training and skills that I am not able to use there. I would like to work on newer cars and maybe be able to specialize in diagnostic work."

FIGURE 5-1 Sending a letter of application and resume can result in a phone call offering a job interview. *Photo by Paul E. Meyers*

"That's good to hear. I called Frank Hopkins at Hillside Community College and he said this is one of your strong areas."

"Yes, it is. Diagnostic work is actually very simple if you know how to use testing equipment."

"Ron, I would like to talk further with you and show you around our shop. Could you come in Saturday morning at 9:00?"

"Yes, I would be happy to. I will see you on Saturday at 9:00, Mr. Young. Thank you for calling."

BEFORE THE INTERVIEW

The *job interview* is a face-to-face meeting between you and an employer. It is generally the last and most important step in the job-seeking process. You will not be invited for an interview unless the employer thinks you may be qualified for the job. Your task is to show the employer that you *are* the person for the job.

An interview gives you a chance to "sell" what you can do for the employer. During the interview, an employer will judge your qualifications, appearance, and behavior. Equally important, the interview gives you a chance to *appraise* the job and the company. It enables you to decide if the position meets your job goals and interests, and whether the employer is the type of company that you want to work for. Before each interview, though, you should

2. This is why references are so important on the resume (Figure 4-7).

CHAPTER 5 Interviewing for a Job ■ 49

take the attitude that the job you are applying for is the one you want. To present yourself in the best possible light, you will need to do several things to prepare for the interview.

Practice Your Interview Skills

You may be a little nervous when you think about going for a job interview. That is normal. To reduce your anxiety and help build your confidence, you may want to role play some practice interviews. Something as important as a job interview deserves advance preparation. You would not go for your driver's license exam without practicing your driving skills, would you?

You may be able to set up a classroom interview situation. Arrange a desk and a couple of chairs like you might find them in an office. The instructor or a fellow student can play the role of an employer. Take turns being interviewed for a *hypothetical* job. Try to make "the interview" as realistic as possible.

Before you practice the interview, though, work together as a group to develop a list of questions for the interviewer to ask. These are some examples of the types of questions the employer may ask:

- I have already read your application form, but tell me something about yourself.
- Do you like school?
- What is your favorite subject? Why?
- What do you like to do in your spare time?
- Tell me why you applied for a job with us.
- How much do you know about the type of work we do here?
- Why do you think you would like this kind of work?
- Have you ever worked on this type of equipment before?
- Were you ever late to work in your last job?
- If I hired you, how long would you expect to stay with us?
- How much do you expect to make?
- What would you want to be doing in five years?
- When will you be available to start work?
- Do you have any questions?

As you can see from these examples, some questions can really put you on the spot if you are

Figure 5-2 Before you practice interviewing, develop a list of questions to ask. *Photo by David W. Tuttle*

3. All students should have an opportunity to be interviewed. If the class is large, perhaps several small groups can be organized to role play an interview. An alternative to role playing would be for students to write out and discuss in class answers to the questions listed.

not prepared for them. By practicing the interview, you will become more aware of what is involved in thinking about a question and answering it aloud. It can be a valuable learning experience to discover, for example, how much you stumble and hesitate. Don't try to memorize answers, but do practice until you can respond easily. Make special efforts to rid your speech of "uhs," "you knows," and similar responses.

Learn About the Company

Find out as much as possible about the job and the company *before* your interview. Start by asking people you know who might have information on the company. From personal contacts you may learn inside information. For example, you might find out about such things as the working conditions or the turnover rate of personnel. Further information may be available from the company itself. Ask about whether the company has any brochures, catalogs, annual reports, or other types of descriptive materials.

Next comes library research. There you can find several directories that tell about corporations by name. A librarian can help you find such references. Some facts to look for include products or services produced, growth rate, standing in the industry, and so on.

If information about the company is not available, find out something about the company's type of industry. Let's say that you are going to interview for a job in a property management firm. Find out what services these firms provide.

When you finish your research, write up a list of questions that you would like to ask about the job or the company. For example, you might ask: "Why did the job become vacant? Will any more training be required? What are the working hours? Who will my supervisor be if I get the job?" It is generally best to avoid asking about salary or benefits. If the information is not provided by the interviewer, you can ask after you have been offered the job.

FIGURE 5-3 An interviewer will be pleased if you have made the effort to learn about the company. *Photo by Paul E. Meyers*

4. Ask students to identify any other unsuitable words or phrases that they may have noticed during the role playing.

5. As you discuss library research, you may wish to assign Activity 1.

6. Ask students to name types or samples of work (photos, drawings, designs, artwork, and so on) that might be appropriate to take along on an interview.

Assemble Needed Materials

Have the materials you plan to take to the interview ready to go. These include the job-lead card, personal data sheet, resume, copies of any correspondence, pen and paper, a list of questions you will ask, and work permit, if needed. Carry all of the materials in a large envelope or briefcase so you won't lose anything.

of time and look around to see how people are dressed. Remember, though, you are dressing for an interview, not the job you'll be doing.

Whatever clothes you decide to wear, they should be clean, pressed, and in good condition. Clothes don't have to be expensive to look neat. Don't forget to clean or shine your shoes. Heavy use of jewelry and other accessories should be avoided.

FIGURE 5-4 If your work is the kind you can show, take samples along to the interview. *Reproduced from Better Homes and Gardens magazine. Copyright Meredith Corporation 1987. All rights reserved.*

Attend to Appearance

Your grooming and dress will influence the interviewer's final decision. Choose clothes that are appropriate for the job setting. Ron, for example, has an interview for a job as an auto mechanic. It is not necessary that he wear a coat and tie. On the other hand, jeans, T-shirt, and sneakers are too casual. Loud colors are never acceptable, nor are fad clothes. If you have doubts about what to wear, ask your work experience coordinator or counselor for advice. Or you might visit the company a day ahead

7. Note that Chapter 11 deals with grooming and dress in more detail. You may wish to integrate portions of Chapter 11 here.

FIGURE 5-5 A clean, neat, well-groomed appearance is important for all job interviews. *Courtesy of Johnson & Wales College*

52 ■ SECTION 1 Preparing for Work

What Would You Do?

You have an allergy to various food products. Occasionally, you unknowingly eat something that causes an allergic reaction. An unpleasant looking skin rash appears on your face and hands. The day before a job interview you have such a reaction. You are very upset and discouraged. You don't want to go to the interview like this. What would you do?

*

Careful grooming is also very important. If you need a haircut, plan ahead to get it done. On the day of the interview, a shower or bath is a must. Also, wash your hair, clean your nails, and brush your teeth. Men should shave or trim beards and mustaches. No heavy smelling colognes or aftershaves, please. Women may use makeup, lipstick, and so on, but they should be used sparingly.

uncomfortable with the situation, then the interviewer should be contacted with an explanation and a request to reschedule the appointment.

Check Last-minute Details

Going to an interview at the wrong place or at the wrong time may seem dumb. People do it all the time, though. Don't miss an interview by making a silly mistake like that. It will help if you write the date, time, and place of the interview on a job-lead card. Check and then double-check the information. You may want to make a trial run so that you will know where the company is located.

If more than a week goes by between the time you made the appointment and the actual interview, then call to *confirm* it. Here is what Ellen did.

"Good morning, Solar Products Company."

"Hello, this is Ellen Simon. I'm calling to confirm my appointment for 10:00 tomorrow with Ms. Han."

"Wait just a moment, I'll check her calendar. Yes, Ms. Simon, she has you down."

"Good. Thank you. I'll be there tomorrow at 10:00."

Plan to arrive at the interviewer's office five to ten minutes ahead of schedule. Introduce yourself and tell why you are there. Don't take anyone with you to the interview. You don't want to give the impression that you can't do things on your own.

8

9

FIGURE 5-6 Don't go to a job interview smelling of cigarette smoke or strong food odors. *Photo by Paul E. Meyers*

* **WWYD Feature A.** If the rash isn't too bad, the student should probably go to the interview and provide an explanation of the nature of the alergy. If the rash is severe and/or the student is very

FIGURE 5-7 Anticipate delays. Leave early for your job interview. *Photo by Paul E. Meyers*

8. Ask students to share any experiences in which they may have missed an appointment, gone to the wrong place, or the like. Discussion should focus on how to avoid such mistakes.

9. To be on the safe side, students should plan to arrive about twenty minutes before the appointment. They should not go to the interviewer's office until shortly before the meeting.

You may have to wait a short time in an outer office or reception area. During that time, you should relax, read, or look over your list of questions. Be pleasant toward others in the reception area. Don't smoke, chew gum, or do anything distracting. The interviewer may later ask for the receptionist's opinion of you.

DURING THE INTERVIEW

You may wonder what type of person the interviewer will be. Unfortunately, you have no way of knowing. If you have five job interviews, you will probably find five completely different personalities. It is not necessary for you to like the interviewer or for the interviewer to like you. The interviewer is looking for the best person to fill a job. You aren't there to be social. You are looking for a job.

10. Prepare yourself to deal with whatever you may find. Remain calm and do your best. If you have prepared well for the interview, you have done your homework up to this point.

FIGURE 5-8 Greet the interviewer with a firm handshake. Avoid limp or bone-crushing handshakes. *Photo by Paul E. Meyers*

10. Ask students who have already had interviews to describe their first impressions of the interviewer.

F·E·A·T·U·R·E

Teleconferencing

◆ ◆ ◆

Video and satellite technology is now making possible a new approach to job interviewing. In October 1984, a company called BPI Source sponsored the first live, nationwide teleconference. Thousands of college students at thirty schools watched ten-minute videos of twenty participating companies. The purpose of the teleconference was to acquaint students with companies looking for graduates.

Eight hour-long programs were telecast to the schools. Program guides that listed the time of each company's telecast were given to students. A student could then choose which presentation to watch. Teleconferencing is an efficient and interesting way to get company information across to large numbers of students.

Because the teleconference was broadcast live, audience members could write down questions to be called to the broadcast site. The most relevant questions were superimposed on the screen and answered by company officials. After the presentation, qualified students were invited to mail in their resumes. Companies then scheduled campus visits to interview selected students.

The approach is currently being used primarily with college students. It is possible that the approach will be used in the future with other groups as well. A related development may be the production of company videos that students can check out at a library and view at home.

FIGURE 5-FEATURE Teleconferencing saves a lot of interviewing time for students and company officials. *Photo by David W. Tuttle*

Teleconferencing. This is an example of an innovation that should be read and discussed in terms of a future trend. You should be alert to any new information that might be used to update this topic. Students might be assigned the task of finding out what recent developments may have evolved in the general area of teleconferencing.

FIGURE 5-9 Be pleasant and friendly but businesslike during the interview. *Reprinted with permission of Communispond, Inc. Management Consultants in Business Communication*

Effective Communication

Let the interviewer set the tone and pace of the interview. Adjust yourself to the style of the interviewer. For example, if the interviewer is serious and businesslike, your style should be similar. If the interviewer is cheerful and outgoing, you may need to brighten up a little. Try to establish a *compatible* relationship with the interviewer.

Communication skills, which are important at every step of the job search, are more so in the job interview. Be sure to listen carefully and speak clearly. Answer each question briefly, but don't give one-word or one-line answers. If you think that the interviewer hasn't understood your answer or that you haven't made yourself clear, try again. Stay on the topic until you are sure that the interviewer has understood your message.

Answer a question only after the interviewer is completely finished. Otherwise, you risk making a bad impression. You may also never find out the exact question or hear important information that may be added to the question.

Listening to the interviewer is as important as speaking thoughtfully and clearly. The ability to listen shows your attentiveness and reflects on your interest in the job. At times, you may want to ask the interviewer the meaning of a word or phrase. Do so. You must understand a question before you can answer it.

Nonverbal Communication

Proper *body language* (nonverbal communication) may help or hinder communication. During the interview, sit comfortably, but don't slouch. Keep your hands on your lap. Don't look at your hands or feet during the interview. Maintain good eye contact throughout the interview, but don't stare. During the interview, keep a pleasant expression on your face.

FIGURE 5-10 What kind of message do you think is conveyed by this body language? *Courtesy of 3M*

FIGURE 5-11 If the interviewer does not already have it, present your resume at some point during the interview. *Photo by Paul E. Meyers*

Also be aware of the interviewer's body language. Watch for nonverbal clues. If the interviewer's body language conveys something negative, think about what you are doing or saying. Then change what needs to be changed.

Asking Questions

An interview involves two-way communications. Of course, the interviewer will ask you questions. Did you know that the interviewer will also expect *you* to ask questions? It is wise to refer to a list of questions you have made beforehand. Hold the list near your lap so you can glance at it as you talk.

Don't be in a hurry to ask questions. Wait until the interviewer invites them. A pause in the conversation once the interview is well underway may be the time for you to bring up your questions. Be careful, though, not to interrupt the interviewer. By all means, if you have not already been invited to do so, request an opportunity to ask your questions before the interview ends.

Your questions should indicate a sincere interest in the company and the job. Good questions are concrete and show that you have prepared for the interview. For example, you might ask, "What opportunities are there to advance within the company?"

Use good judgment in deciding how much time to take up with questions. Try to sense whether or not the interviewer is on a tight schedule. If time seems pressing, ask only your most important questions.

Concluding the Interview

Suppose the interview is almost over. The employer has not said when a decision will be made about the job. What do you do? Ask about it. If the interviewer asks you to call back or supply more information, note it on the job-lead card.

11. Explain and demonstrate different types of body language or assign students this task. It should not be difficult for them to find relevant books and articles.
12. This might also be the time to show samples of any work that was brought along.
13. Ask students to provide other possible questions to ask.

14. A receptionist or secretary may buzz the intercom to signal the interviewer that a specified amount of time has elapsed.

SOUTHWEST REALITY COMPANY
Applicant Evaluation

Name _____ Interview date _____

Position applied for _____

Criteria/comments	Poor	Good	Excellent
1. Appearance:			
2. Poise:			
3. Responses:			
4. Grammar and speech:			
5. Background:			
6. Knowledge of job requirements:			
7. Interest in company:			
8. Potential:			

SUMMARY AND RECOMMENDATION

Strengths:

Weaknesses:

*Based on interview, review of application, and follow-up, should an offer of employment be made? Yes _____ No _____

Date _____ Interviewer _____

FIGURE 5-12 Some interviewers use forms like this to help them rate a job candidate.

Try to get a feeling for when the interview has run its course. The interviewer may stand or simply say right out, "Well, I think that I have enough information about you at this time." To help bring an interview to its conclusion you can ask, "Are there any more questions I can answer?"

Many job applicants fail to ask for the job. This is a big mistake. Tell the interviewer if you want the job. Say something like, "I know I can do the work, Mr. Young, and I would like to have the job."

If the company can't use you, ask about other employers who may need a person with your skills.

Thank the interviewer, shake hands, and leave. On the way out, thank the secretary or receptionist.

AFTER THE INTERVIEW

You can benefit from every interview, no matter what the outcome. Take time to think about the experience as soon as possible after the interview. Review any mistakes that you think you made and consider how you could have avoided them. Could you have been better prepared? Did you mention everything about yourself that the employer needed to know? Think about what you did well. Would these things help you in other interviews?

15. You might have several students role play asking for a job. This is a bold action that many job applicants are reluctant to take.

16. This is another place where you might ask students who have had interviews to share their experiences.

Promptly send a *follow-up letter* to the interviewer. Such a letter may accomplish many things:

1. It helps to build a courteous relationship.
2. Having your letter keeps your name in front of the interviewer.
3. Taking time to write a letter tells the interviewer of your continued interest.
4. The letter allows you to reinforce key points you discussed during the interview.
5. If you forgot to mention something important during the interview, you can put it in your follow-up letter.

A sample follow-up letter is shown in Figure 5-13.

Suppose the interviewer told you that you wouldn't be hired. Or perhaps you are no longer interested in the job. Send a letter to thank the interviewer for considering you.

When writing a follow-up letter, refer to the guidelines given about preparing a letter of application. The rules are similar for both types of letters. If someone helped arrange your interview, send a note of appreciation to him or her. This should be a simple, handwritten thank-you note.

After completing these steps, wait and try to relax. Continue to pursue other job leads in the meantime. If you have not heard from the company in a week, get in touch with them. You can do so sooner if the interviewer indicated that a decision would be made in less than this time.

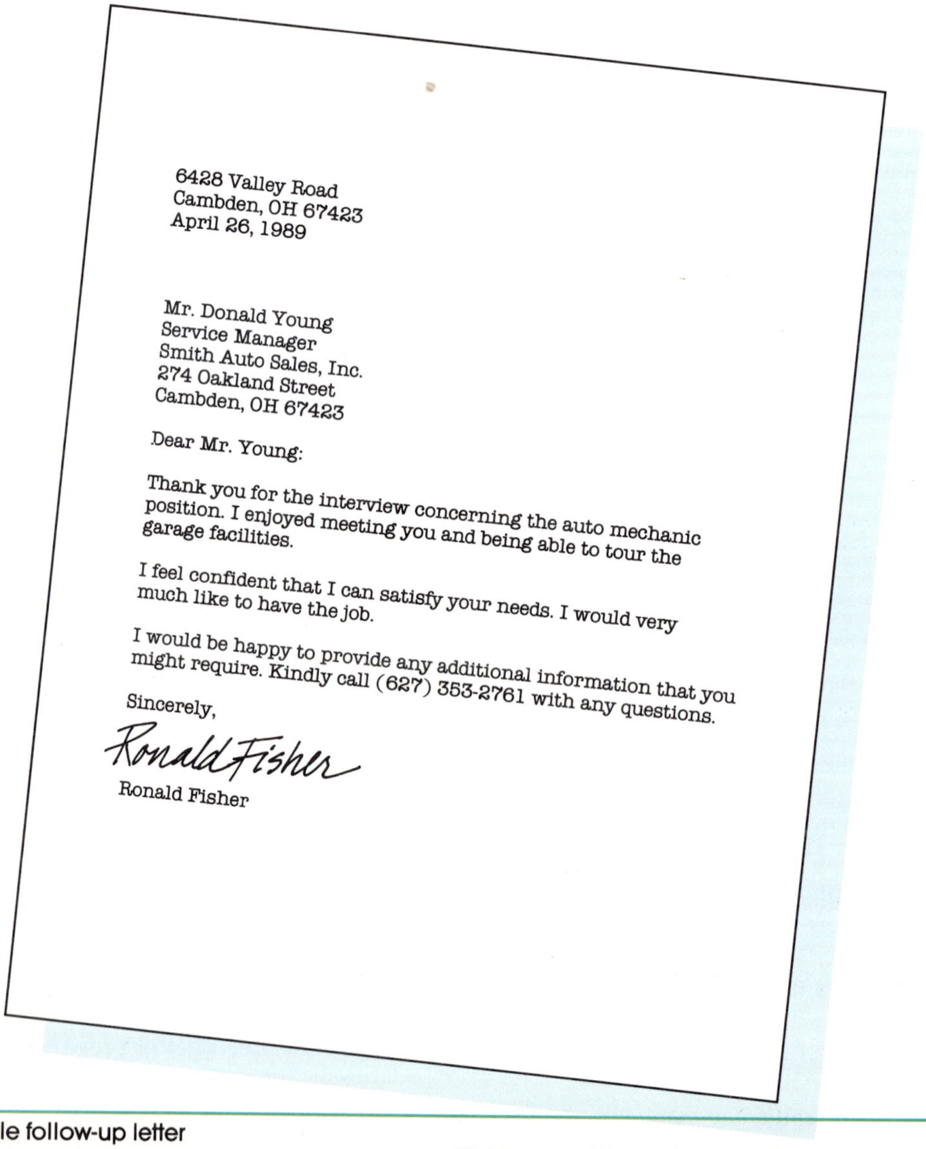

6428 Valley Road
Cambden, OH 67423
April 26, 1989

Mr. Donald Young
Service Manager
Smith Auto Sales, Inc.
274 Oakland Street
Cambden, OH 67423

Dear Mr. Young:

Thank you for the interview concerning the auto mechanic position. I enjoyed meeting you and being able to tour the garage facilities.

I feel confident that I can satisfy your needs. I would very much like to have the job.

I would be happy to provide any additional information that you might require. Kindly call (627) 353-2761 with any questions.

Sincerely,

Ronald Fisher

Ronald Fisher

FIGURE 5-13 Sample follow-up letter

17. You may wish to review the guidelines with the class.
18. Who might be sent a note of appreciation? Show or attach to a bulletin board samples of appropriate thank-you notes.

ACCEPTING OR REJECTING A JOB

You may be hired or rejected during an interview. Usually, though, the employer makes a decision later. Employers like to interview several people for a job before making a choice.

A job offer is generally made by telephone. This gives the employer and the applicant a chance to discuss the details of the job offer. If the *conditions of employment* have not been discussed earlier, now is the time to ask about them. These include such things as working hours, salary, fringe benefits, and so on. You will want to know when you start work and if there is anything special that you need to bring or be prepared to do the first day. For example, you might need to pick up a uniform.

It is possible to be considered for a job at different places at the same time. Let's say that you have been interviewed for jobs at both Burger Barn and Chicken Shack. Burger Barn offers you a job and you accept it. You should phone Chicken Shack and tell them you have taken another job.

What if a company offers you a job you don't want? Be polite. (You never know when you may be contacting them again.) Give a brief explanation of your reasons. Regardless of your reasons *do not* criticize the employer.

What Would You Do?

You have been offered two different jobs. The first job would be acceptable. It is a traditional job for a person of your sex. The second job is a nontraditional job. You would be the only person of your sex out of eight employees who work there. You can't decide which job to take. What would you do?

Not all of your interviews will result in job offers. In fact, most of them probably won't. Dealing with rejection is something we all must learn to do. Being disappointed is normal. Don't, however, react with anger toward an employer. By accepting rejection gracefully, you keep alive your chances for a future job. For example, what happens if the person chosen for the job turns it down? You may be next in line for it.

In all companies, employees come and go. New jobs open. If you are good enough to have been invited for an interview, then you are qualified for a job. Don't get discouraged. Whether at that company or somewhere else, a job will open up for you.

---

19. Some employers will call with a tentative job offer and an invitation to come in and discuss conditions of employment. Or an employer might make a tentative offer by phone and then mail written conditions of employment for consideration.

20. The point here is that Chicken Shack (or other employer) should be informed as soon as a job is accepted. Discuss with students what they should do if Burger Barn offers a job, but they are unsure about accepting it or would rather have a different job. (Have them explain to the caller that they are pleased to have been offered the job, but would like twenty-four hours to think about it before making a final decision.) Caution students about the risk involved in turning down a firm offer to wait for something that may not be forthcoming.

WWYD Feature B. Ask students for examples of traditional and nontraditional jobs (for both genders). Allow them to openly discuss this issue. Encourage students to pursue goals based on interests and aptitudes, not gender, race, or other factors.

21. For other than entry-level jobs, it is quite common for a preferred candidate to turn down a job offer.

CHAPTER REVIEW

Chapter in Brief

- The job interview is generally the last and most important step in the job-seeking process. In preparation for an interview, you should: practice your interview skills, learn about the employer, assemble needed materials, attend to appearance, and check last-minute details.
- During the interview, adjust yourself to the style of the interviewer. Be sure to listen carefully and speak clearly. An interview isn't just one way. Be prepared to ask the interviewer questions. If you want the job, tell the interviewer near the end of the interview.
- After the interview, take time to think about the experience. Review any mistakes you made and consider how to correct them next time. Promptly send a follow-up letter to the interviewer.
- A job offer may be made following the interview or later by phone or letter. Before accepting the offer, make sure you understand the conditions of employment. If you are rejected for a job, accept it gracefully. Don't do anything to close the door on a possible later offer or opportunity.

Words to Know

appraise to evaluate someone or something, such as a potential employer.

body language nonspoken communication through physical movements, expressions, and gestures.

compatible something that is pleasant or agreeable, such as a relationship with a job interviewer.

conditions of employment the specific details of a job offer such as working hours, salary or wages, fringe benefits, and so on.

confirm to verify or make firm, such as calling to confirm (check on) an appointment.

follow-up letter a thank-you letter sent to an interviewer following a job interview.

hypothetical something imagined or pretended, such as a potential job.

job interview a face-to-face meeting between a job seeker and a potential employer.

Questions to Answer

1. A job interview provides you with a chance to do two things. Name them.
2. From the interviewer's standpoint, what is the purpose of the job interview?
3. Name the five things that you should do to prepare for a job interview. Why is each important?

---

1. (a) To sell what you can do for the employer. (b) To appraise the job, the employer, and the company.
2. To determine whether the applicant is the person for the job. To judge the applicant's qualifications, appearance, behavior, and the like.
3. (a) Practice interview skills (to reduce anxiety and help build confidence). (b) Learn about the employer (to be informed and to show intrest). (c) Assemble needed material (to have everything needed for the interview). (d) Attend to appearance (this will influence the interviewer's final decision). (e) Check last-minute details (so you will be at the right place at the right time).

CHAPTER 5 Interviewing for a Job ■ 61

4. Is it necessary that you like the interviewer? Why or why not?
5. Give an example to show how you might adjust your interview style to that of the interviewer.
6. Why shouldn't you give one-word or one-line answers in an interview?
7. What is a major mistake that applicants make at the end of a job interview?
8. What five things may a follow-up letter accomplish?
9. You are being considered for two jobs at the same time. You receive one job offer and accept it. What should you do next?
10. Why is it important to accept a job rejection gracefully?

4. Not necessarily. It is only important that you be able to communicate and that both of you accomplish your respective purposes.
5. If the interviewer is cheerful and outgoing, you may want to brighten up a little.
6. The interviewer will be interested in hearing a more detailed answer or explanation. Also, you don't want to convey the idea that you are nervous or insecure.
7. If interested in the position, they fail to ask for the job.
8. (a) Helps build a courteous relationship. (b) Keeps your name in front of the interviewer. (c) Conveys your continued interest. (d) Reinforces key points discussed during the interview. (e) Mentions something important not covered in the interview.
9. Phone the second party and explain that you have accepted another job.
10. It is a sign of maturity and good manners. Also, it keeps open the possibility for a later offer or opportunity.

Activities to Do

1. Choose a well-known company. Go to a public library and ask a librarian to direct you to information about business corporations. *(Standard and Poor's Register of Corporations* is one resource.) Look up the company that you selected. Write down a half-page or so of information that you think would be important for a job applicant to know about the company. Turn in the paper to your instructor.
2. In class, practice role playing a job interview.
3. If equipment is available, videotape the role-playing interview. View and discuss the tapes later. Seeing yourself on tape can often be quite informative.
4. Prepare a follow-up letter to a hypothetical job interview. Turn it in to your instructor for evaluation.

Topics to Discuss

1. Some class members have probably already had job interviews. People who have had interviews may want to share their experiences with the class. Ask your classmates about things you would like to know regarding a job interview.
2. Despite your best planning efforts, an unexpected emergency or problem arises that prevents you from attending a job interview. How should you handle a situation like this?
3. A person with advanced education or highly marketable skills can often negotiate favorable conditions of employment following a job offer. Discuss realistically how much bargaining power a person has in applying for an entry-level job.

22. An alternative to this would be for the student to write to a company requesting descriptive information. Students could pool the information into some type of resource file maintained in the classroom. Future students could use the resource file as well as add to and update it.
23. Consider giving students the responsibility of planning and managing this activity. Students might be able to borrow videotaping equipment from friends or family members. This can be a very relevant and enjoyable activity for students.
24. Group instruction and individual help will probably be needed in order for students to complete this activity. Rely on experience gained from similar assignments in previous chapters to guide completion of this activity.
25. Experienced class members can share insights at this and several other points throughout the chapter.
26. The nature of the problem or emergency (forgot to get up, car wouldn't start, illness, accident, and so on) will have some influence on how to handle the situation. Generally speaking, though, the best soluiton is to contact the interviewer as soon as possible, honestly explain the circumstance, apologize for missing the meeting, and ask for another appointment.
27. Realistically, a beginning worker has little or no negotiating power and shouldn't expect any.

High Five

DETERMINATION SHOWS THE WAY

Kelly McCormack was born with only one hand, the result of a birth defect. As a child, making friends was difficult. Kelly would often hear children on the playground say, "Go away, you look funny with one hand." She would run home crying because no one would be her friend. The teasing continued throughout elementary and junior high school.

In the ninth grade, Kelly wanted to take a typing class. She went to the teacher to get permission. "You can't type. You don't have enough fingers," the teacher said. Kelly just looked at the teacher and cried. This was the start of a turning point in Kelly's life. She was determined to show the teacher that, given a chance, she could type.

The next year there was a new typing teacher. Again, Kelly asked for permission to enroll in the class. Dr. Mary Haskins, the teacher, recalls that day. "I just looked at her and thought, 'Oh my goodness.' It was obvious that she was severely disabled as far as typing was concerned."

Kelly was so determined that Dr. Haskins agreed to give her a try. The teacher warned her, however, not to expect much. Certainly, she would never be a secretary.

In the typing class, Kelly was left largely to work on her own. Despite early doubts, she kept trying. Before long she had developed a system of her own. She used the five fingers on her left hand to strike most of the keys. She found that her partial right arm could be used to hit the carriage return and similar chores.

After three months of hard and frustrating work, Kelly began to see results. Not only was she learning to type, but her speed was steadily increasing. By the end of the year she was typing 60 words a minute—the fastest in the class.

"Kelly's a very special girl and deserves a lot of credit for her accomplishments," says Dr. Haskins. "I didn't do anything except leave her to work on her own. She has taught me a lesson. Never will I underestimate a student's ability to overcome obstacles."

In the 11th grade, Kelly decided to take Distributive Cooperative Training (DCT). The reason, according to her, "Was to get out of school early." After seeing how active other DCT students were, she decided to get involved. She ran for secretary of the club, and won!

"It was the best thing that ever happened to me," said Kelly. "From then on, I felt good about myself. I felt that people really liked me. I was confident that I was the one for secretary. I talked with other people more, and was happy."

Later in the year, Kelly was encouraged by her DCT Coordinator to run for state secretary. "No way would I win," she thought to herself. But then she began to think that maybe she could do it. She took the plunge and threw her name into the hat. She was frightened though, that nobody would vote for her because she looked different. When all of the votes were counted, Kelly McCormack had become state secretary of the Cooperative Education Clubs of Florida.

"Cooperative education has done a lot for me," says Kelly. "I have learned many things about myself and about leadership and determination. I have learned not to give up—there is always a way."

Kelly also has a good sense of humor. When asked what she considers the toughest part of having only one hand, she replies with a smile, "I have to wear all my rings on one hand."

Section Two

Working on the Job

◆

Chapter 6 Beginning a New Job
Chapter 7 Expectations of Employers
Chapter 8 Worker Rights and Protections
Chapter 9 Human Relations at Work
Chapter 10 Earnings and Job Advancement
Chapter 11 Appearance on the Job

◆

Once you find a job, you will need to turn your thoughts and energies to working on the job. Your first few days and weeks will be busy, exciting, and sometimes confusing. In Chapter 6, you will learn what to expect as you begin a new job. You will also discover how you and your job fit into the overall organizational structure of the company.

After a short adjustment period, you will need to perform the same as other employees. In Chapter 7, you will learn what your employer expects regarding job performance and work habits and attitudes. An employer will evaluate your on-the-job performance. You will learn how such performance evaluations are conducted.

What rights and protections do you have on the job? As a worker, you are entitled to fair and honest treatment regarding wages, hours, and equal pay. You have a right to work in a safe and healthful environment. You are entitled to be treated fairly regardless of your sex, race, or other factors. These are all explained in Chapter 8.

Chapter 9 deals with human relations at work. Your job success will depend on how well you get along with bosses, co-workers, and customers. In addition to working with individuals, you need to be able to work with groups. Guidelines are provided to help you be a more effective member of a work group.

Everyone looks forward to receiving a paycheck. In Chapter 10, you will learn about different forms of compensation and how your paycheck is figured. If you perform well on the job, you can look forward to pay raises and promotions. In this chapter, you will discover what to do in order to advance on the job.

Chapter 11 deals with the importance of a good appearance. No matter what the job, you will be expected to groom and dress properly. A proper appearance, however, varies from job to job. You will learn how to groom and dress in a way that fits your job.

CHAPTER SIX

Beginning a New Job

OUTLINE

Pre-employment Anxiety
Reporting for Work
Orientation to the Workplace
Organizational Structure
Working Under Supervision
Payroll Withholding
Chapter Review

OBJECTIVES

After reading this chapter, you should be able to:
- Recognize that anxiety toward beginning a new job is normal.
- Explain what to expect from an employer when beginning a new job.
- Describe how an organization chart shows the flow of authority and responsibility within an organization.
- List areas for which employers have policies and rules.
- Identify ways to work effectively with a supervisor.
- Illustrate how to fill out a Form W-4.

The job search is over. Your new job is about to start. You will be leaving or at least spending less time in the familiar world of the classroom. The changes you will experience may be scary at first. Remember what it was like going from junior high to high school? A similar experience awaits you now. You are going from the known into the unknown. This can be exciting and frightening at the same time. You are going from high school into the world of work. By taking the time now to learn what to expect, you can prepare yourself for a smooth transition into your new role as a worker.

FIGURE 6-1 Becoming a worker will mark the start of a new phase of your life. *Courtesy of Southern California Edison, G. O'Loughlin*

PRE-EMPLOYMENT ANXIETY

Anxiety is the state of feeling worried or uneasy about what may happen in the future. You may have feelings of anxiety about beginning a new job. Try to relax. Remember that the employer chose your job application from among many others. You were interviewed because the employer thought you were qualified. You were hired because the employer believed you were the best person for the job.

Starting a new job is not like wilderness training. Your employer won't expect you to endure extreme temperatures, sleep on the hard ground, and eat cold beans. Your employer probably isn't going to test you to see if you can make it. Believe it or not, your employer wants you to succeed.

Your employer more than likely understands that you are going through a stressful time. He or she understands that it will take time for you to learn the company's rules, procedures, and any other policies.

4. If caught off guard by such a call, explain that is appropriate to ask the caller to hold while getting a pad and pencil. Better yet, plan ahead and have pad and pencil near the phone.

REPORTING FOR WORK

What you do on the first day of work depends on the type and size of the company you have joined. Let's look at Francine Gordon's first day.

Francine applied for a job at Northeast Electric Power Company. Two weeks later, she received a telephone call from the assistant personnel manager, who offered Francine a job as an equipment operator. Since this was the job Francine wanted, she accepted right away. The assistant personnel manager then told Francine to report to work at 9:30 on Monday morning for a new employee orientation. He also told Francine that a parking decal for her car and a map showing the location of the meeting room would be sent to her in the mail.

Francine arrived at the plant about 9:15 on Monday. A uniformed guard at the entrance motioned for her to stop. Before Francine could say anything, the guard asked her if she was a new employee. The guard pointed out the building entrance and the lot in which she was to park.

What Would You Do?

You have just been hired as a clerk at a grocery store. Your new supervisor tells you to report for work tomorrow at 4:00 sharp. You agree to do this and leave the store. Suddenly you remember that you have to take a make-up exam at school tomorrow afternoon. What would you do?

Francine parked her car and took out her map. She was glad to have the map. The building seemed to be as long as three football fields. She entered the building and walked down the hall. She finally found the correct meeting room. There, Mr. Walsh, the assistant personnel manager, gave Francine a name tag and directed her to a seat.

At 9:35, a woman went to the front of the room. Mr. Walsh introduced here as Mrs. Ramos, the personnel manager. Mrs. Ramos welcomed the twelve new employees and introduced several staff members. Then she gave a fifteen-minute slide presentation about the company. Before seeing the program, Francine had not thought much about the number of people and businesses that depended on Northeast Electric Power Company. She was already feeling proud about working for such an important company.

FIGURE 6-2 Most employers and co-workers will help you adjust to your job. *Photo by Gabe Palmer*

FIGURE 6-3 Some companies have formal orientation sessions. *Photo by Paul E. Meyers*

*WWYD Feature A. Try to reschedule the exam. If this cannot be done, call the employer and explain that you forgot about the test. Ask if you can report to work as soon as the test is completed.

5. Tell students to take the initiative in introducing themselves to company personnel and new co-workers.

66 ■ SECTION 2 Working on the Job

6 Mr. Walsh then took over the meeting. After answering some questions, he passed out a folder to each person. The folder contained a "Policies and Procedures Manual" and many forms. The group filled out forms and discussed the information in the folder for the rest of the day.

Some large companies, such as Northeast Electric Power Company, have a very formal employee orientation program. Because of the large number of employees that Northeast Electric Power Company hires, such a program is efficient. The company can orient several new workers at once. This kind of detailed program assures that all employees have received the same information. Many problems can be prevented when all employees are following the same set of rules.

Now, let's contrast Francine's first day with that of another beginning worker. Denny Liu was hired as a salesclerk at Rogers', a small men's store in North Plaza Mall. Denny learned about the job opening at Rogers' while he was working as a cooperative education student at another mall store. He applied for the job in person. After a short interview with Bob Brown, the manager, he was hired on the spot. Denny agreed to report for work after giving the other store two weeks notice.

Three weeks later Denny arrived for his first day at work. Bob was unlocking the entrance. After greeting each other, Bob and Denny walked to the rear of the store. Along the way, Bob flipped on the lights. Denny smiled to himself. He was amused at how different the back of the shop looked compared to the shop's front display area. Bob pointed toward the coffee pot and asked Denny to start it while he checked the mail.

While the coffee was brewing, Denny and Bob exchanged small talk as Bob sorted the mail. A few minutes later Courtney and Evan, two other employees, came into the shop. Bob introduced Denny to them. They all chatted for a few minutes. Courtney and Evan then went to get the shop ready for its 10:00 opening.

7 A two-weeks notice is generally the minimum amount of time required before leaving a job. Some employers request a longer period. You can leave earlier if the employer concurs.

FIGURE 6-4 At some companies, job orientation is very informal. *Courtesy of SIUC Photocommunications*

6. A company orientation may also include remarks and/or information from a union representative.

CHAPTER 6 Beginning a New Job ■ 67

Bob gave Denny a few forms to sign and a payroll card. He told Denny how to keep track of the number of hours he worked. They then walked around the shop while Bob explained procedures and pointed out features of certain merchandise.

Bob told Denny that he wanted him to begin working at the ties and accessories counter. If the other salesclerks got busy, he was to leave the counter area to help out.

"Denny, you know what goes on in a men's store," Bob said. "If you have questions or need help, ask us. We'll just play it by ear."

By 10:10, Denny had waited on his first customer and made his first sale. Overall, he had a good first day. He had to ask a few questions, and Bob made a few suggestions. Denny knew he was going to like working at Rogers'.

What a difference between Francine's and Denny's first days! Denny spent most of his first day waiting on customers. Francine, on the other hand, spent much of her first day learning more about Northeast Electric Power Company. In fact, Francine didn't actually start work until two weeks later. She spent the first two weeks in class learning how to be an equipment operator.[8]

FIGURE 6-5 In some jobs, employees start performing their duties on their first day at work. *Courtesy of NCR Corporation*

FIGURE 6-6 Some employees spend their first days on the job learning about the company and how to perform their jobs. *Courtesy of Niagara Mohawk Power Corporation*

8. On-the-job training (OJT) is another practice of large employers. This is explained further in Chapter 32.

68 ■ SECTION 2 Working on the Job

Clearly, one person's first day at work may be quite different from another person's first day at work. However, Francine and Denny did many similar things and were provided with similar kinds of information. This was just done in different ways. Can you think of some ways that Francine's and Denny's first days were similar?

What Would You Do?

Upon beginning a new job, you may know very little about a company or its management. This can happen despite your best efforts to research the company and ask thoughtful questions in a job interview. Suppose that during the orientation meeting you discover things about the company that disturb you. Perhaps the company manufactures products that are in conflict with your moral or religious beliefs. Perhaps the company officials have an attitude that is completely different from your own. You begin to wonder if this is the right job for you. What would you do?

*WWYD Feature B. Probably the best action would be to discuss concerns with a parent, school counselor, or religious leader. If the problem is a conflict with moral or religious beliefs, it might be necessary to resign. If it is a matter of concern about company attitudes or methods, you might try out the job for a while before making a final decision.

ORIENTATION TO THE WORKPLACE

During your first days on a new job, you will find out how the company is organized and what the written rules are. You will also begin to learn about the unwritten rules. Information about unwritten rules is included in Chapters 7 and 8. The company will want to know more about you, too. You will have to fill out many forms. The most common one is Form W-4.

Francine and Denny learned many of the same things during their first day on the job. They learned:

- How the workplace was laid out.
- Where they would be working (their workstations).
- How to keep track of hours worked.
- Where to look for posted notices such as work schedules.
- What to do if they needed help or had questions.

9. Have students focus on the routine things they both did, such as getting acquainted, filling out forms, getting their questions answered, and the like.

10. Ask students if they can add anything to this list.
11. Point out that level of authority is generally closely related to pay. The greater the authority, the greater the wages or salary.

These are important things that all workers need to learn during their first day on the job. In the rest of this chapter, you will study other concerns of new workers.

ORGANIZATIONAL STRUCTURE

Every company, business, or school has lines of authority and responsibility. *Authority* has to do with the power to assign work to be done. For instance, a teacher has authority in the classroom. *Responsibility* deals with the duty to carry out a work assignment. In school, for example, you, as a student, are responsible to complete your assignments. The flow of authority and responsibility can be shown in an organization chart.

A sample organization chart for a small kitchen equipment company is shown in Figure 6-7. Each person or group of workers in the organization does different tasks. Note how each level in the organization is responsible to another level. Also note that some workers have more authority than other workers.

When you begin work, you will be given a job title. Where will your job fit into the overall organization? If you start out in an entry-level job, you will probably have a lot of responsibility and little or no authority. You will probably report to a supervisor who will identify work for you to do.

Answering to a supervisor or boss is called reporting to authority. You may do this in two ways. One is *formal reporting*, which is based on rank or the chain of command. For example, Figure 6-7 shows that the production workers formally report to the plant manager.

Another way of reporting to authority is *informal reporting*. This usually involves reporting to a specific person for a short time or for a certain work assignment. Suppose, for example, that you work on the accounting staff for the company shown in Figure 6-7. Your regular supervisor, the vice-president for finance, assigns you to help out the sales manager on a new project. The supervisor tells you to follow what the sales manager tells you to do. In this case, you will be informally reporting to the sales manager for a while.

It is important to follow your company's lines of authority, both formal and informal. Take time to become familiar with these by listening, watching, and asking questions.

12. You may wish to have several students explain where their jobs fit into the organizational structure where they work.

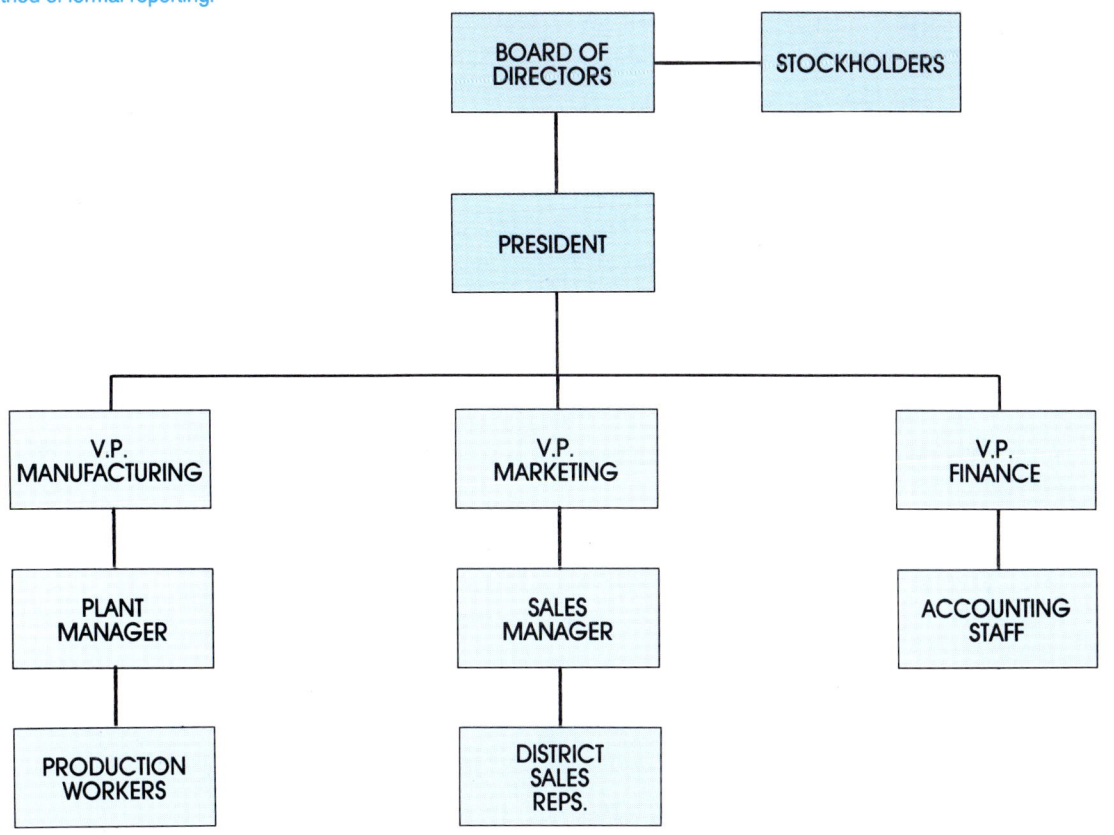

13. Informal reporting may be rare in some organizations. In any event, it is much less common than the normal, day-to-day method of formal reporting.

CHAPTER 6 Beginning a New Job ■ 69

```
                    BOARD OF ─── STOCKHOLDERS
                    DIRECTORS
                        │
                    PRESIDENT
         ┌──────────────┼──────────────┐
        V.P.           V.P.           V.P.
    MANUFACTURING   MARKETING        FINANCE
         │              │              │
       PLANT          SALES        ACCOUNTING
      MANAGER        MANAGER          STAFF
         │              │
     PRODUCTION     DISTRICT
      WORKERS        SALES
                     REPS.
```

FIGURE 6-7 Sample organization chart.

14. Activity 3 directs students to obtain an example of a company policy manual. As you discuss policy manuals here, you might want to assign students the task of bringing in a policy manual.

Policies and Rules

Most companies have written policies and rules. These help the organization to run smoothly. They also ensure that all employees receive equal treatment.

The formal rules often appear in a company *policy manual*. If your company has one, you will be given a copy when you start work. If the workplace is unionized, the policy manual may contain both the employer's and the union's rules.

An employer may also present policies and rules in several other ways. For instance, rules may be explained at a formal meeting or program for new employees, as was done for Francine's orientation. In some cases, important rules appear on a sign or bulletin board somewhere in the work area. Your supervisor or co-workers may also be useful sources of such information.

15. If you don't have one, consider putting up a bulletin board in the classroom. Start using it for the types of communication that students will encounter on the job.

STATE INSURANCE

POLICY NO. 106   DATE: 08/01/89
SUBJECT: NO-SMOKING POLICY
XXXXXXXXXXXXXXXXXXXXXXXXXXXXXXXXXXXXXXXXXXX

State Insurance has established a No-Smoking Policy aimed at protecting the overall health and environment in our workplace.

1. Smoking is not permitted by any person anywhere within State's portion of the building. Person is defined as all State's employees, temporaries, visitors and customers.
2. All potential new hires must be advised of this policy and must abide by it as a condition of employment.
3. Employees in violation of this policy will be subject to the following:
   - First offense: Written reprimand
   - Second offense: 30-day probation
   - Third offense: Two-weeks suspension without pay
   - Fourth offense: Immediate dismissal

FIGURE 6-8 Employees learn about company policies and rules in many different ways.

70 ■ SECTION 2 Working on the Job

Here are some of the most common items for which employers have written policies and rules.

- *Salaries, Wages, and Benefits.* Many employers outline in writing how pay rates, benefits, and raises are decided.
- *Attendance, Absences, and Punctuality.* You must report to work on time every workday unless you have a good reason. If you are going to be late or absent, follow your employer's policy for reporting it. In cases of illness, you may need a medical excuse.
- *Leave.* Most employers provide time off, with and without pay, for various reasons. Find out your employer's policies for sick leave, vacation time, jury-duty leave, and other time off.
- *Work Schedule and Records.* You must follow company rules for hours worked, meals, breaks, and overtime work. This often means clocking in and out on time, *in person.*

17. Some companies issue cash advances so that employees don't have to use their own money for business expenses.

Don had a friend, Kim, clock in for him on mornings he wanted to sleep late. When the boss found out, both Don and Kim almost lost their jobs. If they do this again, the employer's policy is to fire them both.

- *Expenses and Reimbursement.* If you travel on company business or buy materials for company use, those expenses are really company costs. The company should *reimburse* you for them. This means that the company should pay you back the money you spent. Company policy will explain what can be reimbursed and how to go about getting reimbursement.
- *Due Process.* Suppose you have a complaint about something or your boss has a complaint about you. The company may have formal procedures for solving this problem. *Due process* refers to the right to state your case before a decision is made.

FIGURE 6-9 Being too sick to go to work is acceptable. Failing to tell your employer about it is not. *Photo by Paul E. Meyers*

16. Explain what is meant by "jury-duty leave."

18. The courts have generally upheld the principle of due process involving relationships between workers and private employers.

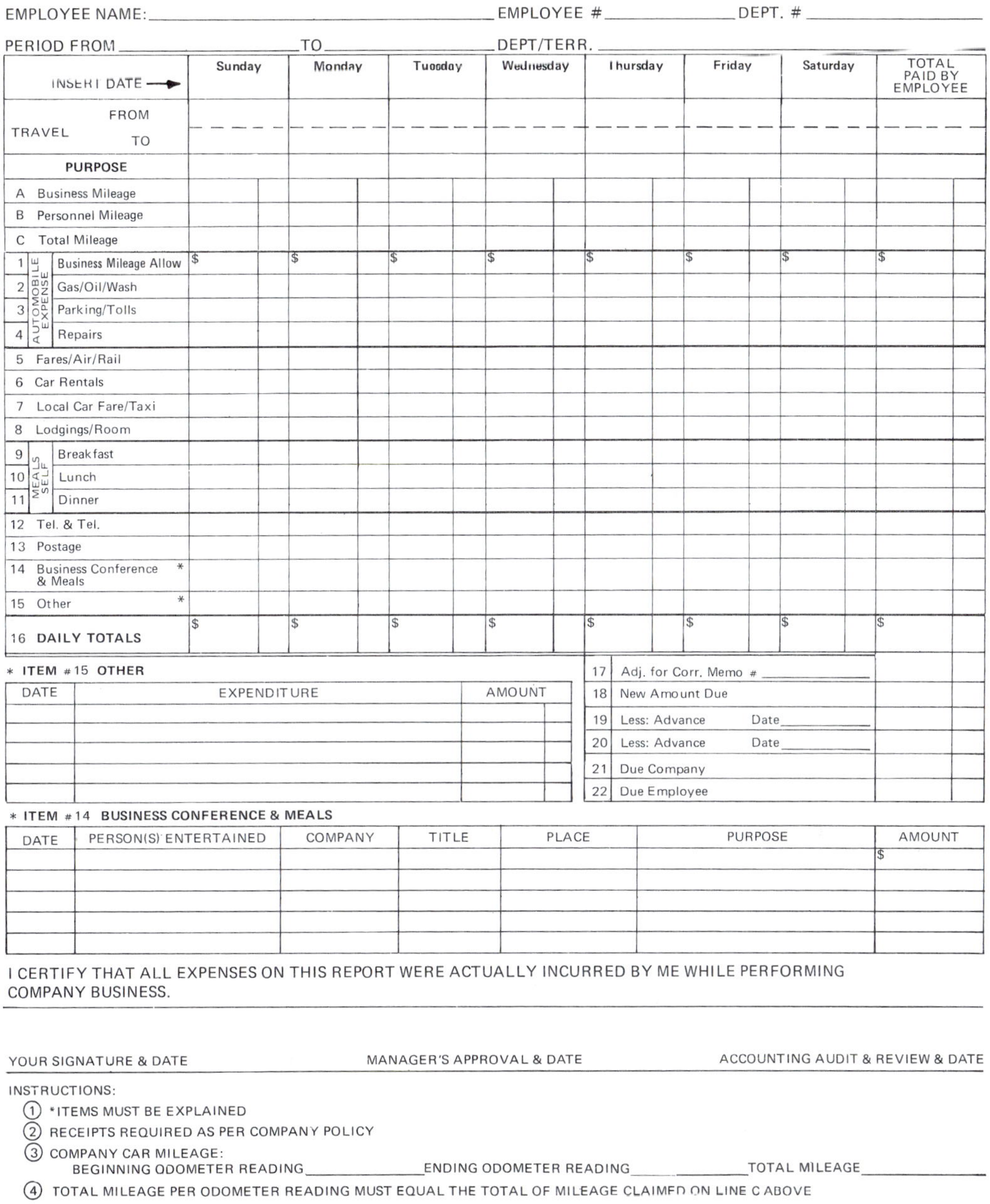
EMPLOYEE NAME: ____ EMPLOYEE # ____ DEPT. # ____

PERIOD FROM ____ TO ____ DEPT/TERR. ____

INSERT DATE →	Sunday	Monday	Tuesday	Wednesday	Thursday	Friday	Saturday	TOTAL PAID BY EMPLOYEE
TRAVEL FROM / TO								
PURPOSE								
A Business Mileage								
B Personnel Mileage								
C Total Mileage								
1 AUTOMOBILE EXPENSE Business Mileage Allow	$	$	$	$	$	$	$	$
2 Gas/Oil/Wash								
3 Parking/Tolls								
4 Repairs								
5 Fares/Air/Rail								
6 Car Rentals								
7 Local Car Fare/Taxi								
8 Lodgings/Room								
9 MEALS SELF Breakfast								
10 Lunch								
11 Dinner								
12 Tel. & Tel.								
13 Postage								
14 Business Conference & Meals *								
15 Other *								
16 DAILY TOTALS	$	$	$	$	$	$	$	$

* ITEM #15 OTHER

DATE	EXPENDITURE	AMOUNT

17 Adj. for Corr. Memo # ____	
18 New Amount Due	
19 Less: Advance Date ____	
20 Less: Advance Date ____	
21 Due Company	
22 Due Employee	

* ITEM #14 BUSINESS CONFERENCE & MEALS

DATE	PERSON(S) ENTERTAINED	COMPANY	TITLE	PLACE	PURPOSE	AMOUNT
						$

I CERTIFY THAT ALL EXPENSES ON THIS REPORT WERE ACTUALLY INCURRED BY ME WHILE PERFORMING COMPANY BUSINESS.

YOUR SIGNATURE & DATE MANAGER'S APPROVAL & DATE ACCOUNTING AUDIT & REVIEW & DATE

INSTRUCTIONS:
① *ITEMS MUST BE EXPLAINED
② RECEIPTS REQUIRED AS PER COMPANY POLICY
③ COMPANY CAR MILEAGE:
BEGINNING ODOMETER READING ____ ENDING ODOMETER READING ____ TOTAL MILEAGE ____
④ TOTAL MILEAGE PER ODOMETER READING MUST EQUAL THE TOTAL OF MILEAGE CLAIMED ON LINE C ABOVE

FIGURE 6-10 If you travel on company business or buy materials for company use, keep accurate expense records. Most companies require them.

19 ■ ***Probation and Review.*** As a new employee, you may work for a period of time on *probation.* During this time, supervisors will carefully evaluate your work and attitude. At the end of your probation period, the employer will decide whether or not to consider you for permanent employment. Once you are a permanent employee, a supervisor will review your performance from time to time. Most employers have written policies about when and how you are to be reviewed.

Read and carefully study your company's policy manual. If you can't find rules covering these items or other items of interest, ask your supervisor about them. You are responsible for obeying all policies and rules. Not knowing the policies and rules is not a good excuse.

19. No negative connotations are implied by the term *probation.* It simply refers to a try-out period.

F•E•A•T•U•R•E

Drug Testing in the Workplace

♦ ♦ ♦

During the orientation to his new job, Frank was surprised to learn that his employer had a drug testing program. After the first month of employment, all workers at Allied Receiving are subject to random drug testing. The purpose of such tests is to identify employees who use illegal (illicit) drugs such as marijuana and cocaine. Not only is the use of such drugs illegal and dangerous, but the drugs have also been linked to accidents, absenteeism, and low productivity. For example, it was found that drugs were a factor in a 1987 train crash that killed 16 passengers and injured 176 others. The engineer had been smoking marijuana.

To identify drug users, employers often require each employee to submit a urine sample for analysis. The analysis can detect traces of cocaine up to two days after the drug was taken. Marijuana has been known to show up in the urine as long as a month after use.

In 1986, the Reagan administration asked all federal agencies to test employees in "sensitive" jobs. Many local governments and private employers followed suit. By 1988, half of the nation's 500 largest corporations had drug testing programs. Testing may be required for job applicants, employed workers, or both. Some employers test workers for "cause"; for instance, if they notice a worker is not performing well. Others test randomly, without announcement and without even suspecting wrongdoing.

Even though drug testing is widely used, the practice remains controversial. Some people claim that the tests are often inaccurate. Others claim that tests violate the Fourth Amendment's prohibition on unreasonable searches. A number of lawsuits have been filed to stop drug testing. It will probably be many years before the courts decide on these issues.

FIGURE 6-FEATURE. Regardless of how you feel about drug testing by employers, certain drugs *are* illegal. *Courtesy of Williamette Industries*

Drug Testing in the Workplace. (a) New types of tests (other than urinalysis) are under development to screen for drugs. (b) At this writing, a number of court cases have been filed regarding the legality of drug testing. Court decisions may alter the practice of drug testing. It may be necessary for you to provide an update on this issue.

Unwritten Rules

Not all of a company's rules are written down. You will gradually learn rules that are not in the policy manual. Some of these rules relate to appearance, work habits, attitudes, and job performance. These rules will be discussed in Chapters 7 and 8.

One unwritten rule that needs to be discussed here relates to how people deal with each other in day-to-day activities. In some cases, managers, supervisors, and employees are very casual. Everyone is on a first-name basis. In other cases, the workers are more formal. All workers may be addressed by last names. Ann Morales, for instance, is called Mrs. Morales, and Paul Cramer is known as Mr. Cramer.

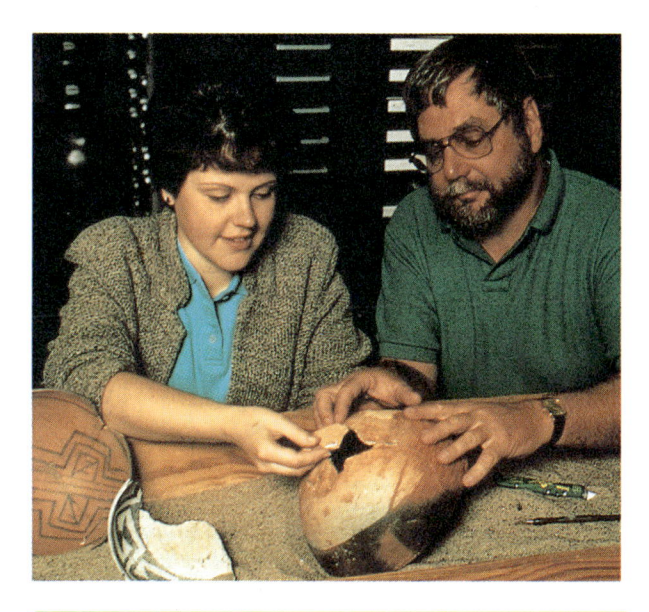

FIGURE 6-11 Even in an informal workplace, don't call supervisors and managers by their first names unless they ask you to. *Courtesy of SIUC Photocommunications*

Some organizations have a formal way of getting work done. Ways of doing things that differ from the accepted way may be frowned upon. In less formal organizations, the most important thing may be getting the work done. How the work gets done may be left to each worker. By paying attention, you will learn how your company expects you to relate to others and to get the work done.

WORKING UNDER SUPERVISION

In the workplace, every employee is responsible to someone else. This is not unlike school. In your job as a student, you are responsible to your teachers. They, in turn, report to the principal, and so on. On the job, unless you are self-employed, you will work under the direction of a *supervisor*. Your supervisor will be responsible for training you and seeing that you learn company rules. He or she will also observe how well you perform on the job. Your success as an employee relates strongly to how well you work under supervision. Some suggestions for getting started on the right foot with your supervisor follow.

- *Use the Supervisor for Communication.* If you want to send messages to someone higher up in the organization, do so through your supervisor.

FIGURE 6-12 Your supervisor is the link between you and higher company officials. *Photo © 1987 Gary Gladstone*

- *Ask the Supervisor for Direction.* Remember, the supervisor is responsible for your work, training and safety. Before starting job tasks for the first time, go over them with the supervisor. For example, you might say, "After I get these cartons unpacked and the contents shelved, then I should come back and see you, right?" Understanding beforehand what you are to do saves everyone time. If you are ever unsure of how to do something, ask for help. Most supervisors respect people who know when to ask for help.

20. Point out that until students learn all the unwritten rules, they should act more formal and conservative.

21. Have students provide examples of types of communication that are transmitted through supervisors. These might include requests for personal leave or notice of grievance.

74 ■ SECTION 2 Working on the Job

- *Don't Ask For or Expect Special Treatment.* Most supervisors are responsible for many workers. All should be treated the same, so don't ask for special favors.
- *Accept and Use the Supervisor's Suggestions.* Your supervisor is more experienced at the work than you. Carla thought she had a better way of doing a job task. Because she was a new worker, though, she kept quiet. Later she learned that there were good reasons, such as safety, for following standard procedures.

PAYROLL WITHHOLDING

Every worker must pay federal income tax. The tax system operates on a pay-as-you-go basis. This means that the employer takes income tax out of each paycheck. The amount of tax the employer withholds depends on three things:

- The amount of money you earn.
- Whether you are married or not (your marital status).
- The number of *allowances* you claim. This refers to the number of tax exemptions you are entitled to claim. For instance, a single person is entitled to one allowance.

Your employer will keep track of how much money you earn. On Form W-4, you will provide information about your marital status and the number of allowances you are entitled to claim.

John Nye is single and only claims one allowance. His completed Form W-4 is shown in Figure 6-13. Christina Comito is a single parent with two children. She claims three allowances—one for herself and one for each child. Based on each employee's earnings and allowances, an employer looks on a table to find how much tax to withhold. For example, in 1988 Christina made $380 per week. Each week, $29.63 was withheld from her paycheck for federal income tax.

Some people may be *exempt* from tax withholdings. This means that they don't have to pay taxes. People who earn less than a certain amount of money in a year are usually exempt. In 1988, for instance, a single person with one allowance who earned less than $4,950 was exempt from paying federal income tax.

FIGURE 6-13 All employers will ask you to fill out one of these forms. A worksheet is provided to help you figure withholding allowances. Most young workers will only need to complete lines B and G of the worksheet.

22. Have students provide examples of special favors. These might include requests to leave early, work a preferred shift, borrow tools or equipment, and so on.

23. Chapter 26 deals with income taxes and how to file an income tax return.

CHAPTER REVIEW

Chapter in Brief

- It is normal to experience some anxiety when beginning a new job. Many companies provide an orientation to help you get started properly. Your employer wants you to be successful on the job.
- One person's first day at work may be quite different from another person's first day. However, most new employees do similar things and are provided with similar kinds of information.
- An organization chart shows the flow of authority and responsibility within an organization. It is important to follow your company's formal and informal lines of authority and responsibility.
- Companies have written policies and rules to help them run smoothly. You are responsible for obeying all policies and rules. Companies also have unwritten rules that you will need to learn.
- On the job, you will probably work under the direction of a supervisor. Use the supervisor for communication and direction. Accept and use the supervisor's suggestions, but don't ask for or expect special treatment.
- Employers are required to withhold money from your paycheck for federal income tax. The amount withheld is based on information that you provide on Form W-4.

Words to Know

allowances the number of tax exemptions one is entitled to.

anxiety a feeling of concern, worry, or unease, such as concern about a forthcoming job interview.

authority the power or rank to give orders or make assignments to others.

due process the legal right to state one's case or point of view before a decision is made.

exempt to be free of something, such as not having to pay taxes.

probation a trial period during which one's performance is being observed and evaluated.

reimburse to pay back money already spent.

responsibility the duty to follow an order or carry out a work assignment.

supervisor a boss; one who gives directions and orders and oversees the work of others.

Questions to Answer

1. What are two reasons why companies like Northeast Electric Power Company conduct employee orientation programs?
2. Which is usually greater for beginning workers, level of authority or level of responsibility?
3. What is the difference between formal reporting and informal reporting?
4. What two purposes do written policies and rules serve in a company?
5. What are the four ways in which a company may communicate policies and rules to employees?
6. What should you do if a subject of interest is not covered in the company's policy manual?
7. Give an example of an area that is often covered by unwritten rules.
8. How is the job of student similar to that of a paid employee?
9. What are four ways to start a good relationship with a supervisor? Briefly explain each.
10. What three things determine the amount of income tax withheld from your paycheck?

Activities to Do

1. Some of your classmates may already have jobs. Ask these people to explain what their orientation to a new job was like. Ask them questions about their experiences on the job.
2. As a group activity, develop an organization chart for the employees in your school. At the top of the chart, start with the school district's board of education. How many levels are there? Suppose a teacher has a complaint about a board policy. To whom would he or she file a complaint? Discuss the process the teacher should follow.
3. Obtain an example of a company policy manual. You may already have one from your job, or perhaps you can borrow one from a family member or a friend. Look through the manuals in class and discuss examples of each of the seven types of policies and rules explained. Do the manuals contain types of policies and rules that are not explained in the chapter? If so, discuss the merits of these policies and rules.
4. Does your school provide students with a written code of conduct or something similar that outlines school policies and rules? If so, discuss how it is similar to a company policy manual. If your school does not have a code of conduct or something similar, discuss possible policies or rules that could go into such a manual.

---

1. (a) It is more efficient to orient a large number of new hires at the same time. (b) It assures that all employees receive the same information.
2. Level of responsibility.
3. *Formal reporting*—based on the chain of command; reporting to the person in the rank above. *Informal reporting*—reporting to a person for a short time or for a certain assignment.
4. (a) Help the organization to run smoothly. (b) Ensure that all employees receive equal treatment.
5. (a) In a company [and/or union] policy manual. (b) Explained during a formal orientation. (c) Posted on a sign or bulletin board in the work area. (d) By supervisors and co-workers.
6. Ask your supervisor.
7. A number of examples could be given regarding appearance, work habits, attitudes, job performance, and interpersonal relations.
8. Both work under supervision and are responsible to a person having higher rank.
9. (a) Use the supervisor for communication, such as sending a message to someone higher in the organization. (b) Ask the supervisor for direction, such as clarifying instructions and asking for help if needed. (c) Don't ask for or expect special treatment, such as leaving work a little early to catch a bus. (d) Accept and use the supervisor's suggestions, such as following standard work and safety procedures.
10. (a) The amount of money earned. (b) Marital status. (c) The number of allowances claimed.

24. Be alert to underscore anything new that was not discussed in the chapter.
25. Students may require assistance with this since they may not be familiar with the organization above the level of principal. An alternative to this assignment is for students to develop an organization chart for where they work.
26. You may wish to provide several examples of policy manuals rather than have students bring them in.
27. If your school has a student code or student handbook, have it available for this activity.

Topics to Discuss

1. What are some of the reasons why employers want new employees to make a quick and successful transition from school to the workplace?
2. Think of an instance in your life in which your anxiety about a situation turned out to be worse than the situation itself. What might this suggest regarding anxiety toward beginning a new job?
3. Some supervisors try not to get too friendly or informal with employees whom they supervise. Do you think this is a good idea or a bad idea? Explain why.
4. Under what circumstances might someone choose to specify an additional amount of withholding on line 5 of Form W-4?

1. The word *employer* is used here in a general way to include manager, owner, boss, supervisor, and related roles.

2. This chapter was written to present the employer's perspective. Throughout the chapter, try to help students understand the employer's position.

CHAPTER SEVEN

Expectations of Employers

OUTLINE
Job Performance
Work Habits and Attitudes
Rating Work Behavior
Chapter Review

OBJECTIVES
After reading this chapter, you should be able to:
- Name and describe the five things that employers expect regarding job performance.
- Name and describe the six things that employers expect regarding work habits and attitudes.
- Describe the purposes of performance evaluation.
- Explain the two-step process of performance evaluation that is used by most large companies.

FIGURE 7-1 An employer has a right to expect a certain level of performance. *Courtesy Lab-Volt Systems, Division Buck Engineering, Inc.*

Everyone needs time to adjust to a new job. After that, you will need to meet the same expectations as other employees. Accepting a job means you make a contract with an employer. You agree to perform certain duties in return for a certain salary or wage. Your responsibility is to do the tasks you were hired to do, in the way and at the time the employer wants them done.

JOB PERFORMANCE

Work organizations either produce goods or provide services. Whether you are involved in producing goods or providing services, your employer will expect certain things from you.

Productivity

Employers expect employees to complete a certain amount of work. The output of a worker is known as *productivity*. Suppose Worker A is more productive than Worker B. This means that Worker A does more work.

Productivity is usually thought of in terms of goods-producing occupations such as welder or bricklayer. Productivity is also important in service occupations. These include barber, flight attendant, salesclerk, and nurse. Whether you hammer nails or wait on tables, the employer will expect you to give a day's worth of work for a day's pay.

Being productive means working at a steady pace during your time on the job. "Goofing off" is never okay. Susan learned this the hard way.

Susan was the sales manager of a small company. She liked her work, but wasted a lot of time. During the workday, she often visited with co-workers and talked on the phone with friends. The boss warned her to manage her time more efficiently. Susan paid no attention. Last week, she was let go.

3. The ten types of goods and services industries are described in Chapter 14 (see Figure 14-4).

4. The term *service-production* is used in labor market information literature, even though the more precise term is *service-providing*.

CHAPTER 7 Expectations of Employers ■ 79

FIGURE 7-2 In some jobs, productivity is easy to see. *Courtesy of Simpson Industries, Inc.*

5. On the chalkboard, label two headings "Goods-Production" and "Service-Production." Ask students to name examples of each. Focus the discussion on outcomes and outputs. Quality of work is explained in the following section.

Quality of Work

An employer expects you to do your work carefully, accurately, and thoroughly. Quality of work means how well a job is performed. Poor work quality may cancel out high productivity. For example, a secretary who types fast but makes a lot of errors isn't doing the job well. Likewise, a production worker who solders many electrical components but whose soldered joints do not hold isn't doing the job well.

The quality of work is very important to a company's success. Customers who receive high-quality goods or services come back for repeat business. This is why employers want their workers to do good work.

Employees who perform high-quality work take *pride* in their work. Pride has to do with feeling proud and satisfied with what you have accomplished. Take the case of Lionel, who works as a physical fitness instructor. He is proud to see his students progress and improve their health.

FIGURE 7-3 Doing quality work can be a source of great pride. You and the employer both benefit. *Courtesy of USX Corporation*

6. Even though *productivity* and *quality of work* are separate things, further illustrate how they are related. Use examples of both goods-production and service-production.

7. Most employers seek high productivity and high quality. Sometimes though, one factor may be compromised slightly to benefit the other. Show examples of this relationship.

80 ■ SECTION 2 Working on the Job

Good Judgment

Have people ever said to you, "Use your head"? What they meant was to think about what you are doing or figure it out yourself. You can't run to a boss every time you have a problem or must make a decision. Your employer will want you to think about a problem and come to the right decision.

Using good *judgment* is a sign of maturity. It is something that employers look for when promoting people to better jobs. If you are known as someone who makes quick decisions and has poor judgment, your time with the company may be short.

What Would You Do?

You have been instructed to call a supplier and order replacement parts for several broken pieces of equipment. You are careful to provide all important information on quantities, part numbers, prices, and the like. After you finish, the supplier asks, "How do you want this shipped?"

"Gee, the boss didn't tell me that," you think. There is no one else in the office to ask. What would you do?

FIGURE 7-4 Do not neglect safety rules and procedures. They are for your protection. *Courtesy of CSX Corporation, Richmond, VA*

8. Ask students of instances in which they may have been told to "use your head."

WWYD Feature A. The situation here relates to using good judgment. One response would be to instruct the supplier to ship the parts in the "normal way" and indicate that you will call back if the boss wants another method. As soon as the boss returns, the employee should explain what was done and then follow-up with the supplier as required.

FIGURE 7-5 Production had to be stopped while broken equipment was checked and repaired. *Courtesy of Miller Electric Mfg. Co. of Appleton, WI*

Safety Consciousness

Many jobs involve working with tools, machines, and equipment. Some of these may be dangerous. For your benefit as well as that of co-workers, the employer will expect you to work safely. Part of being a safe worker is knowing how to do a job. You will have learned this through education or on-the-job training. For instance, if you are working as a carpenter, you should already know how to safely use a circular saw.

Your employer will expect you to perform your job in the way that you have been trained. In addition, the company will probably have safety rules that you will be expected to follow. For example, workers who go to certain areas of the plant may need to wear a hard hat or safety glasses. Or there may be certain containers that workers must use when disposing of cleaning rags or solvents.

If an accident or emergency does happen, you will be expected to follow certain steps. Let's say that a machine part gets stuck in a punch press. Your boss has told you that when this happens you should turn off the machine right away and go for help. Do what you are told. Do not try to fix the problem yourself.

Learn your company's safety rules and procedures. Do this by reading and studying printed company material that you may have. If you have any questions, be sure to ask your boss. Once you know the safety rules, practice them. Knowledge of them alone isn't enough. Additional information on safety will be presented in Chapter 17.

Care of Equipment

An employer often has a lot of money tied up in expensive tools and equipment. You will be expected to take care of them and use them properly. Damaged tools and equipment cost money in two ways. First, the item must be repaired or replaced. Then while the repairs are going on, work time is lost. Should you have questions about tools or equipment, ask them. Not doing so could cause serious problems.

Let's say, for instance, that you are working summers as a farm laborer. The boss asks you if you know how to drive the tractor. You say that you do. The new tractor has some features that are unfamiliar to you. You decide to drive it anyhow. After a few minutes, the tractor stops dead. The mechanic says that your mistake caused several thousand dollars damage to the tractor. Even though the boss fires you because of your carelessness, it could have been worse. In some cases, improper use of tools and equipment injures and kills workers.

---

9. You may wish to integrate here the section from Chapter 17 regarding safety on the job.

10. Ask students to share any personal experiences related to improper care or use of tools and equipment. Discuss how the incident might have been prevented.

Use tools and equipment as if they are your own. Think of them as if you have to pay for repairing or replacing them.

WORK HABITS AND ATTITUDES

Another type of employer expectation has to do with work habits and attitudes. These are the ways employees behave on the job. Poor work habits and a negative attitude are the main reasons most people lose their jobs. You may, for example, be a great hair stylist. You don't keep your job, though, if you cannot get along with your boss, co-workers, or clients.

1. Absent from work too frequently or for questionable reasons.
2. Has to be supervised too much of the time.
3. Takes no initiative when something needs to be done.
4. Isn't very observant, fails to recognize errors or problems.
5. Doesn't listen well.
6. Arrives late or leaves early too often.
7. Doesn't consider the consequences of decisions or actions.
8. Too much socializing with other workers or visitors.
9. Can't accept suggestions or criticism.
10. Doesn't seem to care about doing a job well.

FIGURE 7-6 One study of employers identified these as the ten most serious problems of young, entry-level workers (in rank order).

FIGURE 7-7 Staying home from work because you don't feel like going is not an acceptable reason. *Photo by Paul E. Meyers*

Attendance and Punctuality

To avoid work delays or interruptions, employers expect workers to be on the job regularly (attendance). Let's see what happened on a construction site when a worker "took off" regularly. A crew was building townhouses in the Dallas suburbs. All of the workers showed up unless they had a good reason. Andy frequently missed work. When he was absent, the others covered for him. Sometimes, though, the others were too busy with their own work to do his, too. Andy's work didn't get done on those days. The boss told Andy that if other crew members missed work as he did, the job could shut down. Andy got the point and changed his ways.

Punctuality is also necessary. Workplaces that are open at certain times need employees there to deal with business. An employer's profits and public image may suffer if employees are not there to take care of business. Suppose a restaurant opens for business at 6:00 A.M. If some workers don't arrive until 6:30, customers will get poor service. They will eat elsewhere and tell others to do the same. Be ready to work at starting time, stay until quitting time, and take only the time set aside for lunch periods and breaks. Remember that most workers are not paid for time they miss when they are absent or tardy.

If you must be absent or late, try to tell your supervisor as far ahead as possible. If you get sick one evening, for instance, notify the boss that you will miss work the next day.

Cooperation

"He or she just refuses to cooperate" is a common employer complaint about a worker. *Cooperation* involves getting along with others. One aspect of cooperation is following orders. Another way of saying this is doing what you are told. Since you are likely to be a beginning worker, you will probably receive a lot of orders.

Your job may include many of the boring tasks such as sweeping floors, cleaning equipment, or

11. Make sure students understand the difference between the words *attendance* and *punctuality*.

12. Ask employed students to describe the policy regarding illness and sick leave where they work.

> 13. Point out that the employer is not discriminating nor taking advantage of young workers. Unskilled tasks are routinely assigned to low-paid, entry-level employees.

making coffee. After all, someone has to do them. If you won't, the employer will hire someone who will. So, accept your assignments cheerfully (or at least, willingly) and do your best. If you do so, the employer will notice.

Cooperation also means being able to take criticism. When you accept wages, you agree to do the job the way the employer wants it done. The employer has a right to criticize or correct you. The employer wants you to improve your work performance. (You do too, hopefully.) Accept and profit from constructive criticism. Thank the employer, tell him or her you will improve, and then do so.

Courtesy and cooperation go hand-in-hand. You can build good working relationships by being respectful, friendly, and considerate toward others. A smile or a friendly greeting tells others that you are trying to help create a positive work setting.

Interest and Enthusiasm

Employers like employees who show *interest* and *enthusiasm* toward their work. Such people are often the most productive and cooperative workers. Few people, of course, find everything about their job to be interesting and enjoyable. Do, however, show your enthusiasm for those parts that you do like.

Your company and your co-workers also deserve your interest and enthusiasm. Keep up to date on the company's plans. If your employer has an employee newsletter or company magazine, read it. Try to take part in company social events and activities. You may be just the shortstop the company softball team has been looking for. If help is needed with company charities or service projects, volunteer your time. You, the company, and society will all benefit.

FIGURE 7-8 Entry-level work assignments should be performed cheerfully. *Courtesy of Wal-Mart Stores, Inc. © 1988 Annual Report*

> 14. Ask students to share personal experiences related to participation in company social events and activities.

84 ■ SECTION 2 Working on the Job

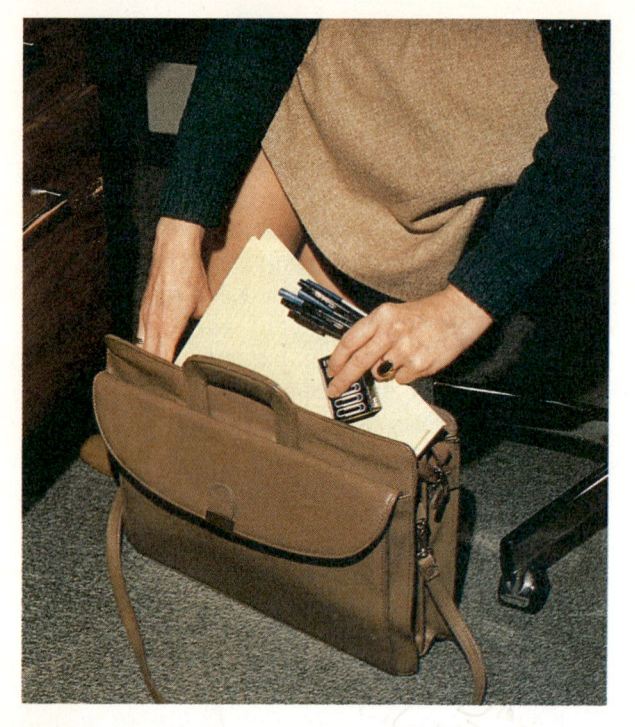

FIGURE 7-9 Customers are not the only shoplifters. *Photo by Paul E. Meyers*

Honesty

Stealing is a serious problem in many businesses and industries. Employers usually deal firmly with theft. Most employees caught stealing are fired. They may face criminal charges as well.

Most stealing involves the theft of money or expensive tools and equipment. But taking office supplies and using the photocopy machine for personal use are also forms of stealing.

Art is an insurance agent. He also serves as secretary of the area's youth soccer association. Over the weekend, he needed to prepare a mailing for the group. So after business on Friday, he loaded up his briefcase with supplies from the company's storeroom. He picked up a typewriter ribbon, a couple of pens, a legal pad, a ream of bond paper, a roll of tape, and a box of envelopes. "They won't miss it," Art thought to himself, "the company made $230 million last year."

Art tried to justify his behavior, but what he did is stealing. Had he been caught, the company would not have been impressed by his excuses. He may have been fired. Surely, his chances for future advancement in the company would have been lessened. You have a promising future. Don't risk it by being like Art.

15. Ask students to provide additional examples of ways in which loyalty toward an employer might be expressed.

WWYD Feature B. This can be a difficult moral decision. Does the employee "rat" on a co-worker? Talking to the co-worker who is taking the money is not advisable. The best alternative is to tell the

What Would You Do?

You and two other employees work as clerks at a Quick-Mart convenience food store. One afternoon you notice that a co-worker lays $.75 from a purchase beside the cash register. You think it is odd that he does not ring it up. When you look back again, the money is gone. Over the next several days, you watch him more closely. You discover that he is stealing money. You wish you had not seen him. You don't know whether to say something to him, tell your boss, or keep quiet. What would you do?

FIGURE 7-10 These workers wear their company name proudly. *Photo by Paul E. Meyers*

Loyalty

Your employer would like you to feel a sense of devotion to the company. This means, for example, that you should not criticize the company when talking with co-workers, friends, or strangers. *Loyalty* means being proud of what you do and where you work. It is believing in your company and defending it, if necessary.

No company, of course, is perfect. If you disagree with a company policy or action, discuss it with your supervisor. If things cannot be worked out, it may be time to find another job.

boss what was observed. The boss will not likely confront the accused without first-hand evidence, which will shift the burden of proof away from the informer.

F•E•A•T•U•R•E

Labor Unions

♦ ♦ ♦

A little less than twenty percent of the American workforce are members of labor unions. A labor union is a group of workers who have joined together to protect their rights. The two main types of unions are craft and industrial. A craft union is made up of skilled workers in a craft or trade, such as plumbers, musicians, or barbers. Workers in the same industry often belong to an industrial union. Perhaps you have heard of the United Auto Workers or the United Mine Workers. These are industrial unions.

Throughout its history, organized labor has fought for three main goals. These have been improvements in:

1) Wages, hours and benefits
2) Job security
3) Safe and healthful working conditions

Unions do other things besides working for these goals. One is to provide apprenticeship programs that teach work skills to young union members. Some unions have hiring halls where workers can go to find out about job openings. Political involvement is often an important labor goal. Unions frequently give money to favorite candidates and provide campaign workers.

The presence and strength of unions varies among geographic areas. Most unions are in the Midwest and Northeast parts of the United States. These areas have large construction, manufacturing, transportation, and mining industries.

An employer that has an agreement with a union is called a union shop. In a union shop, the employer can hire whomever he or she chooses. However, the employee must join the union within a certain period of time. About twenty states, most of them in the South, have so-called "right-to-work" laws that don't allow union shops. These states have open shops in which an employee doesn't have to join a union. Open shops may exist in the other thirty states as well, but employees are often under pressure to unionize.

When you start a job, a co-worker or supervisor may ask you to join a union. Members of the local union must vote on your membership. Usually, though, anyone who applies is accepted. You will probably pay an initiation fee to join and you must pay regular dues.

FIGURE 7-FEATURE This truck driver is a union member. Does he belong to a craft union or an industrial union? *Courtesy of Fluor Daniel Inc.*

---

* *Labor Unions.* This is only a brief introduction to organized labor. If your area has a number of union employers, you may want to expand on this topic. A number of excellent supplemental materials on organized labor may be obtained by writing the American Federation of Labor and Congress of Industrial Organizations, 815 16th Street, N.W., Washington, DC 20006.

86 ■ SECTION 2 Working on the Job

RATING WORK BEHAVIOR

As a student, teachers have been evaluating you for many years. On the job, your employer will also evaluate your work. The evaluation of employees is usually known as *performance evaluation*. The employer rates your job performance, your work habits, and your attitudes.

Purposes of Evaluation

Employee evaluation allows employers to determine how well workers are doing their jobs. Performance evaluations have several purposes.

One purpose is to decide if you deserve a pay raise and how much to give you. Employers know that it is important to provide pay raises as a reward for good work.

Evaluation also helps employees become better workers. This benefits both the employee and the employer. For you, the employee, the feedback you get helps you learn and improve. You find out what your strengths and weaknesses are, and where you may need improvement. For the employer, the evaluation may suggest places where you need more on-the-job training.

Performance evaluation is also known as "merit pay" or "merit raise." About 70 percent of U.S. firms offer some form of performance evaluation.

Finally, evaluation provides a basis for future job assignments. Let's say that an opening exists for a department supervisor. Management might review employee evaluations to see which (if any) employee could be promoted. Or suppose your evaluation results suggest that you would do better in a different job. The employer might then transfer you to another department.

How You Are Evaluated

The way in which you will be evaluated differs from company to company. Donna, who works for a very small company, does not often realize that her boss is evaluating her. From time to time, she and her boss discuss Donna's work over a cup of coffee. All feedback is verbal, no forms are used, and no records are kept.

Most large firms, however, have a standard procedure for employee evaluation. The evaluations usually take place once a year, although every six months is not uncommon.

Most evaluations are done in two steps. Your boss or supervisor fills out an evaluation form. A

FIGURE 7-11 Evaluation in the school classroom or on the job has many of the same purposes. *Photo by Paul E. Meyers*

16. This section is intended to describe how permanent, full-time workers are evaluated. Explain to students (or review) how they will be evaluated.

18. Even though they might not be subjected to it, ask students to describe how employees are evaluated at their places of employment.

19. Public (government) employers tend to follow procedures similar to private employers. Invite a federal or state employer to class to discuss the process.

CHAPTER 7 Expectations of Employers ■ 87

Student-Trainee Evaluation Sheet
COOPERATIVE EDUCATION PROGRAMS

Swinburn Public Schools

Student's Name _____

Training Station _____

Reporting Month _____

Please Return By _____

Supervisor's Name _____

INSTRUCTIONS: Please rate the student by circling the number on each scale below at the point which most accurately describes the student learner's progress to date. (Please feel free to make comments on the back of this paper.)

Categories	OUTSTANDING	ABOVE AVERAGE	AVERAGE	BELOW AVERAGE	UNSATISFACTORY
Personal Appearance	5	4	3	2	1
Attendance and Tardiness	5	4	3	2	1
Rate of Progress	5	4	3	2	1
Follows Directions	5	4	3	2	1
Job Judgment Decision Making	5	4	3	2	1
Attitude Toward Job	5	4	3	2	1
Ability to Get Along with People	5	4	3	2	1
Initiative (Does Things Without Being Told)	5	4	3	2	1
Safety	5	4	3	2	1
Dependability (Overall)	5	4	3	2	1

OUTSTANDING ☐   ABOVE AVERAGE ☐   AVERAGE ☐   BELOW AVERAGE ☐   UNSATISFACTORY ☐

Supervisor's Signature _____ Date _____ Letter Grade _____

Student's Signature _____

FIGURE 7-12 Sample performance evaluation form

sample form is shown in Figure 7-12. Then you meet with the supervisor or boss. The two of you will go over the form and discuss your strengths and weaknesses. The tone of this meeting should be positive and constructive (unless you are doing a really poor job).

20. Collect a number of different evaluation forms from public and private employers for review or display on a bulletin board as you teach this chapter.

The discussion between you and your supervisor will not be one-sided. You should have a chance to discuss what you like and dislike about your current position. This is a good time for you to discuss your future goals. Do not use the time to complain about the job or co-workers, though.

FIGURE 7-13 Approach your work as if you are being evaluated every day. In fact, you are! *Courtesy of Rotary Lift*

After the Evaluation

An evaluation is not just a once-a-year thing. Your boss is continually watching your job performance, work habits, and attitudes. The ratings you receive from time to time result from a process that goes on all the time. This is why it pays to do your best work each and every day.

If you get a negative evaluation, you will need to face up to your shortcomings. Make sure you understand what you can do to correct the problem. Your future in the company will depend on showing that you can improve your work behavior before the next evaluation. If you ignore what your boss tells you, your next evaluation could be your last.

CHAPTER REVIEW

Chapter in Brief

- After a short period of adjustment, you will need to meet the same expectations as other employees. Your responsibility is to do the job tasks in the way and at the time the employer wants them done.
- Your employer will expect the following in terms of your job performance:
    a. *Productivity*—completing a certain amount of work in the time provided.
    b. *Quality of work*—doing your work carefully, accurately, and thoroughly.
    c. *Good judgment*—thinking about a problem and then doing the right thing.
    d. *Safety consciousness*—learning and following safety rules and procedures.
    e. *Care of equipment*—using and handling tools and equipment correctly.
- Another type of employer expectation has to do with work habits and attitudes. Your employer will also expect the following:
    a. *Attendance and punctuality*—showing up for work every day, and on time.
    b. *Cooperation*—getting along with supervisors, co-workers, and customers.
    c. *Interest and enthusiasm*—showing you like and care about your company and co-workers.
    d. *Honesty*—not taking anything owned by the company regardless of what it is worth.
    e. *Loyalty*—believing in and being proud of your company.
- An employer will evaluate your on-the-job performance. Both your job performance and your work habits and attitudes will be evaluated. Employee evaluation allows employers to determine how well workers are doing their jobs.
- Most evaluations are done in two steps. First, your supervisor will fill out an evaluation form. Next, your supervisor will meet with you to go over the ratings. If you get a negative evaluation, you will need to improve your performance before the next rating.

Words to Know

cooperation getting along with and working well with others.

enthusiasm eagerness; a strong interest in something.

honesty a refusal to lie, steal, or mislead in any way.

interest feeling of excitement and involvement.

judgment thinking about a problem and making the right decision.

loyalty faithfulness; believing in and being devoted to something.

performance evaluation the process of judging how well an employee is doing on the job.

pride feeling satisfied with what one has accomplished.
productivity the output of a worker; how much a worker produces on the job.
punctuality being on time.

Questions to Answer

1. Suppose your work always falls below the employer's expectations. What will probably happen?
2. How does the quality of employees' work relate to a company's success?
3. Name three things that an employee can do to perform a job more safely.
4. A damaged tool or piece of equipment may cost an employer in two ways. Explain how.
5. Give three examples of why a person might get fired.
6. What should you do if you must be absent or late to work?
7. List four ways that an employee can be cooperative on the job.
8. Is taking a few stamps and some tape from the company considered stealing? Why or why not?
9. What are the three purposes of employee evaluation from the employer's standpoint?
10. Most companies follow a two-step evaluation procedure. Describe both steps.

Activities to Do

1. Work with your instructor to develop a rating sheet based on the ten items from Figure 7-6. Type the items in random order without the rankings. Make copies of the form. Each person in class should ask one or more employers or supervisors to complete the form. The instructions should ask employers to rank the items from one to ten in terms of what they see as the most serious problems of young workers. Tally the survey results in class and compare them with the rankings shown in Figure 7-6.
2. Assume that you are an employer. What would you do or say to an employee in each of the following situations:
   a. An employee puts the wrong kind of lubricant in a chain saw, causing it to burn up.
   b. An employee calls in sick. As you are going to lunch, you see the person playing tennis.
   c. An employee has been making personal, long-distance calls on company phones.
   d. An employee has been bad-mouthing the company to co-workers.
   Discuss your answers in class.

---

1. You will probably be warned first. Then, you will be fired.
2. Customers or clients who receive quality goods or services will more likely come back for repeat business.
3. (a) Perform the job as trained. (b) Learn and follow company safety rules. (c) Follow stated emergency procedures.
4. (a) The cost of repair or replacement. (b) The lost "downtime" while repairs are being made.
5. Any three examples can be cited related to the six types of work habits and attitudes.
6. Notify your supervisor as far ahead as possible.
7. (a) Follow orders. (b) Accept assignments willingly. (c) Accept criticism. (d) Be courteous toward others.
8. Of course. Taking anything from the company is stealing, regardless of the value.
9. (a) To decide if and how much pay raise to give. (b) To help improve employee performance. (c) To provide a basis for future job assignments.
10. Step one—an evaluation form is completed. Step two—a meeting is held between the boss and the employee to discuss the ratings.

21. Even if the survey results differ from the rankings shown in Figure 7-6, this doesn't diminish the significance of the findings.
22. This activity is intended to make student more aware of the employer's position. These four cases are ones that demonstrate unacceptable employee behavior. The employer would seem to be justified in reprimanding the employee.

Topics to Discuss

1. During the last decade or so, many U.S. companies have moved their manufacturing plants overseas. The reason, they claim, is that U.S. workers are less productive and less concerned about quality than foreign workers. Do you think this is true?
2. Some companies make employees pay for any tools or equipment that they damage or lose. Do you think this practice is fair?
3. Some American manufacturers, particularly in the auto industry, have begun to use Japanese-style management techniques. For instance, workers are given uniforms with the company name on them. Production and management workers all wear the same uniform. This is supposed to help build enthusiasm and loyalty toward the company. Do you think things like this make a difference?
4. As an employee, which would you rather receive: (a) guaranteed 4% annual raise, or (b) the possibility of a raise between 0% and 8% based on the results of an annual evaulation of your performance? Why?

23. Many plants were moved to other countries because of lower labor costs. Economic data, however, does indicate that the U.S. lagged behind Japan, West Germany, and some other countries in productivity during the 1970s and 1980s. By mid-1980, U.S. companies began to respond to the challenge of economic competition and by 1990 led the world in manufacturing productivity. Comparable gains in quality were also achieved.
24. Ask students about the policy on this matter where they work.
25. Many Japanese-style management techniques seem to be working. If any companies using such techniques are located in your area, have students interview some workers and share their findings in class.
26. Students will likely favor (b). Research shows that roughly eighty percent of American workers believe that they are better than average.

CHAPTER EIGHT

Worker Rights and Protections

OUTLINE
Honesty and Respect
Fair Employment Practices
Protection from Discrimination
Worker Safety and Health
Agencies Providing Services to Workers
Chapter Review

OBJECTIVES
After reading this chapter, you should be able to:
- Name and describe the six things that employers owe their workers.
- Discuss the importance of employers treating workers with honesty and respect.
- Name and describe the three types of fair employment practices.
- Explain worker's rights regarding protection from discrimination.
- Explain the roles of employers and workers regarding safety and health in the workplace.
- Identify agencies that deal with workers' complaints.

In Chapter 7, you saw that an employee has certain responsibilities to an employer. An employment contract, however, isn't a one-way deal. Employers also owe certain things to their employees. One of these, of course, is payment for their work. Other things include:

- *Training and Supervision.* An employer should provide the necessary on-the-job training. Once the worker starts the job, the employer should give proper supervision and feedback. Workers need to know what to do, and how well they are performing.
- *Orientation to the Workplace.* A worker deserves to have information about company policies and rules. When these change, the employer should tell its workers.
- *Honesty and Respect.* An employer owes all its workers honesty and respect.
- *Fair Employment Practice.* Laws cover child labor, work hours, and payment of wages. An employer who wants to avoid legal hassles must obey such laws.
- *Protection from Discrimination.* Laws prohibit discrimination against workers.
- *Safety and Health.* Years ago, employers did not have to provide safe working conditions. Many workers paid with their lives. Employers now must follow certain health and safety standards.

The first two responsibilities in the preceding list were discussed in Chapter 6. The four remaining ones will be covered here.

FIGURE 8-1 Most employers treat workers fairly and honestly. *Courtesy Crestmont Federal Savings and Loan Association, Photographer: Ted Cronet*

1. Lordstown and similar episodes in other companies awakened employers to the fact that something was wrong. Employers gradually began to experiment with work redesign methods.

HONESTY AND RESPECT

An employer who pays your salary has a right to tell you what to do as long as it is not unlawful. Most employers and supervisors, however, realize that honesty and respect toward their employees are essential. Workers are not robots. They are human beings with pride and self-worth. The following case about Lordstown shows what can happen when a company forgets about the feelings of its workers.

Lordstown is a city in Ohio where a General Motors assembly plant is located. The plant was built to be the world's fastest, most fully automated auto assembly line. In 1971, the assembly line was producing 104 cars per hour. (The industry average was 55 per hour.) Some GM officials thought that the line could produce even more cars. They cut back workers on the line and increased the number of jobs each person had to do.

The result was that many workers could not keep up with the pace. Some workers were literally riding down the line with the cars as they tried to bolt on parts. Workers complained, but GM officials ignored them. Out of frustration, workers began intentionally leaving pieces off the cars. In some cases, workers inflicted costly damage to the cars. Many cars came off the line with broken windshields, torn upholstery, or other damage. Eventually, the workers went on strike.

Between March 3 and March 24, 1972, approximately 8,000 workers participated in the strike. After three weeks and $150 million in lost production, workers and management agreed to a settlement. The episode at Lordstown marked a turning point in employer-worker relations.

This example illustrates that employers cannot always force workers to do what they want them to do. The best relationship is one where employers treat workers as they wish to be treated. Honesty and respect is the foundation for a good relationship between employers and workers.

FAIR EMPLOYMENT PRACTICES

Many state and federal laws deal with employment practices. A very important federal law is the Fair Labor Standards Act (FLSA). It applies to employers or companies that do business in more than one state and have annual sales of above a certain amount. The FLSA covers three types of practices. These are child labor, wages and hours, and equal pay.

Child Labor

The FLSA includes laws covering workers under the age of eighteen. For instance, people fifteen years and younger cannot work in factories or during school hours. Nor can those under eighteen work in dangerous occupations such as mining.

FIGURE 8-2 Most employees are willing to work hard as long as they are treated fairly. *Courtesy of USX Corporation*

Redesign of work and different relationships between employers and workers result in increased worker satisfaction and greater productivity. Both employers and workers benefit.

2. Emphasize that this was extreme behavior growing out of intense frustration. Sabotage by workers is not condoned.
3. You may wish to assign Activity 1 at this point.

4. Emphasize the primary characteristics of child labor laws: (a) they limit the employment of individuals under a certain age, (b) they restrict the types of occupations that young people may perform, and (c) they limit the hours of employment.
5. Show and explain work permits used by your school.
6. They protect employers from violating child labor laws.

94 ■ SECTION 2 Working on the Job

FIGURE 8-3 At one time, employment of children in factories and mines was common. *Courtesy New York State Archives*

Each of the fifty states also has its own child-labor laws. If both federal and state laws apply to a situation, the employer must obey the stricter standard. For instance, David is seventeen and wants to work at a sawmill in his town. His state's laws would let him work there. Federal law, though, says that such jobs are too dangerous for workers under eighteen. David will have to wait until his next birthday to apply for a mill job.

You read in Chapter 3 that the law is flexible to allow students to take part in work experience education programs. In most states, schools issue work permits to those between fourteen and seventeen years of age. This allows students to work during school hours. The program helps protect the health and welfare of minors. It regulates the types of work they may do and the hours they can work. Can you think of how a work permit benefits employers as well?

Wages and Hours

The FLSA sets standards for minimum wages and maximum hours for most workers in the U.S. Many states also have laws about workers' pay. The *minimum wage* is the lowest wage the law permits employers to pay workers. (Remember, not all employers are covered by this law.) In 1938, the national minimum wage was 25 cents an hour. By January 1, 1981 the figure had risen to $3.35 an hour. Congress periodically raises the minimum wage. Is it still $3.35 an hour?

Perhaps you are muttering that you receive less than minimum wage. If you are a work experience student, chances are that this is true. Because your employer provides your training as well as your job, you probably receive about seventy-five percent of the minimum wage.

The FLSA also sets the length of the *standard work-week*. Time worked beyond forty hours is called

7. Congress may raise the minimum wage at any time. Be alert to any new developments and update this information as appropriate.

8. The standard workweek is eight hours a day, five days a week. But some jobs might have a different workweek such as ten hours a day, four days a week.

FIGURE 8-4 Minimum wage laws do not cover employees of all small businesses. *Photo by David W. Tuttle*

overtime. For overtime hours, employers must pay workers at a rate of 1 1/2 times their regular rate. The discussion of overtime pay in Chapter 10 holds special interest for us all. That material deals with figuring overtime on a paycheck.

What Would You Do?

Your employer asks you to work a few extra hours on Saturday to help him catch up on an important order. Even though you have already put in forty hours this week, you agree to do so. The next week, you eagerly open your pay envelope. You discover that you have been paid straight time for forty-five hours. You call this to the boss' attention. He tells you that he doesn't pay overtime and that you should be glad that you have a job. You aren't satisfied with his explanation. What would you do?

*

WWYD Feature A. This would seem to be a clear violation of the FLSA. Explain the process for resolving a grievance.

Equal Pay

John and Ruth were assistant managers for a small hotel chain. They started working for the chain at the same time. They had equal qualifications. Ruth learned that John was making a lot more money than she was. Ruth tried to figure out the problem. She knew that workers sometimes receive different salaries because of shift work, skill level, and things like that. Ruth ruled out all those reasons. The only difference she could name was that she was a woman. She knew that the Equal Pay Act of 1963 outlawed different wage scales for equal work. This means that workers doing the same job must receive the same wage. An employer may still pay workers different wages based on such things as seniority, skill level, shift worked, and so on. What would you do if you were Ruth?

9

FIGURE 8-5 These workers are paid the same because they are doing equal work. *Designed and produced by Liberia and Associates, photography by Peter Saloutos*

9. Ruth should relate her concern to her employer and ask for an explanation. If the explanation is unsatisfactory, she should pursue the matter with the appropriate government agency.

PROTECTION FROM DISCRIMINATION

As you can see, laws protect workers from being discriminated against. *Discrimination* means treating someone differently than another. For example, if an employer won't hire you only because of your race, that is discrimination. Another example is being "passed over" for promotion because of your sex. So, too, is getting fired because you are older. What about equal treatment in such areas as hiring, promotion, and job security? Laws covering these areas exist. They deal with the broad areas of *equal employment opportunity* and *affirmative action*.

Equal Employment Opportunity

The passage of the Civil Rights Act of 1964 gave the government a strong legal tool to prevent job discrimination. It thus paved the way for equal employment opportunity. Under equal opportunity, employers, unions, and employment agencies cannot discriminate against people because of race, color, religion, sex, or national origin. The Equal Employment Opportunity Commission *(EEOC)* administers the Civil Rights Act and related laws.

SALES
NEWSPAPER SALES REP
A National Newspaper is seeking a sales representative for St. Louis/Kansas City. Responsibilities include the development of retail, vending, corporate and college sales. Excellent salary and benefits. Car provided. Send resume and salary history to:

ARC INC.
78 WEST 5TH STREET
SUITE 100
HICKORY HEIGHTS, OH 45492
ATTENTION: JOHN GOODMAN

Equal Opportunity Employer

FIGURE 8-6 Some companies make it a point to advertise that they are Equal Opportunity Employers.

10. Ask students to provide additional examples of discrimination in employment. Clarify any examples that are confused with affirmative action.

In 1964, Warren Johnson lost his job as a landscaper. His employer had gone out of business. Warren was fifty-six at the time. With his experience, he figured that he would easily find a job. The first two places he applied told him he was "too old." Warren was upset. He could not legally fight the employers. Today, he could fight them.

11. Telling Warren that he was "too old" is overt discrimination. Most discrimination is more subtle and often goes unchallenged because it is very difficult to prove.

12. The term *affirmative action* was first used by President Lyndon Johnson in 1965. It has come to be a more controversial concept than equal employment opportunity (which is the law).

The Age Discrimination Act of 1967 was passed to prohibit discrimination against people between forty and seventy years of age. The Rehabilitation Act of 1973 extended protection to those with physical or mental handicaps. The EEOC also administers both of these laws.

Affirmative Action

Equal employment opportunity laws forbid job discrimination. What about those people who have been victims of past discrimination, though? For instance, many women and other minorities have been unjustly passed over for job promotions. This is an example of a condition that *affirmative action* tries to correct. Affirmative action is not a federal law. Instead, it refers to a series of policies and programs designed to correct *past discrimination*. Most affirmative action programs include special efforts to hire and promote women, minorities, handicapped people, and Vietnam veterans.

FIGURE 8-7 The number of women and minorities has increased in many occupations because of affirmative action programs. *Courtesy Amoco Corporation*

13. Ask students if their place of employment has an affirmative action program. Discuss as appropriate.

14. Before 1971, organized labor was the major advocate for worker safety and health. It was instrumental in OSHA getting passed.

WORKER SAFETY AND HEALTH

Have you seen workers wearing hard hats and safety glasses? Perhaps you have worn such gear yourself. Such equipment helps protect workers from injury. Years ago, many employers were often unconcerned if their employees failed to use safety equipment or otherwise acted unsafely. Some employers even made employees work under unsafe or unhealthful conditions. If workers complained,

15. These are only several of thousands of specific OSHA rules.
16. OSHA also disseminates information to employers about newly discovered safety hazards and new methods of accident prevention.

FIGURE 8-8 It is important to use safety equipment and dispose of wastes properly to keep a workplace safe. *Courtesy Union Pacific Corporation*

17. OSHA has strong legal powers to enforce safety laws, punish offenders, and provide compensation to victims.

CHAPTER 8 Worker Rights and Protections ■ 97

they lost their jobs. In 1971, such situations changed for the better. That year marked the beginning of the Occupational Safety and Health Administration *(OSHA)*. This organization sets and enforces standards for safe and healthful working conditions.

Examples of OSHA rules include the following:

- Each high-radiation area shall contain a sign having the radiation caution symbol and the words: *CAUTION, HIGH-RADIATION AREA*.
- Safety shoes shall conform to certain standards.
- Tools and other metal objects shall be kept away from the top of uncovered batteries.
- Exposed hot water and steam pipes shall be covered with insulating material whenever necessary to protect employees from contact with them.
- All workplaces shall be kept as clean as the nature of the work allows.

All employers having at least one employee must obey OSHA standards. To help employers, OSHA offers free on-site visitations. Most employers welcome suggestions that will create a better work environment. Exceptions exist, though. To discourage these, OSHA makes random inspections as well. If inspectors find hazards, the employer can be fined.

A restaurant server in Kansas complained to her employer that it was too hot in the restaurant's kitchen area. The employer ignored her complaint. She took her complaint to OSHA. When the employer found out, he tried to get even with the server. He threatened her, began giving her the least desirable work, and rearranged her work schedule. The server tried to reason with the employer, but finally quit because of the harrassment.

The server filed a complaint with OSHA. After investigating the case, OSHA ordered the employer to pay the server back wages and to remove all papers about the case from her files. (Most employers keep records on each employee.) OSHA also required the employer to post a notice that advised other employees of the settlement.

Protecting New Workers

New employees have a much higher risk of injury than experienced workers. The Bureau of Labor Statistics (BLS) reports that about half of all work-related injuries occur during the first year of employment. Why are new workers more likely to be hurt?

18. Emphasize the fact that "about half of all work-related injuries occur during the first year of employment." Ask students why they think this is the case.

98 ■ SECTION 2 Working on the Job

Studies show that new workers often do not know enough to protect themselves. The BLS has found that:

- Of 724 workers hurt while using scaffolds, twenty-seven percent said that they had received no information on safety requirements for installing the kind of scaffold on which they were hurt.
- Of 868 workers who suffered head injuries, seventy-one percent said that they had had no instruction about hard hats.
- Of 554 workers hurt while servicing equipment, sixty-one percent said that they were not informed about lockout procedures.

In nearly every type of injury studied by the BLS, the same story is repeated. Workers often do not receive the safety information they need. Or, if they do, they do not apply it.

What Would You Do?

The production machine on which you work was repaired over the weekend. As you begin work on Monday morning, you notice that the safety guard has not been replaced. You immediately go to the supervisor. He tells you to go ahead and get started and he will replace the guard when he gets time. But you don't want to work on the machine unless the safety guard is in place. What would you do?

WWYD Feature B. The machine should not be operated without the safety guard. The boss made an error in judgment. The employee should firmly declare that he/she will not work until the guard is replaced. This will hopefully provoke the desired response from the boss.

What Workers Can Do

During your on-the-job training, your employer is responsible for your safety education. You, too, play an important role. Before starting to work, be sure that you understand all necessary safety measures. If an explanation is unclear, ask again. Practice and use what you have learned. Do not take shortcuts that could endanger your health or safety.

Following are some general safety rules. Can you think of others?

19

- Never use a tool or piece of equipment that lacks a safety guard or has a nonworking one.
- If earplugs or other personal protective devices such as gloves or aprons are required, use them all the time.
- Don't "horse around" or play practical jokes at the workplace.
- Be especially careful when you get tired. This is when accidents are more likely to happen.
- If you work where dangerous substances are used, find out what something is before you handle it.
- Accept responsibility for your own safety on the job.

Besides taking care of their own safety and health, workers should be on the lookout for possible dangers. Employers should correct any problems that employees call to their attention. If an employer doesn't correct a problem, it is up to the employee to call on OSHA for help if needed. OSHA protects your right to complain to your employer, your

20

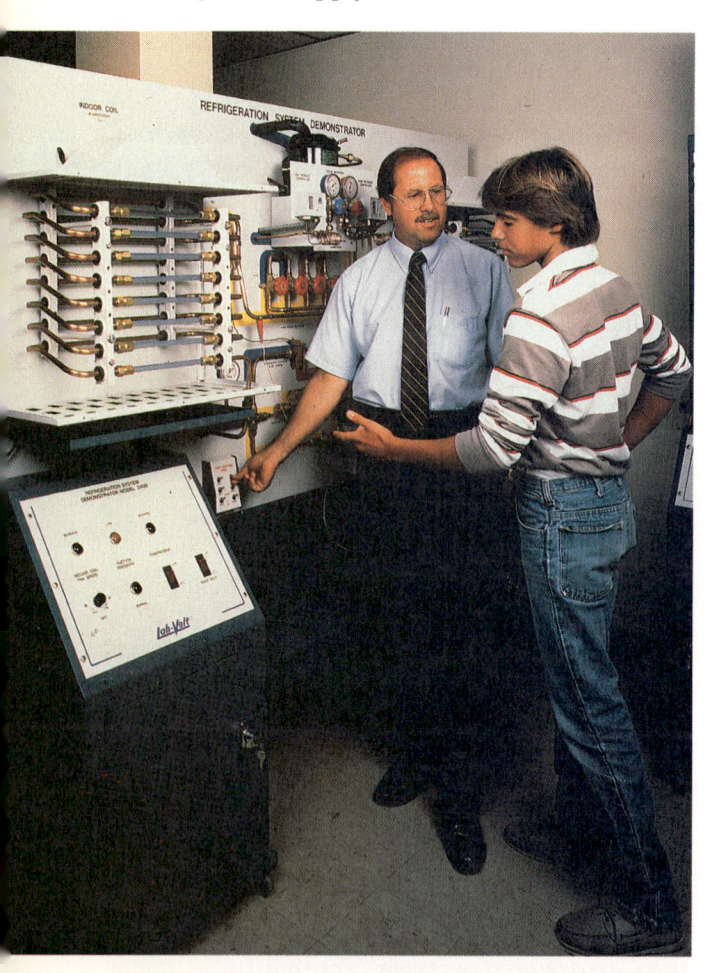

FIGURE 8-9 Ask about anything on the job you don't understand. What you don't know can hurt you. *Courtesy of Lab-Volt Systems Division of Buck Engineering, Inc.*

19. There are an unlimited number of safety rules. You might ask students to name or write on a piece of paper three to five of the most important safety rules that apply to their jobs.

20. Ask students if they have noticed any dangers needing correction where they work.

FIGURE 8-10 Think safety every minute that you are on the job. *Courtesy of SIUC Photocommunications*

union, and to OSHA itself. It is illegal for your employer to punish you for exercising this or any other OSHA right.

AGENCIES PROVIDING SERVICES TO WORKERS

What should you do if you have a work problem dealing with fair employment practices, discrimination, or health and safety? If you are a work experience student, contact your school coordinator. He or she can help solve the problem. Apprentices and union workers can speak to the union representative. Civil service employees also have representatives they can turn to for help. Wherever you work, follow any procedures that may appear in your company's policy manual.

If you do not have certain procedures to follow or anyone else to help you, try to work out the problem with your boss or employer. Ask for a meeting to informally discuss your complaint. Present your point of view and then listen patiently to the other person's side of the story.

21. Provide several representative excerpts from company policy manuals that relate to fair employment practices, discrimination, and health and safety.

FIGURE 8-11 Workers often discover safety hazards. Report them to your boss. *Photo by David W. Tuttle*

F·E·A·T·U·R·E

Collective Bargaining

◆ ◆ ◆

Labor (workers) and management (owners/managers) share a common interest. Both want to see the company grow and succeed. Occasionally, the two groups may disagree regarding wages, benefits, working conditions, or other matters. If the workers are union members, the two sides engage in *collective bargaining* to settle their differences.

In typical collective bargaining, union representatives present demands. Management may accept or reject the demands. It may also make a counteroffer. The two sides often negotiate back and forth for days or even weeks.

Eventually, the two sides agree. The agreement, called a labor contract, is put into writing. The union membership must then vote on the agreement. As a legal document, the labor contract can be enforced in a court of law. The contract usually covers a specified time period such as three years.

After a labor contract is signed, the agreement is put into practice. A contract presents certain rules that labor and management are to follow. Sometimes, though, a complaint or grievance arises over what the rules mean or how they are carried out. For instance, a grievance might result from the firing of a worker or the violation of a safety practice.

The procedure for settling grievances is an important part of the labor contract. An employee with a grievance, along with the union representative, usually discusses the matter with the boss. Most problems are resolved at this level. If the problem is not resolved, the employee may file a complaint with a higher level of management.

FIGURE 8-FEATURE A strike or the threat of a strike is a bargaining tool of labor unions.

Collective Bargaining. Employees working under a collective bargaining agreement are protected by a legally enforceable labor contract (in addition to other federal laws explained in this chapter). A typical contract includes a variety of rules related to worker rights and protections. Obtain a representative union contract and share some specific examples with the class.

FIGURE 8-12 Try to resolve an employment problem informally before contacting an outside agency. *Photo by Paul E. Meyers*

22   If an informal meeting doesn't work, file a formal complaint. Write a letter to the proper company official. State your complaint clearly and briefly. Ask for an answer by a reasonable date. Be polite and businesslike in your letter. Do not make demands. Do ask that the problem be solved. Keep a copy of the letter for your file.

If all of your efforts to solve the problem meet dead ends, you can then turn to outside help. Many federal laws and government agencies protect the rights of workers. A summary of the major types of complaints and agencies that handle them is provided in Figure 8-13. Ask for help at your public library if you have any trouble finding the addresses or phone numbers you need.

Most employers support and respect laws and rules that protect workers. Employers may sometimes overlook a law or rule. Other times, though, an employer violates a law on purpose. In either case, it is up to you to identify and then to report any violations you find. Learn your rights so that you can be in control of your health, safety, and welfare.

22. You may wish to assign Activity 3 at this time.

Type of Complaint	Federal Agency
Child labor Wages and hours	Employment Standards Administration U.S. Department of Labor 200 Constitution Ave., N.W. Washington, D.C. 20210
Equal pay Discrimination based on race, color, religion, sex, national origin, age, or handicap	Equal Employment Opportunity Commission (EEOC) 2401 E St. N.W. Washington, D.C. 20507
Safety and health	Occupational Safety and Health Administration (OSHA) U.S. Department of Labor 200 Constitution Ave., N.W. Washington, D.C. 20210

Note: Federal agencies also maintain state and local offices. Look in the telephone Yellow Pages under "Governmental Offices—Federal."

FIGURE 8-13 These are the primary federal agencies that handle complaints regarding fair employment practices, discrimination, and health and safety.

CHAPTER REVIEW

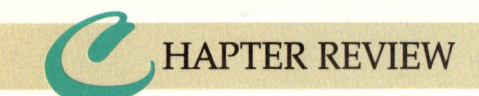

Chapter in Brief

- An employment contract isn't a one-way deal. Employers owe certain things to their employees.
- An employer who pays your salary has a right to give you orders as long as they aren't unlawful. Most employers and supervisors, however, realize that honesty and respect toward their employees are essential.
- Many state and federal laws deal with employment practices. The most important one is the Fair Labor Standards Act (FLSA). The FLSA covers three types of practices: child labor, wages and hours, and equal pay.
- Laws also exist to promote equal treatment in such areas as hiring, promotion, and job security. It is illegal for employers, unions, and employment agencies to discriminate against people because of race, color, religion, sex, national origin, age, or physical or mental handicaps.
- Affirmative action policies and programs have been established to help victims of past discrimination. These include special efforts to hire and promote women, minorities, handicapped people, and Vietnam veterans.
- The Occupational Safety and Health Administration (OSHA) was created in 1971 to set and enforce standards for safe and healthful working conditions. Workers can file a complaint with OSHA if an employer refuses to correct unsafe or unhealthful working conditions.
- New employees have a much higher risk of injury than experienced workers. A reason seems to be that workers often do not receive the safety information they need. Or, if they do, they don't apply it. You play an important role in learning and practicing safety rules.
- If you have a problem at work regarding fair employment practices, discrimination, or health and safety, try to solve it informally. If this doesn't work, file a formal complaint with the proper company official. If this doesn't solve the problem, you can turn to outside agencies for help.

Words to Know

affirmative action a series of government policies and programs designed to correct past discrimination.

discrimination favoring one person as compared to another.

equal employment opportunity the idea that a person cannot be discriminated against in hiring or employment because of age, race, color, religion, sex, national origin, or handicapping condition.

EEOC an acronym for the Equal Employment Opportunity Commission, the government agency that administers the Civil Rights Act of 1964.

minimum wage by law, the lowest hourly wage that can be paid to an employee.

OSHA an acronym for the Occupational Safety and Health Administration, the government agency that sets and enforces standards for safe and healthful working conditions.

overtime time worked beyond the standard forty-hour workweek.

standard workweek by law, the completion of forty hours of work during a seven-day period.

Questions to Answer
1. How does the Lordstown case show an employer's lack of respect toward workers?
2. When federal and state fair labor standards conflict, which law applies? Give an example.
3. Name three things the FLSA covers.
4. What is the purpose of the Equal Pay Act of 1963?
5. The Civil Rights Act of 1964 prevents discrimination on what five things? What things were added in 1967 and 1973?
6. Affirmative action seeks to correct past discrimination. Give an example.
7. To which employers do OSHA rules and standards apply?
8. Why are new employees more likely to be hurt on the job than more experienced workers?
9. To protect your health and safety, what four things should you do before you start to work?
10. Suppose a work problem arises between you and your employer. List the steps that you should follow in trying to correct it.

Activities to Do
1. Find out what your state laws are on child labor, wages and hours, and equal pay. Report your findings to the class.
2. Find out the location of your nearest OSHA office. Pick up or request copies of booklets that explain workers' rights under OSHA. Discuss these in class. After studying them, you may want to make a bulletin board display.
3. Write an imaginary letter to an employer complaining of a work-related problem. Follow the guidelines presented in this chapter. Turn it into your instructor for evaluation.

Topics to Discuss
1. State and federal laws often permit employers to pay worker trainees less than the minimum wage. What is the justification for this? Do you think this is fair?
2. Affirmative action programs give special advantages to groups that were discriminated against in the past. Discuss in class the pros and cons of such programs.
3. Have you ever had a work accident or been hurt on the job? If so, how might it have been prevented? Discuss your answers in class.

---

1. The employer seemed to treat workers as if they were robots. The case illustrates that there are practical limits to the production capabilities of human beings.
2. The one having the stricter standards. For example, if a state law permits a person to work at seventeen, but a federal law specifies eighteen for the same job, then the federal law applies.
3. (a) Child labor. (b) Wages and hours. (c) Equal pay.
4. It outlawed different wage scales for the same type of work (taking into account such things as seniority, skill level, shift work, and so on).
5. (a) Race, color, religion, sex, or national origin. (b) Age added in 1967, and physical/mental handicaps added in 1973.
6. An example would be preference in hiring a minority person from among a pool of equally qualified applicants.
7. All employers having at least one employee must obey OSHA rules and standards.
8. New workers often do not receive the safety information they need. Or, if they do, they don't apply it.
9. (a) Be sure that you understand all safety measures. (b) If an explanation is unclear, ask again. (c) Practice and use what you have learned. (d) Don't take short-cuts.
10. First, enlist the aid of everyone whose job it is to help you. Second, try to work out the problem informally. Third, file a formal complaint. Finally, turn to an outside government agency for help. In all cases, follow procedures that appear in the company's policy manual.

23. Students will probably need direction regarding where to find such information. If you have the relevant materials on hand, an alternative might be to assign students specific parts to summarize and present in class.
24. OSHA has a number of relevant, informative, free materials.
25. The letter may involve any of the six types of things owed employees that were listed at the beginning of this chapter. You may need to give an example or two to help students get started.
26. The justification is that trainees aren't as productive as more experienced workers.

1. Human relations are a two-way street. You influence other people; others influence you.

2. Another characteristic of human relations is that they may be pleasant or unpleasant.

CHAPTER NINE

Human Relations at Work

OUTLINE
Bosses, Co-workers, and Customers
Group Participation
Chapter Review

OBJECTIVES
After reading this chapter, you should be able to:
- Explain the importance of good human relations to success on the job.
- Discuss ways to get along with co-workers.
- Identify three reasons why customers patronize a particular business.
- Discuss ways to participate effectively in a task group.

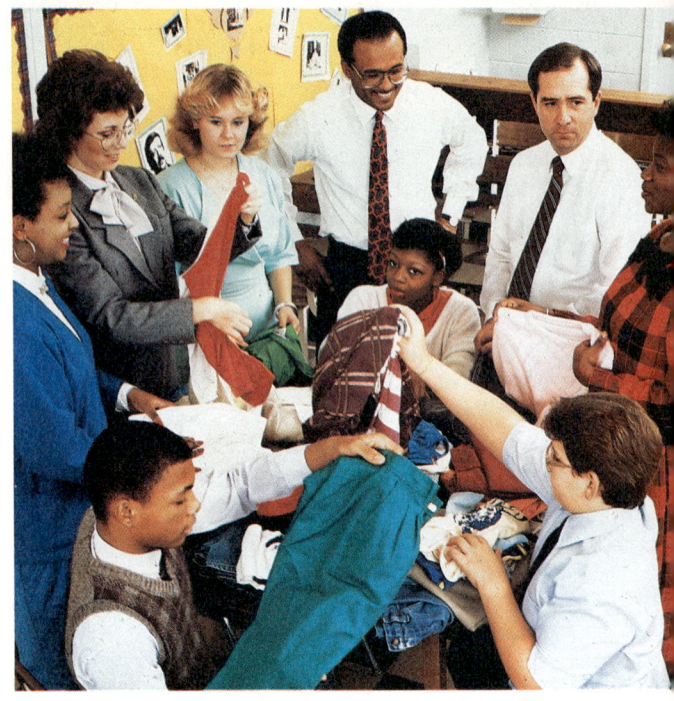

FIGURE 9-1 Relations with others are part of what makes us human. *Courtesy of Ford Motor Company*

You deal with people every day of your life. You may talk, joke, plan, study, argue, and so on. Some of these dealings are more important than others. For instance, you go into a store to buy a quart of milk. Chances are that your conversation with the clerk won't influence life much. On the other hand, a talk with your boss, co-workers, or teacher just might. Your dealings with others influence your happiness and success. They also may affect others. Ask Kevin.

Guy was supposed to pick up his friend Kevin on the way to school. Guy got up late, and in his hurry to get to school, forgot Kevin. So an unhappy Kevin had to walk two miles to school. He got to school late, missed a test, and had to go to detention after school. Guy's mistake caused problems for Kevin.

Some *human relations* are pleasant. Others are very difficult. Unless we become hermits, we can't get away from other people. So we need to learn to deal with many kinds of situations. This is especially true for workers. It's true that most fired workers lose their jobs because they can't get along with others.

BOSSES, CO-WORKERS, AND CUSTOMERS

Suppose you and another student don't get along very well. You find yourselves in the same English class. Chances are that you won't need to work closely with the other student. On the job, though, you may have to work closely all week with someone you really don't like. In such cases, you will both need to put personal feelings aside.

At work we have to deal with all kinds of people. These include bosses, co-workers, and customers. We may like some of these people more than others. Even so, we must try to get along with everyone. Understanding our bosses, co-workers, and customers can make this task easier.

3. Regardless of preferences, however, almost everyone has to learn to interact effectively with others to be successful on the job.

4. Write the word *empathy* on the board. Ask students if they know the meaning of the word (projecting oneself into another's position or situation).

Getting Along with Bosses

Most employees have a boss. The boss may be the company's owner, a crew chief, or a department head. Whoever your boss is, you will need to form a working relationship with him or her (reviewed in Chapters 6 and 7).

Good employees try to understand the boss' position. Being a boss is never easy. How would you feel if you had to fire someone, for instance? Bosses sometimes must do this. They must always provide workers with instructions and helpful criticism. Good bosses act in the interest of the company. They don't act out of friendship. Sometimes, workers and bosses do become friends. Even so, this should not influence their work behavior. The company should still come first. If you and your boss aren't friends, that's fine. You can still have a good relationship. (Some bosses make it a policy not to be friends with people they supervise.)

Getting Along With Co-Workers

Strong friendships depend on *interpersonal attraction*. Think about it. Why do people become your friends? Well, they are probably somewhat like you. We enjoy being with people who are like us in at least some ways. We choose such people for friends, and they choose us. At work, though, interpersonal attraction isn't as important. What *is* important is doing your share of the work and following rules.

FIGURE 9-2 Most students who relate well to teachers also get along with their bosses. *Photo by Dennis Moller*

5. Emphasize the fact that some bosses intentionally maintain a distance between themselves and their employees. It may even be company policy.

FIGURE 9-3 You and your friends have a lot in common. That is one reason why you are friends. *Courtesy of Siena College, Loudonville, NY*

FIGURE 9-4 You can learn a great deal from co-workers. They will probably be glad to share information and advice. *Courtesy Union Pacific Corp.*

As a new worker, you can be sure that your co-workers will be watching you. They will expect you to do your share of the work. Your co-workers probably won't mind helping you out from time to time. They will expect you to do the same when they need help. But your co-workers won't put up with doing their work and yours, too. At least, they won't for very long.

Following the rules is important. Rules make sure that employees in similar jobs receive equal treatment. If you ignore the rules, you are indicating that you are different or better than the other workers. Your co-workers won't like your ignoring the same rules that they are expected to follow.

Sometimes, being different has its place at work. Two examples involve seniority and territorial rights. *Seniority* refers to the length of time someone has worked for a company. Workers with the most seniority have the most privileges. Respecting seniority rules will help you get along with co-workers.

In January, Tina requested to take a week's

6. Rules in the workplace are as necessary as traffic laws are on the highway. Ask students to explain how they are similar.
7. Seniority rules are more formalized under union labor contracts.
8. Ask students if they have encountered or observed the phenomenon of territorial rights where they work.

9. Appearance on the job is discussed in detail in Chapter 11.

vacation during the first week in June. Mrs. Soria, the boss, came to talk to her. It turned out that Sven, who had the same job title as Tina, wanted the same week off. Mrs. Soria told Tina that she couldn't do without both of them that week. Since Sven had been there two years longer than Tina, he would get to take that week. Tina thanked Mrs. Soria for telling her. She then started to think about choosing some other week.

In a work setting, certain unwritten rules about *territorial rights* may develop. Some workers come to feel that they control a certain office, area, or sales territory. When you are on their turf, they expect you to behave as they wish. An example might be that you are not to bring food into a certain person's office. Or, maybe you aren't supposed to use someone's tools without asking permission first. Be alert for such things. Try to respect others' territorial rights.

Doing your share of the work and following the rules lead to good feelings among co-workers. Other ways to maintain good relationships with co-workers include the following:

- *Appearance.* Maintain good personal hygiene and grooming. Don't underdress or overdress.
- *Courtesy.* Be pleasant, friendly, and courteous. Don't force relationships with co-workers. In time, some may become your friends.
- *Attitude.* Be positive. Don't complain about your job. Clint sometimes gets tired of being a "go-fer" for everyone in the shop. He doesn't let it discourage him, though. Clint is glad to have a job, and looks forward to a promotion soon.
- *Interest.* Show interest in the job. Pay attention to what co-workers are doing and show them that you feel their interests are important.
- *Loyalty.* Don't criticize the company or gossip about bosses or co-workers. Those you talk to will wonder what you are saying about them!
- *Tolerance.* Try to tolerate the opinions, habits, and behaviors of co-workers. Being different is all right. Martha, for instance, is a vegetarian. She eats bean, cucumber and alfalfa sandwiches for lunch. Through her, some co-workers have learned more about good eating habits.

FIGURE 9-5 **Try to avoid being a LIFO (Last In to work and First Out at quitting time).** *Photo by Paul E. Meyers*

10. Make sure students understand the slang term *go-fer* meaning to "go for," "go get," or "go after." Remind students that many of their co-workers were also "go-fers" at one time.

11. Ask students if they have learned anything or gained any greater insights as a result of working with people who may be different from themselves.

F ◆ E ◆ A ◆ T ◆ U ◆ R ◆ E

Relating to Workaholics

◆ ◆ ◆

At some point in your career, you may work for or with a workaholic (or become one yourself). Understanding and getting along with workaholics is a special case in human relations.

Workaholics are people who are addicted to their work. They love their work. They live their work. They find it very difficult to ever leave their work. In her book *Workaholics*, Marilyn Machlowitz provides two examples of workaholics. An elderly attorney sat at his desk working while his office building was on fire. He ignored the fire and sirens until he was forcibly removed by firefighters. A pregnant publicist felt labor pains. She rushed to her doctor's office. When she found out that delivery was still hours away, she went back to work.

Workaholics exist in every occupation. It's not necessary to be employed to be one. Many homemakers are workaholics. As a group, workaholics are surprisingly happy. They are doing what they love. They can't seem to get enough of it. If they are in the right job, they can be extremely productive.

There is another side to the workaholic at work. According to Machlowitz, workaholics may be among the world's worst workers. They suffer few ills themselves. But they often wind up doing damage to their companies. They often create a pressure-cooker atmosphere. They demand a great deal. They expect everyone to be as dedicated to work as they are.

Workaholics often have difficulty delegating work to others. They tend to be critical of coworkers. Even their high energy level causes problems. Workaholics may try to do everything themselves.

FIGURE 9-FEATURE Workaholics work hard and play hard. *Courtesy of United Telecom, Inc.*

As you see, it can be difficult to work with a workaholic. The truth is, says Machlowitz, that workaholics are better suited to be entrepreneurs. They just don't do well in a business organization managing people.

---

* *Relating to Workaholics.* Being addicted to one's work is a type of compulsion. Unlike addiction to drinking or gambling, though, addiction to work is much less self-destructive. Workaholics, as pointed out, are often happy and productive. The problem with workaholics is that they tend to be difficult to manage, to work with, and to work for. Ask students if they know anyone who is a workaholic.

12. Being a person who others can call on for help.
13. Many of the "What Would You Do" features in this book involve questions of ethics and ethical behavior.

CHAPTER 9 Human Relations at Work ■ 109

What Would You Do?

You have been cutting and styling Mrs. Laird's hair for about six months. You are beginning to dread her coming into the shop. You like Mrs. Laird, but her young son is a terror. You wish she wouldn't bring him along. He is loud and obnoxious and disturbs the other patrons. He always wants something from his mother and cries when he doesn't get his way. You don't want to make Mrs. Laird angry, but something has to be done about the boy. What would you do?

*WWYD Feature A. Mrs. Laird should be told that her son is creating problems and that if he can't behave, he should be left at home.

Without customers, a company can't stay in business. Relationships between employees and customers are important to the success of a business. Let's look at some reasons why a customer deals with a certain business. We will also give some hints as to how employees can encourage customers to return.

FIGURE 9-6 Sometimes, walking away from an argument is the best thing to do. You can talk about the problem later. *Photo by Paul E. Meyers*

- *Maturity.* Be agreeable and avoid arguments. If conflicts do arise with co-workers, talk them out.
- *Dependability.* Always do what you say you will do. Quinn agreed to work overtime on Saturday afternoons. Last Saturday would have been a great sailing day. Quinn went to work because he had given his word. He would have preferred to have gone to the bay.
- *Openness.* Be open to suggestions and change. Ask co-workers for advice and offer to help them.
- *Ethics.* Don't try to get ahead at the expense of others. Heather is the department's most creative layout artist. She lets her work speak for itself. Heather never criticizes the other artists' work to make herself look better.

Getting Along With Customers

The purpose of a business is to make a profit. Some businesses sell goods such as clothing, hardware, or autos. Other businesses sell services. Examples of services include insurance, haircuts, and dry cleaning. A business sells its goods or services to customers. Not all customers are called by that name. An accountant may speak of *clients,* and a nurse of *patients.* What about users of library services? In a sense, they are customers of a service, even though they don't pay for it. Librarians call their customers *patrons.*

14. Write "goods" and "services" on the board and ask students to provide several examples of each.

FIGURE 9-7 Some businesses advertise that the customer is always right. *Photo by David W. Tuttle*

15. Government services should also follow the guidelines for getting along with customers.

110 ■ SECTION 2 Working on the Job

One reason why customers *patronize* a business is that they like the product or service provided. Leigh, for instance, goes to Andrews-Evans because she likes their almond ice cream. Rafael has his hair cut at Rich's because he likes Rich's work. Customers who patronize a business have certain wants or needs. A competent worker who treats customers well encourages business.

Darcy is a landscaper for Sunrise Nursery. Last month, Mr. Clements, a client, said he wanted some more flowers and shrubs around his house. He didn't have anything special in mind. So Darcy said she would think about it and call him. She did so and then made an appointment with Mr. Clements. Darcy brought with her everything Mr. Clements would need before making a decision. Her efforts paid off. She got that job and other new customers in the neighborhood.

Businesses that provide services after a sale also encourage customers. The services may include such things as product repair, refunds, or quick processing of a claim. Let's look at a couple of contrasting examples.

A customer is returning a defective product to a store. Here is the conversation between the customer and a salesclerk:

"I bought this clock-radio a couple of weeks ago. For some reason, the alarm doesn't work."

"Did you drop it or something?"

"No, it just quit on its own."

16. Ask students if they can add to this list of things regarding "services after a sale."

FIGURE 9-8 Treat customers like you would want to be treated. *Courtesy of Delta Air Lines, Inc.*

17. Ask students if they have ever been involved in an interaction like the one described in the preceding example (almost everyone has).

"Are you sure it's broken? Maybe you're not setting it properly."

"I can assure you that I know how to set it."

"Did you buy it here?"

"Of course, I bought it here. You can see that the box has your sales sticker on it."

"Do you have the receipt?"

It is easy to see the direction this conversation took. Here is a conversation between another customer and a second salesclerk:

"I bought this food processor here some time ago and now it has quit working."

"I'm sorry you have had a problem. Do you remember about when you bought it?"

"Yes, it was right after Christmas. Here is the receipt."

"Good. The warranty is still valid. Why don't you go pick out another one, while I write up an exchange ticket."

"This is the same model and price, but it's a different color."

"Is that color OK?"

"Yes, I actually like it better."

"Well, that worked out well, didn't it? Will you please sign this form, while I put it in a bag for you? You shouldn't have any trouble with this one. Come back and see us."

A third reason customers return to a business is because of what is called *goodwill*. These are the little things about a business. Examples include reputation, honesty, and attitude toward customers. Employees promote goodwill in many ways.

- Jana calls as many customers as possible by name. She also knows which ones like to be called by their first names and which by their last.
- Ingmar knows that a lot of people come into the store just to look around. He makes them feel welcome and then stays back until they ask for or seem to need help.
- Many adults come into Mia's store to buy toys or gifts for their children or young friends. They seem to appreciate it when she offers suggestions about the items that children like best.
- Some customers at the ice cream shop where Cleveland works have trouble deciding what flavor they want. He offers uncertain customers free samples.
- Jillian remembers what it was like when she was in college and didn't have much money. Her restaurant is the most popular one in the campus town. Why? Heaping plates of good food, of course.

18. Ask students if they can add to this list of examples of *goodwill*.

CHAPTER 9 Human Relations at Work ■ 111

GROUP PARTICIPATION

Most people, at least some of the time, work in groups. These are called *task groups* (or work groups). Groups are often formed to brainstorm a new product, discuss quality control problems, or plan a new sales strategy. There is a trend in business and industry to use more and different types of task groups. But do groups really perform better than individuals?

19. Work groups have been used in business and industry for a long time. The increasing use of Japanese-style management techniques has resulted in increased awareness and greater use of groups in promoting participative management (quality circles being the best known example).

FIGURE 9-9 This vocational youth organization is a task group. How many task groups are you a part of? *Photo by David W. Tuttle*

Groups are generally superior to most individuals at many (but not all) tasks. A school newspaper, for example, benefits by having different people write columns on current events, club activities, sports, and the like. It would be hard for one person to write

20. Research on task groups indicates that a group can make a better decision or produce a better product than the *average* group member. Groups, however, have their limitations.

FIGURE 9-10 Big jobs require a lot of workers. *Courtesy 1988 Campaign, United Way of Northeastern New York, Inc. Photography: Corporate Graphics, Resource, Inc. Billboard: Whiteco-Metrocom*

about all these things. For tasks requiring a lot of effort, groups are faster than individuals. An example would be building a house. Following are guidelines for working effectively in a group.

- *Show Your Readiness to Help the Group.* A group depends on the willingness of each member to accomplish its work. Do your share of the work on a regular basis. And volunteer your effort from time-to-time for special group projects.
- *Accept the Role the Group Gives You.* Groups have leaders and followers. Followers are often in greater demand. Pitch in and do whatever the group needs, whether it is recording minutes, stuffing envelopes, or cleaning up after a meeting.
- *Carry Out Your Role as Best You Can.* Sports teams often have role players who go into the game to

What Would You Do?

You enjoy being in the club and are always eager to help out. In fact, you probably do more than anyone else. It is getting to the point that whenever something needs to be done, club members automatically look to you. You have been asked a number of times recently to sub for someone who has other plans. Some of the club members seem to be taking advantage of your willingness to always pitch in. What would you do?

* *WWYD Feature B.* The individual needs to learn how to be more assertive.

21. Ask students to provide examples of valuable role players in a work group (where they work, if possible).

do certain things. Can you think of examples? Role players make a valuable contribution to a team or a group. Do your job well and you and the group will both benefit.

- *Share Your Views With Others.* Don't hold back on a good idea or suggestion. Your solution may be perfect. Offer your feelings and opinions, even if they differ from what others think. Groups sometimes make poor decisions or choices. If you believe this is the case, say so.
- *Don't Dominate Meetings.* Someone who talks too much irritates other group members. Don't overpower others, even though you may have the right answers or the best ideas.
- *Accept Group Decisions.* Offer your views when a group is discussing something. But once the group makes a decision, don't argue about it.
- *Encourage Other Members.* Doing your best on a job will encourage others to do likewise. A kind word from time to time always helps. Remember to pass out compliments and congratulations for a job well done.
- *Think of Solutions, Not Past Problems.* Suppose you have a fight with a family member. Dwelling on the problem won't help. Thinking of how to solve it will. The same is true in task groups. Focus on finding solutions to problems.
- *Be Proud of Group Success.* Completing a hard task, or winning a game is very satisfying. Should success come, enjoy it with your fellow members.

Getting along well with others is an important work and life skill. As a skill, it must be learned and practiced.

FIGURE 9-11 Each worker in a task group must fulfill his or her assigned role. *Courtesy Westinghouse Electric Corporation*

22. Sometimes it is difficult to accept a group decision. Remember, groups tend to make a better decision than the average group member. Groups don't always make the best decision, though.

23. Emphasize the fact that human relations skills must be learned and practiced.

CHAPTER REVIEW

Chapter in Brief

- Human relations are very important to job success. Most fired workers lose their jobs because they can't get along with others.
- Bosses act in the interest of the company. They don't act out of friendship. Workers and bosses sometimes do become friends. It is more important, though, to learn to work effectively with the boss than to become friends.
- Doing your share of the work and following the rules lead to good feelings among co-workers. Other ways of maintaining good relationships with co-workers include:
  a. *Appearance.* Maintain good personal hygiene, grooming, and dress.
  b. *Courtesy.* Be pleasant, friendly, and courteous.
  c. *Attitude.* Be positive and don't complain about your job.
  d. *Interest.* Show interest in the job and what your co-workers are doing.
  e. *Loyalty.* Don't criticize the company or gossip about bosses or co-workers.
  f. *Tolerance.* Try to tolerate the opinions, habits, and behaviors of co-workers.
  g. *Maturity.* Be agreeable and avoid arguments.
  h. *Dependability.* Always do what you say you will do.
  i. *Openness.* Be open to suggestions and change.
  j. *Ethics.* Don't try to get ahead at the expense of others.
- Relationships between employees and customers are important to the success of a business. Customers deal with a certain business for several reasons. One is that customers like the product or service provided. A second reason is the types of follow-up services provided. A third is the goodwill provided.
- Most people work in groups from time to time. Do the following to be an effective group member:
  a. Show your readiness to help the group.
  b. Accept the role a group gives you.
  c. Carry out your role as best you can.
  d. Share your views with others.
  e. Don't dominate meetings.
  f. Accept group decisions.
  g. Encourage other members.
  h. Think of solutions, not past problems.
  i. Be proud of group success.
- Effective human relations is a skill. As a skill, it must be learned and practiced.

Words to Know

clients the business customers of a professional worker.

goodwill acts of kindness, consideration, or assistance.

human relations interactions among people.

interpersonal attraction a tendency to be drawn to another person because of similar characteristics and preferences.

patients persons under treatment or care by a medical practitioner.

patronize to trade with or give one's business to a certain individual or company.

patrons customers of certain service-producing businesses or institutions.

seniority the length of time someone has worked for a company.

task group a work group formed to accomplish a particular objective.

territorial rights unwritten rules concerning respect for the property and territory of others.

Questions to Answer
1. Why do most workers lose their jobs?
2. How important is it for you to be friends with the boss?
3. Name two ways to start out on the right foot with co-workers.
4. How should you relate to a co-worker whose opinions, habits, or behavior are different from yours?
5. What should you do if a co-worker offers advice or suggestions?
6. What are the three reasons why customers deal with a certain business?
7. Why is it important to know how to work in groups?
8. Groups are generally superior to most individuals at many tasks. Give an example.
9. What should you do if a task leader assigns you a job to do?
10. When is the best time to provide an opinion regarding a group decision?

Activities to Do
1. Identify a human relations problem that you have had with another student or a co-worker. What was the nature of the problem? Based on what you have learned in this chapter, how could you have helped avoid the problem? Share your answers in class.
2. This chapter gave several reasons why customers deal with certain businesses. Think about your favorite businesses. Can you add any reasons to those the text gives? As a class, list the reasons on the board.
3. Invite an employer who uses task groups to speak. Ask the person to talk about how to get along in task groups. Prepare a list of questions beforehand.

Topics to Discuss
1. Human relations skills are also important for bosses. What does it take (beyond being a good co-worker) to be an effective boss?
2. Even though people work in groups, they still like to maintain their individuality. What are some of the ways that people express their individuality on the job?
3. Certain occupations like police officers, nurses, and attorneys deal with people who are often emotionally upset. What types of special human relations skills do these people need? What other occupations require these skills?

1. Because they can't get along with bosses, co-workers, or customers.
2. Bosses and employees sometimes become friends. However, it is not an essential condition. Being able to work together is what's important.
3. (a) Do your share of the work. (b) Follow the rules.
4. There is nothing fundamentally wrong with being different. Try to tolerate the opinions, habits, and behaviors of co-workers.
5. Be open to the advice and suggestions of co-workers.
6. (a) They like the product or service. (b) The follow-up services provided. (c) The "little things" (goodwill) that are provided.
7. There is a trend toward more and more task groups being used in the workplace.
8. For tasks requiring great diversity, and for tasks requiring a lot of effort.
9. Accept the role and do your best to carry it out.
10. During the time that the decision is under discussion.

24. You may wish to review the three reasons why customers patronize a business that were explained in the chapter.
25. Any type of task group would be satisfactory. Students might find a quality circle to be particularly interesting.
26. The skills to get along with co-workers and customers are essentially the same human relations skills needed to be a boss. The intent here is to see if students can name any additional skills. Chapter 18 describes characteristics of effective leaders, which include several types of human relations skills.
27. One way of expressing individuality is territorial rights, which were discussed in the chapter. Perhaps students can provide additional examples.
28. Additional human relations skills might include sensitivity to the needs of others, patience and caring, and the ability to inspire trust and confidence. Additional occupations are counselors, social workers, clergy, special education teachers, and undertakers. Students may be able to name other skills and occupations.

1. Students should check the statement of earnings.
2. Illustrate the example on the board. Assign several sample problems.
3. Illustrate the example on the board. Assign several sample problems. Also, point out that some workers may receive "double time" for working holidays or other special occasions.

CHAPTER TEN

Earnings and Job Advancement

OUTLINE
Your Job Earnings
Your Paycheck
Pay Raises
Job Advancement
Chapter Review

OBJECTIVES
After reading this chapter, you should be able to:
- Identify and describe different forms of compensation.
- Describe how a paycheck is figured.
- State three guidelines regarding working for a pay raise.
- Identify the most common reasons for changing jobs.
- Explain what to do when voluntarily leaving a job.

FIGURE 10-1 Payday is most people's favorite day. *Photo by Paul E. Meyers*

1

When you get paid, you will receive a paycheck and an attached statement of earnings. Some people cash or deposit their paycheck and throw away the pay statement. This is not a good idea. You may have lost money because of an error. Or too much money may have been withheld for certain deductions. In this chapter, you will learn about how your earnings are figured and about different types of payroll deductions. You will also learn about pay raises, promotions, and what is involved in changing jobs.

YOUR JOB EARNINGS
The amount of your paycheck depends on how you are paid and on the deductions taken out. How do you know if your paycheck is accurate? Read on.

Forms of Compensation
The total amount of income and benefits you receive makes up your *compensation*. Employees are compensated in many ways.

Wages. Most workers receive a set hourly wage. To arrive at the amount of pay, the hourly wage is multiplied by the number of hours worked. For example, if Sean receives $5.30 an hour and he works a 40-hour week, his weekly wages are $212.00 ($5.30 × 40). Most hourly workers are paid weekly.

For working over 40 hours a week, most hourly

2

4. Salaried workers who put in the additional hours, however, often receive greater merit raises.

116

CHAPTER 10 Earnings and Job Advancement ■ 117

paid weekly. Others receive checks every other week. Some people must really plan ahead! They get paid only once a month. Salaried workers may put in more than 40 hours a week. Even so, they may not receive any extra pay. Do you think this is fair?

Piece-rate. In this method, the worker is paid for the amount of work performed. A sewing machine operator, for example, might be paid $.50 for each piece of goods completed. If 112 such pieces were done in one day, the worker would get $56.00 (112 × $.50) for that day.

FIGURE 10-2 Most hourly workers punch a time clock. The employer usually "docks" pay if the worker is late or leaves early. *Product of Simplex Time Recorder Co., Gardner, MA*

FIGURE 10-3 These farm workers are paid for the amount of fruit they pick. *Courtesy of Produce News*

workers get *overtime pay.* The overtime wage is usually 1½ times the normal hourly wage. Let's say that Sean worked 45 hours one week. He would receive $5.30 an hour for the first 40 hours and $7.95 ($5.30 × 1½) for the five extra hours. His weekly wages would be $251.75 ($212.00 + 39.75).

Salary. Some workers receive a salary instead of an hourly wage. The salary is paid per month or per year. Teachers' salaries are usually a certain amount for nine or ten months. Some salaried workers are

Commissions. Most sales workers receive all or part of their compensation through commissions. A commission is an amount the worker receives for making a sale. Real estate agents and insurance brokers are some workers that receive commissions. Can you name others?

Most commissions are a certain percentage of the total sale. Rita Yang, for example, is a real estate agent. She gets a two percent commission on each house she sells. (If she owned the agency, she would get six percent or more.) Last week, Rita sold a house

5. Illustrate the example on the board. Assign several sample problems.

6. Ask students to name additional occupations that typically receive commissions (most are marketing and sales occupations).

FIGURE 10-4 Servers sometimes get half of their total pay in tips. *Photo by David W. Tuttle*

for $116,000. This meant a $2,320 commission ($116,000 × 0.02). She doesn't do that every day, though.

Tips. Some workers receive a minimum hourly wage and earn the rest of their compensation from tips. Examples include restaurant servers, porters, and cab drivers. Can you think of any others? A *tip* (or gratuity) is an amount of money given in return for a favor or service. (Tips is an acronym for the phrase "to insure prompt service.")

Bonuses. A bonus is extra money a company gives workers as a gift or a reward for good work. Most bonuses come from employers that are willing to share some of the company profits. For instance, in March 1988, Ford Motor Company distributed $635 million in profit sharing to salaried and hourly workers. The payout was the largest ever by a major U.S. corporation for a single year. Each hourly worker received a bonus check averaging $3,700.

Fringe Benefits. Fringe benefits are indirect forms of compensation. That is, they are given instead of cash. Do you or your family members get company-paid insurance? How about paid holidays, vacations, and sick days? These are the most common fringe benefits. If you don't get fringe benefits, don't be discouraged. Most entry-level and part-time jobs offer few fringe benefits. Chances are you will get some later.

F·E·A·T·U·R·E

Employer-Sponsored Child-Care Assistance

◆ ◆ ◆

About 70 percent of women between the ages of twenty and forty-four are employed. This number is expected to increase to 80 percent by 1995. Over half of these women are mothers. This has led to child-care assistance becoming the hot new fringe benefit.

The number of employers offering some type of child-care service has increased about 500 percent since 1982. More programs are on the way. In San Francisco, an ordinance was passed recently requiring developers in that city to include space for child care in new downtown office buildings. In Monterey Park, California, Union Bank opened a new service center in 1986. The office included a separate 5,000-square-foot child-care facility with a staff of twelve located just 200 feet from the main building. The AFL-CIO has passed a resolution backing employer-union sponsored child-care centers.

The major reason that companies offer child-care assistance is to attract and hold good employees. For instance, one department head turned down a job across town that offered a large salary increase. She put it this way: "I spend the lunch hour with my six-month-old son. They couldn't put a price tag on having my child within a few minutes of me."

Child-care assistance is an expensive undertaking. Very few companies pay 100 percent of the costs. Usually, employees pay tuition that amounts to about one-third to one-half of the cost of private, community child-care. Experts predict that more employers will offer child-care assistance in the future.

FIGURE 10-FEATURE Employer-sponsored child-care assistance has grown as more and more mothers with young children have joined the workforce. *Courtesy of Unisource*

Employer-sponsored Child-care Assistance. This summarizes a relevant problem for both working parents and employers and illustrates a growing trend. Ask students about child-care assistance where they work. Be alert to new information in newspapers and magazines that can be used to update this topic.

120 ■ SECTION 2 Working on the Job

YOUR PAYCHECK

When you get your first check, look it over carefully. Make sure that your name is spelled right and your address and social security number are correct. Even employers make mistakes!

Your first paycheck may surprise you. Most new workers don't take home the pay they expect. Why is this so? You are right if you said that the employer has taken money out for certain reasons. Let's go back and see how the employer figures your earnings.

The amount of salary or wages that you earn during a certain time period is your *gross pay*. For example, if you work 20 hours a week at $4.85 an hour, your gross pay is $97.00 (20 × $4.85). From this amount, certain *deductions* are made for taxes, retirement, and so on. After these deductions are subtracted from your gross pay, you are left with *net pay* or take-home pay.

A pay statement or *statement of earnings* attached to your paycheck shows your gross pay, deductions, and net pay. A sample pay statement for a person paid weekly is shown in Figure 10-6.

Payroll deductions are of many types. The employer must take out (withhold) some of them. Other deductions, though, depend on what you request the employer to withhold. The most common types of payroll deductions are:

■ *Income Taxes.* Your employer must withhold federal income tax from your earnings and send it to the federal government. When you start your job, you will need to fill out a Form W-4. (This was covered in Chapter 6.) Based on your

FIGURE 10-5 Examine your paycheck and pay statement each pay period. Ask your boss or supervisor about anything you don't understand.

FIRST TRUST CORPORATION
2 COMPUTER DRIVE   TROY, NY 12347   Pay Statement

Co. Code	Department	File No.	Clock No./ID.	Name	Pay Period ENDING	Pay Date
5XQ	301712	35637	05502	Roberts, Esther	01/24/89	01/22/89

Hours/Units	Rate	Earnings	Type	Deduction	Type	Deduction	Type
40	452 00	452 00	REG B	2 63	DENTAL	16 95	HEALTH

This Pay	Gross	Fed. With. Tax	Social Security	State With. Tax	City With. Tax	Sui/Dis	Net Pay
	452 00	67 71	33 50	15 06	60		315.55
YTD	1317 31	198 29	98 93	42 60	1 80		

FIGURE 10-6 Sample pay statement or statement of earnings

12. Refer students to Figure 10-6 and illustrate gross pay, deductions, and net pay on the board. You may wish to assign Activity 2 at this time.

CHAPTER 10 Earnings and Job Advancement ■ 121

answers on the form, the employer figures the amount of federal tax to withhold each payday. Depending on where you live, the employer may withhold state and local taxes, too.

■ *FICA.* The acronym *FICA* stands for *Federal Insurance Contributions Act* tax. It's better known as the Social Security tax. Most jobs in the United States are part of the federal Social Security program. Both you and your employer pay into this fund. Social Security is discussed further in Chapter 27. Notice in Figure 10-6 that the employer withheld $33.50 for Social Security from Esther Roberts' paycheck.

FIGURE 10-8 Many employers let their employees buy U.S. Savings Bonds through payroll deductions.

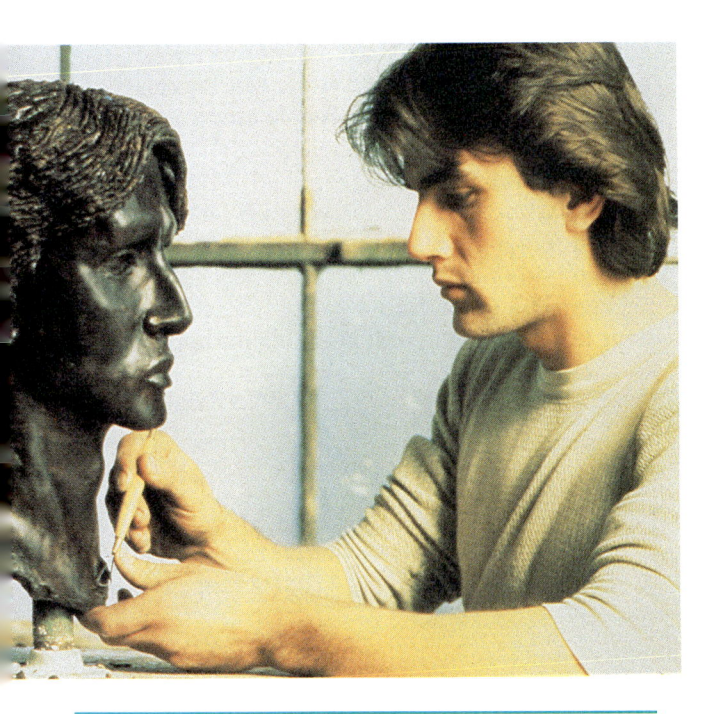

FIGURE 10-7 Self-employed people, such as this sculptor, have twice the FICA deduction as employees of a company. *Courtesy of SIUC Photocommunications*

■ *Insurance.* Many employers offer group life and health insurance programs to full-time employees. Employers often pay all or part of the insurance cost. If you must pay, the employer may withhold the premium from your paycheck. Esther Roberts' employer contributes 70% toward health insurance and provides free life insurance. Esther Roberts pays $16.95 per week for health insurance, family coverage, $2.63 for optional dental insurance and $.60 for supplemental income and disability coverage.

■ *Union Dues.* Most union members can pay their dues through payroll deductions.

■ *Charity.* Many workers donate to charity through payroll deductions. A common example is The United Way.

■ *Savings.* Do you find it hard to save? If so, see if your employer can withhold money for savings. For instance, the employer may be willing to deduct money for a savings account or U.S. Savings Bonds.

When you start a job, the employer should explain your deductions to you. If no one does, ask. After all, the deductions are your money.

13. Do you have state and/or local income taxes in your area?
14. In 1990, the tax rate was 7.65% on the first $54,000 of earnings.
15. The six most common types of deductions are described here. You may wish to mention others or ask students to name additional examples.

122 ■ SECTION 2 Working on the Job

16. Make sure students understand the difference between an *incentive* and a *reward*.

What Would You Do?

Each payday you carefully go over your check. Several times, you have found mistakes in which you were underpaid. The boss always apologizes and makes the correction. This payday, however, you discover that you have been overpaid by $20. You share this information with a co-worker. He tells you to forget it, since you have probably been cheated out of more than $20 by the company. You have been thinking about this all weekend. What would you do?

*

PAY RAISES

16 Pay raises benefit both employees and their employers. As an employee, the idea of a pay raise may provide you with an *incentive* to do a good job. After getting the raise, you may feel better about your job. This, in turn, may make you continue to improve your work.

Improved work makes employees more valuable to the company. Most companies want to keep their good employees. So they give them raises. Good workers who don't get raises may go elsewhere.

Alice worked in the claims department of an insurance company for over three years. Eight other people worked in the same department. Alice was clearly the best worker. One of her co-workers said that Alice always did the work of two people.

All workers in the department get regular pay raises. Last year, Alice was upset when she got the same raise as the other workers. Her boss could have gotten her a higher raise.

Alice made an appointment to discuss a raise with Ms. Lorch, her boss. Alice asked why she kept getting the same average raise as everyone else even though she did more work. Ms. Lorch agreed that Alice was the most valuable employee in the department. But she explained that if she gave Alice a higher raise, it would create bad feelings within the department. That was enough for Alice. She started looking for another job. It didn't take her long to find one either. 17

Later, a friend at the old job told Alice that things have not been going well in the claims department.

FIGURE 10-9 You probably work harder on the job if your efforts pay off. The same is true at school. *Photo by David W. Tuttle*

* WWYD Feature A. The employee should inform the boss about the $20 overpayment. The boss and the employee should be held to the same standards of conduct.

17. Ask students if they think that giving Alice a higher raise would "create bad feelings."

18. Raises are also very dependent on the economy. Ask students to provide illustrations of this concept.

CHAPTER 10 Earnings and Job Advancement ■ 123

want a pay raise because they are not making as much money as they would like. An employer won't be impressed by a worker who asks for a raise because he or she wants to buy a VCR, for instance.

When asking for a pay raise, tell the boss why you deserve one. Steve, for example, pointed out to his boss that sales had increased eighteen percent since he started working in the department.

Ask for a raise when the company is doing well and the boss has had a good week. Your timing should be right in yet another way. Don't ask for a raise during a time when you should be working. Ask for an appointment to discuss a raise during break, lunch, or after work.

FIGURE 10-10 Alice now works for an employer who rewards hard work and quality effort. *Courtesy of Simpson Industries, Inc.*

Alice's replacement can't do the amount of work that Alice could. The new person also makes a lot of errors, something that Alice seldom did. One day the friend heard Ms. Lorch say that she wished she had Alice back.

Getting a Pay Raise

In many jobs, employees receive *automatic raises* every six months, twelve months, and so on. All employees may get the same dollar amount or the same percentage amount. In some cases, the amount of the raise depends on the type of job. Production employees may get higher raises than office workers, for instance.

Some employers give *merit raises* instead of, or in addition to, automatic raises. A merit raise is based on the amount and quality of an employee's work. Most employers use a performance evaluation to determine these.

Not all employers have a set policy on pay raises. In such cases, it may be up to the employer to decide when an employee deserves a raise. Or the employee may be expected to ask for a raise. This type of situation is common in small businesses.

Suppose that you decide to ask for a raise. First of all, if you are a new employee, don't expect one until after you have learned the job and shown that you can do it well. You must earn a raise. Some workers

19. Recall that performance evaluation was discussed in Chapter 7.
20. Ask students if there is a set policy on pay raises where they work.

FIGURE 10-11 What would you say if you were the boss and someone interrupted your work to ask for a raise? *Photo by Paul E. Meyers*

When you meet with the boss, ask what workers must do to get a pay raise. If you have done all those things, tell the boss. Be clear. Talk about exactly what you have done. If the boss says there is no rule for granting raises, present your case. When asking for a raise, show confidence and respect. If you are turned down, don't argue with the decision. Just say that you will keep working hard and hope that you get a raise later. If you feel strongly that you deserve a raise, you may want to follow Alice's example.

21. Emphasize that beginning workers should not expect a pay raise until they have learned the job and can do it well.
22. You may wish to assign Activity 4 at this time.

124 ■ SECTION 2 Working on the Job

JOB ADVANCEMENT

Most people start working in a low-paying, entry-level job. An entry-level job is a good way to earn money and gain valuable experience. Usually, though, an entry-level job isn't one that you want to keep forever. You may want to advance within the company or move to a better job in another company.

Job Promotions

A *promotion* is an advancement from one position to another within a company. The new position usually brings a new title, more money, and more responsibility. Some promotions also bring the chance to supervise others. Opportunities for promotion differ among occupations and industries. For example, most workers in skilled trades have less chance for promotion than do sales reps. Large businesses offer more chances for promotion than do small ones.

Promotion opportunities occur for two reasons: (1) a new position is created within the company; or (2) a vacancy occurs because someone was promoted or left the company. How can you put yourself in line for a promotion? You can begin during the job interview. Ask, "What are my chances for advancement if I perform well?" Suppose you work where you can advance. Do the best work you can every day. Employers notice workers who do their jobs well and get along with others.

Even if you are an A-1 employee, remember that promotions take time. Employers want to watch you over a period of time. Even when an employer thinks you are ready, an opening may not yet exist. Or a worker who has the same job as you may have more seniority. If so, the person with more seniority will probably get promoted first.

While many people want promotions, not all of us want to be the boss or have a better job. A higher level job is not for everyone. Seymour knows this now.

23. Or an entry-level job may reveal the need or awaken the desire for more education or training. Career decision-making will be dealt with in Chapter 12.

24. Ask students what opportunities for promotion exist where they work.

25. Advancement may also depend on completing additional education or training.

FIGURE 10-12 To be promoted on some jobs, a worker may need to take a written or performance test. *Photo by Paul E. Meyers*

26. You may wish to discuss Topic 3 at this time.

When the job of office manager opened up, Seymour's co-workers encouraged him to apply. He was the most experienced accounting clerk in the company, got along with everyone, and knew the business well. He applied for the job and got it.

Seymour soon found out that being an office manager was different than he had thought. He had to assign work, manage the office budget, make on-the-spot decisions, and do many other things. To get everything done, he began to come to work early and stay late. Once he started giving orders, Seymour sensed tension between himself and the other employees. His most painful moment was when his boss ordered him to fire one of the clerk typists.

Seymour isn't alone. All occupations have people like him. They are great workers, but aren't suited to be supervisors. No matter what your job, try to work toward something that you will like. For many workers, that is the job they have now.

FIGURE 10-13 Not everyone is suited to be a manager or boss. *Photo by Paul E. Meyers*

Changing Jobs

Years ago, most people stayed in a job for most of their working lives. Things have changed since then. While some people stay on the same job, most of us don't. The most common reasons for changing jobs are:

- *Lack of Opportunity with Present Employer.* You may be in a dead-end job that offers little chance for pay raises and promotions.

27. Ask students to provide examples to illustrate how workers may like their occupations but dislike their jobs.

CHAPTER 10 Earnings and Job Advancement ■ 125

What Would You Do?

You have been working at a farm implement dealership since your senior year in high school. You like the job and the people who work there. The business, however, is barely making enough profit to stay alive. You have only had one small raise in three years. You have been laid off a couple of months each winter. The prospects for additional raises or promotions don't look good. You understand the dealer's financial problems, but you have your future to think about. What would you do?

- *Better Opportunity Elsewhere.* Perhaps you like the job you have, but another company offers you something you would like even better. Often such a change involves a pay raise.

- *Dislike for Present Occupation or Job.* Not everything looks as good up close as it did from afar. Perhaps you thought you would really enjoy the occupation you are in. After doing it for a while, you see that you were wrong. It's just not what you want to do the rest of your life. You may want to train for another occupation.

  Or, you may like your occupation (what you do) but dislike your job (where you work). In this case, changing jobs is probably the answer.

- *Change in Personal or Family Situation.* You may need to quit a job because of such things as illness or a move to a new area.

- *Loss of Job.* Perhaps your company slows down and lays you off. Maybe the employer even goes out of business. These things aren't your fault. Being fired probably is. Either way, you are out of a job.

No matter what the reason, plan the change carefully if you can. Don't make a quick decision. Some workers get angry and quit. Later, most of these people regret what they did. Earlier in the chapter, you read about Alice being turned down for a raise. It would have been a mistake for her to quit on the spot. Instead, she made sure she had a new job first. Another mistake would have been to threaten her boss with the statement, "If you don't give me a raise, I'm going to quit." What do you think would have happend then?

WWYD Feature B. Future prospects look grim. The employee should probably begin looking for a new job.

Once you have decided to leave, find out if the company has rules about quitting a job. If so, follow them. If not, give your employer *at least a two-week notice.* Tell your boss *before* you mention it to your co-workers. Follow up your verbal notice with a written *letter of resignation,* Figure 10-14.

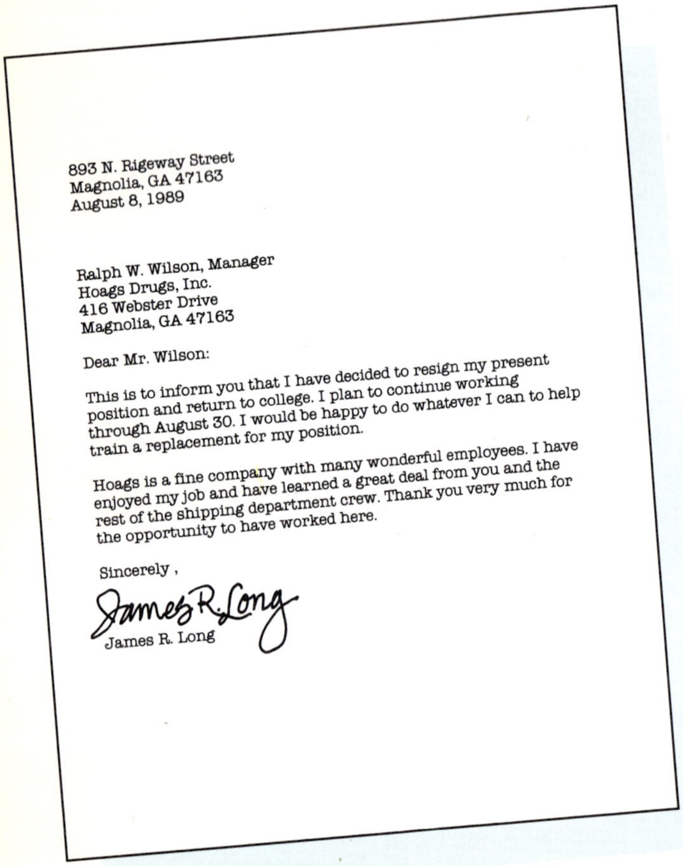

>   893 N. Rigeway Street
>   Magnolia, GA 47163
>   August 8, 1989
>
>   Ralph W. Wilson, Manager
>   Hoags Drugs, Inc.
>   416 Webster Drive
>   Magnolia, GA 47163
>
>   Dear Mr. Wilson:
>
>   This is to inform you that I have decided to resign my present position and return to college. I plan to continue working through August 30. I would be happy to do whatever I can to help train a replacement for my position.
>
>   Hoags is a fine company with many wonderful employees. I have enjoyed my job and have learned a great deal from you and the rest of the shipping department crew. Thank you very much for the opportunity to have worked here.
>
>   Sincerely,
>   *James R. Long*
>   James R. Long

FIGURE 10-14 Sample letter of resignation

Such a letter should contain the following points: (a) the fact that you are leaving, (b) a date when you plan to leave, (c) the reason you are leaving, (d) an offer to help train your replacement, and (e) a thank-you for the chance to work there.

Once you have told your employer you are leaving, don't let up. Do your job as best you can through the last day. Don't criticize your boss on the last day or brag to your co-workers about your new job. Your employer will watch and evaluate you through your last day. Try to leave on good terms with your employer.

Being Fired

Being fired is much different than leaving a job on your own. Some employers may ask you to leave, but give you the chance to resign. Remember that resigning will make it easier for you to find another job. If you are fired outright, try to turn disaster into a learning experience. Never make the same mistake twice.

The following people were fired. Each, however, learned from the experience.

- Phyllis was fired, but wasn't sure why. It would have been easy for her to never go back. Instead, she made an appointment with her former boss to find out why she was fired. After learning about some of her poor work habits, she decided to improve on her next job.
- Theo was let go because he didn't have the skills for the job. He decided to start classes at the community college.
- Sharlene lost her job because of too many absences. She didn't think the boss would fire her. When the boss did, Sharlene was shocked. She will do her best to see that it won't happen again.
- Ed was told that he had a bad attitude. It was true. He couldn't get along with the boss, co-workers, or customers. Ed talked over the situation with a good friend who helped him understand what he was doing wrong. Ed now sees that he was carrying a chip on his shoulder.

If you have made mistakes like Phyllis, Theo, Sharlene, or Ed, admit them. Don't lie to yourself or blame someone else. The best approach, though, is not to do things that result in getting fired. Use what you have learned in this and earlier chapters to be a more effective worker.

---

28. Ask students about the rules for quitting a job where they work.
29. You may wish to assign Activity 3 at this time. Provide group instruction and individual assistance as required.
30. Ask students if any of them would care to share an experience in which they were fired from a job. Focus on what was learned from the incident.

CHAPTER REVIEW

Chapter in Brief

- The amount of your paycheck depends on how you are paid and on the deductions taken out. Employees are compensated in many ways. These include: wages, salary, piece-rate, commissions, tips, bonuses, and fringe benefits.
- The total amount of salary or wages that you earn is your gross pay. From this, certain deductions are made. After deductions are subtracted from the gross pay, you are left with net pay.
- The most common types of payroll deductions are: income taxes, FICA, insurance, union dues, charity, and savings.
- Pay raises benefit both employees and employers. Some workers receive automatic raises every so often. Merit raises may be given instead of or in addition to automatic raises. Not all employers have a set policy on pay raises.
- A promotion is an advancement from one position to another. Opportunities for promotion differ among occupations and employers. Getting a promotion usually takes time and is based on outstanding performance.
- People frequently change jobs. There are many different reasons for changing a job. No matter what the reason, try to plan a job change carefully. Try to leave on good terms with your employer. Follow company guidelines for resigning and leaving a job.
- Some people are fired or given a chance to resign. If this happens to you, try to learn from the experience.

Words to Know

automatic raise a regular pay raise received by all employees.

compensation the total amount of income and benefits received from a job.

deductions certain amounts that are withheld from the paycheck of an employee.

gross pay the amount of salary or wages earned for a certain period before deductions are withheld.

incentive something to work toward; a potential reward.

letter of resignation a letter by an employee notifying an employer of the intent to quit a job.

merit raise a pay raise that is based on job performance.

net pay the amount on a paycheck; the take-home pay of an employee after deductions are subtracted from gross pay.

overtime pay the wage received for working overtime, usually 1½ times the normal hourly wage.

promotion an advancement to a higher-level job within a company.

statement of earnings a pay statement; the attachment to a paycheck that shows gross pay, deductions, and net pay.

Questions to Answer

1. The amount of money you receive from your paycheck depends on two things. Name them.
2. List and briefly explain each form of compensation.
3. What type of workers are most likely to be paid on commission?
4. Which payroll deductions are generally automatic? Which ones are optional?
5. What is the FICA tax?
6. Why is it important to check your pay statement often?
7. Name two reasons why promotion opportunities occur.
8. Is a promotion for everyone? Why or why not?
9. List five common reasons for changing jobs.
10. Why is it best to leave a job on good terms with your employer?

Activities to Do

1. Suppose that you earn $4.80 an hour. One week, you work 48 hours. You are paid the normal rate for the first 40 hours, and time-and-a-half for overtime. What is your gross pay for the week?
2. Nat earns $200 a week salary plus a 5% commission on his total sales. This month his sales amounted to $18,500. His deductions are as follows:
   - Federal income tax, $188.50
   - State sales tax, $37.46
   - FICA, $121.61
   - Credit union, $48.00
   - Charity, $25.00

   Based on these figures, what is Nat's gross pay for the month? How much are his total deductions? What is his net pay?
3. Let's say that you are going to leave your job for a better one. Write a sample letter of resignation. Turn it in to your teacher for evaluation.
4. Plan the conversation you would have with your supervisor to ask for a raise. Role play this situation beforehand.

Topics to Discuss

1. If you were a salesperson, would you rather be paid a salary or a straight commission? Discuss the advantages and disadvantages of each.
2. In recent years, workers in a number of industries have been forced to take pay cuts and give up benefits in order to save their jobs. Would you be willing to take a pay cut to keep a job?
3. Do you think that you would like to be a supervisor? Why or why not?
4. The decision to change jobs and move elsewhere is often complicated for married couples who both work. Discuss how you might feel in giving up a good job in order to move with your spouse.

---

1. (a) How you are paid. (b) The amount of deductions.
2. *Wages*—a set hourly figure. *Salary*—a set amount paid weekly, biweekly, or monthly. *Piece-rate*—payment based on the amount of work performed. *Commissions*—an amount, usually a percentage, based on the amount of sales achieved. *Tips*—an amount of money given in return for a favor or service. *Bonuses*—extra money given as a gift or reward. *Fringe benefits*—indirect forms of compensation such as insurance, paid vacations, and so on.
3. Sales agents of various types.
4. *Automatic*—income taxes, FICA, or other retirement. *Optional*—insurance, union dues (usually required, but optional in terms of witholding), charity, savings.
5. Social Security tax.
6. A mistake might have occurred in figuring wages or deductions.
7. (a) A new position is created within the company. (b) A vacancy occurs because someone was promoted or left the company.
8. Not necessarily. Some people are happy with what they are doing. Some people don't deal well with additional responsibilities.
9. (a) Lack of opportunity with present employer. (b) Better opportunity elsewhere. (c) Dislike for present occupation or job. (d) Change in personal or family situation. (e) Loss of job.
10. When you apply for a new job, the potential employer may call your previous employer for information about you.

31. Gross pay is $249.60.
32. Gross pay is $1,725; deductions are $420.57; net pay is $1,304.43.
33. The letter should include the five points explained.
34. A salary is guaranteed; hard work and outstanding performance may go unrewarded. Hard work and outstanding performance may result in high commissions; no commissions are earned unless sales are made.
35. Students are prone to say no. Help students to empathize with a worker who has to support self and family.
36. With the majority of women now employed in the labor force, this is increasingly becoming a problem. Also, the woman is often the one who has the chance to move.

1. Emphasize the point about how an employee's appearance may convey a certain image. For this reason, many employers insist on well-groomed employees.
2. Emphasize how personal hygiene is a prerequisite to good grooming.

CHAPTER ELEVEN

Appearance on the Job

OUTLINE

Grooming and Appearance
Dressing for the Job
Chapter Review

OBJECTIVES

After reading this chapter, you should be able to:
- Explain why good hygiene, grooming, and proper dress are important on the job.
- List five rules for good grooming and appearance.
- Describe the benefits of good posture.
- Summarize guidelines on dressing for the job.

Howard had been on his job for only ten days when Mr. Bedrava, the boss, called him in. "Howard," Mr. Bedrava began, "Your appearance and grooming impressed me a lot when I interviewed you for this job. In fact, that's one of the reasons I hired you. But since you've started work, your looks have changed. Some of your co-workers have complained about body odor, too. I'm disappointed. I don't want our customers to think that your appearance is an indication of how we do business. Please think about cleaning up your act. I hope we won't have to talk about this again."

This straight talk embarrassed Howard. "Gee, I'm sorry," said Howard. "I didn't think it mattered that much how warehouse workers looked. I see what you're saying, though. A lot of people *do* see me in this job. Thanks for giving me another chance."

Like Mr. Bedrava, most employers and bosses take note of their employees' appearance. In fact, many performance evaluations have a section on appearance. No matter what your job, your employer will expect you to groom and dress properly.

FIGURE 11-1 These people are dressed appropriately for their jobs. *Courtesy of Delta Air Lines, Inc.*

GROOMING AND APPEARANCE

An appropriate appearance on the job begins with *personal hygiene*. In most jobs, being clean is not enough. It is also necessary to be neat and attractive as well. This is what *grooming* is all about. Rules for personal hygiene apply to everyone. What is considered to be attractive or good grooming varies from person to person and job to job. For instance, a hairstyle that looks good on one person may not suit another. What is considered to be proper makeup in one job setting may be inappropriate in another. Some of the following grooming tips may apply to you and your job situation, while others may not.

129

*WWYD Feature A. The solution here is to trim the nails.

130 ■ SECTION 2 Working on the Job

What Would You Do?

You have always wanted long, polished nails. One Saturday you go to the Sculptured Nails Salon for artificial nails. You think they are gorgeous. Back at work on Monday, things aren't so good. The longer nails interfere with your keyboarding. Your work has slowed down and you are making more mistakes. The supervisor has noticed also. She has suggested that you have the nails trimmed. "I can't," you think. "I paid a lot of money for these nails." What would you do?

5. The onset of puberty and accompanying hormone changes result in the need for teenagers to be more alert to possible body odors.

Shaving

A grooming decision for men is whether to be clean shaven or to grow a mustache or beard. Going to work with a growth of stubble is not a good choice. Should you choose to grow facial hair, start during a vacation. If you do grow a mustache or beard, shave your neck and the uncovered parts of the face. Weekly trims are in order, too.

Deodorants and Antiperspirants

Even after bathing, underarm perspiration odor can develop quickly. To control this, many people use a deodorant (for odor) or an antiperspirant (for wetness). Choose whatever fits your needs.

Wendy, a Houston realtor, has always perspired heavily. Moving to Texas made her problem even worse. Deodorant was no longer enough. Perspiration stains on her clothing embarrassed Wendy—especially when she was with clients. Antiperspirants reduced the amount of perspiration—and Wendy's embarrassment.

Skin Care and Cosmetics

Your skin may need care beyond daily bathing. The most common problem is dry skin. In colder climates, heated homes and low humidity cause the skin to become dry and itchy. In such cases, moisturize your skin often with lotion.

Hairstyling

For most jobs, hair should be neat, trimmed, and not too faddish. Beyond this, how you wear your hair is up to you. Whatever style you choose, hair should be neatly combed or brushed.

A hairstylist can help you choose a style that goes best with your features and your type of hair. When deciding on a hairstyle, be sure to think about the amount of care it will need. Twila chose a style that required her to roll it every day. She soon tired of the routine. After a while, Twila chose a style that was easier to care for.

FIGURE 11-2 The best hairstyle is one that compliments your features and hair characteristics. *Photo by David W. Tuttle*

3. Ask students if any of them have had hairstyles that require an excessive degree of care.
4. Some employers may prohibit mustaches or beards.
6. Grooming aids for daily use (deodorants, shaving creams, body lotions, and so on) differ widely in price. Encourage students to try store brands.

F·E·A·T·U·R·E

Sun Protection

♦ ♦ ♦

FIGURE 11-FEATURE Too much sun when you are young may cause skin problems later. *Courtesy of New York State Department of Commerce*

Jobs requiring outdoor work pose a special skin care problem. Long-term exposure to the sun will cause your skin to become wrinkled and leathery. Premature aging of the skin isn't the main problem, though. Dermatologists believe that continued exposure to the sun leads to skin cancer. The process can be likened to filling up a bottle with liquid. Each day's sun gets added to a lifetime's worth of exposure. After enough exposure, skin cancer may result.

The National Cancer Institute estimates that more than 300,000 cases of skin cancer occur each year in the United States. Between one and two percent of the cases result in death. Death rates for skin cancer have increased ten times in the last sixty years. The rate of increase is expected to continue.

What should you do if you have to work in the sun for long periods of time? The best protection is to keep the skin covered. Wear a hat, long-sleeved shirt, and long pants. What also works are special lotions and creams called *sunscreens*. These are rated according to a numerical "sun protection factor" (SPF). A lotion with a SPF of 2, for example allows you to stay in the sun two times longer than you could without any protection. Many dermatologists, however, recommend nothing less than a SPF of 15, especially on the face. Sunscreens aren't just for weekends on the beach. They should be used each day that you are outside exposed to the sun.

*Sun Protection. This feature describes a job-related health hazard that is too frequently presented only as a cosmetic or beauty problem. It is often difficult to get young people to accept the seriousness of excess sun exposure. Concentrate on explaining SPF ratings and how easy sunscreens are to use.

132 ■ SECTION 2 Working on the Job

Hands may need special attention. Abused hands get rough, sore, and look bad. To help heal and soothe rough, sore hands, use hand lotion often. This applies to both men and women.

Many women choose to use cosmetics or beauty aids to improve their appearance. If you do, don't overdo them. Too much makeup can dry out the skin and cause irritation. Cosmetic counters in large department stores often have people who can advise you on proper cosmetic use.

CORRECT POSTURE   **INCORRECT POSTURE**

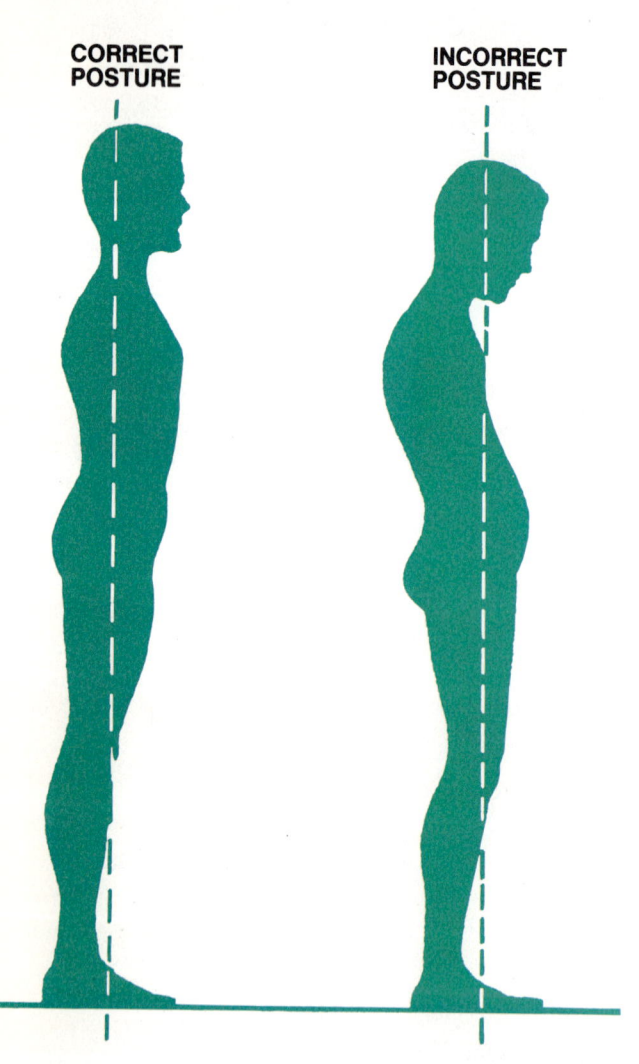

FIGURE 11-3 Difference between correct and incorrect posture

9. Ask how many students wear uniforms on their jobs.
10. Ask students to describe expectations regarding dress where they work.

Posture

Matthew is always clean and well groomed. His poor posture, however, ruins his appearance. *Posture* is the way you stand, walk and sit. Like Matt, people with poor posture have a stooping head and shoulders and a belly that sticks out. They appear to be lazy and lacking in self-confidence. This may be untrue, but poor posture sends out the wrong message.

A person with good posture appears to be poised and self-confident. Good posture, like good grooming, is necessary if you want to make a good impression on the job. Good posture also makes you feel better and helps fight fatigue. The difference between correct and incorrect posture is shown in Figure 11-3.

What Would You Do?

You just started a co-op job at a large savings and loan association. You are aware of how important it is to look good on the job. Everyone at work dresses so nicely. But you only have a couple of decent outfits. You don't have the money to go out and buy a lot of new clothes. You feel very self-conscious at work. You know you look more like a student than a real employee. You are thinking about looking for a new job where you could wear a uniform or more casual clothes. What would you do?

DRESSING FOR THE JOB

Clothes are important to your overall appearance on the job. Some jobs require a uniform. If yours does, make sure the uniform you wear is *always* clean and pressed.

If your job doesn't require a uniform, deciding how to dress will be more difficult. On most jobs, however, the employer expects workers to dress in a certain way. A bank teller, for instance, is supposed to look professional. For a man, this usually means a suit (or nice slacks and jacket), together with a dress shirt and tie. For women, professional dress includes a suit or dress, or a nice skirt, blouse, or sweater. If in doubt, notice what the other employees wear. If you have any questions, ask your boss. Here are several rules:

---

7. Poor posture should not be confused with orthopedic problems or problems of aging (osteoporosis).
8. Ask students to provide examples of how good posture may help prevent fatigue on the job (at a keyboard, driving a vehicle, and so on).

* *WWYD Feature B.* This illustrates a common problem for beginning workers. Emphasize that keeping clothes clean and neat is the first requisite.

FIGURE 11-4 Deciding how to dress is easier if your job requires a uniform. *Courtesy of Johnson & Wales College*

- *Wear What Fits Your Job.* Think about your type of job. Will you get dirty and greasy? Will you need protection from sun, wind, rain, or cold? Will you be handling food? Buy the type of clothing that is best suited for the work you will do.

11. Ask students if any of their jobs have special requirements regarding dress. Many probably relate to safety and/or hygiene.

- *Wear What Looks Good On You.* Within the expectations or requirements for the job, wear clothes that look good on you. Don't try to dress like someone else. Choose clothes that best match your physical features and personality.

12. Ask students if they have a favorite mode of dress or a favorite color(s). Are there colors or styles they wear that frequently earn compliments?

FIGURE 11-5 This person's outfit is well coordinated for a pleasing appearance. *Photo by Paul E. Meyers*

- *Plan Your Wardrobe Carefully.* You won't be able to buy your entire *wardrobe* all at once. So build around a number of basic items. For instance, a pair of gray slacks will go with many different shirts, blouses, or sweaters. You can wear a navy blazer formally or informally. Fad clothes may be fun off the job. But, unless such clothes are required on your job, don't wear them to work.

- *Learn How to Coordinate Clothes.* Teach yourself how to mix and match your clothes. For instance, don't wear a plaid shirt or blouse with a different plaid slacks. Libraries have magazines and books that can help you learn about fashion.

- *Choose Quality, Well-made Clothing.* The most expensive clothes are not always the best quality. Nor are clothes with a popular name or label always the best. Compare clothes and prices in many different stores before you decide to buy. After all, you will live with your choice for a long time.

- *Take Proper Care of Your Clothes.* Think about clothing care before you buy. Easy-care fabrics are more practical than ones that require frequent ironing or dry-cleaning. Don't go to work in clothes that look as if you slept in them. To prevent heavy wrinkling, hang up or fold clothes properly. If wrinkles do appear, iron them. Dirty clothes are out, too. Clothes have attached tags that tell how to care for them. Follow the instructions carefully.

13. The topics in this section dealing with choosing a wardrobe, coordinating clothes, comparison shopping, and clothing care might benefit from having the assistance of a resource person (see Activity 2). An alternative to an external person would be to invite a home economics teacher or perhaps some home economics students to meet with the class.

Michele's clothes are well chosen and fit her nicely. She is careless, however, in taking care of them. Her winter coats have been missing buttons for two years. Today, she wore a dress that has a ripped arm seam. In spite of her nice clothes, Michele often looks sloppy. Her co-workers joke about her appearance.

It's a fact that the way you look influences how other people see you. Your appearance will greatly influence your job success. Everyone can look good. Remember that a winning appearance depends more on knowledge and effort than it does on physical beauty.

FIGURE 11-6 Proper care will keep your clothes neater and save you money at the dry cleaners. *Photo by Paul E. Meyers*

CHAPTER REVIEW

Chapter in Brief

- No matter what your job, your employer will expect you to groom and dress properly. What is considered to be a good appearance, however, varies from job to job.
- In addition to personal hygiene, grooming is important on the job. Hair should be neat, trimmed, and not too faddish. Beyond this, how you wear your hair is up to you. A grooming decision for men is whether to be clean shaven or to grow a mustache or beard. To control underarm odor, use a deodorant or antiperspirant. Your skin may need care beyond daily bathing. Women should use cosmetics and other beauty aids properly.
- Posture is the way you stand, walk, and sit. Good posture, like good grooming, is necessary if you want to make a good impression on the job.
- Clothes are important to your overall appearance on the job. Wear what fits your job. Wear what looks good on you. Plan your wardrobe carefully. Learn how to coordinate clothes. Choose quality, well-made clothes and take proper care of them.

Words to Know

grooming maintaining a neat, attractive appearance.

personal hygiene keeping one's body clean and healthy.

posture the position of a person's body while standing, walking, or sitting.

sunscreen a special lotion used to protect the skin from the sun's ultraviolet rays.

wardrobe wearing apparel; one's clothing.

Questions to Answer

1. Why was Mr. Bedrava so concerned about Howard's poor hygiene and grooming?
2. For most jobs, what is the basic rule about hairstyles?
3. Suppose Kyie, a medical laboratory technician, wants to grow a beard. When should he start?
4. What is the purpose of a deodorant? An antiperspirant?
5. What are the possible dangers of too much sun exposure? How can you prevent overexposure?
6. How does good posture help you to make a good impression on the job?
7. If you aren't sure about how to dress on the job, what two things might you do?
8. List the six basic rules for clothing choice, wear, and care.

1. Employers don't want customers to think that the poor appearance of an employee is an indication of how the business is run.
2. Hair should be neat, trimmed, and not too faddish. Within these guidelines, wear whatever style looks good on you.
3. During a vacation so that he won't have to go to work with a growth of stubble.
4. A *deodorant* kills the germs that cause odor. An *antiperspirant* reduces the amount of perspiration.
5. Long-term exposure to the sun can lead to skin cancer. Wear protective clothing and use a sunscreen.
6. Good posture conveys an appearance of poise and self-confidence.
7. (a) Notice what other employees wear. (b) Ask your boss or supervisor.
8. (a) Wear what fits your job. (b) Wear what looks good on you. (c) Plan your wardrobe carefully. (d) Learn how to coordinate clothes. (e) Choose quality, well-made clothing. (f) Take proper care of clothes.

Activities to Do

1. Invite a hairstylist to class to discuss hair care and hairstyling as they relate to appearance on the job.
2. Invite a clothing store representative to class to discuss how to make the most of a basic wardrobe.
3. Prepare a bulletin board that shows proper dress and appearance for different occupations. Each person in the class should contribute something from a magazine or other source. Try to show occupations for which students in the class are preparing.
4. The sunscreens contained in suntan products are rated by numbers. The numbers correspond to the degree of protection provided. Prepare a chart or poster explaining the numbering system.

Topics to Discuss

1. What are your feelings toward someone who has poor personal hygiene or inappropriate appearance? Pretend that you have a friend or co-worker with such a problem. Discuss your feelings and how you might go about telling the person.
2. Good appearance varies from job to job. Discuss different examples. Give examples that illustrate both different grooming practices and different types of dress.
3. Hairstyles, use of beauty aids, and clothing styles often differ from one region of the country to another. Perhaps you have lived or traveled in regions different from where you live now. Discuss some of these differences.

14. Be sensitive to different hair-care needs in relation to gender and race.
15. Sun protection factor (SPF) numbers have increased steadily since they were first introduced. In early 1990, the highest available SPF was 50. A local druggist or dermatologist might be able to provide a SPF chart.

High Five

OFFICE EDUCATION MAKES A DIFFERENCE

The career of Frederick Korb got off to a rocky start. During his sophomore year in high school, he worked at a local restaurant. He made the mistake of stealing money from his employer and was caught. The employer decided not to prosecute. But as punishment, Korb had to pay back the money and perform community service work.

The next year, he enrolled in an Office Education program. He obtained a cooperative education job as a bank teller. The job entailed cashing checks, taking deposits, making withdrawals, and balancing the cash drawer. He handled thousands of dollars in cash daily, while waiting on customers. According to Korb, Office Education "saved him."

Korb notes that Office Education "prepares students for the real world" with its combination of work and study. He feels that he has gained "real experience and knowledge of how to work with the public." It has helped motivate him to want a "good education" in addition to a "good job." But most of all he says, "I've learned self-respect."

In addition to working at the bank during his junior and senior years, Korb was active in Business Professionals of America. This is the vocational student organization for individuals in business and Office Education. He competed in business-type contests, planned and managed conferences, and spoke before various youth and business groups. He was president of the state association and served as parliamentarian of the national organization.

In February 1988, Korb was invited to testify before the Illinois State Board of Education. He emphasized that Cooperative Vocational Education can make a difference and credited the program for helping him turn himself around. One board member, in commenting on Korb's testimony, noted that his story helps translate "a lot of dollars and cents into human terms."

Section Three

Career Planning

Chapter 12 Career Decision-making
Chapter 13 Information About Your Self
Chapter 14 Career Information

Throughout your lifetime, you will be faced with making educational and occupational decisions. The more important the decision, the more time and effort you should spend on it. In Chapter 12, you will learn how to use a five-step process of decision-making. By using a systematic approach, you can gain greater control over your life. Your chances of being satisfied with the decision will also be increased.

Occupational decision-making should be based on self-information. By learning more about what you like to do (interests), what you are able to do (aptitudes), and what you believe is important (work values), you will make better choices about what you want to be. These three types of self-information (interests, aptitudes, work values) are explained in Chapter 13.

Occupational information is also an important part of decision-making. The ways in which information about occupations and industries is collected, classified, and disseminated are explained in Chapter 14. The most useful and up-to-date occupational resource is the *Occupational Outlook Handbook (OOH)*. You will learn in this chapter how to use the OOH to conduct an occupational search.

1. *Career decision-making* refers to making choices about work roles. Such choices involve decisions about jobs (where to work) and occupations (what to do).

2. Karen has a part-time job. She has already made at least one career decision.

CHAPTER TWELVE

Career Decision-making

OUTLINE
The Decision-making Process
Individuals and Decision-making
Other Influences on Decision-making
Chapter Review

OBJECTIVES
After reading this chapter, you should be able to:
- Discuss instances in which an organized decision-making process is needed.
- List and summarize each step in the decision-making process.
- Identify and describe different decision-making styles.
- Discuss the need to accept responsibility for career planning.
- Explain how previous decisions, environment and experience, and real-world restrictions influence decision-making.

FIGURE 12-1 What should a person do when she likes her job, but would also like to go to college? *Photo by David W. Tuttle*

3. The immediate career decision confronting Karen is what to do when her co-op job comes to an end.

During the past year, Karen has worked part-time in a local clothing store as part of a cooperative vocational education program. Since the store is rather small, she has learned many different skills.

Karen sells, prices merchandise, operates the cash register, and prepares advertising. From time to time, she helps with payroll records and tax reports. Her window display for an Easter sales promotion brought many compliments from customers and co-workers. Her most interesting experience to date was going with the store manager on a buying trip.

The store manager has already offered her a full-time job after graduation. Karen had planned to go away to college. She can't decide whether to turn down the offer of a full-time job or go to college. What should she do? How should she go about making her decision?

THE DECISION-MAKING PROCESS

Decision-making involves choosing between two or more choices or *alternatives.* Some people make no effort to identify the choices available to them. Be aware that choosing not to decide is also a choice. Most everyday decisions such as "What shall I wear today?" are made without much thought. But decisions like the one facing Karen are not this easy

4. Emphasize that the more important the decision, the more likely it is that a systematic approach is needed.

5. The five-step process shown in Figure 12-3 is representative.
6. Emphasize that a *problem* is simply a situation requiring a solution. Problems are not necessarily negative situations.

CHAPTER 12 Career Decision-making ■ 141

to make. She needs to follow a systematic decision-making process that will help her organize important information and make the decision that is best for her.

A simple five-step decision-making process is shown in Figure 12-3 and explained in the following paragraphs. The same steps are followed whether you are making a decision about a career, choosing a college, or buying a used car.

Defining the Problem

The term *problem* here refers to a question in need of a solution. The decision-making process begins when you become aware of a problem and see the need to make a decision. Perhaps the problem is broad and long-range such as, "What are my goals in life?" Maybe it is an intermediate-range problem such as "What occupation do I want to prepare for?" A problem like "How can I earn some money to pay for Saturday's date?" is an immediate one.

Karen has partially answered her long-range goal in that she would like to work in some area related to business after graduation. She still must answer the more immediate problem of whether to continue working at the clothing store. After making a choice, she may have to decide on future educational plans.

Gathering Information

Once the problem is known, gather the necessary information. You can't make a good decision without it. Unfortunately, how do you know how much information is enough? You don't. The amount of information you gather and the time you spend gathering it should be related to how important the decision is. In other words, *the more important the decision, the greater the amount of information needed.*

To help decide whether to continue working at the clothing store, Karen made an appointment with Mrs. Enrico, the store manager. She explained to Mrs. Enrico that she liked retail sales and her job at the clothing store. She also explained that she wanted to go to college. Mrs. Enrico was very understanding and encouraging. She told Karen what she could expect over the next several years in terms of responsibilities and salary at the store. She also gave Karen the choice of working at the store part-time.

Evaluating the Information

In this step, you organize the information you have gathered into categories. You then identify the pros and cons of each possible choice. A rating scale

FIGURE 12-2 Not all decisions require a formal decision-making process. *Photo by Paul E. Meyers*

Step 1: Define Problem
Become aware of the need to make a decision. Identify the problem.

↓

Step 2: Gather Information
Obtain information about the problem.

↓

Step 3: Evaluate Information
Weigh information to arrive at a list of acceptable alternatives.

↓

Step 4: Make Choice
Select the alternative that leads to the most desirable result and has the highest possibility of success.

↓

Step 5: Take Action
Put your choice into action and commit yourself to making the decision work.

↓

FIGURE 12-3 Learning this five-step process can help you to better plan your future career.

7. Encourage students to define the problem as a question. For example, "What am I going to do after high school graduation?"

8. Collect information on at least three alternatives and if you continue to uncover the same or similar alternatives, you probably have collected enough information.

142 ■ SECTION 3 Career Planning

or checklist may be of help as you do this.

After talking to Mrs. Enrico, Karen wrote down the three choices she had:

1. Work full-time at the store and not go to college.
2. Quit the job at the store and go away to college.
3. Go to the nearby community college part-time and work at the store part-time.

For each alternative, Karen wrote down as many advantages and disadvantages she could think of. For instance, if she chose 1, Karen would have a full-time salary. She could probably buy the car she had been wanting. On the other hand, she might want to change jobs someday. In that case, a degree would be a strong advantage. She also went over the alternatives with her parents to see if they could add any information.

Making a Choice

At this point, you choose one of your alternatives. Making a choice is often difficult because rather than choosing between desirable and undesirable alternatives, you must choose from among several desirable alternatives.

WWYD Feature A. Select a "double specialization" or select one alternative as a "major specialization" and the other as a "minor specialization."

What Would You Do?

You plan to go to a business school next year. You have already applied and been accepted. Now, you are using a decision-making process to choose a program of study. You have collected a lot of information and given the problem a great deal of thought. The difficulty is that you like two programs (specializations) equally well. What would you do?

It was finally time for Karen to choose. She decided on choice 3—working part-time and going to college part-time. By working, she could pay for her education without having to borrow money. Going to a community college would also be a lot cheaper than a four-year school, since she could live at home. And who knows? Maybe she will want to transfer to a four-year college in two years.

Taking Action

At this point, you begin to carry out the alternative you chose in step four. Suppose that you have weighed alternatives and decided to seek a job in a distant city. The first thing to do before you leave home is to find a job in the new place.

Taking action also involves committing yourself to making the decision work. In moving to a new city, for example, it might be a while before you find a job there. It would be easy to give up. Stick with

FIGURE 12-4 Some people aren't accepted by the college of their choice. Not all "good" decisions turn out the way you want them to. *Photo by David W. Tuttle*

9. Alternative 3 is new. In gathering and evaluating information, additional alternatives are often revealed.

10. Emphasize the difficulty in choosing from among several desirable alternatives. Ask students if they have even been confronted with such a choice.

11. Taking action and following through depend on persistence and maintaining a positive attitude.

CHAPTER 12 Career Decision-making ■ 143

your job search, but make sure your expectations are realistic.

Having made her choice, Karen informed her parents and Mrs. Enrico. They all agreed with Karen's decision and thought that she was wise to have made it. Karen felt good about having put the decision behind her. Now it was time for her to start deciding what courses to take in school.

Occupational Decision-making

Let's see how the decision-making process might be used in making an occupational choice. As each step is explained, refer occasionally to Figure 12-5. The first step is defining the problem. In this case, the question is: "Which occupation should I choose?"

In step two, you collect information. In choosing an occupation, information about your own (self) characteristics and occupations are required. The three major types of self-information are interests, aptitudes, and work values. (You will learn more about self-information in Chapter 13.) You will use self-information to develop a preliminary list of occupational alternatives. You will then explore each occupation on the list. (In Chapter 14, you will learn how to do an occupational search.)

In the third step, you consider the information and *eliminate* those occupations that are unacceptable for one reason or another. A form like the one shown in Figure 12-6 is helpful at this point.

By the fourth step, you have only a few alternatives left. Each of the choices seems to be equally

13. Notice that Step 2 may involve collecting several types of information and may occur over an extended period of time. Information gathering may also involve both vicarious and experiential approaches.

Step 1: Define Problem
Which occupation should I choose?

↓

Step 2: Gather Information
- Identify interests and aptitudes.
- Develop a list of occupational alternatives based on self-information.
- Collect occupational information.

↓

Step 3: Evaluate Information
- Compare and evaluate occupational information.
- Evaluate own feelings and attitudes.
- Eliminate unacceptable occupational alternatives.

↓

Step 4: Make Choice
Based on your work values and career goals, choose the occupation that seems best to you now.

↓

Step 5: Take Action
Begin a job search or enroll in an appropriate educational program that will prepare you for the occupation.

↓

FIGURE 12-5 This is how the decision-making process is applied to making an occupational choice.

12. Ask students if they have ever felt a sense of relief upon making a tough decision.

CHECKLIST FOR EVALUATING POSSIBLE OCCUPATIONAL ALTERNATIVES

Name of occupation _____

	Yes	No	Not Sure
1. The nature of the work involved in this occupation is the type I'd *like to do*.			
2. I believe I have the *ability to do well* in this occupation.			
3. This occupation involves doing work that is *important to me*.			
4. The typical *working conditions* for this occupation are acceptable to me.			
5. I'm willing to complete the necessary *education* or *training requirements* to qualify for this occupation.			
6. I have the *educational background* to be admitted to any required education or training program.			
7. The future *employment outlook* for this occupation is good.			
8. I would be satisfied with the *amount of earnings* that is typical for this occupation.			
9. There are other *related occupations* in which I could work after learning this occupation.			
10. I believe I have *enough information* about this occupation to make a decision.			

On a scale of 1 (low) to 10 (high), I'd give this occupation a final ranking of _____

FIGURE 12-6 This is an example of a checklist that can help you evaluate alternatives.

14. Choosing involves both *selection* and *elimination*.

144 ■ SECTION 3 Career Planning

desirable. You may be happy with any one of the choices. What you try to do, though, is choose the one alternative that seems best at this time. There is no guarantee that your choice will work out. But you still must choose based upon your best judgment.

Once you have made a decision, you are ready to put your choice into action. Starting a cooperative education program is an example of taking action. Perhaps you are not sure what type of educational program will meet your needs. If this is the case, you should start the decision-making process again. This time the problem is "What type of educational program should I choose?"

During any of the five steps, you may wish to seek help from a counselor, teacher, parent, or other adult. Talking about goals and alternatives often helps people make decisions. The final decision, though, will be yours.

16. Learning and using a decision-making process is not something mastered in one class period. You may find it desirable to return to Figures 12-3 and 12-4 many times.

FIGURE 12-7 The hardest choices to make are between alternatives that are equally desirable. These individuals considered both agricultural technology and horticulture. *Photos by Paul E. Meyers*

15. Progression from Step 3 to Step 4 is more of a continuous process than is progression between other steps.

*WWYD Feature B. If the student has sound reasons for wanting to change majors, the additional time and effort are probably worth it.

CHAPTER 12 Career Decision-making ■ 145

What Would You Do?

You are attending a two-year technical institute, majoring in automotive technology. After two semesters, you have decided to change your major to machine tool technology. The counselor says you can make the change. But you will have to take overload hours and attend an additional semester beyond two years. You are anxious to finish school and begin work. You can't decide whether the additional time and effort will be worthwhile. What would you do?

INDIVIDUALS AND DECISION-MAKING

The decision-making process is a tool. How well you use this tool depends largely on your style of decision-making, and your willingness to accept responsibility and take action.

Decision-making Styles

In watching a baseball game, you will notice that players have different batting styles. For example, one batter will move quickly into the batter's box, crowd the plate, and swing at the first ball that comes near the strike zone. Another batter will delay stepping into the box, stand deep in the batter's box, step out of the box if the pitcher is too slow, and won't swing until the pitch is exactly right.

People also have different *decision-making styles.* These styles are gained over a long period of time. Seven styles of decision-making are most common.

The Agonizer. These people collect a lot of information and spend a lot of time evaluating it. In fact, they spend so much time doing this that they end up not knowing what to do! They get overwhelmed with all the data.

The Mystic. Have you heard someone say a decision was made because it "feels right." Such a decision is based on *intuition* or hunch. Some people make most of their choices this way.

The Fatalist. These people don't believe that they have much control over their choices. So, they don't spend much time gathering information.

Joyce's parents insist that she live at home and attend the local university. They will pay her tuition and expenses if she does this. Joyce will be an education major even though the school's education department is weak. State University, 200 miles away, has a strong department. Joyce, an excellent student, would like to go there. But she is convinced that she has no choice.

The Evader. John is a junior in high school. He has taken a general program of study because he has made no career decision. He hopes that by delaying long enough, the problem will go away. In its worst form, this style of decision-making is known as "the ostrich style." Ostriches stick their heads in the sand. John is behaving like an ostrich. He hasn't made any career decision at all.

The Plunger. These people eagerly make decisions. In fact, they are usually too eager to do so. The plunger frequently chooses the first alternative that comes to mind.

The Submissive. "What do you want me to do?" Sound familiar? Such people always want someone else to make a decision for them. If no one will make the decision for them, submissives will make it themselves based on what they think someone else would want them to do.

The Planner. These people are likely to use a good decision-making strategy. They are thorough and weigh all the information. Such people seek to maintain a balance between facts and emotions. Is this your decision-making style?

FIGURE 12-8 What type of decision-making style is being used here? *Courtesy of Sears, Roebuck and Company*

17. Concentrate on helping students to recognize differences in the way people approach decision-making. Obviously, the planner is the preferred style.

18. You may wish to assign Activity 2 at this time.

146 ■ SECTION 3 Career Planning

Benefits of Good Planning

Being a planner can have several benefits. For instance, it can increase your chances of being satisfied with your decision. By *collecting information about a number of alternatives* and carefully weighing the facts, you increase the chances of choosing what is best for you.

Using an organized decision-making process will provide you with more choices. A skilled decision-maker usually develops many alternatives from which to choose. Having several alternatives gives you more freedom than if you had only one or two.

Taking Charge of Your Life

The benefits of successful decision-making are achieved only if the process is used. And that depends on your willingness to accept responsibility for making decisions and for taking action to carry them out.

19. Research suggests that "accepting responsibility for what happens to you" is *a* key factor, if not *the* key factor in a successful career.

A very important part of growing up is accepting responsibility for what happens to you. This doesn't mean that luck, natural ability, family advantages, or discrimination do not play a part. It is clear that they do. For instance, John Kennedy's being elected President of the United States was certainly helped by the wealth and name he inherited from his family. And the success of Ted Williams at baseball was influenced by his nearly perfect eyesight.

On the other hand, it is possible to identify many examples of famous or successful people who did not have these advantages or who had only average ability. Success and happiness often depend on the choices you make.

Too many people blame someone or something for what happens to them. For example, in conversations about grades, students often say things like: "Mr. Anderson *gave me* a D in English." In truth, teachers don't give grades at all. Teachers simply

FIGURE 12-9 It is easy to blame someone else for your shortcomings. *Photo by David W. Tuttle*

20. Ask students to provide examples of how luck, natural ability, family advantage, and discrimination may *help* or *hinder* one's career.

F•E•A•T•U•R•E

Envy in the Workplace

This chapter has stressed that success and happiness depend on your own efforts. This doesn't mean, however, that other people cannot help or hinder you. In her book, *The Snow White Syndrome,* Betsy Cohen points out that envy is often a by-product of success. *Envy* is dislike or hatred. In the fairy tale, Snow-White's beauty led the Wicked Queen to try to kill her.

Unfortunately, envy exists in the workplace. The more successful you are, the more envy you are likely to cause. In the workplace, an envious person can hurt you. This is because your success often depends on others' cooperation. If someone is envious, he or she can make you look bad. Here are some ways that envy is expressed:

- "Forgetting" instructions or deadlines.
- Gossiping or lying behind your back.
- Being continually late, stubborn, or resistant.
- Clever put-downs.
- Excessive compliments and flattery.
- Outright destruction of your work.

Envious people act to control you. They want to bring you back to their level. To avoid being a victim of envy, learn to recognize it. Try to develop a tolerance for it. Don't make it worse by flaunting your strengths. Be considerate toward co-workers. Build on the other person's achievements. Remember that envy reflects what other people may see, not the real you.

If you are ambitious and aspire to be successful, be prepared to face envy. It exists in many workplaces. If you achieve success, someone is probably going to be envious.

FIGURE 12-FEATURE Help deter envy by cooperating with, rather than competing with, co-workers. *Photo by Liane Enkelis*

Envy in the Workplace. Ask students if they have ever perceived instances of envy either at school or in the workplace. Have they ever been victims or perpetrators of envy? Perhaps students can add to the list of ways that envy is expressed.

FIGURE 12-10 Experiences in school or extracurricular activities often influence later career choices, whether it is on the school newspaper or the swim team. *Courtesy of Gerry Trafficanda (photographer) McCann-Erickson Inc.*

assign grades to student's work. If you receive an A, you have earned it. The same is true if you receive a D.

OTHER INFLUENCES ON DECISION-MAKING

We have discussed how information, decision-making style, and willingness to accept responsibility all influence decision-making. Now, let's discuss three more factors related to decision-making. These are previous decisions, environment and experience, and real-world restrictions.

Previous Decisions

One decision may influence later ones. To illustrate, let's consider the case of Dee Dee, a tenth-grade student who is deciding what courses to take next year. She picks a health occupations course. By making this decision, Dee Dee will begin to move *toward* a health career and *away* from such fields as business, food service, and auto mechanics. Her decision isn't final, though. Dee Dee may change direction later—even as an adult. Important choices that influence later career decisions include selecting school courses and college majors, gaining work experience, marrying, and joining the military.

Environment and Experience

Your *environment* is your surroundings. It includes your family, your neighborhood, your friends, your school, your church, and the like. Your *experiences* are what you do and what happens to you in your environment. Environmental and experience factors may strongly influence your choices. Let's see what influenced Sandra Campbell.

Sandra Campbell decided to become a veterinary assistant. Her decision was heavily influenced by three environmental and experience factors. She grew up on a farm where she developed a love for animals. She worked part-time at her uncle's animal hospital and enjoyed that experience. And she lives near a community college that offers the only veterinary assistant's program in the state.

Real-world Restrictions

There are a number of *reality factors* over which we have little control that often influence decisions. These are persons, events, or situations that exist. Sam would like to be a musician, but the reality is that he would have trouble supporting himself. So he chooses another occupation and plays for parties on the weekend. Someday he may be able to work as a musician full-time.

21. Ask students to give examples of how they may have "earned" a low grade.
22. You may wish to discuss Topic 3 at this time.
23. Ask students to provide examples of how environment and experiences may have influenced their choices.

Often what appear to be real-world restrictions are not. For instance, Sarah didn't think she would have enough money to attend a certain school. She was happy when the school gave her the scholarship she applied for. That, and a student loan, will get her through the program.

Other reality factors include age, experience, qualifications, abilities, physical characteristics, and so on. For example, someone with poor eyesight can't become a commercial airline pilot. In making career decisions, everyone faces real-world restrictions. When you face such a situation, either try harder or choose another alternative.

FIGURE 12-11 Ways can be found around many of life's roadblocks. *Photo by Kenneth Deitcher*

24. The "success stories" used to open each section of this book provide illustrations of how individuals have overcome reality factors and other limitations. Discuss as appropriate.

CHAPTER REVIEW

Chapter in Brief

- Decision-making involves choosing between two or more alternatives. The more important the decision, the more time and effort should be devoted to it. Decision-making involves the following five steps:
    1. Defining the problem
    2. Gathering information
    3. Evaluating the information
    4. Making a choice
    5. Taking action

    In making an occupational decision, step two involves collecting information about self-characteristics and occupations. During any of the five steps, you may wish to seek help from a counselor, teacher, parent, or other adult.

- How well you use the decision-making process depends on your style of decision-making, and your willingness to accept responsibility and take action. Seven styles of decision-making are common: the agonizer, the mystic, the fatalist, the evader, the plunger, the submissive, and the planner. The planner is the preferred style.

- Being a planner can have several benefits. It can increase your chances of being satisfied with your decision. It can provide you with more choices. It will help you gain greater control over your life.

- A very important part of growing up is accepting responsibility for what happens to you. Your success and happiness will depend largely on the choices you make. Too many people blame someone or something for what happens to them.

- Three other factors also influence decision-making. These are previous decisions, environment and experience, and real-world restrictions.

Words to Know

alternatives the choices or options available in making a decision.

decision-making the process of choosing between two or more alternatives or options.

decision-making styles the typical manner in which a person makes a decision.

environment the sum total of one's surroundings.

experiences the sum total of events that compose an individual's life.

intuition a feeling or hunch.

problem a question in need of a solution or answer.

reality factors those persons, events, or situations that are real and present, such as the high cost of going to an Ivy League college.

CHAPTER 12 Career Decision-making ■ 151

Questions to Answer
1. When is a systematic decision-making process best used?
2. Name and briefly explain each step in the decision-making process.
3. In choosing an occupation, two types of information are collected in step two. Name them.
4. Identify the decision-making style that is described below:
   a. These people delay making a career decision.
   b. These people get overwhelmed with all the data.
   c. These people choose the first alternative that comes to mind.
   d. These people make decisions based on what they think someone else would want them to do.
5. Which is the best type of decision-making style to use?
6. Using a decision-making process can have several benefits. Name three.
7. Explain what is meant by the phrase "accepting responsibility for what happens to you."
8. Give an example to illustrate how previous decisions may influence later ones.
9. What is the difference between your environment and your experiences?
10. Name three reality factors that can limit career decisions.

Activities to Do
1. You have probably used a problem-solving method in one of your science or math classes. Compare the problem-solving method with the decision-making process. How are they similar and different? Discuss your answers in class.
2. Find out which type of decision-making style is most common in your class. Be honest and write on a piece of scrap paper which of the seven styles you use. (No names on papers.) Summarize results on the board and discuss the outcome in class.
3. Groups as well as individuals can use the decision-making process. As a class, apply the decision-making method to a real or hypothetical situation. For example, what type of computer would be best for use in the class?

Topics to Discuss
1. Identify and discuss a variety of situations in which a systematic decision-making process should be used.
2. How is an occupational decision different from a job decision?
3. Decisions are influenced by previous decisions made and not made. Identify and discuss some of the important decisions you have made and not made. How did they turn out? Might the outcome have been different had you used a systematic decision-making process?
4. Do you believe that you have the power to influence the direction of your life and career?
5. We tend to think of reality factors as negative things such as not having enough money or lacking qualifications. Can you think of positive reality factors that also limit or restrict choices?

---

1. The more important the decision, the greater the need to use a systematic decision-making approach.
2. *Defining the problem*—becoming aware of the need to make a decision and identifying the problem. *Gathering information*—collecting data related to the problem. *Evaluating the information*—weighing information to arrive at a list of acceptable alternatives. *Making a choice*—selecting the alternative that leads to the most desirable result and has the greatest likelihood of success. *Taking action*—putting the choice into action and committing yourself to making the decision work.
3. (a) Self-information. (b) Occupational information.
4. (a) Evader. (b) Agonizer. (c) Plunger. (d) Submissive.
5. The planner.
6. (a) Can increase your chances of being satisfied with the choice. (b) Will provide you with more choices. (c) Allows greater control over your life.
7. It means that you can't leave it up to someone else to take care of you and make decisions for you. You must take action to influence the direction of your life.
8. Choosing to take a health occupations course moves you in the direction of a health career and away from other fields. Many other examples could be cited.
9. *Environment* refers to your surroundings. *Experiences* are what you do and what happens to you in your environment.
10. There are many, including lack of money, physical limitations or handicaps, age, experience, qualifications, abilities, and the like.

25. A problem-solving strategy always leads to the same, correct solution. In decision-making, the solution will vary according to individual differences among decision-makers.
26. Occupational decisions involve choosing *what one wants to do*. Job decisions involve choosing *where one wants to work* (review Chapter 1). Choosing a job comes *after* one has learned an occupation; the exception is for entry-level jobs (including co-op) that do not require prior occupational training.
27. A Brooke Shields or a Michael Jackson has restrictions imposed upon them as a result of fame and fortune. Ask students to provide other illustrations.

1. The word *self* is used here as a noun, not a pronoun.
2. It may be idealistic to think that individuals can choose occupations that they like, are good at, and involve important work.
4. Interests, aptitudes, and work values are the three primary types of self-information used in occupational and educational decision-making.

CHAPTER THIRTEEN

Information About Your Self

OUTLINE
Types of Self-information
Relationships Among Self-information Factors
Self and Other Life Roles
Chapter Review

OBJECTIVES
After reading this chapter, you should be able to:
- Discuss how self-information can help you make more satisfying occupational decisions.
- Name and describe the three types of self-information.
- Describe how interests, aptitudes and work values are measured.
- Explain how interests, aptitudes, and work values may be similar or different.
- Illustrate how interests, aptitudes, and work values may be expressed outside of one's job.

3. This is a simple definition for an abstract concept. There is a large body of sophisticated psychological literature on *self* and *self-concept*.

If you are in your teens, you can look forward to forty or more years of working. That is a long time—especially if you work at an occupation that you dislike. Wouldn't you like to have an occupation that you enjoy doing, that you are good at, and that involves work that is important to you?

Before you select an occupation, you should first answer the question, "Who am I?" Information about your *self* can help you make more satisfying career decisions. The self is what you are—your personal characteristics or traits.

152

FIGURE 13-1 Your self is much more than what you see in a mirror. *Photo by David W. Tuttle*

In this chapter, you will learn to relate information about your self to occupational decisions. By learning more about what you like to do, what you are able to do, and what you believe is important, you will make better choices about what you want to be.

TYPES OF SELF-INFORMATION
When making an occupational decision, you should have information about your interests, aptitudes, and work values.

Interests
We all make choices based on likes and dislikes. We choose from different types of food, music, clothes, hobbies, and so on because we enjoy one thing more than another. For instance, if you enjoy Chinese food, you may choose to go to Chinese restaurants when eating out. If you dislike Greek food, you probably won't go to many Greek restaurants. Things that we like to do are called *interests*. William, for instance, enjoys hunting, fishing, camping, and hiking. His interests relate to outdoor activities.

5. Ask students to name or list several of their interests.
6. Have students name several occupations that are suggested by their interests.

FIGURE 13-2 What type of interests would you say this person has? *Photo by Paul E. Meyers*

Your interests can lead to occupations that might suit you. William's interest in the outdoors suggests that he would do well in such occupations as forester, game warden, or recreation worker.

Debbie likes working with her microcomputer. She enjoys creating computer graphics. Debbie is also experimenting with a program that will play music on the computer. What kinds of occupations do you think Debbie might be suited for?

By thinking about your likes and dislikes, you are taking the first step toward learning about yourself. Do you prefer indoor or outdoor activities? Would you rather work alone or with people? Do you like to work with tools and machines or data and figures? Do you enjoy music or art?

School courses and activities can offer clues to occupations that might be of interest. What school subjects do you like best? Think about school activities such as clubs, plays, musicals, and fund-raising events. Don't forget about hobbies. What do activities and hobbies reveal about your interests?

Vera, for example, belongs to the Journalism Club and works on the staffs of the yearbook and school newspaper. English has always been her favorite school subject. All of Vera's interests point in the direction of a career in the communications field.

7. Debbie's interests suggest some type of occupation involving the creative application of computers, such as computer animator.

		L	?	D
02.01	Develop chemical processes to solve technical problems	—	—	—
	Analyze data on weather conditions	—	—	—
	Develop methods to control air or water pollution	—	—	—
02.02	Study causes of animal diseases	—	—	—
	Develop methods for growing better crops	—	—	—
	Develop new techniques to process foods	—	—	—
02.03	Examine teeth and treat dental problems...........................	—	—	—
	Diagnose and treat sick animals	—	—	—
	Give medical treatment to people.......	—	—	—
02.04	Prepare medicines according to prescription	—	—	—
	Study blood samples using a microscope	—	—	—
	Test ore samples for gold or silver content	—	—	—
03.01	Manage a beef or dairy ranch..........	—	—	—
	Operate a commercial fish farm	—	—	—
	Manage the use and development of forest lands.......................	—	—	—

Source: *Interest Checklist*, U.S. Employment Service, 1979

FIGURE 13-3 Here are sample items from the *Interest Checklist*.

8. Have students name school courses, school activities, and hobbies that they like. Discuss how these suggest possible occupations of interest.

154 ■ SECTION 3 Career Planning

Rather than only thinking about your interests, you might want to complete an occupational interest inventory. An interest inventory contains a list of work activities. For each activity, you indicate if you like it, dislike it, or don't know. Figure 13-3 shows several statements taken from the *Interest Checklist.*

An interest inventory is not a test. There are no right or wrong answers. However, responses to the items need to be carefully interpreted. Assistance from a teacher or counselor is usually required.

Chances are that your answers will form a pattern. Let's see how the *Interest Checklist* can help you identify occupational interests. Go back to Figure 13-3. You will see that the statements of work activities are listed in groups of three. To the left of each group is a four-digit number. This number corresponds to one of 66 work groups found in a government publication called the *Guide for Occupational Exploration (GOE).* Copies are in many school libraries.

Let's say that you marked "like" for the three work activities in group "02.04." Work group 02.04 is called "Laboratory Technology." This means that you have shown an interest in work activities relating to laboratory technology.

Once you have identified a work group (or groups) of interest, you can go to the *GOE* for more information. The *GOE* explains each work group and lists occupations in that group. Occupations in the Laboratory Technology group include, for example, Medical Technologist, Food Tester, Seed Analyst, and Film Laboratory Technician.

The results of an interest inventory do not mean that the occupations you find are the only ones for you. They simply represent alternatives that you should investigate. Learn more about the suggested occupations and others as well. And learn more about your self. Don't base your occupational choice solely on the results of an interest inventory.

11. This is only one illustration of how responses to an interest inventory may be used to initiate occupational exploration. Many other applications are available from commercial book and test publishers.

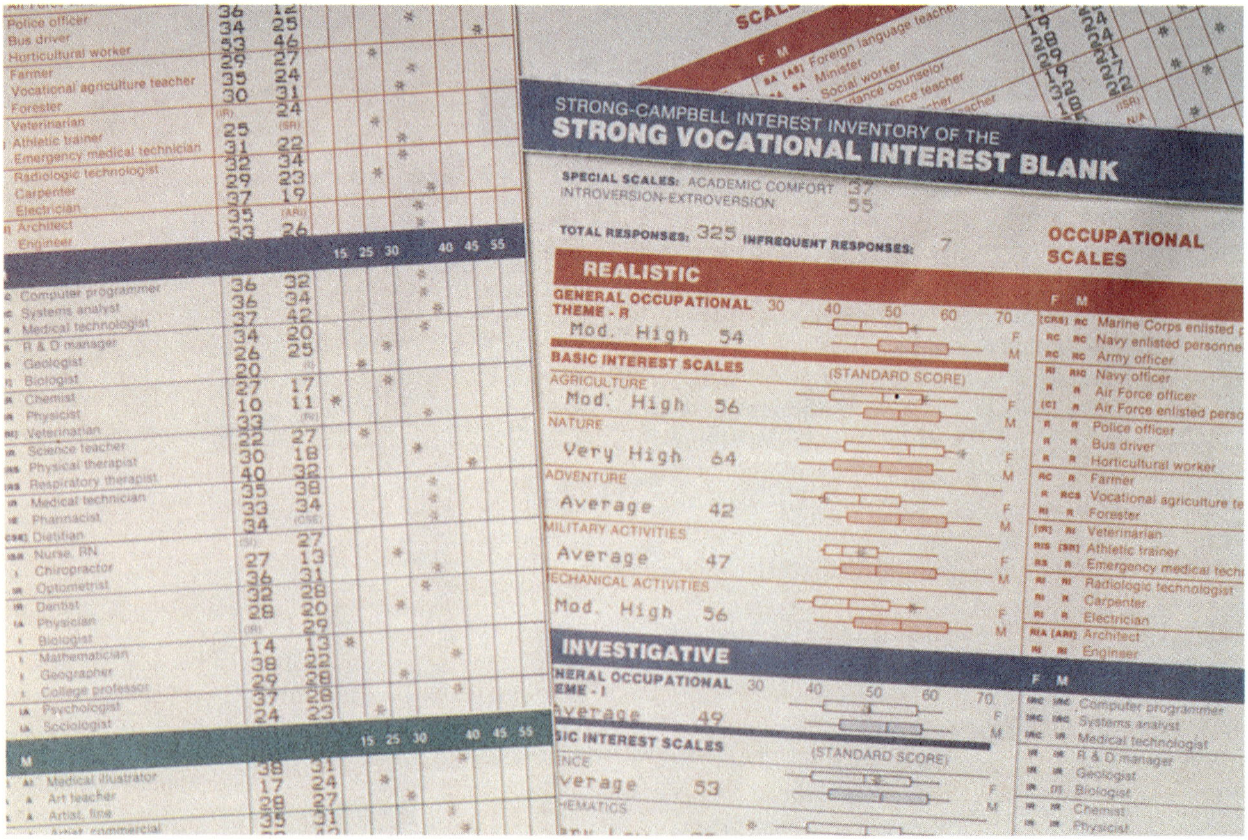

FIGURE 13-4 Some interest inventories provide a printout that explains the results. *Photo by Paul E. Meyers*

9. The *Interest Checklist* was developed by the U.S. Department of Labor in 1979 as a counseling aid. It is in the public domain and can be duplicated for classroom use.

10. Emphasize that an interest inventory is not a test and that there are no right and wrong answers.

12. The value of an interest inventory is to point the way for follow-up exploration. Also emphasize that interests are only one of several types of self-information.

13. The definition here is consistent with that used for the *Armed Services Vocational Aptitude Battery (ASVAB)*—probably the most widely used aptitude measure.

CHAPTER 13 Information About Your Self ■ 155

FIGURE 13-5 The Armed Services use aptitude tests to help place military recruits into appropriate training programs. *Courtesy of U.S. Navy Recruiting*

What Would You Do?

You have always been interested in electronic gadgets. You enjoy taking things apart to find out how they work. The two electronics courses you took were your favorite courses. This year, you are working as a co-op student at Apollo TV and Electronics. Most of your time is spent as a "go-fer" helping to install antennas and satellite dishes. Occasionally, you get to do a minor repair job like clean the heads on a VCR or solder a loose connection on a radio receiver. The job is nothing like you thought it would be. You are beginning to wonder if you made the wrong occupational decision. What would you do?

*WWYD Feature A. In this case, the student hasn't yet had the opportunity to perform tasks representative of an electronics technician.

Aptitudes

Are there occupations that you are interested in, but you wonder if you would do well in them? Terrance, for instance, thinks that he might like to be an architect. But he isn't sure if he has the ability to become one. He needs to look at his *aptitudes*. An aptitude is a developed ability. Your aptitudes represent things you are good at doing.

Terrance can get some idea about his aptitudes by looking at his grades. He has taken algebra and geometry and done well in both. Architects need math ability. Also, his art teacher has said that Terrance has a talent for designing and illustrating. Terrance thought about the two mechanical drawing courses he took. He got an A in both. Overall, it seems that Terrance might do well in his occupation of interest.

How else can you find out if you are suited for a certain occupation? Well, you can take an aptitude test. These tests are ones that measure how well you *should* be able to do in a certain field. An

14. Ask students to provide examples of how their grades in school courses might suggest aptitudes.

156 ■ SECTION 3 Career Planning

aptitude test does not tell you how well you *actually* will do or are doing. Scores on an aptitude test will give you an idea of how well you *might* do. The six most common aptitudes covered by the tests are:

1. Verbal aptitude—using words well.
2. Numerical aptitude—doing math quickly and accurately.
3. Clerical speed and accuracy—picking out letters or words quickly, and arranging number and letter combinations in order.
4. Manual dexterity—moving the hands easily and skillfully.
5. Mechanical reasoning—understanding mechanical principles, how things work, and how tools are used.
6. Spatial visualization—forming mental pictures of the shape, size, and position of objects.

1. Which two words have the same meaning?
   (a) open (b) happy (c) glad (d) green
2. Which two words have the opposite meaning?
   (a) old (b) dry (c) cold (d) young
3. Add (+)
   766
   11
   (A) 677 (B) 755 (C) 777 (D) 656
4. Julie works 8 hours a day, 40 hours a week. She earns $4.20 an hour. How much does she earn each week?
   (A) 120.00 (C) 151.80
   (B) 133.80 (D) 168.00
5. At the left is a drawing of a flat piece of metal. Which object at the right can be made from this piece of metal?

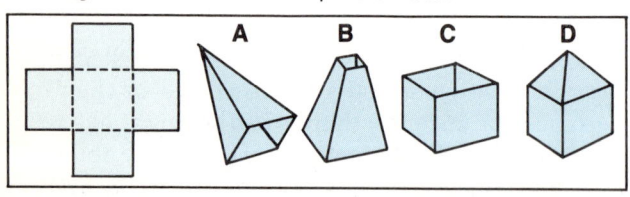

Which pairs of names are the same (S) and which are different (D)?

6. W. W. Jason...W. W. Jason
7. Johnson & Johnson...Johnson & Johnsen
8. Harold Jones Co....Harold Jones and Co.

For questions 9 through 12 find the lettered figure exactly like the numbered figure.

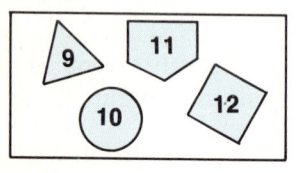

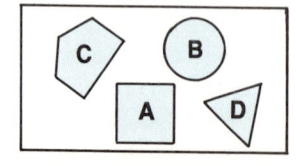

Source: Doing Your Best on Aptitude Tests, GPO, 1976

The types of questions included in an aptitude test vary widely depending on the aptitude being measured. Several different examples are shown in Figure 13-6. Each question has only one correct answer.

A separate score is given for each aptitude that is being tested. The scores are often reported as percentile ranks. For example, Joe received a percentile rank of 85 on Mechanical Reasoning. This means that out of every 100 people who took the test, Joe scored better than 84 of them.

Your teacher or counselor will help you interpret your aptitude test results. After you speak with him or her, the rest will be up to you.

SEE IF YOU MARKED YOUR ANSWERS LIKE THIS

If your answers are not the same as these, go back over the test to find out why.

1. a-b a-c a-d **b-c** b-d c-d
2. a-b a-c **a-d** b-c b-d c-d
3. A B **C** D
4. A B C **D**
5. A B **C** D
6. **S** D
7. S **D**
8. S **D**
9. A B C **D**
10. A **B** C D
11. A B **C** D
12. **A** B C D

FIGURE 13-6 Here are sample aptitude test questions.

15. An aptitude test is a measure of performance in various areas. Based on performance, predictions can be made regarding an individual's potential in an occupation.
16. Ask students to relate the examples of test questions shown in Figure 13-6 to the types of aptitudes listed previously. For example, items 1 and 2 assess verbal ability.
17. Do not confuse the term *percentile,* which is a rank, with *percent.* A person might answer 90 out of 100 items correctly (90%), but rank at the 95 (or some other) percentile.

18. Aptitudes can be used to initiate occupational exploration or to help narrow down a list of occupational alternatives.
19. Distinguish between cultural values and work values.

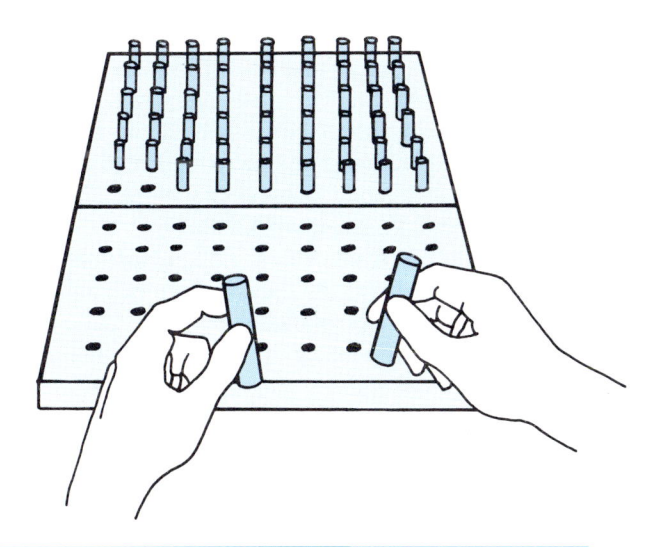

FIGURE 13-7 Some aptitude tests require you to work with your hands.

Work Values

Values are attitudes and beliefs about things we think are important in life. For instance, Americans believe strongly in the right of free speech. This is a basic democratic value that we think is important.

Values that relate to work and career are called *work values*. These are feelings about the importance or worth of an activity or occupation. For instance, if you would like to have an occupation in which you could help other people, you are expressing a value for a certain kind of work.

Work values can also be thought of as needs that we try to meet in our work. For example, Fred gave up a good job with a large insurance company to start his own business. He did so because he wanted to make his own decisions. For Fred, the need for independence was not being met in his former job.

What are some work values? Following are several examples.

- Altruism—helping other people.
- Creativity—inventing things, designing products, or developing new ideas.
- Achievement—having feelings of accomplishment from doing a job well.
- Independence—being able to work in your own way.
- Prestige—wanting to be looked up to.
- Money—earning enough to buy the things you want.
- Security—having a steady job even in hard times.
- Surroundings—being in a pleasant work environment.
- Variety—having the opportunity to do many types of tasks.

FIGURE 13-8 For these Peace Corps volunteers, helping others is more important than pleasant surroundings or making money. *Photos by David W. Tuttle*

20. Given a list of things to do (or be), which one is the highest priority for you? This is a reflection of your work values.
21. This is another relevant way (meeting needs) of explaining work values.
22. Some authors may specify additional types of work values.

158 ■ SECTION 3 Career Planning

You can identify your work values by taking a work values measure. Such measures generally include statements describing things that people look for in their work. The following examples, drawn from *The Values Scale,*[1] show the types of items included in an inventory.

You read each statement and indicate how important it is to you according to a four-point rating scale:

1. means of little or no importance.
2. means of some importance.
3. means important.
4. means very important.

It is now or will in the future be important for me to:

5. help people with problems.
8. discover, develop, or design new things.
23. know that my efforts will show.
42. have a regular income.
65. do something at which I am really good.

[1]Super, Donald E. and Nevill, Dorothy D. *The Values Scale.* Palo Alto, CA: Consulting Psychologists Press, 1985.

The Values Scale consists of 106 such items. Interpretation of this measure is very simple. For instance, questions 23 and 65 in the example relate to the *Achievement* work value. Let's say that you assigned a rating of 4 to questions 23 and 65. This means that work that gives you a feeling of achievement is very important. Most occupations, of course, involve several kinds of work values.

Unlike interest inventories and aptitude tests, the results of a work values measure are not as easily related to specific occupations. This is because work values come from feelings that are more personal. As a result, work values scores are not as useful in helping to identify which occupations to explore. A work values measure is better used in step four of the decision-making process than in step two (refer back to Figure 12-5). You will recall that step four is one in which you make a choice from among a small number of desirable occupational alternatives. Knowledge of work values can help you make final career choices that will lead to your future goals.

23. Research has suggested that work values tend to be less relevant than interests or aptitudes as a factor in adolescent occupational decision-making. Conversely, work values tend to be more important for adults.

FIGURE 13-9 Which work value do you think is important to this person? *Courtesy of SIUC Photocommunications*

*WWYD Feature B. A work values measure can reveal what characteristics of work are important to an individual. Such information can be beneficial in career planning and decision-making. However, an individual must be willing to accept responsibility for making decisions and for taking action to carry them out.

What Would You Do?

You have completed a work values measure. In going over the results with the counselor, you learn that your highest rated values are money, independence, and prestige. It is true. You would like to be wealthy, independent, and have people look up to you.

"Big deal," you think. "Now all I have to do is go out and find someone that will give me an important job and pay me a lot of money. That's a joke. Work values measures are a waste of time. I will probably end up working in the mines like the rest of my family." If you felt like this person, what would you do?

Earl took a work values measure which suggested that altruism, security, and surroundings are important to him. These results tend to confirm his interest in becoming a technology education teacher. Norma found out that creativity and variety are the most important values for her. She is leaning toward becoming a floral designer or interior designer.

RELATIONSHIPS AMONG SELF-INFORMATION FACTORS

Interests, aptitudes, and work values relate to each other. Sometimes they agree and sometimes they conflict. For some people, interests, aptitudes, and work values may all point to the same choice. Robert, for example, wants to be a fashion designer. He has been interested in fashion design ever since he was a child. He has the aptitude, having already won several ribbons and awards in design competitions. Fashion design is usually done in pleasant surroundings, which is important to Robert.

For other people, though, interest, aptitudes, and work values may seem to point in different directions. This is not unusual. Nor is it something to worry about. Jean, for example, has a high aptitude for mechanical reasoning and manual dexterity. But mechanical principles and using tools and machines don't interest her much. What she really wants to do is some type of work that is mentally challenging and involves working with people.

Suppose *your* information conflicts. Choose based on the interest, aptitude, or work value that means

24. It is a reality that interests, aptitudes, and work values interact in different ways for different individuals. Career counseling is desirable following any type of career assessment activity.

CHAPTER 13 Information About Your Self ■ 159

FIGURE 13-10 This person is an excellent coach even though he never played football himself. *Courtesy of Skjold Photographs*

FIGURE 13-11 Even though you know what occupation you want, it may not be achievable. Some occupations are very competitive and exclude all but a few highly talented people. *Courtesy of Lockheed Corporation (Photographer: Eric Schulzinger)*

the most to you. Then, try out your choice and see how it works. If you are not satisfied, look for something else. Your first occupational choice doesn't have to be a permanent one. You can learn from your decisions. Each decision you make will provide you with information that will help you make better decisions in the future.

25. Self-awareness is best thought of as a continuing, long-term process.

F·E·A·T·U·R·E

Mid-career Change

♦ ♦ ♦

Information about your self can help you make more satisfying occupational decisions. For young people, interests and aptitudes tend to be the more meaningful types of self-information. For adults, however, work values are usually the most important factor. An estimated six to ten percent of U.S. workers over age twenty-four voluntarily change occupations every year. The main reason is to pursue work values not presently being met.

Earl, for example, was an engineer for a large manufacturing company. After fifteen years, he had climbed the corporate ladder to become a manager. But he found he was working harder and enjoying it less. So, at age thirty-seven he left the company to become a community college instructor. He hoped to gain more freedom in his work and spend more time with his family.

Arlene and her husband, Joe, owned and managed an automotive parts business for ten years. She had always been fascinated by the stock market. At age forty, she decided to leave the family business to train as a stockbroker. She now says it was the best move she ever made.

Mid-career changes are usually brought on by the desire for greater earnings, achievement, or happiness. Or simply the realization that one isn't suited for a certain occupation. Usually it's a combination of age, unhappiness, and a feeling of being trapped in an occupation.

Changing occupations, however, is not something to be taken lightly. It involves considerable risk. It can lead to a sharp drop in income, and lots of insecurity and anxiety. Mid-career decisions are usually successful if they are well-planned and based on good self-information.

FIGURE 13-FEATURE People often continue to make educational and occupational decisions throughout their lifetime. *Photo by Paul E. Meyers*

Mid-career Change. Emphasize these characteristics about mid-career change: (a) work values and other self-characteristics may change over time, (b) people can and do successfully change occupations, and (c) a formal decision-making process should be employed before making a career change.

26. This section illustrates how people can express themselves outside of (or in addition to) their jobs.

FIGURE 13-12 You might be surprised by the occupations these people have. *Courtesy of Ford Motor Company*

SELF AND OTHER LIFE ROLES

An occupation can be a very important part of your life. However, it is only one part of a total *lifestyle*. *Life roles* in addition to worker may include those of citizen, spouse, parent, and student. Many people lead happy and productive lives even though their jobs don't satisfy all of their interests, aptitudes, and work values. People pursue hobbies, sports, and leisure activities. Many people also participate in organizations, clubs, church, and the like. Let's take a look at some examples.

Gregorio works as a heavy equipment operator. His work is okay, but his first love is old cars. He has a 1931 Model A Ford that he has been restoring for about six years. He found the car rusting away in a junkyard. For Gregorio, working on his Model A is a satisfying hobby and a major source of enjoyment.

Marcy is a personnel officer of a large company and really enjoys her work. She also is a very talented artist. Marcy manages to set aside about ten hours each week to work on her painting. By continuing to paint, she can satisfy her strong need for creative expression.

CHAPTER 13 Information About Your Self ■ 161

Bill is a manufacturing sales representative and a former minor league baseball player. He is successful in his work, but misses being involved in baseball. To satisfy his interests, Bill coaches a little league baseball team. He is a good coach and teacher of baseball. His young players respect him for taking the time to help them. They are not aware, however, that he gets more enjoyment out of it than they do.

Yvonne is an operating room nurse. She helps during surgery. Her job involves a great deal of stress and anxiety. Yvonne sometimes wishes that the job was less demanding. To help her deal with the stress, she sings in the church choir. Singing allows her to satisfy interests and abilities that she doesn't use on her job.

All of these people have found ways to express themselves outside of their jobs. You may be fortunate enough to work at an occupation that uses all your interests, aptitudes, and work values. If not, many outside activities can provide you with outlets for expressing your self.

FIGURE 13-13 Gregorio works as a heavy-equipment operator. *Courtesy of NYNEX*

27. The activities of Gregorio, Marcy, Bill, and Yvonne illustrate how people may express themselves in unpaid work.

162 ■ SECTION 3 Career Planning

CHAPTER REVIEW

Chapter in Brief

- Before you choose an occupation, first answer the question, "Who am I?" Such information about your self can help you make a more satisfying occupational decision. When making an occupational decision, you should have information about your interests, aptitudes, and work values.
- Things that you like to do are called interests. You can identify your interests by thinking about your likes and dislikes or by taking an interest inventory. Interests can be related to occupations that you may wish to investigate or explore.
- An aptitude is a developed ability. Your aptitudes represent things you are good at doing. Like interests, aptitudes can be related to occupations. By knowing your aptitudes, you can get some idea of occupations that you might be good at.
- Work values are your feelings about the importance or worth of an activity or occupation. Knowledge of work values are not as useful as interests and aptitudes in identifying occupations to explore. But you can use your work values to help you make a final choice from among a number of desirable occupational or educational alternatives.
- Interests, aptitudes, and work values sometimes all agree. When this happens, decision-making is not difficult. In other cases, interests, aptitudes, and work values conflict. This is not unusual, nor is it something to worry about. If the information conflicts, base your choice on the interest, aptitude, or work value that means the most to you. Then, try out your choice and see how it works.
- You may be fortunate enough to work at a job that uses all your interests, aptitudes, and work values. If not, outside activities (hobbies, sports, clubs, church) can provide you with a variety of outlets for expressing your self.

Words to Know

aptitudes developed abilities; those things that one is good at doing.

interests things that you like to do; preferences for certain kinds of work activities.

life roles the various parts of one's life, such as citizen, parent, spouse, worker, and so on.

lifestyle the way in which a person lives.

self what you are; your personal characteristics or traits.

work values attitudes and beliefs about the importance of various work activities.

Questions to Answer

1. What is the first question to ask yourself before choosing an occupation?
2. There are three types of self-information used in career decision-making. Name them.
3. What does participation in school activities reveal about your self?

---

1. "Who am I?" Such information can help you make more satisfying educational and occupational decisions.
2. (a) Interests. (b) Aptitudes. (c) Work values.
3. Participation in clubs, plays, musicals, vocational student organizations, and so on, are indicative of your interests.

4. Why is it incorrect to call an interest inventory a "test"?
5. Without taking an aptitude test, how can you find out about your aptitudes?
6. If you are good at diagnosing and repairing auto engines, what two aptitudes do you have?
7. Name three occupations that would be suitable for a person who values independence.
8. At what point in the career decision-making process is knowledge of work values important? Explain.
9. What should you do if your interests, aptitudes, and work values point in different directions?
10. Why do people often pursue hobbies and other activities very different from what they do in their jobs?

4. Because there are no right or wrong answers.
5. Your grades tend to reveal something about your aptitudes. A good grade in a subject generally means that you have an aptitude for it.
6. *Mechanical reasoning* (to diagnose) and *manual dexterity* (to repair the engine).
7. Hundreds of occupations allow for a high degree of independence. These include most sales agents, farmers, self-employed businesspersons, public relations specialists, postsecondary teachers, journalists, and so on.
8. Step four. This is one in which a choice is made from among a small number of desirable alternatives. Knowledge of work values helps you to prioritize alternatives.
9. This is not unusual, nor is it something to be overly concerned about. Select the occupation based on the interest, aptitude, or work value that means the most to you.
10. In order to express interests, aptitudes, or work values not being used on the job.

Activities to Do
1. Make an appointment with the school guidance counselor to review your student records. Find out if you have taken any type of interest, aptitude, or work values inventory or test. If you have, ask the counselor to interpret the results for you.
2. To what extent are your interests, aptitudes, and work values being met in your work experience job? Rate the job in the terms of your overall satisfaction on a scale of 1 (low) to 10 (high). What are you doing or can you do to express interests, aptitudes, and work values not being met on your job? Discuss your answers in class.
3. Perhaps your teacher or counselor can arrange to have you take an interest inventory, aptitude test, and work values measure. If so, such information can be helpful to you in later occupational exploration and career decision-making.

28. Rather than have each student contact the counselor individually, you may wish to work with the counselor to arrange a more efficient process—say coming to class and meeting with students, both as a group and individually.
29. Also, remind students that one of the objectives of work experience education is to help confirm present interests and goals or discover new ones.

Topics to Discuss
1. This chapter has explained self-information in relation to occupational decision-making. Discuss how self-information may also be used to assist in making educational decisions.
2. As you mature, new interests develop and old ones are left behind. Think of examples of how your interests have changed from the time when you were younger. What does this suggest in terms of your occupational interests?
3. Self-information can help you identify occupations that you might wish to do. Discuss why it is important to investigate and explore these occupations prior to making a final decision.

30. Knowledge of interests, aptitudes, and work values can be related to college majors or other educational alternatives in the same way as for occupations.
31. Interests do change with maturity. However, research has shown that adolescent interests are surprisingly stable over time. Work values are more likely to change with maturity.
32. Self-assessment using paper-and-pencil measures can be insightful. However, active exploration and work experience are required to test and validate interests, aptitudes, and work values.

1. Career information includes information about occupations, industries, jobs, and educational alternatives. Occupations and industries are covered in this chapter.

2. An aptitude measure can also be used to identify relevant occupations to explore.

CHAPTER FOURTEEN

Career Information

OUTLINE

The World of Work
Tomorrow's Jobs
Exploring Occupations
Chapter Review

OBJECTIVES

After reading this chapter, you should be able to:

- Explain how occupations and industries are grouped.
- Describe trends in the growth of goods and service industries.
- Discuss reasons for the rapid growth of service industries.
- Identify occupations having the fastest rate of growth and those having the greatest numerical increase during 1986-2000.
- Use the *Occupational Outlook Handbook* to conduct an occupational search.

The school guidance counselor gave Mel an interest inventory. The results suggested that Mel might like certain occupations. These were electrician, aircraft mechanic, refrigeration mechanic, and tool and die maker.

These indeed are occupations that appeal to Mel, but he doesn't know very much about them. He wonders for example, what workers in those occupations actually do. How much education or training do they need? Do the occupations have a good outlook for the future? How much money do people in such occupations earn? To answer his questions, Mel needs to collect information about these occupations. Learning how to use resources on occupational information is an important part of career decision-making.

164

FIGURE 14-1 Using occupational information is similar to using a dictionary, encyclopedia, or other reference work. *Courtesy of SIUC Photocommunications*

3. Ask students if they can add to this list of things one might wish to know about an occupation.

THE WORLD OF WORK

By the year 2000, it is estimated that 139 million people will be employed in the United States labor force. People work in hundreds of different types of offices, stores, factories, mines, farms and other workplaces. Workers are employed in over 35,000 different occupations! This network of occupations and workplaces (industries) is often called the *world of work*.

Because of the large number of occupations and industries, special grouping systems make it easier to collect and publish information about the world of work. A group is a collection of two or more things that are alike in some way. For example, rock, country, and classical are types of music. Groups are sometimes labeled as "categories," "classifications," "families," or "clusters."

4. Point out how the school library uses the Dewey Decimal System to maintain its book collection in an orderly fashion.

FIGURE 14-2 Without a way to classify different occupations and industries, it is difficult to understand the world of work. *Courtesy of New York Convention and Visitors Bureau, Inc.*

About a dozen different systems classify information about the world of work. The two most important classifications are occupational and industrial.

Classifying Occupations

In recent years, the U.S. Department of Commerce has been developing a grouping system called the *Standard Occupational Classification* (SOC) system. The SOC classifies occupations based on the type of work performed. For instance, the Mechanics and Repairers division includes workers who maintain and repair various kinds of machines and equipment. These include motor vehicles, appliances, communication equipment, electrical and electronic equipment, and related equipment and machines.

Occupational Groups	Sample Occupations
1. Managerial and Management-Related Occupations	accountants, bank officers, health inspectors, purchasing agents, school administrators, insurance underwriters
2. Engineers, Surveyors, and Architects	architects, drafters, surveyors, engineers, cartographers
3. Natural, Computer, and Mathematical Scientists	computer systems analysts, chemists, geologists, meteorologists, statisticians
4. Lawyers, Social Scientists, Social Workers, and Religious Workers	psychologists, social workers, ministers, lawyers, economists
5. Teachers, Librarians, and Counselors	elementary teachers, secondary teachers, professors, librarians, counselors
6. Health Diagnosing and Treating Practitioners	chiropractors, dentists, optometrists, physicians, veterinarians
7. Registered Nurses, Pharmacists, Dietitians, Therapists, and Physical Assistants	dietitians, pharmacists, registered nurses, speech pathologists, physical therapists
8. Health Technologists and Technicians	dental hygienists, surgical technicians, health record technicians, licensed practical nurses, radiologic technologists
9. Writers, Artists, and Entertainers	radio and TV announcers, photographers, dancers, musicians, commercial artists
10. Technologists and Technicians, Except Health	air traffic controllers, legal assistants, broadcast technicians, electronics technicians, computer programmers
11. Marketing and Sales Occupations	cashiers, insurance agents, real estate brokers, travel agents, securities sales workers
12. Administrative Support Occupations, Including Clerical	bank tellers, bookkeepers, secretaries, telephone operators, postal clerks
13. Service Occupations	firefighters, correction officers, chefs, barbers, flight attendants
14. Agricultural, Forestry, Fishing, and Related Occupations	farmers, ranchers, animal caretakers, timbercutters, gardeners
15. Mechanics, Installers, and Repairers	automotive mechanics, appliance repairers, millwrights, office machine repairers, TV service technicians
16. Construction Trades and Extractive Occupations	carpenters, bricklayers, electricians, coal miners, rotary drill operators
17. Production Occupations	meatcutters, typesetters, dental laboratory technicians, machine tool operators, welders
18. Transportation and Material Moving Occupations	pilots, truckdrivers, construction machinery operators, oil pumpers, locomotive engineers
19. Handlers, Equipment Cleaners, Helpers and Laborers	construction laborers, dock hands, garbage collectors, parking attendants, vehicle cleaners
20. Job Opportunities in the Armed Forces	officers, sonar operators, missile engineers, troop leaders, ship captains, navigators, demolition experts, and thousands of occupations with the same title as in the civilian sector

NOTE: The SOC actually consists of 22 divisions, but only these 20 are used in the *Occupational Outlook Handbook*.

FIGURE 14-3 This is the major way the federal government classifies occupations.

The SOC consists of the twenty divisions shown in Figure 14-3. These divisions are used as the basis for the *Occupational Outlook Handbook (OOH)*. The *OOH* is an excellent resource for occupational information. You will learn more about the *OOH* later in this chapter.

5. "Precision Production Occupations" and "Production Working Occupations" are combined in the *OOH*. "Miscellaneous Occupations," is not used in the *OOH*.

Classifying Industries

Another important grouping system is the *Standard Industrial Classification* (SIC). The SIC basically describes where people work. It is a grouping of different workplaces according to the type of product produced or service provided. The Manu-

CHAPTER 14 Career Information ■ 167

All industries can be divided into two sectors, service-producing and goods-producing.

- Goods-producing industries
- Service-producing industries

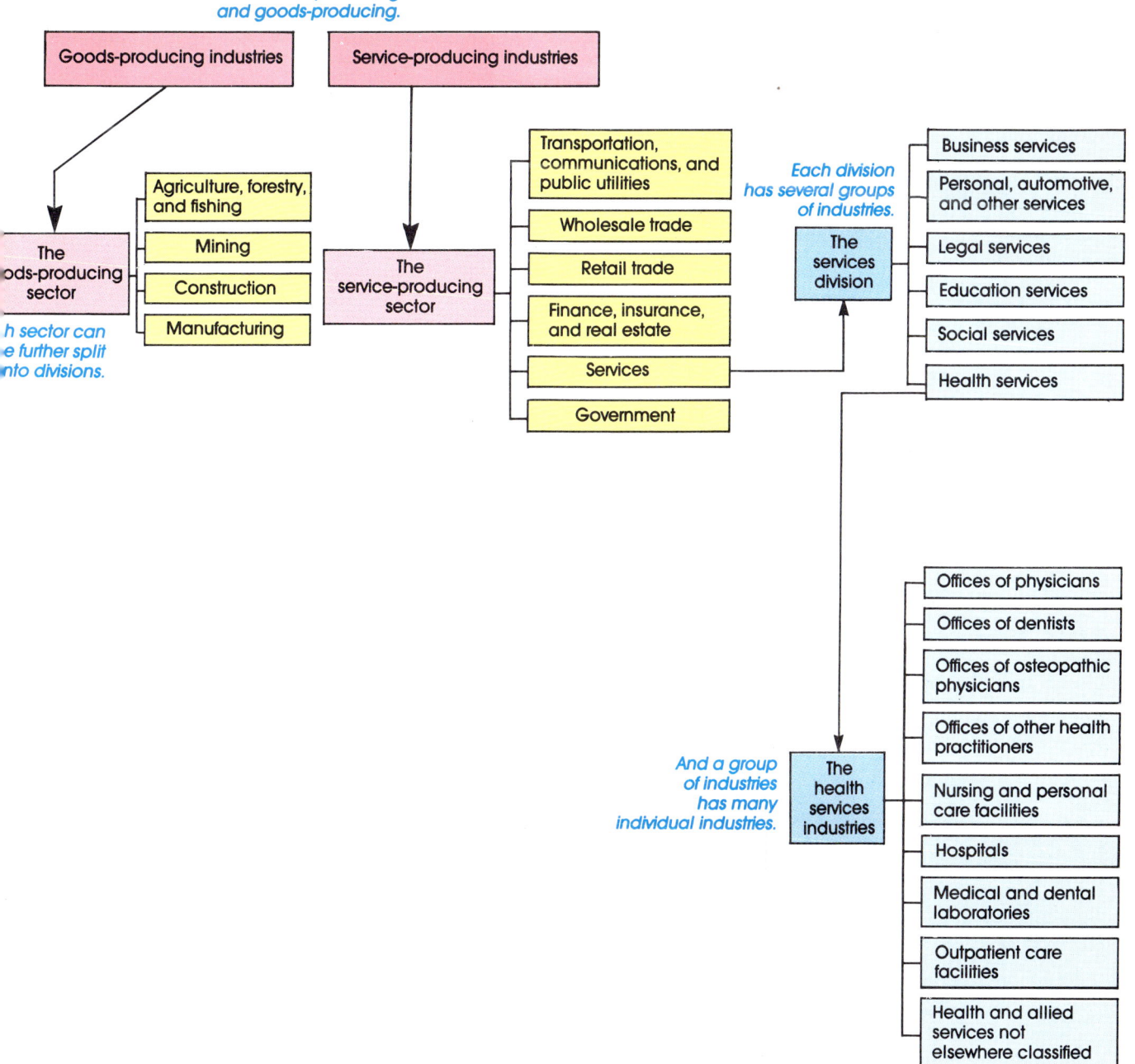

Each sector can be further split into divisions.

The goods-producing sector:
- Agriculture, forestry, and fishing
- Mining
- Construction
- Manufacturing

The service-producing sector:
- Transportation, communications, and public utilities
- Wholesale trade
- Retail trade
- Finance, insurance, and real estate
- Services
- Government

Each division has several groups of industries.

The services division:
- Business services
- Personal, automotive, and other services
- Legal services
- Education services
- Social services
- Health services

And a group of industries has many individual industries.

The health services industries:
- Offices of physicians
- Offices of dentists
- Offices of osteopathic physicians
- Offices of other health practitioners
- Nursing and personal care facilities
- Hospitals
- Medical and dental laboratories
- Outpatient care facilities
- Health and allied services not elsewhere classified

FIGURE 14-4 In the SIC system, industries are classified by sector, division, and group.

facturing division, for instance, includes industries that use machines or chemical processes to change materials or substances into new products. In the SIC system, all places of employment are called *industries*. In other words, hospitals, schools, food stores, restaurants, banks, and hundreds of other types of workplaces are industries. The SIC system is divided into the two broad categories and ten major divisions shown in Figure 14-4. It is important to understand the SOC and SIC classifications. This is because the government collects and reports information this way. The following section provides illustrations of how the SOC and SIC are used.

6. Emphasize that all places of employment are called *industries*. It may be awkward at first, but please use this standard terminology.

7. Be alert to articles and news reports regarding economic and employment data and trends. The ten SIC divisions are used as the basis for communicating such information.

168 ■ SECTION 3 Career Planning

TOMORROW'S JOBS

To project future job trends, the Bureau of Labor Statistics analyzes population patterns, economic and social change, and technology. By their nature, job projections are only educated guesses. But such projections can help you know about future opportunities in industries and occupations of interest. After all, you may not want to train for an occupation that will be in little demand.

Changing Employment in Industries

Since about 1960, employment in service-producing industries has been increasing at a faster rate than employment in goods-producing industries. About seven of every ten jobs are in service industries such as health care, trade, education, repair and maintenance, transportation, banking, and insurance.

Rising incomes, higher living standards, and an aging population have helped contribute to the rapid growth of service industries. The result has been greater demand for health care, entertainment, and business and financial services. People with higher incomes may spend heavily on eating out, personal fitness, recreation and the like. The large group of "baby boomers" (76 million) born between 1946 and 1964 are also using more health services. In addition, the growth of cities and suburbs has brought a need for more local government services.

Through the year 2000, employment is expected to increase faster in service-producing industries than in goods-producing ones. In fact, service-producing industries are expected to account for almost all new jobs between now and 2000, Figure 14-6. Employment in these industries is expected to increase to 95.7 million jobs, an increase of 20 million over 1986.

9. A new edition of the *Occupational Outlook Handbook* is published every two years. You might want to duplicate and discuss in class the section on "Tomorrow's Jobs."

10. Take time to explain and discuss Figures 14-3 through 14-10. These contain very important concepts and information.

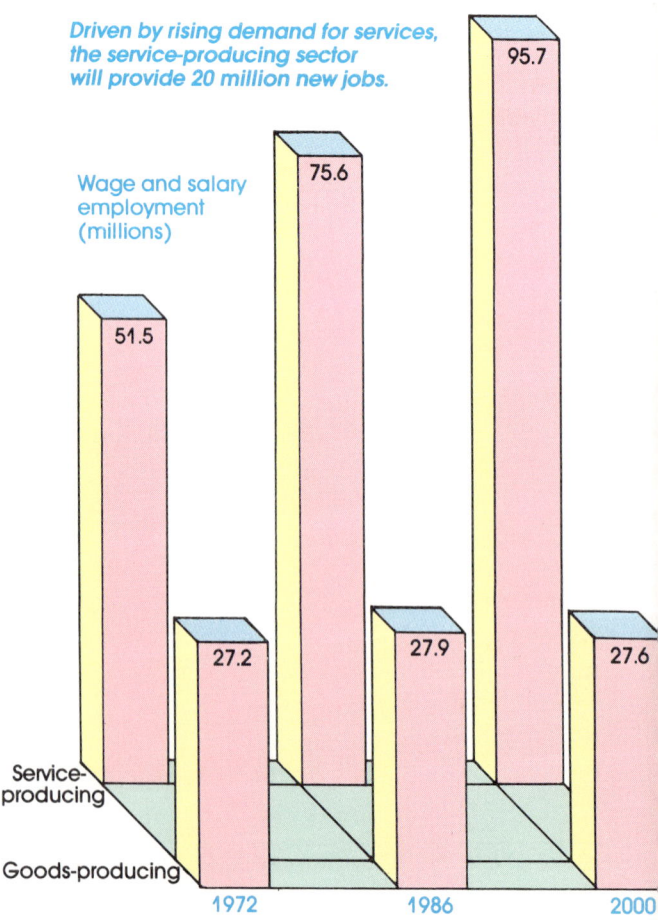

Driven by rising demand for services, the service-producing sector will provide 20 million new jobs.

Wage and salary employment (millions)

Year	Service-producing	Goods-producing
1972	51.5	27.2
1986	75.6	27.9
2000	95.7	27.6

Employment trends among the industry divisions in the service-producing and goods-producing sectors will be very different, reflecting the types of goods and services purchased by individuals, businesses, and governments.

FIGURE 14-5 Industries providing services will continue to employ an increasing percentage of the work force. *Courtesy of Contel Corporation*

FIGURE 14-6 The service-producing sector will account for nearly all new jobs between now and 2000.

8. To illustrate the importance and relevance of the SIC and SOC systems, look in the current *Occupational Outlook Handbook* for the special feature on "Tomorrow's Jobs."

11. Emphasize the fact that virtually all new jobs in the next decade will be in the service sector. Ask how many students are currently employed in service industries.

F·E·A·T·U·R·E

Military Occupations

♦ ♦ ♦

The largest employer in the country is the military services (Army, Navy, Air Force, Marine Corps, Coast Guard). In late-1980, about 2.2 million persons were on active duty in the Armed Forces. In addition, over 2 million persons were in military reserve units.

The major occupational groups for active military personnel are shown in the accompanying table. Nearly three out of every ten enlisted persons are involved with electrical, electronic, mechanical, and related equipment. This reflects the highly technical and mechanical nature of the military. Officers (about five percent of all military personnel) are concentrated in administration, medical specialities, and directing combat activities.

Military life is more disciplined and structured than civilian life. There are dress and grooming requirements. Certain formalities, such as saluting officers and obeying military laws and regulations, must be followed.

Hours and working conditions vary. Most military personnel usually work eight hours a day, five or five and one-half days a week. Some assignments, however, require night and weekend work, or being on call at all hours. All may require a lot of travel and periodic relocation.

The military offers a wide range of employment and training opportunities. Future opportunities should be excellent in all branches of the service. Military personnel have greater job security than their civilian counterparts. Satisfactory job performance generally assures one of steady earnings and advancement. A section on Military Occupations may be found in the *Occupational Outlook Handbook*. A separate resource called the *Military Career Guide* is also available.

Military enlisted personnel by broad occupational category

(Percent distribution)

Occupational Category

Transportation and material handling	23
Administrative	16
Combat specialty	15
Vehicle and machine mechanics	12
Electronic and electrical equipment repair	10
Service	8
Engineering, scientific, and technical	6
Health care	4
Machine operators and precision workers	3
Construction	1
Media and public affairs	1
Human services	1
Total	100

Source: Occupational Outlook Handbook: 1988-89 Edition.

FIGURE 14-FEATURE The military is composed of these major occupational groups.

*Military Occupations. A short-term enlistment or a career in the military is a sound choice for many young men and women (women are eligible to enter eighty-eight percent of all military specialties). The Department of Defense has produced a resource entitled the *Military Career Guide* that is the Armed Forces equivalent of the *OOH*. Contact (or invite to class) a local military recruiter to obtain a free copy. The recruiter can also explain use of the ASVAB (aptitude test) and related occupational resources.

Some industries will grow more rapidly than others.

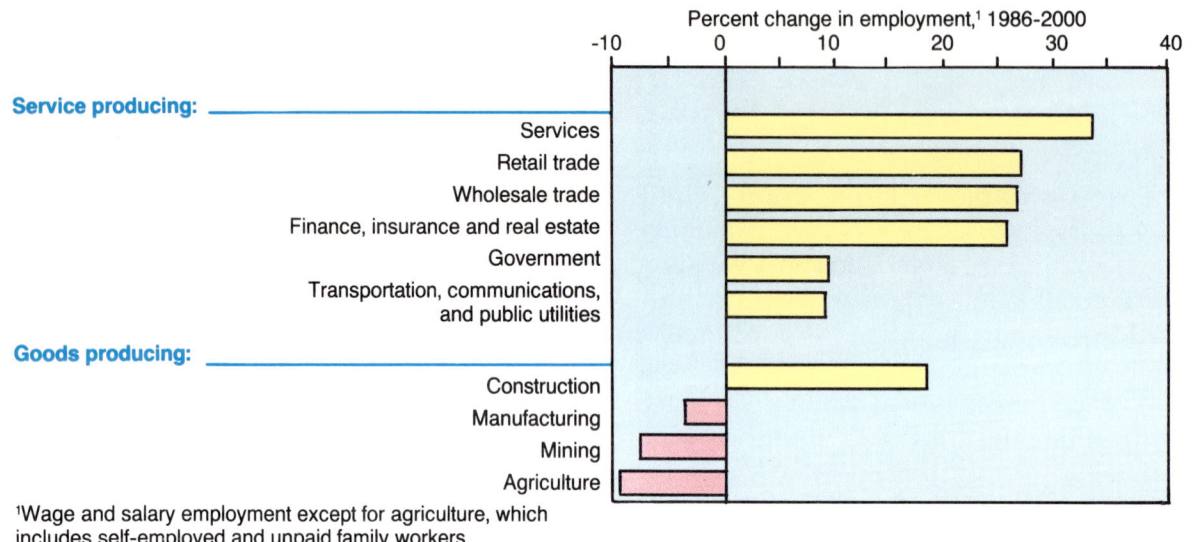

Percent change in employment,[1] 1986-2000

Service producing:
- Services
- Retail trade
- Wholesale trade
- Finance, insurance and real estate
- Government
- Transportation, communications, and public utilities

Goods producing:
- Construction
- Manufacturing
- Mining
- Agriculture

[1] Wage and salary employment except for agriculture, which includes self-employed and unpaid family workers.
SOURCE: Bureau of Labor Statistics

12. All states now receive federal funds to disseminate career information through what is called the State Occupational Information Coordinating Committee (SOICC). Your SOICC should have a wide variety of information to share, including information on employment growth for specific occupations. A listing of SOICCs is in the Appendix of the *Occupational Outlook Handbook*.

FIGURE 14-7 Through the year 2000, changes in employment will vary widely among industries.

Within industries, growth will vary widely, Figure 14-7. It will be the greatest in Services and Retail Trade. In the goods-producing sector, construction is the only division that will grow as a whole.

Luis wants to be a forest conservationist. He was discouraged to read that the agriculture, forestry, and fishing industry will probably decline in the future. Upon reading further, however, he found that the demand for some occupations in the group (such as forest conservationist) will remain steady.

Changing Employment in Occupations

Future employment growth will vary greatly among the occupations included in the twenty SOC divisions. Therefore, it is better to examine the outlook for specific occupations than for different occupational groups.

Information about projected trends is useful in several ways. It might, for instance, suggest to a person planning a career that he or she select a field for which future employment is expected to grow. On the other hand, it might suggest to a worker in a

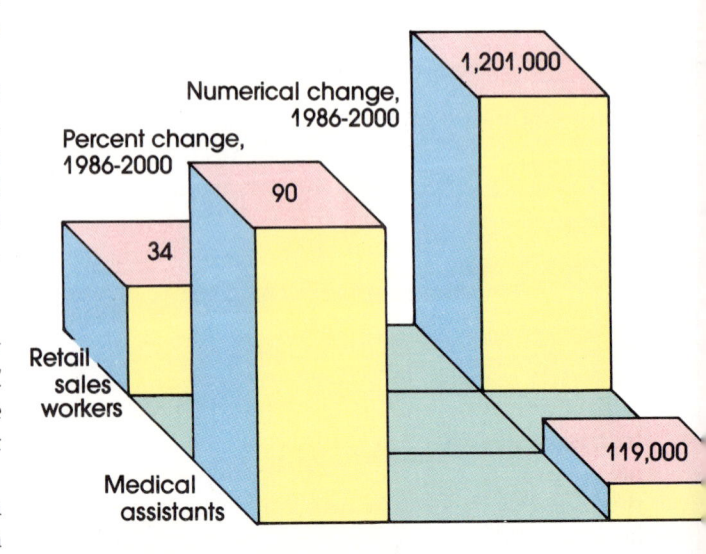

FIGURE 14-8 When assessing future job opportunities, both the rate of growth and the number of new jobs need to be considered.

(Retail sales workers: Percent change 34, Numerical change 1,201,000; Medical assistants: Percent change 90, Numerical change 119,000)

CHAPTER 14 Career Information ■ 171

Growth of employment, 1986-2000 (percent)
Average of all occupations

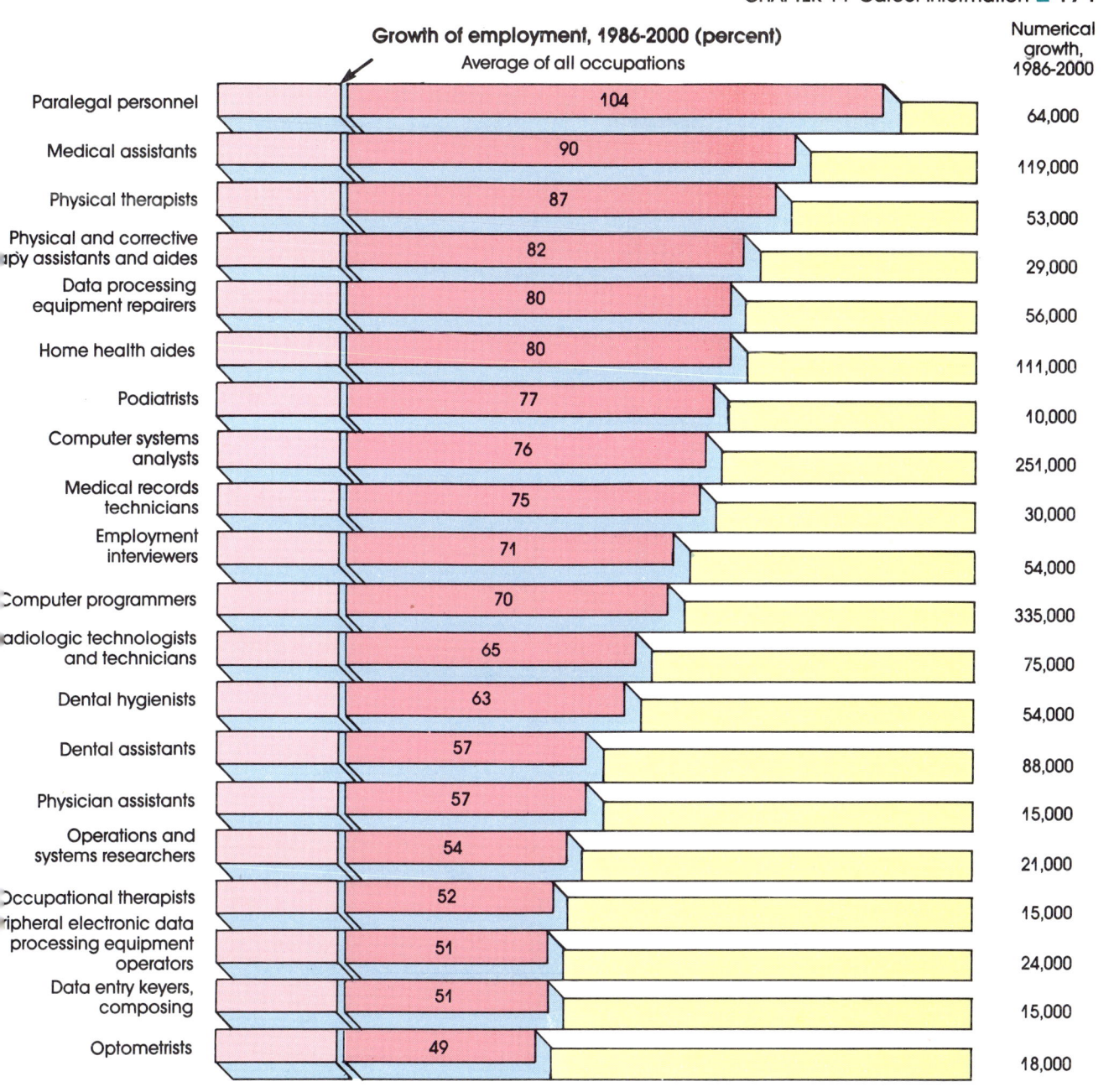

Occupation	Growth %	Numerical growth, 1986-2000
Paralegal personnel	104	64,000
Medical assistants	90	119,000
Physical therapists	87	53,000
Physical and corrective therapy assistants and aides	82	29,000
Data processing equipment repairers	80	56,000
Home health aides	80	111,000
Podiatrists	77	10,000
Computer systems analysts	76	251,000
Medical records technicians	75	30,000
Employment interviewers	71	54,000
Computer programmers	70	335,000
Radiologic technologists and technicians	65	75,000
Dental hygienists	63	54,000
Dental assistants	57	88,000
Physician assistants	57	15,000
Operations and systems researchers	54	21,000
Occupational therapists	52	15,000
Peripheral electronic data processing equipment operators	51	24,000
Data entry keyers, composing	51	15,000
Optometrists	49	18,000

FIGURE 14-9 The twenty fastest growing occupations, 1986-2000

declining industry that he or she consider retraining for a different field.

To obtain a complete picture of occupational trends, you will need to know two things. One is the *rate of growth* (percent) of an occupation. The other is the *numerical increase* of workers. The relationship between rate of growth and size of change for two occupations is shown in Figure 14-8.

From the chart, you can see that between 1986 and 2000 the rate of growth for medical assistants will increase by ninety percent. Yet, the number of *new* jobs for medical assistants between 1986 and 2000 will only be about 119,000. On the other hand, the growth rate for retail sales workers will increase only about thirty-four percent. But the actual number of *new* jobs in that area between 1986 and 2000 will be about 1,201,000. Study the chart in Figure 14-8 until you understand the difference.

Figure 14-9 shows the occupations that are projected to have the fastest growth rate between 1986

13. Make sure all students understand the concepts in Figure 14-8 regarding "rate of growth" and "numerical increase." This is essential to understanding Figures 14-9 and 14-10.

172 ■ SECTION 3 Career Planning

and 2000. You can see that health-related occupations will account for twelve of the twenty fastest growing ones. Overall, Figure 14-9 shows that the fastest growing occupations will be those requiring a college degree or some type of technical training. Why do you think that most of the occupations are in the health field?

In Figure 14-10, the twenty-seven occupations

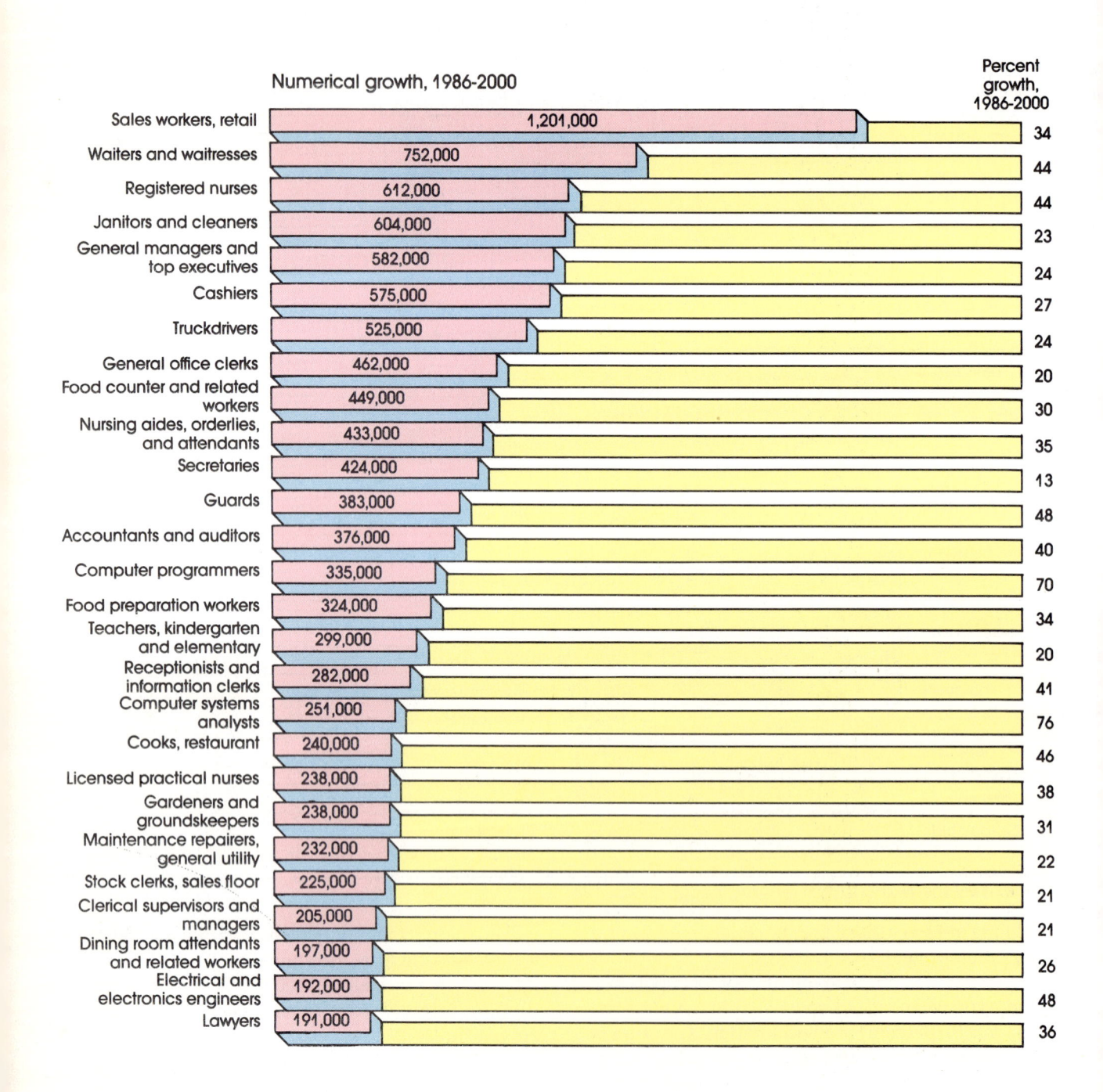

Occupation	Numerical growth, 1986-2000	Percent growth, 1986-2000
Sales workers, retail	1,201,000	34
Waiters and waitresses	752,000	44
Registered nurses	612,000	44
Janitors and cleaners	604,000	23
General managers and top executives	582,000	24
Cashiers	575,000	27
Truckdrivers	525,000	24
General office clerks	462,000	20
Food counter and related workers	449,000	30
Nursing aides, orderlies, and attendants	433,000	35
Secretaries	424,000	13
Guards	383,000	48
Accountants and auditors	376,000	40
Computer programmers	335,000	70
Food preparation workers	324,000	34
Teachers, kindergarten and elementary	299,000	20
Receptionists and information clerks	282,000	41
Computer systems analysts	251,000	76
Cooks, restaurant	240,000	46
Licensed practical nurses	238,000	38
Gardeners and groundskeepers	238,000	31
Maintenance repairers, general utility	232,000	22
Stock clerks, sales floor	225,000	21
Clerical supervisors and managers	205,000	21
Dining room attendants and related workers	197,000	26
Electrical and electronics engineers	192,000	48
Lawyers	191,000	36

FIGURE 14-10 Occupations with the largest increase in number of new jobs, 1986-2000

14. The major reason is that the seventy-six million baby-boomers born between 1946 and 1964 will be getting older and will require more medical services.

*WWYD Feature A. Being a full-time homemaker is a valid and important career goal. However, about seventy percent of women between the ages of twenty and forty-four are employed.

CHAPTER 14 Career Information ■ 173

shown are projected to have the greatest actual growth in number of jobs during the period 1986 to 2000. Note that most new jobs will be within service industries.

Another important fact shown in Figure 14-10 is that most new jobs will require on-the-job training or skills learned through vocational and technical education. Only about seven of the twenty-seven occupations are ones that normally require a college degree.

What Would You Do?

You have read so much recently about work, career decision-making, and occupations. You have found it to be interesting. You guess that you will probably work after leaving high school. However, what you really hope to do someday is to be a wife, mother, and homemaker. You are afraid to even mention it, because you think other students might laugh at you. What would you do?

EXPLORING OCCUPATIONS

With the information you now have about yourself and job trends, you are ready to start an occupational search. Many resources exist to help you. One of the easiest to use is the *Occupational Outlook Handbook (OOH)*.

15

Why is it useful to know how to use the *OOH*? Well, the *OOH* is available in more guidance offices and public libraries nationwide than any other occupational resource. And since the *OOH* is revised every two years, the information included is up to date.

Using the Occupational Outlook Handbook

The occupations included in the *OOH* are mostly ones in small (but growing) fields. Most of the occupations require some degree of education or training beyond high school. The *OOH* describes about 225 occupations in detail. These occupations comprise eighty percent of the labor force. A listing of about 125 additional occupations is provided in the appendix. These comprise an additional ten

16

FIGURE 14-11 Learn to use the *Occupational Outlook Handbook*. It contains factual, up-to-date information. *Photo by Paul E. Meyers*

15. It is desirable to have multiple copies of the *OOH* in your classroom or school library. If they aren't available, ask the school librarian for help in securing some.

16. The *OOH* contains information on occupations that comprise about ninety percent of all jobs. This will encompass the interests and aptitudes of most students.

OCCUPATIONAL SEARCH FORM

TITLE OF OCCUPATION: _____

NATURE OF THE WORK

A. List five major tasks that workers in this occupation perform.

1. _____
2. _____
3. _____
4. _____
5. _____

WORKING CONDITIONS

B. What are the normal working hours? _____

C. Describe the typical working conditions. _____

D. Are there any unpleasant or dangerous aspects to this occupation? _____

EMPLOYMENT

E. In 19____, how many jobs were in this occupation? _____

F. In what type of industries or locations do people in this occupation work? _____

TRAINING, OTHER QUALIFICATIONS, AND ADVANCEMENT

G. What is the preferred or required level of education or training? _____

H. Is licensure or certification required? _____

I. Are any special abilities or qualifications recommended or required? _____

J. What opportunities are there for advancement? _____

JOB OUTLOOK

K. Check (✓) the statement in each column below that best describes the future outlook for this occupation.

Change in Employment	**Opportunities and Competition**
____ faster than average growth	____ very good to excellent opportunities
____ average growth	____ good opportunities
____ slower than average growth	____ may face competition
____ little change	____ keen competition
____ decline	

EARNINGS

L. The average yearly starting salary in 19____ was $ _____.

M. In 19 ____, the average yearly earnings ranged from $ _____ to $ _____.
   (low)   (high)

RELATED OCCUPATIONS

N. List the titles of any other related occupations.

1. _____
2. _____
3. _____
4. _____
5. _____
6. _____
7. _____
8. _____

SOURCES OF ADDITIONAL INFORMATION

O. List the names and addresses of places where further information may be obtained. _____

_____
_____
_____
_____
_____
_____
_____
_____
_____

What is the source of this information? *Occupational Outlook Handbook:* 19 ____/____ Edition, pages _____.

FIGURE 14-12 This form allows you to summarize information from the eight parts of a typical OOH occupational description.

---

percent of the labor force. Each occupational description in the *OOH* is set up as follows:

1. Nature of the work
2. Working conditions
3. Employment
4. Training, other qualifications, and advancement
5. Job outlook
6. Earnings
7. Related occupations
8. Sources of additional information

Having the same information about each occupation makes it easier to do comparisons.

Doing a Search

Let's say you are following the five-step decision-making process explained in Chapter 12. In step two, you used self-information to come up with a list of occupations that might suit you. Now it is time to learn more about each of your choices. Such a study is called an *occupational search*. In doing a search, it is helpful to use a form like the one shown in Figure 14-12. That way you can organize information from each of the occupational descriptions. Your instructor will provide you with copies of the form.

Now get a copy of the most recent edition of the *OOH*. At the top of your form, write the name of the occupation. Then turn to the "Index to Occupations" near the end of the *OOH*. This will give you the page numbers that discuss your occupation. As you read the *occupational description,* fill out your search form. Feel free to make notes on the form or add other information that you think is important. Repeat this process for as many occupations as you want to research.

---

17. Photocopy several representative occupational descriptions from the *OOH*. Use a marker to highlight the eight parts. Attach to a bulletin board and call students' attention to them.

18. You may wish to assign Activity 1 at this time. Note that the form in Figure 14-12 parallels the eight types of information provided for each *OOH* occupational description.

176 ■ SECTION 3 Career Planning

What Would You Do?

You have identified three occupations that you want to learn more about. You get an *Occupational Outlook Handbook (OOH)* and look up information on the first occupation. You copy down important facts and data for later study. You follow the same procedure for the second occupation. For the third occupation, however, no information is available in the *OOH*. What would you do?

* *WWYD Feature B.* It was noted earlier that the *OOH* does not contain information on all occupations. A teacher or counselor should be able to help locate information in another resource.

After you have finished collecting information, compare and evaluate your information. For help in doing this, refer back to Figure 12-6, "Checklist for Evaluating Possible Occupational Alternatives."

20. Explain and demonstrate any other resources that you may have access to (see also Activity 3).

Other Sources of Career Information

The *OOH* isn't the only available resource. Many publishing companies produce resources to be used in occupational exploration and decision-making. Your teacher or career counselor may introduce you to such materials. Or you may find them on your own. (Librarians will be glad to help you.)

The greatest change in the use of occupational information is the development of computerized information systems. Many high schools, community and junior colleges, career centers, and Job Service offices have access to such systems. Most of you have or will be using a computer at some point in your decision-making.

It doesn't matter whether you use a book or a computer to find occupational information. The important thing is that you find it. A thorough occupational search will expose you to many possible choices. From these, you can make your decision. Good decisions, like the one you are trying to make, come through complete, up-to-date information.

FIGURE 14-13 Computers are becoming widely used to provide occupational information. *Courtesy of NYNEX Corp./Bill Varie © 1988*

19. Make copies of this form and have them available. Note that the items in Figure 12-6 parallel the eight types of information found in the *OOH* occupational descriptions.

21. There is a wide variety of computer software available for career planning and decision-making. Contact your SOICC for more information.

CHAPTER REVIEW

Chapter in Brief

- The network of occupations and industries is called the world of work. Because of the number of different occupations and industries, grouping systems are used to organize information about the world of work. The two most important grouping systems are the *Standard Occupational Classification* (SOC) and the *Standard Industrial Classification* (SIC).
- The SOC classifies occupations according to the type of work performed. The SOC divisions are used as the basis for the *Occupational Outlook Handbook*. The SIC describes where people work. In the SIC system, all places of employment are called industries.
- About seven out of every ten jobs are in service industries. Through the year 2000, employment is expected to increase faster in service-producing industries than in goods-producing ones. Services are supposed to account for about all new jobs between now and 2000.
- To understand occupational trends, it is necessary to look at both rate of growth and numerical increase of workers. The fastest growing occupations are health-related. But the occupations with the largest increase in number of jobs are primarily low-skilled and semi-skilled service occupations.
- The *Occupational Outlook Handbook (OOH)* is a very important resource that you need to learn how to use. The *OOH* contains detailed occupational descriptions for about 225 occupations. These comprise eighty percent of the labor force. Follow the recommended procedure in conducting an occupational search.

Words to Know

goods-producing industries those companies and businesses, such as manufacturing, construction, mining, and agriculture, that produce some type of a product.

industries places of employment such as factories, hospitals, restaurants, banks, and so on.

occupational description information about a specific occupation that explains what the work is like.

Occupational Outlook Handbook (OOH) a printed resource produced by the government that provides occupational information.

occupational search collecting information about an occupation of interest using some type of printed resource or data base.

service-producing industries those companies and businesses that produce (provide) some type of personal or business service, such as transportation, finance, insurance, trade, and so on.

178 ■ SECTION 3 Career Planning

Standard Industrial Classification (SIC) a system of grouping industries according to the type of product or service produced.

Standard Occupational Classification (SOC) a system of grouping occupations based on the type of work performed.

world of work an informal phrase used to describe the network of industries and occupations.

Questions to Answer

1. Why are classification systems used to organize information about the world of work?
2. In the SOC system, how are occupations grouped? In the SIC system, how are industries grouped?
3. What type of industries are projected to grow the fastest? Explain why.
4. How can projections about future occupational trends help you in career decision-making?
5. To understand future occupational trends, it is necessary to know two types of information. Name them.
6. What characteristics do the fastest growing occupations shown in Figure 14-9 have in common?
7. How many of the occupations with the largest growth shown in Figure 14-10 require a college degree?
8. Why is it useful to know how to use the *OOH*?
9. Does the *OOH* contain information on all occupations? Explain.
10. Every occupational description in the *OOH* contains eight kinds of information. Name them.

Activities to Do

1. Use an *Occupational Outlook Handbook* and copies of Figure 14-12 to conduct an occupational search. (Your instructor can arrange to have copies of the form duplicated.) Follow the steps described in this chapter.
2. After completing an occupational search, you may want to collect first-hand information about a given occupation. With the help of your teacher or counselor, identify a person who works in your occupation of interest. Interview the person to find out his or her feelings about the occupation. If possible, also arrange to visit his or her place of employment.
   Before the interview, work with classmates to develop an interview form. Going over the information that you have already collected on the occupational search form may help you identify the types of questions you want to ask.
   After the interview, report to the class on what you have learned. Discuss whether the interview confirmed or changed your interest in the occupation.
3. Invite your school guidance counselor to class. Ask the counselor to describe and demonstrate any additional career information resources located in your school's guidance office, library, or career center.

1. There are so many different occupations and industries that classification systems are needed in order to be able to collect and publish information about the world of work.
2. SOC—classifies occupations based on the type of work performed. SIC—classifies industries based on where people work.
3. Service industries. Because of the increasing demand for personal, business, and government services.
4. By revealing which occupations are expected to grow, resulting in greater opportunities for employment.
5. (a) The growth rate of an occupation. (b) The actual increase in number of anticipated jobs.
6. Twelve of the twenty provide health services; six of the twenty are in the computer field.
7. Only about twenty-five percent of them are ones that require or give preference to college graduates.
8. It is more readily available in schools and public libraries than any other occupational resource. It is up-to-date (revised every two years) and easy to use.
9. No. Detailed occupational descriptions are provided for 225 occupations, comprising about eighty percent of the labor force.
10. (a) Nature of the work. (b) Working conditions. (c) Employment. (d) Training, other qualifications, and advancement. (e) Job outlook. (f) Earnings. (g) Related occupations. (h) Sources of additional information.

22. Teachers and students have found this to be a very relevant and worthwhile activity.

Topics to Discuss

1. If you are really interested in a particular occupation, how concerned should you be about its future job outlook?
2. How do civilian occupations differ from those in the military?
3. To make a good occupational decision, you should consider several types of information (nature of the work, working conditions, job outlook earnings, and so on). In the final analysis, however, there are very few perfect occupations. Most occupational decisions involve a compromise among various factors. Provide examples and discuss how occupational decision-making involves compromise.

23. Over seventy-five percent of all military occupations have counterparts in the civilian labor force.

High Five

GETTING INVOLVED

Patty Hendrickson's career in business began at a very young age. She explains that, "I have always been a business major, since about age four when I had my first lemonade stand. I also set up a store and sold candy. I became even more interested in business during my freshman year when I went to my first typing class."

In high school, Patty was active in the Future Business Leaders of America-Phi Beta Lambda (FBLA-PBL). She says, "FBLA was a wonderful high school education in itself. It is easy to read or hear about concepts, but FBLA-PBL was a 'real-life' practice arena." She served as both State and National President of FBLA and State President of PBL. She says that, "FBLA was the best decision I ever made in my life."

She graduated from Eastern Illinois University with a degree in finance and is currently pursuing an MBA degree at the University of Wisconsin-La Crosse. She served as a March of Dimes National Youth Council member and was appointed by President Reagan to the National Council on Vocational Education. She is an enthusiastic supporter of vocational education, saying that, "I just owe so much to vocational education. I am a product of it."

Patty is a licensed insurance broker and registered representative for securities sales. She has recently started her own consulting firm, H&F Consulting in Holmen, Wisconsin. In addition, she has written several hundred training modules that are used in her leadership training workshops.

A number of her business clients include vocational student organizations. She engineers activities and presentations for team and individual growth, which demonstrate that leadership can be a "fun" responsibility. Her involvement in a vocational student organization helped her to develop leadership skills. Looking back at her own experience, she encourages students to "get involved... it is a great way to learn and practice leadership skills."

Section Four

Success Skills

Chapter 15 Communication Skills
Chapter 16 Math and Measurement Skills
Chapter 17 Safety Skills
Chapter 18 Leadership Skills
Chapter 19 Computer Skills
Chapter 20 Entrepreneurial Skills

To be successful on the job, you need occupational skills, employability skills, and basic academic skills. The first two types of skills were explained in previous chapters. Communication skills, one type of academic skills, is dealt with in Chapter 15. Communication involves listening, speaking, reading, and writing. A second type of academic skills, math and measurement skills, is reviewed in Chapter 16.

Chapter 17 describes types and causes of accidents. For teenagers and young adults, accidents are the leading cause of death. You will examine things to do and avoid in order to prevent accidents at home, school, on the job, and elsewhere. Safety is everyone's business.

Leadership is the process of influencing people to accomplish the goals of an organization. In Chapter 18, you will learn about six characteristics of leaders. Vocational student organizations are presented as ways to help students develop leadership skills. The last part of the chapter deals with parliamentary procedures. These are rules used by business and other groups to conduct effective meetings.

Do you know how to use a computer? If not, you may be lacking one of the most important job skills of the future. In Chapter 19, you will learn about the importance of keyboarding skills. What a computer is and how it works will be explained. Application of computers in the workplace will also be illustrated. The chapter concludes with predictions about the future of computers in the workplace.

In the future, you may work as an employee for someone or go into business for yourself. Owning your own business is explored in Chapter 20. You will learn about the advantages and disadvantages of entrepreneurship and what it takes to operate a successful business.

1. The three categories are useful as a basis for discussion and instruction. In reality, however, the three skills are inseparable in the performance of most occupational tasks.

CHAPTER FIFTEEN

Communication Skills

OUTLINE
Listening
Speaking
Reading
Writing
Chapter Review

OBJECTIVES
After reading this chapter, you should be able to:
- State guidelines for good listening.
- Discuss rules for effective speaking.
- Identify ways to improve reading skills.
- Explain why writing is the most important form of business communication.
- Illustrate different forms of business communication.

FIGURE 15-1 Some occupations require considerable use of communication skills. *Courtesy of Ford Motor Company*

1   To be successful on the job, you need three types of skills: (a) occupational skills, (b) employability skills, and (c) basic academic skills. Occupational skills are the technical or manual abilities unique to a certain occupation. People learn these skills through vocational education or other education and training programs. Certain skills such as honesty, good grooming, and a positive attitude are required in all jobs. These are called employability skills. You read about employability skills in Chapters 7, 9, and 11.

2   Workers need basic academic skills, too. Leon learned this during his first week as a stockhandler at Meadows Garden Center. He thought that all he would have to do is care for the plants—he was mistaken. Mrs. Wilkinson, Leon's boss, often had to correct his grammar, spelling, and math. She told him that workers need many kinds of skills. Knowing how to do the work itself isn't enough. Many employers feel as Mrs. Wilkinson does.

2. Ask students if their employer has ever had to correct their communication or math skills.

182

CHAPTER 15 Communication Skills ■ 183

FIGURE 15-2 This person missed an important meeting. He thought the boss said "2:30" instead of "10:30." *Photo by Paul E. Meyers*

This chapter deals with communication skills, one type of academic skills. *Communication* involves sending information, ideas, or feelings from one person to another. This is done through language. Language may be spoken or written. Before communication can take place, a receiver must understand the language. Communication, therefore, involves writing, reading, listening, and speaking.

According to *Effective Business Communication*, typical workers spend about seventy percent of their workday hours communicating. About forty-five percent of communication time is spent listening; thirty percent, speaking; sixteen percent, reading; and nine percent, writing. In the following material, we will examine these four skills.

3. The percentages are less important than making students aware of the fact that a typical worker spends a large proportion of time communicating.

LISTENING

Communication links the working world. Listening may be its weakest link. It has been said that poor listening costs employers billions of dollars every year.

Poor listening takes many forms. For instance, the boss told Murray to send the district sales agents both of the new price lists. A couple of days after Murray sent the report, the phones started ringing. The agents wondered where their price lists were. Murray knew he had goofed. He sent out a second mailing right away. By not following directions, he cost the company time and money. Common causes of poor listening include distractions, prejudging and overstimulation, and partial listening.

Distractions

Have you ever thought of something else while someone was talking? It's often hard *not* to do this. Most of us talk at a rate of about 125 words per minute. The average mind can handle about 600 to 800 words per minute. This means that there is a gap between the rate at which people are able to speak and the rate at which listeners are capable of thinking. Therefore, the mind tends to wonder.

A *distraction* is something that you notice while you are listening to someone talk. For instance, suppose you are talking to the boss and someone turns on a noisy machine. Perhaps the workplace lighting flickers on and off. Your mind might pay attention to the distraction. Other common distractions are telephone calls, changes in temperature, and the appearance of a new smell. What kinds of problems could these cause later?

Prejudging and Overstimulation

Sometimes listeners try to outguess the speaker. This is called *prejudging*. Here is an example. Mrs. Krause asked to meet with the salesclerks a few minutes before the store opened. Carla began to feel nervous. She thought that Mrs. Krause was going to criticize her for something she had done. She started to think what her answer would be. Mrs. Krause just wanted to review check-approval policies. Carla had prejudged what Mrs. Krause was going to say. As it turned out, Mrs. Krause complimented Carla. She was the only one who was doing that task correctly!

Another cause of poor listening is called *overstimulation*. A listener becomes too eager to respond to the speaker, as shown in the following example. Mr. Costa was demonstrating to Lee and the other apprentices how to adjust an air compressor and spray gun. He said that enamel requires a higher air pressure than lacquer. He misspoke—lacquer requires higher air pressure.

Lee caught the error and couldn't wait to correct him. But Lee was so eager to point out the mistake that she didn't pay attention to the rest of the demonstration.

Partial Listening

This can take several forms, including fragmented listening and pretend listening. *Fragmented listening* is when the listener listens only for certain things. For example, Harold works as a graphic artist for a large department store. Twice a year, the store manager talks to all employees about company goals. The only time Harold pays attention is when the manager says something about the art department.

Pretend listening is when the listener either doesn't care what is going on or is waiting for a turn to talk. Margo is a maintenance worker for the same company as Harold. She thinks it is a waste of time for maintenance workers to attend the store manager's presentation. Though she pretends to listen, she thinks about everything but company plans and goals. By not concentrating on the message being delivered, Harold and Margo miss very important information.

Following are a number of guidelines for good

FIGURE 15-3 Vocational student organizations provide many opportunities for individuals to develop communication skills. *Courtesy of Muhlenberg Co. AVEC KY HOSA*

8. Consider developing and duplicating an actual rating sheet for these eight guidelines. For each guideline, have students rate themselves "usually," "sometimes," or "never."

listening. Rate yourself in terms of how good a listener you are. You should:

1. Have a questioning attitude. Good listeners want to understand what is being said.
2. Concentrate on what is being said. Listening requires effort and active participation.
3. Eliminate distractions by turning off noisy machines, closing doors, moving closer to the speaker, and so on.
4. Use your eyes as well as your ears and mind. Facial expressions and body language are often as important as what is said.
5. Listen "between the lines" for what the speaker *doesn't* say. The Coldwell Company's president told workers that someone had bought the company. Though he didn't say so, it sounded as if the plant might be relocated.
6. Get all the facts before evaluating it or reacting to it.
7. Write down important things before you forget them.
8. Ask questions if you don't understand something.

SPEAKING

Effective speaking requires correct pronunciation, clear enunciation, use of standard English, and good grammar. Each of these will be summarized. A section on telephone skills is also included.

Correct Pronunciation

Most words have several syllables. For instance, the word *advertisement* has four syllables: ad-ver-tise-ment. Correct *pronunciation* means saying the proper sound for each syllable and accenting the right syllable. Thus, the word *advertisement* is actually pronounced as "ad-vur'-tiz-ment." The accent is on the second syllable. Also, notice that the third syllable is pronounced as "tiz" rather than "tise."

Clear Enunciation

Clear enunciation means speaking distinctly. Many people, for instance, don't enunciate contractions such as "we're." That is, they say "we're" like "weer." How do you say "we're"? Poor enunciation and bad pronunciation often go together. As a result, words like "are" and "our" often sound alike. The same is true for "fire" and "far." Say these two pairs of words out loud to find out how clearly you enunciate.

9. Caution students about prejudging.
10. It is good to review and discuss speaking skills here. This should be a continuing concern throughout the course.

CHAPTER 15 Communication Skills ■ 185

FIGURE 15-4 Try to speak like TV newscasters. They use standard English. *Courtesy of Knight-Ridder Inc.*

11. Review and illustrate how words are divided into syllables. Write down and maintain a list of words that you hear students mispronounce frequently. Use such words here as examples.
12. Do have students say the pairs of words out loud to illustrate differences in enunciation. Ask students if they can provide additional examples.

FEATURE

Eliminating Gobbledygook

♦ ♦ ♦

The term *gobbledygook* was coined years ago by a Texas congressman. He had been reading government reports mixed with bloated, empty words. Gobbledygook, then, refers to "wordy, vague, unclear language." This language disorder is found in education, government, science, and all other fields. Here are some examples:

- *Articulate*—talking to one another.
- *Vertical insertion*—invasion by paratroopers.
- *Social-expression product*—greeting card.
- *Protein spill*—to vomit.
- *Experienced car*—used car.
- *Guest-relations facility*—restroom.

Gobbledygook seems to be used for several reasons. Sometimes, people want to make common things seem more important. So an elevator operator becomes a *vertical-transportation-corps member*. A toothpick becomes a *wood interdental stimulator*.

Jargon is sometimes used to discourage or hide the truth. In one medical report, a *therapeutic misadventure* was used to refer to an operation that killed the patient. An airline's report referred to a plane crash as the *involuntary conversion of a 727*.

Gobbledygook should never be used. It lowers the value of language. It makes words and ideas more difficult to understand. Clear, simple speaking and writing are always the best approaches. Word pollution, like other forms of pollution, needs to be cleaned up.

*

FIGURE 15-FEATURE Some advertising intentionally uses gobbledygook to increase the appeal of a product. *Courtesy of Harris & Company and Sears, Roebuck and Co. 1987 Annual Report*

---

*Eliminating Gobbledygook. You can have fun with this topic. Perhaps you can provide additional examples of gobbledygook for students to decipher. Or assign students to bring in examples. Do, however, summarize by noting the importance of clear, concise language.

13. You may wish to assign Activity 2 at this time.
14. Point out that TV newscasters are good models for the use of standard English.

CHAPTER 15 Communication Skills ■ 187

FIGURE 15-5 Some words and phrases used in your peer group may not be appropriate in the workplace. *Courtesy of Siena College, Loudonville, NY*

Use of Standard English

American English takes many forms. One is the informal slang that many teenagers use. Can you give examples of some of these words? It's fun to speak like this with friends. Informal slang is nonstandard English. So is poor grammar. *Standard English,* on the other hand, is the customary form of language used by the majority of Americans. Most employers will expect you to use standard English on the job.

Rules of Good Grammar

Since grade school, you have studied *grammar* in language arts and English classes. A language's grammar is a set of rules about correct speaking and writing. All languages have dozens of rules.

Grammar rules are pretty easy to understand. Even so, many people continue to say things like "they ain't here" instead of "they aren't here." Can you think of reasons why people break so many grammar rules when they speak?

Why should you use good grammar? Well, your getting and keeping a job may depend on it! How you speak makes an impression on an employer. Suppose you are interviewing people for a job. Two applicants have strong job skills. One says things such as "I done it" and "I couldn't find it nowhere." The other person speaks correctly. Whom would you hire? Poor grammar may create doubt in an employer's mind about your ability. It can also turn away customers and clients.

Telephone Skills

In Chapter 4, you learned how to use the telephone as part of a job search. Proper use of the telephone is also required on the job. An employee represents the company in a business transaction. An employee's time also costs the business money. Therefore, an effective speaker conducts telephone conversations with *courtesy* and *efficiency*.

When answering a business call, you should observe these guidelines:

■ Answer in a pleasant, helpful tone of voice. Identify the company at once. For example,

15. A variety of commercial and noncommercial supplemental materials have been developed for teaching grammar and other communication skills within vocational education.
16. Rather than attempt to review rules of grammar here, the emphasis is on awareness of the importance of good grammar.
17. You may wish to review these pages in Chapter 4.
18. For each guideline, ask students how they have been instructed to do it (or what they have observed) where they work.

188 ▪ SECTION 4 Success Skills

"Hello, Edwards and Company" or "Edwards and Company, may I help you?"
- Listen attentively as the caller gives the reason for calling. Be prepared to record a phone message. If you take a message, record complete information, i.e., date and time, caller's name and number, nature of the call, the follow-up action required.
- Route the call to the person best able to meet the caller's need. An appropriate response would be, "Thank you, I'll transfer you to Mr. Weber, our sales manager."
- If the caller wants to talk to a specific person, you might ask, "May I tell her who is calling?"
- Often, the desired person will not be able to accept the call. In this case, your response might be, "I'm sorry, Mrs. Knight is away from her desk. May I ask her to return your call?"
- Always fulfill your promise to the caller. Pass on the message, track down the correct information, return the call yourself, or whatever else is required.
- Pleasantly conclude all calls; for example, "Thank you for calling."

Similar courtesies should be used when placing a business call. Follow these rules:

- Before placing a call, have your purpose clearly in mind. Write down the points you want to make. Have any necessary reference material at hand.
- If you are placing an order, complete a written order form beforehand.
- Identify yourself at once and state your reason for calling. For example, "Hello, this is Arnold Swartz at Midwest Publishers. I'm calling to inquire if our order is ready to be picked up."
- If necessary, name the person or department with whom you want to do business. After identifying yourself, state something like, "I would like to speak with Mr. Sullivan in the service department."
- Your call should be direct and businesslike. But don't forget to talk in a warm and friendly tone.

READING

Like listening, reading is a way to receive information. Both require concentration and understanding. More so than listening, however, reading also requires recognizing words before you can understand their meaning. To show this, look at the three lines in Figure 15-6. The first line is Spanish; the

19. You may wish to role play some specific situations involved in answering or placing a call.

20. Have students keep a diary of new words they encounter on the job. Or require them to turn in once a week a list of five (or more) new words used in a sentence.

1. ¿ Sabe usted quién es el maestro? (phrase in Spanish)

2.  [shorthand symbol] (phrase in shorthand)

3. Do you know who the teacher is? (phrase in English)

FIGURE 15-6

second is shorthand; and the third is English. These three lines say the same thing! You may understand only the third line. Some of you may understand only lines 1 and 3, and so on. Language is like a code. Unless you can recognize and attach meaning to it, you can't understand it.

Let's see if you can recognize and understand these four English words: *glabella, larrikin, neap,* and *scrieve.* Are any of them familiar to you? Probably not. The words might as well be written in Italian (unless, of course, you know that language). This points out the importance of *vocabulary.* Your vocabulary is the total of all the words you know. You can't understand what you read unless you know the meaning of the words used.

Improve Your Vocabulary

Your vocabulary already consists of thousands of different words. Keep adding new words to your vocabulary. Don't just pass over words that you don't know. As you find new words, look up their meanings in a dictionary. After you learn a word, use it in your speaking and writing. Vocabulary-building is a lifelong task.

Practice Reading

Because reading is a skill, people can improve it through practice. Reading newspapers and magazines are good ways to practice. So, too, is reading material in your field of work. Not only will you improve your reading, you will also be learning at the same time.

It's pretty boring to read things that aren't interesting to you. Of course, we all must do some of this. On your own time, though, follow your interests, hobbies, and so on. If you don't want to spend a lot of money, check out materials from the public library.

21. You may wish to assign Activity 4 at this time. The objective is to encourage reading.

CHAPTER 15 Communication Skills ■ 189

FIGURE 15-7 The more you read, the more your reading skills will improve. *Courtesy of Siena College, Loudonville, NY*

What Would You Do?

You recognize that you should probably read more books. On a number of occasions, you have checked books out of the library. Each time, you begin a book eager to read it. However, it is not long before you lose interest and put it aside. You feel guilty about not sticking with a book until it is finished. What would you do?

*

WRITING

Most workers spend less time writing than listening, speaking, or reading. Even so, writing is probably the most important form of business communication. This is because it is good business to keep permanent records of all business operations, transactions, and agreements. Denny learned this the hard way.

Denny was asked to answer the phone while the boss stepped out for a moment. He took two calls and left messages on her desk. A few moments after she returned, Denny saw the boss approaching.

"Who are these messages from?" she said. "I can't read them."

What could Denny say?

Written communication takes place within a company and between organizations. *Internal* communication takes the form of notes, business forms, and memorandums. *External* communication mainly takes the form of business letters.

Notes and Business Forms

A note is the most informal type of written business communication. Many notes are short hand-

WWYD Feature A. Perhaps the student hasn't found any books yet related to her/his interests. A librarian could be asked for advice.

190 ■ SECTION 4 Success Skills

23. Emphasize that neatness, correct spelling, and accuracy are the keys to completing business forms and notes.

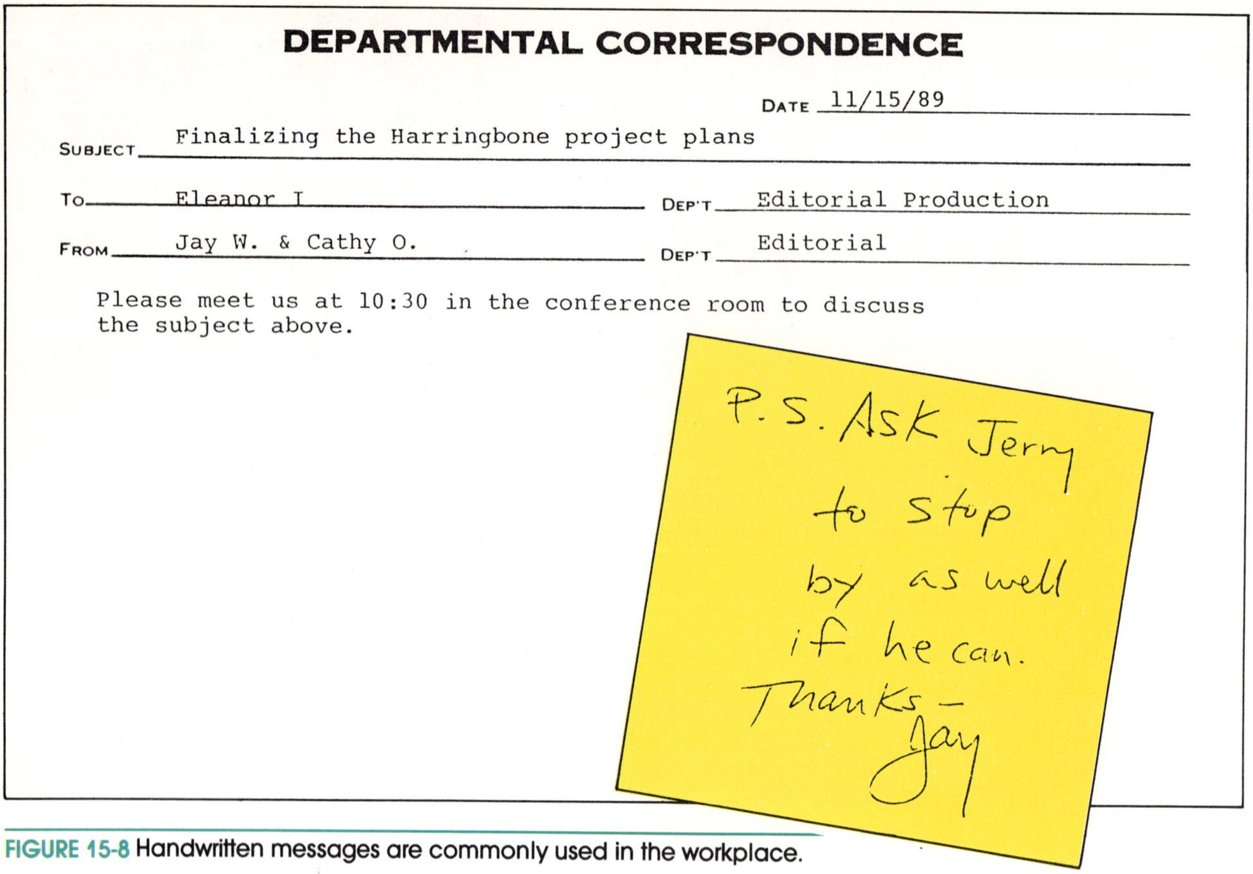

DEPARTMENTAL CORRESPONDENCE

DATE 11/15/89

SUBJECT: Finalizing the Harringbone project plans

TO: Eleanor I.   DEP'T: Editorial Production

FROM: Jay W. & Cathy O.   DEP'T: Editorial

Please meet us at 10:30 in the conference room to discuss the subject above.

P.S. Ask Jerry to stop by as well if he can. Thanks — Jay

FIGURE 15-8 Handwritten messages are commonly used in the workplace.

written messages. They are frequently attached to some other written message, Figure 15-8. A wide variety of preprinted notes are used in business to record phone messages, route information, send directions, and so on.

Business forms are another type of written communication. Businesses use preprinted forms to record business operations. Some examples of common business forms include:

- Petty cash form
- Sales call report
- Purchase order
- Quotation form
- Job work order
- Stock requisition
- Packing list
- Receiving form
- Production form
- Invoice

Notes and business forms are usually simple to complete. However, they need to be readable and accurate. For a message to be readable, write (or type) it neatly. Spell words correctly. If you aren't sure about the spelling of a word, check a dictionary. Finally, always check over written messages for possible errors before transmitting them.

What Would You Do?

You come home from school grumbling about the grade you received on a written assignment. The teacher always marks off for misspelled words regardless of how good the paper is otherwise. You tell your sister, Amy, that you don't think it is fair.

"If I were you, I wouldn't worry about it," says Amy. "You don't have to be concerned about spelling when you get out of school. At work, we have word processors that use software that automatically identifies and then corrects any spelling errors." What would you do?

22. Ask students to provide examples of preprinted notes and forms where they work.

WWYD Feature B. Computer software has made it easier to identify and correct spelling errors. However, there are many overriding reasons why one should learn to spell.

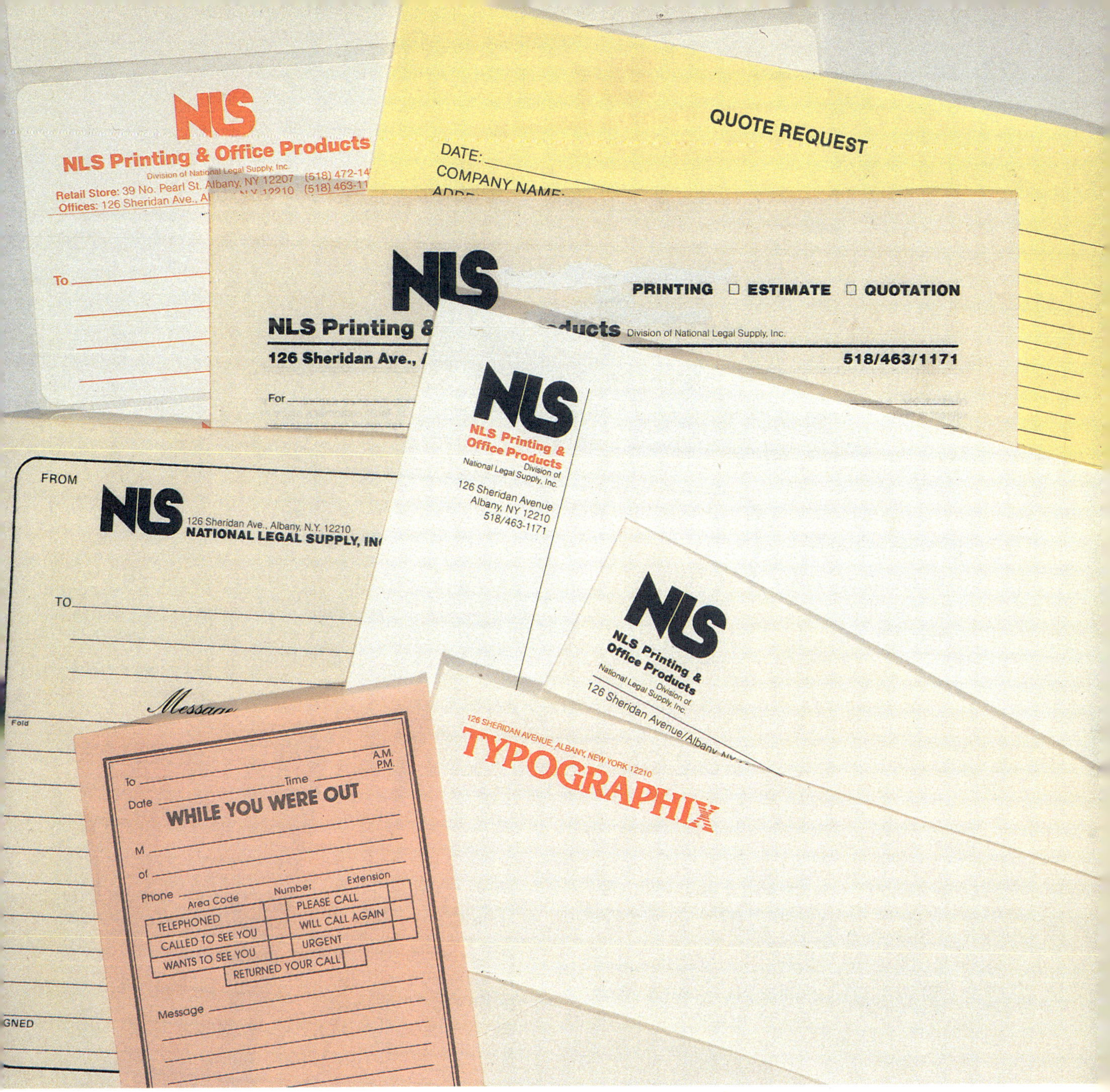

FIGURE 15-9 Businesses use a variety of preprinted forms. *Courtesy of NLS Printing and Office Products, Albany, NY*

Memorandums

Within companies, memorandums are the main form of written communication. Memorandums are also called "memos." Memos carry messages upward, downward, and across departmental lines. For instance, a stockclerk may write a memo to a boss. The boss may respond with a memo to the department. Or the boss may send a memo to someone in another department.

24. Point out that memos may also be handwritten on preprinted forms.

Most memos deal with daily business matters. They are usually brief. Their tone tends to be rather informal. Memos are used to communicate four types of information:

1. Instructions or explanations
2. Announcements and reports
3. Requests for information, action, or reaction
4. Answers to requests

MEMORANDUM

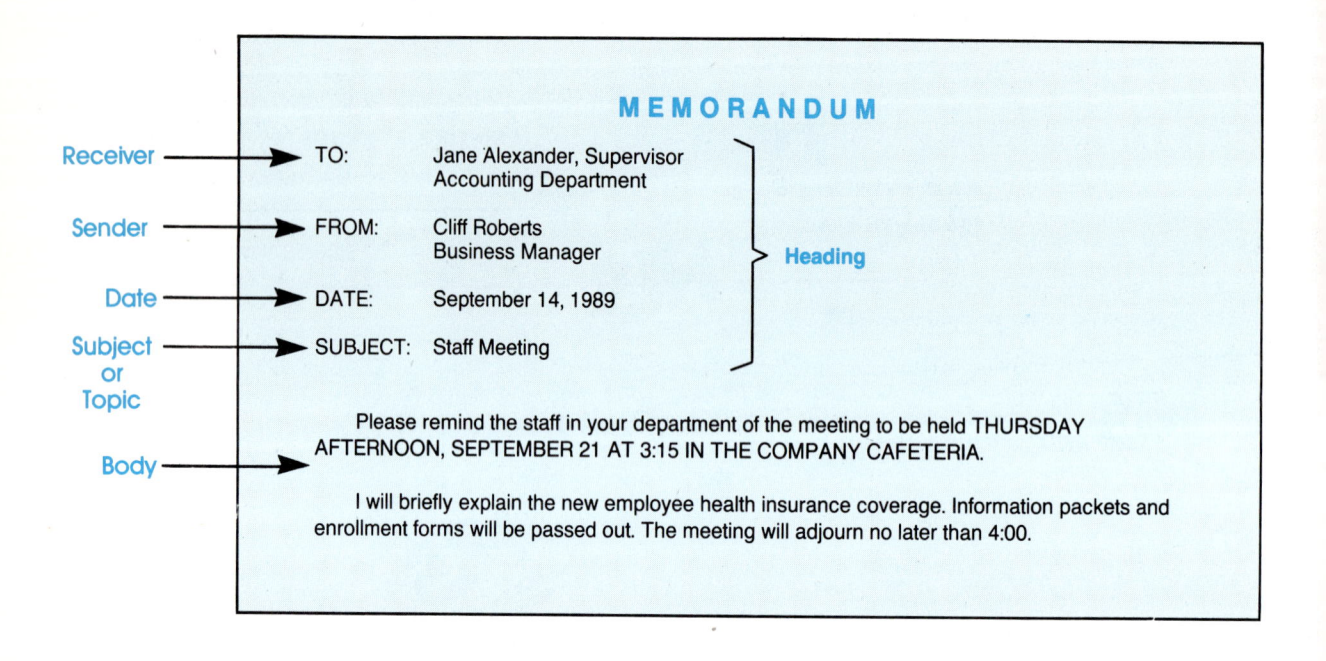

Receiver →	TO:	Jane Alexander, Supervisor Accounting Department
Sender →	FROM:	Cliff Roberts Business Manager
Date →	DATE:	September 14, 1989
Subject or Topic →	SUBJECT:	Staff Meeting

(Heading)

Body →

Please remind the staff in your department of the meeting to be held THURSDAY AFTERNOON, SEPTEMBER 21 AT 3:15 IN THE COMPANY CAFETERIA.

I will briefly explain the new employee health insurance coverage. Information packets and enrollment forms will be passed out. The meeting will adjourn no later than 4:00.

FIGURE 15-10 A typical interoffice memo. The major parts are labeled.

25. The memo shown in Figure 15-10 primarily conveys instructions and explanations.

A typical memo with its major parts labeled is shown in Figure 15-10. What type(s) of information does it communicate?

Little introductory information is necessary in a memo. But the first paragraph is often used to explain the purpose of the memo. A memo is usually limited to one main topic. Headings, underlining, or capitalization of words can be used to call attention to key points.

Busines Letters

Why are business letters so common when it is so easy to place phone calls? Phone calls aren't permanent records. Business letters are. In many cases, someone follows up a phone call with a business letter.

The average worker is more likely to write notes and memos on the job than business letters. Even so, it is still important to know how to write a good business letter. You saw in earlier chapters, for example, several cases where people wrote business

26. You may wish to assign Activity 3 at this time.
27. Ask students to describe the types of written communication they perform on the job.

28. Note that the letter shown in Figure 15-11 contains guidelines for writing business letters.

letters during a job search. A good business letter should:

- Communicate a clear message.
- Convey a professional, businesslike tone.
- Be well organized.
- Use correct grammar, spelling, and punctuation.
- Have an attractive appearance.

A sample letter with its major parts labeled is shown in Figure 15-11. The letter uses what is called a "modified block style." Most parts of the letter begin at the left margin except for the date, complimentary close, and signature line which begin at the center of the page. In a "block style" letter, all lines (except a printed letterhead) begin at the left margin.

When writing a business letter, make a draft copy first. Then, rewrite the letter as necessary. Before sending it, read the letter carefully for errors. As a final step, make a copy for your records. If you are using a word processor, save the letter on disk.

29. Have students evaluate a previously written letter in terms of the guidelines provided in this section. Rewrite a sample letter as appropriate.

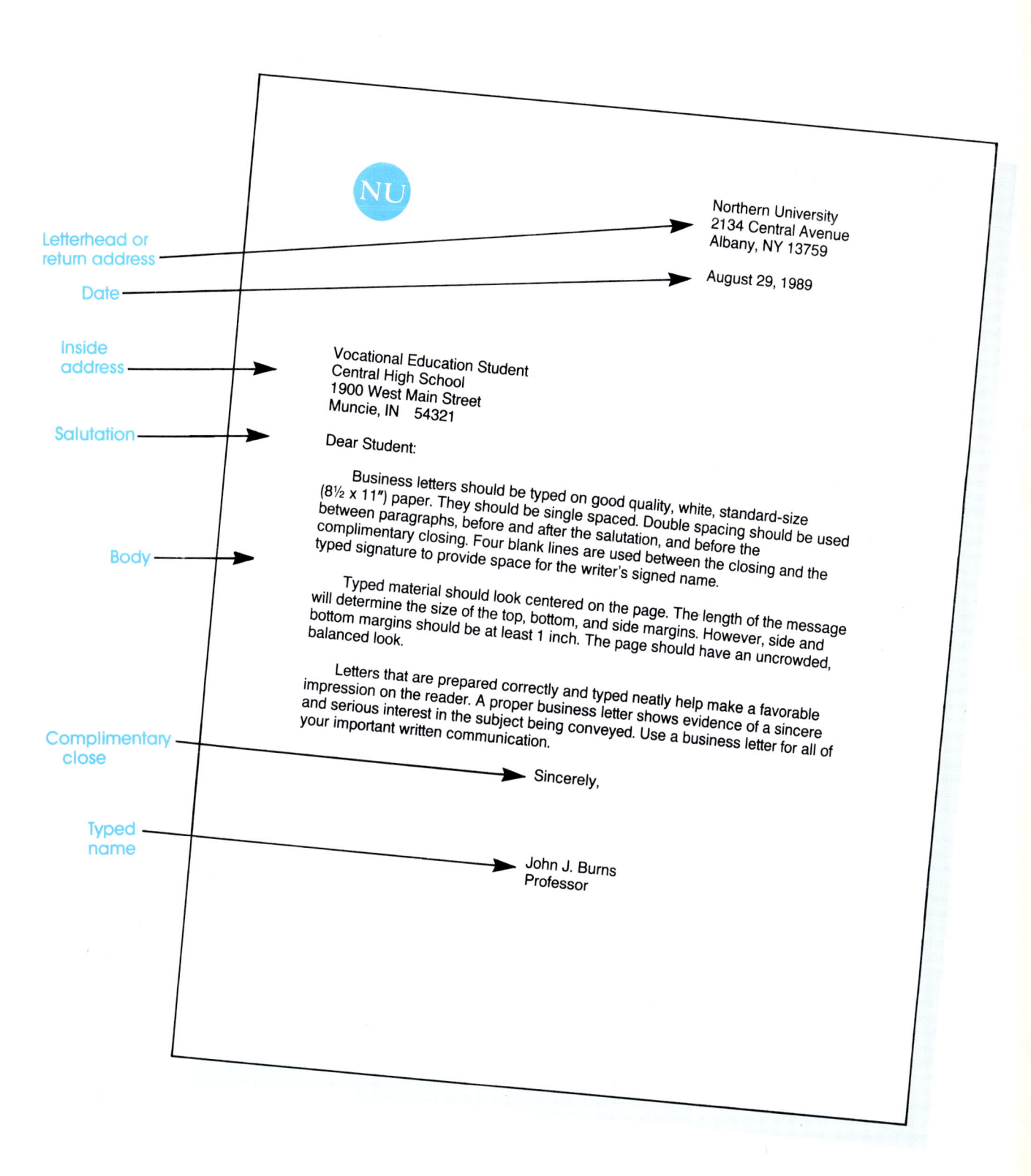

CHAPTER 15 Communication Skills ■ 193

Letterhead or return address → Northern University
2134 Central Avenue
Albany, NY 13759

Date → August 29, 1989

Inside address → Vocational Education Student
Central High School
1900 West Main Street
Muncie, IN 54321

Salutation → Dear Student:

Body → Business letters should be typed on good quality, white, standard-size (8½ x 11") paper. They should be single spaced. Double spacing should be used between paragraphs, before and after the salutation, and before the complimentary closing. Four blank lines are used between the closing and the typed signature to provide space for the writer's signed name.

Typed material should look centered on the page. The length of the message will determine the size of the top, bottom, and side margins. However, side and bottom margins should be at least 1 inch. The page should have an uncrowded, balanced look.

Letters that are prepared correctly and typed neatly help make a favorable impression on the reader. A proper business letter shows evidence of a sincere and serious interest in the subject being conveyed. Use a business letter for all of your important written communication.

Complimentary close → Sincerely,

Typed name → John J. Burns
Professor

FIGURE 15-11 Main parts of a business letter

CHAPTER REVIEW

Chapter in Brief

- In addition to occupational and employability skills, basic academic skills are required for job success.
- Communication links the working world. Listening may be its weakest link. Common causes of poor listening include distractions, prejudging and overstimulation, and partial listening.
- Effective speaking requires correct pronunciation, clear enunciation, use of standard English, and good grammar. An important application of effective speech is use of the telephone.
- Reading requires recognizing words before you can understand their meaning. Therefore, effective readers need a large vocabulary. Because reading is a skill, it can be improved through practice.
- Writing is probably the most important form of business communication. It is good business to keep records of what goes on. Internal communication within a company takes the form of notes, business forms, and memorandums. External communication between organizations mainly takes the form of business letters.

Words to Know

communication sending information, ideas, or feelings from one person to another.

distractions things that draw attention away from what one is doing.

enunciation speaking and pronouncing words clearly.

grammar a set of rules about correct speaking and writing.

pronunciation the way in which words are spoken.

standard English the usual form of language used by the majority of Americans.

vocabulary the total of words known by an individual.

Questions to Answer

1. What three types of skills are needed to be successful on the job?
2. Which type of communication skill is used most by the average worker? Which type is used least?
3. Name and provide an example of each of the four common causes of poor listening.
4. When listening, what does it mean to have a "questioning attitude"?
5. What are the four things required to be an effective speaker?
6. In what ways are listening and reading the same?
7. List two ways to improve reading skills.
8. Why is writing the most important form of business communication?
9. Memos are used to communicate four types of information. Name them.
10. What four steps should be followed in writing a business letter?

1. (a) Occupational skills. (b) Employability skills. (c) Basic academic skills.
2. The most—listening; least—writing.
3. *Distractions*—a loud noise takes your mind away from listening. *Prejudging*—assuming that you know what the speaker is about to say. *Overstimulation*—becoming so eager to ask a question that the rest of the speaker's comments are not heard. *Partial listening*—listening only for those things that directly relate to your job and ignoring the rest of the presentation.
4. Listening with a conscious focus on "What is the speaker saying, or what is the speaker trying to tell me?"
5. 'a) Correct pronunciation. (b) Clear enunciation. (c) Use of standard English. (d) Good grammar.
6. Both are ways to receive information.
7. (a) Improve your vocabulary. (b) Practice reading.
8. It is standard business practice to keep permanent records of all business operations, transactions, and agreements.
9. (a) Instructions or explanations. (b) Announcements and reports. (c) Requests for information, action, or reaction. (d) Answers to requests.
10. (a) First, write a draft copy. (b) Rewrite the letter as necessary. (c) Read the letter carefully for errors before sending it. (d) Keep a copy for your records.

Activities to Do

1. Throughout your school years, you have probably taken several achievement tests. Make an appointment with the school counselor to review your performance regarding language and communication skills. If you have done average or better on such tests, you probably have the basic communication skills for most entry-level jobs. If your skills are below average, ask the counselor for suggestions on how to improve your skills.
2. Keep a list for one day of slang words and phrases that you hear classmates and other people using. The next day, share the list with the class. Discuss what words and phrases of standard English could be substituted for them.
3. Assume that you are in charge of organizing the annual company picnic. Write a pretend memo to company employees. The memo should provide all important details about the picnic. Turn the memo in to your teacher for evaluation.
4. List several of your hobbies or recreational interests. Go to the library and find out what books are available on these subjects. Choose a book and read it. Make a short oral report to the class about the book you read.
5. For some individuals, giving a presentation to co-workers or a speech to a community group is part of their job. Effective public speaking depends on: (a) knowing the subject, and (b) preparing the presentation. Give a five-minute speech to the class concerning some aspect of your job that you know well. Follow these guidelines:
    a. Select a subject that you can explain well in five minutes.
    b. Outline the main points to be covered. Write them down on note cards.
    c. Practice the speech beforehand so that it will not be too short or too long.
    d. Give the speech with confidence and enthusiasm.
    Afterward, discuss the strengths and weaknesses of each speech.

Topics to Discuss

1. Computers, robots, and other forms of technology are changing many types of occupations and businesses. How is business communication changing as a result of new technology?
2. There are geographic differences in the way people use language. You may have lived or traveled in areas different from where you now live. Discuss some of the interesting and colorful words and phrases that people use in different parts of the country.
3. An *acronym* is a word formed from the first letter of consecutive words. An example is ASAP (as soon as possible). Identify and discuss some of the acronyms that are used in personal and business communication.

---

30. Rather than have each student contact the counselor individually, you may wish to work with the counselor to arrange a more efficient process—say coming to class and meeting with students, both as a group and individually.
31. Also promote reading by keeping a variety of magazines in the classroom. Bring in your old copies and ask teachers and students to do the same. Encourage students to take magazines home for evening and weekend reading.
32. You may need to provide several examples of appropriate topics. Provide additional instruction on giving a speech as needed.

33. Ask students to provide examples from where they work.
34. This can be informative, but deal sensitively with racial and ethnic differences.
35. Also, have students share acronyms that are unique to their jobs.

1. Ask students what kinds of math they use on the job.
2. There is a wide variety of commercial and noncommercial text materials for teaching these skills within vocational education. If your students are weak in this area, you may wish to augment this chapter with additional materials.

CHAPTER SIXTEEN

Math and Measurement Skills

OUTLINE
Basic Math
Basic Measurement
Systems of Measure
Chapter Review

OBJECTIVES
After reading this chapter, you should be able to:
- Identify occupations requiring math and measurement skills.
- Apply math skills to computation of: total purchase amount, trade discount, cash discount, markup, sales tax, and markdown.
- Calculate surface measures and volume measures.
- Convert measures from one unit to another.

1 Like communication skills, math is also important on the job. Some occupations use more math than others. A carpenter, for instance, uses math more than an aerobics instructor. Math is taught from early grade school through high school. We assume here that you have already learned basic math and measurement skills. This material does not seek to introduce new math content. Rather, it shows how basic math and measurement skills are used in the workplace.

BASIC MATH
The following examples show some common uses of arithmetic. Sometimes this is called "busi-

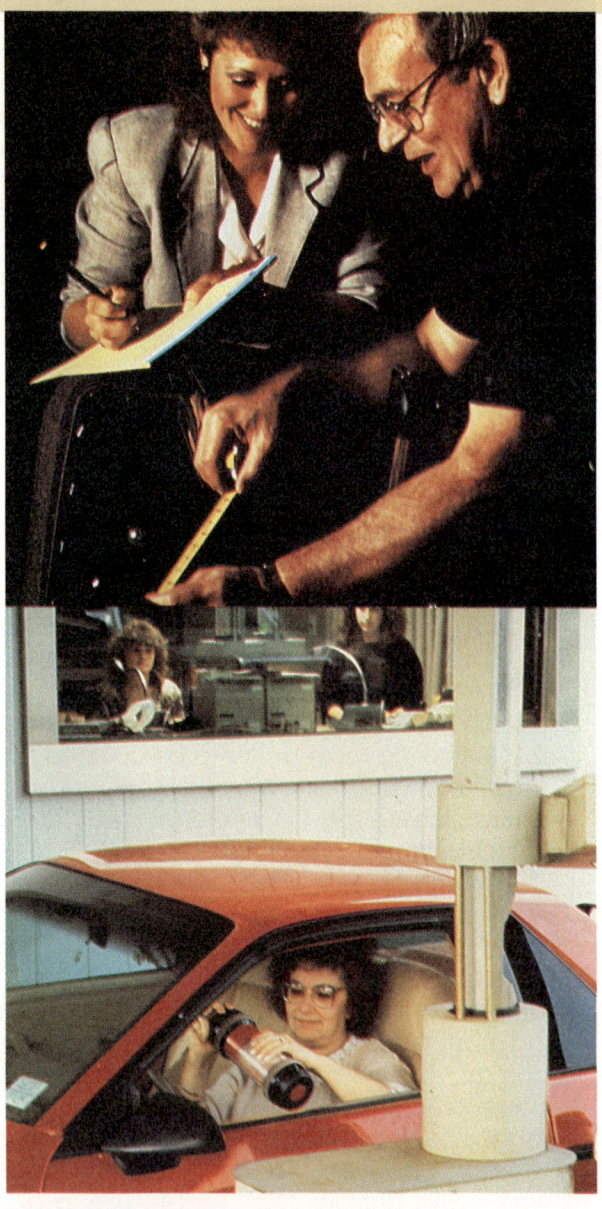

FIGURE 16-1 The type of math used on the job varies from worker to worker. *Courtesy of Boise Cascade Corporation and Crestmont Federal Savings and Loan Association (Photographer: Ted Cronet)*

ness math." The next part of the chapter deals with basic measurement. This is sometimes called "vocational math" or "shop math." In later chapters of the book, you will apply math skills again. You will figure interest and taxes, do comparison shopping, and other so-called "consumer math."

3. Note that both math and measurement skills are reviewed in this chapter. Adapt instruction of this material to meet the needs of your students.

196

4. Many of the examples used in this chapter are quite simple. This is an accurate reflection of the workplace, in which a great deal of simple math is employed.

What Would You Do?

In observing your boss, you are surprised at the amount of math that she uses. She seems to constantly be analyzing sales data and entering numbers into a calculator. You would like to be able to move up in the company, or perhaps own a small store of your own someday. However, math has always been your weakest subject. You wonder whether you would be able to perform the math part of the business. What would you do?

*WWYD Feature A. The required business math is probably something that can be learned on the job. If math is an obstacle to advancement, however, the person should pursue additional training.

Total Purchase Amount

Most of your purchases involve single items. For instance, you buy a pair of running shoes for $44.95. The total amount of your purchase is easy to figure:

CHAPTER 16 Math and Measurement Skills ■ 197

1 × $44.95 = $44.95. In most states, you must add sales tax, too.

Businesses, however, often buy large numbers of the same item. A sporting goods store, for example, might buy dozens of pairs of running shoes. To find the total amount of the purchase, multiply the number of items by the price of one item (unit price).

PROBLEM: Figure the total amount of a purchase of 24 pairs of shoes at $32.95 each, 15 pairs of socks at $1.49 each, and 3 dozen shoelaces at $0.79 each.

SOLUTION: Quantity × Unit Price = Amount

Shoes:	24 × $32.95 =	$790.80
Socks:	15 × $ 1.49 =	22.35
Laces:	36 × $ 0.79 =	28.44
	Total Amount	$841.59

This skill is important for people who prepare invoices. An *invoice* is a bill for goods. Look at Figure 16-2.

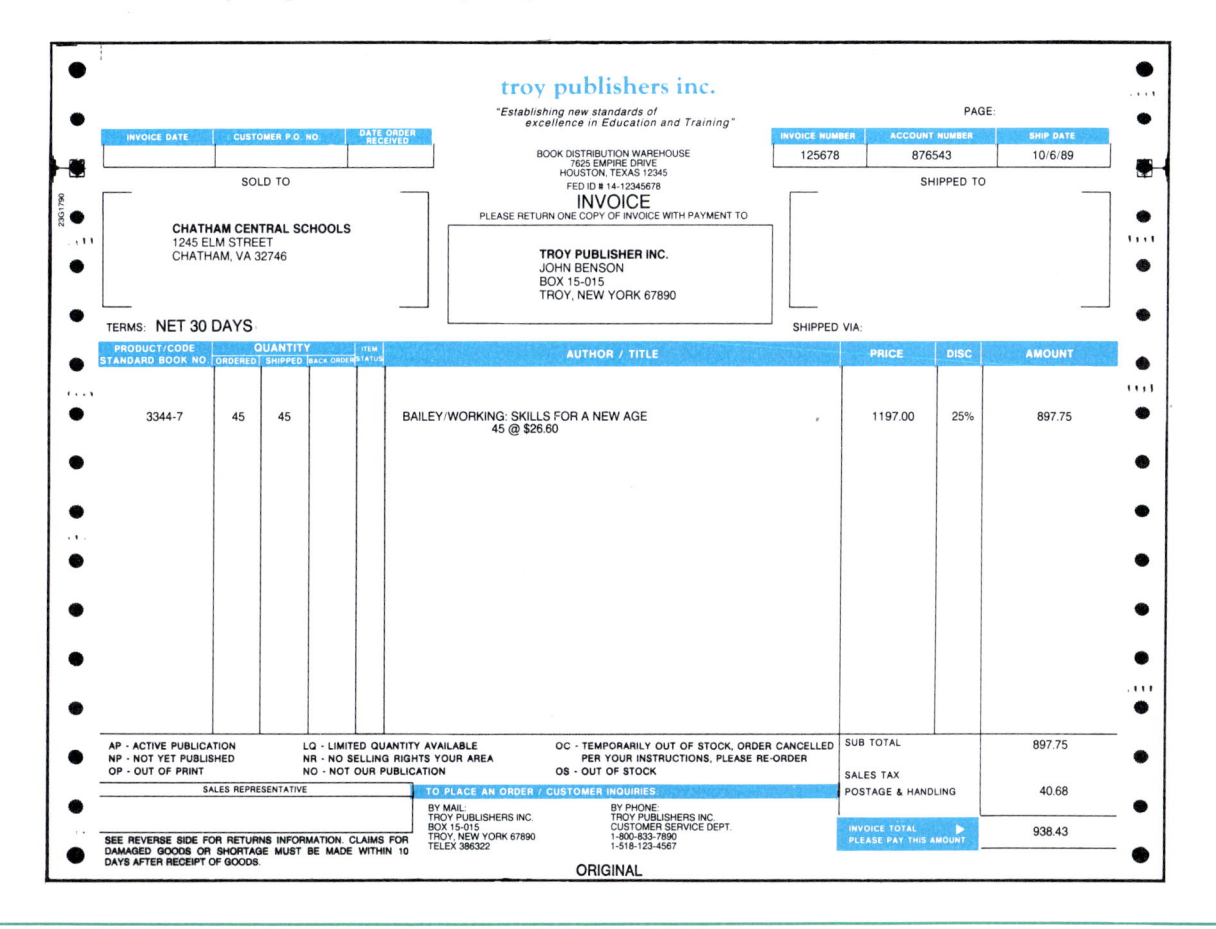

FIGURE 16-2 Invoice preparation is a common application of math in the workplace.

5. A recommended approach for teaching the math skills on these pages is to name the type of skill; e.g., total purchase amount, and describe how it is used in the workplace.

6. A distinction is often made between a bill and an invoice. A *bill* is a statement for services performed, while an *invoice* is a statement for goods that have been sold.

198 ■ SECTION 4 Success Skills

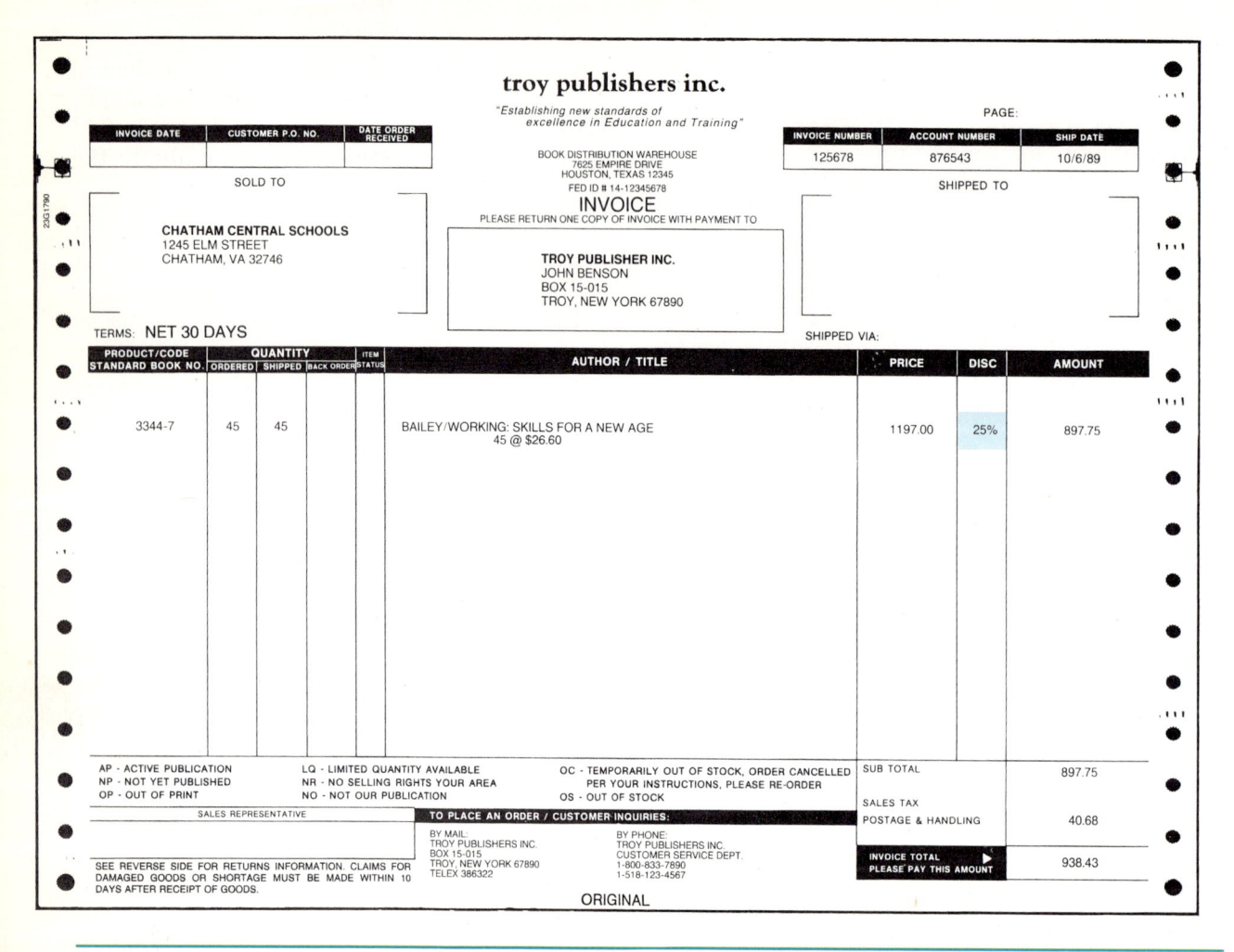

troy publishers inc.
"Establishing new standards of excellence in Education and Training"

INVOICE DATE	CUSTOMER P.O. NO.	DATE ORDER RECEIVED		INVOICE NUMBER	ACCOUNT NUMBER	SHIP DATE
				125678	876543	10/6/89

BOOK DISTRIBUTION WAREHOUSE
7625 EMPIRE DRIVE
HOUSTON, TEXAS 12345
FED ID # 14-12345678

INVOICE
PLEASE RETURN ONE COPY OF INVOICE WITH PAYMENT TO

SOLD TO
CHATHAM CENTRAL SCHOOLS
1245 ELM STREET
CHATHAM, VA 32746

TROY PUBLISHER INC.
JOHN BENSON
BOX 15-015
TROY, NEW YORK 67890

SHIPPED TO

TERMS: NET 30 DAYS   SHIPPED VIA:

PRODUCT/CODE STANDARD BOOK NO.	QUANTITY ORDERED	SHIPPED	BACK ORDER	ITEM STATUS	AUTHOR / TITLE	PRICE	DISC	AMOUNT
3344-7	45	45			BAILEY/WORKING: SKILLS FOR A NEW AGE 45 @ $26.60	1197.00	25%	897.75

AP - ACTIVE PUBLICATION   LQ - LIMITED QUANTITY AVAILABLE   OC - TEMPORARILY OUT OF STOCK, ORDER CANCELLED PER YOUR INSTRUCTIONS, PLEASE RE-ORDER
NP - NOT YET PUBLISHED   NR - NO SELLING RIGHTS YOUR AREA
OP - OUT OF PRINT   NO - NOT OUR PUBLICATION   OS - OUT OF STOCK

SUB TOTAL		897.75
SALES TAX		
POSTAGE & HANDLING		40.68
INVOICE TOTAL PLEASE PAY THIS AMOUNT		938.43

SALES REPRESENTATIVE

TO PLACE AN ORDER / CUSTOMER INQUIRIES:
BY MAIL: TROY PUBLISHERS INC. BOX 15-015 TROY, NEW YORK 67890 TELEX 386322
BY PHONE: TROY PUBLISHERS INC. CUSTOMER SERVICE DEPT. 1-800-833-7890 1-518-123-4567

SEE REVERSE SIDE FOR RETURNS INFORMATION. CLAIMS FOR DAMAGED GOODS OR SHORTAGE MUST BE MADE WITHIN 10 DAYS AFTER RECEIPT OF GOODS.

ORIGINAL

FIGURE 16-3 The percent discount is stated on the invoice.

7. The term *trade discount* originally referred to a discount given only to those members of the same trade. Today, it has a wider meaning and refers to any large discount from list price.

Trade Discount

A *trade discount* is a deduction from the catalog (list) price of an item. Trade discounts are usually given to retailers to enable them to sell merchandise at a greater profit. In some cases, buyers get special discounts when ordering large numbers of something. The trade discount is a percentage of the list price.

PROBLEM: An office desk is listed in a catalog at $680. Business customers can buy the desk at a trade discount of 30%. How much will a business have to pay for the desk? (What the business pays is the net purchase price.)

SOLUTION: 30% = 0.30

8. For math purposes, trade discounts are equivalent to quantity and sale discounts.

9. This is sometimes called *terms of payment*. The terms might be expressed as 4/10, 2/20, or n/30. This means that a 4% discount can be taken if paid within 10 days; 2% if paid within 20 days. The expression n/30 means the net amount is due within 30 days.

$680.00
× 0.30
$204.00 Discount

$680.00
−204.00
$476.00 Net purchase price

Cash Discount

Every sale between a business buyer and seller involves *terms*. The terms state the time limit within which the buyer must pay. A common term of sale is "net due in 30 days." This means that the buyer has 30 days in which to pay the bill. After 30 days, the buyer must pay the price plus interest.

10. The vendor gives terms to encourage prompt payment. Conversely, interest may be charged on accounts that are past due.

To encourage prompt payment, the seller may offer a *cash discount* of several percent (say 3%). A cash discount benefits both the buyer and seller. The buyer saves money, while the seller has the payment instead of an unpaid account. (The seller also has business expenses to pay.)

> **PROBLEM**: An invoice for $510 has terms of net due in 30 days with a 3% discount given for payment within 10 days. What is the amount of payment if made promptly?
>
> **SOLUTION**: 3% = 0.03
>
> $510.00
> × 0.03
> $ 15.30 Discount
>
> $510.00
> - 15.30
> $494.70 Net amount of payment

Markup

A retailer buys goods from a supplier to resell. Remember the running shoes? The price the store paid is called the cost price. To make money, the retailer then added an amount *(markup)* to the cost price. (Selling price = cost price + markup.)

> **PROBLEM**: An item cost $28.00; its selling price is $35.00. How much is the markup?
>
> **SOLUTION**:
>
> $35.00 Selling price
> -28.00 Cost price
> $ 7.00 Markup
>
> **PROBLEM**: Based on the cost price, what is the percent of markup?
>
> **SOLUTION**:
>
> $$\frac{\$7.00 \text{ (markup)}}{\$28.00 \text{ (cost price)}} = 0.25 \text{ or } 25\%$$

Businesses know how much markup will give them enough money to cover expenses and make a fair profit, so they add markup to the item before trying to sell it.

> **PROBLEM**: A radio costs $42.00 and will be sold at a markup of 30% of the cost price. What is the selling price?

> **SOLUTION**:
>
> $42.00 Cost price
> × 0.30 Markup
> $12.60
>
> $42.00 Cost price
> +12.60 Markup
> $54.60 Selling price

Sales Tax

Most states and cities have sales tax on many goods and services. Sales taxes usually range between one and seven percent. The sales tax is added on to the purchase price of goods and services.

FIGURE 16-4 Most cash registers figure sales tax automatically. *Courtesy of NCR Corporation*

---

11. This is also called *markon* or *margin on sales*.
12. Some businesses use selling price as the base for markup.
13. Sales tax within a state may vary. For instance, in New York, the sales tax is 7% but in New York City it is 8¼%.

PROBLEM: Someone buys a sweater for $28.00 and a pair of slacks for $36.00. A 5% sales tax is added to the purchase price. What is the total amount of the purchase?

SOLUTION:

$28.00
+36.00
$64.00 Purchase price

+ 3.20 ($64.00 × 0.05) Sales tax
$67.20 Total amount

Markdown

Most retail stores have periodic sales to move slow-selling merchandise, clear out end-of-season goods, or attract customers to the store. A reduction in the selling price of a product is called a *markdown*. The markdown is usually expressed as a percent.

PROBLEM: A merchant is having a sale on all summer swimwear at 40% off (markdown). What is the sale price of a swimsuit that used to cost $45.00?

SOLUTION:

$45.00 Original price
×0.40 Markdown
$18.00

$45.00 Original price
-18.00 Markdown
$27.00 Sale price

BASIC MEASUREMENT

Measurement is the act of determining the dimension, quantity, or degree of something. The object can be volume, area, distance, degrees, time, energy, or weight. Measurement answers the question "how much." It does so in a uniform and standardized way. This means, for example, that all inches are the same length. Many workers need to use measurement on their jobs. Such occupations include nurses, dental technicians, carpenters, drafters, machinists, and sheet metal workers. Can you name others?

FIGURE 16-5 Dozens of different types of measurement tools are used in the workplace. *Photo by Paul E. Meyers*

14. The sales tax that applies depends on the *place of delivery*.
15. The markdown based on the net selling price (new, reduced price) is $18.00 ÷ $27.00 = 0.67 or 67%.
16. This material on measurement may be more or less relevant than the previous material on business math. Adapt your instruction accordingly.
17. The science of measurement is called *metrology*. Early units of measurement were based on the sizes of body parts.
18. Ask students to name other occupations.

F•E•A•T•U•R•E

Calculator Review

♦ ♦ ♦

The calculator has become an essential tool in the workplace. You should be able to use one. Let's review the operation of a calculator and practice some basic skills.

A calculator has number buttons and command buttons. The arrangement of the buttons will vary among different models.

⑦ ⑧ ⑨   ÷ DIVIDE
④ ⑤ ⑥   × TIMES
① ② ③   − MINUS
   ⓪   + PLUS
                = EQUALS

Push CE if you make a mistake in your last entry.

Push C if you make a mistake and want to redo the problem.

Turn on the calculator. To add 34 and 57, push ③ ④ + ⑤ ⑦ =

The answer appears on the screen: 91.

Complete the following addition and subtraction problems.

1. 48 + 21 = 69
2. 56 + 32 = 88
3. 64 - 8 = 56
4. 26 - 19 = 7
5. 73 + 0 = 73
6. 97 - 38 = 59

Complete the following multiplication and division problems.

7. 135 ÷ 7 = 19.29
8. 27 × 6 = 162
9. 214 × 52 = 11,128
10. 72 × 76 = 5,472
11. 50 ÷ 4 = 12.5
12. 110 ÷ 18 = 6.11

The calculator has no commas and no dollar signs. To add $3,618 and $4,192, push

③ ⑥ ① ⑧ + ④ ① ⑨ ② =

The screen shows: 7810.

Write in the dollar sign and comma: $7,810.

FIGURE 16-FEATURE Calculators save a lot of time and effort. But you still have to know how to use math. *Courtesy of Sears, Roebuck and Co. 1987 Annual Report*

Calculate the following problems. Remember to write in the dollar signs and commas.

13. $6,043 + 1,675 = $7,718
14. $5,461 - 4,813 = $ 648
15. $7,286 × 24 = $174,864
16. $3,012 / 72 = $41.83

Many calculators have these additional buttons.

MR button reads or displays the memory number.

MC button clears the memory number to zero.

[M+] button enters or adds to the memory number.

[M-] button subtracts from the memory number.

Placing a number in memory is useful for figuring sales tax, markup, and markdown. If you want to add a sales tax of 3.5%, push [3][.][5][M+]. To calculate the tax on $54.95, push [5][4][.][9][5][×][MR][%]

The answer is [1.92325], or $1.92.

Calculate a tax of 3.5% on the following amounts:

17. $86.75   18. $119.95   19. $5.50   20. 2,320.40
    ($3.04)   ($4.20)   ($0.19)   ($81.21)

If the tax increases from 3.5% to 4.0%, the actual increase is 0.5%. To increase the tax by that amount, push [.][5][M+]

To decrease the tax by 1.25%, push [1][.][2][5][M-]

Clear the memory when you have finished. *

*Calculator Review. This is a simple review of the basics in using a calculator. The activity can be done in class or as a homework assignment. Provide individualized instruction and supplemental activities as required.

Surface Measurement

Being able to calculate the surface measures of areas and perimeters is necessary on many jobs. Construction workers, for example, must figure perimeter and area measures in order to know how much concrete, lumber, and other materials to order. Workers in the printing industry must figure perimeters and areas to cut specific sizes of paper stock.

A *perimeter* of an object is the distance around it. It is measured in any standard linear unit, including miles, feet, inches, kilometers, meters, centimeters, or millimeters. Find it by adding together the length of the outer edges of the figure for most shapes. For circles and some irregular figures, you will need to use simple formulas.

The rectangle is a four-sided object having a right angle (90°) at each corner. The page you are reading is a rectangle, most walls and floors are rectangles, even a square is a rectangle, Figure 16-6.

Rectangles have two pairs of sides. Each pair is equal in length. To find the perimeter, you add together the lengths of all sides. Suppose you are building a fence to enclose a dog kennel. Using the measurements shown in Figure 16-6, you add the length of the two 20-foot sides together with the length of the two 5-foot sides to find that the perimeter is 50. Thus, you need 50 feet of fencing to build the kennel. If all sides were of equal length, you could have found the perimeter by multiplying the length of one side by four.

The perimeter of a circle is called the *circumference*. To find the circumference, you must know the diameter or the radius of a circle. A circle with a radius of 8 inches and a diameter of 16 inches is shown in Figure 16-7. To find the circumference, you must use a formula.

The formula is:

Circumference (C) = 3.14 × Diameter (D)

(NOTE: The 3.14 does not change.)

Common Rectangles

[Figure showing four rectangles of various sizes, the rightmost labeled with 20' length and 5' height]

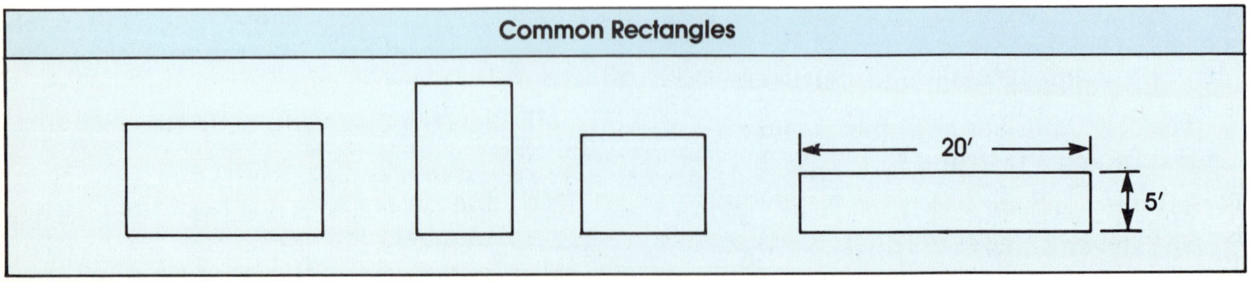

FIGURE 16-6 The rectangle is the most familiar geometric shape.

19. In construction, additional material is often ordered to account for measurement error and waste.
20. Emphasize that the radius is always one-half of the diameter.

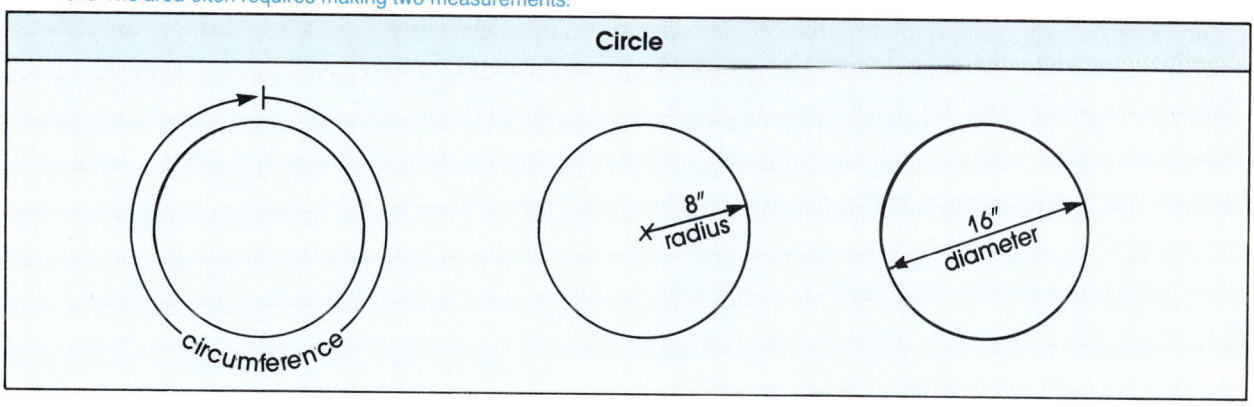

21. The constant 3.14 is called pi.
22. The *length* of anything can be found by making one measurement. The *area* often requires making two measurements.

Circle

FIGURE 16-7 The main dimensions of a circle are the circumference, radius, and diameter.

Let's say that you are going to form and install an exhaust duct in a woodworking shop. Using the dimensions shown in Figure 16-7, how wide of a piece of sheet metal will you need to roll it into a 16-inch diameter cylinder?

Step 1: Set up the formula: C = 3.14 × D

Step 2: Place values into the formula and multiply:
C = 3.14 × 16 inches
C = 50.24 inches

You will need a piece of sheet metal 50.24 inches wide plus a little extra for the seam.

The same process in reverse will help you to determine the diameter or radius of a circle if you know the circumference. To find the diameter, you divide the circumference by 3.14. For example, the diameter of a circle with a circumference of 35 feet is 11.15 feet (D = 35 ÷ 3.14).

An *area* is the number of square units of space on the surface of the figure enclosed by the perimeter. Area calculation uses several simple formulas, each of which is suited to a certain geometric shape. Areas are given in units of square measure such as square feet, square inches, or square meters.

For rectangles, the formula for determining area is:

Area = length × width or A = l × w

For example, the area of a rectangular room that is 8-feet long and 12-feet wide is 96 square feet (8 × 12 = 96). If the room were square with each side being 12 feet, then the area would be 144 square feet (12 × 12 = 144).

23. The word *area* comes from a Latin word meaning "threshing floor." The early Romans probably related the size of the floor to a certain quantity of grain.

FIGURE 16-8 This carpet layer has to make accurate measurements. *Courtesy of C.H. Masland and Sons Carpet Company*

To find the area of a circle, you again use a formula that contains the constant, 3.14, as well as the value of the radius. The formula is written as:

Area (A) = 3.14 × r^2

The r^2 means the radius is squared. In other words, you multiply the radius of the circle by itself before multiplying it by 3.14. The symbol for squaring is a 2 that is placed slightly above and following the number to be squared. For example, the radius of 4 squared (r^2) is 4 × 4 or 16.

204 ■ SECTION 4 Success Skills

Suppose you are going to pour a round concrete pad for a storage tank. To figure the concrete needed, you first must figure the area. The radius of the pad is 8 feet. You would work the problem in the following steps:

Step 1: Set up the equation.
$A = 3.14 \times r^2$

Step 2: Place values into the formula and multiply:
$A = 3.14 \times 8^2$
$A = 3.14 \times 64$
$A = 200.96$ square feet

Volume Measurement

Like perimeters and areas, volume measures are often used on the job. Volume is the amount of space an object takes up. It can be expressed in units of cubic measure such as cubic inches, cubic yards, and cubic feet. It can also be given in units such as gallons, quarts, ounces, and bushels.

To figure the volume of a figure that contains all right angles, such as a rectangle or square, the formula is:

Volume = length × width × height or $V = l \times w \times h$

FIGURE 16-9 Concrete, sand, gravel, and some other construction materials are sold by the cubic yard. *Courtesy of GE, photo by Mark Homan Studios*

24. Only the three most common area measurements are dealt with here (rectangle, square, and circle). Figure other types of area measurements at your discretion.

25. Finding the *volume,* or capacity of something, often requires making three measurements.

26. Volume measures are sometimes described in terms of how they are used, such as "dry" measures or "wet" measures. Ask students to provide examples.

27. For a square box (i.e., cube), the formula is simply $V = s^3$.
28. Only the volume of rectangular objects is dealt with here. Figure other types of volume at your discretion.

So, for example, to find the volume of a rectangular box that is 4-feet long, 2-feet wide, and 1-foot high, you multiply $4 \times 2 \times 1$, which equals 8 cubic feet.

If the dimensions are in different units, they have to be converted to the same unit of measurement before multiplying. Let's say that you are going to lay a 6-inch gravel base in a ditch before installing a sewer pipe. The ditch is 30-inches wide and 150-feet long.

Step 1: Set up the equation:
$V = l \times w \times h$

Step 2: Place values into the formula:
V = 150 feet × 30 inches × 6 inches

Step 3: Convert all measures to the same units. In this case use feet.
V = 150 feet × 2.5 feet × 0.5 foot

Step 4: Multiply:
V = 187.5 cubic feet

You would need 187.5 cubic feet of gravel. However, since gravel is usually sold by the cubic yard, you need to divide 187.5 by 9 (one cubic yard contains 9 cubic feet). How many yards of gravel would you need?

What Would You Do?

You have just finished preparing the site for pouring a concrete patio. You overhear the boss saying that the job will probably require about 10 yards of concrete. That doesn't sound right to you. So you make a quick calculation. You come up with 12 yards. You want to tell the boss he is wrong, but you are not sure how he will react. What would you do?

SYSTEMS OF MEASURE

To be effective on the job, you should be able to work with the basic units of measure in the conventional (or English) and metric systems. You should be familiar with procedures for converting measures from one unit to another within the same system. You also need to be able to convert measures from the conventional system to the metric system and vice versa.

You are probably most familiar with the conventional system of measure. It is the one used most often in the United States. Conventional units of measure and their relationship to each other are shown in Figure 16-10.

Conventional System Units of Measure

Linear Units
1 foot = 12 inches
1 yard = 3 feet or 36 inches
1 mile = 5,280 feet or 1,760 yards

Weight Units
1 pound = 16 ounces
2,000 pounds = 1 ton
1 pint = 1 pound

Area Units
1 square foot = 144 square inches
1 square yard = 9 square feet
1 square mile = 3,097,600 square yards

Time Units
1 minute = 60 seconds
1 hour = 60 minutes
1 day = 24 hours

Volume Units
1 gallon = 231 cubic inches
1 cubic foot = 7 1/2 gallons
1 cubic foot (water) = 62 1/2 pounds
1 gallon (water) = 8 1/3 pounds
1 bushel (struck) = 2,150.5 cubic inches
1 bushel (heaped) = 2,747.7 cubic inches
1 cubic foot = 1,728 cubic inches
1 cubic yard = 27 cubic feet

FIGURE 16-10 Conventional System units of measure

29. You would need 20.83 (rounded off to 21) yards of gravel.
30. Ask how many students have to perform tasks involving converting measures from one unit to another.

* *WWYD Feature B.* The person should politely call the error to the boss' attention. He probably would appreciate it.

Within the same unit or type of conventional measure, conversion to equivalent measures usually involves division or multiplication. For example, to find the number of cubic feet required to hold 20 gallons of water, you would divide the 20 gallons by the conversion equivalent of 7.5 gallons per cubic foot:

$20 \div 7.5 = 3.67$ cubic feet

To find the number of square feet in 20 square yards, you would multiply 20 yards by the 9 square feet per yard:

$20 \times 9 = 180$ square feet

Most of the world, except for the United States, uses the metric system of measure. However, Congress passed a trade bill in 1988 that requires all federal agencies to convert to the metric system by 1992. This means, for example, that if the Justice Department wants to buy paper, it must be measured in centimeters, not inches. If the Department of Defense wants to buy gasoline, it must do so in liters, not gallons.

This law won't force private companies to convert to the metric system. It seems likely, however, that it will encourage them to do so. Currently, some occupations and industries use the metric system a lot. The fields of medicine, engineering, and science are examples. Metric system units of measure are shown in Figure 16-11.

31. Ask students why they think the requirement to convert to the metric system was included in the 1988 trade bill. (To facilitate international trade and to make the U.S. more economically competitive.)

Conversions between and across units of measure in the metric system are in whole numbers and are divisible by 10. This is a major advantage over the conventional system of measure. For example, each centimeter is simply 10 millimeters and 20 cubic centimeters is equal to 20 milliliters. To find how many meters there are in 86.2 kilometers, you only have to multiply by 1,000:

86.2 kilometers $\times$ 1,000 = 86,200 meters

There are times on the job when you will work with both conventional and metric units of measure. It often becomes necessary to convert measurements from one system to another. To do so, you can use the conversion chart shown in Figure 16-12.

Let's say that you want to express 30 square feet in terms of square meters. Since 1 square foot is about 0.09 square meter, you must multiply the number of square feet by 0.09:

$30 \text{ ft}^2 \times 0.09 = 2.70 \text{ m}^2$

The conversion chart is very useful to make quick and easy conversions from metric to conventional and from conventional to metric. However, keep in mind that the converted values will be only *approximate*. If greater accuracy is needed you should consult a table that has the conversion values listed to three decimal points.

32. Conversion from metric to conventional, and vice versa, takes time and costs a company money. This is a good illustration of why the metric provision was included in the 1988 trade law.

Metric System Units of Measure

Linear Units
1 millimeter (mm) = 0.001 meter
1 centimeter (cm) = 0.01 meter
1 decimeter = 0.1 meter
1 meter = 10 decimeters, 100 centimeters, 1,000 millimeters
1 kilometer = 1,000 meters

Weight Units
1 milligram = 0.001 gram
1 centigram = 0.01 gram
1 decigram = 0.01 gram
1 gram = 1,000 milligrams, 100 centigrams, 10 decigrams
1 kilogram = 1,000 grams

Area Units
1 square centimeter = 100 square millimeters
1 square meter = 10,000 square centimeters
1 square kiliometer = 1,000,000 square meters

Volume Units
1 milliliter = 1 cubic centimeter
1 milliliter = 0.001 liter
1 centiliter = 0.01 liter
1 deciliter = 0.01 liter
1 liter = 1,000 milliliters, 100 centiliters, 10 deciliters
1 kiloliter = 1,000 liters

FIGURE 16-11 Metric system units of measure

CHAPTER 16 Math and Measurement Skills ■ 207

FROM METRIC TO CONVENTIONAL

Symbol	When You Know	Multiply by	To Find	Symbol
LENGTH				
mm	millimeters	0.04	inches	in
cm	centimeters	0.4	inches	in
m	meters	3.3	feet	ft
m	meters	1.1	yards	yd
km	kilometers	0.6	miles	mi
AREA				
cm²	square centimeters	0.16	square inches	in²
m²	square meters	1.2	square yards	yd²
km²	square kilometers	0.4	square miles	mi²
ha	hectares (10,000 m²)	2.5	acres	
MASS (weight)				
g	grams	0.035	ounces	oz
kg	kilograms	2.2	pounds	lb
t	tonnes (1,000 kg)	1.1	short tons	
VOLUME				
ml	milliliters	0.03	fluid ounces	fl oz
l	liters	2.1	pints	pt
l	liters	1.06	quarts	qt
l	liters	0.26	gallons	gal
m³	cubic meters	35	cubic feet	ft³
m³	cubic meters	1.3	cubic yards	yd³
TEMPERATURE (exact)				
°C	Celsius temperature	9/5 (then add 32)	Fahrenheit temperature	°F

FROM CONVENTIONAL TO METRIC

Symbol	When You Know	Multiply by	To Find	Symbol
in	inches	2.5	centimeters	cm
ft	feet	30	centimeters	cm
yd	yards	0.9	meters	m
mi	miles	1.6	kilometers	km
AREA				
in²	square inches	6.5	square centimeters	cm²
ft²	square feet	0.09	square meters	m²
yd²	square yards	0.8	square meters	m²
mi²	square miles	2.6	square kilometers	km²
	acres	0.4	hectares	ha
MASS (weight)				
oz	ounces	28	grams	g
lb	pounds	0.45	kilograms	kg
	short tons (2,000 lb)	0.9	tonnes	t
VOLUME				
tsp	teaspoons	5	milliliters	ml
Tbsp	tablespoons	15	milliliters	ml
fl oz	fluid ounces	30	milliliters	ml
c	cups	0.24	liters	l
pt	pints	0.47	liters	l
qt	quarts	0.95	liters	l
gal	gallons	3.8	liters	l
ft³	cubic feet	0.03	cubic meters	m³
yd²	cubic yards	0.76	cubic meters	m²
TEMPERATURE (exact)				
°F	Fahrenheit temperature	5/9 (after subtracting 32)	Celsius temperature	°C

FIGURE 16-12 Approximate conversion charts

CHAPTER REVIEW

Chapter in Brief

- Basic math and measurement skills are used by many workers. One type of math skill is often called "business math." This involves being able to figure: (a) total purchase amount, (b) trade discount, (c) cash discount, (d) markup, (e) sales tax, and (f) markdown.
- Basic measurement skills are often called "shop math." This involves being able to perform surface measurement (perimeter and area) and volume measurement.
- Most countries, except for the U.S., use the metric system of measure. Even so, some occupational fields use the metric system a lot.
- You should be familiar with procedures for converting measures from one unit to another within the same system. You also need to be able to convert measures from the conventional system to the metric system and vice versa.

Words to Know

area the number of square units of space on the surface of a figure enclosed by the perimeter.

cash discount a discount of several percent offered to the buyer to encourage early payment on an account.

circumference the perimeter of a circle.

invoice a bill for goods; an itemized statement of merchandise sent to a purchaser.

markdown a reduction in the selling price of a product.

markup an amount added by a retailer to the cost price of goods that allows it to cover expenses and make a fair profit.

measurement the act of determining the dimension, quantity, or degree of something.

perimeter the distance around the outside of an object.

terms terms of sale; the time limit within which the buyer must pay for merchandise received from the seller.

trade discount a deduction from the catalog (list) price of an item.

Questions to Answer

1. Calculating such things as total purchase amount, trade discount, markup, and sales tax is often called "business math." Why is it called this?
2. How does a cash discount benefit a buyer? How does it benefit a seller?
3. A contractor is billed $1,850 for lumber with a cash discount of 5% offered for payment within 10 days. How much money would be saved by paying immediately?
4. What is the difference between the cost price and the selling price of a product?
5. What is the selling price of a dress that costs $60 and is marked up 40%? Later, the dress is put on sale at a markdown of 25%. What is the sale price of the dress?
6. Why are uniform and standardized measures necessary in business and industry?

---

1. Because this is the type of math used most frequently in business operations and transactions.
2. By paying early, the buyer saves money. The seller benefits by having the cash use for other transactions.
3. $92.50
4. Markup.
5. Selling price—$84.00; sale price—$63.00
6. Without uniform and standard measures, the economic activities of production and consumption would be in a state of chaos. For example, consider the problem for consumers if service stations sold gasoline in different size "gallons."

7. How many 4 foot × 8 foot sheets of plywood are needed to cover a 16 foot × 32 foot roof?
8. How many cubic feet of storage space is contained in a warehouse that is 40 yards long and 15 yards wide and has 12-foot ceilings?
9. Name the two common systems of measure. Which system is used by most countries in the world?
10. The temperature is 78 degrees Farenheit. How many degrees Celsius is this?

Activities to Do

1. For your co-op or work experience job, list all the ways that you use math and measurement skills. Then, in class, compare your list with other students. What skills does the class find are the most common?
2. For the classroom in which you are meeting, perform the necessary measurements and calculations to answer the following questions.
   a. What is the perimeter of the classroom?
   b. How much area of floor space is contained within the classroom?
   c. How much area of wall space is taken up by window and door openings?
   d. How much volume is contained within the classroom?
   e. Identify a circular-shaped object in the classroom such as a wastebasket. What is the circumference of it?
3. Identify as many occupations as possible that might make the types of calculations performed in Activity 2.
4. How many kilometers do you travel to work each day? What is the average distance for the entire class?
5. To find the average of a set of numbers, you can add them on a calculator and divide by the total number. For example:

   $(140 + 145 + 146 + 149 + 144 + 146) \div 6 = 145$

   The average is 145. Another way to find the average is to pick a "benchmark" number less than or equal to the smallest number. In the preceding example, 140 is the benchmark. Now, add the difference between each number and the benchmark. Then find the average of the difference.

   $(0 + 5 + 6 + 9 + 4 + 6) \div 6 = 5$

   The average difference is 5. Add this to the benchmark and you get 145. This shortcut can save you a lot of time. Often, you can add the numbers in your head without using a calculator. Using benchmarks, find the averages of the following numbers:

   a. Prices of $200, $220, $210, $215, and $230.
   b. Lengths of 47 inches, 46 inches, 51 inches, 45 inches, 52 inches, 46 inches, and 49 inches.
   c. Temperatures of 80, 72, 75, 74, 73, 77, 81, and 76.

---

7. 16 sheets.
8. 64,800 cubic feet
9. (a) Conventional (or English) and metric. (b) Metric is most used.
10. 26 (25.5) degrees Celsius.

33. The common skills will likely vary from class to class depending upon the nature of students' jobs.
34. The intent here is simply to have students apply measurement skills. Expand or limit this exercise as you see fit.
35. (a) Benchmark is 200; average difference is 15. (b) Benchmark is 45; average difference is 3. (c) Benchmark is 72; average difference is 4.

Topics to Discuss

1. Calculators, computers, cash registers, and other machines automaticlaly perform many math calculations on the job. This being the case, how important is it that you be able to perform math by hand?
2. Should the United States convert to the metric system? Discuss the advantages and disadvantages.
3. In "rough carpentry" work, measurements within 1/4 inch are considered "accurate." Other jobs, such as installing cabinets, require more accurate measurement. Discuss and give examples of how standareds of accuracy in measurement vary among different occupations.
4. How much is the sales tax in your state? What types of goods and services does it cover?

36. Some type of calculating machine is used most of the time. But there will always be occasions when it must be done by hand. Perhaps students can provide examples.
37. The major disadvantages are the cost, training required, and the inconvenience involved in converting. The major advantage is compatability with the rest of the world. Advocates say that the metric system is also more logical and easier to learn and use.

CHAPTER SEVENTEEN

Safety Skills

OUTLINE
Accidents
Personal Safety
Public Safety
Chapter Review

OBJECTIVES
After reading this chapter, you should be able to:
- Describe the nature of accidents according to type and class.
- Discuss rules for personal safety in the home, at school, on the job, in recreation, and on the road.
- Explain what to do in a flood, tornado, hurricane, and earthquake.
- Name examples of government agencies and private organizations that promote public safety.
- State the three *E*'s of safety.

Safety experts define an *accident* as an unplanned event often resulting in personal injury, property damage, or both. Accidents rank fourth behind heart disease, cancer, and stroke as a cause of death among the general public. For teenagers and young adults, however, *accidents are the leading cause of death*.

Even though accidents are unexpected, this doesn't mean that they occur by chance. Almost all accidents can be prevented by eliminating unsafe behavior and conditions and by following basic safety rules. In this chapter, you will learn more about accidents and what you can do to prevent them.

1. That accidents are the leading cause of death for teens and young adults is a grim fact. This underscores the importance of the material in this chapter.

Unsafe Conditions
- Lack of proper protective clothing and gear
- Unrealistic/inappropriate production schedules
- Unguarded tools and equipment
- Defective/antiquated tools and equipment
- Poorly layed-out work areas and storage space
- Clutter from poor housekeeping
- Lack of safety training, emphasis, and policy
- Improper lighting, ventilation, and noise control
- Failure to provide supervision
- Failure to heighten safety awareness
- Unnecessary exposure to hazardous substances
- Poor design
- Temperature and humidity extremes

Unsafe Actions
- Removing safety devices
- Using the wrong tools or using defective tools
- Using tools/equipment without authority or training
- Following improper work procedures
- Failure to spot, report, and remove hazards
- Failure to provide, attend to, or adhere to supervision
- Distractions/inattention while working
- Rushing to complete job...or using equipment at improper speed
- Failure to take safety seriously
- Fatigue
- Attempts to repair equipment while it is in use
- Failure to observe rules for lifting, fire safety, materials handling, and so forth
- Wearing improper clothing

(Source: *Basic Safety I: Apprentice Related Training Module.* Raleigh, North Carolina: CONSERVA, Inc., 1982, page 11.)

FIGURE 17-1 Sample unsafe conditions and actions. Note that each problem has a human cause and that each is correctable.

211

ACCIDENTS

In an average year, accidents kill nearly 94,000 Americans and injure about 9 million more. Accidents and injuries are estimated to cost the nation about $118 billion annually. There is no way to calculate the cost of human lives. Data on accidents are reported by type and class.

Type of accidents refers to the cause of accidents. The leading causes of accidental death in the U.S. are shown in Figure 17-2. For people under seventy-five, motor vehicles lead as a cause of accidental death. For young people between fifteen and twenty-four, about two-thirds of accidental deaths are caused by motor vehicles.

Types of Accidents	Number of Deaths
Motor vehicle	47,900
Falls	11,000
Drowning	5,600
Poisoning	4,900
Fires	4,800
Choking	3,600
Firearms	1,800
All other types	14,400
Total	94,000

FIGURE 17-2 Major causes of accidental death in the United States *Courtesy of National Safety Council. Accident Facts, 1987 Edition*

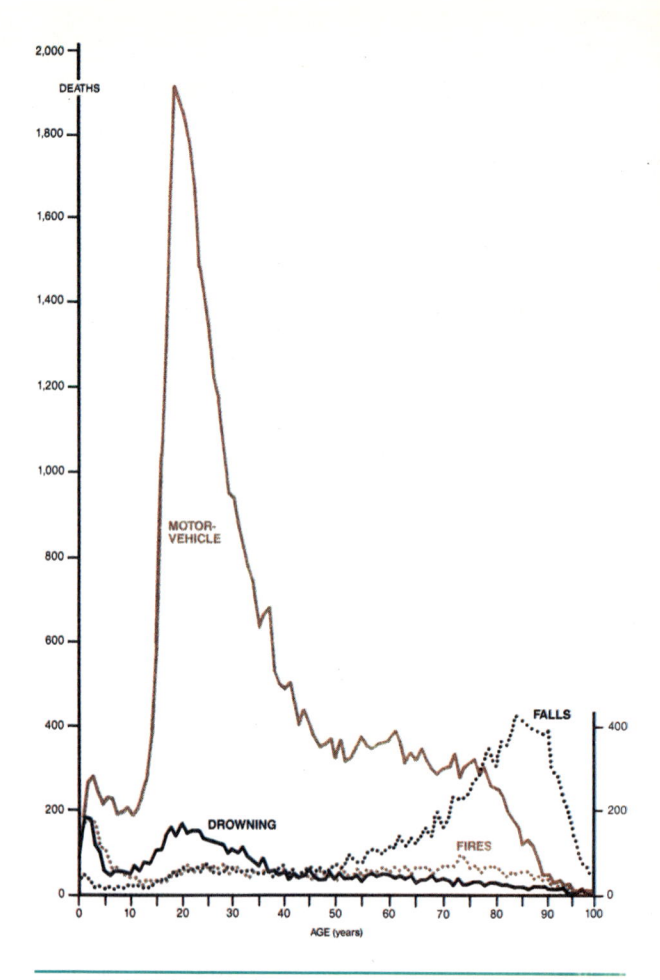

FIGURE 17-3 Leading causes of accidental death by age *Courtesy of National Safety Council. Accident Facts, 1987 Edition*

The second-highest cause of accidental death varies in different age groups. Up to forty-four years, it is drownings; forty-five to seventy-four years, falls. For people over seventy-five, falls are the leading cause of accidental death, followed by motor vehicle accidents.

Class of accidents refers to where the accident occurs. More accidents take place on roads and highways (motor vehicles, bicycles, and pedestrian accidents) than any other class. Home accidents are second, followed by accidents in public places. Accidents at work trail far behind. Over the last fifty years, accidental deaths at home, in public places, and at work have declined significantly. The accidental death rate on roads and highways, however, has increased steadily.

2. The source is entitled *Accident Facts* by the National Safety Council. Order a copy by writing Customer Service, National Safety Council, 444 N. Michigan Ave., Chicago, IL 60611.

3. Make sure students understand the difference between *type* (cause, kind) and *class* (location) of accident.

PERSONAL SAFETY

Safety is freedom from harm or the danger of harm. The word *safety* also refers to the precautions taken to prevent accidents. In this section, you will examine some of the things to do and avoid in order to prevent accidents at home, school, on the job, and elsewhere.

In the Home

You probably consider your home a safe place. But about one-fourth of all accidental deaths and about one-third of all disabling injuries occur in and around the home. This translates into one death every twenty-six minutes and one disabling injury every ten seconds. A *disabling injury* is one causing death, permanent disability, or any degree of

4. It is somewhat strange to call both a temporary total disability and one causing death a *disabling injury*. However, the National Safety Council defines the term this way.

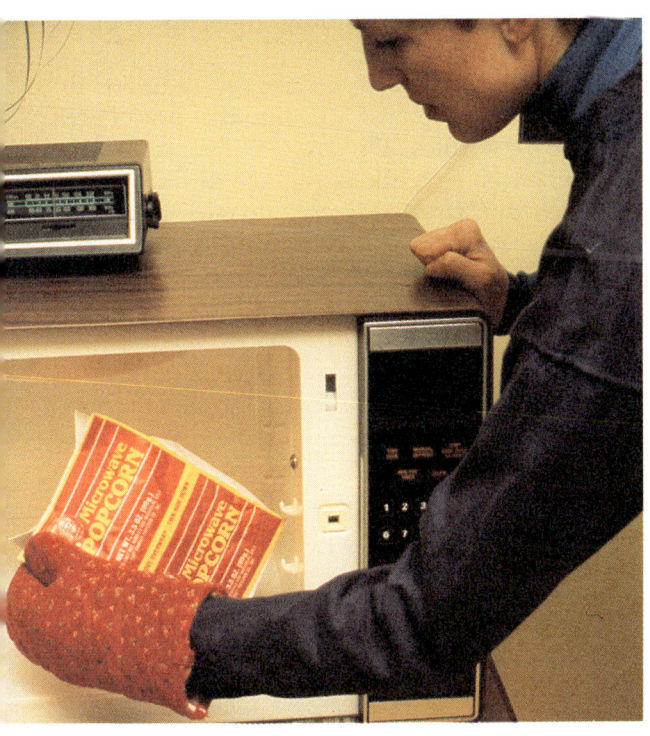

5. Ask students if they have ever had an accident because of poor housekeeping.

CHAPTER 17 Safety Skills ■ 213

FIGURE 17-4 Microwave ovens create tremendous internal temperatures in foods. Be cautious of escaping steam when opening microwave popcorn and other packaged foods. *Photo by Paul E. Meyers*

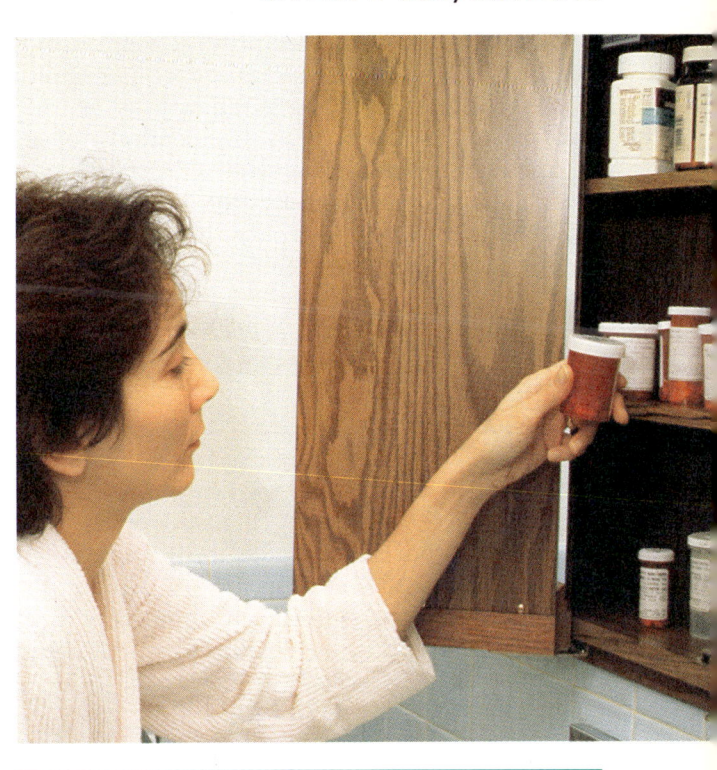

FIGURE 17-5 Never use old or unlabeled medicine or take another person's medicine. *Photo by Paul E. Meyers*

temporary total disability beyond the day of the accident. In addition, millions of people suffer minor (but painful) cuts, burns, and bruises.

Good housekeeping is one of the most important safety defenses. Keep everything in its proper place. Do not leave shoes, toys, books, or other objects on floors and stairs where someone could trip over them. Put kitchen knives and utensils, tools, and household cleaners away immediately after you have used them.

In many homes, the kitchen is the busiest and most dangerous room. Climbing and reaching cause many accidents. Use a ladder or a firm chair to reach objects in high places. Store appliances and other heavy objects on low shelves. Turn pot handles toward the back of the range to avoid burns and scalds. To prevent cuts, keep kitchen knives in a rack, not loose in a drawer. Kitchens often have types of floor coverings that can become very slick when wet. Immediately wipe up water, grease, or anything else spilled on the floor.

Falls are also one of the worst dangers in the bathroom. Install nonslip strips in the tub or shower and provide handrails to prevent falls while bathing.

6. Lawn mowers are now required to have devices that automatically stop the blade whenever the operator's hands are removed from the handle (commercial mowers are exempt).

Water is an excellent conductor of electricity. Dry your hands thoroughly before using a hair dryer, razor, or other electrical appliance. A plugged-in radio could *electrocute* you if it falls into water. Unless radios, TVs, and stereos are battery operated, keep them out of the bathroom.

In the yard, lawn mowers are the cause of many injuries. Wear a shirt, pants, and heavy work shoes when operating a mower. Be alert to anything lying on the ground that might be thrown by running over it. Wear safety goggles when using string-type weed cutters.

At School

State and local laws require schools to meet certain health and safety standards. Beyond these, school officials try to make the environment as safe as possible. They conduct safety programs for students and teachers. Regular drills are conducted to prepare for fire, weather, earthquake, or other types of emergencies. Teachers provide instruction regarding proper safety practices in their particular subjects.

Accidents in school most commonly occur in

7. Look around the classroom. You may see evidence of safety information or safety devices. Identify same.

gyms and on athletic fields, in vocational shops, science labs, and art rooms. It is your responsibility to work with teachers and to follow their instructions in these types of classes. Accidents also occur in corridors, on stairways, and in regular classrooms. Many accidents result from students rushing to get to the next class or to go home. Stay to the right in corridors and on stairs. Don't run, crowd, or shove. In classrooms, keep your feet out of the aisles. Don't throw pens, pencils, or paper clips, which can cause serious eye injuries.

On the Job

Workplace safety has improved greatly over the years. In 1910, about 20,000 workers in the U.S. lost their lives on the job. Today, the workforce is over twice as large, but the accidental death rate is about half. Still, over 10,000 workers are killed and about 1.8 million disabling injuries occur annually while at work. Your safety responsibilities as an employee are:

1. *Learn and Obey Rules.* Supervisors and experienced workers have learned best how to do the job. Listen, observe, and follow their instructions. Always obey rules and regulations for shop or office safety practices.
2. *Consult Procedures.* If you don't know how to do something, stop and consult the procedures manual or rules. Or ask your supervisor or experienced co-workers.
3. *Watch for Hazards.* Many companies depend on employee assistance in identifying safety hazards and in changing safety procedures. Think about what you are doing. As you observe safety hazards or have ideas for improvements, make them known.
4. *Report Accidents and Injuries.* Accident reports are one of the best means of identifying safety hazards that need to be corrected. Participate in accident and injury reporting and investigation. Insurance benefits to the injured person sometimes depend on this.
5. *Become Involved.* Encourage other workers to act and work safely. Try to set a good example for other workers. Volunteer to participate in the shop, department, or company safety committee.
6. *Perform as Trained.* This is your most important responsibility regarding safety. Use the correct tools to perform your tasks. Allow enough time

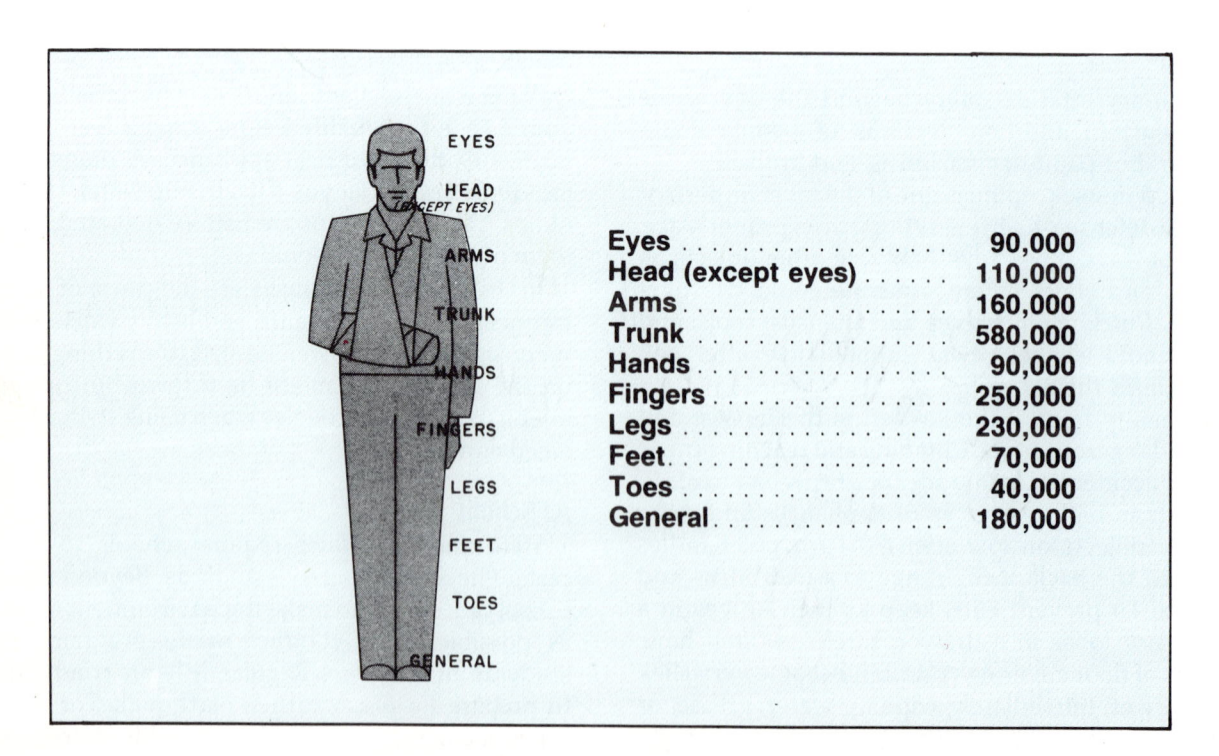

Body Part	Number
Eyes	90,000
Head (except eyes)	110,000
Arms	160,000
Trunk	580,000
Hands	90,000
Fingers	250,000
Legs	230,000
Feet	70,000
Toes	40,000
General	180,000

FIGURE 17-6 Part of body injured in work accident *Courtesy of National Safety Council. Accident Facts, 1987 Edition*

8. Many accidents result from silly pranks and thoughtless acts that are not intended to be harmful.
9. You may wish to assign Activity 1 at this time.
10. Ask students if they can add other responsibilities to this list.

CHAPTER 17 Safety Skills ■ 215

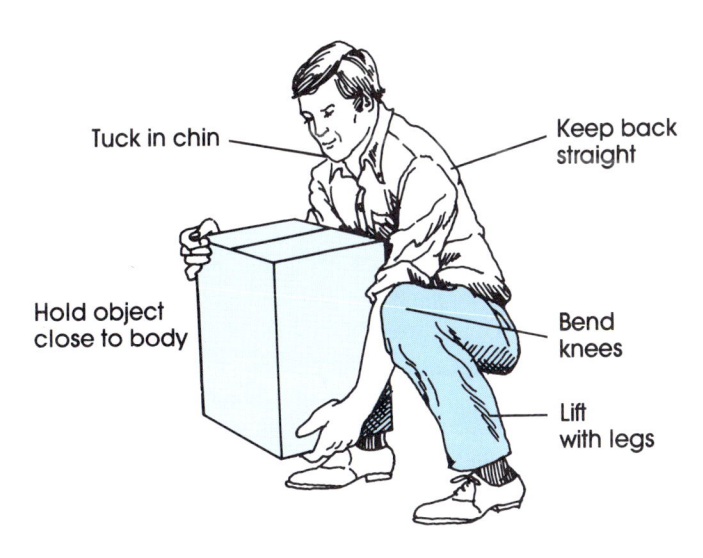

FIGURE 17-7 Safe lifting is an important part of job safety. This shows the proper way to lift a heavy object.

to finish safely. Avoid distractions. Follow operating procedures for using equipment and perform tasks according to training specifications. Do not operate machinery or drive under the influence of alcohol, drugs, or certain medications. Be neat and practice good housekeeping.

What Would You Do?

It is your turn to work the Saturday evening shift. Normally, you don't mind working until 9:00 P.M. Tonight, though, you badly want to see the game. If you hurry, you may be able to see the last half.

At quitting time, you quickly lock the door and start cleaning up. It only takes you a few minutes to wipe off the tables, clean the counter, and empty the trash. By 9:15, you are on your way.

As you arrive at the gym, the image of a coffee pot flashes through your mind. Coffee pot!!! Did you remember to turn off the coffee pot? You think so, but you aren't sure. What would you do?

* *WWYD Feature A.* In matters of safety, extra effort is required. The person should return to work to make sure that the coffee pot is turned off.

In Recreation

Many types of outdoor recreation have some element of hazard. The major causes of accidents are inexperience, overconfidence, and fatigue. General rules for safe recreation include keeping physically fit, learning the basic skills of the particular activity, selecting a safe play area, using proper equipment and dress, avoiding overexertion, and never taking chances. Some activities present special problems.

Drownings are the third major cause of fatal accidents. Anyone who goes in, on, or near the water should learn how to swim. Two important rules to follow are never to swim alone and always be aware of your limitations.

FIGURE 17-8 When people are having fun, they often don't think of safety. *Courtesy of Outboard Marine Corporation*

Boating accidents have become an increasing problem. The chief causes of boating accidents are speeding, poor judgment, and recklessness. Operator fault is a factor in half the boating casualties.

11. Available types of outdoor recreation vary from region to region. Focus on those activities that are unique to your part of the country.

F·E·A·T·U·R·E

Safety-belt Laws Start to Click

♦♦♦

In 1972, Australia became the first nation to require front seat occupants of automobiles to wear safety belts. Since then thirty other nations (including Great Britain, Canada, France, West Germany, Japan, and the U.S.S.R.) have put safety-belt-use laws on the books. The United States is the only industrialized nation in the world that doesn't require its citizens to buckle up.

Even though there is no federal safety-belt law in the United States, many states have passed their own safety-belt laws. The first state law took effect in New York on January 1, 1985. By early 1989, twenty-eight states and the District of Columbia had such legislation. All fifty states require infants and small children to be secured in safety belts while in cars.

The simple reason behind safety-belt laws is that they save lives and help prevent serious injury. In the thirty countries with national safety-belt-use laws, traffic deaths have dropped an average of twenty-five percent. Reductions in serious injuries have been even greater.

For Americans, the benefits of safety-belt-use laws would be substantial. It has been estimated that at least half of the people killed every year would survive by buckling up. The majority of the 1,800,000 disabling injuries could be reduced to scratches, cuts, and bruises. Most of the millions of "minor" traffic injuries could be avoided altogether. Traffic deaths and injuries are costing nearly $120 billion a year in lost wages, medical expenses, insurance costs, and property damage. These costs could be cut sharply through safety belt use.

What more of a reason do you need to wear a safety belt!

FIGURE 17-FEATURE Here is why you should always buckle up when you drive. *Photo courtesy of National Highway Traffic Safety Administration © 1988 U.S. DOT*

Safety-belt Laws Start to Click. Emphasize that the data demonstrate overwhelmingly the value of safety belts. Encourage discussion of this important subject.

Boaters should know the safety limitations of their craft and never exceed the safe speed. The U.S. Coast Guard establishes and enforces boating regulations. A boat operator should learn and follow such regulations.

Rifles, pistols, and shotguns are deadly weapons. Never point a gun at anyone. Guns should be unloaded before cleaning or storing. All firearms should be kept in a locked case or cabinet. Ammunition should be stored away from the firearms in a locked container.

On the Road

Automobiles and roads are built to be safer than ever before. More people are using seat belts. As a result, the death rate has dropped in relation to the number of miles driven. The current rate of less than three deaths per 100 million miles of travel compares with the rate of about seven deaths in 1950. But the actual number of accidents and deaths keeps rising. This is due to the fact that there are more drivers and more autos on the road every year.

The causes of traffic accidents are difficult to determine. A number of things contribute to every accident. Improper driving of some kind is involved in about ninety percent of all accidents. This includes speeding, failure to yield the right-of-way, following too closely, and driving left of the center line. Alcohol is a factor in at least fifty percent of fatal accidents. Unsafe vehicles are a factor in at least ten percent of accidents.

Pamela can't wait for classes to begin next semester. She will be enrolled in driver education. She looks forward to learning how to drive and being able to use the family car. She is wise to take driver education. It is one of the most valuable tools in traffic safety. People who have taken driver education have fewer accidents.

12

You can help prevent auto accidents and injury by following common-sense rules. Use seat belts every time you drive. Follow the speed limit. Adjust your speed to traffic and weather conditions. Be a courteous driver. Stay a safe distance behind other vehicles and signal when you plan to turn or change lanes. Never drive under the influence of drugs or alcohol. Keep your car in good running order.

	Type and Location	No. of Deaths	Date of Disaster
Floods:	Galveston tidal wave	6,000	Sept. 8, 1900
	Johnstown, Pa.	2,209	May 31, 1889
	Ohio and Indiana	732	Mar. 28, 1913
	St. Francis, Calif., dam burst	450	Mar. 13, 1928
	Ohio and Mississippi River valleys	380	Jan. 22, 1937
Hurricanes:	Florida	1,833	Sept. 16-17, 1928
	New England	657	Sept. 21, 1938
	Louisiana	500	Sept. 29, 1915
	Florida	409	Sept. 1-2, 1935
	Louisiana and Texas	395	June 27-28, 1957
Tornadoes:	Illinois	606	Mar. 18, 1925
	Mississippi, Alabama, Georgia	402	Apr. 2-7, 1936
	Southern and Midwestern states	307	Apr. 3, 1974
	Ind., Ohio, Mich., Ill. and Wis.	272	Apr. 11, 1965
	Ark., Tenn., Mo., Miss. and Ala.	229	Mar. 21-22, 1952
Earth-quakes:	San Francisco earthquake and fire	452	Apr. 18, 1906
	Alaskan earthquake-tsunami hit Hawaii, Calif.	173	Apr. 1, 1946
	Long Beach, Calif., earthquake	120	Mar. 10, 1933
	Alaskan earthquake and tsunami	117	Mar. 27, 1964
	San Fernando-Los Angeles, Calif., earthquake	64	Feb. 9, 1971

Source: World Almanac, National Transportation Safety Board, National Weather Service, National Fire Protection Association, Chicago Historical Society, American Red Cross, U.S. Bureau of Mines, National Oceanic and Atmospheric Administration, and city and state Boards of Health.

FIGURE 17-9 Largest U.S. disasters. Why have there been fewer deaths in recent years during such disasters? *Courtesy of National Safety Council. Accident Facts, 1987 Edition*

12. People who get good grades also have fewer accidents. Ask students why (good students tend to exercise better judgment and to be more conscientious, knowledgeable, and alert).

218 ■ SECTION 4 Success Skills

What Would You Do?

You have had a great time at the picnic. The weather was good and the food was delicious. You enjoyed seeing your old friends. It is now time to hop in the car for the long drive home.

About half-way back to the city, the sky starts to darken. The wind begins to blow, and you see lightning in the distance. After a few more miles, the first drops of rain hit the windshield. The rain is soon coming down in torrents. It is only 4:30, but it is so dark that you have to turn on the headlights. The windshield wipers are going full-speed. Even so, you can barely see the center line. You wonder what would happen if you had to stop suddenly. You would like to pull off the highway, but are not very familiar with the road. What would you do?

*WWYD Feature B. The best thing to do would probably be to proceed with caution until a safe place is found to turn off and wait out the storm.

Emergency Situations

Many accidents and deaths result from natural disasters. Such tragedies often strike suddenly. You can lessen the risks, however, if you know what to do during a flood, tornado, hurricane, or earthquake. Some safety rules apply to all natural disasters.

Flood conditions typically build up over hours and days. Leave a flood area as soon as a warning is announced. Don't be caught in a low-lying area. After returning from a flood, have electrical wiring and appliances checked before using them. Boil drinking water until health officials say that the water supply is safe.

Tornados occur most frequently in late spring and early summer. Be alert to threatening weather during these periods. If you hear a warning or see a tornado coming, go to a basement or inside room without windows. If you can't move to another room, get under a heavy table or lie flat on the floor. If you are in a car, don't try to outrun the tornado. Get out of the car and lie in a ditch.

Hurricane forecasting has improved tremendously in recent years. Weather bureaus work closely with local radio and TV stations to broadcast information about hurricanes and other weather-related problems. After learning of a hurricane warning, keep your radio or TV on for further information. Follow the instructions of local officials regarding what to do. After the storm, avoid loose electrical power lines and report them immediately to the power company.

Earthquakes are the most sudden of any natural disaster. In an earthquake, you must react within seconds to the danger. If you are indoors, take cover under a table or desk. If you are outside, move away from buildings or other structures where you might be struck by falling objects. If you are in a car, stop immediately in a safe area and stay in the car.

PUBLIC SAFETY

Safety is everyone's business. The role of employers was explained in Chapter 8. In this chapter, you have learned about the individual's safety responsibilities. In the following section, you will learn what government agencies and private organizations do in working for public safety.

FIGURE 17-10 Street and sidewalk maintenance is a simple example of safety activities by local governments. *Courtesy of Martin Marietta Corporation*

13. Again, types of natural disasters vary from region to region. Ask students to share any relevant experiences involving natural disasters.

14. Call attention to Figure 17-9 regarding the largest U.S. disasters. In recent decades improved forecasting and early warning systems have helped to prevent many deaths and injuries.

Public safety refers to all efforts by federal, state, and local governments to protect persons and property. These include legislation, such as traffic ordinances and building codes, and regulatory activities, such as control of air pollution. Police and fire protection services are examples of public safety. The schools and public transportation systems also play important safety roles. For instance, if you have flown in a commercial airliner, you know that the flight attendants provide safety instruction before each departure.

Government Agencies

Many agencies of the United States government are devoted to safety. Following are several examples. The Consumer Product Safety Commission protects consumers from unsafe household goods. The National Transportation Safety Board works to ensure the safety of all types of transportation. The Federal Aviation Administration creates and enforces air safety regulations. Safety in motor vehicles is the responsibility of the National Highway Traffic Safety Administration. Earlier in Chapter 8, you learned how the Occupational Safety and Health Administration works to reduce hazardous job conditions. Most state, county, and city governments also have departments concerned with safety and health.

Private Organizations

A number of nonprofit, private organizations engage in activities to promote personal and public safety. Following are the most common. The National Safety Council collects and distributes information on every aspect of accident prevention. It publishes the *National Safety News* and other magazines; issues pamphlets, bulletins, and posters; and aids in developing community safety programs. The American Red Cross conducts instructions in first aid and in water safety. It also issues safety information. Underwriters Laboratories tests and certifies electrical appliances, automobile and boat safety equipment, and burglar and fire alarms.

The Three *E*'s of Safety

The three *E*'s of safety are engineering, education, and enforcement. Proper *engineering* of buildings, highways, machines, and appliances eliminates many accident hazards. Through *education*, people can be made aware of the accident problem and the ways to prevent them. *Enforcement* of safety rules prevents many accidents. The three *E*'s of safety require expenditures of time and money. But these are small compared with the savings in human suffering, compensation costs, medical expenses, and lost time.

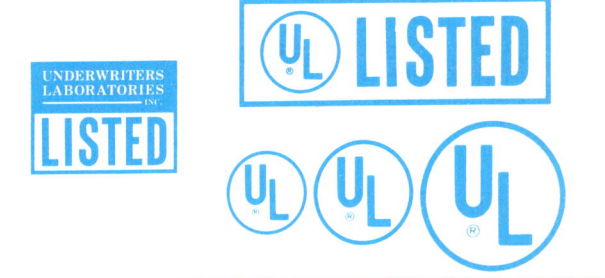

FIGURE 17-11 A *UL* seal on a product means that it has been checked for safety from fire, electric shock, and other hazards. *Courtesy of Underwriters Laboratories*

15. You may wish to assign Activity 5 at this time.

CHAPTER REVIEW

Chapter in Brief

- An accident is an unplanned event. Accidents are the leading cause of death for teenagers and young adults. Almost all accidents can be prevented by eliminating unsafe behavior and conditions and by following basic safety rules.
- Accidents are reported by type and class. The leading type (cause) of accidental death is motor vehicles. More accidents take place on roads and highways than any other class (location).
- Safety refers to the precautions you take to prevent accidents. Know and practice rules for personal safety in the home, at school, on the job, in recreation, and on the road.
- Natural disasters often strike suddenly. You can lessen the risks if you know what to do during a flood, tornado, hurricane, and earthquake. Some safety rules apply to all natural disasters.
- Safety is everyone's business. Individuals and employers have a major responsibility for personal safety. Many agencies of the federal government and a number of private organizations are devoted to public and personal safety.
- The three *E's* of safety are engineering, education, and enforcement. The costs of safety are small compared with the savings in human suffering, compensation costs, medical expenses, and lost time.

Words to Know

accident an unplanned event often resulting in personal injury, property damage, or both.

disabling injury an injury causing death, permanent disability, or any degree of temporary total disability beyond the day of the accident.

electrocute to cause death by electric shock.

natural disaster an uncontrollable event in nature that destroys life or property.

public safety all efforts by federal, state, and local governments to protect persons and property.

safety freedom from harm or the danger of harm.

Questions to Answer

1. What is the leading cause of death among teenagers and young adults?
2. What is the leading type (cause) of accidental death in the United States? Where (class) do most accidents occur?
3. Give three examples of how good housekeeping helps prevent home accidents.
4. What is the most important thing you can do on the job regarding safety?
5. Name the major causes of outdoor recreation accidents.
6. The number of accidents and deaths on the road has increased despite safer autos and roads. Why?
7. What types of improper driving practices cause auto accidents?
8. How do natural disasters differ from other types of accidents?

1. Accidents generally; motor vehicle accidents specifically.
2. Leading *type* (cause) of death is by motor vehicle; leading *class* (where) of death is on roads and highways.
3. Many examples could be cited. For instance, keeping everything in its proper place.
4. Perform as trained.
5. Inexperience, overconfidence, and fatigue.
6. There are simply more drivers and more autos on the road every year.
7. Speeding, failure to yield the right-of-way, following too closely, and driving left of the center line.
8. Because they occur in nature, they cannot be prevented.

9. Give two examples of government public safety efforts.
10. What are the three *E's* of safety?

Activities to Do

1. The instructor will divide the class into small groups. Each group will be assigned the responsibility of preparing a bulletin board display on workplace safety. The display should be changed periodically until each group has completed its assignment.
2. Assume that you are at a party where some of the people have been drinking. The driver of your car has had too much to drink, but he insists on driving home. Do you allow him to do so? Do you ride with him? Role play this situation in which one person is the driver and the rest of the class are people at the party.
3. Have you heard of the organization called Students Against Drunk Driving (SADD)? Perhaps you have a chapter in your school or community. Invite a representative of SADD to the class to explain about the organization. Your class might take the lead in getting a chapter started in your school, if you don't already have one.
4. Assume that a cook trainee badly cut her hand in the kitchen. She had to be taken to the emergency room for stitches. Try to estimate the total cost of this accident. Remember to include lost wages of the injured person and the driver, medical bills, lost productivity, and anything else you can think of.
5. Many government agencies and private organizations work in the field of personal and public safety. Select one of the organizations below, read about it in an encyclopedia or other source, and prepare a short written report.
   - National Transportation Safety Board
   - Federal Aviation Administration
   - National Highway Traffic Safety Administration
   - Consumer Product Safety Commission
   - Occupational Safety and Health Administration
   - United States Fire Administration
   - Nuclear Regulatory Commission
   - U.S. Coast Guard
   - Federal Railroad Administration
   - U.S. Forest Service
   - Mine Safety and Health Administration
   - National Bureau of Standards
   - National Safety Council
   - American Red Cross
   - National Fire Protection Association
   - Underwriters Laboratories
   - American Association of Automotive Medicine
   - Insurance Institute for Highway Safety
   - American Industrial Hygiene Association
   - American Society of Safety Engineers

9. Two common ones are: (a) traffic ordinances, and (b) police protection. Other examples could be cited.
10. (a) Engineering. (b) Education. (c) Enforcement.

16. Also related to controlling alcohol use, some schools organize special activities for prom night and graduation. How do students feel about such activities?
17. The actual figures are less important than promoting awareness of the overall costs of accidents.

Topics to Discuss

1. You probably were not aware of the large number of safety agencies and organizations shown in the preceding list. Why do you think so many different groups are working to improve personal and public safety?
2. Discuss all of the things your employer does to promote safety. Name as many things as you can. All class members should contribute. Your instructor may ask you to bring in copies of safety manuals or other printed material provided by the employer.
3. Think of an accident you had at home, school, work, or in recreation. What was the cause? Discuss how the accident might have been avoided.
4. Why do you think that the U.S. is the only industrialized country in the world that doesn't have a national safety-belt law?

18. Because accidents touch so many people and because safety is everyone's concern.
19. It is more difficult to arrive at a consensus in a diverse, pluralistic democracy like the U.S.

1. Begin this chapter by asking students to identify people they consider to be leaders. Raise the question of whether leadership is different from celebrity, office, status, and wealth.

2. Leadership is also different from management, which is defined as "planning, organizing, staffing, directing, and controlling." Differentiate between "leaders" and "managers."

CHAPTER EIGHTEEN

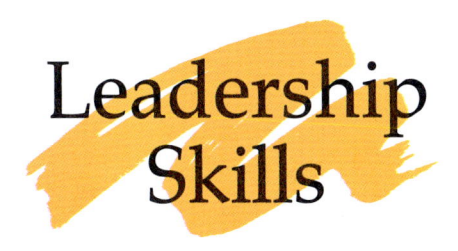

Leadership Skills

OUTLINE
Organizational Leadership
Vocational Student Organizations
Parliamentary Procedure
Chapter Review

OBJECTIVES
After reading this chapter, you should be able to:
- Define what is meant by leadership.
- Name and illustrate six types of leadership behaviors.
- Explain the purposes of a vocational student organization.
- Identify types of vocational student organizations.
- Demonstrate knowledge of parliamentary procedure.

FIGURE 18-1 Being a famous celebrity doesn't necessarily mean one is a leader. *Photo courtesy of The National Broadcasting Company, Inc.*

When you hear the word *leadership,* what do you think of? Many people think of a particular person, such as a high government official, a sports figure, a person of wealth, or a prominent celebrity. This view equates leadership with status, wealth, office, and celebrity. But are all such people leaders? Of course not. In this chapter, a different view of leadership is provided.

ORGANIZATIONAL LEADERSHIP
Dozens of books have been written on the subject of leadership. One book indicates that more than 350 definitions of leadership exist. We focus here on only one part of leadership. That is leadership within an organization.

Organizations are oriented toward achieving certain goals. An insurance company, for example, exists to sell insurance, meet needs of customers, and make a profit. This goal orientation is important for our definition of leadership. *Leadership* is the process of influencing people so as to accomplish the goals of the organization.

A number of writers have described the characteristics of effective leaders. John Zenger, president of a leadership training firm, identifies six types of leadership skills. They are summarized in the following paragraphs.[1] These represent actions and behaviors that most leaders seem to share in common. As you read them, however, keep in mind that a given leader might not be strong in all of them. Also, be aware that leaders may exhibit these characteristics in different ways.

[1] Zenger, J.H. "Leadership: Management's Better Half," *Training,* December 1985, pp. 44-53.

223

Leaders Are Good Communicators

Leaders enjoy communicating and use every opportunity to convey their message. A leader's message often has to be repeated again and again. Leaders are effective in large meetings or in one-on-one discussions. Some rely on written or other forms of communication. For instance, using models or drawings to get a point across. Leaders view information as something to be shared, not to be hoarded. They use interaction with others to gather and give information.

A leader is not always the person in charge of a meeting or an organization. You can often identify the leader of a group by the way he or she communicates: Who is most persuasive? Who speaks with knowledge and authority? Who is able to express what others have been trying to say? Who do others really listen to? Who talks last on the subject?

> 3. If one unit or department in an organization stands out—look for an effective leader. A department head or supervisor is often doing something different from other managers.

FIGURE 18-2 Leadership often arises from members within an organization. *Courtesy of Muhlenberg Co. AVEC KY HOSA*

Not all leaders are naturally gifted communicators. Lincoln and Gandhi were basically shy people. Deep beliefs about their missions drove them into the limelight. Lincoln and Gandhi gained the skill of communicating through self-discipline. They never shied away from communicating their vision and beliefs.

> 4. Strong beliefs and convictions often result in leaders overcoming their own shyness or preference for anonymity to take bold action.

> 5. An example of how leaders encourage others is John Kennedy's famous statement—"Ask not what your country can do for you; ask what you can do for your country."

Leaders Develop Committed Followers

The best leaders recognize that they can't do everything themselves. Leaders involve others. They ask for advice, information, and solutions to problems. Once given, they provide positive feedback. They help make the people in the organization feel responsible for what happens.

By involving people, leaders encourage them to be self-reliant and to practice self-management. An example of this is the use of task groups that was discussed in Chapter 9. Leaders understand the power of groups and what groups can accomplish. They meet frequently with their groups to encourage them and create a strong team spirit.

Leaders recognize that people are more productive if you help them to advance. Leaders share credit with their associates. Good work is praised and rewarded. Leaders foster and thrive on the success of others.

> 6. This characteristic of leadership is also found in outstanding teachers. High accomplishment, however, is resisted by some students and employees. This results in leaders often being disliked.

FIGURE 18-3 Leaders prepare and run effective meetings. *Courtesy of Muhlenberg Co. AVEC KY HOSA*

Leaders Inspire High Accomplishments

Leaders are not satisfied with "average" and won't tolerate poor workmanship or shoddy performance. They challenge people to stretch and reach new heights. They set high standards and expect high-quality performance. At the same time, however, leaders tolerate honest mistakes.

> 7. Sometimes, though, leaders also have to "push" people on.
> 8. Note the words *frequently* and *often*. Be reminded that leadership can be described in terms of general characteristics.

CHAPTER 18 Leadership Skills ■ 225

Edwin Land, founder of Polaroid, said: "The first thing you naturally do is teach the person to feel that the undertaking is manifestly important and nearly impossible.... That draws out the kind of drives that make people strong." The leader's style *pulls* rather than *pushes* people on.

Leaders Are Role Models

Many individuals earn a position of leadership because of their prior skills and successes. Leaders should represent the values of the units they lead. A captain of an athletic team is frequently the star player. A district sales manager is often a super salesperson.

Leaders know that people copy their behavior. If they work harder, the group will pick up the pace. If they slow down, the group pace slackens. Leaders send a clear signal by their own behavior. During Chrysler's financial crisis, every employee was aware that Chairperson Iacocca cut his own salary to $1 per year.

Contrast Iacocca's example with that of another executive whose company faced a similar financial crisis. He called the employees together to inform them of layoffs and budget cuts. After the presentation, he flew in a private jet to a fancy resort for a weekend of golf. Workers resented his behavior. The company's financial problems grew worse as a result of low employee morale and reduced productivity. The executive was later fired.

Leaders Search Out Key Issues and Problems

Leaders are good at uncovering and solving difficult problems. They want to know as much as possible about the matter. They ask tough questions such as: "How did this happen?" "How long has this been going on?" "What is being done to correct this?" "Who is responsible for it?"

Leaders know how to focus attention on an issue or problem. For instance, Du Pont requires every lost-time accident to be reported to the chairperson on a daily basis. This has helped make the entire company more safety-conscious.

The president of National Semiconductor wanted to turn around the performance of a particular division. So he moved his desk next to the division's general manager. This was a clear signal that improvement was expected.

Leaders Are Involved in External Relations

Leaders don't stay chained to their desks. Leaders represent the organization and serve as links to the outside world. They get involved with outside groups. They participate in professional or trade associations. They are in frequent contact with other businesses and other leaders. They get involved in community activities and service organizations.

Summary

Only a few people will lead nations. Many more will lead companies, departments, or small groups. Some people start out with better developed abilities than others. But what have been described here as leadership characteristics can be learned by everyone. The next section describes a type of organization that can help you to develop leadership skills.

VOCATIONAL STUDENT ORGANIZATIONS

Vocational student organizations (VSO) are nonprofit, national organizations with state and local chapters. They are supported primarily by student-paid dues. Each organization is linked with an occupational

FIGURE 18-4 Prior success is often, but not always, a forerunner to later leadership. *Photo by David W. Tuttle*

F•E•A•T•U•R•E

Trade and Professional Associations

♦ ♦ ♦

Trade and professional associations have been around for thousands of years. They are an important part of our economic, social, and working lives. A trade association seeks to advance common business interests of members. The common interest may be growing cotton or manufacturing boats. As with unions, individuals join trade associations to accomplish goals that no one individual or company could achieve alone. A trade association tries to make the public aware of its product or service.

Trade associations exist in almost every form of business. For example, have you heard of the National Potato Chip and Snack Food Association? Some trade associations cover a business function such as manufacturing, distribution, or retailing. For instance, several retail stores may form a trade association. Other trade associations are based on the types of goods or services produced. Peanut farmers, service station operators, or restaurant owners, for example, may form an association. The size of trade associations varies widely. The Motor Vehicle Manufacturers has only a few members. On the other hand, the National Automobile Dealers Association has several thousand members.

The most important goal of a trade association is more income from its product or service. Activities of trade associations may include advertising, sponsoring research on new products, or promoting high standards. To get their message out, the group may publish pamphlets or sponsor tours. It may also publish a magazine for members and hold yearly conventions. For some trade associations, lobbying for favorable laws is a major activity. To pay for these activities, trade associations collect dues from members.

A professional association or society is made up of people having a common background in an occupation. Examples are teacher, pilot, secretary, electronic technician, dental assistant, and chef. Members often need to have an academic degree, license, or certificate to join an association. Professional associations seek to inform members about new developments and issues. They publish journals and hold meetings and conventions.

More than 2,000 professional associations exist. They range from accountants to zoo directors. Such associations provide members with opportunities for continuing education and leadership development. Some associations have student memberships. If a professional association related to your occupation is available, join it.

FIGURE 18-FEATURE Cooperative advertising is a familiar activity of trade associations. *Courtesy of the Catfish Institute*

Trade and Professional Associations. Associations encourage leadership and provide opportunities to exercise leadership. Vocational student organizations themselves can be called professional associations. Have students identify other trade and professional associations related to their occupational interest or specialty.

CHAPTER 18 Leadership Skills ■ 227

area such as business, home economics, or health occupations. These organizations function as an integral part of vocational education.

Specific goals and objectives vary from one organization to another. But all have similar overall purposes to develop leadership skills and good citizenship. The organizations provide students with opportunities to function as junior members of the profession. Students apply skills learned in the classroom and interact with others in the occupational area. They develop a respect for the occupation and its *code of ethics* (rules for professional practice and behavior). Other outcomes include providing service, developing decision-making skills, and building confidence.

The national organization generally produces written guides for teacher/advisors, student handbooks, and promotional materials. In addition, the organization may sponsor national conferences,

FIGURE 18-5 Vocational student organizations supplement, enrich, and strengthen the curriculum. *Courtesy of Vocational Industrial Clubs of America, Health Occupations Students of America, Future Homemakers of America and Distributive Education Clubs of America*

14

15

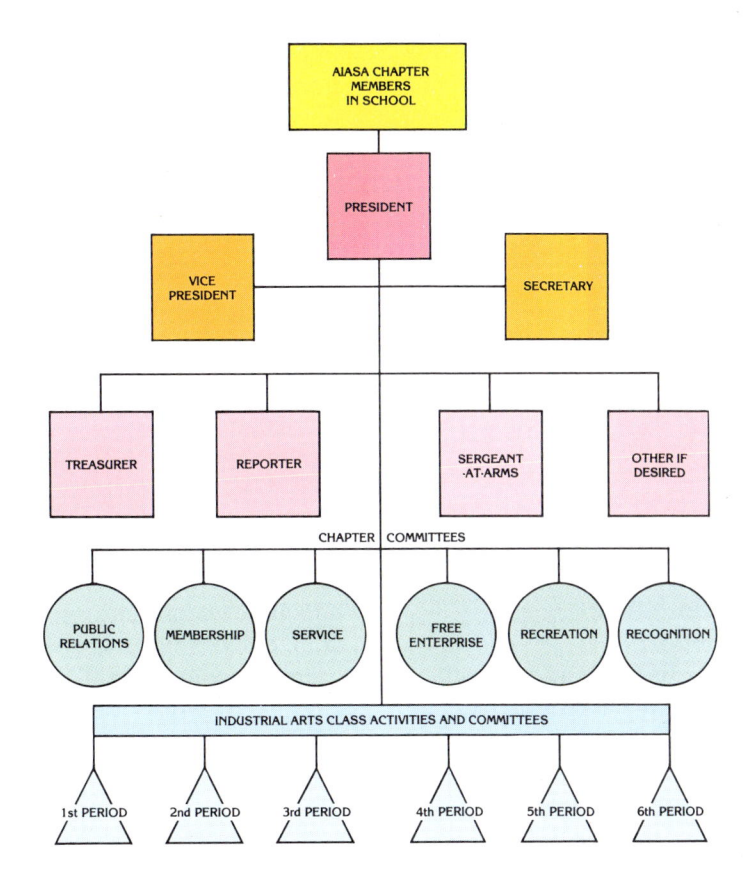

Note: The American Industrial Arts Student Association (AIASA) has changed its name to Technology Student Association (TSA).

FIGURE 18-6 This sample organizational chart shows how a local vocational student organization chapter might be structured. *Courtesy of Technology Student Association*

14. Provide an example of a written code of ethics.
15. You may want to digress from the text and describe the nature of VSOs in your school. Involve other instructors as appropriate.

Perhaps have student representatives explain their respective VSOs (refer to Activity 2).

leadership development workshops, competitive contests, and award programs. Following is a brief profile of each VSO.

Technology Student Association (TSA)

TSA is devoted to industrial arts/technology students at the elementary, junior high, and high school levels. Prior to June 1988, the organization was called the American Industrial Arts Student Association. Activities are designed to develop the leadership and personal abilities of students as they relate to the industrial and technical world. TSA assists students in making informed and meaningful career choices.

Business Professionals of America (BPA)

Prior to July 1988, BPA was known as the Office Education Association. The name was changed to reflect the fact that business education is incorporating new and expanding areas such as mid-management and entrepreneurship. The BPA is for students enrolled in business and office education programs at the secondary and postsecondary levels. Its goal is to prepare students for rewarding and successful careers in business and as business leaders.

Distributive Education Clubs of America (DECA)

DECA is an organization for future leaders in marketing, merchandising, and management. One purpose of the organization is to contribute to occupational competence in distributive education. It also promotes understanding and appreciation for the responsibilities of citizenship in a free-enterprise system. Membership in the following divisions are available: high school, two-year post-secondary, college, alumni, and professional.

Future Business Leaders of America— Phi Beta Lambda, Inc. (FBLA-PBL)

FBLA-PBL seeks to bring business and education together in a positive working relationship. The purpose of FBLA is to develop vocational and career supportive competencies and to promote civic and personal responsibilities. It is for secondary students in business and office education. The purpose of FBLA-PBL is to provide opportunities for junior college and college students to develop competencies for business and office occupations or business teacher education.

National FFA Organization

First known as the Future Farmers of America (FFA), this group changed its name in November 1988. It was founded in 1928 to make instruction more interesting and more practical by combining work experience, competitive livestock judging, and agricultural leadership development activities with classroom instruction. It is part of the high school vocational agriculture/agribusiness instruction program preparing students for careers in agriculture. The National FFA Organization encourages entrepreneurship, better work attitudes, and responsible citizenship.

Future Homemakers of America/Home Economics Related Occupations (FHA/HERO)

These two closely related organizations are for young men and women in home economics at the junior high and high school levels. Their purpose is to help youth assume active roles in society in areas of personal growth, family life, vocational preparation, and community involvement. FHA is the only in-school student organization with the family as its central focus. HERO chapters emphasize preparation for home economics occupations.

Health Occupations Students of America (HOSA)

The health care system needs workers who are technically skilled, people oriented, and capable of providing leadership as a member of a team. The focus of HOSA is to enhance the delivery of quality health care and to promote health care careers. It is for secondary, postsecondary and adult students enrolled in health occupations.

Vocational Industrial Clubs of America (VICA)

VICA is for students in trade, industrial, technical, and health occupations programs in high schools and junior/community colleges. VICA offers leadership, citizenship, and character development programs to complement the student's skill training. Dignity of work, high standards in trade ethics, workmanship, scholarship, and safety are emphasized.

PARLIAMENTARY PROCEDURE

Parliamentary procedure is a way to conduct a meeting in a fair and orderly manner. It is called "parliamentary" because it comes from the rules and customs of the British Parliament. The United

FIGURE 18-7 The U.S. Congress and other lawmaking bodies follow parliamentary procedure. *Courtesy of New York State Senate*

Officers and Committees

An organization usually elects a president (or chair), a vice-president, a secretary, and a treasurer. Some groups also elect a sergeant-at-arms or other officers. The president presides at meetings and supervises the work of other officers and committees. The vice-president assists the president and chairs meetings when the president is absent. The secretary notifies members of meetings, keeps the minutes, and takes care of all correspondence and committee reports. The treasurer keeps a record of income and expenses and prepares the financial reports. The sergeant-at-arms maintains order during meetings.

What Would You Do?

Several friends approach you saying that they would like to nominate you for office in a vocational student organization. You are pleased that they respect your ability. If you were elected, it would mean extra work and responsibility. You aren't sure that you have the time or could do the job. What would you do?

States Congress and other lawmaking bodies follow parliamentary procedure. The rules are used in simpler form by business and professional groups, school organizations, and social clubs. The basic principles of parliamentary procedure are majority rule, protection of the minority, and the orderly consideration of one subject at a time.

Bylaws

An organization operating according to parliamentary procedure adopts a set of bylaws. The *bylaws* define the basic characteristics of the organization and describe how it will operate. They describe qualifications for membership and procedures for selection of members. The bylaws state the duties of officers and how they will be elected. They also state how committees will be formed and what their functions will be. All members of an organization should be provided with a copy of the bylaws.

*WWYD Feature A. It is normal to question one's ability. This is an opportunity to learn and grow—the student should go for it.

Most organizations elect officers once a year. This is often done at the first meeting of the new year. A member may nominate a fellow member. Usually, after two or more people have been nominated, the voting takes place by secret ballot. The person receiving the majority vote is the elected officer. A *majority* is a vote of at least one more than half of the people who vote.

Certain duties of an organization are handled by committees. Most organizations have two types of committees. One type, standing committee, deals with regular and continuing matters, such as membership and finance. A second type, special committee, is formed whenever necessary to work on a specific matter. Examples might be to plan a social event or to revise the bylaws. Special committees break up when their task is done. Committees are either appointed or elected according to the bylaws.

19. Some organizations have a seperate *constitution*. Because the two documents tend to overlap, many organizations adopt a single document known only as the bylaws.

20. Name other examples of officers (e.g., historian, reporter, parliamentarian) and committees per your own VSO.
21. When and how are officers elected in your organization(s)?

PARTS OF A CHAPTER MEETING

It is customary for every group to adopt a standard order of business for the meeting. When the organization's by-laws do not provide for or require a specific order, the following is in order.

1. **Call To Order**
   "Will the meeting please come to order."

2. **Roll Call**
   "Will the secretary please call the roll."

3. **Reading and Approval of Minutes**
   "Will the secretary please read the minutes of the last meeting." The minutes are read and the chairman asks:

   "Are there any corrections to the minutes?" The chair pauses to hear any corrections offered, if there are none, the chair says, "There being no corrections, the minutes will stand approved as read."

   If there are corrections, the chair recognizes the correction(s) and asks, "Are there further corrections to the minutes?" If there are none, the chair states, "There being no further corrections, the minutes will stand approved as corrected."

4. **Adoption of Agenda**
   This step is provided to insure that (1) all persons are aware of what has been proposed for discussion at the meeting; (2) that all persons are given the opportunity to have whatever matter(s) they feel is (are) important to the organization placed on the agenda for discussion; and (3) to provide a limit to and order for the matters to be discussed at the meeting.

   To achieve this, the presiding officer states, "The following items are proposed for discussion at this meeting." After reading the list of proposed agenda items, the presiding officer asks, "Are there other matters that should be discussed at this meeting?" If there are additional matters requiring discussion, the chair places them in their proper positions on the agenda.

   The chair, after insuring that all pertinent matters will come before the meeting, reads the entire agenda and states, "There being no other matters that should come before this meeting, the agenda for this meeting will stand as read."

5. **Report of Officers and Standing Committees**
   Officers, boards, or standing committees should be called upon to report in the order in which they are mentioned in the constitution or by-laws of the organization.

6. **Report of Special Committees**

7. **Unfinished Business**
   "We have now come to unfinished business. Our agenda lists the following matters as unfinished business." The chair reads from the agenda and states, "We will hear these matters in the order in which they have been mentioned."

8. **New Business**
   "We have now come to new business. Our agenda lists the following items as new business . . ." (Chair reads from the agenda). He states, "We will hear them in the order in which they were mentioned."

9. **Program**
   Programs such as exhibitions, demonstrations, etc., which are incidental to the business meeting, will be scheduled for presentation at this time.

10. **Adjournment**

    Unqualified form:

    Proposer moves for adjournment; motion is seconded; chairperson calls for a vote; action depends upon majority vote. The motion cannot be discussed.

    Qualified form:

    Proposer moves for adjournment within a definite time or adjournment to meet again at a specified time; motion is seconded; the chair calls for discussion; a vote is taken; action depends upon majority vote; can allow for legal continuation of the meeting.

Note: The American Industrial Arts Student Association (AIASA) has changed its name to Technology Student Association (TSA).

FIGURE 18-8 Typical parts of a chapter meeting *Courtesy of Technology Student Association*

Holding a Meeting

Most organizations require that a quorum be present before a meeting may begin. A *quorum* is a majority of the total membership. An organizations' bylaws usually provide for an *order of business*. This is the series of steps covered in a meeting. A standard order of business is shown in Figure 18-8. An actual meeting proceeds according to a list of items to be taken care of called an *agenda*. A typical agenda for a vocational youth organization is shown in Figure 18-9.

22. Call attention to the order of business shown in Figure 18-9 and the sample agenda shown in Figure 18-10. Note the similarities and differences.

PLANNING AND CONDUCTING A MEETING

Planning and conducting a meeting are two tasks that every member should be able to perform correctly and with ease. To do this, certain knowledge and skills should become part of your repertoire.

The President, with assistant from the chapter officers, should meet prior to the time of the regularly scheduled meeting to plan the business to come before the membership. Minutes from the previous meeting should be examined so that any unfinished business can be ascertained and noted for discussion at the upcoming meeting.

The agenda is a listing of those activities to be engaged in and those items of business to be brought before the membership for discussion at the next meeting. A standard order of business is used when preparing an agenda. You should be aware of and apply the order of business in the planning and conducting of all meetings. A typical chapter agenda is shown below.

SCHOOL CHAPTER AGENDA

DATE: September 16,
TIME: 1:30 p.m.
PLACE: Mills Godwin High School

I. **CALL TO ORDER**

II. **OPENING CEREMONY** (Roll call, introduction of visitors)
- Visitors: Mr. Joseph Long, Miss Laura East

III. **READING OF MINUTES**

IV. **OFFICER AND STANDING COMMITTEE REPORTS**
- Treasurer's Report
- Enterprising/Finance Committee to report on fund-raising activities

V. **SPECIAL COMMITTEE REPORTS** (none)

VI. **UNFINISHED BUSINESS**
- Halloween Dance to be held October 30 — Selection of Band

VII. **NEW BUSINESS**
- The purchase of AIASA blazers for chapter officers

VIII. **ANNOUNCEMENTS**
- Members who have not turned in their money for the trip to Washington, D.C. must do so today.
- The Executive Committee will meet on September 25 in the Industrial Arts Lab at 12:00 noon. Bring your lunch with you. Milk will be served.

IX. **PROGRAM**
- Miss Laura East, from the State AIASA office, will speak on the Virginia AIASA Annual Conference to be held in May.

X. **CLOSING CEREMONY**

Note: The American Industrial Arts Student Association (AIASA) has changed its name to Technology Student Association (TSA).

FIGURE 18-9 A typical chapter agenda *Courtesy of Technology Student Association*

An important part of any business meeting involves making, discussing, and disposing of motions. A *motion* is a brief statement of a proposed action. There are four types of motions:

1. *Main motions* are the tools used to introduce new business.
2. *Secondary motions* provide ways of modifying or disposing of main motions.
3. *Incidental motions* arise out of business being conducted.
4. *Privileged motions* deal with the welfare of the group, rather than any specific proposal.

23. The four types of motions and their use are not something that is learned instantly. The material can be studied and discussed, but application is essential to mastery (refer to Activity 4).

ACTION	STATEMENT
Privileged Motions	
Adjourn the meeting	"I move that we adjourn."
Recess the meeting	"I move we recess until..."
Secondary Motions	
Postpone consideration of a matter without voting on it	"I move we table the motion."
End debate	"I move the previous question."
Have a matter studied further	"I move we refer this matter to a committee."
Amend a motion	"I move that this motion be amended by..."
Main Motions	
Introduce business	"I move that..."
Resume consideration of a previously tabled motion	"I move we take from the table..."
Reconsider a matter already disposed of	"I move we reconsider our action relative to..."
Incidental Motions	
Raise a question about parliamentary procedure	"Point of order."
Withdraw a motion	"I ask permission to withdraw the motion."
Seek information about the matter at hand	"Point of information."

FIGURE 18-10 Common motions listed in order of their rank of priority

The most common motions are summarized in Figure 18-10. The motions are listed in order of their *precedence* or rank of priority. When considering a main motion, secondary motion, or privileged motion, no motion listed below it may be introduced. Any motion listed above it, however, can be introduced. Incidental motions have no precedence. They must be decided or disposed of before returning to the business under consideration. Different rules apply to a motion regarding whether a second is needed, whether the motion is debatable, whether it can be amended, and so on. An organization often has a *parliamentarian* to advise the presiding officer (chair) on matters of procedure. Even though motions differ, the general procedure is the same.

To make a motion, a member obtains the floor by rising and addressing the chair. The chair recognizes the member by announcing his or her name. The motion is stated, followed by a second. The chair restates the motion for the benefit of all members. It is then open to debate (discussion). Debate continues until all members who wish to speak

FIGURE 18-11 Each motion must be disposed of in some way before another item of business can be taken up.
Photo by Paul E. Meyers

What Would You Do?

The vocational student organization to which you belong has had a successful year in fund-raising. You are meeting today to discuss how to spend the chapter's money. A motion is on the floor to authorize spending the money for a party. The discussion suggests that there is a lot of support for the motion. You too would enjoy a party, but think that it is an inappropriate way to use the money. You aren't sure about whether to speak against the motion. An alternative would be to amend the motion to use only a portion of the funds for a party. What would you do?

*

have had an opportunity. Members then vote on the motion. Those who approve the motion say "Aye"; those against the motion say "No." If the majority of members vote to accept the motion, it is approved.

Parliamentary procedure does not have to be mysterious and complicated. However, it is something that takes time to learn. One of the best ways to learn it is to join and participate in a vocational student organization.

25

25. Give students an opportunity to ask any remaining questions they may have about local VSOs. Have descriptive information available or help students obtain it. This chapter provides a good point of departure for getting students enrolled and involved in a VSO.

* *WWYD Feature B.* The person should express her/his views and speak against the motion. Perhaps one dissenting voice will encourage others to speak out. The essence of parliamentary procedure is debating issues.

CHAPTER REVIEW

Chapter in Brief

- Leadership can be defined as the process of influencing people so as to accomplish the goals of the organization. John Zenger identifies six types of leadership characteristics:
  1. Leaders are good communicators.
  2. Leaders develop committed followers.
  3. Leaders inspire high accomplishments.
  4. Leaders are role models.
  5. Leaders search out key issues and problems.
  6. Leaders are involved in external relations.

  Leadership characteristics can be learned by everyone.

- Vocational student organizations function as an integral part of the vocational education curriculum. Each VSO is linked with an occupational area. The organizations provide students with opportunities to function as junior members of the profession. Students apply skills learned in the classroom and interact with others in the occupational area.

- Parliamentary procedure is a way to conduct a meeting in a fair and orderly manner. The rules are used by business and professional groups, school organizations, and social clubs. The basic principles of parliamentary procedure are majority rule, protection of the minority, and the orderly consideration of one subject at a time.

- Bylaws define the basic characteristics of the organization and describe how it will operate. An organization usually elects a president, vice president, secretary, and treasurer. Certain duties of an organization are handled by standing and special committees.
- An important part of any business meeting involves making, discussing, and disposing of motions. There are four types of motions: main motions, secondary motions, incidental motions, and privileged motions. Each motion must be disposed of in some way before another item of business can be taken up.

Words to Know

agenda the list of items to be followed in an actual business meeting.

bylaws printed information that defines the basic characteristics of an organization and describes how it will operate.

code of ethics rules for professional practice and behavior.

leadership the process of influencing people so as to accomplish the goals of the organization.

majority a vote of at least one more than half of the people who vote.

motion a statement of proposed action by a participant in a business meeting.

order of business a standard series of steps followed in a business meeting.

parliamentarian the individual in an organization who advises the chair on matters regarding correct parliamentary procedure.

parliamentary procedure the formal rules used to conduct a meeting in a fair and orderly manner.

precedence the order of priority among the four types of motions used in a business meeting.

quorum a majority of the total membership of an organization.

vocational student organization (VSO) nonprofit, national organization with state and local chapters that exists to develop leadership skills and good citizenship among members. Each organization is composed of vocational students interested in a specific occupational area.

Questions to Answer

1. Organizations are oriented toward achieving certain goals. Name an organization (other than the example in the book) and list two of its goals.
2. In what way is information viewed by a leader?
3. How do leaders involve other members of the organization?
4. Give an example of how a leader can serve as a role model.
5. What are the general purposes of a vocational student organization?
6. What types of activities are conducted by vocational student organizations?
7. What are the three basic principles of parliamentary procedure?
8. Identify and explain the two types of committees.

---

1. Any number of organizations could be cited. You might have students name the organization where they work, or perhaps a VSO.
2. As something to be shared, not to be hoarded.
3. By asking for advice, information, and solutions to problems.
4. One example is by working hard. Other examples could be cited.
5. The general purposes of a VSO are to develop leadership skills and good citizenship.
6. Activities include national conferences, leadership development workshops, contests, and award programs.
7. (a) Majority rule. (b) Protection of the minority. (c) The orderly consideration of one subject at a time.
8. *Standing*—deals with regular and continuing matters such as membership and finance. *Special*—formed whenever necessary to work on a specific matter.

9. Name and describe the four types of motions.
10. Explain how a motion is introduced for debate.

Activities to Do
1. Identify a famous person who has been referred to as a leader. Rate her or him in relation to each of the six characteristics discussed in this chapter. Use a scale of "high," "average," and "low." What is the overall rating? As described in this chapter, could the person be called a leader?
2. Find out the types of vocational student organizations available in your school. For each one, list the qualifications for membership. Invite a representative from each organization to talk to the class. Select an organization of interest and join it.
3. If a vocational student organization is not available in your occupational area, write the national office to find out how to start one. Your instructor can provide the address. Initiating a VSO chapter would provide an excellent opportunity to demonstrate your leadership.
4. Practice parliamentary procedure by role playing a meeting in class. Elect a class president, vice president, and secretary. The officers should then develop an agenda. The secretary should prepare and distribute the agenda. Conduct an actual meeting according to the agenda. Concentrate on making, discussing, and disposing of sample motions.

Topics of Discuss
1. A characteristic of leaders is that they are able to develop committed followers. There are instances throughout history in which individuals have been able to develop committed followers for illegal or immoral purposes. Think of some historic or present examples. Should such people be called "leaders"?
2. A person may be named head of an organization or be elected to an office without being a leader. Discuss some of the things, other than leadership, that allow people to rise in an organization.
3. Strong leaders may be scattered throughout an organization. Identify and discuss as many examples as you can.
4. You have probably been involved in meetings or discussions that dragged on endlessly without anything being accomplished. Discuss how proper use of parliamentary procedure might have prevented that from happening.
5. It has been said that, "If you want to manage somebody, manage yourself." Discuss the meaning of this phrase.

---

9. *Main motions*—used to introduce new business. *Secondary motions*—provide ways of modifying or disposing of main motions. *Incidental motions*—arise out of business being conducted. *Privileged motions*—deal with the welfare of the group.
10. A member obtains the floor by rising and addressing the chair. After being recognized, the member introduces the motion by stating, "I move that...," or uses other appropriate language depending upon the intent of the motion.

26. This can be done individually or as a class activity.
27. Getting a VSO chapter started in your school would be a terrific leadership activity.

28. By our definition (influencing people to accomplish the goals of the organization), a person like Adolph Hitler or Charles Manson (or other cult figure) could be called a "leader." Leadership, then, can be positive or negative.
29. Being a solid, dependable manager often results in promotion. So to is seniority frequently rewarded. Sometimes, a person may be a "compromise choice," a "company man," or a "good ole boy." A person can also rise in an organization through devious means.
30. If students can't answer this, call their attention to Figure 18-11. Have them review privileged and secondary motions to stimulate thinking. (A motion to adjourn the meeting is one simple, direct way to potentially end discussion.)

1. Students may vary considerably among school districts and even among classes regarding their prior familiarity with computers. Adapt your instruction of this chapter accordingly.
2. The 1983 report of The National Commission on Excellence in Education *(A Nation at Risk)* was among the first to declare computer literacy as one of the "New Basics."

CHAPTER NINETEEN

Computer Skills

OUTLINE
Keyboarding Skills
How Computers Work
Computers in the Workplace
The Future of Computers
Chapter Review

OBJECTIVES
After reading this chapter, you should be able to:
- Explain the importance of keyboarding skills.
- Name and describe the five sections of a computer.
- Summarize how a computer works.
- Show awareness of the role computers play in the workplace.
- Discuss the possible future impact of computers.

FIGURE 19-1 The first electronic digital computer called ENIAC began operating in 1946. It weighed 30 tons and took up 15,000 square feet of floor space. *Courtesy of IBM Archives*

3. This is often called "applications software."
4. The most familiar type of computer is the personal computer (PC). Point out, however, that entire computers on miniature chips are an integral part of common, electronic household and business appliances, from coffee pots to paper copiers.

The previous four chapters deal with knowledges and skills that have always been important on the job. To those we must now add what is called *computer literacy*. Computer literacy is a general knowledge of what computers are, how they work, and what they can be used for. Chances are that your future work will involve some contact with computers.

KEYBOARDING SKILLS

Wayne graduated from high school without learning anything about computers. He lost out on several good jobs after interviewers learned that he couldn't use a computer. Wayne got the message and signed up for an adult-ed course in computers. In that class, he learned enough to be able to do simple operations and to run ready-to-use *software*.

He got a job in the parts department of a plumbing supply business. In his job, Wayne uses a computer more often than a pen. He orders parts, does billings, keeps inventory, and does dozens of other tasks on the computer. He wonders what it must have been like in the parts department before the computers arrived.

A *computer* is an electronic tool. Like other tools, it helps people do various kinds of work. It can do simple arithmetic and can solve complex mathematical problems. With an optical device, it can read a printed page and write (display) text and graphics

236

5. Computers can "read, write, and talk."
6. Many keyboards are "enhanced" with additional function and numeric keys.

CHAPTER 19 Computer Skills ■ 237

on a screen. If it has a voice synthesizer, it can even "talk." It can direct equipment to do work. Unlike people, a computer can work twenty-four hours a day without getting tired. It runs on little electricity and seldom breaks down. It can store vast amounts of information and can communicate with its human user. Perhaps the computer's greatest benefit is its ability to work at very high speeds.

Like Wayne, you will probably need to learn *keyboarding skills* (if you haven't already). A keyboard is the part of a computer that looks like a typewriter. Most keyboard terminals are connected to a TV-like screen.

The arrangement of letters and numbers on the keyboard is the same as for a typewriter. You can use the computer keyboard to write a letter or report. The preparation of letters, memos, and other documents is called *word processing*.

Keyboarding, however, involves more than using the computer as a typewriter. The keyboard terminal directs the computer's operation. Various keys send commands to the computer. For example, one key is labeled ESC. It stands for "ESCape." Most often the ESC key clears data from the screen.

Another characteristic of a keyboard is that the letter and number keys are sometimes used for different things. If you want to type the number "3," you press that key. Some computers that have color graphics use numbers to represent different colors, too. For instance, pressing the "3" key may let you choose the color purple.

Keys are also pressed in different combinations to send commands to the computer. For instance, you can stop many computers by pressing the "CTRL" key and then the "S" key. These examples show only a few of the uses of the keyboard. A keyboard's operation will vary depending on the type of computer and the software used.

Though keyboards differ in their operation, basic commands and procedures are similar. Knowing how to keyboard will prove to be a valuable skill. No matter what type of business or industry you work in, you will benefit by knowing how to use a computer keyboard.

FIGURE 19-2 Many high schools now offer word processing classes. Students learn how to "keyboard" instead of how to "type." *Courtesy of Johnson & Wales College*

7. A chart, transparency or actual keyboard would be useful at this point to illustrate keyboard characteristics.
8. Ask students how many of them use computers on the job. Discuss the types of applications.

HOW COMPUTERS WORK

9   In very simple terms, the computer does work in three steps: (a) it receives instructions, (b) it does tasks according to instructions provided, and (c) it shares the results. These three steps are shown in Figure 19-3.

INPUT → PROCESSING → OUTPUT

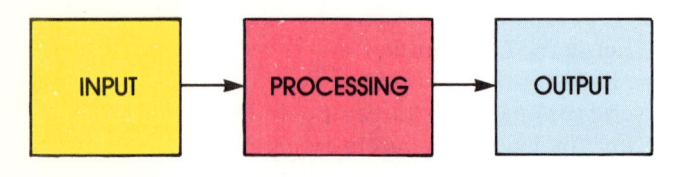

FIGURE 19-3

The computer solves problems much as people do. For instance, let's compare how you and the computer would add 20 + 43, Figure 19-4.

You receive information by either reading or hearing the numbers.	INPUT	The computer receives the information in the form of electronic signals.
You draw upon your knowledge of arithmetic which is in your memory. You bring together the data (20, 43) and the method (addition) and come up with the answer.	PROCESSING	The computer draws upon a program stored in its memory. Bringing the data from input and the instructions from memory, the computer adds the numbers.
You report the results (63) by writing down the answer or saying it out loud.	OUTPUT	The computer changes the results from electronic language to human language. It presents the results in print, sound, or other form.

FIGURE 19-4

Now let's go beyond this simple explanation. To do this, we will need to relabel the second step and divide it into three sections. The input-processing-output sequence now appears as shown in Figure 19-5.

CENTRAL PROCESSING UNIT

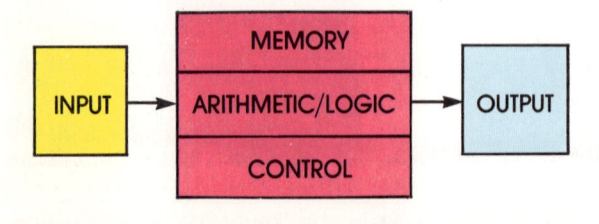

INPUT → [MEMORY / ARITHMETIC/LOGIC / CONTROL] → OUTPUT

FIGURE 19-5

9. The intent here is to demystify how computers work. Computers are very sophisticated, electronic machines. But their operation is conceptually quite simple.

What Would You Do?

You are very interested in computers. You have subscribed to a computer magazine to learn more about them. You are saving money to buy a PC. But, the more you read, the more confusing it gets. There are so many different brand names and models to choose from. When you do get close to making a decision, you read that a newer, more powerful, and cheaper model will be out soon. Should you buy or continue to wait? What would you do?

*WWYD Feature A. It appears that computer technology will continue to evolve rapidly for some time. Buy a state-of-the-art machine that has the capability for expansion.

10. If you are knowledgeable about computers, an optional activity would be to remove the cover from a PC and point out the five sections of a computer.

We now have the workings of a modern computer. A computer has five sections: (a) input, (b) memory, (c) arithmetic and logic, (d) control, and (e) output.

Input

The input section of a computer takes information and changes it into electronic signals the computer can use. Various devices can input data. Perhaps the most common is a keyboard. As the operator types letters or numbers on the keyboard, they appear on the screen. This allows the operator to check the data.

Sometimes the monitor is used with a light pen that allows the user to draw on the screen. Other kinds of input devices include magnetic tapes and discs and punched cards and paper tape. A telephone can even be hooked up to a computer through the use of a *modem*.

Two kinds of information are fed into the computer input. One is called a *program*. A program consists of instructions on how to solve a certain problem or do a certain task. The second kind of information consists of the facts and figures the program must use. From the input, the program and data go to the memory section of the computer.

CHAPTER 19 Computer Skills ■ 239

```c
/* Demonstrate a simple program with input and output */
#include <stdio.h>
#include <math.h>

main( void )
{
  char ch;

  printf("\nPress a single key and then the <ENTER> key");
  ch = getchar();

  printf("You pressed the '%c' key - Its ASCII code is %3d",ch,ch);
  printf("\n");
```

Output:

Press a single key and then the <ENTER> key: *g*

You pressed the 'g' key - Its ASCII code is 103

FIGURE 19-7 This is a simple program with input and output. *Reprinted from Marek/Seabrook, Programming in C © Delmar Publishers Inc., 1989*

FIGURE 19-6 How many input and output devices do you see here? *Courtesy of IBM Corporation*

11. Ask students to name other input devices (mouse, optical scanner, another computer, and so on).

Memory

The memory section is the part of the computer system that records and stores the data. This data stays in memory until other parts of the computer need it.

The memory section actually has two parts. One part is permanent memory. It is called *ROM,* which stands for *r*ead-*o*nly *m*emory. The manufacturer pre-programs the ROM. It tells the computer to do different things. What these things are depends on the uses of the computer.

The other part of the memory is working memory. It is called *RAM* (*r*andom-*a*ccess *m*emory). This part stores both current programs and data being processed. Whenever the computer is turned off, it erases all RAM data.

FIGURE 19-8 This tiny semiconductor (chip) contains thousands of microscopic electronic circuits. Each circuit serves as a memory cell. *Courtesy of Lockheed Corporation (Photographer: William James Warren)*

12. Some manufacturers permanently store applications software in memory also.

Arithmetic and Logic

The arithmetic and logic section is the heart of the computer. It does all the computer's math operations.

The arithmetic and logic section adds, subtracts, multiplies, divides, and compares numbers. To do complex calculations, the four operations combine into a number of steps as the program directs. This section also processes words. It does these tasks at speeds measured in millionths of a second.

The arithmetic and logic section receives its input from the memory section. After processing, the data returns to the memory section. There it will be ready for use when needed.

Control

Part of the program of instructions a computer receives goes to the control section. The control section directs the other four sections of the computer.

Based on the program, the control section decides when to accept data from which input device. It chooses when to send information from the input to memory and when to send it to the arithmetic and logic section. It decides when to call up a program and data from storage. And it decides when the computer's work should go to the output.

Output

The output section changes data from electronic language into forms that people can understand. Most output is either displayed, printed, or stored.

FIGURE 19-9 A printer is one of the most useful output devices. *Courtesy of © Tandy Corporation*

13. This section describes a computer in terms of sequential operations (see Figure 19-3). In practice, there is continuous interaction of data, instructions, and control signals.
14. Computers are so fast that output may occur virtually simultaneously with input.
15. Arrange a computer-controlled robot demonstration.

16. This section is intended to illustrate variious applications of computers in the workplace. Be alert to new information in newspapers and magazines.

CHAPTER 19 Computer Skills ■ 241

FIGURE 19-10 Computers are used in business and industry. *Courtesy of Westinghouse Electric Corporation*

Output can appear on the same monitor that displayed the input data. A printer may also "type" the output. Sometimes magnetic tapes and discs store the data. Output devices are often the same as input ones.

Some computer systems transmit output as spoken words or music. Output can also consist of instructions that tell machines to do certain kinds of work (such as robots).

15

COMPUTERS IN THE WORKPLACE

16 Computers play a very important role in our working world. Following is only a sample of their varied uses.

Business and Industry

Many offices now do routine office tasks by computer. These may include checking inventories and managing payrolls. In many offices, the typewriter is disappearing in favor of the word processor. And in some offices, even the secretary is disappearing! That is, some secretaries are staying home to do their work.

Many companies are experimenting with what is called *telecommuting*. This refers to a work station in an employee's home. Work assignments go to the employee via a phone modem. The employee does the work on a microcomputer and then relays it back to the office.

17

Telecommuting offers new job opportunities to many people. One 45-year-old man who is paralyzed with polio had never held a job. He got a computer and learned how to program. Now, he does programming at home for a large drugstore chain.

American auto manufacturing was once considered to be the best in the world. By 1980, however, the auto industry had many problems, including recession, foreign competition, and high interest rates. The four major U.S. auto companies reported losses of $4.2 billion that year. Auto companies launched a $70 billion spending program to modernize production. Computers and robots appeared. They began to do hundreds of tasks such as precision welding, painting, and alignment. In only a few years, production costs went down and quality improved. Some auto experts think that U.S. cars are once again among the best in the world. The computer played an important role in this recovery.

18

17. The number of people working at home linked to the workplace via a computer is steadily increasing. Ask students if they know someone who does this.

18. A field trip or video showing the use of robots in manufacturing would be an interesting activity.

FIGURE 19-11 Computers are used to launch, guide, and land spacecraft. *Courtesy of Lockheed Corporation (Photographer: William James Warren)*

What Would You Do?

You work for your grandparents in a small, family-owned business. After taking a computer course in school, you have become aware of what computers can do. You see a number of ways that a computer could be used in the business. You suggest to your grandfather that he buy a computer.

"Son, we don't have the money to buy an expensive computer," he says. "Besides, the old-fashioned way has been working just fine for years."

You are disappointed, but still believe that a computer would be a wise investment. What would you do?

* *WWYD Feature B.* Perhaps Grandfather would be more receptive if he could be shown specifically what a computer costs and what it could save in time and money.

Government

The federal government was the earliest user of computers. Today, the government couldn't operate without computers. The Census Bureau relies on computers to update population figures. The Internal Revenue Service uses computers to check more than 125 million tax returns per year. The FBI uses computers to compare a suspect's fingerprints with those in a computer data base. Computers are a vital part of the radar defense system that guards the United States. They also launch, guide, and land spacecraft.

Communications

A writer doing a story used to rely only on printed reference materials. Now, the writer may have a computer and modem linked to an electronic data base. Data bases may provide general or specialized information. Some data bases cover

19. Some public libraries have replaced their card catalogs with computers and electronic files. A visit to an electronic library would make an interesting field trip.

stock prices or airline schedules. Others deal with movie reviews. What's more, the information in an electronic data base is up-to-date. With printed reference materials, the data is probably a year or more old on the day it comes off the press.

Other uses of computers in communications include computer-to-computer hookups that allow mail to be sent electronically. Computers also route telephone calls automatically without the need for a human operator. The computer even tells you when you dial a wrong number.

Transportation

The transportation industry relies on computing systems for controlling and planning the use of trains, aircraft, ships, and highway traffic. Railroad companies use computers to keep track of equipment scattered over many locations. Many cities in the United States have computerized traffic lights that change according to how much traffic is flowing. One of the most important uses of computers is in air traffic control. Here, computers keep track of the location of incoming and departing planes. A computer simulator helps train airline pilots and ship captains.

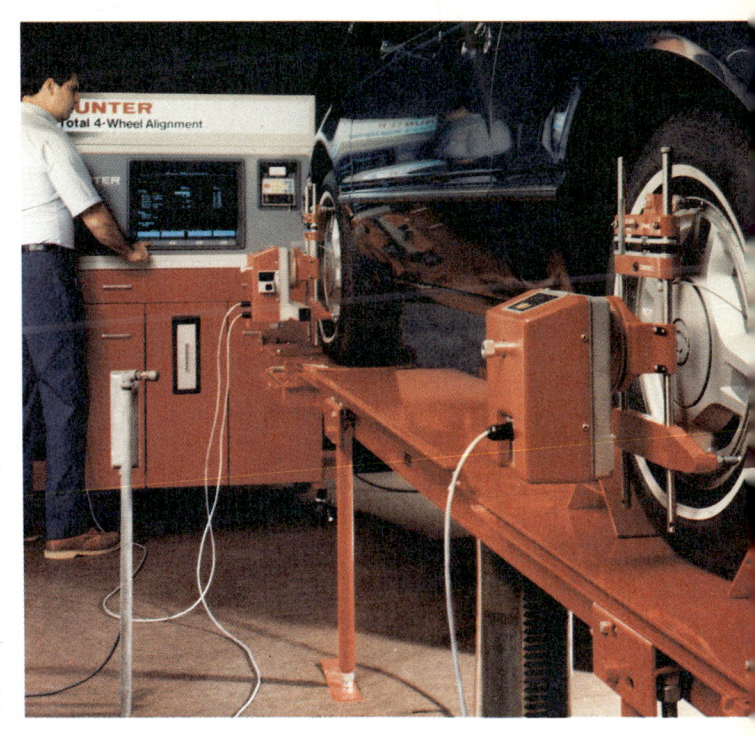

FIGURE 19-13 Computers are used in testing vehicle systems. *Courtesy of Hunter Engineerig Co.*

FIGURE 19-12 Electronic data bases provide up-to-date information. *Photo by Paul E. Meyers*

FIGURE 19-14 Computers are used to teach students from kindergarten through graduate school. *Courtesy of IBM Corporation*

Education

You can probably see many uses of computers in your school. Computers help teach students from kindergarten through graduate school. Guidance counselors also are using computers to help students plan careers.

Isiah made an appointment at the career center for a session on "self-guided career exploration." When he arrived at the career center, a worker directed him to a computer terminal. He "booted up" a floppy disk and completed an interest inventory. When he finished, a profile of his interests was printed out. The computer also gave him a list of occupations he might wish to explore.

He then met with a counselor who helped him interpret his profile. Later, he returned to the computer for printouts on several occupations that interested him. He also got a listing of schools in his state that provided training in those occupations.

Other school personnel also use computers. Administrators plan course schedules, keep track of teachers' assignments, and store records of students' grades. Coaches use the computer to keep team and individual statistics in all sports. The school dietitian plans the lunch menu and stores recipes on the computer.

Science and Engineering

All science occupations rely on computers. Chemists and physicists use computers to control and check laboratory instruments and to analyze data. Through computers, astronomers guide telescopes and process photos of planets and other objects in space. In biology labs, computer-controlled machines scan and measure slides of genes and blood cells. Meteorologists use computers to track and study weather patterns.

Without computers, it would be impossible for engineers to do certain problems. Architectural and

FIGURE 19-15 Computers are used for science and engineering. *Courtesy of Westinghouse Electric Corporation*

20. You may wish to assign Activity 1 at this time.

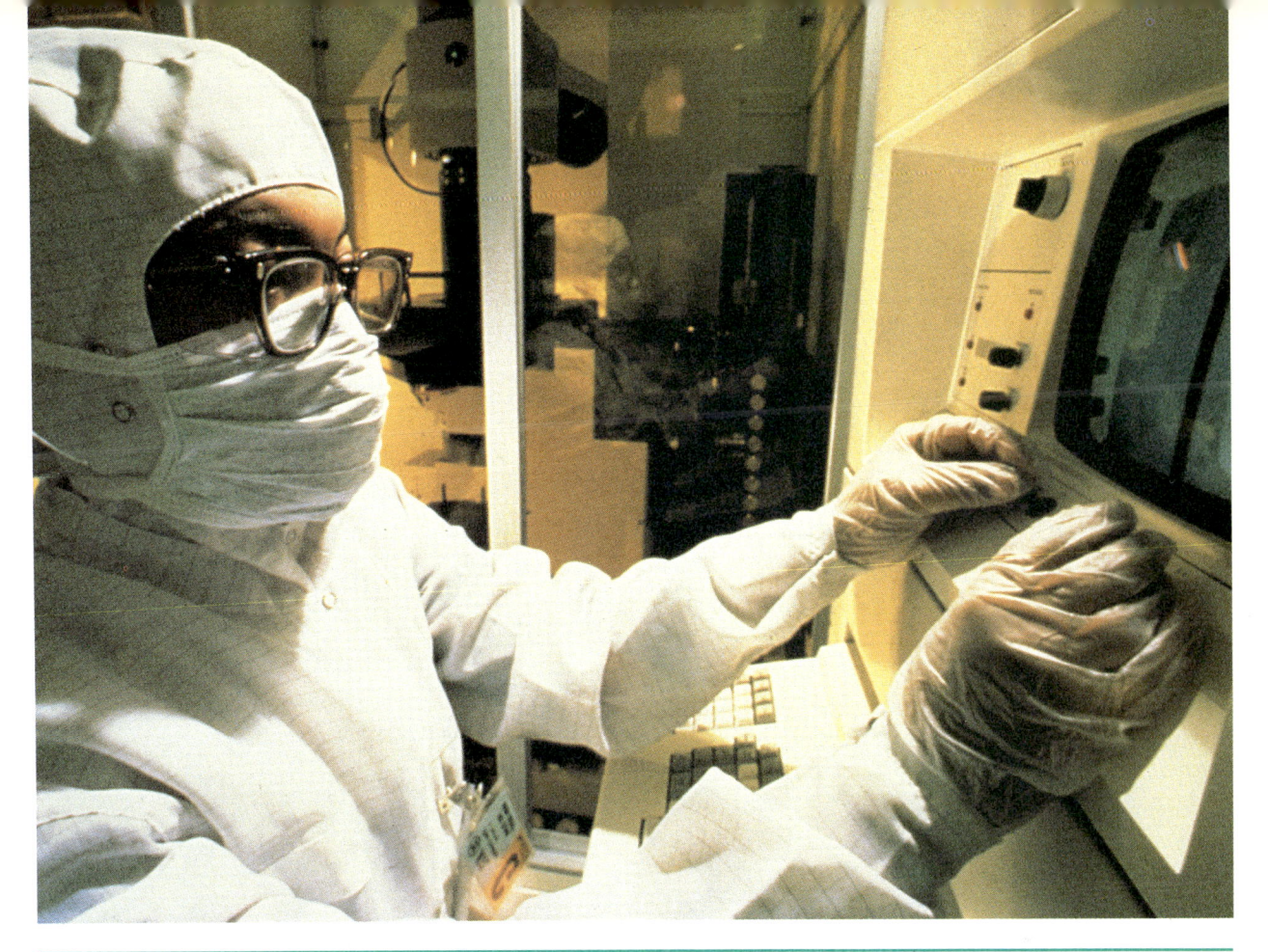

FIGURE 19-16 Doctors use computers to help them perform many tasks. *Courtesy of Westinghouse Electric Corporation*

civil engineers use computers to design bridges and other structures. They even use computers to make actual drawings. Before road construction starts, computers often analyze photographs. The results help people decide exactly where the roads should go.

Medicine

In medicine, computer use began with keeping records. Now, doctors use the computer as a diagnostic tool. One clinic has computers in each doctor's office. The computers are connected to a master network. The network contains some 4,000 symptoms for more than 500 diseases. When a doctor types a list of symptoms into the computer, it prints out a list of possible diseases.

Computers are also a help in the care and treatment of patients. Computers can control heart pacemakers. Computers can also pump measured quantities of insulin into diabetics. They can test blood samples for hundreds of different allergies. In the future, computers may stimulate deadened muscles with electric impulses. This may allow many paralyzed people to walk.

Dr. Evers uses her computer for information on various drugs. By typing in the word *rhinitis* (inflammation of the nose), she can get a list of medications from among 1,500 drugs.

THE FUTURE OF COMPUTERS

The rapid development of computer technology should continue in the future. Computers will get smaller, more powerful, and less expensive. At the same time, computers will become easier to use. Programming will be simpler and it will become possible to give spoken commands to computers. All of these changes will have a great impact on the workplace. Predicting the future is risky. However, the following changes seem likely:

- The number of occupations that require computer literacy and keyboarding skills will continue to increase. Eventually, most occupations will involve computer use.

21. All of these "future changes" are, to a degree, already occurring. Ask students to provide specific illustrations of each trend.

F·E·A·T·U·R·E

The Workerless Factory

Traditional manufacturing methods are based on the idea of mass production. In mass production, machines are set up to perform a single task, for instance, drilling holes in a metal casting. After setup, hundreds or thousands of parts are drilled and stockpiled. The setup is then changed to a new operation.

Mass production is an efficient, low-cost way to produce parts made over and over. However, it becomes less efficient and more costly for small quantities, or for parts that need frequent retooling. This is where a new approach called "flexible manufacturing system" (FMS) comes in.

The FMS is a totally automated system linking production machines, computers, and robots. The advantage of the FMS is that it can make many different kinds of parts in varying amounts. It can also switch from one operation to another almost instantly. For example, in one tractor manufacturing plant, machines are programmed to work on a transmission and a clutch housing at the same time.

Another manufacturer uses the FMS to make up to 2,000 variations of forty basic models of an electric meter. A locomotive plant makes a motor frame in sixteen hours rather than the sixteen days it used to take. A computer manufacturer uses the FMS to turn out laptop computers in less than six minutes without being handled by a single worker.

Labor requirements for the FMS are vastly different than for conventional systems. A company that manufactures planes uses only nineteen people (including maintenance worker) to run the eight-machine FMS through three shifts. With conventional methods, twenty-four production machines and seventy-two workers would be needed to get the same output.

The FMS does have drawbacks. The system takes a long time to "debug" before full-scale production can begin. And because the system is so tied together, a failure at one stage can shut down the entire process. Probably the biggest drawback is cost. In 1990, the average cost for one FMS was about $4 million. For small companies employing fewer than fifty workers, the cost is out of the question.

FIGURE 19-FEATURE With flexible manufacturing systems (FMS), self-propelled carts are often used to move parts from station to station. *Courtesy of Eaton-Kenway, Inc.*

The Workerless Factory. This is an elaboration of one application of computers in the manufacturing industry. Industrial giants like Caterpillar, Boeing, Lockheed, General Electric, John Deere, IBM, and Mack Trucks have installed FMSs. Some Technology programs in universities and community colleges have installed smaller versions for training purposes.

- Employment in areas involving computers and robots will increase dramatically. One source, for instance, estimates that two million robot technicians will be working by the year 2000.
- Computer technology will create many new industries and occupations. (Try to guess what some of these might be.)
- Electronics will surpass auto manufacturing and oil as the world's largest industry.
- The use of industrial robots will expand from the assembly line to all phases of manufacturing. In the totally automated factory of the future, robots will replace humans in many cases.
- The automation of offices and other service industries will increase. In the office of the future, most communication will be carried out electronically. Electronic storage and transmission of information will lead to the "paperless office."
- Major shifts in job patterns will occur. Computers and robots may eliminate as many as twenty-five percent of present jobs.
- Technology can also create new jobs. Many experts believe that, in the long run, technology will produce more jobs than it takes away.
- Workers losing their jobs to automation must be willing to retrain. To keep up with new technology, all workers will need continuing education and training.

You live in a very exciting time. Not since the Industrial Revolution has the workplace undergone such changes. Indeed, some people are calling the modern era of electronics the "second industrial revolution." The computer is leading this revolution. Your generation will be the first to grow up in the world of the computer.

How much knowledge and experience do you have with computers? If it is limited, think about doing something to correct it. Take a course or try to get a friend to start teaching you keyboarding skills. Not being able to use a computer could hold you back from getting or advancing in a job.

22. You may be able to add other likely changes. Since change is occurring rapidly, be alert to new information that can be used to update this section.

CHAPTER REVIEW

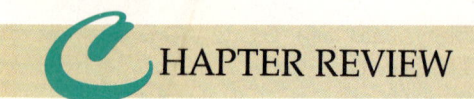

Chapter in Brief

- Computer literacy is a general knowledge of what computers are, how they work, and what they can be used for. A computer is an electronic tool. It helps people do various kinds of work.
- A keyboard is the part of a computer that looks like a typewriter. Keyboards are similar in terms of basic commands and procedures. You will benefit by knowing how to use a computer keyboard.
- The computer does work in three steps: it receives instructions, it does tasks according to instructions provided, and it shares the results. This is called the input-processing-output sequence.
- A computer has five sections as follows:
  1. *Input.* This section takes information and changes it into electronic signals the computer can use.
  2. *Memory.* This section records and stores the data. One part is permanent memory (ROM). The other part is working memory (RAM).
  3. *Arithmetic and logic.* This is the heart of the computer. It does all of the computer's math and logic functions.
  4. *Control.* This section directs the other four sections of the computer.
  5. *Output.* This section changes data from electronic language into understandable forms.
- Computers play a very important role in the working world. They are used in all major fields of work.
- The rapid development of computer technology should continue in the future. The number of occupations that require computer literacy and keyboarding skills will increase. If your knowledge of computers is limited, think about doing something to correct it.

Words to Know

computer an electronic tool that can store and process data, and can direct the work of other tools.

computer literacy a general knowledge of what computers are, how they work, and what they can be used for.

keyboarding skills the ability to operate a computer by use of the typewriter-like keyboard terminal.

modem an electronic device that allows computers to be linked through standard telephone lines.

program coded instructions that cause a computer to perform a certain task. *See also* software.

RAM an acronym for random-access memory; the working memory in a computer.

ROM an acronym for read-only memory; the permanent memory in a computer.

software the electronic instructions and programs that direct a computer to perform certain applications.

telecommuting an application of computers in which an employee, based at home (or other location), receives assignments and returns completed work via a phone modem.

Questions to Answer
1. Name two characteristics of a computer keyboard.
2. What are the three major steps in the operation of a computer?
3. List the five sections of a computer. Then briefly tell what each section does.
4. Name five different types of input devices.
5. What is the difference between ROM and RAM?
6. Name two computer output devices.
7. Rewrite the following steps in the proper sequence:
    a. Processed data returned to memory
    b. Numbers typed into keyboard
    c. Processed data shown on monitor
    d. Stored data moved for processing
    e. Calculations performed
    f. Typed data stored in memory
8. How might telecommuting benefit a homebound person?
9. How does the FBI use computers?
10. How does safe air travel depend on computers?
11. How might an athletic coach use a computer?
12. How will computers likely change in the future?

Activities to Do
1. Identify as many ways as you can that computers are being used in your school. Don't limit your answers to just instruction.
2. Choose an occupation in which you are interested. Find out how workers in that occupation use computers. Present your findings in an oral report to the class.
3. The increasing popularity of computers has led to many new occupations and new businesses. Look in the Yellow Pages of your phone book to find out the numbers and types of different computer businesses in your area. Also, examine the classified section of your Sunday newspaper. How many job ads can you find for computer-related occupations? Discuss your findings in class.
4. Identify as many sources as possible in your school or community regarding how you might learn or improve your computer skills.

Topics to Discuss
1. Computer critics say that computers are putting too many people out of work. They believe that someday computers will take over most of what workers now do. Do you agree? Discuss in class the human costs and benefits of computers.
2. People are often reluctant to use new technology such as computers. Why do you think this is so? How might you change the attitude of someone who feels this way?
3. In what types of occupations do computers have the greatest potential use? The least potential use? Explain your answers.

---

1. Any two of the following: (a) The arrangement of letters and numbers on the keyboard is the same as for a typewriter. (b) The keyboard terminal directs the computer's operation. (c) Letter and number keys are used for different purposes. (d) Keys are pressed in different combinations to send commands to the computer.
2. (a) Input. (b) Processing. (c) Output.
3. (a) *Input* — takes information and changes it into electronic signals that the computer can use. (b) *Memory* — records and stores the data. (c) *Arithmetic and logic*—does all of the computer's math and logic functions. (d) *Control*—directs the other four sections of the computer. (e) *Output*—changes data from electronic language into understandable forms.
4. Any five of the following: keyboard, light pen, magnetic tapes and discs, punched cards, paper tape, modem, mouse, joy stick, another computer, and so on.
5. ROM is permanent memory; RAM is working memory.
6. Any two of the following: monitor, printer, magnetic tapes and discs, punched cards, paper tape, modem, another computer, and so on.
7. Proper sequence is b, f, d, e, a, c.
8. It can offer new job opportunities by linking the person up to an external employer via a computer and modem.
9. One way is to check fingerprints against those in a data base. Other examples could be cited.
10. One way is to track the location of incoming and departing planes. Other examples could be cited.
11. One way is to keep team and individual statistics. Other examples could be cited.
12. It is likely that they will become smaller, more powerful, and less expensive.

23. Have students make a bulletin board display of computer-related job openings.
24. There is a normal tendency for people to avoid things about which they are unfamiliar. Old habits are often barriers to change. A good way to change attitudes is to show someone how easy a computer is to use. Or, how useful one can be.
25. The greatest potential use tends to be in those occupations dealing with large amounts of knowledge and information (recall the Chapter 1 feature about the Information Age). The least potential use is probably in human service occupations such as direct patient care, counseling, teaching, social work, and the like.

1. For most teens, going into business for themselves is unrealistic. The aim of this chapter is to make students aware of entrepreneurship as a future possibility. On the other hand, a number of successful businesses have been established by young people (see Discussion Topic 3). Ask students if they know of any such businesses.

CHAPTER TWENTY

Entrepreneurial Skills

OUTLINE
Nature of Small Business
Advantages and Disadvantages of Self-employment
Ingredients for Success
Are You the Type?
Choosing a Business
Chapter Review

OBJECTIVES
After reading this chapter, you should be able to:
- Name contributions that small business makes to our society.
- Discuss advantages and disadvantages of self-employment.
- Outline what it is like to own and operate a small business.
- Identify ingredients necessary for a successful business.
- Evaluate own self-employment traits.
- Describe factors to consider in choosing a business.

FIGURE 20-1 After completing her education and working eight years for someone else, this woman decided to open her own shop. *Courtesy of © Tandy Corporation*

FIGURE 20-2 Many small businesses are in services, such as this technician servicing a car. *Photo by Ruby Gold*

1 As a cooperative education or work experience student, you are working in a business owned or managed by someone else. In the future, you may continue to work as an employee for another person. Or you may decide to become an *entrepreneur*. An entrepreneur is someone who runs his or her own small business. The person is *self-employed*.

250

F·E·A·T·U·R·E

The Growth of Small Business

FIGURE 20-FEATURE The stock of many small businesses is bought and sold the same as giant corporations. *Courtesy of New York Stock Exchange*

The first settlers to this country arrived from Europe. They came seeking freedom to live, speak, work, and worship. Many Colonial Americans chose business as a way of life. These early business persons were some of the first to speak out against British rule. Paul Revere, for example, was a silversmith before he became a revolutionary. Almost everyone who signed the Declaration of Independence was a businessperson or professional of some kind. For these individuals, the ideal of "life, liberty, and the pursuit of happiness" included the freedom to be one's own boss.

For about a century after the Revolutionary War, small business people and farmers provided most of the country's goods and services. Thousands of hardworking businessmen and women realized the American dream. They helped to lay the foundation for the Industrial Revolution of the late 1800s.

Machines invented during the Industrial Revolution led to the building of great factories. Gradually, more people went to work in cotton mills, steel mills, auto assembly plants, and other manufacturing industries.

In recent years, the economy has changed from an emphasis on goods production to providing services. An important fact about this change is that service businesses are more likely to be small businesses. Small businesses are being incorporated at a rate about twice the number from a decade earlier. No one knows how many proprietorships and partnerships are being formed. The trend, however, is clearly that more and more people are going into business for themselves.

The Growth of Small Business. This feature illustrates the role played by business persons throughout our history. Democratic values and the spirit of entrepreneurship are very compatible.

NATURE OF SMALL BUSINESS

Small businesses are found in agriculture, construction, sales, services, and every other type of industry. They are located throughout the country. Many are in big cities, but a large number are in small towns. Small businesses are as scattered and different as the people who own them.

Importance of Small Business

Small business makes many important contributions to our society. One is the creation of new jobs. As new businesses begin and expand, they hire new workers. About two-thirds of all new jobs are provided by businesses employing fewer than twenty people.

Another contribution is that small businesses often recycle old buildings. It is not unusual, for example, to find a restaurant or a dry cleaners housed in what used to be a service station. Can you think of examples in your town or neighborhood?

A third contribution is that small business provides opportunities for women and minorities to get started in business. About thirty-two percent of all self-employed people are females and seven percent are minorities. The percentage for both groups is increasing steadily each year.

The most important contribution of small business comes from new inventions, products, and services. Many of the great success stories of American business have been the result of people who had a new idea or a better way of doing things.

During the summer of 1976, Steven Jobs and his friend Stephen Wozniak developed a new microcomputer. They worked in the garage of Jobs' parents. In August, the 20-year-old Jobs took a bus to Atlantic City to demonstrate his machine at a computer show. After the show, Jobs took twenty orders back to his home in California. Apple Computer Company was born!

FIGURE 20-3 By age 23, Steve Jobs had a net worth of $1 million. By age 25, it was over $100 million. *Courtesy of Marketing Communications (NEXT)*

2. The federal government defines a small business as one that employs less than 500 people. In this chapter, small business simply refers to someone who is self-employed.

FIGURE 20-4 Small businesses provide opportunities for many young people to launch a business. *Photo by David W. Tuttle*

CHAPTER 20 Entrepreneurial Skills ■ 253

Form of Organization

A business can be organized in one of three ways: proprietorship, partnership, or corporation.

Proprietorship. This is the simplest and most common form. A *proprietorship* is a business owned by one person, who receives all the profits. The owner may have employees.

Partnership. A partnership is a business that has two or more co-owners. In fact, *partnerships* often come about because proprietors need additional money or want help running the business. Owners in a partnership share in both the company's management and its profits.

Corporation. A *corporation* is very different from the other two forms. In return for a fee paid to the state, a corporation receives a charter, which allows the business to carry on certain activities. The owners of a corporation are called *stockholders* and they elect a *board of directors*. The board, in turn, makes major decisions about the company and hires the company president.

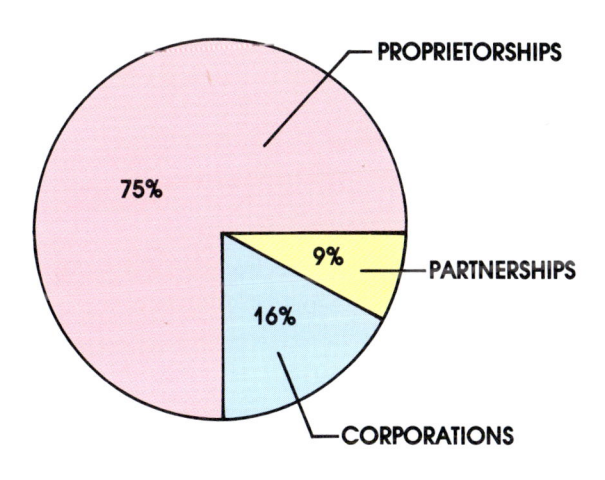

FIGURE 20-5 Proprietorships make up about seventy-five percent of all small business.

4. Ask students to provide illustrations of why a sole proprietor might form a partnership. (A creative artist needs a partner to manage the finances. An inventor needs capital to get a new product into production.)

FIGURE 20-6 Many proprietorships and partnerships are family owned and operated, such as this small business. *Photo by David W. Tuttle*

5. We tend to think of corporations as being large companies. However, a corporation may consist of only several people. Point out that stock in a corporation may be held privately, as opposed to being publicly traded.

254 ■ SECTION 4 Success Skills

What Would You Do?

The company you work for is losing business to foreign competition. The owner says he just can't compete if he has to continue paying high labor costs. He is looking for a buyer. If he can't sell the business, he is going to shut it down.

A group of employees has been meeting to try to help find a solution. One option being considered is for the employees to buy the company and run it themselves. This has been done successfully in a few businesses. If you were in a situation like this, what would you do?

*

* *WWYD Feature A.* One source estimated that in 1990 there were about 1,500 employee stock ownership plans (ESOP), triple the number a decade earlier.

about the benefits of self-employment. Here is what they told us:

"I never really liked working for other people. I like to try new things. That can be a problem when you are an employee. In my business, I can take full advantage of new ideas that appeal to me."

"Being self-employed, I can make my decisions quickly. I used to work for a large corporation where decision-making was very slow."

"I enjoy having a flexible schedule. Last week, my wife took two vacation days. I arranged my schedule so we could go camping."

FIGURE 20-8 The desire for independence is a major reason why people go into business for themselves. *Photo courtesy of Eagle Press & Graphics Inc.*

"In the shop where I worked, I did only one task. Now I can work on a project from beginning to end. I can use *all* my skills. And, I am working toward goals that are important to me."

"I am proud to be a business owner. Four years ago, we opened this small supermarket. We now have three, which will belong to our kids someday."

"When you work for yourself, no one can fire you!"

6

All work situations have negative points. Self-employment is no exception:

"In the beginning, the appliance-repair business brought in little money. But we still had to pay rent and other expenses."

FIGURE 20-7 Advances in technology have created many new opportunities. *Courtesy of AMETEK, Inc.*

ADVANTAGES AND DISADVANTAGES OF SELF-EMPLOYMENT

Being self-employed is different from working for someone else. Before starting a business, you should consider the advantages and disadvantages of working for yourself. We asked some entrepreneurs

6. Ask students if they can name additional benefits of self-employment. You may wish to assign Activity 3 at this time.

7. Ask students if they can name additional negative aspects of self-employment.

CHAPTER 20 Entrepreneurial Skills ■ 255

No one person can represent the experiences of all entrepreneurs. The following case study will give you a good idea of the advantages and disadvantages of self-employment. The workday of Ann Kirsten (the person in this case study) shows many of the freedoms, uncertainties, and responsibilities shared by small business owners.

Self-Employment Case Study

As an entrepreneur, Ann Kirsten does many types of work tasks. In a large business, each work task would probably be done by a single person. As you read this piece, which has been reprinted and slightly adapted from the *Occupational Outlook Quarterly*, keep in mind the variety of things that Ann has to be able to do.

The Day Begins. On a typical workday, Ann Kirsten of Washington, D.C. arrives at the Emporium, her small gift and card shop, at about 10 A.M. Stepping inside, she takes a sharp owner's look around the store, which holds a miscellaneous assortment of wares: crystal salad bowls, candles, neckties, placemats, scented soap, and toys are among the many items in stock.

FIGURE 20-9 Unfortunately, many small businesses do not succeed. Why? *Photo by Paul E. Meyers*

"I am a free-lance graphic artist. My income varies a lot. It is either 'feast' or 'famine' it seems."

"We are store owners in a one-industry town. As soon as the plant started laying off, we were affected. And it wasn't our fault! If this keeps on, we may have to close. We would lose the money we have put into the business. And we could lose our house and other property, too. We are hoping for the best."

"Being self-employed is high pressure. All the decisions are my responsibility. If I make a major mistake, all of us around here could be out of work."

"I often put in sixty- or seventy-hour weeks."

Even when you are self-employed, you will not be your own boss entirely. No matter what business you choose, you must satisfy your customers. And your *creditors* and your competitors will influence what you do. For instance, suppose the store down the street has a two-for-one sale. You may have to do the same at your store, too. The law also touches your business. Health authorities and insurance people will expect you to meet certain standards and to follow certain regulations. You will have to abide by wage and hour laws and keep proper tax and business records as well.

8. Discuss how a competitor may influence one's business practices. An example is a "gas war."

FIGURE 20-10 This shop doesn't open until 11 A.M., but it is open until 7 P.M. and the owner works six days a week. *Photo by David W. Tuttle*

9. An entrepreneur is often a jack-of-all-trades. Ask students to explain this term. (A person who can do passable work at various trades.)

The Emporium opens at 11 A.M. and Kirsten hurries to make sure everything is in order. She makes a fresh pot of coffee—a bonus for early customers—and checks to see that the store's shelves are well-stocked and tidy. Spotting a few gaps, she tells the two full-time salesclerks who have just arrived to shelve supplies of candle holders and ashtrays. She also instructs the employees to unpack a recently arrived carton of stainless steel serving bowls, tag them with the prices she has determined, and display them near the coffee mugs.

Answering the Mail. Satisfied that everything is in order, Kirsten takes the morning mail upstairs to a small room filled with so many cardboard boxes that it looks more like a stockroom than an executive office. Settling down at her old wooden desk, she opens the mail, taking special note of new merchandise catalogs, bills, and a customer check that has bounced. She answers some of the letters and files the rest into appropriate piles for future action.

Kirsten spends the rest of the morning in her office filling out several government forms required of self-employed persons. She is interrupted by a telephone call from a *supplier* who regrets that Kirsten's latest order will be delayed for three weeks. Annoyed but unable to do anything about the shipment date, Kirsten shrugs off the incident.

Unexpected Caller. A few minutes later, a sales representative unexpectedly walks in and tries to sell Kirsten a new line of paper placemats and napkins. Kirsten generally buys her merchandise from *wholesale houses* in New York City (which she visits about six times a year). But occasionally, she does buy from a visiting salesperson. Today she declines, however, believing that her current line of paper table items is adequate. Kirsten takes her time about making this decision, since her income hinges on her ability to make sound judgments about what her customers will buy. If she invests in an item that doesn't sell, she loses money.

Waiting on Customers. At 1 P.M., Kirsten goes back downstairs to relieve her clerks during their

FIGURE 20-11 Correspondence and other types of paperwork are a required part of all small business. *Photo by David W. Tuttle*

10. Many entrepreneurs maintain an office at home where they work after the business has closed. Or the business itself may be in the home.
11. Point out that when Kirsten takes time off from work, she is probably borrowing time that will need to be paid back later.
12. Kirsten's accountant is probably a self-employed person also.

FIGURE 20-12 Being able to leave the business for a short while to jog, run errands, or have lunch with a friend may be one advantage of self-employment. *Photo by David W. Tuttle*

lunch hours. Before starting the Emporium seven years ago, Kirsten enjoyed a fifteen-year career in public relations. She likes working with people and enjoys waiting on and talking to customers.

The clerks return and Kirsten grabs a quick lunch at a neighborhood delicatessen before running a business errand at the post office. She then takes time out for a haircut. Inasmuch as she is her own boss, Kirsten can take time off whenever she wants. Generally, however, she is reluctant to spend too much time away from the store, since there is always so much work there to be done.

Bookkeeping, too! Back at the office, Kirsten goes over the books with her accountant, who keeps track of income and outgo and evaluates the store's performance. Looking at recent sales income and expenses, Kirsten briefly remembers the days when she received a fixed yearly income. In those days, she regularly collected a paycheck from which her employers had already withheld money for State and Federal income taxes. Her share of payments for Social Security benefits, a health insurance plan, and other programs that assured her income during old age or periods of sickness had also been deducted. And like most employers, the organizations for which she worked had paid part of the cost of these benefits.

Looking over the books, Kirsten is happy to see a good rate of profit. If the store's income had not met expenses for the last several months, she would have to make up the difference out of her own savings. This rarely occurs nowadays, but, like many new businesses, the Emporium lost money during its first several months of operation.

Kirsten recalls, too, how she had to borrow money to start the business and persuade a lender that she could succeed. Then there had been the years of meeting payments on the borrowed money as well as interest for its use. These payments had to be made regularly, for a merchant is helpless without a good credit rating. As she looked back, Kirsten was gratified to see that it had all paid off.

End of a Long Day. Kirsten finishes conferring with her accountant at 6 P.M. and then goes downstairs to help wait on customers until the shop closes at 7. Several boxes of merchandise have arrived during the day, and Kirsten stays for an hour after closing to unpack and shelve a few items. She generally puts in at least a nine-hour workday—not counting "time off" when she reads magazines to keep up with buying trends or thinks about new ideas for the store—and works six days a week.

Every once in a while, Kirsten remembers the days when she was salaried and worked a forty-

13. A new business has to plan for the probability that it will actually lose money for a certain period of time.

14. During the Christmas season, Kirsten may work more like twelve hours a day.

258 ■ SECTION 4 Success Skills

17. Write the Small Business Administration, 1441 L. Street, N.W., Washington, DC 20416 for information about publications and services that they provide.

weaknesses. The traits needed by a self-employed person are:

1. Ability to take action when needed.
2. Ability to lead others.
3. Being dependable and trustworthy.
4. Being a good organizer.
5. Ability to work hard.
6. Ability to make good decisions.
7. Having a positive attitude.
8. Being honest and open.
9. Ability to accomplish goals.
10. Desire to succeed.
11. Willingness to take risks.

FIGURE 20-13 The satisfaction that comes from being self-employed often makes up for the long hours and other disadvantages. *Photo by David W. Tuttle*

15. Recall that a sole proprietor can possibly compensate for some shortcomings by forming a partnership or corporation.

hour, Monday-through-Friday week. She strongly believes, however, that the present freedom and challenge of being her own boss and the knowledge that her efforts are paying off in money that goes into her own pocket more than make up for the long hours and other disadvantages.

INGREDIENTS FOR SUCCESS

A successful business requires more than just interest and a desire to make money. Studies of businesses and conversations with business owners suggest that three things are necessary for a successful business: the right personality, know-how, and money.

Personality

Not everyone has the personality needed for self-employment. Success in business is not based on wishful thinking. If you want to be your own boss, you need to be honest about your strengths and

16. Return to Chapter 2 to review how Terry got started in his own business.

FIGURE 20-14 The traits required to be a good student or school leader are similar to those needed by entrepreneurs. *Photo by David W. Tuttle*

Know-how

Self-employed people need some knowledge in various areas of business. These include finance, economics, management, marketing, accounting, and commercial law. Business know-how is usually learned through coursework and on-the-job training. Before starting out on their own, most entrepreneurs work in others' businesses.

FIGURE 20-15 Many entrepreneurs, such as this store owner, take classes to sharpen their skills. *Photo by David W. Tuttle*

Pat King started his own restaurant last year. He had worked many years as a manager for a national chain before making his decision. Even after their business is started, many owners enroll in management training programs and take workshops and study materials provided by the Small Business Administration (SBA).

The SBA is an agency of the federal government. Its purpose is to encourage, assist, and protect the interests of small business. The SBA produces and distributes low-cost management assistance publications and conducts management workshops and courses. The agency also makes loans to small businesses. Your public librarian can help you find the location of the nearest SBA office.

Before starting a business in a trade, technical, or professional career, it is necessary to learn the required skills. For example, Kerry and Jill got training in electronics, worked for someone else, then started their own electronics repair business.

Another way to get business know-how is to buy a *franchise*. A franchise is a contract with a large company to sell goods and services within a certain area. Some well known franchises are 7-Eleven Food Stores, H.R. Block, Domino Pizza, and Holiday Inn. Franchise fees range from several thousand dollars to several hundred thousand dollars.

Money

The third key to successful self-employment is money. An entrepreneur must have enough capital (money) to start a business. Often this money can be borrowed from banks and other lending institutions. Business owners must pay rent, utilities, and other operating expenses. Equipment and supplies must be purchased. *Retailers* must be able to buy a large enough supply of merchandise to attract and hold customers. Any employees must be paid first. And, of course, there must be enough left over for the owner's salary.

The cost of going into business depends on the type of business, the location, size, and other factors. Often, the business that can be started with a small amount of money is also the business with the least potential for profit. On the other hand, businesses with good profit potential are out of the reach of most people because of the money required to begin.

Most small businesses start out slowly. It takes time for a new business to establish a reputation

18. You may wish to assign Activity 4 at this time.
19. It is often easier for an entrepreneur having a skilled trade (e.g., mechanic, hair stylist, computer repairer) to meet some capital requirements through her/his own efforts than it is for an owner of a retail business (say a yogurt shop) that is essentially dependent on the product to sell itself.

and build up a supply of loyal customers. The Small Business Administration says that it takes four to six months for some businesses to be self-supporting. Others take even longer. Unfortunately, some businesses never succeed and must close.

FIGURE 20-16 If you need to borrow money to start a business, the lender will expect to see a sound business plan. *Photo by Paul E. Meyers*

20. You may wish to conduct Activity 5 at this time. This can be a very relevant and informative activity.

ARE YOU THE TYPE?

To succeed in business, you must honestly evaluate your strengths and weaknesses. You will be your most important employee. If you recognize that you are weak in a certain area, you may be able to find a partner or hire an employee to help you. The exercise shown in Figure 20-17 will help you to see if you have the traits needed for self-employment.

How did you do? Count up the number of *YES* answers. If most of your answers are *YES*, you may have what it takes to run your own business. Review your answers again. Make sure you didn't answer *YES* because of wishful thinking.

If you have several *NO* or *NOT SURE* answers, you should probably not risk your money and your time in starting a business. You should recognize, however, that you can take steps to improve yourself and increase your chances of success.

21. Another good activity would be to administer the *Self-Directed Search* (SDS). This is a type of interest inventory, the outcome of which is an indication of one's "occupational personality."

ENTREPRENEUR RATING SCALE

1. I am a self-starter. I get things done. — YES   NOT SURE   NO
2. I like people. I can get along with just about anybody. — YES   NOT SURE   NO
3. I am a leader. I can get most people to go along when I start something. — YES   NOT SURE   NO
4. I like to take charge of things and see them through. — YES   NOT SURE   NO
5. I like to have a plan before I start. I'm usually the one to get things lined up when our group wants to do something. — YES   NOT SURE   NO
6. I like working hard for something I want. — YES   NOT SURE   NO
7. I can make up my mind in a hurry if I want to. — YES   NOT SURE   NO
8. People can trust me. I do what I say. — YES   NOT SURE   NO
9. If I make up my mind to do something, I'll see it through. — YES   NOT SURE   NO
10. I am always careful to write things down and to keep good records. — YES   NOT SURE   NO

(Adapted from: *Starting and Managing a Small Business of Your Own.* 1982). SBA—public domain.

FIGURE 20-17 Complete this exercise to see whether you have the traits to be an entrepreneur. (Do not write in this book.)

CHOOSING A BUSINESS

If you are serious about going into business, you will first need to identify what business you want to be in. You need to be clear about the kind of business even though you may not know exactly which one. For example, you may be sure you want to go into retailing, but not know what sort of store to open. Or you may decide that some other business is better than the one you originally considered. The time to change your mind is before you start a business, not after.

You might also begin by writing out a summary of your background and experience. Include what you learned on jobs, in school, and from hobbies (that relate to your business interests). Then write down what you would like to do. Try to match up

For more information about the SDS, write Psychological Assessment Resources, Inc., P.O. Box 998, Odessa, FL 33556.

CHAPTER 20 Entrepreneurial Skills ■ 261

what you have done with what you would like to do. If you don't like the business you choose, your lack of interest will probably lead to failure.

The more experience and training you have, the better your chances of success. So pick a field you know the most about. The best way to learn about a business is through actual experience. Seek a job working for somebody else in the business you are considering. Try to pick a well-managed, successful company. Once hired, learn as much management know-how as you possibly can.

22. This section provides a good overview of the many considerations involved in going into business. There are many ways to go about it. However, emphasize that even under the best of circumstances, self-employment is still a risky proposition.

What Would You Do?

You are a very good auto mechanic and take pride in your work. You can diagnose difficult problems that other mechanics often can't solve. Customers also know your work is good. Many of them specifically request that you work on their cars. This irritates some of your co-workers.

Recently several customers have remarked that you are too good of a mechanic to work for someone else. They say you ought to consider starting your own business. What would you do? *

FIGURE 20-18 Developing a salable skill is an excellent first step toward becoming an entrepreneur. *Courtesy of GE, photo by Mark Homan Studios*

23. Working for someone else first is probably the most common route to entrepreneurship.

* *WWYD Feature B.* Having a marketplace skill and a good reputation for quality work are two strong assets on which to build a business.

Education will help, too. While there may be no educational requirements for starting your own business, the more schooling you have, the better equipped you should be. For example, in most businesses, you must know how to figure interest and discounts, keep simple and accurate records, and take care of correspondence. How might you learn these skills in school?

Get all the facts you can about the kind of business you want to start. Find out what the appropriate trade association is, what it publishes, and what assistance it offers. Visit similar businesses to get a first-hand idea of how they operate. Read magazines, newspapers, and newsletters on the subject. Collect as much information as possible from other sources, even the competition. Talk with the local Chamber of Commerce, local business groups, banks, and the like.

Next, try to determine whether potential customers need or want the type of business in which you are interested. Don't take anything for granted. Even if certain products and services meet certain needs, people may want something different.

The business you are thinking about should be in tune with the trends of the time. Choose a field in which growth is expected. You will need to study a lot and seek advice from people who are in a position to know. Successful business owners are those who can make accurate predictions about the future.

FIGURE 20-19 This transportation business fulfilled a need that existing businesses weren't meeting. *Photo by Paul E. Meyers*

CHAPTER REVIEW

Chapter in Brief

- Small businesses are found in every type of industry. They make many important contributions to our society. Small business creates new jobs, recycles old buildings, provides opportunities for women and minorities, and creates many new products and services. A business can be organized as a proprietorship, partnership, or corporation.
- Self-employment has many advantages and many disadvantages. Entrepreneurs work for themselves, make their own decisions, have a flexible schedule, do a variety of tasks, and take pride in owning their own business. On the other hand, entrepreneurs have big responsibilities, work long hours, have fluctuating incomes, and risk the possibility of failing. The case study of Ann Kirsten illustrates many of the advantages and disadvantages.
- Being a successful businessperson requires the right personality, know-how, and money. Before considering starting a business, you should honestly evaluate your strengths and weaknesses. Not everyone is suited to owning their own business.
- If you are serious about going into business, pick a field you know the most about. The more experience and training you have, the better your chances of success. Find out all you can about the kind of business you want to start. Try to determine whether potential customers need or want the type of business in which you are interested. Choose a field in which growth is expected. Successful business owners are those who can make accurate predictions about the future.

Words to Know

board of directors individuals elected by the shareholders to assume responsibility for the management of their company.

charter a legal document giving a corporation permission to conduct certain business activities.

corporation a form of business organization in which shareholders own the business and elect a board of directors to manage the company.

creditors persons or companies to whom money is due.

entrepreneur one who runs her/his own business; a self-employed person.

franchise a contract with a parent company to use its name and sell goods or services within a certain area.

partnership a form of business organization in which two or more persons co-own the business.

proprietorship a form of business organization in which one person owns the business.

retailers businesses that sell directly to the consumer.

self-employed an individual who owns and operates a business; an entrepreneur.

stockholders individuals who purchase stock, or shares of ownership in a company.

supplier a person or agency that distributes goods to retailers.

wholesale houses businesses that sell to retailers rather than to consumers. *See also* supplier.

Questions to Answer

1. Why isn't there such a thing as a typical small business?
2. Name the four important contributions that small business makes to our society.
3. Name and briefly explain the three forms of business organization.
4. Give four advantages and four disadvantages of self-employment.
5. Ann Kirsten performs many different types of work tasks such as supervising employees and ordering new merchandise. Name five additional work tasks she performs.
6. Name the three main ingredients that are necessary for self-employment.
7. What is the SBA and what does it do?
8. Are you the type of person who might be a successful entrepreneur? Why or why not?
9. Why is the first six months often crucial in getting a new business started?
10. Why is having a trade or a technical skill a good first step in becoming an entrepreneur?

Activities to Do

1. You learned earlier that the most important contribution of small business is new inventions, products, and services. With your classmates, try to identify as many inventions, products, and services as you can that small businesses have introduced in the last several years.
2. Select someone who has achieved success in a business that he or she started. (A good resource is *Entrepreneurial Megabucks,* which contains a list of the 100 greatest entrepreneurs over the past twenty-five years.) After gathering information, write a two- to three-page biography. Turn in the paper to your teacher.
3. Contact two or three small business owners in your community and explain to them you are working on a class project. Ask them to identify the main reason for going into business. In class, pool your findings and discuss the results.
4. Check the reference section of your local public library for copies of franchise directories. (A good source is the *Franchise Opportunities Handbook* published by the U.S. Government Printing Office. It lists all the franchises available in the USA and people to contact for more information.) Select a franchise in which you are interested. Write to the franchisor and ask for their franchise package for prospective owners. Report your findings to the class.
5. Arrange with your instructor to duplicate copies of the "Entrepreneur Rating Scale" shown in Figure 20-17. Complete one yourself. Next, give one to a parent or family member and one to your supervisor at work and ask them to rate you. Compare ratings to see how well they agree. Discuss the results with your teacher.

---

1. Because small businesses vary greatly in terms of size, type of industry, form of organization, characteristics of owners, and so on.
2. (a) Creates new jobs. (b) Recycles old buildings and vacant businesses. (c) Provides opportunities for women and minorities. (d) Creates new inventions, products, and services.
3. (a) *Proprietorship*—owned by one person. (b) *Partnership*—has two or more co-owners. (c) *Corporation*—operates in accordance with a state charter. May be owned by one person or thousands of stockholders.
4. *Advantages*—working for oneself, can make own decisions, quickly, have flexible schedule, do a variety of tasks, have pride in ownership, can't be fired. *Disadvantages*—takes a while to become self-supporting, income may fluctuate, business affected by competition and by overall state of the economy, pressure and responsibility, long hours.
5. Additional work tasks include: writes correspondence, completes government forms, meets with suppliers and salespeople, waits on customers, maintains accounts and financial records, reads trade information, plans for the future.
6. (a) Right personality. (b) Know-how. (c) Money.
7. An agency of the federal government whose purpose is to encourage, assist, and protect the interests of small business.
8. based on study of Figure 20-17. See also Activity 5.
9. It takes a period of time for a new business to become known, develop loyal customers, and become self-supporting.
10. With a skill, you already have something salable. You probably also have a good idea of the market for such a skill, and perhaps a group of clients or customers.

24. This may be difficult to do on a national level. Focus on those products and services introduced in your local region. The telephone Yellow Pages can be used as a resource.
25. You might want to type and distribute a list of entrepreneurs for students to select from. Encyclopedias are probably the most readily available resource to use.

Topics to Discuss

1. New businesses are often started because they provide something better or different. Name and discuss products and services that you are dissatisfied with that could possibly lead to the creation of a new business.
2. Think about recent trends and how society is changing. Discuss the types of businesses that are likely to be successful five years from now. Provide reasons for your predictions.
3. During the late 1970s and early 1980s, dozens of young computer and software whizzes became millionaires while still in their teens. How were they able to accomplish so much at such a young age?

26. Brainstorm as many products and services as you can. Maybe you will come up with a winner.
27. Precede the discussion by reviewing the section on "Tomorrow's Jobs" in Chapter 14.
28. Creativity, imagination, and inventiveness are often more important than age or prior experience for achieving success in a new, emerging field.

High Five

FROM CATTLE TO COUNTRY MUSIC

George Strait was born near the small southwest Texas settlement of Poteet. His father was a junior high school mathematics teacher. "It wasn't exactly a country music upbringing," he recalls. "My dad didn't even have a record player, and when he listened to the radio, it was usually the news or the cow market reports. If a song happened to come on, I never paid much attention to what it was."

In high school, Strait was active in Future Farmers of America. He was on the chapter livestock judging team, participated in the parliamentary procedure contest, and received leadership training, including public speaking through chapter activities. He also played cornet and was occasionally the lead singer in, he says, "some of your basic high school garage bands. We'd play 'Gloria,' 'Louie, Louie,' and other music like that."

He spent a couple of uneventful semesters at Southwest Texas State University before joining the army. He was stationed in Hawaii, and worked in the payroll department. When the base commander organized a country band, Strait applied for the job. The music of Hank Williams, George Jones, and other country artists soon became his favorite style of music.

After the army, he returned to Texas and reenrolled in college. He finished his degree in agricultural education, becoming certified to teach vocational agriculture. While still in college, he put together his Ace in the Hole Band and began performing in local clubs.

After graduation, he tried to balance the duties of raising a family, working a job as a cattle ranch manager, and performing nights in dance halls. This was a very difficult and frustrating period for him. Strait made several unsuccessful trips to Nashville during these years.

After playing music for about seven years, he began to think that he wasn't good enough to make it as a musician. He accepted a job with a company that designed cattle pens, but at the last moment he decided to try music for one more year. About six months after Strait had almost given up on music, a record promoter landed him a contract with MCA/Nashville.

It would take Strait several more years to reach superstar status. By 1985 he was the Country Music Association's Male Vocalist of the Year. The award was repeated in 1986 and again in 1989. Twenty of his singles have reached Number One. All ten of his albums have sold gold (500,000), with two reaching platinum status (1 million). When he is not singing, Strait runs a cattle ranch in southern Texas.

Section Five

Managing Your Money

Chapter 21 Our Economic World
Chapter 22 The Consumer in the Marketplace
Chapter 23 Banking and Credit
Chapter 24 Budgeting, Saving, and Investing Money
Chapter 25 Insuring Against Loss
Chapter 26 Taxes and Taxation
Chapter 27 Social Security

In Chapter 21, you will learn about economics and the American free enterprise system. Economics is the study of how goods and services are produced, distributed, and used.

A consumer is someone who buys or uses goods and services. In Chapter 22, you will learn about consuming and your rights and responsibilities as a consumer.

Checking accounts are one of the most commonly used banking services. How to open and manage a checking account is explained in Chapter 23.

A person's financial well-being is related to how they spend and manage money. In Chapter 24, you will learn how to get the greatest benefit from your money by developing and using a budget. The chapter also deals with saving and investing money.

People buy insurance to protect themselves from risk due to fire, accident, illness, or other catastrophe. In Chapter 25, you will learn about health, life, home, and auto insurance.

In Chapter 26, you will learn about taxation and types of taxes. A tax is a required contribution of money that people make to the government.

Government programs that help people meet social and economic needs are called social security. The six most common types of social security programs are explained in Chapter 27.

CHAPTER TWENTY-ONE

Our Economic World

OUTLINE
Principles of Economics
Economic Systems
The American Free Enterprise System
Economic Growth
Economic Freedom
Chapter Review

OBJECTIVES
After reading this chapter, you should be able to:
- List the four factors of production.
- Explain the circular flow of economic activity.
- Illustrate how supply and demand influence market prices.
- Name and describe the two basic types of economic systems.
- Summarize characteristics of the American free enterprise system.
- Name the three things required for economic growth.
- Discuss types of economic freedom that you enjoy.

Over 120 million people are employed in the workforce. They work in hundreds of thousands of offices, stores, factories, farms, and other places. These men and women produce trillions of dollars worth of goods and services a year. This activity occurs without the government telling people where to work or what to produce.

FIGURE 21-1 The strength of America is due largely to the efforts of individual citizens. *Courtesy of Ford Motor Company and Sears Roebuck and Co., 1987 Annual Report*

268

1. Economics can be a very sophisticated subject. Concentrate on helping students to learn the basic concepts and vocabulary. The overall aim of this chapter is better understanding by students of their roles and responsibilities as consumers and producers.

CHAPTER 21 Our Economic World ■ 269

The main reason why our system works so well is that people are free to make economic decisions and to improve their financial well-being. To continue to succeed, our economy needs the support of all of us. You have responsibilities as both consumers and producers. In this chapter, you will learn about the American economic system and your part in it.

PRINCIPLES OF ECONOMICS

Economics is the study of how goods and services are produced, distributed, and used. Economics is also concerned with how people and governments choose what they buy from among the many things they want. You probably don't have much trouble spending your paycheck. The hard part involves making choices from among the many things you need and want. Federal, state, and local governments have the same types of choices to make.

The city of Centerville, for example, would like to build a new swimming pool at the city park. However, there is not enough money left in the budget after the city pays employees' salaries and bills. These expenses include street maintenance, garbage collection, and snow removal. A city, like an individual or family, has only so much money to spend.

Factors of Production

Meeting the needs of people and nations from what is available leads to the economic activity called *production*. Production takes place when a farmer grows corn, a nurse cares for a patient, or a barber cuts hair. In one way or another, all production involves the following four resources.

Natural Resources. Materials provided by nature are important to production. Soil, water, mineral deposits, and forests are all examples of a nation's resources. Human beings do not create them.

2. The term *economy* comes from the Greek word *Oikonomia* which means "household management."

FIGURE 21-2 Economics is an important part of our lives. Millions of economic choices are made every day. *Photo by Robert McKendrick. Courtesy of Underwriters Laboratories Inc.*

FIGURE 21-3 The United States is lucky to have an abundance of natural resources. *Courtesy of USX*

3. Note that production involves both "producing goods" and "producing services."

270 ■ SECTION 5 Managing Your Money

6. Use Figure 21-6 in explaining and discussing the circular flow. Trace the circular flow from the perspective of both "the public" and "business and industry."

FIGURE 21-4 A Japanese trainer working in an American auto assembly plant is common during production start-up operations. Combined with training programs in Japan, Japanese trainers travel to America to train the American workers. *Courtesy of Toyota Manufacturing, U.S.A., Inc.*

4 *Labor.* Labor includes all of the people employed in the workforce. Both the skill of the workforce and the amount of labor help to determine the amount of production.

Capital. Most people think of capital as money. To the economist, however, capital (sometimes called capital goods) is any person-made means of production. Tools, machines, and factories are examples of capital goods. Capital used skillfully can greatly increase productivity.

Management. Management refers to the people who organize and direct the other three factors. In Chapter 20, we called this entrepreneurship. Managers assume the risk of operating a business. Good organization and management apply to both one-person businesses and large corporations.

4. Labor includes both physical and mental effort.
5. Point out that consumption involves "consuming goods" and "consuming services."

Consumption

Several kinds of economic activities help people satisfy their needs and wants. Production is one such activity. A second kind of economic activity is *consumption*. This is the process of using goods and services that have been produced. Buying a pair of shoes, drinking a soda, and going to a movie are all different kinds of consumption. All of us are consumers.

There is a close relationship between consumers and producers. This is called the circular flow of economic activity. Here is how the circular flow works. Suppose that you work in the business or industry shown in Figure 21-6. The inside bottom arrow shows that you give your services to a producer who employs you. The business or in-

7. Ask students to name some of the markets in which they have participated in the last several days.

8. The law of supply and demand works two ways: (a) demand influences supply (heavy demand outstrips short supply), and (b) supply influences demand (plentiful supply stimulates sales; i.e., demand). Ask students to provide illustrations of each.

CHAPTER 21 Our Economic World ■ 271

dustry (producer) gives you wages for your work as indicated by the outside bottom arrow. But you also receive goods and services from producers, as the inside top arrow shows. For these goods and services, you pay money to producers, as indicated by the outside top arrow.

The Market

Whenever goods and services are bought and sold, a *market* is created. A market may be a neighborhood grocery store or an international grain market. Buyers and sellers may meet in person, or they may conduct their business by telephone, mail, or satellite transmission.

In a free economy, market prices rise and fall according to *supply* and *demand*. When the demand is greater than the supply, the seller will often raise the price of the goods or service. This encourages the producer to provide a greater supply of goods or services. Eventually, the supply begins to catch up with the demand. If the supply becomes greater than the demand, the seller may lower the price to help get rid of the excess supply. This situation happened with computer games in the early 1980s. When companies first introduced computer games, there was a great demand for them. Most games were selling in the $35-$40 range. Several years later, consumer interest lessened. There was an oversupply of games on the market. As a result, prices were slashed to $10 or less.

FIGURE 21-5 This farmer is involved in both production and consumption. Can you explain how? *Courtesy of Deere & Company*

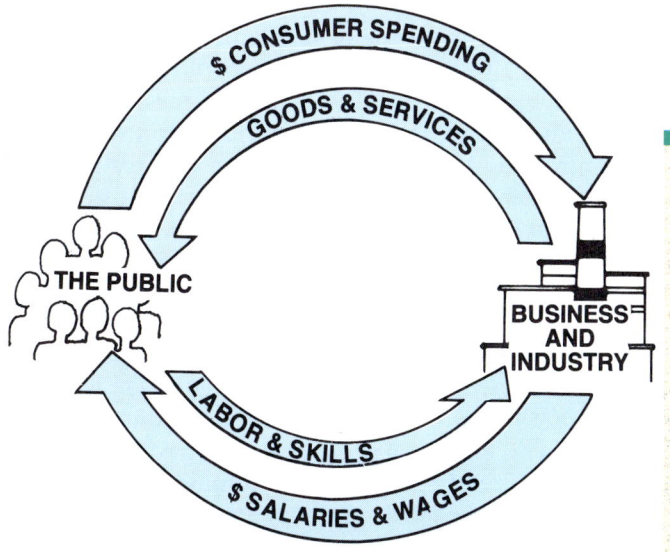

FIGURE 21-6 A circular flow of goods, services, and money takes place between consumers and producers.

What Would You Do?

A new brand of exercise shoes has just been introduced. They are "hot." Merchants can hardly keep them in stock. You go to the store to buy some. You love the shoes, but are shocked by the price. They are about $25 more than the shoes you usually buy. You would have to charge them since you don't have enough cash. Your mom suggests that you wait a few months until the price comes down. You doubt that they will be any cheaper later on. What would you do?

* *WWYD Feature A.* The law of supply and demand is a very reliable phenomenon. The price will undoubtedly come down at some point.

272 ■ SECTION 5 Managing Your Money

10. Under the influence of General Secretary Gorbachev, the Soviet Union has recently instituted economic reforms *(perestroika),* which seem to be moving the Soviet economy

FIGURE 21-7 In a centrally planned economy, shortages of consumer goods are common. *Photo by Edith Raviola*

In a market, *competition* helps to keep prices down. Suppose there is only one seller for a product or service. Prices will be high. Consumers have no real choice. But if there are many sellers, each competes with the other. Shoppers benefit from the lower prices that result.

ECONOMIC SYSTEMS

Countries don't solve their basic economic problems in the same ways. There are different economic systems. One major type is the centrally planned economy. Under this system, the people have no voice in economic decision-making. A central authority (government) owns all resources and sets wages. The group in power also controls all production and distribution. For example, the central government decides how much production should be devoted to consumer goods such as automobiles and washing machines.

9. You may wish to conduct Activity 1 at this time.

A second major type of economic system is free enterprise. In such an economy, people and industries can do more or less as they please. Private individuals and industries own and control the resources and means of production and distribution. People can work for themselves or they can sell their labor to someone else for wages. Consumers can buy and sell as they choose. Such buying and selling creates markets where supply and demand influence prices.

In actual practice, neither of these economies is ever found in a pure form. The Soviet Union leans heavily toward the centrally planned economy. In spite of this fact, Soviet consumers are free to decide how to spend their incomes. And some goods may be privately owned.

The United States leans heavily toward the free enterprise economy. The government, however, owns many resources and runs various industries.

more in the direction of free enterprise. Update the effects of *perestroika* at your discretion.

FIGURE 21-8 A wide variety of consumer goods is more typically found in a free enterprise economy. *Photo by Ruby Gold*

FIGURE 21-9 State governments are also driven by the profit motive. This state run lottery provides millions of dollars for education. *Photo by Ruby Gold*

It also controls certain prices. In addition, laws prohibit companies from making unsafe products. Both the Soviet Union and the United States, then, are "mixed economies."

THE AMERICAN FREE ENTERPRISE SYSTEM

The United States is said to have a free enterprise economy, even though it doesn't exist in a pure form. For the most part, the American economy runs by itself. People and industries make most of their own economic decisions. Let's look more closely at this system.

Private Ownership[11]

Suppose you go to a busy part of your town or city. You stop for an oil change at a shop owned by a friend. He says your car will be ready in half an hour. Since it is time for lunch, you go next door to a café to eat. You have just observed two examples of private ownership. For the most part, people can set up any legal kind of business they wish.

Profit Motive

All business owners want to make as much money as possible. To at least stay in operation, businesses must make a profit. Not all of them succeed.

Gino was surprised to learn that one of his favorite restaurants was going out of business. The restaurant had been owned by the same family for more than thirty years. The food was excellent and fairly priced. The restaurant seemed to have many loyal customers.

Since Gino had wanted to own a restaurant, he checked into buying it. In examining the financial records of the business, Gino discovered why it was being sold. Mr. Colletti, the owner, may have known how to prepare good food, but his knowledge of running a business was sadly outdated.

Gino figured that the costs of operation were about twenty percent higher than they should have been. He concluded that by using good business practices such as wholesale buying, quantity purchasing, and control of overhead he could make a good profit. What's more, he could do it without sacrificing quality or service.

Competition

Jenny wanted to buy a certain brand and style of shoes. Each store that carried the shoes wanted a different price. What did Jenny do? She bought

---

11. Private ownership is used here as the antithesis of government ownership. Private ownership, of course, includes ownership by individuals and corporations.

F·E·A·T·U·R·E

Counterfeit Goods Undercut the Economy

Few consumers are aware that they may be buying counterfeit goods. An estimated 250 different fake products have flooded the market. These include jewelry, jeans, handbags, auto parts, toys, electronic appliances, perfumes, and even prescription medicine. Products are often made to imitate popular and high status items such as Rolex watches, Izod knit shirts, Opium perfume, Cabbage Patch dolls, and Apple computers.

The economic toll is staggering. Counterfeit goods cut into company profits and reduce taxes paid. Fake products are estimated to cost the nation more than 100,000 jobs each year. Health and safety are also major concerns. Imagine driving around with fake brake shoes on your car! The death of a helicopter pilot was linked to the failure of a fake rotor assembly part. Many people are taking drugs and using health care products that contain ineffective or wrong ingredients.

Here is an example of how fake products are produced and distributed. A dishonest importer signs up a foreign manufacturer to make a shoddy oil filter. The manufacturer produces the filters. They are packaged into large crates generically labeled "oil filters" to pass U.S. Customs. The importer receives the filters and packs them in boxes printed with a real brand name. They are sold to a legitimate wholesaler as "overstock." The wholesaler (who is unaware they are fake) sells to reputable retail outlets. Consumers then come along and buy the phony filters at gas stations, auto dealers, chain stores, and the like.

There are a number of things you can do to protect yourself. Be wary when looking for hard-to-get toys and other fad items. When shopping for a product having a high status trademark, read labels carefully and pay close attention to workmanship. Look for sloppy printing, misspelled words, and altered logos on packages. Don't buy a product when the packaging is missing or not up to standard. For example, expensive watches that are sold in plastic pouches or plain boxes. Be cautious of products sold at "flea markets" or by street vendors. Buy at reputable businesses. If you do happen to get taken, you will be more likely to get a refund.

FIGURE 21-FEATURE Products are often made to imitate popular and prestigious merchandise such as this wrist watch. *Courtesy of Rolex Watch U.S.A., Inc.*

* *Counterfeit Goods Undercut the Economy.* The relevance of this feature is the economic impact of counterfeit goods. Emphasize the economic loss in profits, taxes, and jobs. Try to obtain examples of counterfeit goods to illustrate.

from the store where she would get the most for her money. If one company had a *monopoly* on the shoe business, Jenny would not have had a choice. A monopoly is exclusive control over the supply of a product or service. Every pair of shoes in all the stores would have been the same price.

Free enterprise needs competition. It forces producers to be efficient and encourages a wide variety of goods and services. Competition is so important to the American economy that the government has passed laws to forbid monopolies.

Freedom of Choice

You have already read that people having certain resources can start a business. They are not the only ones who have choices. Consumers and workers do too.

Consumer choices influence the types of goods and services produced. For instance, if consumers stop buying a certain product, it will probably disappear from store shelves. Buyers also help determine the prices of goods. Marketers will price as highly as they think the market will bear. If they are wrong, prices will fall. Prices also go down if heavy competition appears.

A similar situation exists with workers. They seek to be paid as much as possible. In a free enterprise economy, they are able to work for whomever they choose. And people who want to change jobs can do so.

Profit and competition help control this system. Some say that in free enterprise, markets are self-regulated. This means that supply and demand help set prices for goods and wages for workers.

FIGURE 21-11 United States citizens are the world's greatest consumers of goods and services. *Photo by Ruby Gold*

ECONOMIC GROWTH

The United States economy has grown steadily throughout the years. In order for this growth to continue, several things must occur. First, a portion of the nation's resources must be used to produce capital goods. Second, individuals and businesses must use a portion of their income for savings and investments. Third, the nation must use a portion of its resources for education and training. These influences on economic growth will now be illustrated.

You have read about the factors of production. As you will recall, these are natural resources, labor, capital, and management. Companies use these factors to provide both capital goods and consumer goods. But a country can't grow if it uses all of its resources to produce consumer goods and services.

FIGURE 21-10 Why do you think the price keeps going down? *Photo by Ruby Gold*

12. Have students name or bring to class an example of advertising in which the element of competition is clearly evident.

13. These things can be thought of as three types of economic "investments." Illustrate and discuss each one.

FIGURE 21-12 To remain competitive, manufacturing industries modernize plants and equipment regularly. *Courtesy of LTV Aircraft Products Group*

These don't produce anything of further value. Think about it. Once you buy them, a pair of jeans loses value. Capital goods, on the other hand, create future economic worth. Suppose a trucking company puts money into new rigs and loading docks. Workers use the docks over and over to load goods onto the trucks. These, in turn, carry cargo to distant markets.

When buying new capital goods, businesses often borrow money. For example, Mrs. Luna decides to add on to her flower shop. She doesn't have all the funds she needs. The bank gives her a loan. Where does First City Bank get this money? It comes from deposits from people like you. When the savings rate is high, banks have more money to lend businesses. The economy can grow.

14. Assign Activity 2 at this time. Have students chart the GNP since 1970 to illustrate periods of prosperity and recession.

*WWYD Feature B. Employment is very much affected by fluctuations in the business cycle. The person would be advised to build up some savings in anticipation of a possible recession.

Capital goods produce value. So do workers and managers. Offering further training to employees benefits a business. Skilled workers and managers contribute to future production and growth. Many employers pay for this education.

Patterns of Economic Growth

A free enterprise economy goes through various cycles. Tracing these shifts is like following the path of a roller coaster. A period of expanding economic growth is known as *prosperity*. During these good times, unemployment is low. Workers receive steady pay raises because companies make high profits. Since so many people are working, they buy many consumer items. This leads to increasing production. The supply of goods meets the demand, so prices stay down.

A downturn in the economy is called a *recession*. Let's see what can happen. Suppose there is a strong national feeling that the economy will turn bad. While scared consumers save more of their incomes, goods stack up on shelves. Companies make production cutbacks, which lead to worker layoffs. Young persons seeking their first jobs can't find work. People then have less money to spend, so they buy even fewer goods.

If a recession gets worse, a *depression* can result. In this situation, very large numbers of people become unemployed. Consumers purchase only what they really need. Business failures increase. Production drops further and even more workers lose their jobs.

Major fluctuations in economic growth have occurred for decades. Yet, there is much disagreement (even among economists) regarding causes and solutions. Many heated national debates result from disagreement among politicians and others over inflation, recession, and unemployment.

Inflation

A serious problem of our economic system is often *inflation*. This is when prices of goods and services rise rapidly. A *slight* upward trend in prices is very typical of free enterprise and isn't very serious. Wages usually increase along with prices. When prices go up much faster than wages, though, money loses some of its value. Let's see how this can happen. Workers at The Jiffy Company don't think

What Would You Do?

Business has been great at the shop where you work. You received a raise and are working a lot of overtime. You are using the extra money to buy clothes and other things you have always wanted. One day at break, you are showing a co-worker the picture of a new watch you put on layaway.

"It's neat," he says. "But if I were you, I wouldn't spend all of my paycheck. Good times won't last forever."

"I thought business was good," you say.

"It is," he responds. "This is the way it always is before things slow down and we get laid off."

You haven't thought about that. You wonder if you should go ahead and buy the expensive watch. What would you do?

FIGURE 21-13 Ask a parent or other adult how much they paid for a movie ticket at your age. The increase is due largely to inflation. *Photo by Ruby Gold*

15. Conduct Activity 3 at this time. An alternative would be to show a film or video. Perhaps the school librarian or AV Director could help you locate something on the Great Depression.

16. The outcomes of local, state, and national elections are often influenced by prevailing economic conditions. Ask students to provide examples.

their wages are keeping up with the cost of living. Through their union, employees bargain for pay increases. To cover the raises, the company raises the prices of its products. Consumers buying a Jiffy Food Processor, for example, will now pay more for it. If there are price increases throughout the economy, Jiffy's workers will continue to seek higher wages.

What causes inflation? There is no single, easy answer. However, economists generally agree that the following factors fuel inflation:

1. Excessive consumer demand
2. Government spending and *deficits*
3. Increased energy costs
4. Decreased productivity
5. Government regulations
6. Fear of future inflation

Even though the causes are complex, inflation can be curbed. All segments of society, including government, business, labor, and consumers, must work together to control it.

ECONOMIC FREEDOM

You have learned that in a free enterprise system, individuals make most of the economic decisions. Another way of saying this is that people in a market economy enjoy economic freedom. Economic freedom is a collection of the following rights, which allow people to make free choices:

1. The right to choose an occupation.
2. The right to change occupations or jobs.
3. The right to engage in business and to make a profit.
4. The right to spend money as one chooses.
5. The right to offer our goods or services at a price we decide.
6. The right to reject prices on goods or services we may want to buy.
7. The right to use property and wealth to produce income.
8. The right to succeed, limited only by one's ambition and ability.

17. Ask students to provide specific illustrations of the six inflation factors.

FIGURE 21-14 When you graduate from high school or college, you will have many choices to make about your future. Not everyone in the world is as fortunate. *Courtesy of Siena College, Loudonville, NY*

Economic freedom is not available to everyone in the world. Like other freedoms, people often take economic freedom for granted. Economic freedom can be lost or weakened if individuals, businesses, and governments fail to act as responsible consumers and producers.

18. These can also be characterized as personal economic choices. Each person is free to make choices, but must decide what he/she wants and set goals.

CHAPTER REVIEW

Chapter in Brief

- Economics is the study of how goods and services are produced, distributed, and used. Economics mainly deals with how things that people need and want are made and brought to them. It is also concerned with how people and governments choose what they buy from among the many things they want.
- Meeting the needs of people and nations from what is available leads to the economic activity called production. All production involves four resources: natural resources, labor, capital, and management.
- Consumption is the process of using goods and services that have been produced. All of us are consumers. Consumers and producers are linked together by what is called the circular flow of economic activity.
- Whenever goods and services are bought and sold, a market is created. In a market, competition helps to keep prices down.
- There are two major types of economic systems. In a centrally planned economy, the government owns all resources and controls production and distribution. In a free enterprise economy, private individuals and companies own most of the resources and control production and distribution.
- The American free enterprise system has four main characteristics: private ownership, profit motive, competition, and freedom of choice. The system runs largely by itself without government interference.
- In order for economic growth to continue, several things must occur. First, a portion of the nation's resources must be used to produce capital goods. Second, individuals and businesses must use a portion of their income for savings and investment. Third, the nation must use a portion of its resources for education and training.
- A free enterprise economy goes through various cycles. A period of expanding economic growth is known as prosperity. A downturn in the economy is called a recession. A very serious recession can lead to a depression.
- Inflation is when prices of goods and services rise too rapidly. This problem is caused by many factors, including: excessive consumer demand, government spending, increased energy costs, decresed productivity, government regulations, and fear of future inflation.
- Economic freedom is not available to everyone in the world. It can be lost or weakened if individuals, businesses, and governments fail to act as responsible consumers and producers.

Words to Know

competition the efforts of sellers to win potential customers.

consumption the process of using goods and services that have been produced.

deficits when the government spends more than it takes in.

demand the willingness of consumers to spend money for goods and services (when demand increases, the price generally goes up).

depression a severe recession marked by stagnant business activity, scarcity of goods and money, and high unemployment.

economics the study of how goods and services are produced, distributed, and used.

inflation a sharp increase in the cost of goods and services.

market marketplace; the place where buyers and sellers meet to conduct business.

monopoly exclusive control of the supply of any goods or service in a given market.

production the making of goods available for human needs and wants.

prosperity a period of expanding economic growth.

recession a period of declining economic growth.

supply the amount of goods available for sale (when the supply is plentiful, the price generally decreases).

Questions to Answer

1. What is the most important economic issue with which individuals and governments must deal?
2. All production involves four factors. Name them and briefly describe each one.
3. What phrase is used to describe the relationship between consumers and producers?
4. Explain how market prices rise and fall as a result of supply and demand.
5. Name two differences between a centrally planned economy and a free enterprise economy.
6. List the four characteristics of free enterprise.
7. Why is it important for individuals and businesses to save and invest money?
8. Why is it important for companies to invest in training for workers and managers?
9. The economic growth of a free market economy goes through cycles like the path of a roller coaster. Give an example.
10. How do the following factors contribute to inflation: (a) government spending, and (b) decreased productivity?

1. Making choices from among the many needs and wants.
2. (a) *Natural resources*—materials provided by nature. (b) *Labor*—number of workers and skills of the workforce. (c) *Capital*—tools, machines, factories, and other means of production. (d) *Management*—people who organize and direct the other three factors.
3. The circular flow of economic activity.
4. If the supply is greater than the demand, prices usually fall. When the demand is greater than the supply, prices often go up.
5. *Centrally planned*—government owns resources, government controls production, people have no voice in economic decision-making. *Free enterprise*—individuals own resources, individuals control production, people have great influence in economic decision-making.
6. (a) Private ownership. (b) Profit motive. (c) Competition. (d) Freedom of choice.
7. Saving and investing provides one pool of funds that business can borrow and use for expansion.
8. Skilled workers and managers contribute to future production and growth.
9. The roller coaster path can best be shown on a graph. Expanding economic growth is shown as peaks on the graph. Declining economic growth is shown as valleys on the graph.
10. *Government spending* contributes to inflation by increasing demand for commodities (including money). *Decreased productivity* contributes to inflation by raising the cost of producing goods and services.

Activities to Do

1. As a class, identify someone in your community who has lived in a country with a centrally planned economy. Invite the person to class to share personal experiences. Before the person arrives, prepare questions that you want to ask.
2. You often read or hear news reports about the gross national product (GNP). What is the GNP? How is it figured? How is the GNP used as a measurement of economic growth? Use encyclopedias or other resources to answer these questions.
3. Does someone you know remember The Great Depression? As a class, invite some people to speak about what it was like. Be sure to prepare questions ahead of time.

Topics to Discuss

1. The early 1980s was a very difficult period for automakers. There were low sales and foreign competition. Large companies such as General Motors, Ford, and Chrysler lost billions of dollars. Thousands of autoworkers lost their jobs. Yet, during this period, the price of new cars continued to rise. This seems to differ from what we have learned about the law of supply and demand. Discuss this situation in class.
2. You have learned that inflation's causes are many. Discuss how the following individuals might contribute to inflation:
   - A union leader negotiating a labor contract.
   - A merchant setting prices for goods.
   - A factory worker assembling car parts.
   - A consumer shopping for a video cassette recorder.
   - An elected official preparing a new budget.
3. What are some of the things the government often does during periods of recession to help stimulate the economy and relieve unemployment?

---

19. The early 1980s was a period of double-digit inflation caused primarily by a dramatic increase in the price of oil. Because so much of the economy is dependent on energy, auto prices went up independent of demand.
20. (a) Union leader might demand excessive wage increases. (b) Merchant might price goods too high. (c) Factory worker might work less productively. (d) Consumer might want a "hot" item in short supply. (e) Elected official might propose higher expenditures than revenues.
21. During a recession, the government often lowers interest rates, cuts taxes, and provides job training programs. Perhaps students can name other things.

1. Recall that the nature of a market was described in Chapter 21.
2. Consumer skills include skills dealt with in previous chapters: interpersonal skills (9), decision-making skills (12), communication skills (15), and math and measurement skills (16).

CHAPTER TWENTY-TWO

The Consumer in the Marketplace

OUTLINE
You as a Consumer
What is Consuming?
Advertising and the Consumer
Consumer Rights
Consumer Responsibilities
Consumer Complaints
Chapter Review

OBJECTIVES
After reading this chapter, you should be able to:
- Give examples of goods and services that are consumed.
- Name and describe the three stages involved in consuming goods and services.
- Identify different advertising techniques.
- Discuss types of consumer rights.
- Describe responsibilities of consumers.
- Summarize steps to take in dealing with consumer problems.

FIGURE 22-1 Suppose you were hungry. Choosing one of these restaurants would require some consumer decision-making. *Courtesy of NY Convention & Visitors Bureau*

1   A market is anywhere two or more parties come together to buy and sell. At one time, the market was a clearing along the river. There were few goods to buy and little choice available.

Now, the market may be a department store, service station, grocery store, movie theater, or barber shop. All markets operate basically the same. That is, sellers wish to attract buyers and then make a profit on the sale. Buyers, on the other hand, look for good quality at a low price.

As a buyer, you will make decisions all your life. Today, you may choose between two brands of shampoo. In a few years, you may need to make more important choices, such as which house to buy. Making a mistake then could be very costly. By learning wise consumer skills now, you might save yourself problems later.   2

3. Make sure students understand the difference between *wants* and *needs* by asking them to provide examples of each.

282

4. For major purchases, students should use a formal decision-making strategy. You may wish to review Figure 12-3.

YOU AS A CONSUMER

A *consumer* is someone who buys or uses goods and services. Goods are articles that are produced or manufactured. Some goods, such as food, are used up almost immediately. Other goods last for many years. For instance, do you know someone who has an old car that runs well? A house is also a type of good. If properly built and maintained, a house may last for a long time.

Services differ from goods. Services involve the payment of money to people and to businesses for work performed. Having a suit dry cleaned and getting a haircut are personal services. We pay fees to doctors, dentists, and lawyers in exchange for their knowledge and skills. Buying life insurance or obtaining a credit card involves the use of business services. Many common services that we use are for maintenance and repair work, such as having an automobile tuned up or a TV fixed. Entertainment and recreation are also types of services that we often purchase.

Money buys food, clothing, and other necessities of life. We also buy goods and services that we want but may not need. A pair of designer jeans and a concert ticket are examples of things that we may want. People often use the term *need* when they really mean *want*. To say that you need a new pair of designer jeans to wear to the game is probably not true. You may want the jeans, but you do not actually need them. Needs are necessities; wants are luxuries.

FIGURE 22-2 Many of us *want* to own a camera. But, for a photographer, having a camera is a *need*. Photo by Paul E. Meyers

5. Bring to class or assign students to go to the school or public library to peruse copies of *Consumer Reports*. Show other consumer magazines as appropriate.

CHAPTER 22 The Consumer in the Marketplace ■ 283

WHAT IS CONSUMING?

Being a consumer is more than simply paying money for something. Consuming involves three stages—choosing, buying, and using.

Making Choices

Buying always involves choosing or making choices. You have to eat in order to stay alive, so that really is not a choice. However, you *do* have to make decisions about what you eat. Do you eat a balanced diet or only frozen pizzas and soft drinks? Do you prepare meals at home or eat in restaurants? Are you like Mike? He often skips meals in order to spend money on movie tickets.

Sometimes, you have to choose between two similar products or services. Suppose you are going to buy a pair of shoes. The two pairs of shoes you like vary in price and quality. How do you decide which pair to buy? Some choices involve different kinds of products or services. Let's say you would like to have a perm and a sweater. But you only have enough money for one of these. Which will you decide to buy? Another type of choice is that between spending your money or saving it. This may be the most difficult choice of all. If you save some of your money, it will mean doing without some things that you would like to have now.

Buying Wisely

This stage begins once you have decided to buy. Knowledge and planning are very important to wise buying. There are several ways to learn about different products and services. You can talk with friends and family, attend special classes, and read consumer magazines. *Consumer Reports* is perhaps the best-known consumer magazine. It rates various products in terms of price, quality, and other factors. Knowing which products are rated highly can save you shopping time as well as money. There are still other things you can do to be a good shopper.

Bill Martin is a wise consumer. Let's see how he saves money on food and clothing. First of all, Bill never shops for food when he is hungry. He knows that when he is hungry he tends to buy food on impulse. To avoid exceeding his food budget, Bill plans what he will buy. He writes everything on a list and follows it. Bill knows that the grocery stores in his town run sales on Tuesdays and Wednesdays, so he shops then when possible. He buys *generic products* when he can because the quality is good and the prices are lower.

6. Explain the difference between *brand name* (DelMonte, Kraft, Campbells), *store brand* (Safeway, Kroger, Walgreen), and *generic* (product name only) products.

284 ■ SECTION 5 Managing Your Money

FIGURE 22-3 Public libraries generally subscribe to a variety of consumer magazines. Consult such materials before making a major purchase. *Photo by Paul E. Meyers*

*WWYD Feature A. Some people do have a negative attitude toward generic foods. Generic brands *are* often lower in quality than brand names. However, the nutritional value is generally about the same. Advise students to try store brands and generics and decide for themselves.

What Would You Do?

You live in the city where you work and share an apartment with several friends. You all pool grocery money and take turns shopping and cooking. You are more thrifty than your roommates. You often buy store brands and generics rather than more expensive brand name foods. As you are unloading groceries, one of your roommates comes into the kitchen.

"What's this stuff," she bellows. "I'm not eating this generic junk. We can afford to buy some decent food."

What would you do?

*

7. You may wish to assign Activity 1 at this time.

8. Throughout this chapter, encourage students to share personal experiences regarding comparison shopping, using credit,

Large sizes of cereal and canned food are often good buys, and Bill is always sure to use up these products. If some of the food is wasted, a large size isn't a bargain. Last week, Bill saw some dented cans in a bin. He passed the bin without buying because the food might have been spoiled. Buying spoiled food, no matter how cheap, is no bargain.

Recently, Bill went to a department store to look for a new shirt. He found four he liked, but rejected two right away. The care label on one said "dry clean only." Over several years, dry cleaning can be expensive. The other rejected shirt was 100 percent cotton and would need to be ironed. Of the two remaining shirts, one was better made than the other.

However, before buying the better-made shirt, Bill decided to do some *comparison shopping*. He first checked prices in a mail-order catalog. They were slightly cheaper than the store's, but he would have to wait for the shirt to be delivered in the mail. He would also have to pay postage. Then Bill saw a discount store's newspaper ad for shirts. When Bill reached the store, a clerk was putting shirts on a shelf. Two of them were exactly what Bill wanted. The labels showed they were *brand-name* shirts. Best of all, the shirts were on sale for 25 percent off.

Buying wisely also involves the careful use of credit. Some businesses may sell products cheaper when you pay cash. If you do charge a purchase, it is important to know how much more the product or service will cost you. Usually, if you pay within a certain amount of time, the credit is free. If you don't pay right away, though, credit may be expensive.

Using Goods and Services Properly

Wise consuming doesn't end after you bring a product home. If a product is ruined because of carelessness, you have wasted money. Treat products like you want them to last forever. Suppose you just bought a new hair dryer. Be sure to save the receipt in case you have to return the product. Then, read the instructions carefully *before* trying it out. Once you are sure the item works, check the carton for the *warranty* card. A warranty is a guarantee or promise that a product is free from defects. Fill out the card and send it in right away.

You are now ready to enjoy your new hair dryer. Always use it according to directions. Remember that if you misuse a product, *you* are responsible for any damage. The company that made the hair dryer won't honor the warranty on a misused product.

problems with faulty appliances, being a wise consumer of services, and the like. Everyone probably has a "horror" or "success" story to share.

FIGURE 22-4 By comparison shopping, you can get more value for your money. *Courtesy of Sears, Roebuck and Co. 1987 Annual Report*

FIGURE 22-5 It is easy to say "charge it," but remember that the bill will arrive later. *Photo by Information/ Education Inc.*

Being a wise consumer of services is also important. For example, the price of an oil change may vary by ten dollars or more depending on where you have a car serviced. Watch for advertising by automobile dealers, discount stores, service stations, and tire and appliance service centers. Such businesses frequently lower the price on oil changes simply to increase business and get you into their store. Or if you want to save the most money, buy the oil and filter at a discount store and change it yourself.

ADVERTISING AND THE CONSUMER

Sellers of goods and services use *advertising* to attract potential buyers. Advertising is any type of public notice or message. It is all around us. It is in newspapers and magazines. Ads also appear on TV, buses, signs, and billboards. Do you receive advertising in the mail? (That form is called *direct-mail advertising*.)

9. Have students bring in all of the direct-mail advertising received at home (ask permission to do so). Compare and discuss the different approaches used by advertisers.

9

F·E·A·T·U·R·E

Buying a Used Car

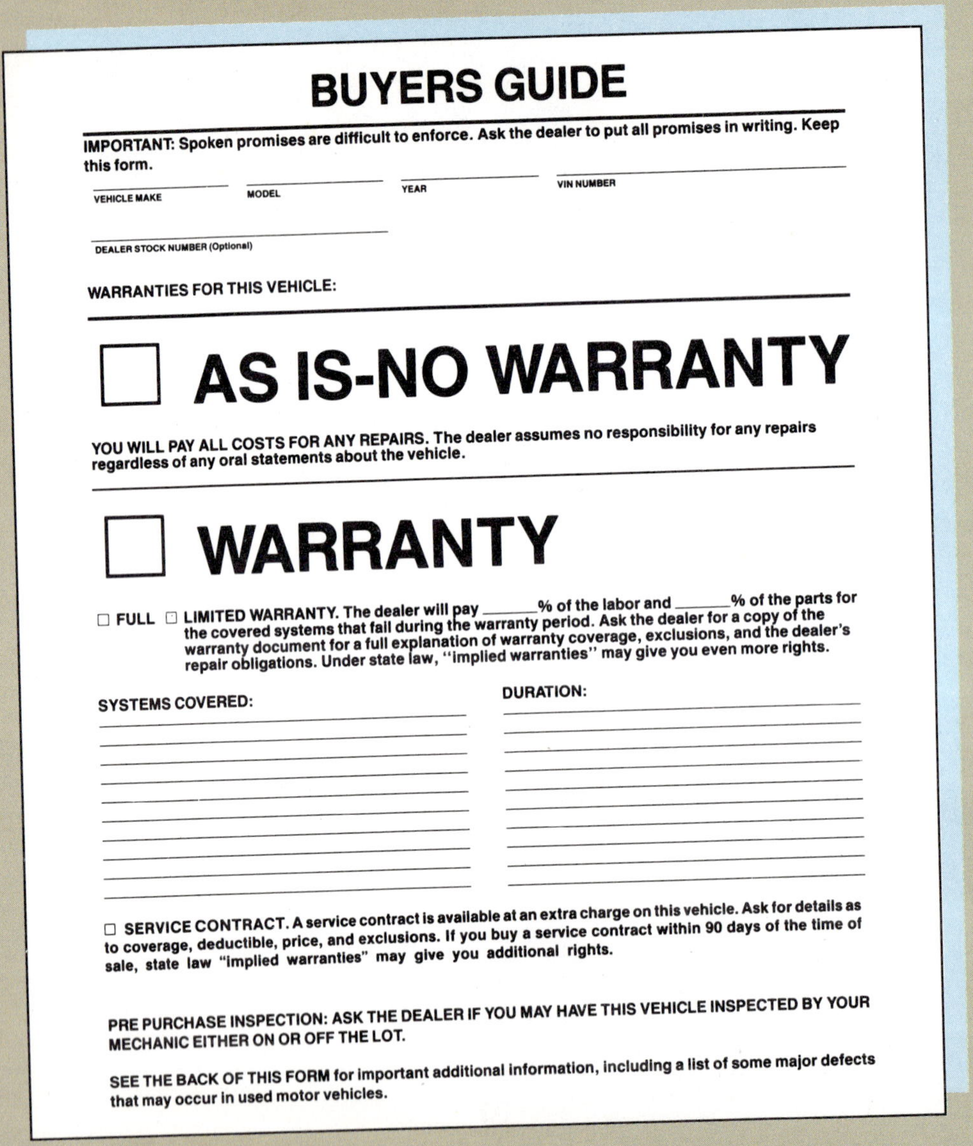

BUYERS GUIDE

IMPORTANT: Spoken promises are difficult to enforce. Ask the dealer to put all promises in writing. Keep this form.

VEHICLE MAKE _____ MODEL _____ YEAR _____ VIN NUMBER _____

DEALER STOCK NUMBER (Optional) _____

WARRANTIES FOR THIS VEHICLE:

☐ **AS IS-NO WARRANTY**

YOU WILL PAY ALL COSTS FOR ANY REPAIRS. The dealer assumes no responsibility for any repairs regardless of any oral statements about the vehicle.

☐ **WARRANTY**

☐ FULL ☐ LIMITED WARRANTY. The dealer will pay _____ % of the labor and _____ % of the parts for the covered systems that fail during the warranty period. Ask the dealer for a copy of the warranty document for a full explanation of warranty coverage, exclusions, and the dealer's repair obligations. Under state law, "implied warranties" may give you even more rights.

SYSTEMS COVERED: _____   **DURATION:** _____

☐ SERVICE CONTRACT. A service contract is available at an extra charge on this vehicle. Ask for details as to coverage, deductible, price, and exclusions. If you buy a service contract within 90 days of the time of sale, state law "implied warranties" may give you additional rights.

PRE PURCHASE INSPECTION: ASK THE DEALER IF YOU MAY HAVE THIS VEHICLE INSPECTED BY YOUR MECHANIC EITHER ON OR OFF THE LOT.

SEE THE BACK OF THIS FORM for important additional information, including a list of some major defects that may occur in used motor vehicles.

FIGURE 22-FEATURE Information contained on the Buyers Guide becomes a legal part of the sales contract for a used car. *Courtesy of Reynolds & Reynolds*

For most of us, car ownership begins by buying a used car. In fact, used car sales outnumber new car sales by about two to one. Many people simply cannot afford the cost of buying a new car. Others, though, actually prefer a used car to a new one. They say that used cars are a much better value for the money.

The majority of used cars are bought from private owners, new car dealers, used car dealers, and auto rental companies. Each has advantages and disadvantages. A good car at a fair price may be found through any of the four sources. New car dealers, however, are probably the best overall source. New car dealers sell used autos that have been traded in on new ones. They usually keep only the newer and better cars on their lots. Cars are usually reconditioned and offered with some type of warranty. The dealer wants you to be satisfied and come back later and buy a new car. However, used car prices at a new car dealership are usually higher than elsewhere. This is because of the greater cost of doing business.

Once you have located a car that interests you, make a careful inspection. You don't have to be an expert on cars to spot major problems. Look for body damage and signs of rust. Look under the car for holes in the exhaust system and for evidence of fluids leaking from engine, radiator, transmission, or brakes. Drive the car and listen for noises, rattles, and vibrations. Note anything about which you feel suspicious or uncomfortable. Not all problems are serious. But you need to find out what things will need to be fixed or replaced if you decide to buy.

A careful examination of a used car and a test drive should help you to eliminate unacceptable ones. Before agreeing to buy, however, take several more steps:

1. Get an idea of the price for the year and model car that you are considering. Check the *Official Used Car Guide* published by the National Automobile Dealers Association. The NADA guide can be found at most credit unions, banks, and public libraries.
2. Confirm the mileage. The law requires that the seller provide the buyer with a signed statement indicating the current mileage. Anyone who illegally tampers with an odometer, or who fails to provide the required disclosure statement may be sued.
3. Take it to a mechanic for an inspection. You should not rely solely on your judgment about a car. Hidden problems in the engine, transmission, or rear axle are of the most concern because these are costly to repair.
4. Contact the previous owner. Federal law requires dealers to have this information. Most reputable dealers will give you the name and phone number of this person. Call the person and explain that you are thinking about buying his or her previous car. You may be surprised at how cooperative and honest this person can be.
5. Check out the warranty. In May 1985, a new Federal Trade Commission rule took effect. The rule requires sellers of used cars (except private owners) to place a large "Buyers Guide" window sticker on each car. The guide makes clear what type of warranty is provided with the car. Many consumer experts say not to buy a used car "as is." Get a warranty, even if it is just for thirty days. A warranty provides important financial and legal protection.

Now you are ready to finalize the deal. Most buyers and salespeople expect to haggle a little over the price. However, don't expect the salesperson to lower the price much. Or don't expect the seller to do a lot of free repairs as part of the deal. The margin of profit on a used car is fairly low.

Dealers try to make it easy for you to buy a car by providing financing. However, their rates will often be higher than you can find elsewhere. Don't be afraid to tell the salesperson that you will get your own financing. To hold the car, you may be required to leave a small deposit.

Once you pay for the car, it is yours. You will then need to arrange for insurance, license plates, and a new title. After that you can slip behind the wheel, buckle up, and take your car for a cruise. Drive carefully.

Buying a Used Car. This is a high-interest topic for many young people. Conduct Activity 5 and Discussion Topic 6 concurrent with discussion of this feature. If possible, have available a copy of the

Official Used Car Guide. A library, credit union, or auto dealer might be willing to donate several out-of-date issues for instructional purposes.

288 ■ SECTION 5 Managing Your Money

FIGURE 22-6 How does an advertising sign such as this benefit the community? *Photo by Paul E. Meyers*

Advertising is very important for both the seller and the consumer. From a business point of view, the purpose of advertising is to sell goods and services. For consumers, advertising provides information about goods and services for sale.

What are some ways that advertising helps you, the consumer? Well, suppose you see two newspaper ads for A-1 Tents. One store's price is cheaper than the other's. Without leaving your home, you can decide where to buy the tent at the best price. This way, you don't have to go from store to store to check prices. You will save time and money.

The next day, you hear a radio spot in which the announcer talks about a bargain tune-up at Smith's Garage. A while later, you see an ad in the window of Pope's Auto. On the same tune-up, they offer a better price than Smith's. Again, by comparing advertising, you are able to save money.

Do you complain about ads on radio and TV? Without advertising, many of your favorite programs would go off the air. This is because most of the costs of producing these programs are paid for by advertising. Newspapers and magazines are also operated with money made through advertising. As you can see, without advertising our world would be quite different than it is now.

FIGURE 22-7 Advertising can be very expensive. Advertisers had to pay $675,000 for each thirty-second spot during the 1989 Super Bowl. *Photo by Paul E. Meyers*

10. Point out that "comparing advertising" is a form of "comparison shopping."

CHAPTER 22 The Consumer in the Marketplace ■ 289

11. Ask students if any of them have been seduced by advertising to buy a product or service that they later regretted.

Advertising also has disadvantages. Consumers pay for it. The cost of advertising often ranges from zero to five percent of the selling price of a product or service. So $0.50 of a $10 price tag could be advertising costs.

Advertising can be expensive in yet other ways. It can convince us to buy things we may not actually need. Jason knows this—now.

Jason had been saving his hard-earned money for a used motorcycle. He already had $250. Last winter, he kept seeing ads for leather coats. Jason already had a nice coat, but many of his friends had leather ones. They were nice. On the way to the bank one day, Jason passed the clothing store and went in. He entered with $250 and left with a leather coat and a few dollars. After several weeks, he was sorry he had not saved the money. Jason had to start saving for a motorcycle all over again.

Sometimes, we do need a product or service. There may be so many ads for it that we have trouble deciding. Consumers might make choices based on false advertising claims. Most advertisers, though, are honest. A few do make false promises or cheat the public in other ways. How to deal with such situations is discussed later in this chapter.

Advertising Techniques

To get us to remember their products or services, advertisers use such means as pictures, slogans, and jingles. In fact, we may often use a brand name to refer to a whole class of products. For example, how many times have you heard the brand name "Scotch tape" used instead of cellophane tape? Also, how about Kleenex tissues, Xerox copies, and Levis jeans? Can you think of other examples?

Once people are familiar with a product's name, they may buy it. But advertisers don't take chances. To achieve their aims, advertisers use proven methods such as the following.

Endorsements. Famous people present the advertising message. For example, a famous athlete may tell you she uses a Whammo tennis racquet. If the racquet is good enough for her, it should suit you. Right? That is how the advertiser wants you to think.

Familiarity. You hear a jingle, musical theme, or slogan over and over. The advertiser wants you to become familiar with a product and remember it.

Association. This approach often is seen during the holiday season. Here is an example. A horse-drawn sleigh passes by a beautiful, snow-covered

12. Have students provide additional examples of brand names that are used to refer to a whole class of products.

Profile in Quality #9: *To many people the quality of a car is the dependability of the car. Not just when it's new, but thousands of miles down the road. Ford's quality is well documented. In nationwide surveys, for 7 years running, owners of Lincoln, Mercury and Ford cars and light trucks have reported fewer problems, on average, than owners of any other vehicles designed and built in North America.* This dependability is backed by Ford Motor Company's 6 year/60,000 mile powertrain warranty.***

One more reason Ford Motor Company has designed and built the highest quality American cars and trucks for 7 years running.

Quality is Job 1.

FORD · LINCOLN · MERCURY · FORD TRUCKS · FORD TRACTORS

*Based on an average of owner-reported problems in a series of surveys of '81–'87 models designed and built in North America.
Restrictions and deductible apply. Ask your dealer for a copy of this limited warranty. **Buckle up—Together we can save lives.

FIGURE 22-8 To attract your attention, advertisers use many techniques. *Courtesy of Ford Motor Company*

landscape. This pleasant scene is then associated with the product being advertised.

Goodwill. Some advertisers work hard to create a good public image. They may provide health tips or engage in other activities. A major fast-food restaurant chain, for example, paid for the swimming and diving facility used at a recent Olympic Games.

Successful Living. These approaches appeal to people's desire for success, wealth, status, or beauty. For instance, one manufacturer of men's shoes uses the advertising phrase "Shades of the Sophisticated Man." The message is that you will be more sophisticated if you wear their shoes.

Emotional Appeal. Many ads contain messages related to happiness, friendship, and other pleasant emotions. "Buy a diamond for someone you love" is a theme that frequently appears.

13. You may wish to assign Activity 2 at this time. An alternative would be to have students name examples of products or services as each type of advertising is discussed.

290 ■ SECTION 5 Managing Your Money

Eric Heiden. Cardmember since 1980.

FIVE GOLD MEDALS · SPEED SKATING

1980 GAMES · LAKE PLACID, NY

FIGURE 22-9 Which type of advertising technique is used here? *Courtesy of American Express Travel Related Services Company, Inc.*

Economic Appeal. Messages about spending, saving, and making money are featured in many ads. An example is, "No money down, no payments until after Christmas."

Conformity. In this approach, you are encouraged to buy something because others have it. You may hear "Our product is used by millions of satisfied customers." An example of a slightly different approach is, "By using this camera, you, too, can be an expert photographer."

Scare Tactics. We all want to avoid unpleasant situations, such as danger and embarrassment. Who wouldn't want to prevent an auto accident?

14. You may wish to conduct Activity 3 at this time. Do inform the winning company of the class' choice. Companies have been known to reply with free samples or discount coupons.

Sure-Grip tires will keep you from having one. This advertiser wants you to think you may have an accident if you don't use its products.

Intellectual Appeal. Many products claim to help you become more informed or better educated. Or they appeal to your intelligence. Does the following sound familiar? "Smart people have found this dishwashing soap to be the better product."

Health and Comfort. This approach is used in ads for products such as aspirin, skin creams, and vitamins. The ads tell you how the product will make you healthier or feel better.

FIGURE 22-10 Have you noticed how advertising for health care products often changes with the season? For example, ads for cold remedies in the winter and sunburn lotions in the summer. *Courtesy of Plough, Inc.*

Sales Traps to Avoid

There is nothing wrong with advertising as long as it is honest. If you dislike an ad's message, you can choose not to buy. Problems occur when the advertising is misleading. Be alert to the following deceptive (misleading) practices.

15. In addition to being misleading, some of the practices may be illegal, depending upon the state in which they occur.

*WWYD Feature B. The person should politely ask to speak with the store manager. Unless the advertised price is unreasonably low, the store manager will probably honor the price.

CHAPTER 22 The Consumer in the Marketplace ■ 291

False Pricing. When consumers see an item that has been marked down, they naturally believe it's a bargain. Sale prices are usually lower than the regular ones. However, some merchants will raise the regular price on a sales ticket *before* marking it down. Let's say that the suggested price for a watch is $60. After the seller changes the price tag to read $100, the price is then "marked down" to $60. A consumer buys it believing that $40 has been saved. The truth is that the watch was bought at the regular price.

Bait and Switch. This occurs when an ad offers a product or service that is not available. For example, a butcher shop advertises a cut of meat at a bargain price. When you get to the store, you find out that the meat has all been sold. Or maybe they had none to begin with. The ad was used as "bait" to get you to the store. The clerk then tries to show you a more expensive cut (the "switch").

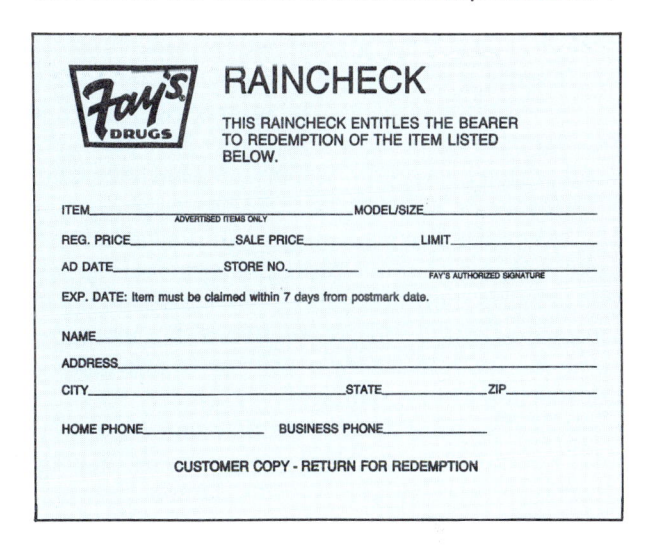

FIGURE 22-11 Merchants who sell out of an advertised product often give "rainchecks." What does this mean? *Courtesy of Fay's Drug Company, Inc.*

"lasting 50% longer." Look carefully at such ads. Are the advertisers keeping facts from you? Do they tell you *how* a product has been improved? If so, does what they say make sense? If a product is said to last longer, ask yourself "Longer than what?" Your question might not have an answer.

Other ads use words such as "stain resistant" or "never needs ironing." The terms used may have several meanings. For example, a coat that is "stain-resistant" can't be expected to resist *all* stains. Ads

What Would You Do?

You see an advertisement in the paper for an item you have wanted. You stick the ad in your pocket and head for the store. You find the item on the store's shelf and take it to the checkout counter. The clerk rings up the item at the regular price. You point out that the item is on sale. The clerk brushes off your comment and says that the ad in the paper is in error. What would you do?

Referral Sales Plans. A few sellers of services and expensive products use this technique. How does it work? Suppose someone contacts you about siding for your house. You are offered a "special introductory deal" on new siding. The seller explains that you will receive a bonus of $100 for each new purchaser you refer to them. Unfortunately, you pay the full price for the siding job. You then discover that it is very difficult to find customers for the builder. Their bad reputation is probably known. The sellers may even have left town. Most consumers are never able to earn their bonus money.

Unclear, Untrue, and Overstated Claims. Some products are advertised as being "improved" or

FIGURE 22-12 Not all salespeople use high-pressure tactics. This salesperson is providing advice and suggestions to people planning a deck project. *Photo by David W. Tuttle*

16. A reputable merchant will often offer a "raincheck" for products that are temporarily out of stock.
17. Emphasize to students that they should not automatically distrust all advertising, but that they should view advertising with a skeptical and questioning attitude.

that say a product is "guaranteed" are often unclear and untrue. If you are told a product is guaranteed, make sure the *guarantee* is in writing. Another problem phrase is "lasts a lifetime." Few products do. If a claim for a product seems too good to be true, it probably isn't true.

Clever Sales Tactics. You have studied an ad and believe that it's not misleading. Wise consumerism doesn't stop there. Remember that salespeople use various techniques to get you to buy. For instance, some salespeople use high-pressure or fast-talking approaches. Others flatter you or are very friendly because they want to make it difficult for you to say "no." Sometimes, a salesperson who is having trouble getting you to buy will turn you over to a second salesperson. A favorite sales trick is to say that "the price is going up tomorrow." A similar line is "this is the last item available."

18. Actually, it wasn't until the 1960s that a lot of Federal consumer legislation was passed. A key event was a message delivered before Congress by President Kennedy in 1962 in which he

CONSUMER RIGHTS

Consumers have not always had rights. Until this century, there were few laws to protect buyers. If consumers bought defective products, it was their problem. Since they had no legal responsibility, producers often paid little attention to safety and quality. After many consumers were harmed by unsafe products and faulty merchandise, the public began to demand tougher standards.

Laws now require manufacturers to make safety their concern. Consumers have a right to expect that what they buy is safe. Laws also now protect consumers who buy faulty merchandise. After an item is sold, the producer must stand behind it. Consumer rights regarding credit, interest rates, insurance, housing, and so on, are discussed throughout the remainder of Section 5.

Cathy bought a Brewbetter coffeemaker. After

FIGURE 22-13 One of the earliest consumer advocates was Ralph Nader. His book entitled *Unsafe at Any Speed* contributed to establishing laws requiring that manufacturers make safety their concern. *Courtesy of Chevrolet Motor Division*

proclaimed a *Consumer Bill of Rights.* This was an era in which the phrase "caveat emptor" (let the buyer beware) gave way to "caveat venditor" (let the seller beware).

19. Ask students if they have ever had an experience regarding a product recall.

CHAPTER 22 The Consumer in the Marketplace ■ 293

she had used it for several months, she read a *recall* notice in the newspaper. Many people had reported problems with the product. It had even caused several fires. When Cathy took the coffeemaker back to the seller, she got a new one.

Laws protect buyers in another way. When purchasing a good or service, consumers must have choices. At one time, a single company could control an industry, such as oil. This is referred to as a monopoly. You learned about monopolies in Chapter 21. The company could charge whatever it wanted and consumers had to pay. Laws keep these situations from happening now.

Until the 1960s, there wasn't much information available about products and services. People often bought according to what they had heard from advertisers and friends. Now the government and many private associations and businesses provide a wide variety of consumer information and services. Smart shoppers take advantage of their right to obtain consumer information.

CONSUMER RESPONSIBILITIES

Along with consumer rights come responsibilities. First of all, you owe it to yourself to learn how to choose, buy, and use goods and services. This chapter has given you some tips on wise consuming. In the remaining chapters of Section 5 of this text, you will read more about smart shopping. Your study of consumerism won't end here though. Such learning is a lifelong process.

Assertiveness

To protect yourself and other consumers, you have a responsibility to speak out. Be *assertive*. If you think a business hasn't behaved properly, speak politely but firmly to a salesperson. Whenever you are not satisfied with the salesperson's response, see the manager. Should you continue to receive poor products and services, take your business elsewhere. Buying goods and services is somewhat like casting a vote. Through the things that you buy (or don't buy), you vote for or against a business.

Honesty

You expect businesses to be fair and honest with you at all times. As a responsible consumer, you should also be fair and honest. You may not realize it, but all consumers pay a penalty for a few dishonest people. When a person steals from a department store, for example, the store may suffer a temporary loss. However, to make up for this loss (and others), the store will raise its prices.

20. A young person who is assertive runs the risk of being misunderstood. Caution students about this.

FIGURE 22-14 Shoplifting is a serious crime and adds to the cost of consumer goods.

CONSUMER COMPLAINTS

Most of the time, you will be satisfied with goods and services you purchase. Sometimes, however, you may be disappointed. Here is a list of the most common consumer problems.

- Difficulties in getting a product repaired or replaced as promised in the warranty.
- Misleading advertising, labeling, or packaging.
- Defective products. For example, a cassette tape may break the first time you use it.
- Being overcharged for a product or service.
- Poor service or work of bad quality.
- Goods that were ordered and paid for but never received.
- Errors in computerized billing.

Suppose such a situation happens to you. How will you solve it?

21. Stealing is only one type of dishonesty. Another is returning a product for exchange that you ruined. Have students name additional examples.

Before Complaining

If you have a consumer *complaint,* don't write a nasty letter or hire a lawyer. In fact, you should never write a nasty letter to a business! Do review the whole situation and try to resolve it in the simplest manner possible.

Save Everything. Keep track of all paperwork related to what you buy. This includes copies of order forms, receipts, and warranties. It is difficult to settle a complaint without proof of purchase.

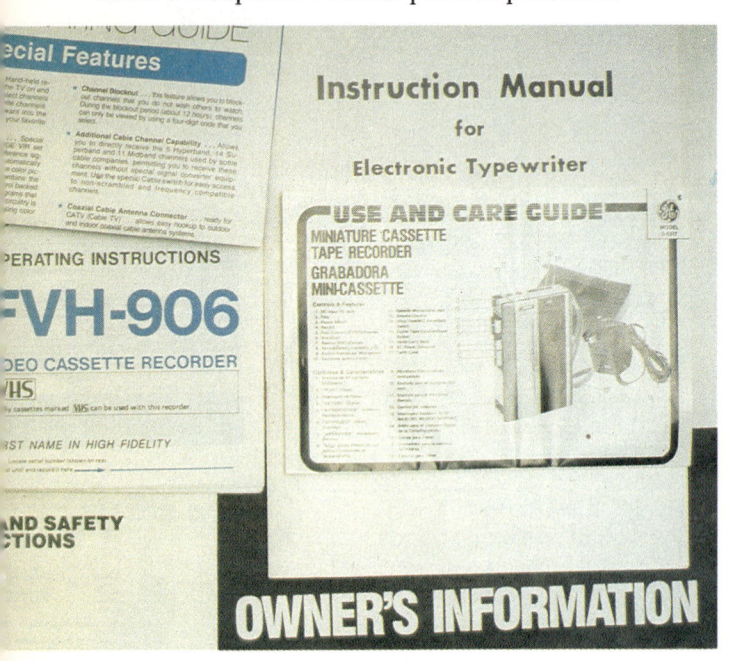

FIGURE 22-15 By following instructions in owners' manuals, you can extend the life of many products. *Photo by Paul E. Meyers*

Think it Through. You may have a faded blouse or a broken tool, but who is at fault? The reason the blouse faded was because you washed it with hot water instead of cold. The tool broke because you used it improperly. You should not expect the seller or manufacturer to replace such a product.

Many products don't work properly because people fail to follow instructions. This is often true for electrical appliances. If a product doesn't do what it should, reread the instruction book. Look at the product again. Ask a friend or family member to do the same. *Then* return the item or call a repairperson.

Give the Seller a Chance. If you know there is a problem and you aren't at fault, take the product back to where you bought it. Make sure you have the receipt and anything else you might need. Be prepared to explain the nature of your problem. Think over what you want the merchant to do. For example, do you want a replacement, a refund, or do you want the product repaired?

Ask to see someone who can handle your problem. Many larger stores have a complaint (or customer service) department. If so, go there. Explain your case to the person in charge. Don't be either too timid or too aggressive. Usually, if you are fair and reasonable, the other person will be also. You may be surprised at how quickly the problem is resolved. Sellers don't want to lose customers.

Making a Formal Complaint

If the local merchant can't or won't help you, the next step is to complain to the manufacturer. Ask the seller how to contact the manufacturer. If you can't get this information, check the product. It should have the manufacturer's name and address. If you can't find the address, ask your local librarian for help.

When you don't have the name of a person at the company, address the letter to the Customer Service Department. The Better Business Bureau says that a complaint letter should contain the following information:

- *What You Bought.* Describe the product. Does the item have a size and color? Is there a serial number?
- *Where You Bought It.* Give the complete address of the seller.
- *When You Bought It.* The date of purchase is important.
- *How You Paid For It.* Specify how you paid for the item. Did you use cash, a check, a credit card, or a money order? Attach copies of necessary papers. (Never send originals.) Paperwork may include receipts, cancelled checks, and sales contracts.
- *What the Problem Is.* Let the facts speak for themselves.
- *What You Want.* Do you want a refund? Would you like them to repair the item? Be clear.

---

22. A valuable resource to have available for this section is a *free* publication entitled *Consumer's Resource Handbook.* Get it by writing the Consumer Information Center, Pueblo, Colorado 81009.

23. Some companies like L.L. Bean and WalMart have a policy of accepting returns at any time for any reason. You and students might be able to name additional examples. Discuss why companies are willing to do this.

CHAPTER 22 The Consumer in the Marketplace ■ 295

1436 Lincoln Road
Waterton, MI   67459
June 12, 1989

Mr. Gerald Morris
Customer Service Manager
Barkley Tackle Company
1003 Seventh Street
Henderson, WI 37849

Dear Mr. Morris:

On June 7, 1989, I purchased a 5'6" Barkley casting rod (Model No. 96) at Lunker Sporting Goods Store in Waterton, MI. The selling price was $29.95, which I paid in cash. Attached find a photocopy of the receipt.

Several days later, I used the rod for the first time. As I tried to make a routine cast, the rod snapped in half. I had only used it for about an hour.

I then took the rod back to the store and explained what had happened. I was told by the store manager, Mr. Robert Stark, that the rod was not guaranteed. I insisted that I had used it only once, but he said there was nothing he could do.

I'm very sorry that the rod broke, but I do not believe that I was at fault. I have always used Barkley fishing products without any previous problems. This is to request that you provide me with a replacement rod or a refund. I'm sure you will agree that this problem should not have happened.

Sincerely yours,

Brad Corder

Brad Corder

FIGURE 22-16 A sample letter of complaint

Make a copy of the letter for yourself. You should receive a response within two or three weeks. If you don't, contact your local Better Business Bureau or consumer rights group for help.

24. The previously mentioned *Consumer's Resource Handbook* lists hundreds of public agencies and private companies to contact for help in resolving a consumer complaint. The booklet also has a good sample of a complaint letter.

25. You may wish to assign Activity 4 at this time.

CHAPTER REVIEW

Chapter in Brief

- A consumer is someone who buys or uses goods and services. Goods are articles that are produced or manufactured. Services involve the payment of money to people and businesses for work performed.
- Being a consumer is more than simply paying money for something. Consuming involves three stages: making choices, buying wisely, and using goods and services properly.
- Advertising is important for both sellers and consumers. For the seller, the purpose of advertising is to aid in selling goods and services. For the consumer, advertising provides information about goods and services for sale. Sellers use various advertising techniques to accomplish their purpose.
- There is nothing wrong with advertising as long as it is honest. Problems occur when the advertising is misleading. Always be on the lookout for misleading advertising practices such as: false pricing; bait and switch; referral sales plans; and unclear, untrue, and overstated claims.
- A number of steps have been taken to protect the rights of consumers. Laws have been passed regarding safety, faulty merchandise, and competition in the marketplace. Government and private agencies also provide a wide variety of consumer information and services.
- Along with consumer rights come responsibilities. You owe it to yourself to learn how to choose, buy, and use goods and services. You have a responsibility to speak out regarding poor products and services. You should also be fair and honest in your business dealings.
- Sometime, you will probably have a consumer complaint. Try to resolve the problem in the simplest manner possible. Make a formal complaint, if simpler approaches do not work. Be business-like in your efforts to resolve a consumer complaint.

Words to Know

advertising a public notice or message intended to aid in the sale of a product or service.

assertive firmly and positively stating one's position or point of view.

brand name nationally known brand; a product made or sold by a well-known company.

comparison shopping the process of finding out the cost of a product or service at several different places before making a decision to buy.

complaint an expression of dissatisfaction with a product or service.

consumer someone who buys or uses goods and services.

direct-mail advertising advertising that is sent to potential customers through the mail.

generic products goods that state only the common name of the product on the label.

guarantee a pledge that something is exactly as stated or advertised. *See* warranty.

CHAPTER 22 The Consumer in the Marketplace ■ 297

recall to call back; a request to return something.

warranty a guarantee; a promise that the product is free from defects.

Questions to Answer
1. How are the goals of a buyer and seller different?
2. What is a need? A want?
3. The process of consuming has three stages. Name and briefly describe these three stages.
4. Give three reasons why Bill Martin is a wise consumer.
5. Why should you use and care for a product properly?
6. Advertising has advantages and disadvantages for consumers. Name two of each.
7. Which type of advertising technique is used in each of the following ads:
   a. A famous person speaks for the product.
   b. A company provides athletic uniforms with their name on them.
   c. A company explains how their product will make you more attractive.
   d. You are told how a certain service will save you money.
   e. An accident or other dangerous situation is shown.
8. What is meant by "bait and switch"? Give an example.
9. What are your rights and responsibilities as a consumer? Name two of each.
10. How is buying a product or service similar to casting a vote?
11. What should you do before writing a formal letter of complaint?
12. What six points should be included in a complaint letter?

1. The *buyer* wants a good quality product at a low price. The *seller* wants to make a good profit on the sale.
2. A *need* is something you must have, such as food, shelter, or clothing. A *want* is something you desire, but which is not necessary or essential.
3. (a) *Choosing*—making choices about if and what to buy. (b) *Buying*—how to go about buying something. (c) *Using*—using and caring for a product properly.
4. Any three of the following: doesn't shop for food when hungry, plans what he buys, buys sale items, buys generic products whenever appropriate, often buys larger size items, bypasses defective goods, considers need for laundering and care when buying clothing, does comparison shopping.
5. Improper use and care can ruin or shorten the life of a product.
6. Any two of these. *Advantages*—provides information; helps one do comparison shopping, thus saving time and money; helps pay for products and services used and enjoyed. *Disadvantages*—cost of advertising is included in the price paid for goods and services; can influence one to buy things not needed; too many ads can make choosing more difficult; can sometimes be misleading.
7. (a) Endorsements. (b) Goodwill. (c) Successful living. (d) Economic appeal. (e) Scare tactics.
8. It refers to using "bait" (the ad) to get you into the store in quest of a nonexistent or unsatisfactory product. Once there, the seller tries to get you to "switch" to something else.
9. *Consumer rights*—protection from unsafe products; protection from faulty merchandise; opportunity to make choices without being subjected to monopolies; access to consumer information. *Consumer responsibilities*—to learn how to choose, buy, and use goods and services; to be assertive in protecting your and other's rights; to be honest and fair in business dealings.
10. The decision to buy or not to buy is a vote for or against a certain product or business.
11. Try to resolve it in the simplest possible manner. Think it through yourself and give the seller a chance to handle it.
12. (a) What you bought. (b) Where you bought it. (c) When you bought it. (d) How you paid for it. (e) What the problem is. (f) What you want.

298 ■ SECTION 5 Managing Your Money

Activities to Do

1. Prepare a list of five different grocery items. Then visit a number of different stores (at least three) and record the price of each item. What were your findings? Which store is the most expensive? The least expensive? Which stores carry generic brands? Were those items priced lower than brand-name products?
2. Find examples of the advertising techniques discussed in this chapter (endorsements, familiarity, association, and so on). You will probably need to do this over several days. Pool your ads with classmates. Choose the best ads for a bulletin-board display.
3. Conduct an election for your class' or school's favorite TV commercial. Nominate candidates. Prepare an election ballot and circulate it to classmates. Count the ballot and declare a winner. Send a letter to the winning company explaining what the class has done.
4. Think of a problem you have had with a product or service. Write a sample complaint letter to the manufacturer. Follow the guidelines provided in the chapter. Turn in the letter to your teacher.
5. As a class activity, develop a list of things to look for in buying a used car. Include things to examine visually and through a test drive.

Topics to Discuss

1. Think of a major purchase you have made recently. Did you do comparison shopping before buying the item? If so, explain how you went about it. If not, explain why.
2. Until recently, doctors and lawyers have been prohibited from advertising their services. It is still a controversial issue. What is your opinion on this practice?
3. Have you ever ruined a new product by failing to read or follow instructions? If so, discuss your experience in class.
4. You have probably heard someone say that buying a certain thing is "false economy." What does this phrase mean? Discuss examples of consumer practices that illustrate false economy.
5. Have you ever been cheated by a dishonest seller or misleading advertising? If so, discuss your experiences in class.
6. You or other members of the class have probably bought used cars. Car owners should share experiences in order to learn more about buying a used car. Discuss the following questions: Where was the car bought? Was a fair price paid for the car? Were any hidden problems discovered after the sale? Was the car covered by a warranty? You can probably think of additional questions.

26. Before discussing this, bring to class several examples of advertising by doctors and lawyers. A lot of such advertising consists of little more than an "announcement" of available services.
27. *False economy* essentially means that the product or service is not a good value. It may be cheaper initially, but will not last as long as something more expensive. A similar phrase is: "you get what you pay for."

CHAPTER TWENTY-THREE

Banking and Credit

OUTLINE
Financial Institutions and Services
Checking Accounts
Managing a Checking Account
Credit and Its Use
Chapter Review

OBJECTIVES
After reading this chapter, you should be able to:
- Name and describe the four major types of financial institutions.
- Describe how to open a checking account.
- Illustrate how to write and endorse a check.
- Illustrate how to maintain a check register and reconcile a bank statement.
- Illustrate how to make a bank deposit.
- Discuss how electronic banking may change money management.
- Name and describe the two basic types of credit.
- Calculate the cost of credit.

As you grow older, your use of money will probably change. Rather than pay cash for all of your purchases, you will find that it is often more convenient to write a check. There may also be times when you don't wish to use cash or a check. In those cases, you may want to use credit instead. The credit you use may be in the form of a loan or a charge purchase. Knowing how to use checking, credit, and other financial services are important life skills for everyone.

1. These four types of financial institutions are more similar than different.

FIGURE 23-1 It is not a good idea to carry around large amounts of cash. Deposit your paycheck in a checking account. *Photo by Paul E. Meyers*

FINANCIAL INSTITUTIONS AND SERVICES
A bank used to be the place to go when you wanted to save money, borrow money, or open a checking account. Today, there are four major types of financial institutions that provide these services and others.

Commercial Banks
Commercial banks may also be known as "bank and trust companies" or "community banks." Commercial banks are the most common type of financial institution. They are *full-service banks*, which offer a variety of services. These include checking and saving accounts, loans, safe deposit boxes, money orders, travelers checks, and so on. Borrowers and savers can find almost every convenience and service in these places.

300 ■ SECTION 5 Managing Your Money

FIGURE 23-2 Look for this seal where you bank. It means that your money is insured if the bank should fail. *Photo by Paul E. Meyers*

Mutual Savings Banks

These began early in the nineteenth century in order to service ordinary people that commercial banks often overlooked. In theory, mutual savings banks are owned by their depositors. However, a board of trustees directs the bank's operations and acts in the interest of the depositors. There are only about eighteen states that charter mutual savings banks.

Such banks generally provide the same services as commercial banks. In addition, they offer some of the services of a savings and loan association. One of the main attractions of mutual savings banks is that they often pay a slightly higher rate of interest than commercial banks.

FIGURE 23-3 The names of many mutual savings banks include words like *farmers, merchants, peoples,* and so on. Do you know why? *Courtesy of Dime Savings Bank of New York*

2. Many mutual savings banks have interesting names (see Figure 23-3). Are there any noteworthy ones in your area?

3. FSLIC (which insures S & L deposits) is technically insolvent. Some type of major restructuring is probably in order. Update this subject as appropriate.

Savings and Loan Associations

Other names for these institutions are "building and loan associations," "cooperative banks," "savings associations," and "homestead associations." They started in the early 1800s when people pooled their savings. Each, then, in turn, could borrow enough money to build a house. Savings and loan associations are now in all states. Such institutions provide more home mortgage business (home loans) than all other lenders combined.

Credit Unions

Credit unions (CUs) are nonprofit savings and loan cooperative associations. They are made up of people who have something in common. This could be a place of employment, a union membership, or the like. For example, all employees of a particular school district might form a credit union. Members govern the credit unions. They only accept savings from and make loans to those who belong. At the end of the year, a well-run credit union often has a surplus to distribute to its members.

Credit unions provide savings accounts, consumer loans, and financial counseling. A convenient feature of CUs is that members can often make deposits and loan payments through payroll deductions.

FIGURE 23-4 Deposits in a credit union are insured by the NCUA rather than the FDIC. *Courtesy of National Credit Union Administration*

Changes in Financial Institutions

During the early 1980s, many banking laws were changed to allow financial institutions to be more competitive. Now financial institutions can pay higher rates of interest than before. Another result

4. How many students work at companies that have credit unions?
5. You may wish to assign Activity 1 at this time.

FIGURE 23-5 In one year, Teresa Romero saved $60 in service charges and earned $28 in interest by moving her checking account to a different institution. She is treating herself to a new radio with the money she saved. *Courtesy © Tandy Corporation*

of the changes is that the four major types of financial institutions have begun to offer similar services.

Financial institutions now actively compete for business. This is good news for the consumer. It means, however, that consumers should shop around and compare services, charges, and rates of interest. This will ensure that they get the best deal.

The experience of Teresa Romero is a good case in point. When Teresa learned that her bank was raising the service charge on checking accounts, she began to ask about charges elsewhere. She discovered that she was eligible to join the credit union where her mother worked. After becoming a member, she received no-cost checking. In addition, she was paid monthly interest on her checking account balance.

CHECKING ACCOUNTS

Checking accounts are one of the most commonly used banking services. Checking accounts have two main advantages: safety and convenience. Checks provide a safe and convenient way to pay bills. It is unsafe to carry large amounts of cash. Also, keeping large amounts of money at home is unwise. Michael found this out.

Michael never thought he needed a checking account. He liked to go to the bank on Friday evenings and cash his paycheck. He then paid for all of his purchases in cash. The cash he didn't carry with him was kept inside an empty tennis ball can that was stored on the hall closet shelf. No one would ever think of looking there for money, he thought.

Michael returned from a movie late on Friday night to discover that his apartment had been burglarized. His portable color TV and VCR were the only things he noticed that were missing. As he sat down on the couch to think about what to do, he remembered his money. He went to the hall closet. As he opened the closet door, an empty tennis ball can rolled off the top shelf.

6. Ask how many students already have a checking account.

302 ■ SECTION 5 Managing Your Money

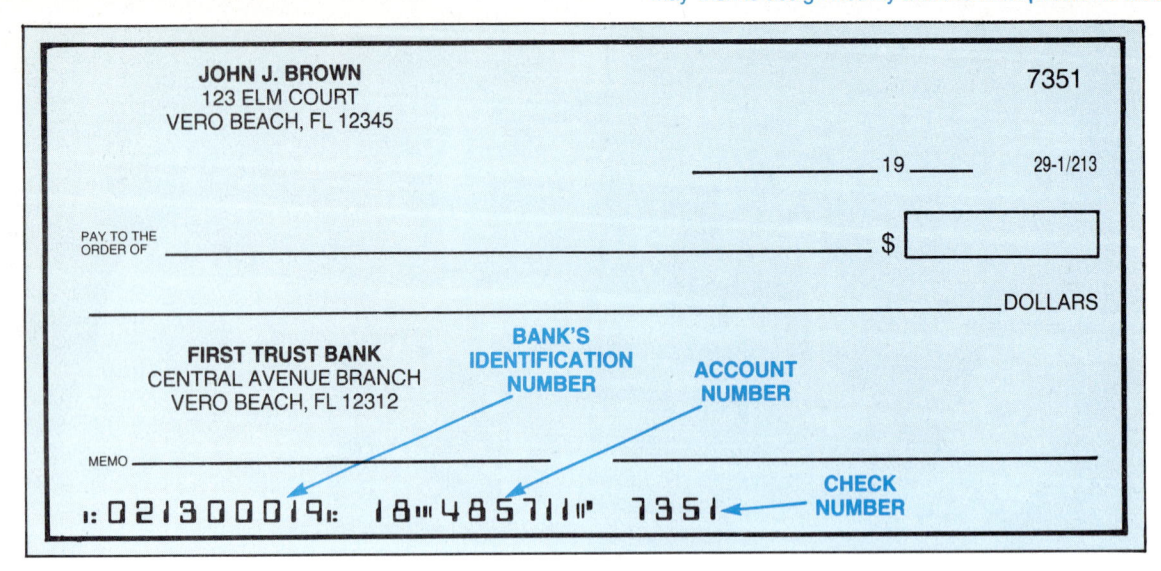

8. "Regular" and "special" is one convenient way of classifying types of checking accounts. There are many variations. You may wish to assign Activity 2 at this time. *(Note: As students*

```
                JOHN J. BROWN                                    7351
                123 ELM COURT
                VERO BEACH, FL 12345
                                                _____ 19 ____   29-1/213

   PAY TO THE
   ORDER OF _____ $ [        ]

   _____ DOLLARS

        FIRST TRUST BANK       BANK'S
        CENTRAL AVENUE BRANCH  IDENTIFICATION   ACCOUNT
        VERO BEACH, FL 12312   NUMBER           NUMBER

   MEMO _____
                                                   CHECK
                                                   NUMBER
        ⑈021300019⑉  18⑈485711⑊   7351 ◄——
```

FIGURE 23-6 The coded numbers at the bottom of the check are read by a computer. This permits the check to be processed rapidly.

He had insurance to cover the cost of replacing the TV and VCR. But he was heartsick to lose the money he needed to live on the rest of the month. Needless to say, Michael opened a checking account the next time he got paid.

Checks can be used as freely as cash. Unlike cash, however, only the person to whom the check is made out can get the money. A second advantage of checks is that they make it easier to keep good financial records. A canceled check is legal proof of payment. Be sure to save your canceled checks.

Without the use of checks, our economic system couldn't function. Individuals and businesses write billions of checks each year. A very elaborate national system allows millions of checks to be processed daily. Let's see how the system works.

Assume that you take your car in for repairs and the bill comes to $45. Rather than pay the mechanic in cash, you write a check. That is, you write instructions to your bank, the American National Bank, to deduct $45 from your account and pay it to Joe's Garage. Joe then takes your check to his bank, Mid-America Bank, where he deposits the check. His account is credited in the amount of $45.

The Mid-America Bank does not collect payment directly from the American National Bank. It would be ridiculous for a bank to pay separately for every check written by a customer and receive separate payment for every check credited to a customer's account. Instead, a bank sends all of its checks to a centralized clearinghouse. The checks are added up at the clearinghouse each day. Each individual bank then makes or receives just one daily payment to or from its fellow banks.

After the check has been cleared, it is returned to the American National Bank where the bank subtracts $45 from your account. The check is stamped "paid" and will be returned to you later along with other canceled checks.

Types of Checking Accounts

In the past, banks offered only two basic types of checking accounts: regular and special. A regular account, often called a minimum balance account, requires that the customer maintain a certain minimum balance. As long as the minimum balance is in the account, there is no extra charge. If the balance drops below the minimum amount, however, the customer will have to pay a service charge. Regular accounts are often advertised as "free checking accounts."

A second basic type of checking account is the special account, often called a cost-per-check account. With this type of account, you pay a flat monthly service charge plus another 20 to 25 cents for each check you write. Special accounts are for people who only write a few checks each month. A young person opening his or her first checking account should carefully consider this type of account.

One of the newest types of checking accounts is an interest-bearing account called a *Negotiable Order*

7. Operation of the Federal Reserve System is an interesting subject. Ask your school librarian or AV Director for help in locating a film or video about the Federal Reserve.

collect information about checking accounts from different financial institutions, have them also collect data about savings accounts to be used in Chapter 24.)

9. Point out that the minimum balance can be thought of as a savings account. That is, one institution assesses a $4.00 monthly service charge if the balance drops below $400. By maintaining the minimum balance, you can "save" $48.00 per year in service charges. This is the equivalent of a 12 percent return on investment.

CHAPTER 23 Banking and Credit ■ 303

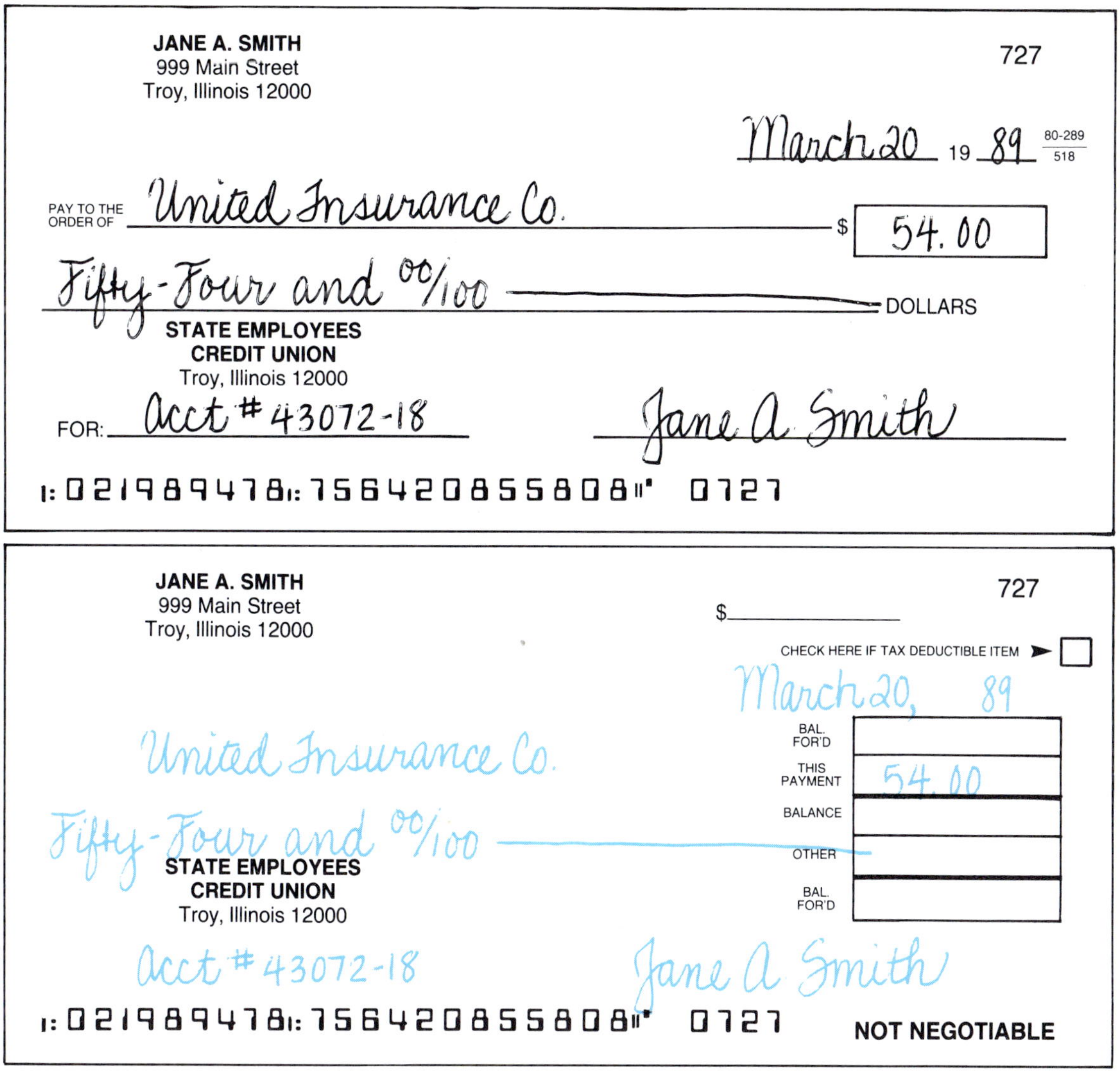

FIGURE 23-7 Some banks and credit unions don't return canceled checks. Rather, a *two-part* check form is used to provide a record of the transaction.

of Withdrawal (NOW) account. These started with savings and loan associations and are now offered by many commercial and savings banks also. A withdrawal order is just like a check, except that it is written against a savings account rather than a checking account. Your money earns interest up to the day the order clears. However, most NOW accounts require that you maintain a balance of at least several hundred dollars.

A growing number of credit unions offer a type of checking account called a *share-draft account*. It is very similar to a NOW account. You write drafts (checks) against a credit union savings account.

FIGURE 23-8 A NOW account provides the earnings of a savings account, plus the convenience of a checking account. *Courtesy of Dime Savings Bank of NY*

304 ■ SECTION 5 Managing Your Money

Your money earns interest until the draft clears. Many credit unions have no monthly service charges at all. However, to earn interest on the account, the credit union often requires a minimum balance of $500 to $750.

If abused, a checking account can become very expensive. For example, if you write a check for more than you have in your account (an *overdraft*), the check will be returned. Your bank will then charge you a fee for every check that "bounces." If you write a check to someone, and decide to "stop payment" on it, the bank will usually charge you for this also. As you are shopping around for a place to open a checking account, request an information sheet that describes all of the institution's services and charges.

Opening a Checking Account

Once you have decided on a bank and checking account plan, opening an account is very simple. You need only fill out a *signature card*, Figure 23-9. The signature card asks for your name, address, phone number, social security number, and similar data. At the end of the card, there is a place for your signature. The signature that you put on the card should be your legal name, not a nickname.

MANAGING A CHECKING ACCOUNT

Maintaining an accurate up-to-date checkbook requires knowledge and practice of a few important rules. Here are some important steps and guidelines to follow.

the account, charge for an initial supply of checks, and/or assess a monthly service charge regardless of whether the account is used.

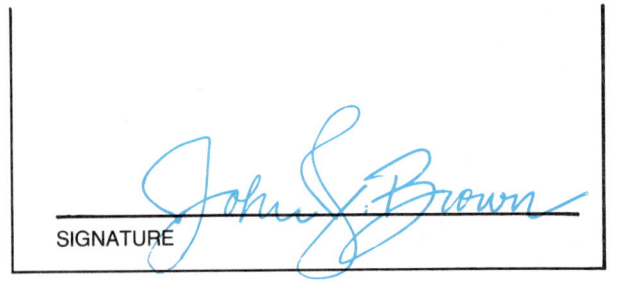

FIGURE 23-9 A signature card is a legal document that spells out the formal relationship between you and the financial institution.

Writing a Check

A blank check requires five kinds of information. One additional kind is optional. Each of these will now be discussed. Refer to Figure 23-10 as you read about each part.

Date. Record the date on the check. This will help you keep accurate records. Never date a check ahead of time *(postdating)* because you don't have enough money in your account. If the payee cashes the check, you might overdraw the account.

Payee. The person or institution to whom you write the check is the *payee*. It is proper to ask someone how they would like the check made out. On their bills, many businesses indicate how to write the check. If the name is a long one, it is acceptabe to abbreviate. However, use common abbreviations, such as "Inc.," "Co.," and "Assoc."

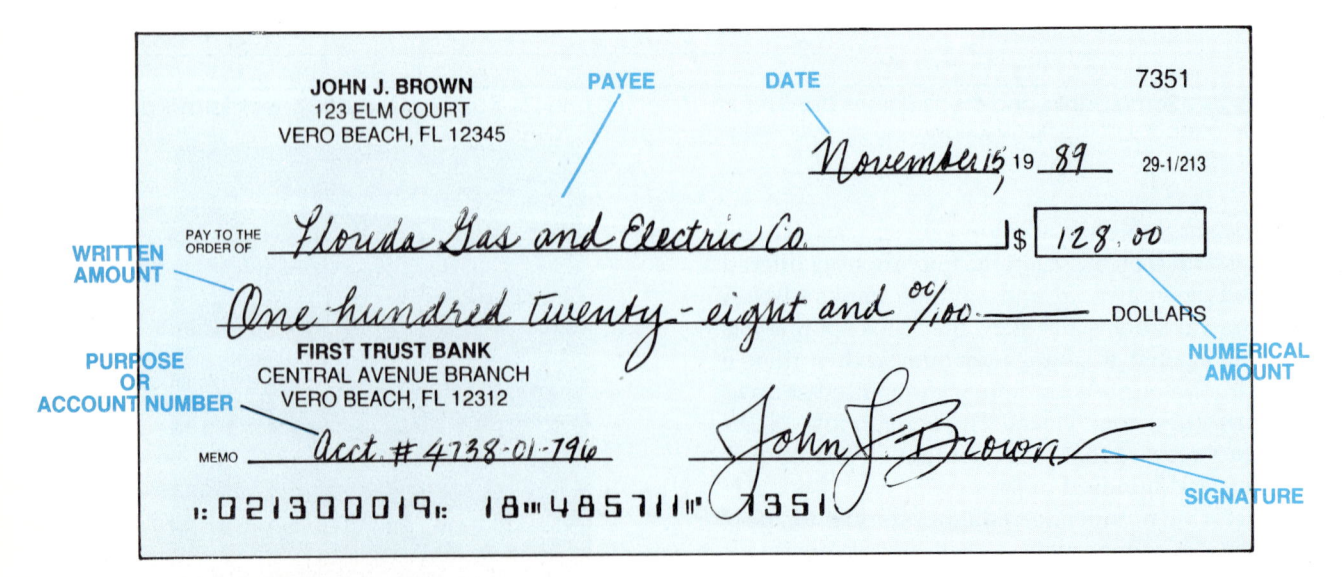

FIGURE 23-10 A correctly written check.

10. Even though it is easy to open a checking account, caution students not to do so until they are sure they need one. Remind them that an institution may require a certain deposit to open

11. Prepare an overhead transparency of a blank check to use in explaining this part. Also, duplicate a sheet containing samples of blank checks for students to practice filling out.

12. These are the basic guidelines for filling out checks. You may wish to add others.

Numerical Amount. You record the amount of the check in two places. At the end of the line where you fill in the name of the payee, you write the amount of the check in dollars and cents. For example, "$10.50." If the check is for under a dollar, put a "0" in front of the decimal point and insert the word *cents* "$0.85 cents." To keep someone from altering the check easily, place the figures close to the dollar sign.

Written Amount. On the long line near the middle of the check, you will see the word *Dollars.* Here you write out the same amount that you earlier wrote in numerals. Use this form: "Ten and 50/100" or Fifty-three and 00/100." If the amount is less than one dollar, write in "Only eighty-five cents" and draw a line through the word *Dollars.* If there is any blank space left after you have written in the amount, draw a wavy line between the written amount and the word *Dollars.* Otherwise, someone might alter the check. If there is ever a difference between the numerical amount and the written amount, the written amount is the legal one. Generally, however, a bank will contact the writer before it will accept a check with differing amounts.

Purpose. In the lower left-hand portion of a check, there is a space that's indicated as "For" or "Memo." This space doesn't have to be filled out. But it is always a good idea to do so. This is where you indicate the purpose of the check. For example, "auto tune-up" or "birthday gift." In paying bills, some companies may ask you to write a policy or account number on the check. Next to "Memo" or "For," you would write "Acct. #4738-01-796" if that were your number. Routinely filling in this line can help you later as you review a budget or prepare an income tax return.

Signature. The bottom right-hand portion of the check is where you sign your name. Sign it exactly as it appears on the signature card you filled out when you opened the account. Don't use the words *Mr., Miss, Mrs.,* or *Ms.* as part of a signature.

In addition to following the procedure discussed for filling out checks, also keep in mind the following guidelines:

- Even though it is legal, don't use a pencil to write a check. Anyone could alter your check.
- You can write a check to yourself and cash it. Simply write "Cash" as the payee and present it to the bank. (Some banks might also ask you to sign the back of the check.)
- If you make an error on a check, don't correct it. Instead write "VOID" across the face of the check and file it with your canceled checks. Then make out a new check. Remember to write "VOID" in your register, too.
- Don't sign a blank check and let someone else fill in the amount.
- Don't leave your checkbook or blank checks in a place where someone can take them.
- Don't loan a blank check to someone because they have forgotten theirs. The bank's computer will read *your* electronic number and subtract the money from your account.

13. Have on hand several examples of check registers to demonstrate differences.

What Would You Do?

You like having a checking account, but the checkbook is just something else to carry. You often put it in the glove box of your car. It is safe enough since you always keep the car locked. After a movie one evening, you return to your car to find that it has been burglarized. Your stereo is gone and so is the checkbook. You are very upset and don't know what to do next. What would you do?

Keeping a Check Register

After you open an account, you will receive a supply of imprinted checks and a separate *check register.* The register is where you keep a record of checks written, deposits, and other transactions. One checkbook style has a check stub attached to the check itself. There is no separate check register. However, the check register style is the most popular.

A common mistake people make in maintaining a checking account is not recording checks in the register. This often happens when someone is in a hurry. Get in the habit of filling out the check register *at the time you write a check.* If you don't, you won't know the correct balance and might overdraw the account.

Overdrawing a checking account can be very embarrassing. One day Jackie Brown got a phone call from her friend Barbara who worked at The Clothes Rack. Barbara called about a check that Jackie had written to buy a new outfit. The bank had returned the check to the store because of "Insufficient Funds." Jackie was humiliated.

*WWYD Feature A. The first thing is to call the police and report the theft. Next, call the bank and have them stop payment on all future checks written on the account. This will protect against any loss.

306 ■ SECTION 5 Managing Your Money

In looking over her check register, Jackie found that she had not recorded a check written to the gas company. It was near the end of the month when she wrote a $53.46 check to The Clothes Rack. There was only $46.20 in her account and the check "bounced." Jackie immediately took another check to Barbara.

Figure 23-11 shows two common ways to maintain a check register. Study each part of the illustration. Both ways work well, so choose the one that you prefer. The column next to the "payment/debit" column may be used to check off items cleared when you balance a statement. Or, if you prefer, you can indicate in this column which items are tax deductible (T).

Endorsing a Check

Suppose a friend writes you a check. What do you do with it? You take it to your bank and endorse it there. An *endorsement* is your signature on the back/left side of a check. Your written name enables a bank to cash the check. There are three common types of endorsement: blank, restrictive, and full. See Figure 23-12.

ONE-LINE ENTRY

NUMBER	DATE	DESCRIPTION OF TRANSACTION	PAYMENT/DEBIT (−)	✓ T	FEE (IF ANY) (−)	DEPOSIT/CREDIT (+)	BALANCE 282 34
7341	3/25	Cash	150 00			255 67	388 01
7342	3/25	Florida Telephone	25 00				363 01
7343	3/27	Metropolitan Life Ins.	8 70				354 31
7344	3/27	John Hancock Ins.	5 78				348 53
7345	3/27	Capital Cablevision	19 75				328 78
7346	3/27	State Bank	400 00			305 67	234 45
7347	4/1	Chrysler Credit Corp.	257 62			485 45	462 28
7348	4/1	Town and Country Motel	68 00				394 28
7349	4/1	Fairway Supermarket	36 11				358 17
7350	4/3	Linens and Things	90 91				267 26

TWO-LINE ENTRY

NUMBER	DATE	DESCRIPTION OF TRANSACTION	PAYMENT/DEBIT (−)	✓ T	FEE (IF ANY) (−)	DEPOSIT/CREDIT (+)	BALANCE 282 34
7341	3/25	Cash	150 00				150 00
		Car repair					132 34
Deposit	3/25	Deposit Check				255 67	255 67
							388 01
7342	3/25	Florida Telephone	25 00				25 00
		Telephone Bill					363 01
7343	3/27	Metropolitan Life Ins.	8 70				8 70
		Insurance					354 31
7344	3/27	John Hancock Ins	5 78				5 78
		Insurance					348 53
7345	3/27	Capital Cablevision	19 75				19 75
							328 78

FIGURE 23-11 Maintaining a check register is not difficult. However, you must be accurate and pay attention to detail.

14. Point out that check registers may differ slightly depending upon the supplier. Instructions are provided along with the check register.

A **blank endorsement** is simply your written signature. Once you have signed a check, it can be treated as cash. Anyone can then present it to the bank for payment. So, never endorse a check until you are ready to cash it.

Jill Yount

A **restrictive endorsement** is a message and a signature that restricts the use of the check. The most common restrictive endorsement is "For deposit only." This is usually used when you wish to send a check by mail to a bank for deposit. With this message, the check can't be used for any other purpose.

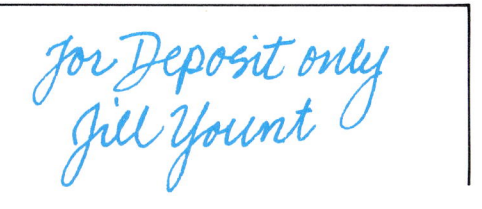

*For Deposit only
Jill Yount*

A **full endorsement** is used when you want to pay someone else with a check that is made out to you. This is done by writing "Pay to the order of _____" and then signing your name. This endorsement transfers the right of payment from you to a new payee.

*Pay to the Order
of Sharon Weber
Jill Yount*

FIGURE 23-12 Different forms of endorsement are used for different purposes.

Endorse a check exactly as it is made out. Do this even if your name is improper or misspelled. When there is an error, you endorse the check first as is, followed by the correct way. For example, suppose a check to Sharon Robbins is made out incorrectly to "Sharon Robins." She would first endorse it as "Sharon Robins" followed by "Sharon Robbins." Or a check to Skip Turner would be endorsed "Skip Turner" followed by "James A. Turner."

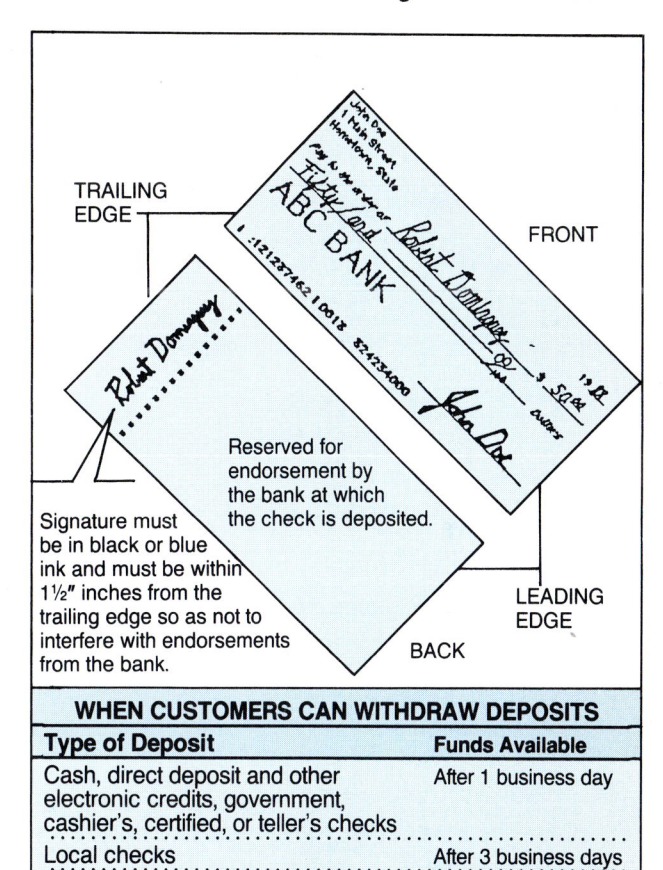

Signature must be in black or blue ink and must be within 1½" inches from the trailing edge so as not to interfere with endorsements from the bank.

Reserved for endorsement by the bank at which the check is deposited.

WHEN CUSTOMERS CAN WITHDRAW DEPOSITS	
Type of Deposit	**Funds Available**
Cash, direct deposit and other electronic credits, government, cashier's, certified, or teller's checks	After 1 business day
Local checks	After 3 business days
Out of town checks, deposits at ATM not owned by customers institution	After 7 business days

Source: FDIC

FIGURE 23-13 Follow these new check endorsing requirements.

A new federal law went into effect September 1, 1988. It guarantees customers of financial institutions timely access to money they deposit. The law also requires customers to use new uniform standards to endorse checks, Figure 23-13. If you fail to follow the guidelines, you will still get your money. But it could take longer.

Making a Deposit

The process of putting money into a checking account is known as "making a deposit." To do this, you fill out the preprinted *deposit ticket* that comes with your supply of checks. A deposit ticket is used to deposit any combination of currency, coins, or checks. In making a deposit, a portion of the deposit can be received in cash, if desired. Figure 23-14 shows a completed deposit ticket.

15. Many employers provide the option of direct deposit of payroll checks.

DEPOSIT TICKET

JOHN J. BROWN
123 Elm Court
Vero Beach, FL 12345

DATE *November 15,* 19 *89*

CASH →	32	00
LIST CHECKS SINGLY	76	18
TOTAL FROM OTHER SIDE		
TOTAL ITEMS TOTAL	108	18

29-1/213

USE OTHER SIDE FOR ADDITIONAL LISTING. ENTER TOTAL HERE

BE SURE EACH ITEM IS PROPERLY ENDORSED

FIRST TRUST BANK
Central Avenue Branch
Vero Beach, FL 12312

⑆021300019⑆ 18⵿485711⵿

CHECKS AND OTHER ITEMS ARE RECEIVED FOR DEPOSIT SUBJECT TO THE PROVISIONS OF THE UNIFORM COMMERCIAL CODE OR ANY APPLICABLE COLLECTION AGREEMENT.

FIGURE 23-14 A completed deposit ticket

FIRST TRUST BANK
Central Avenue Branch
Vero Beach, FL 12312

JOHN J. BROWN
123 Elm Court
Vero Beach, FL 12345

PAGE 1 OF 1

002 613 CY

13435711
6134357116

STATEMENT OF YOUR ACCOUNT(S) FOR PERIOD 11-15-88 THROUGH 12-13-88
****
SUMMARY OF REGULAR ACCOUNT # 18 485711

```
BALANCE LAST STATEMENT            502.10
DEPOSITS AND OTHER ADDITIONS     1910.78
CHECKS AND OTHER SUBTRACTIONS    1306.12
BALANCE THIS STATEMENT           1106.76      TAXPAYER ID NUMBER   123 45 6789
```

DATE	TYPE OF TRANSACTION	CHECKS SUBTRACTIONS	ADDITIONS	BALANCE
11-15	BEGINNING BALANCE			502.10
11-18	DEPOSIT		405.24	907.34
11-22	CHECKS POSTED (3)	67.20		840.14
11-23	DEPOSIT		650.15	1472.54
11-23	CHECKS POSTED (1)	17.75		
11-25	CHECKS POSTED (4)	519.45		953.09
11-28	CHECKS POSTED (1)	44.00		909.09
11-29	CHECKS POSTED (3)	47.20		861.89
11-30	DEPOSIT		305.24	
11-30	CHECKS POSTED (1)	50.00		1117.13
12-05	CHECKS POSTED (3)	363.27		753.86
12-06	CHECKS POSTED (1)	149.69		604.17
12-07	DEPOSIT		305.24	909.41
12-08	CHECKS POSTED (1)	4.00		905.41
12-09	CHECKS POSTED (1)	43.56		861.85
12-12	DEPOSIT		244.91	1106.76

CHECKS POSTED   (* INDICATES SEQUENCE BREAK)

CHECK	AMOUNT	DATE	CHECK	AMOUNT	DATE	CHECK	AMOUNT	DATE
7242	50.00	11-30	7249	21.20	11-29	7255	16.00	11-29
7243	44.00	11-28	7250	8.70	11-25	7256	10.00	11-29
7244	17.75	11-23	7251	47.20	11-22	7257	13.27	12-05
7245	10.00	11-22	7252	10.00	11-22	7258	43.56	12-09
7246	400.00	11-25	7253	17.66	11-25	7259	300.00	12-05
7247	50.00	12-05	7254	93.09	11-25	7260	149.69	12-06
7248	4.00	12-08						

FIGURE 23-15 A bank statement is a monthly summary of all transactions.

CHAPTER 23 Banking and Credit ■ 309

16. At the time of deposit, some institutions will immediately enter the deposit into a computer and then return a printout to the customer showing the deposit and current account balance.

When you make a deposit, the bank will return to you a receipt showing the amount of the deposit. Check this to make sure it agrees with the amount you wrote in the deposit ticket. Record the deposit right away in your check register.

Balancing a Statement

Once a month, the bank will send you a packet that includes a *statement of account* and the canceled checks that you wrote. Canceled checks are not returned if you have the type of checks shown in Figure 23-7. The statement is a summary of all your transactions for a given period. It includes the following:

- The amount of each check and the date the bank received it.
- The deposits you made.
- Any service charges.
- Beginning and ending balances.

Study the example shown in Figure 23-15.

The process of comparing the statement with your check register is known as "balancing a checkbook." (In some cases, the word *reconciling* may be used instead.) Instructions for how to balance your account are usually printed on the back of the statement, Figure 23-16. Follow each step exactly as described. If you have a problem that you can't figure out, don't wait until you receive the next statement. Rather, go to the bank right away and ask someone to help you.

After you have balanced your checkbook, make any necessary changes in the register. For example, you may need to record an amount for service charges or for an overdraft.

Electronic Banking

In the future, electronic banking may change the way you manage money. *Electronic banking* is a broad

17.

18.

"It's Easy to Balance Your Account" - Follow the instructions and use the reconcilement form below.

Reconcilement Instructions:

- Check off each paid check on your checkbook stub or register.
- Be sure that all **checks posted** and **other subtractions** shown on your checking account have been subtracted from your checkbook balance and that all **deposits** and **additions** have been added.
- List and total under "Checks Outstanding" all checks not paid by the Bank during this statement period.
- Fill in the ending balance shown on this statement.
- Add the deposits made after the close of this period.
- Deduct the checks still outstanding.
- The result should be the same as the balance remaining in your checkbook.

Checks Outstanding							Reconcilement Form
Check No. or Date	Amount	Check No. or Date	Amount	Check No. or Date	Amount	
	$	Total Forwarded	$	Total Forwarded	$	Balance as of this statement, shown on front. $
						Add Deposits not yet shown on front
						Total $
						Subtract Total Checks Outstanding $
						This Result should agree with your checkbook balance $
Total or Carry Forward		Total or Carry Forward		Total		

Please Examine at Once.
Your account will be considered correct if no report is received by our auditors in 14 days; except that matters involving your line of credit or electronic transfer(s) must be reported within 60 days (see above).

FIGURE 23-16 Following this step-by-step procedure will allow you to keep your account in balance.

17. You may wish to conduct Activity 4 at this time. Develop a realistic, sample problem.

18. Add relevance to the topic of electronic banking by picking up descriptive information regarding available services at financial institutions in your area.

310 ■ SECTION 5 Managing Your Money

FIGURE 23-17 Automated teller machines (ATM) are the most common type of electronic banking. *Courtesy of Goldome*

term used to describe various types of electronic fund transfers (EFT). There are four common types of EFT services:

1. *Automated Teller Machines.* Twenty-four-hour electronic terminals that permit you to bank at your convenience. You simply insert your personal EFT card in the machine to withdraw cash, make deposits, or transfer funds between accounts.
2. *Pay-by-Phone Systems.* Permit you to telephone your bank and instruct it to pay certain bills or to transfer funds between accounts.
3. *Direct Deposits or Withdrawals.* Allow you to authorize deposits such as a paycheck to your account on a regular basis. You can also arrange to have regular bills such as insurance premiums and rent payments paid automatically.
4. *Point-of-Sale Transfers.* Let you pay for retail

19. A plastic *debit card*, similar in appearance to a credit card, is used for most EFT services.

purchases with your EFT card. This is similar to a credit card except that money for the purchase is immediately transferred from your bank account. Electronic banking can be very convenient. A possible disadvantage, however, is that your EFT card and personal identification number is used for all transactions. If it should be lost or stolen, you must immediately notify your bank. With EFT, you also need to carefully examine receipts and monthly statements for errors. At the time you open an EFT account, your bank will provide you with written information on your rights and responsibilities.

CREDIT AND ITS USE

Credit refers to the receipt of money, goods, or services in exchange for a promise to pay. People may get credit in the form of loans. This form is called loan credit. Sales credit is also available. In this type, consumers can delay their payments for goods and services.

Loan Credit

Loan credit involves money borrowed in order to buy something. Most of these loans are for major expenses. Borrowers may not have cash on hand to pay for a house, car, or college education. The buyer usually gets a loan at one place and spends the cash in another. For example, you may secure a loan from a credit union. You will then use the money to buy a car at a local dealer.

FIGURE 23-18 Without loan credit, it would be impossible for most people to buy a house or car. *Courtesy of Ford Motor Company*

20. In recent years, home equity loans have become increasingly common. This is a slightly different type of loan credit. Briefly explain the nature of a home equity loan.

F·E·A·T·U·R·E

Your Credit History

♦ ♦ ♦

Whenever you apply for credit, the potential merchant or lender will usually request a credit report on you. Such information is obtained from a credit bureau. A credit bureau is a private organization that provides information to businesses regarding the credit history of customers. Merchants pay a fee for this service. There are 1,400 credit bureaus across the country. About half the adult population is on file in one of them.

Your credit file contains four major types of information.

1. Personal information such as name, address, previous addresses, marital status, and number of dependents.
2. Information about your salary, spouse's salary, and other income.
3. The status of your current accounts. What kinds of loans you now have. How well you pay your bills. This information can remain in your file for seven years.
4. Any court judgments or liens against you. A lien is a charge against your property for failure to pay a debt. Accounts turned over to a collection agency are also noted.

The credit bureau only compiles information and provides it to the merchant. The merchant or lender than makes a judgment about how credit worthy you are.

Federal law gives you the right to know what information is in your file. If you are refused credit on the basis of a credit bureau report, the merchant must give you the name and address of the bureau. You are entitled to obtain a free credit report from them. If you disagree with information in the file, the credit bureau must reinvestigate. Information that can't be backed up must be taken out.

Even if you aren't turned down for credit, you may want to look at your file. A local bank or merchant can tell you the name of the credit bureau nearest you. Write or call them to ask how to obtain a credit report. You will probably be charged a fee up to $10. After you read the report, you can ask to have missing information added to the file.

If you move, don't think you can escape from credit history. Your file moves with you to another credit bureau. One of the reasons merchants use credit bureaus is because people move so often.

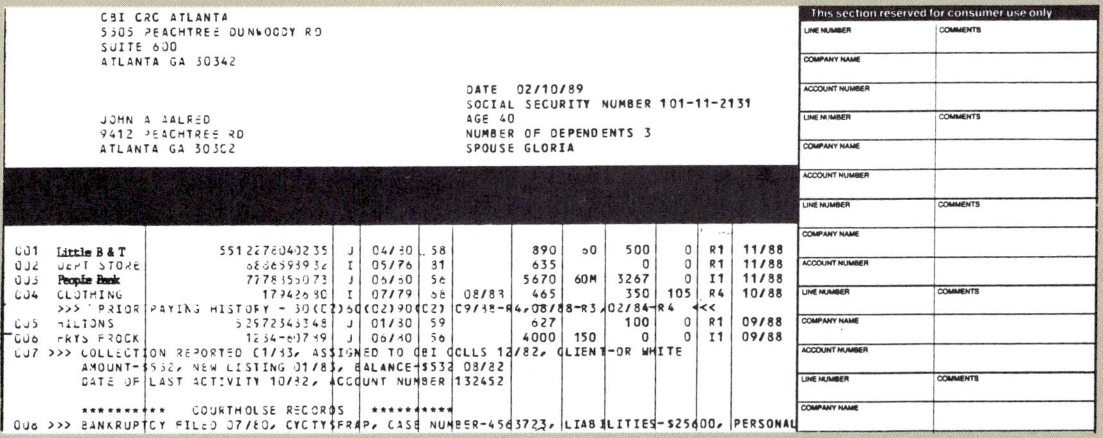

FIGURE 23-FEATURE People should know what is included in their credit bureau file. *Courtesy of CBI/Equifax*

* *Your Credit History.* Students are often surprised to discover that a credit bureau maintains records of people's credit histories. In your discussion, emphasize the following: (a) the importance of timely payments on a credit account to maintain a good credit record, (b) how to obtain a credit report, and (c) how to correct and/or add to a credit file.

Buyers generally pay back loan credit in equal installments over a fixed time period. In the case of the auto loan, you might pay installments of $150 for 36 months.

Sales Credit

When using loan credit, you borrow money. Sales credit, however, allows you to obtain goods and services immediately. You can then delay paying until later. There are three main types of sales credit: open charge accounts, revolving charge accounts, and installment accounts.

Many businesses provide open charge accounts to customers with good credit ratings. Don Marshall has a charge account at Polk's Department Store. One day, he decides to charge two sweaters there. After telling the clerk he is making a charge purchase, Don presents his charge plate. He signs a receipt and then takes home his purchase. The bill arrives a few weeks later.

The revolving charge is probably the most common form of consumer sales credit. Most of these are credit card accounts issued by chain stores, oil companies, and banks. The latter cards have such names as VISA, MasterCard, and Discover. With them, you can charge a number of goods and services. These include restaurant meals, airline tickets, and auto repairs.

22. Credit card interest rates vary depending upon the company. Provide examples. Point out that an annual fee may also be required. You may wish to assign Activity 5 at this time.

FIGURE 23-19 Stores are eager for customers to open charge accounts. Do you know why? *Photo by Joe Schuyler*

FIGURE 23-20 Installment contracts generally give the seller the right to repossess an item if payments aren't made. *Courtesy of American Automobile Association*

21. Help students better understand these three types of sales credit by using local illustrations and examples. Also, ask students for same.

23. You may wish to assign Activity 6 at this time.

24. Annual interest is easily determined by dividing the finance charge ($20) by the amount borrowed ($200). For APR, however, the calculations are laborious.

Like Don, credit card customers receive a monthly statement of all transactions. Don paid his entire bill. He could also have made a minimum payment or some other amount. But had he done that, he would have paid a finance charge. What percent of interest is paid on credit card purchases?

Installment accounts are the third major type of sales credit. People may use these to buy items that exceed the credit line of revolving charge accounts. Stores that don't honor credit cards may offer installment plans. Examples of items sometimes bought this way include furniture and home appliances.

The customer usually makes a small down payment. An installment contract that details payment terms for the balance is signed. The contract usually calls for fixed monthly payments and a finance charge. Installments are paid over several months or a few years. Finance charges are often higher than those for revolving accounts.

The Cost of Credit

The cost of credit varies from place to place. Fortunately, the law requires lenders to tell you in writing before you sign an agreement how much the charges will be. To understand the agreement, you will need to know the terms *finance charge* and *annual percentage rate*.

The *finance charge* is the total dollar amount you pay for using credit. It includes interest, service charges, insurance premiums, and other fees. For example, borrowing $100 for a year might cost you $15 in interest. If there is also a service charge of $2, the finance charge will be $17.

The *annual percentage rate* (APR) is the percentage cost of credit on a yearly basis. Suppose you borrow $200 for one year and pay a finance charge of $20. If you keep the entire $200 for 12 months and then

What Would You Do?

You are excited about buying your first car. You got a good deal and the finance rate is reasonable. The last step is to sign the installment sale contract. In going over the contract, you discover that the amount financed includes charges for "credit life and disability insurance" and "extended warranty." You ask the salesperson about the charges. He says they are optional, but that most people buy them. They only add a few dollars to the monthly payment. You aren't sure whether you need them. What would you do?

pay it back in one lump sum, you are paying an APR of 10 percent. However, if you repay the $200 and finance charge in 12 equal monthly installments (a total of $220), you don't really get to use the $200 for the whole year. In fact, you get to use less and less of the $200 each month. In this case, the $20 charge for credit amounts to an APR of 18 percent.

The APR is your key to comparing credit costs regardless of the amount of credit or the repayment period. All lenders (such as banks, stores, and credit card companies) must state the cost of their credit in terms of both the finance charge and APR. The law says you must be aware of this information before signing a credit contract.

To actually compare credit costs, you must take into account the APR and the length of the loan. Let's assume you are buying a car for $7,500. You pay $1,500 down and borrow $6,000. The relationship among three different credit arrangements is shown in Figure 23-21.

* *WWYD Feature B*. It is not true that "most people" buy them. The decision is an individual one involving a comparison of costs against benefits. Two guidelines are relevant: (a) if needed at all, cheaper insurance is probably available elsewhere, and (b) an extended warranty generally makes sense only for a used car.

25. Explain the general concept of APR by developing this example on the board. Show month-by-month how the available credit amount is reduced with each monthly payment. ($220 borrowed for 12 months equals a monthly payment of $18.33. Payment is made for first month leaving a balance of $201.67. Payment for second month leaves $183.34. Continue until twelfth payment of $18.37 is made.)

	APR	Length of Loan	Monthly Payment	Total Finance Charge	Total Cost
Creditor A	14%	3 years	$205.07	$1,382.52	**$7,382.52**
Creditor B	14%	4 years	**$163.96**	$1,870.08	$7,870.08
Creditor C	15%	4 years	$166.98	$2,015.04	$8,015.04

FIGURE 23-21 The cost of credit varies according to the APR and the length of the loan.

26. Refer students to Figure 23-21 and explain the three different credit arrangements illustrated in the text.

The lowest total loan cost is available from Creditor A. If you are looking for a lower monthly payment, you can get that by paying the loan back in four years instead of three. However, the lower monthly payment from Creditor B will add $487.56 to the total finance charge. If the four-year loan is only available from Creditor C, the 15 percent APR will add another $144.96 to the finance charge.

Other terms, such as the size of the down payment, will also make a difference in the cost of credit. Be sure to consider all aspects of a loan before making a choice.

CHAPTER REVIEW

Chapter in Brief

- There are four major types of financial institutions: commercial banks, mutual savings banks, savings and loan associations, and credit unions. Recent changes in laws governing financial institutions now allow all of them to offer similar kinds of services. Increased competition among financial institutions is good news for consumers.
- Checking accounts are one of the most commonly used banking services. Checking accounts have the advantages of safety and convenience. There are four types of checking accounts: regular (minimum blanace), special (cost-per-check), negotiable order of withdrawal (NOW), and share-draft account.
- A blank check requires several kinds of information: date, payee, numerical amount, written amount, purpose (optional), and signature. Learn how to correctly write a check.
- The check register is where you keep a record of checks written, deposits made, and other transactions. A common mistake is not recording checks in the register. Overdrawing a checking account can be very embarrassing.
- An endorsement is a signature and a message to the bank to cash, deposit, or transfer the check to someone else. There are three kinds of endorsements: blank, restrictive, and full.
- Once a month, the bank will send you a statement of account. The process of comparing the statement with your check register is known as balancing (or reconciling) a checkbook.
- Credit refers to the receipt of money, goods, or services in exchange for a promise to pay. Credit may be in the form of loan credit or sales credit. There are three main types of sales credit: open charge accounts, revolving charge accounts, and installment accounts.
- The finance charge is the total dollar amount you pay for using credit. The annual percentage rate (APR) is the percentage cost of credit on a yearly basis. The APR is your key to comparing credit costs regardless of the amount of credit or the repayment period.

CHAPTER 23 Banking and Credit ■ 315

Words to Know

annual percentage rate (APR) the percentage cost of credit on a yearly basis.

automated teller machine (ATM) one type of electronic banking in which a plastic card is used in an electronic terminal to withdraw cash, make deposits, or transfer funds to another account.

check register a ruled form used to record all of the transactions that occur in a checking account.

credit the receipt of money, goods, or services in exchange for a promise to pay at a later time.

deposit ticket a preprinted form used to make a deposit in a checking account.

electronic banking a broad term used to describe various types of electronic fund transfers.

endorsement a signature on the back of a check used to cash or transfer ownership of the check.

finance charge the total dollar amount paid for the use of credit.

full-service bank one that offers customers a full range of financial conveniences and services.

negotiable order of withdrawal (NOW) a type of interest-bearing checking account in which a withdrawal order (check) is written against a savings account rather than a checking account.

overdraft a check written for an amount greater than is available in the account.

payee the person or agency to whom a check is written.

postdating placing a date on a check that is ahead of the current date.

share-draft account a type of checking account in which a draft (check) is written against a credit union savings account.

signature card a form that is completed to open a checking account.

statement of account a summary of all of the transactions completed in a checking account for a given time period.

Questions to Answer

1. There are four major types of financial institutions. Name and briefly describe them.
2. What are the two main advantages of having a checking account?
3. Explain the basic difference between a regular checking account and a special checking account.
4. Name the five kinds of information you have to write on a check.
5. How should you endorse a check if your name is misspelled on the face of the check?
6. What is a mistake people often make with their check registers? How can this mistake be prevented?
7. In simple terms, what is the purpose of balancing a bank statement?
8. Name and briefly describe the four types of EFT services.

1. (a) *Commercial banks*—most common type of financial institution offering a variety of services. (b) *Mutual savings banks*—similar to commercial banks but often pay higher interest rates. Owned by depositors. (c) *Savings and loan associations*—largest provider of home mortgages. (d) *Credit unions*—nonprofit savings and loan cooperative associations. Restricted to credit union members.
2. (a) Safety. (b) Convenience.
3. *Regular* accounts usually require a certain minimum balance to be maintained. *Special* accounts are for people who only write a few checks per month. A charge is made for each check written.
4. (a) Date. (b) Payee. (c) Numerical amount. (d) Written amount. (e) Signature.
5. First, endorse it exactly as made out. Then, directly below, endorse it with the correct spelling.
6. Failing to record checks in the register. By getting in the habit of filling out the register each time a check is written.
7. To compare the statement of account with the check register.
8. (a) *Automated teller machines*—twenty-four-hour electronic terminals that permit personal banking. (b) *Pay-by-phone systems*—pay bills and transfer funds by phone. (c) *Direct*

316 ■ SECTION 5 Managing Your Money

9. There are two forms of credit. Name and briefly explain each type.
10. What are the three basic types of sales credit?
11. What does the finance charge include?
12. What is the practical purpose of the APR?
13. Let's say you bought a new car for which you paid $2,000 down and made monthly payments of $178.60 for three years. What was the total cost of the car?

Activities to Do

1. As a class, survey the types of financial institutions in your community, suburb, or region of the city. How many institutions are there? Classify each according to the four types of institutions discussed earlier. Which is the most common type of financial institution in your area?
2. A group of several students should visit at least three different financial institutions. Collect information about the types of checking accounts offered. How many different types of accounts did they discover? Which type of account best meets your needs in terms of both cost and convenience? Discuss your answers in class.
3. Ask a parent or other person to allow you to perform the following tasks for them:
   a. Write a check.
   b. Record a transaction in a check register.
   c. Make a deposit to a checking account.
4. The instructor will provide a sample statement of account and check register. Follow the procedure shown in Figure 23-16 to reconcile the bank statement.
5. Obtain an application for a credit card at a financial institution or other business. Read the application carefully and answer the following questions:
   a. Is the card free or is an annual fee required?
   b. What is the APR?
   c. How is the finance charge figured?
   d. What is the credit limit?
   e. What is the minimum monthly payment required?
6. Find out the interest rates being charged in your area for consumer loans. Compare the rates for a number of different sources, such as savings and loan associations, commercial banks, and finance companies. Which one offers the best rates?

---

deposits and withdrawals—automatic deposit of paycheck and payment of bills. (d) *Point-of-sale transfers*—instant payment of retail purchases.

9. (a) *Loan credit*—money borrowed in order to buy something. (b) *Sales credit*—charge accounts in which goods or services are received and payment is made later.
10. (a) Open charge accounts. (b) Revolving charge accounts. (c) Installment accounts.
11. Includes interest, service charge, insurance premium, and any other added fees.
12. It allows consumers to compare credit costs among different lenders regardless of the amount of credit or repayment period.
13. Total cost of $8,429.60.

27. This can be done by using the telephone Yellow Pages (all will probably be included under the heading "banks"). The accuracy of the classification is less important than making students aware of the different types of institutions that exist in their region.
28. Information could also be requested by mail or phone—a good opportunity to use communication skills.
29. Students will need to do this on their own. Encourage them to do so.
30. You could collect several applications or have students do so.
31. There probably won't be much difference among banks, S & Ls, and credit unions. However, this activity will provide a good opportunity to make students aware of the higher interest rates charged by finance companies.

Topics to Discuss

1. Discuss advantages and disadvantages of electronic banking.
2. Some futurists are saying that we are headed for a "checkless" or "moneyless" society. Do you think this time will ever come?
3. Many people like to order merchandise from mail order catalogs. Which of the following methods of payment are the safest and offer the greatest consumer protection: money order, check, credit card? Discuss reasons for your answer.
4. A young person applying for credit is often required to have a parent or other adult co-sign the application. What does this mean? Do you think the requirement is fair?

32. Electronic banking is a big step toward such a society. The trend will likely continue.
33. All are safe as methods of payment. However, a credit card purchase provides you with greater protection in resolving a consumer problem.
34. It means that the co-signer is responsible for the debt if the credit holder defaults. Even if it seems unfair, it is a reasonable requirement given the greater credit risk involved.

1. Emphasize the principle that how you spend your income is often as important as how much you earn.

2. Refer students to Figure 24-2 and explain how to use the form.

CHAPTER TWENTY-FOUR

Budgeting, Saving, and Investing Money

OUTLINE
Income and Spending Patterns
Developing and Using a Budget
Saving Money
Types of Savings Accounts
Figuring Interest Rates
Investing Money
Chapter Review

OBJECTIVES
After reading this chapter, you should be able to:
- Identify personal income and spending patterns.
- Name and describe the four steps involved in developing and using a budget.
- Discuss the importance of setting aside a portion of income for savings.
- Name and describe the two basic types of savings accounts.
- Compute interest rate returns on savings.
- Explain the following types of investments: stocks, bonds, and money market funds.

FIGURE 24-1 Don't allow the habits of childhood to carry over into your adult life. *Photo by Paul E. Meyers*

People often refer to someone's financial status by use of such terms as *rich*, *middle class* and *poor*. Financial well-being, of course, is related to how much money you earn. The way in which you spend money, however, is also important.

Many people who earn average incomes live comfortably and securely. They have learned how to get the greatest benefit from their money. Wise money management depends on knowledge and skill in the areas of budgeting, saving, and perhaps investing money.

INCOME AND SPENDING PATTERNS

A good first step in learning how to manage money is to find out where your money is coming from (income), and where it is going (expenditures). You will do this by maintaining a record of *income* and *expenditures*. A simple form for doing this is shown in Figure 24-2. You can use a form to cover a week or any time period you choose.

To fill out a form such as this one, begin by inserting the total amount of cash on hand at the beginning of the week. (Don't include savings.) Then, start keeping detailed records of all income and expenditures. For income, include take-home pay as well as tips and any money you receive from gifts or allowances. In the column provided, list all

318

RECORD OF INCOME AND EXPENDITURES

Week Feb 4-10, 19 89

Cash on hand 28.00

Date	Item	Income	Expenditure
4	Allowance - lunch money	18.00	
4	School lunch ticket		7.50
5	Gas in car		5.00
6	Babysitting	8.00	
7	Basketball game		1.50
	Soda and snack afterward		1.50
8	Movie w/friends		3.50
	Pizza afterward		3.00
9	Shopping (new record)		7.95
10	Personal Care Items		2.30

End of week cash balance 21.75   Totals 26.00   32.25

FIGURE 24-2 Records like these can help you determine patterns of income and expenditures.

expenditures, regardless of how small. At the end of the week, total up all income and expenditures.

How much money is left at week's end? It should equal initial cash at hand plus or minus income and

320 ■ SECTION 5 Managing Your Money

expenditures. Say your initial cash at hand was $75. You spent $50 and your aunt sent you $15 as a birthday gift. The end-of-week cash balance would be $40.

3   Once you have kept your records for a few weeks, figure your average income and expenditures. Add up all the income for the period and then divide by the number of weeks covered. Do the same for expenditures. Keeping a record of income and expenditures over a period of time can help you to understand your financial condition and spending habits. You can then use this information to help set up a budget for yourself.

What Would You Do?

Everyone at work seems to be talking about the new state lottery. Eric says he is going to spend $10 a week on lottery tickets. Shelly is going to buy one ticket, but thinks it is foolish to spend more than a dollar. Ollie says the odds of winning are so great that spending even a dollar is throwing money away. Ruth says that lotteries and other forms of gambling are morally wrong.

Winning the lottery would sure be the answer to your budget problems. But there are a lot of good reasons not to play the lottery. What would you do?

* *WWYD Feature A.* If you have a lottery in your state, what are the age requirements? Allow students to discuss their views toward lotteries. People who play should probably be like Shelly.

FIGURE 24-3 Everyone who earns a paycheck should have a plan for spending his or her money. *Photo by David W. Tuttle*

DEVELOPING AND USING A BUDGET

A *budget* is a plan for managing income and expenditures. Such a spending plan will help you get the most benefit from your earnings. The four steps involved in developing a budget are:

1. Establishing goals
2. Estimating income and expenditures
3. Setting up the budget
4. Following and revising it

The process is similar for everyone—individuals and families, young people and adults.

Establishing Goals

Goals should be set before you work out the details of your budget. Identify what you need and want. As you decide on goals, discuss them with

3. You may wish to assign Activity 1 at this time.

your family. If the budget is for a family, all family members should participate. Goals should be kept realistic in relation to present and expected future income.

To focus on your goals, list them according to time periods. Be as specific as possible. Bear in mind that there are short-range, medium-range, and long-range goals.

Naturally, goals change along with situations. For example, if you are single and live at home, your goals are probably different than they will be when you leave home. If you marry, your goals will change again, as they will if you have children. With two persons working, the family goals may be different than they would be if only one were working, and so on.

Once you have decided on your goals, write them down. Save your list. You will need to refer to it as you plan the budget.

4. Financial goal setting may not be relevant to a young person who is still supported by parents. Emphasize that a budget is a tool to help achieve future needs and wants.

5. You may wish to assign Activity 2 at this time.
6. Point out that this is the benefit of having maintained a record of income and expenditures.

CHAPTER 24 Budgeting, Saving, and Investing ■ 321

PERSONAL (OR FAMILY) GOALS
Goals for this year: _____
_____
_____
Goals for the next five years: _____
_____
_____
Long-term goals: _____
_____
_____

FIGURE 24-4 Write out your financial goals so that you will know what you are working toward.

Estimating Income and Expenditures

Once you have decided on goals, estimate your income and expenditures. A budget may cover any convenient budget period. Most people like to plan a budget around how often they get paid, such as weekly, bimonthly, or monthly.

If you have kept records of income and expenditures for a four- to six-week period, you should be able to arrive at fairly close estimates. If the budget is for a family, records of income and expenditures should be kept over a three- to six-month period. Figure out your average income per budget period. Now review. Did you include all regular income such as wages, salary, and tips? How about variable income, such as bonuses, gifts, interest, and dividends.

Individuals whose income varies present special problems. Examples of such people include seasonal workers, salespeople on commission, farmers, and other self-employed people. In these cases, it is usually better to base the budget estimates slightly below the average income. It is always easier to spend the extra money than it is to come up with a shortage.

FIGURE 24-5 Financial goals should benefit *all* family members. *Photo by David W. Tuttle*

322 ■ SECTION 5 Managing Your Money

Ann is a sales representative who earns most of her income from commissions. The more she sells, the more she earns. During the last six months, her income has been about thirty percent above normal. Business has been so good that she decided to trade her old car in on a new one. She can make payments with the extra commissions she is earning.

She got a call today at the office from one of her best clients. "Hello, Ann, this is Cliff at Dramon Corporation. I'm afraid I'll have to cancel that big order you wrote up for me last week. My field representatives are telling me that business is starting to slow down. We could be moving into a recession."

What if an economic slowdown is on the way? Ann's future commissions will probably fall. Ann now wishes she hadn't gone in debt for the new car.

Regarding expenditures, your previous records should help you identify the major categories of items. Next, review the list to make sure you haven't left out a seasonal expenditure or some other item that doesn't show up in your records. A checkbook register together with bills and receipts can help you remember such information.

As you review your record of expenditures, decide whether to continue your present spending pattern or to make changes. If you are satisfied with how you have used your money, allow similar amounts in your budget estimates. Suppose your records point out poor buying habits or overspending. In that case, you must decide to make changes.

Setting Up the Budget

Now that you have established your financial goals and have estimated income and expenditures, you are ready to set up your spending plan. The sample budget form shown in Figure 24-7 consists of three main parts.

The first part of the budget is for savings. It is important to set aside this money as soon as you are paid. If you wait until the end of the budget period, there may be nothing left for savings. You should save a regular amount of income for use in an emergency. For a family, the amount should equal *at least* one month's total income. Once you have reached your figure set aside for emergencies, start shifting money to savings goals and investments.

8. Many different approaches to budgeting are found in the literature. This sample budget, adapted from a USDA publication, is fairly representative.

FIGURE 24-6 Farmers often have a big check at harvest time. But there is often a long time between paychecks. *Courtesy of Elanco Products Company, Makers of Treflan* ®

7. A drop in income will probably not jeopardize Ann's ability to make car payments. However, she may have to make reductions in other areas of her budget.

9. Make an overhead transparency of the budget form to use in explaining budgeting.

HOUSEHOLD BUDGET FORM

Month __Jan.__ 19 __89__   Estimated Income $ __1220.00__

Expenditure	Estimate	Actual	Difference (+ or -)
Savings			
Emergency reserve	30	30	0
Goals	50	30	+20
Regular Expenses			
Rent or mortgage payments	270	270	0
Auto payment	70	70	0
Utilities	150	181	-31
Credit or loan payments	40	40	0
Insurance	50	50	0
Other ( )			
Variable Expenses			
Food and beverage	300	295	+5
Clothing	40	67	-27
Transportation	70	65	+5
Household	30	30	0
Medical care	25	18	+7
Entertainment	40	48	-8
Gifts and contributions	30	25	+5
Taxes	25	25	0
Other ( )			
TOTALS	1220	1244	-24

FIGURE 24-7 Using a budget form like this can improve the quality of your life and contribute to meeting future goals.

The next two parts of the budget include regular and variable expenditures. *Regular expenditures,* sometimes called fixed expenditures, are those essential monthly payments that are usually the same amount each month. *Variable expenditures* are day-to-day living expenses. They may change depending on the time of year, spending habits, and so on. Here is a list of common regular and variable expenditures.[10]

10. Authors differ slightly regarding what is included under regular (fixed) and variable expenditures. It is appropriate to modify this general approach to meet individual needs.

Regular Expenditures

- **Rent or Mortgage Payment.** This fixed expenditure covers your basic housing needs. Renters pay their landlord. Buyers of a property make payments to the lender that granted the mortgage. A mortgage payment usually includes amounts for property taxes and insurance.
- **Utilities.** These include such services as electricity, telephone, gas, and water. *Even though these*

FIGURE 24-8 To save money, you have to learn to do without some of the things that you would like to have. *Photo by Paul E. Meyers*

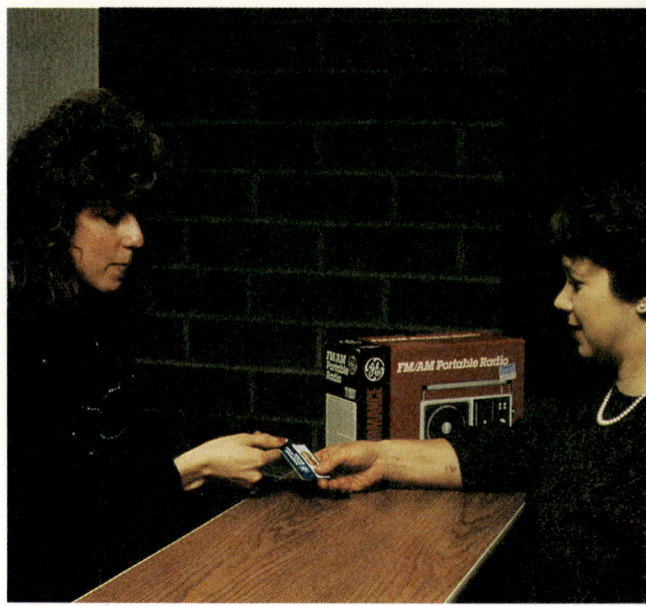

FIGURE 24-9 Don't use that charge card unless it is for a budgeted expenditure. *Photo by Paul E. Meyers*

amounts vary, you should list them as regular expenses because they are essential monthly payments. Suppose you have trouble deciding how much to budget for utilities? Check with the utility companies. Many of them have a plan whereby you can pay a fixed amount each month based on your average utility usage.
- *Insurance.* Include here all insurance premiums not covered by payroll withholding and mortgage payments. Life and auto insurance are two common examples.
- *Auto Payment.* This is an optional expenditure. However, many people make monthly installment payments on an auto loan.
- *Credit or Loan Payments.* These are also optional expenditures. They may include payments on charge accounts or student loans, for example.

Variable Expenditures

Food and Beverage. This includes food and beverages purchased for home use as well as essential meals eaten away from home, such as school lunches. Optional purchases, such as a snack after the game, should be listed under "Entertainment."
- *Clothing.* Include here the cost of buying new clothing. Be sure to also consider expenditures for repairs, alterations, dry cleaning, and laundry charges.
- *Transportation.* Include here the cost of using public transportation. If you own a vehicle, be sure to consider expenditures for gas, oil, repairs, tolls, and license plates.
- *Household.* This includes the cost of buying and maintaining furniture and home appliances. (Furniture payments could be included in "credit payments.") If you rent, the owners may or may not provide furniture. Everyone, though, must buy cleaning supplies. And homeowners may have extra expenses, such as paint, and lawn-care products.
- *Medical Care.* You can plan ahead for some of your medical care. For example, you know if you have to take regular medication or have periodic

F·E·A·T·U·R·E

Credit Billing Blues

It is difficult enough to manage a budget without being billed for things you don't owe. They can be taken care of, however, if you know how to use the *Fair Credit Billing Act.* To be protected under the law, here is what you need to do:

1. Write the bank or merchant who issued the credit. A telephone call *does not* trigger the legal safeguards provided under the Act. Your notice must be received within sixty days after the bill containing the error was mailed. Include in the letter your name and account number; the date; type, and dollar amount of the incorrect charge; and why you think there was a mistake.
2. Send the letter to the correct place. Don't put your letter in the same envelope as your payment. Your bill will usually explain where you should address inquiries. You may wish to send a certified letter to make sure the creditor receives it.

If you follow the preceding procedure, the creditor is required to acknowledge your letter in writing within thirty days after it is received. The alleged error must be investigated. Within ninety days, the mistake must be corrected or you must be given an explanation and proof of why the bill is accurate.

If you continue to have problems, you should contact your local or state consumer protection agency. Under the law, the creditor cannot close your account just because you disputed a bill. *

FIGURE 24-FEATURE Review your monthly statement carefully. Credit billing errors do occur. *Photo by Paul E. Meyers*

* *Credit Billing Blues.* Everyone who uses credit should be aware of their rights. Creditors are required to provide written information about billing rights at the time credit is issued. Also, such information is typically provided on the back of monthly statements. Show and discuss several examples.

326 ■ SECTION 5 Managing Your Money

12. Perhaps students might have other suggestions about how to allocate income.

Following and Revising the Budget

Following a budget involves the *allocation* of income to various budgeted items, and keeping accurate records of expenditures. One way to allocate income is simply to deposit all or most of the income in a checking account. You can then write checks for items as necessary. Another common way of allocating income is to first cash the paycheck. After you have divided the cash according to budget categories, place it in separate envelopes. These should be labeled with the names of your main budget headings. You then take money out of the envelopes as needed.

FIGURE 24-10 If you know how, you can save money by doing your own home repairs and maintenance. *Courtesy of The Pillsbury Company*

check-ups. Try to set aside some money for variable medical and dental expenses not covered by insurance.
- *Entertainment.* This includes vacations, hobbies, concert tickets, sporting events, and the like. If you had children, babysitting might be a related expense.
- *Gifts and Contributions.* Besides gifts, be sure to consider contributions to charity, churches, and political parties.
- *Taxes.* Include here amounts for taxes not withheld from your paycheck or included in a mortgage payment. Keep in mind that it is often necessary to pay extra income taxes at the end of the year.

These items are the expenditures that most families have. You should feel free to *add or subtract items as necessary.* If you choose, *rearrange them in a way that works best for you.* Once you have developed a list of expenditures for your budget, enter on the budget form a dollar amount for each item. The total of all items in the "Estimate" column should equal the amount of "Estimated Income."

11. You may wish to conduct Activity 3 at this time. Prepare and duplicate the budget form shown in Figure 24-7. Conduct Activity 4 as appropriate.

FIGURE 24-11 Don't develop a budget and then forget it. Follow it. *Photo by Paul E. Meyers*

A good choice is probably a combination of the two methods. Place most of your paycheck in a checking account. The remaining is kept on hand for frequent purchases. Regardless of which method you use, you must refer to the budget often. Otherwise, your spending plan is useless.

Keeping accurate records is an important part of maintaining a budget. Because you will probably pay them by check, major expenditures are easy to keep track of. Be sure, though, to write everything in your check register. Small cash purchases can be another matter. Because you make so many of them, it is tempting to ignore them. Failure to note these items makes your budget useless.

13. Maintaining a budget is largely dependent on developing daily record-keeping habits and setting aside time periodically to synthesize records and evaluate performance.

14. Financial matters are a major source of stress in people's lives and a factor related to family and marital instability, illness, alcohol and drug use, and other problems. A budget can't compensate for unemployment or an inadequate income, but will help people to gain a *greater degree of control* over their personal and family finances.

CHAPTER 24 Budgeting, Saving, and Investing ■ 327

What Would You Do?

You have done your best to develop and follow a budget. You are careful to stick to budget estimates. But every month there is an unexpected expense. It never seems to be the same type of expenditure. One month it is a car repair, the next month a medical bill, another month an increase in insurance, and so on. You are very frustrated and about ready to "trash-can" the budget. What would you do?*

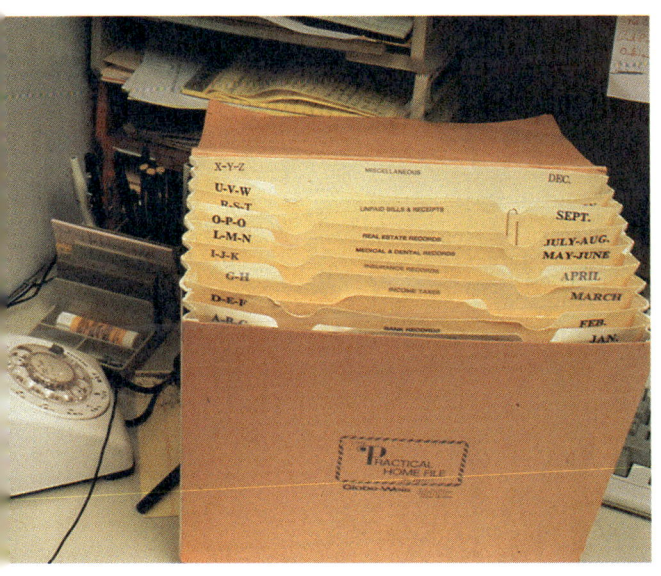

FIGURE 24-12 An expandable folder like this can help you to maintain your budget. *Photo by Paul E. Meyers*

So, to account for cash purchases, use a form such as the one shown in Figure 24-2. If that form doesn't meet your needs, modify it or develop a new one. Another approach is to get an expandable manila file and label each pocket according to the items in the budget. You can use this file to keep track of receipts. To jot down items for which you do not have a receipt, keep a notepad and pen near the file. All family members who spend money should get in the habit of saving and filing.

At the end of the budget period, collect your receipts and records. Then, transfer the information to the budget form column labeled "Actual." Write in the total amount spent for each *line item* in the budget. In the next column, record the difference between the "Estimate" and the "Actual" amounts. (Refer to Figure 24-7.) For example, if you estimated $70 for transportation, but only spent $65, write in "+$5." However, suppose you spent $85. In that case, you would put down "-$15."

After you have filled in all information, add up the totals for the "Actual" and "Difference" columns. Now you must face up to reality. How does your spending compare to your estimates? If the figures are similar, you should be proud of yourself. If not, try to find the problem. Perhaps your estimates weren't accurate or realistic. Or, maybe the estimates were good, but you had trouble sticking to them. If there is a problem with the estimates, revise them. When the problem is with you, resolve to do a better job next time.

You should not expect to have a perfect budget the first time you set one up. A budget is something you must keep working and reworking. Even after you arrive at a budget that is right for you, you will need to change it from time to time.

SAVING MONEY

If all of your paycheck goes for bills, you are working for someone else! Ask Ralph. On the first of the month when he gets paid, Ralph writes checks for all of his monthly payments. Checks go for rent,

FIGURE 24-13 In several thousand miles, Ralph's car will need a new set of tires. If Ralph saves a portion of his paycheck, he will have the money to buy new tires when they are needed. *Photo by David W. Tuttle*

* *WWYD Feature B*. Managing money is difficult. There are often more expenses than income. But this is precisely why budgeting is desirable. The alternative of not having a budget is worse.

328 ■ SECTION 5 Managing Your Money

16. Encourage students to consider different institutions for their checking and savings accounts. Convenience is a factor, however, that should also be taken into account.

Happy New Yields!

Open one of these First American CDs and get a high rate and yield. Plus, get an extra 1/2% bonus and an even higher yield if you already have—or open—a deposit account with us.*
These high rates also apply to IRAs! Call or visit any of our 42 conveniently located offices today!

	1 YEAR CD		2 YEAR CD	
Bonus!	**8.02%** BONUS Annual Yield	**7.79%** Bonus Annual Rate	**8.37%** BONUS Annual Yield	**8.12%** Bonus Annual Rate
	7.49% Annual Yield	7.29% Annual Rate	7.84% Annual Yield	7.62% Annual Rate

If you prefer immediate access to your money while still earning a high return, invest in our...

MONEY MARKET ACCOUNT!*

5.69% Annual Yield / **5.55%** Annual Rate

* Personal and corporate accounts only to $100,000. To qualify, depositors to these CDs must open or currently have one of the following at First American: a checking, passbook, statement savings, NOW, Super NOW, or Money Market account (certain minimum balances apply). $1000 minimum deposit on CDs; $500 minimum deposit on IRAs (1 and 2 year CDs only). With CDs only, principal and interest must remain on deposit one full year to earn the annual yields shown. Interest compounded and credited quarterly. Substantial penalty for early withdrawal. All rates and yields subject to change without notice. Offer may be withdrawn at any time. $1000 minimum deposit on Money Market account. ** 1/2% bonus not applicable.

The Professionals with the Personal Touch.

1stAMERICAN
FIRST AMERICAN BANK OF NEW YORK

Call any one of these branches in your area: Member FDIC

Main Office 447-4700. **Albany: Central Ave.** 453-1647, **Delaware Ave.** 453-1656, **New Scotland Ave.** 453-1627, **South Pearl St.** 453-1637, **State St.** 453-1609, **Washington Ave.** 453-1641, **Western Ave.** 453-1600. **Clifton Park** 371-2294. **Colonie: Central Ave.** 453-1651, **Wolf Rd.** 453-1612. **East Greenbush** 453-1616. **Elsmere** 453-1603. **Glenmont** 453-1635. **Guilderland** 453-1624. **Latham** 453-1659. **Rensselaer** 453-1632. **Rotterdam** 355-0025. **Schenectady: State St.** 372-4415, **Woodlawn** 377-2271. **Troy** 453-1619. **West Sand Lake** 674-2866.

FIGURE 24-14 Financial institutions, like other businesses, use a variety of advertising techniques to attract new customers. *Courtesy First American Bank of New York*

15. This is an advantage of payroll deduction in which money for savings can be set aside before it is received (see Discussion Topic 4).

17. Newspaper advertising (particularly weekend editions) is often a good source of information about savings institutions and interest rates.

*WWYD Feature C. There would be nothing wrong with switching banks and receiving a free gift as long as the new account earned equal or greater interest.

a car payment, utilities, and various credit card accounts. After putting aside amounts for groceries and insurance, Ralph has little left. He keeps his fingers crossed every month. Ralph knows that an illness or emergency would be a financial disaster.

One weekend at a family gathering, Ralph was talking about finances with his Uncle John. Uncle John, a banker, listened patiently until Ralph had finished. Then he said, "Ralph, you must learn to *pay yourself first.*" What Uncle John meant was that Ralph should reward himself for working. He should take a portion "off the top" of his paycheck and put it into savings.

The word *savings* refers to cash that has been set aside in a bank account. There are two reasons to do this. First of all, you will have some funds to meet a financial emergency. Suppose Ralph follows his uncle's advice and opens a savings account. Then should his old car need urgent repairs, Ralph won't wonder how he will pay for them. Secondly, a savings account allows you to achieve financial goals. Ralph, for example, may want to save toward a compact disc player.

Where to Save

In Chapter 23, you read about the four types of financial institutions offering checking accounts. Those institutions—commercial banks, mutual savings banks, savings and loan associations, and credit unions—accept savings deposits as well. Bear in mind that it is not necessary to have both checking and savings accounts at the same place. Do some comparison shopping. Teresa Romero did.

You may also remember from Chapter 23 how Teresa Romero saved money on her checking account by moving it to a credit union. So, when it came time to open a savings account, she reviewed the material she had already collected about financial services.

After comparing various plans and interest rates, Teresa decided to open a savings account at a mutual savings bank. It is close to her home and doesn't close until 8:00 P.M. on Friday evenings. Her money, on which she receives a good interest rate, is insured. She can withdraw funds at any time. Teresa is satisfied to know that she is using her money wisely.

Because of certain changes in federal and state regulations, institutions now offer about the same types of services. Shop carefully for the right ones for you. You have many choices. For example, even

within one institution, you may discover a variety of savings plans. In the end, your efforts will gain you more interest for your savings dollars.

What Would You Do?

You see an ad in the newspaper regarding the grand opening of a new mutual savings bank. The bank is offering a clock radio to new customers who deposit a certain amount. You already have a passbook account and a CD at another bank. But you are considering switching banks to get a free gift. What would you do?

TYPES OF SAVINGS ACCOUNTS

Financial institutions may advertise many different savings account plans. These plans are generally of two basic types: regular savings accounts and time deposits.

Regular Savings Accounts

Regular savings accounts, also called "passbook accounts," are very convenient and flexible. You can make deposits and withdrawals at any time. These accounts get their name from the passbook used for recording deposits, withdrawals, and in-

FIGURE 24-15 What is the purpose of a savings account passbook? *Photo by Paul E. Meyers*

information may have been collected while completing activities for Chapter 23 related to checking services.

18. "Regular" and "time deposits" are convenient ways of classifying types of saving accounts. There are many variations. You may wish to assign Activity 5 at this time. Actually, such

SECTION 5 ■ Managing Your Money

terest payments. Some regular accounts, however, are being converted to computerized statements. A statement may be provided at the time a transaction is made. A summary statement may also be mailed monthly or quarterly to the customer.

It is easy to open a regular savings account. You simply sign a signature card and make a deposit. An individual account number will be assigned, and the institution will give you a passbook or an identification card for your account.

Regular savings accounts offer safety, convenience, and *liquidity*. In return for these benefits, depositors receive slightly less interest than they would on other accounts. The lower return is due to the fact that passbook accounts are expensive for institutions to service.

19. Discuss variations of passbook accounts that are found in your area.

SAVINGS WITHDRAWAL FORM

SAVINGS DEPOSIT FORM

FIGURE 24-16 Special forms are usually used for making deposits and withdrawals.

20. Remind students that it is foolish to have a checking or savings account in an institution that is not federally insured (FDIC, NCUA, FSLIC).

21. The term *CD* is almost synonymous with time deposits.
22. Competition is forcing savings institutions to become more flexible regarding penalties for early withdrawal.

Time Deposits

If you can deposit a lump-sum amount for a longer period of time, you may be interested in time deposits. These special accounts may be called certificates of deposit (CD) or they may have names such as "Golden Passbook Accounts" or "Bonus Savings Accounts."

Most time deposits work in the same way. A depositor puts in money for a fixed period of time. This may be six months, one year, or longer. The saver agrees not to withdraw money from the account during that period. In return for agreeing not to withdraw the money for a fixed period of time, the institution pays a higher rate of interest. Also, the longer the saver agrees to keep the money in the account, the higher the rate of interest will be, Figure 24-17. What if the depositor *needs* to withdraw the funds? It can be done, but the interest rate will be greatly reduced.

First Trust Bank
Central Avenue Branch
Vero Beach, FL 12312

SUBJECT TO CHANGE

DEPOSIT RATES EFFECTIVE ——— May 3, 1989

THRU ——— May 9, 1989

Type	Minimum	Current Rates
Time Deposits 32 - 91 days	$500	6.30
Time Deposits 92 days - 1 year	$500	6.55
Time Deposits 13 - 18 months	$500	6.65
Time Deposits 19 - 30 months	$500	7.25
Time Deposits 31 - 48 months	$500	7.45
Time Deposits over 48 months	$500	7.75

FIGURE 24-17 This is an example of how time deposits vary according to different time periods.

23. All four factors described influence interest rates. Carefully explain each.

Time deposit accounts often require a minimum deposit. The advantages of time deposits are that they are safe and provide a guaranteed rate of return for a fixed time period. On the negative side, they don't permit deposits and withdrawals and aren't as liquid.

24. Work a sample problem on the board and then assign additional practice problems.

25. To figure out how long it will take for your money to double, divide 72 by the rate of interest earned. For example, 72 ÷ 10% = 7.2 years; 72 ÷ 8% = 9 years; 72 ÷ 5% = 14.4 years.

FIGURING INTEREST RATES

Determining the best interest rates for different savings plans requires effort on your part. To start, look at this newspaper ad:

> Save more at University Bank. 5¼% interest compounded daily, paid quarterly on passbook savings. Yield 5.390.

From the ad, you learn the amounts of the annual interest rate (5¼%) and annual percentage yield (5.390). University Bank also tells you how often interest is compounded (daily) and when interest is paid (quarterly). Let's now discuss these four points in detail.

Annual Interest Rate

The law requires banks and other financial institutions to clearly state in their ads the true annual interest rate paid on savings. In the preceding ad, the figure "5¼%" is the annual interest rate. This means that on each $100 of savings, the institution pays you $5.25 in interest. Interest rates are figured by multiplying rate times time in years times principal (0.0525 × 1 × $100 = $5.25).

Frequency of Interest Compounding

It is easy to understand the annual interest rate. You want the most interest for your money. But the highest advertised annual rate may not be the best deal. More important than the interest rate is how often the interest is compounded. When an institution adds interest, an account's balance rises. There is then more money to earn interest later. This process is called *compounding*. A 6-percent interest rate that is compounded annually is one in which the interest is added every 12 months. So if $100 is in your account, $106 will be the balance after one year. At the end of the second year, you will have $112.36. The institution figured that interest rate on $106. How much, then, would you earn the third year?

If the interest rate of 6 percent on $100 is compounded semiannually, you will have $103 at the end of six months. After a year, you will have $106.09, and at the end of two years, $112.55. The more often the interest compounds, the more money you make. Figure 24-18 shows how the value of a $1,000 deposit varies according to the rate of compounding.

Interest Pay Periods

How often does the financial institution credit

26. Work out the examples provided here on the board and then assign additional practice problems.
27. Refer students to Figure 24-18. Pose questions such as: How

CHAPTER 24 Budgeting, Saving, and Investing ■ 331

Frequency of compounding	After 1 year	After 5 years	After 10 years	After 20 years
Daily	1,054.67	1,304.90	1,702.76	2,899.41
Quarterly	1,053.54	1,297.96	1,684.70	2,838.20
Semiannually	1,053.19	1,295.78	1,679.05	2,819.21
Annually	1,052.50	1,291.55	1,668.10	2,782.54

FIGURE 24-18 More frequent interest compounding results in higher returns. The figures are based on a $1,000 deposit at 5¼ percent.

much more is earned after one year for daily compounding versus annual compounding? ($2.17) For ten years? ($34.66) Continue as appropriate.

interest to your account? The ad for University Bank says that they compound interest daily and pay it four times a year (quarterly). Should you close the account in mid-quarter, you would lose all the interest for that three-month period. You may want to look instead for an account that pays interest from day-of-deposit to day-of-withdrawal.

Annual Percentage Yield

When comparing one savings account with another, it is useful to know the annual percentage yield, or APY. That figure will tell you the actual yearly interest rate per $100 left on deposit. The number takes into account both the rates for annual interest and compounding. In general, the higher the APY, the better the deal you receive. Refer to Figure 24-19.

5¼%, compounded	APY
Daily	5.47%
Quarterly	5.35%
Semiannually	5.32%
Annually	5.25%

FIGURE 24-19 The APY is the best indicator of how much interest you will earn.

Other Information

The four factors discussed here aren't the only ones that influence savings interest. One bank ad, for instance, contained this statement: "Deposits made by the tenth of the month earn interest from the first. Interest is figured on the low balance per month and there must be a balance at interest-paying days in order to earn interest."

28. Emphasize that APY has the same significance as APR (Chapter 23) in making financial decisions. You may wish to assign Activity 6 at this time.

332 ■ SECTION 5 Managing Your Money

This example illustrates only one of the many different methods that savings institutions use to compute interest. However, if you know the basic principles of figuring interest rates, you should be able to understand and compare the methods used by different institutions.

If you shop around, remember that savings institutions may differ a great deal as to how they figure interest. Try to narrow down your choices to a few institutions offering the highest APY. Speak with bank personnel about requirements. Your best choice will probably be the institution having the highest APY and the fewest restrictions and penalties.

Following this advice will bring you financial rewards. Why settle for just any institution? It is *your* money. Study Figures 24-20 and 24-21 to see how different amounts of savings can grow according to different interest rates and time periods.

> 29. Have available or assign students to bring in newspaper advertising that illustrates different APYs. Compare and discuss different rates.

Weekly deposit	After 1 year	After 3 years	After 5 years	After 10 years	After 20 years
$ 5	$ 267.16	$ 845.95	$1,489.54	$ 3,431.69	$ 9,265.67
10	534.32	1,691.89	2,979.08	6,863.37	18,531.35
15	801.48	2,537.84	4,468.62	10,295.06	27,797.02
20	1,068.63	3,383.79	5,958.17	13,726.74	37,062.70
25	1,335.79	4,229.74	7,447.71	17,158.43	46,328.37

FIGURE 24-20 Over the years, a small amount of savings can add up to a large amount. (Based on 5¼ percent interest, compounded daily.)

> 30. Remind students that inflation will reduce the "real value" of long-term savings (illustrate why). Nonetheless, compound interest on savings is a remarkable phenomenon.

Interest rate	After 1 year	After 3 years	After 5 years	After 10 years	After 20 years
4½%	$615.13	$1,932.88	$3,376.53	$7,618.34	$19,641.57
5	616.84	1,948.41	3,422.06	7,831.35	20,832.93
5¼	617.70	1,956.25	3,445.16	7,940.88	21,463.05
5½	618.55	1,964.11	3,468.42	8,052.13	22,115.27
6	620.28	1,979.99	3,515.63	8,281.10	23,496.83
6½	622.01	1,996.02	3,563.61	8,518.04	24,982.45
7	623.74	2,012.22	3,612.46	8,763.73	26,583.82
7½	625.48	2,028.60	3,662.20	9,018.48	28,310.47
8	627.23	2,045.16	3,712.83	9,282.67	30,173.06

FIGURE 24-21 This shows the importance of shopping around for the highest rates.

> 31. Realistically, investing money is a less relevant subject for young people than saving money. However, an understanding of basic terms and concepts is a good foundation to build upon.

> 32. Emphasize that the element of risk is present in many investments. Many newspapers report degree of risk along with performance when listing different investments.

INVESTING MONEY

Investing is the process of using money not required for personal and family needs to increase overall financial worth. Investing is different from savings in that investing is a long-term financial strategy. Money for investing comes from funds left *after* meeting basic expenditures and short- and medium-range savings goals.

The investor wants to make as much money as possible. In order to make a lot of money, though, there is usually a risk of losing money. For example, buying stock in a new, unproved company is very risky. High-risk investments, however, can sometimes produce big payoff. Let's take another example. Buying bonds of a large, financially stable corporation involves a relatively low risk. However, lower risk investments generally produce smaller profits.

What Would You Do?

At a family holiday gathering, you overhear a conversation about investing. It seems that a friend of your uncle's is forming a partnership to start a new company. Uncle Bill is very excited. He has already committed $20,000 to the venture. He claims that he is going to make a fortune. Several other family members are interested. Maybe you can get in on the deal also. What would you do?

> * WWYD Feature D. New companies are very risky ventures and should be avoided by all but the most experienced investors.

In investing, you must learn to balance risks. Probably the best way to balance risks is to *diversify* investments. This means to spread out money over several different types of investment options. Let's now examine three popular types of investments: stocks, bonds, and money market funds.

Stocks

One of the most popular forms of investment is the purchase of shares of *stock*. When you buy stock in a company, you are buying part of the ownership of that company. Shares of stock vary in price from a few dollars a share to a few hundred dollars. Stock is most often sold in 100-share lots.

> 33. The New York Stock Exchange has developed a set of high school teaching materials called *Taking Stock in the Future*.

FIGURE 24-22 Collectibles like coins, stamps, antiques, and art are another form of investment. However, these are risky and not recommended for beginners. *Photo by Paul E. Meyers*

Stocks are usually bought from individuals called *brokers* who specialize in selling stocks and other investments. Stock prices vary from day to day. The purchase price for a stock is the current selling price plus a small fee, called a *commission*, charged by the broker.

You can make money on stocks through *dividends*, through *capital gain*, or both. Dividends are the profits that a company divides among the stockholders. Let's say you bought stock in a company for $24 a share. If the company paid 50 cents a share dividend each quarter, you would make $2 a year on each share of stock that you owned. The return on your investment would be 8.3 percent.

Capital gain refers to an increase in the selling price of the stock. For example, if the stock you bought at $24 increased in price to $30 a share, the capital gain would be $6 per share. In this case, your return on investment would be 25 percent.

Instead of buying individual stocks, you can purchase shares of stock in a *mutual fund*. A mutual fund is an investment company that pools the money of thousands of investors and buys a collection of stocks called a *portfolio*. The advantage of a mutual fund is that prices do not vary as much as those for an individual stock. Like individual stocks, profits on mutual funds can be derived from dividends, capital gains, or both. Mutual funds are generally recommended over individual stocks for the beginner and for the small investor.

34. Work the two examples regarding dividends and capital gains on the board. Conduct Activity 7.
35. You may wish to assign Activity 8 at this time.

FIGURE 24-23 A stock certificate is evidence of your ownership in a particular company. *Photo by Paul E. Meyers*

36. Bonds are sometimes called *securities* (evidence of debt), while stocks are called *equities* (ownership in a company).

Bonds

You have learned that stock represents shares of actual ownership in a company. *Bonds* represent a loan to a company or government agency. Let's say a large corporation needed 10 million dollars to expand its plant. One way to raise the money would be to sell shares of stock in the company. Another way would be to issue bonds. A bond is a pledge to repay the borrowed sum plus a certain amount of interest.

To be more specific, Lunar Manufacturing Company issues $1,000 bonds paying 8.5 percent interest with a maturity date of 2010. If you purchase one of these bonds, Lunar Manufacturing Company will pay you $85 interest per year until 2010, at which time they will return your $1,000 dollars.

Bonds issued by private companies such as Lunar Manufacturing Company are called corporate bonds. Government agencies also issue bonds to raise money for roads, schools, sewer systems, and so on. Those issued by state, city, county, and other units of local government are called municipal bonds. When the federal government issues bonds, they are known as government bonds. The idea behind all bonds is the same. They are a piece of paper that represents a promise to repay a specific borrowed amount in the future along with a fixed interest rate.

Bonds can be purchased through the same brokers that sell stocks. Like stocks, bonds are available

37. The most familiar government bond is the U.S. Savings Bond. Pick up brochures at a bank or credit union and share with students.

individually or through mutual funds that specialize in bonds.

Money Market Funds

This is a type of mutual fund run by an investment company or a financial institution. Money is pooled from many investors and used to purchase short-term corporate notes, U.S. treasury notes, and certificates of deposit. The objective is usually to earn the highest possible safe interest rate. *Money market funds* provide a way for the small investor to take advantage of the higher interest rates that were once available only to the large investor. Most funds require a minimum deposit (often as little as a few hundred dollars).

Money market shares can be purchased directly from an investment firm, through a financial institution, or from a broker. The interest rates on these funds go up and down according to the general economy. Unless offered by financial institutions, money market funds are not insured or guaranteed, but they are regarded as very safe. Shares in these funds can be sold (redeemed) at any time.

Investing is part of an overall process of budgeting and saving money. Decide on your personal or family goals and stick to them. Don't get greedy. Stay away from hot tips that promise instant wealth. To avoid losing money, be wary and investigate any investment very carefully before turning over any money.

FIGURE 24-24 The federal government is the largest borrower in the country. It borrows money by selling savings bonds and other securities. *Photo by Paul E. Meyers*

38. Activity 5 asks students to collect savings information. If completed, such material probably also contains information about money market accounts.

39. Caution students that investment claims of instant wealth or huge profits should be viewed with skepticism.

CHAPTER REVIEW

Chapter in Brief

- A good first step in learning how to manage money is to identify sources of income and spending. You will do this by maintaining a record of income and expenditures. This will help you understand your financial condition and spending habits. Such information is then used to set up a budget.
- A budget is a plan for managing income and expenditures. Such a spending plan will help you get the most benefit from your earnings. The four steps involved in developing a budget are: establishing goals, estimating income and expenditures, setting up the budget, and following and revising the budget.
- Goals should be set before you work out the details of your budget. List goals according to different time periods. Goals should be realistic and achievable. Write them down and use them to plan the budget.
- Once you have decided on goals, estimate your income and expenditures. Base estimates on actual records. Budget periods are usually planned around how often one gets paid (weekly, bimonthly, monthly, or the like).
- A budget consists of three main parts: savings, regular (fixed) expenses, and variable expenses. Items can be added or subtracted from these three parts or rearranged in a way that works best for you.
- Following a budget involves allocation of income to various budgeted items. A good way to do this is to place most of your paycheck in a checking account. Write checks for larger expenses. Keep the remaining cash on hand for frequent purchases. Keeping accurate records is an important part of maintaining a budget.
- You shouldn't expect to have a perfect budget the first time you set one up. A budget is something you must keep working and reworking until it "fits."
- Savings refers to cash that has been set aside in a bank account. Savings are important for two reasons. First, to have funds for a financial emergency. Second, to meet personal and family financial goals.
- There are two basic types of savings accounts. With a regular savings account (passbook account), you can make deposits and withdrawals at any time. They offer safety, convenience, and liquidity. A time deposit account is where you deposit a certain lump sum for a fixed period of time. They are safe and offer a higher rate of return than passbook accounts.
- Interest earned on savings depends on the annual interest rate, frequency of compounding, and when the interest is paid. In comparing savings options, it is useful to know the annual percentage yield (APY). Generally, the higher the APY, the better the deal.

- Investing is the process of using money not required for personal and family needs to increase overall financial worth. Investing involves the risk of losing money. A good way to balance risks is to diversify investments.
- There are three popular types of investments. Investing in stocks involves buying shares of actual ownership in a company. Money on stocks can be made through dividends, capital gains, or both. Another way to invest is to purchase paper certificates called bonds, which provide a fixed interest rate. Bonds represent a loan to a private company or government agency. Money market funds are a type of mutual fund that invests in corporate and government notes and certificates of deposit. Money market rates vary monthly according to overall interest rate trends.

Words to Know

allocation the process of distributing income to the various items in a budget.

bonds interest-bearing certificates issued by a government or corporation.

brokers individuals who specialize in selling stock and other financial investments.

budget a plan for managing income and expenditures.

capital gain an increase in the selling price of a stock.

commission a fee paid to a broker upon purchase of a stock.

compounding compound interest; a process in which interest is periodically added to the account balance, causing savings to steadily grow.

diversify to spread out money over several different types of investment options.

dividends company profits that are divided among the stockholders.

expenditures money that is spent.

income money coming in.

investing using money not required for personal and family needs to increase overall financial worth.

line item a single entry in a budget; a budgeted item.

liquidity easily converted into cash.

money market fund a type of mutual fund in which the pooled funds are used to buy interest-bearing notes and certificates of deposit.

mutual fund an investment company that pools the money of many investors and buys a collection of stocks or bonds.

portfolio a collection of stocks or bonds.

regular (fixed) expenditures in budgeting, those essential payments that are about the same amount each month.

savings cash set aside in a bank account to be used for financial emergencies and goals.

stocks shares of ownership in a company.

variable expenditures in budgeting, day-to-day living expenses.

Questions to Answer

1. Two factors influence a person's or family's financial well-being. Name them.
2. What is the purpose of keeping a record of income and expenditures?
3. What four steps are involved in developing a budget?
4. How does goal setting differ for a single person and a married person?

1. (a) The amount of money earned. (b) How money is spent.
2. To find out where money is coming from (income) and where it is going (expenditures). Such information is used to help set up a budget.
3. (a) Establishing goals. (b) Estimating income and expenditures. (c) Setting up the budget. (d) Following and revising the budget.
4. A married person needs to set goals and make financial decisions in terms of what is best for the entire family.

5. Why is the first part of a budget devoted to savings?
6. Explain how to allocate income to budgeted items.
7. In following a budget, you might discover that your actual expenditures are quite different from your estimated expenditures. What two things might cause this problem?
8. Explain what is meant by the phrase "pay yourself first."
9. There are two reasons to set aside savings. Name them.
10. What are the two basic types of savings accounts? Briefly describe each.
11. On what two things is the annual percentage yield (APY) based?
12. How is investing different from saving money?
13. What is the basic difference between a stock and a bond?
14. Name the type of bond issued by a private company. By a local government.
15. What is the main advantage offered by a money market fund?

Activities to Do

1. Write down income and expenditures on a form similar to Figure 24-2. Keep records for a week. Then, study them. List at least three things you noticed about your spending. Discuss your findings in class.
2. Think about your financial goals. Write down your financial goal(s) for the next year. Then note your financial goals for the next five years. Discuss your goals in class. How do they compare to your classmates' goals? Also discuss how your goals might be different if you and your classmates were all five years older.
3. Consider the case of a family consisting of a husband, wife, and one young child. Assume the family's net monthly income is $1,500.00. As a group in-class activity, prepare an estimated budget for this family. Use or adapt the budget form shown in Figure 24-7.
4. After completing Activity 3, invite a qualified person to class to review the budget. Ask him or her to examine and discuss your class' budget for the family.
5. In groups of two or three, visit several different financial institutions in your area and collect information on their regular (passbook) savings account. (Or individuals or teams could be assigned to visit specific institutions.) Compare the alternatives with respect to: (a) interest rate paid, (b) how the interest is computed, (c) when the interest is paid, (d) annual percentage yield, (e) minimum size of deposit, (f) service charges, and (g) rules and restrictions. You may wish to prepare some type of a chart to help you compare alternatives. Discuss your findings in class.
6. Let's assume that you deposited $500 in a savings account paying 6 percent annual interest. You do not disturb the money for a year. Interest is compounded quarterly. At the end of a year, how much money is in the account? What is the annual percentage yield?
7. Let's assume you bought 100 shares of stock at $25 a share. The stock pays a 40-cent dividend each year. How much total dividend do you receive in two years?

---

5. To emphasize the importance of saving money. Unless money for savings is set aside early, there may be nothing left later.
6. One way is to deposit most of the income in a checking account and write checks for items as necessary. The remaining cash is kept on hand for frequent purchases.
7. (a) Estimates were not accurate or realistic. (b) You have trouble sticking to the budgeted amounts.
8. Taking a portion "off the top" of one's paycheck and placing the money into a savings account.
9. (a) To meet financial emergencies. (b) To achieve financial goals.
10. (a) *Regular savings account*—one in which deposits and withdrawals can be made at any time. (b) *Time deposits*—money is deposited for a fixed period of time. Minimum amount often required. Usually a penalty for early withdrawal of funds.
11. (a) Annual interest rate. (b) Frequency of interest compounding.
12. Investing is the process of using money not required for personal or family needs to increase overall financial worth. Investing is a long-term financial strategy.
13. A *stock* represents part ownership in a company; a *bond* is simply a loan of money to a government or corporation.
14. (a) Corporate bond. (b) Municipal bond.
15. Provides a way for small investors to earn higher interest rates than could be earned on their own.

40. Information could also be collected by mail or phone.
41. Quarterly interest of $7.50, $7.61, $7.73, and $7.84 totals $530.68 at end of year—APY of 6.14%.
42. $40 per year—$80 for the two years (annual yield of 1.6%).

8. Locate the listings for the New York Stock Exchange in the financial section of a newspaper. Select a stock of interest in the listing and answer the following questions: (a) Does the stock pay a dividend? If so, how much? If so, what is the yield? (b) How many shares were sold the previous day? (c) What were the previous day's high, low, and closing prices? (d) What was the net change? (e) What does the "P/E Ratio" stand for?

Topics to Discuss

1. Philanthropy is the act of giving away money. How do you feel about giving money to charity?
2. A big problem for the federal government is staying within a budget. The government routinely spends more than it takes in (called deficit spending). Why do you think this is the case?
3. It is not unusual to read about the financial difficulties of high-paid professional athletes, entertainers, and other famous people. What are some of the "problems" created by fame and instant wealth?
4. What is the advantage of using payroll deductions to save and invest money? Are payroll savings and investment options available where you work?
5. Have you ever saved money over a long period of time and then used it to buy something? Describe how it made you feel to accomplish a savings goal.
6. There is an old saying that "you shouldn't invest more in stocks than you can afford to lose." How true do you think this statement is?

---

43. You may wish to photocopy and duplicate a section from the stock listings to use here.
44. It has been written about John D. Rockefeller, that out of the allowance he gave his children, he required them to save one-third and give one-third to charity.
45. The prices of stocks fluctuate and there is always the risk of losing money. However, the average return on stock investments over time is about 9%.

1. The idea of insurance can be traced back thousands of years. Goods were loaned to Babylonian traders at an interest rate of 25% of the value of the ship and its cargo. If the goods were lost, the trader was not required to repay the loan. In a sense, the high rate of interest was the trader's payment for insurance. For more interesting history, consult an encyclopedia.

2. Insurance companies employ people called *actuaries* who work with sophisticated mathematical models to determine expected losses.

CHAPTER TWENTY-FIVE

Insuring Against Loss

OUTLINE
Nature of Insurance
Health Insurance
Life Insurance
Home Insurance
Auto Insurance
Chapter Review

OBJECTIVES
After reading this chapter, you should be able to:
- Explain the basic idea of insurance.
- Name and describe the five types of health insurance.
- Summarize the advantages and disadvantages of term and cash-value life insurance.
- Outline different characteristics of home insurance.
- Name and describe the six types of auto insurance coverage.
- Identify factors that influence the cost of auto insurance.

Making a major purchase, such as a home or car, is very costly. Once you have bought such items, you don't want to lose them. Things do happen, though. Suppose you purchase a new car. A week later, you park in the lot of the local library. When you leave the library, the car is gone. The next day, the police call to say your car has been found. Your joy disappears upon learning that the car was badly wrecked.

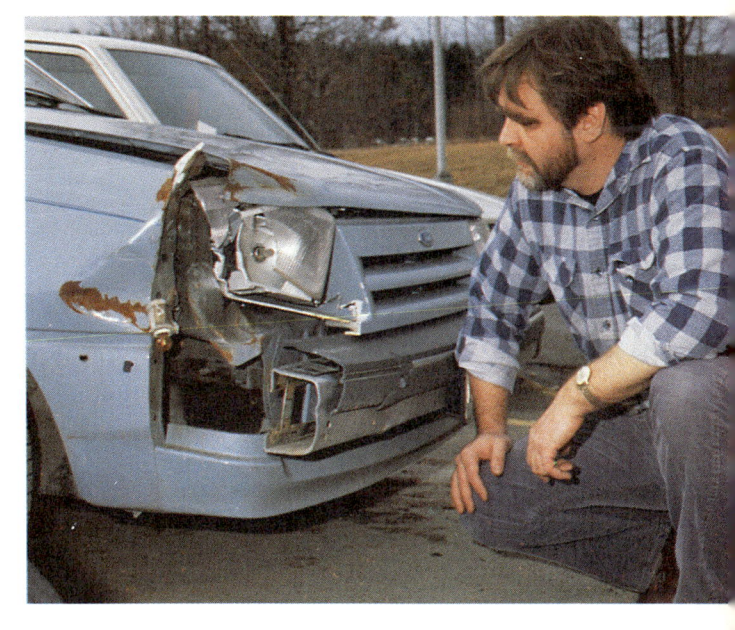

FIGURE 25-1 Steve bought this car new a month ago. He is glad he has insurance. *Photo by David W. Tuttle*

Deciding if you need insurance, evaluating different policies, and comparing costs and coverage can be difficult. This chapter will help answer your questions. The material will deal with the nature of insurance, and then discuss the specifics of the four most important kinds of insurance: health, life, home, and auto.

NATURE OF INSURANCE

Throughout history, people have used insurance to protect themselves from *risk* due to fire, accident, or other *catastrophe*. Few people can bear such catastrophes without serious hardship. Society, as well, may suffer from an unexpected loss. For instance, if someone dies, the community may need to support a dependent family. When a building burns and a business is forced into bankruptcy, creditors lose money and employees their jobs.

The basic idea of insurance is that a large group of individuals pay a yearly premium that goes into a common fund. When disaster strikes one member of the group, the pooled funds pay for the loss. Insurance shifts probable loss from the individual to the group.

FIGURE 25-2 The first mutual fire insurance company was founded in 1752 with the help of Benjamin Franklin. *Courtesy of The Franklin Institute*

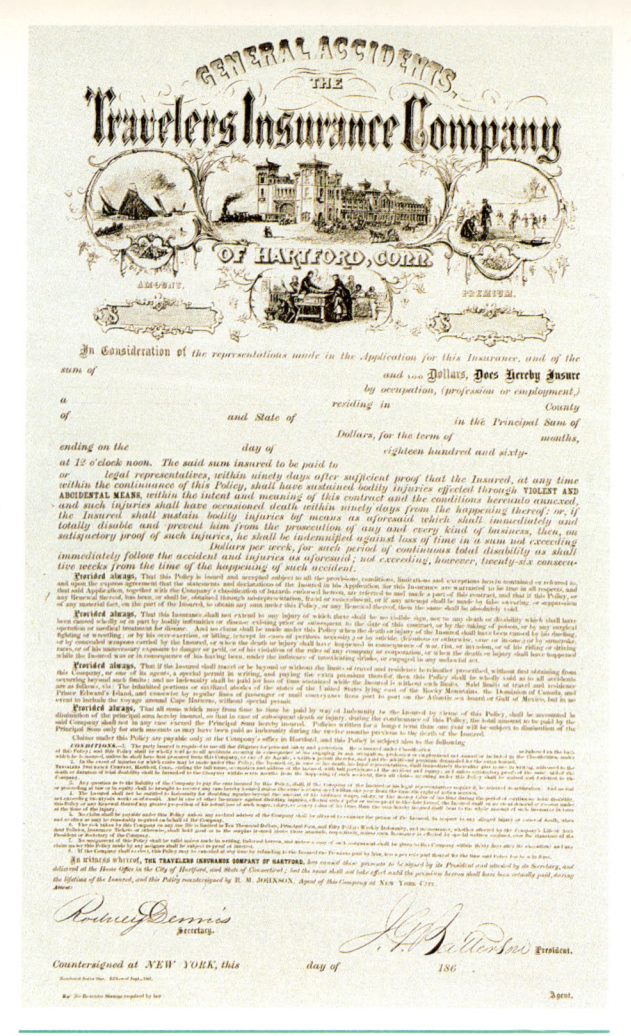

FIGURE 25-3 The first accident policy in the U.S. was sold in 1863 by the Travelers Insurance Company. It covered James Bolton during a two-block walk from his home to the post office. The premium was two cents. *Courtesy of Archive, The Travelers Companies*

3. Famous athletes and entertainers often insure parts of their bodies (quarterback's arm, singer's voice, and so on) against permanent injury and resultant loss of income.

In simple terms, when you buy insurance, you are substituting a known expenditure (insurance premium) for protection against risk of a large uncertain loss. The kinds of risks against which people seek protection may be grouped in this way:

- *Personal Risks.* These are catastrophes affecting individuals. Examples include accident, illness, disability, and unemployment.
- *Property Risks.* There is always the possibility that property will be damaged or destroyed. Losses include such things as automobile accidents, natural disasters, fire, and vandalism.
- *Liability Risks.* Certain events may affect the person or property of others. Injury may result from an automobile accident that you caused. Or a visitor to your home might be hurt.

4. Find out what the average cost of a semi-private hospital room is in your area.

In addition to providing protection against financial loss, insurance gives people greater peace of mind. Knowing that you have minimized your risks can contribute to your emotional security.

HEALTH INSURANCE

The purpose of health insurance is to pay expenses resulting from illness or accident. This is probably the most necessary form of insurance because the expenses resulting from illness or accident can be enormous. The costs, for example, of a minor surgery and several days in a hospital are likely to be several thousand dollars. Major surgery and an extended hospital stay can amount to tens of thousands of dollars.

Jim was painting the house. He fell about twenty feet from a ladder. Jim was badly injured. Over the

5. Family health insurance coverage for a dependent child often terminates at age nineteen (twenty-three for a full-time student). Individual policies differ.

*WWYD Feature A. People who see a doctor frequently (say for allergy shots) and/or who purchase a lot of prescription medicines often favor an HMO.

next five years, he was in the hospital twenty-two times for surgery and other medical care. His total medical expenses were nearly a million dollars. This is a rare case, but it does show why insurance is so important.

Most people obtain health insurance through some type of group plan. This may be through an employer, union, or professional association. The group policy may only cover the individual enrolled, or it may include dependents as well. Persons not eligible for group coverage may buy individual plans. However, group plans usually provide more coverage and are less expensive than individual plans.

In the traditional approach to health insurance, an insurance company pays a doctor or hospital for services performed in treating an illness or accident. Routine office visits are not covered. During the last decade or so, the *health maintenance organization* (HMO) has been growing. It is an alternative to traditional health insurance. Members in an HMO (or the employer) pay a regular fee as they would for an insurance policy. The difference, however, is that HMO members are entitled to unlimited professional services and treatment. This includes regular office visits and checkups as well as treatment for illness and accidents.

What Would You Do?

You are employed as a library assistant at one of the state universities. You have received information about the new health insurance plan that covers all state employees. Beginning June 1, you will have the choice of continuing with the regular health insurance or switching to a new HMO option. The premium, which is paid by the state, is the same for both plans. You aren't sure which plan to select. What would you do?

Even though regular insurance plans protect against huge medical expenses, most of them are not free. A typical health insurance plan, for example, might require you to pay the first $100 for a hospital stay (called a *deductible*) and 20 percent of the remaining amount. Many policies contain a

6. Because of the increasing popularity of HMOs, you may wish to provide supplemental information here.

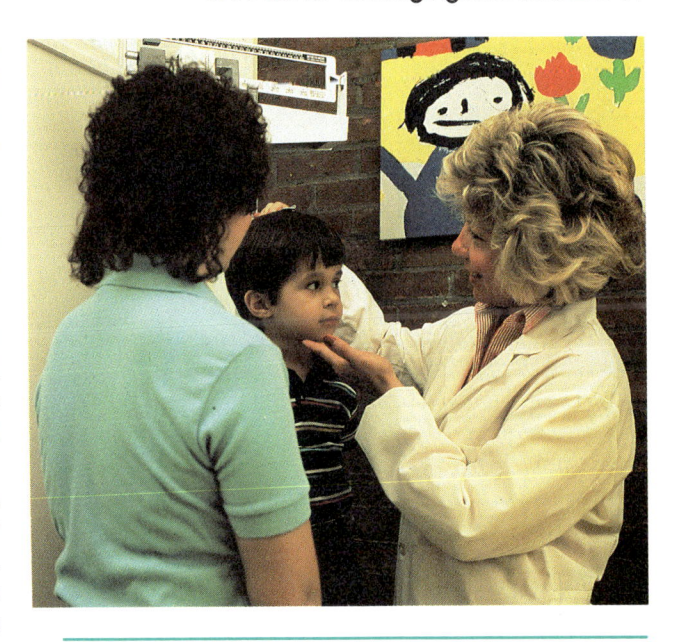

FIGURE 25-4 HMOs focus on preventative health care. The idea is to avoid more serious problems and higher insurance costs later. *Courtesy of Empire Blue Cross and Blue Shield*

stop-loss provision, which prevents your out-of-pocket expenses from rising above a certain amount.

Health insurance packages usually cover hospital, surgical, medical, and major medical expenses. If you want disability insurance, though, you will have to buy a special policy. For full-time employees, employers often pay all or part of the cost of health insurance.

FIGURE 25-5 Some health insurance plans provide coverage for dental and vision expenses. *Courtesy Sears, Roebuck and Company, 1987 Annual Report*

7. Provide several concrete examples of deductibles and stop-loss provisions.

Hospital Expense

This coverage provides for hospital charges such as room and meals, operating room use, laboratory fees, and drugs. The policy may specify a certain maximum-per-day room charge or may limit the number of days in the hospital the policy will cover. This type of health insurance is the most common.

Surgical Expense

Coverage here involves a wide variety of medical procedures and operations, ranging from sewing up a cut to replacing a heart valve. Depending on the procedure, it may be performed on an inpatient or outpatient basis. A policy may contain a list of covered surgical procedures and the amount that will be paid for each one.

Medical Expense

Medical expense, also known as physician's expense, is usually combined with hospital and surgical-expense insurance. The three together form what is known as *basic* coverage. Medical expense coverage pays for the doctor's medical visits while the patient is in a hospital. Some policies provide benefits for home and office visits as well.

Major Medical Expense

This type of insurance protects against huge expenses resulting from a serious illness or accident. Covered expenses generally include the same types of charges as those for basic coverage. Major medical contains a *co-insurance* feature that requires a policyholder to share in the expenses beyond the deductible amount. One of the most common plans is an "80-20" policy in which the insurance company pays 80 percent and the policyholder takes care of the other 20 percent.

In one group plan, for example, the insurance company pays 80 percent of the first $15,000 of covered expenses and 100 percent thereafter up to a maximum of $250,000.

Disability Coverage

Paying benefits to someone unable to work because of illness or injury is the purpose of disability insurance. The coverage is sometimes called loss-of-income insurance. A typical policy may pay between fifty and seventy-five percent of the worker's normal earnings for a specified period. This insurance may not be as important for people already covered by such benefits as paid sick leave, workers' compensation, and social security.

8. You probably are a member of some health insurance group and have a booklet that explains the nature of the coverage. Have the booklet available for reference.

9. Many policies now require that certain types of minor surgery be performed on an *ambulatory* basis ("same-day surgery," "outpatient surgery," "surgicenters").

Helen was in a hurry to get to work and failed to notice that a light rain had fallen and then frozen during the night. As she stepped from the covered porch onto the sidewalk, she slipped and fell. She cried out in pain. A neighbor who was leaving for work at the same time saw her fall. He helped her into the house and called an ambulance.

Helen's injury was diagnosed as a broken hip. Surgery on the hip was required, followed by a long period of rest and physical therapy. It was six months before Helen was able to return to work. Fortunately, she had a disability insurance policy that provided her with income while she couldn't work. Without the disability policy, she would have had to dip into her retirement savings.

10. Work on the board several sample problems involving 80-20 co-insurance. You may also wish to conduct Activity 1 at this time.

FIGURE 25-6 Self-employed people need the protection of disability coverage. What whould happen to the business if this man got sick? *Photo by Paul E. Meyers*

LIFE INSURANCE

Life insurance involves a contract written between an insurance company and a policyholder. The document specifies an amount of money *(face value)* to be paid in the event of the policyholder's death. Also stated in the contract is the price of the policy *(premium)* and the name of the person *(bene-*

11. Indeed, these are forms of disability insurance.
12. You may wish to assign Activity 2 at this time.

F•E•A•T•U•R•E

Walk-in Medical Clinics

What would you do if you severely cut yourself while slicing vegetables? Or if you woke up on a Sunday morning with a bad earache and high fever. You would probably head for the emergency room of the nearest hospital. Some people are now beginning to have another option. It is called the walk-in medical clinic.

These new health clinics are one of the hottest trends in medical care. Thousands of them have sprung up across the country in the last several years. Regional and nationwide chains are being created just like fast-food restaurants. They are legitimate medical facilities staffed by licensed doctors and other professional personnel. They are providing competition and changing the way we make decisions about medical treatment.

The clinics take patients without appointments. They are open twelve-to-sixteen (some twenty-four) hours a day, seven days a week. They can treat most typical illnesses or accidents. But they don't do major surgery or handle serious emergencies like auto accidents. Fees for a normal visit are the same or slightly less than those for a regular doctor. For emergency treatment, however, the clinics can be substantially less. Treatment of a cut requiring stitches, for example, can be a third to a half of what is charged by a hospital emergency room. Health insurance usually covers such emergency treatment.

FIGURE 25-FEATURE Walk-in medical clinics provide competition for traditional clinics and hospitals. This may help to hold down costs for medical treatment and health insurance. *Courtesy of Healthshield—The Community Health Plan*

Cost and convenience, however, are not the whole story. In our mobile society, many people don't have a regular physician. When they need a doctor, walk-in clinics can provide that service.

* Walk-in Medical Clinics. This describes a growing trend in the health care industry. In 1990, there were about 3,000 such clinics nationwide. Are there any in your area? Have any students gone to one?

ficiary) to whom the death benefits are to be paid. The main purpose of life insurance is to provide financial security for dependents after the insured's death.

Individuals differ in terms of their need for life insurance. A young, single person without dependents, for example, has little need for life insurance. All that may be required is a small policy to pay funeral expenses and to cover outstanding debts.

People with children have the greatest need for life insurance. If the wage earner (or wage earners) should die, the family would need an income to pay day-to-day living expenses. Insurance would help a family member or friend raise surviving children and perhaps provide them with higher education.

Traditionally, the primary wage earner has been the man of the house. Today, however, women often earn as much or more than their husbands. Many women are head of the household. They have great insurance needs. Even a person not working outside the home should be insured in order to cover added expenses in the event of death.

As with health insurance, both group and individual life insurance policies are available. Most life insurance, though, is in the form of individual policies. Two basic types of life insurance are available: term and cash value.

Term Insurance

Term insurance is often called pure insurance because it provides protection only. The policy has no cash value or loan value. People buy term insurance for a specified period of time. Under term insurance, you pay as long as you need the coverage. Then you drop the policy or it terminates automatically. For example, you might purchase a twenty-five-year policy to provide protection while you are making big house payments and your children are growing up.

As you grow older, the likelihood of your dying increases. This is why term insurance premiums go up as you age. Premiums are low at first and then increase steadily throughout the course of your life. By the time you reach age sixty, you may be paying fifteen times what the same amount of protection

FIGURE 25-7 Women have the same needs for life insurance as men do. *Courtesy of Marriott Corporation*

13. Children below the age of 21 are often insured for a nominal amount as part of a parent's life insurance policy.

14. Ask students to identify some of the added expenses that might result from the death of a full-time homemaker (child-care, housekeeping, laundry, and so on).

15. A common form of term insurance is five-year renewable term in which the premium remains constant for five years before being raised.

IMPORTANT—Please print or type all data except signature

PAYROLL DEDUCTION AUTHORIZATION

INSTRUCTIONS— 1. Form to be completed for each application. All necessary data to be filled in. Agent must indicate correct frequency and total amount for all coverage purchased and the date first deduction is to take place. The first deduction must be the earliest possible date deduction can be made.
2. EMPLOYER'S COPY IS TO BE FORWARDED TO BOOKKEEPER IMMEDIATELY SO DEDUCTIONS CAN COMMENCE
3. Agent's copy is to be retained by agent for his/her records.
4. Home Office copy is to be forwarded to Home Office Underwriting with the application and is to be used to (1) verify amount of coverage purchased, and (2) determine the contract date for all policies issued.

NAME OF EMPLOYEE *(Last, First, Middle Initial)* | SOCIAL SECURITY NUMBER | PAYROLL OR DEPT. NUMBER

NAME OF INSURED *(If other than Employee)* | NAME OF EMPLOYER

I hereby authorize my above named employer or successor to deduct from my wages the amount stated below as consideration for contracts issued by The Travelers Insurance Company.

AMOUNT OF DEDUCTION
WEEKLY $ ________ BI WEEKLY $ ________ SEMI MONTHLY $ ________ MONTHLY $ ________

Date of first deduction ________________, 19 ____ | Monthly Premium billed by The Travelers Insurance Company * $ ________

It is understood that my employer will forward each month such amounts as may be billed by The Travelers Insurance Company, Hartford, Connecticut and pay the amounts thereof on my behalf, as they fall due during the continuance of my employment or until this authorization is revoked by me by written notice to said employer.

________________, 19 ____ ________________________
(Date Signed) *(Signature of Employee)*

***In all instances the monthly premium billed by The Travelers is the amount that is to be remitted to The Travelers Billing and Collection 8NB.**

L-9329 REV. 9-88 PRINTED IN U.S.A. The Travelers **EMPLOYER'S COPY**

FIGURE 25-8 Life insurance can often be purchased through payroll deduction. *Courtesy of The Travelers Companies*

cost you at age eighteen.

In the example just described, the face value of the policy remains steady and the premium increases yearly. Such insurance is called *level term.* Another type, called *decreasing term* insurance, works differently. In that kind of policy, the premium remains steady, but the face value decreases yearly. In year one, for example, you might have a face value of $50,000. In year two, it drops to $48,000; year three to $46,000; and so on.

Cash-value Insurance

Under cash-value insurance, protection is teamed with the gradual buildup of a savings account. Cash-value insurance is also called permanent insurance because when the policy is paid up after a certain number of years, the policyholder owns the insurance. For example, if you purchase a plan called life paid-up at sixty-five, you pay premiums until you are sixty-five. At that point, you have a permanent policy that will pay the face value upon your death. Other names for cash-value insurance are whole, ordinary, and straight life insurance.

The premium and the face value for cash-value insurance remain the same each year. You pay the same premiums for as long as you live. Or you can purchase plans that are paid up in twenty or thirty years. A portion of the premium is set aside and accumulates in a type of savings account. The interest rate, however, is usually less than other forms of savings. If the policy is dropped, the cash value is returned to the policyholder. 16

Which Type to Buy?

There are advantages and disadvantages to both term and cash-value insurance. The primary advantage of term insurance is that it is less expensive than cash-value insurance. But with cash-value

16. The monetary worth of a cash-value policy is usually called the cash surrender value.

17. You may wish to assign Activity 3 at this time.

19. A fall by a guest is one of the more common accidents. Ask students to provide additional examples of accidents or injuries that might result in liability claims.

346 ■ SECTION 5 Managing Your Money

insurance, you have protection combined with savings.

Most experts on the subject (who do not work for insurance companies) seem to agree that term insurance is the better value. They point out that the main purpose of life insurance is protection. About the only way young people can realistically afford the amount of insurance necessary to protect their families is to purchase term insurance. You may want to buy term insurance and save the difference between that and cash-value insurance. Later, you may want to consider cash-value insurance as part of an overall life insurance program. But don't get saddled with a big policy and a big premium at a time when you can least afford it.

How Much Insurance Will You Need?

The amount of life insurance coverage depends on your personal situation and what you want to protect. The needs of a young, single person are very different from those of someone with a family, or a middle-aged couple who have their home paid for and their children raised. Some insurance agents provide the general guideline that you need insurance equal to about four to eight times your annual income.

1. Fire or lightning.
2. Windstorm or hail.
3. Explosion.
4. Riot or civil commotion.
5. Aircraft.
6. Vehicles.
7. Smoke.
8. Vandalism or malicious mischief.
9. Theft.
10. Damage by glass or safety glazing material which is part of a building.
11. Volcanic eruption.
12. Falling objects.
13. Weight of ice, snow, or sleet.
14. Accidental discharge or overflow of water or steam from within a plumbing, heating, air conditioning, or automatic fire protective sprinkler system or from within a household appliance.
15. Sudden and accidental tearing apart, cracking, burning, or bulging of a steam or hot water heating system, an air conditioning or automatic fire protective sprinkler system, or an appliance for heating water.
16. Freezing of a plumbing, heating, air conditioning, or automatic fire protective sprinkler system, or of a household appliance.
17. Sudden and accidental damage from artificially generated electrical current (does not include loss to a tube, transistor, or similar electronic component).

FIGURE 25-10 These are the perils against which properties are insured. The first eleven represent what is called basic homeowners insurance. *Courtesy of Insurance Information Institute*

HOME INSURANCE

For most people, a home is the largest expenditure in their budget. In addition to the home itself, household furnishings and personal belongings represent a sizable investment. For this reason, it is very important to protect a home and the contents against damage or loss. The basis for all home insurance policies is coverage against the various damages or *perils* shown in Figure 25-10.

Another important feature of home insurance policies is the provision for living expenses. For example, the Alfano's home was damaged by a storm and they couldn't live in it. The insurance company paid for the family's lodgings, meals, and related expenses elsewhere until the house was livable again.

Liability coverage is also a part of home insurance policies. The most important type of *liability* coverage is personal liability, which protects you against a claim or lawsuit resulting from an accident or injury occurring on your property. The same coverage will also protect you if someone in your family causes an injury away from home.

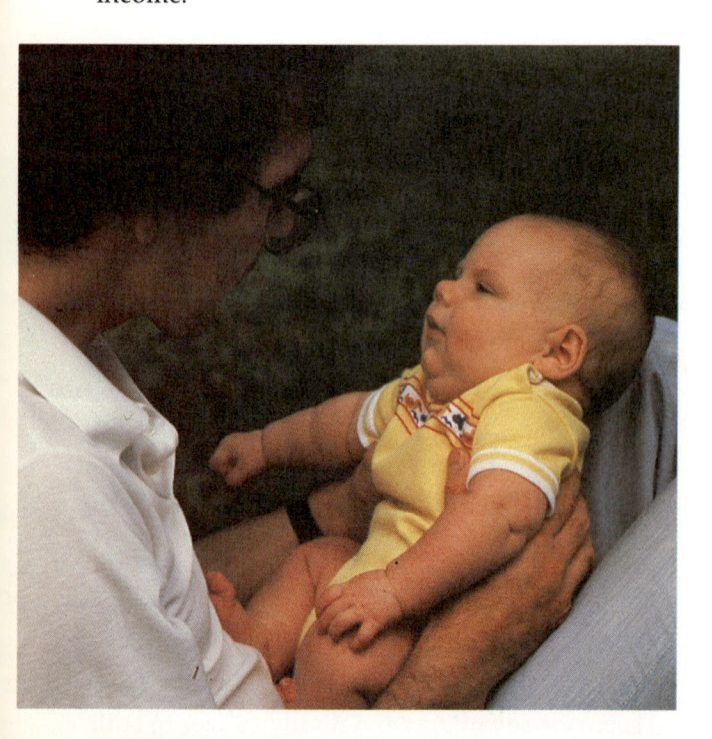

FIGURE 25-9 As your personal situation changes, so does your need for life insurance. *Photo by Edith Raviola*

18. Consider a couple in their early twenties who have one child and make $30,000 a year. They probably need the higher figure—$240,000 of coverage.

20. Even a minor kitchen fire can cause enormous smoke damage and inconvenience. Have any students been involved in such a misfortune?

21. You may wish to assign Activity 4 at this time.
22. Ask how many have been involved in an auto accident. Additional ones have probably been involved as passengers.

FIGURE 25-11 If the family pet attacked a neighbor, would your liability insurance cover you? *Photo by Paul E. Meyers*

To meet the varying needs of customers, insurance companies have developed various kinds of homeowners insurance. Whether you live in a house, apartment, mobile home, or condominium, there is a policy designed for you. Ann and Mark learned this fact the hard way.

Ann and Mark were newlyweds who had just moved into their first apartment. They were awakened one night by the sound of a fire alarm. They got up quickly, threw on coats, grabbed the puppy, and fled the apartment. As they raced down the back exit, they heard the siren of the fire truck coming. The fire was on the floor above theirs.

The fire company put out the blaze in a few minutes. It wasn't a serious fire, but there was a lot of smoke and water damage. All of Ann's and Mark's clothes and upholstered furniture was ruined.

The next day the couple went to the apartment manager's office to find out about getting their clothes and furniture replaced. The manager told them that his insurance only covered damage to the building. Apartment tenants have to carry insurance on their personal property. Ann and Mark were upset. They had assumed that the building owner carried insurance that also covered their property. They should have had a renter's policy. The fire proved to be a costly lesson for Ann and Mark regarding the need to understand home insurance.

What Would You Do?

You have just moved into an apartment with a couple of friends. As you unpack, one of your roommates asks if you have purchased renter's insurance. You laugh and say that you don't have enough possessions to worry about insurance.

"You'd be surprised," says your roommate. "It would cost quite a bit of money to replace everything in this room."

"I'll think about it," you say. "But I really can't afford insurance for a couple of months." If you were in this situation, what would you do?

*WWYD Feature B. The implication of the roommate's comment is that the person has a number of possessions that should be insured. A monthly or quarterly premium for a renter's policy would probably not be prohibitive.

AUTO INSURANCE

The topic of auto insurance is very important to young people. Unfortunately, they are the ones who most need it. Drivers under age twenty-five are involved in about a third of all auto accidents.

Everyone who drives a motor vehicle is responsible for operating it safely and paying for any damage the vehicle might cause. All states now have what are called financial-responsibility laws that require drivers to pay for damages they cause to persons or property. Rather than risk having to come up with thousands of dollars as a result of an accident, most people buy insurance to show proof of financial responsibility. About half of the states have laws specifically requiring registered automobile owners to have liability insurance of some kind.

Types of Auto Insurance Coverage

An auto policy may provide six basic types of coverage:

Bodily Injury Liability. This coverage applies if you kill or injure someone in an accident in which

20
21
22
23
24

23. Point out that it is not illegal to drive without insurance in those states not having financial-responsibility laws. But it is very risky to do so. Even wealthy people need liability insurance.
24. Take care to fully explain and discuss these six types of coverage. Photocopy and duplicate a sample policy to illustrate how to read an auto policy.

you are at fault. The person may be a pedestrian, a rider in your car, or someone in another car. The policy covers bodily injury expenses and claims, including your legal expenses if you are sued.

Property Damage Liability. What if you damage another person's car or property? This type of insurance won't repair your car, but it will cover the other person's car or property. Property damage liability also provides legal expenses should you be taken to court.

Protection Against Uninsured Motorists. This coverage applies to bodily injuries that you may suffer as a result of a hit-and-run accident. The policy also covers you in the event of an accident in which the other driver doesn't have insurance.

Keith was sitting in his car at a stoplight waiting for the light to change. Suddenly, a car from behind smashed into him. The other driver was adjusting the radio and not paying attention to the intersection ahead. Keith's car was badly damaged.

The police came and filled out an accident report. They gave Andy, the other driver, a traffic citation for reckless driving. Keith and Andy exchanged information regarding addresses, phone numbers, and so on. Andy said that he couldn't remember the name of his insurance company, but that he would call Keith later with the information. The call never came.

In the meantime, Keith contacted his insurance company. They told him to go ahead and have his car fixed and they would collect from Andy's insurance company. As it turned out, Andy didn't have auto insurance. However, since Keith was covered by uninsured motorists' protection, his insurance company assumed the cost of having the car repaired.

As for Andy, he was found to be in violation of the state Motorists' Responsibility Law. His driver's license and automobile registration were taken away. In order to get them back, Andy will have to pay Keith's insurance company the $1,200 it cost to repair Keith's car.

Medical Payments. Under this coverage, your insurance company agrees to pay medical expenses resulting from accidental injury. Medical insurance includes you and family member whether in your car or someone else's. It also applies if you are struck by a car. Payment is made regardless of who is at fault.

Auto Collision. Your car is covered by this type of insurance. The insurance company will pay to have your car repaired or replaced regardless of who is at

25. Point out that state financial-responsiblity laws do not require collision or comprehensive coverage.
26. You may wish to conduct Activity 5 at this time.
27. Some motorcycle policies are written so that policyholders don't have to pay for coverage during the winter months when the bike isn't ridden (cold weather regions only).

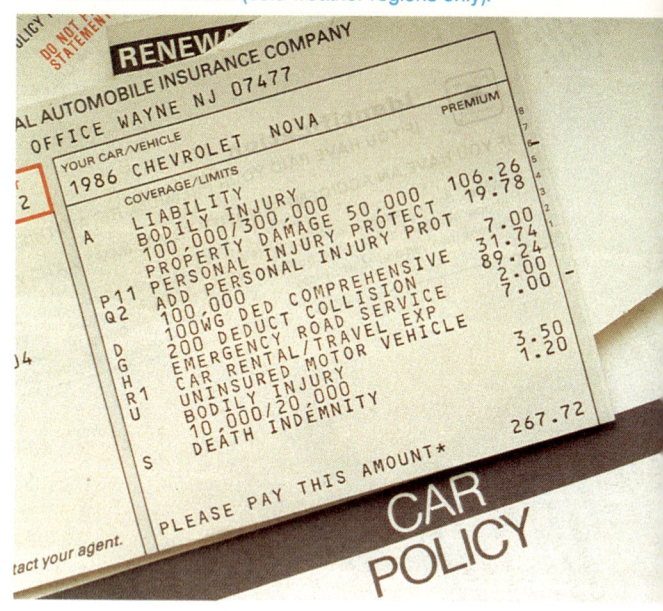

FIGURE 25-12 This is a typical automobile insurance policy. Note the six common types of coverage. *Photo by Paul E. Meyers*

fault. Keep in mind, though, that collision insurance doesn't cover repairs greater than the actual cash value of the car. Collision is the most expensive form of coverage. Most collision insurance is sold with a deductible (usually $200 or $250).

Auto Comprehensive. This coverage protects your car against loss from theft, vandalism, fire, windstorms, and other perils listed in the policy. If your car is damaged in an accident, collision, not comprehensive, will cover it.

The Cost of Auto Insurance

Basic rates for automobile insurance vary from area to area. Each state is divided into rating territories that indicate the losses paid in various parts of the state. The price of insurance is then set based on the loss experience of the rating territory. This means that rates in an area having heavy losses will be higher than in places where losses aren't so great.

Many factors influence the price of insurance. These include the year, make, and model of the car. The sex, age, marital status, and driving record of the operator are also factors. In addition, driving a car a long distance every day will raise premiums. If you have more than one vehicle insured, you might receive a discount.

Even though you can't do much about influencing basic insurance rates, you do have some control

FIGURE 25-13 Auto insurance rates are very high for sports cars like this. *Courtesy of Chevrolet Motor Division*

over the final cost. How many types of coverage do you wish to have? The first four mentioned previously are too important not to have. However, whether you purchase collision or comprehensive depends on how much your auto is worth. It would be foolish to have collision on an old car worth only a few hundred dollars.

You can also reduce the cost of car insurance by choosing higher deductibles. For example, raising the deductible on collision or comprehensive coverage from $100 to $250 can save you about twenty percent. With some companies, if you take driver education or have good grades, you are eligible for discounts.

Motorcycle insurance is similar in coverage to that for cars. By knowing the basics of auto insurance, you should have no trouble understanding policies covering motorcycles.

No-fault Insurance

A problem for insurance companies is determining who is at fault in an accident. This process often requires the service of lawyers and may lead to long delays and expensive legal fees. Courts award generous compensation to some victims. Others receive little or nothing.

In order to reduce time, costs, and provide fair settlements to victims, about half of the states have developed what is called no-fault insurance. Under the no-fault system, each person's losses and expenses are paid for by his or her insurance company regardless of who caused the accident. Lawsuits are permitted only under certain conditions.

No one enjoys paying insurance premiums, especially for something that you don't see or may never use. Don't, however, be tempted to take a chance and go without insurance. You only have to have one big loss to realize why it is so important to have insurance protection.

FIGURE 25-14 No-fault insurance is designed to help eliminate expensive legal battles.

28. Ask students for their opinions regarding no-fault insurance. You may also wish to assign Activity 6 at this time.

CHAPTER REVIEW

Chapter in Brief

- Insurance shifts probable loss from the individual to the group. The basic idea of insurance is that a large group of individuals pay a yearly premium that goes into a common fund. When disaster strikes one member of the group, the pooled funds pay for the loss. People buy insurance to protect themselves against three types of risks: personal, property, and liability.
- The purpose of health insurance is to pay expenses resulting from illness or accident. The expenses resulting from illness or accident can be enormous. There are four major types of health insurance: hospital, surgical, medical, and major medical. These are usually sold together in various combinations of health insurance packages. A fifth type of health insurance, disability, is usually sold separately. It provides income to people who are out of work because of illness or injury.
- The main purpose of life insurance is to provide financial security for dependents after the insured's death. The two basic types of life insurance are term and cash value. Term insurance provides protection at a low cost. It has no cash or loan value. Cash-value insurance provides protection along with the gradual buildup of a savings account. The amount of life insurance coverage you need depends on your personal situation and what you want to protect.
- For most people, a home and its contents is their most valuable investment. For this reason, it is very important to protect a home and contents against damage or loss. An important feature of home insurance is the provision for living expenses. This pays for food and lodging while your home is being rebuilt or repaired. Liability coverage is also important. It protects you against a claim or lawsuit for an accident or injury occurring on your property. There are various kinds of homeowners insurance, depending on type of coverage desired and whether you live in a home, apartment, condominium, or other dwelling.
- All states have financial responsibliity laws requiring drivers to pay for damages caused to persons or property. Most people buy insurance for this purpose. An auto policy may provide six types of coverage: bodily injury liability, property damage liability, protection against uninsured motorists, medical payments, auto collision, and auto comprehensive.
- The cost of auto insurance varies from one geographic area to another. Rates are also influenced by a number of factors, including the year, make, and model of car; driving record of operator; distance driven daily; type of coverage and deductibles desired; and so on. About half of the states have no-fault auto insurance. This pays for losses and expenses regardless of who caused the accident.

Words to Know

beneficiary the person to whom the death benefits from a life insurance policy are to be paid.

catastrophe a sudden disaster or misfortune.

co-insurance a provision of health insurance in which the insured person is required to share in the expenses (typically 20 percent) beyond the deductible amount.

deductible a provision of insurance in which the insured person is required to pay a certain initial amount before the insurance company pays the balance.

face value regarding life insurance, the amount of money that is paid in the event of the insured's death.

HMO an acronym for health maintenance organization; a type of insurance in which unlimited group health care is provided for a fixed monthly or yearly fee.

liability that for which one is responsible, such as an accident occurring in your home.

perils the possible damages from which one seeks protection through the purchase of home insurance.

premium the cost of an insurance policy.

risk the chance of an accident or loss.

stop-loss provision a condition of health insurance that limits the amount of the bill for which the insured person is responsible.

Questions to Answer

1. Explain how insurance shifts probable loss from the individual to the group.
2. Insurance protects against three kinds of risks. Name them.
3. What is meant by basic health insurance coverage? What is major medical coverage?
4. Which individuals are most in need of disability coverage?
5. Describe an advantage and a disadvantage of both term and cash-value insurance.
6. Which type of term insurance has the same face value throughout the life of the policy?
7. What four things are usually covered by a homeowners insurance policy?
8. Which type of auto insurance coverage applies to the following situations:
   a. You run into someone's parked auto.
   b. Your car is damaged when you back into a utility pole.
   c. A tree falls on your car during a windstorm.
9. Name four factors that influence the cost of auto insurance.
10. Explain the idea underlying no-fault auto insurance.

1. A large group of individuals pay a yearly premium that goes into a common fund. When disaster strikes, the pooled funds pay for the loss.
2. (a) Personal. (b) Property. (c) Liability.
3. (a) *Basic* coverage is a term used to describe a health insurance package consisting of hospital, surgical, and expense coverage. (b) *Major medical* includes the same types of coverage as basic, but it protects against huge expenses resulting from a serious illness or accident.
4. People not already covered by sick leave, workers' compensation, or social security. And peole who are self-employed.
5. TERM: *Advantages*—cheapest protection available; can buy for a short period of time. *Disadvantages*—premium increases with age; no cash or loan value. CASH VALUE: *Advantages*—permanent insurance; provides cash and loan value; premium stays the same. Disadvantages—initially more expensive to buy; return on investment is usually less than other forms of savings or investments.
6. Level term insurance.
7. (a) Home itself. (b) Furnishings and personal belongings. (c) Living expenses. (d) Liability.
8. (a) Property damage liability. (b) Auto collision. (c) Auto comprehensive.
9. Any four of the following: where you live; year, make, and model of car; sex, age, and marital status of driver; driving record of operator; coverages and deductibles chosen; number of cars insured; whether you have had driver education; grades of driver.
10. Each person's losses and expenses are paid for by his or her insurance company regardless of who caused the accident. The purpose of no-fault insurance is to prevent long delays and reduce costs.

352 ■ SECTION 5 Managing Your Money

Activities to Do

1. Mrs. Owen has just recovered from a serious illness. Her hospital stay resulted in a bill of $12,340. She has health insurance that contains the following provisions:
   a. A $100 deductible for each hospital visit.
   b. Co-insurance in which the plan pays 80 percent of the next $5,000, and 100% of the costs thereafter.
   How much of the bill does Mrs. Owen have to pay?
2. As a class, obtain a policy or descriptive information about disability insurance. What types of illnesses and injury does the insurance cover? How much will the policy provide? What is the cost of the policy?
3. As a class, obtain cost estimates for a twenty-year-old individual on three different $50,000 face-value policies of the following types:
   a. Five-year renewable level-term plan
   b. Thirty-year decreasing term plan
   c. Thirty-year cash-value plan
   What is the annual cost for each plan at age 20, 30, 40, and 50? What is the average yearly cost for insurance over the thirty-year period? Is this a fair way to compare the cost of life insurance? What other factors (if any) need to be taken into consideration?
4. Obtain a policy or descriptive information about renter's insurance. What does the policy cover? How much is the annual premium? Does a young person moving into an apartment for the first time need such insurance? Why or why not?
5. Arrange to have an insurance agent or broker visit the class to discuss auto insurance. Ask him or her to discuss how rates are established and how final premiums are computed. Ask for recommendations about liability, medical payments, and uninsured motorists' coverage. Ask him or her to discuss the pros and cons of having comprehensive and collision coverage. If you wish, also find out how to decide between different levels of deductibles.
6. Learn your state's requirements for auto insurance coverage. Also, is no-fault insurance available in your state?

Topics to Discuss

1. Hospitals have traditionally been operated as nonprofit community agencies. More and more hospitals and clinics are now being operated as private businesses. Why have these changes come about? What is your opinion of health providers becoming businesspersons?
2. People differ in terms of their need for life insurance. Identify and discuss family situations in which there is the greatest need for life insurance.
3. Home insurance perils are related to where you live. Identify and discuss different perils that are more common in one part of the country than another.
4. In what ways can you help to control the amount you pay for auto insurance?

---

29. Mrs. Owen pays $1,100.
30. Cost is a good way to compare the same type of policy among different companies. But cost alone is somewhat misleading in comparing term against permanent life because of the cash value of the latter. Two important considerations are: (a) One could probably earn a higher return on investment than that earned with permanent insurance; but (b) Permanent insurance is a form of "forced saving," without which, some people would not save. Ask students for other factors.
31. A young person who sets up housekeeping and begins to acquire material possessions beyond clothing and personal items probably has need for renter's insurance.
32. Some hospitals and clinics have been forced to close or go private because of lack of funds. Private medical facilities are operated to make money the same as any other business.
33. Any individual who has others dependent upon her/him for support needs life insurance. Students should be able to provide several examples.
34. There are many examples: snow and ice damage in northern regions, hurricanes on the east coast, floods along the Mississippi and other rivers, and so on.
35. There are quite a number of ways, such as raising the deductible on collision or comprehensive coverage. Have students name as many others as they can.

WWYD Feature A. Refer students to Figure 6-13. To be exempt from withholding, the instructions say "Read line 6 of the certificate below to see if you can claim exempt status. If exempt, only complete the certificate; but do not complete lines 4 and 5." Few students meet all three conditions in line 6. Point out, however, that if the person doesn't owe any taxes he/she will get a refund.

CHAPTER TWENTY-SIX

Taxes and Taxation

OUTLINE

Taxation
Types of Taxes
The Federal Income Tax
Filing an Income Tax Return
Chapter Review

OBJECTIVES

After reading this chapter, you should be able to:
- Explain the purpose of taxes.
- Identify and explain the major types of taxes.
- Illustrate the difference between a graduated tax and a flat tax.
- Summarize the general process by which the amount of income tax is determined.
- Complete a Form 1040EZ.

John Nye had just completed two weeks on his new job. He could hardly wait to get his first real paycheck. His supervisor handed him the check as he was leaving on Friday afternoon. He took the paycheck and put it into his jacket pocket, not wanting to appear too excited.

After he got on the bus headed for home, John unfolded the paycheck and looked at it. He was disappointed. He had known that deductions would be taken from his paycheck. But he hadn't realized the amount would be so large.

When he got home, John asked his mother why he had to pay taxes. "After all," he said, "I don't make very much money." John's mother explained how every citizen is expected to pay part of the cost of government. Mrs. Nye also explained the types of

1. Ask students how they reacted to their first paycheck.
2. Not all deductions, of course, are for taxes.
3. A local government may be a county, village, town, or city.

FIGURE 26-1 Most homeowners pay local property taxes. What is the largest expenditure included in this real estate tax bill?

taxes, and John's future need to file an income-tax return. This chapter will help you to understand more about the purpose and types of taxes.

What Would You Do?

You are working about fifteen hours a week as part of a work experience program. In looking over your pay statement, you discover that money has been withheld for federal and state income taxes. You try to recall back to the time you filled out Form W-4 "Employee's Withholding Allowance Certificate." You think that you claimed exemption from withholding because you don't expect to owe any taxes this year. Perhaps you made a mistake on Form W-4. What would you do?

TAXATION

Local, state, and federal are the three levels of U.S. government. These units of government provide a

353

354 ■ SECTION 5 Managing Your Money

wide variety of services. Supporting schools, building and maintaining roads, and providing for the nation's defense are examples. The process by which the expenses of government are paid is called *taxation*.

Purpose of Taxes

A *tax* is a compulsory (required) contribution of money people make to the government. Calling a tax compulsory helps to distinguish it from other types of payments. For example, when you buy a postage stamp you are paying for a government service. The difference between that purchase and taxation is that you aren't required to buy a stamp. The main purpose of taxation is to raise *revenue* to pay the cost of government. Most taxes are revenue taxes.

$1,024,328,000,000

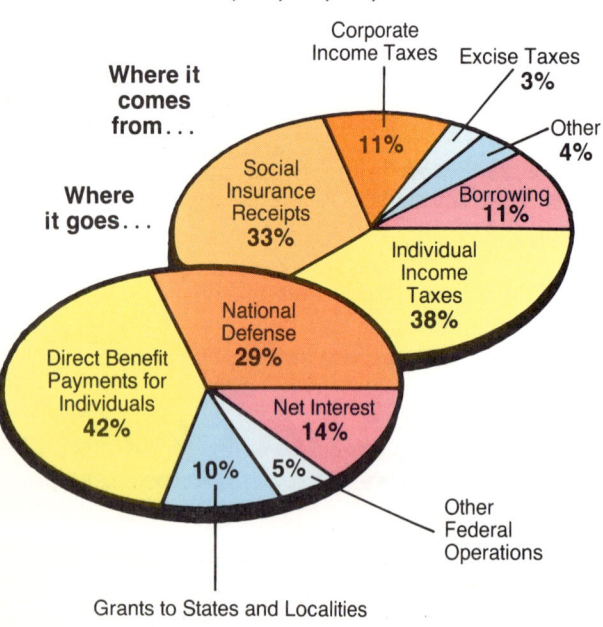

Where it comes from...
- Corporate Income Taxes 11%
- Excise Taxes 3%
- Other 4%
- Borrowing 11%
- Individual Income Taxes 38%
- Social Insurance Receipts 33%

Where it goes...
- National Defense 29%
- Direct Benefit Payments for Individuals 42%
- Net Interest 14%
- Grants to States and Localities 10%
- Other Federal Operations 5%

FIGURE 26-2 This is how the federal government raises and spends money.

Direct and Indirect Taxes

For centuries, governments have used direct and indirect ways of raising money. A direct tax is paid directly to the government. Examples include paycheck deductions and property taxes.

If you buy gasoline, you pay an indirect tax. The oil company pays tax on the gasoline it produces. These increased costs are then passed on to you at

4. Taxes are not usually labeled "direct" or "indirect." This is simply a useful way to help students better understand the nature of taxes.
5. If your state has an income tax, what is the rate?
6. Recall from Chapter 10 that this is called FICA tax.
7. If your state has a sales tax, what is the rate? Do you also have a local sales tax?

FIGURE 26-3 How much tax is included in the cost of gasoline where you live? *Photo by Paul E. Meyers*

the pumps. Passing on taxes to the consumer is known as "shifting the tax burden."

Sometimes, a direct tax can become an indirect tax. Karen's landlord told her that the rent was going up $20 a month. When she ask why, Karen learned that property taxes on the building had risen about $600 last year. What the owner did was to pass the property taxes (a direct tax) on to Karen and other renters in the form of an indirect tax.

The consumer is often aware of indirect taxes. When you buy gasoline, for example, the price you pay for excise tax is clearly shown on the pump. Or, when you buy automobile tires, the bill will list the amount of federal excise tax.

Some kinds of indirect taxes are "hidden." For instance, the price you pay for a stereo receiver includes taxes paid on the labor and raw materials used to produce the product. Taxes were collected on the factory and equipment used in manufacturing. Shipping costs to get the product to market include taxes paid by the transportation company. In fact, hidden taxes may make up as much as twenty percent of the cost of goods you buy.

TYPES OF TAXES

Individuals and businesses pay a variety of direct and indirect taxes for the purpose of raising revenue. The major types of taxes are: income; payroll; sales and excise; and estate, inheritance, and gift.

8. The excise tax is a type of "consumption" tax designed to generate additional revenue. The rationale seems to be that people who purchase such items can afford to pay a little extra.

9. No tax is paid on an average family's estate (only on gross estates over $600,000). Thirty-three states have estate taxes, and eighteen have inheritance taxes.

Income Taxes

You pay taxes on the money you earn and businesses are taxed on their profits. Governments collect the majority of taxes in this manner. The federal government, most state governments, and a few local governments collect income taxes. You pay income taxes not only on salary, wages, and tips, but on savings and investment income as well.

Payroll

Income taxes pay for the overall costs of government. Payroll taxes, however, only go to support social security insurance programs. If you work for an employer covered by social security, both you and the employer make a contribution. These funds will help to provide you with a retirement income and other benefits. Some workers, such as teachers and government employees, pay into a state retirement program rather than into social security. You will learn more about social security in the next chapter.

FIGURE 26-4 In most states, sales tax is not collected on food and medicine. *Courtesy of Esselte Business Systems Inc.*

Sales and Excise Taxes

Most state governments and some local ones have a *sales* tax. When you buy something, a few cents per dollar is added to the amount of the sale. Taxes on large items can be very high. For instance, on a car purchase, the sales tax can amount to several hundred dollars.

Excise taxes are a type of sales tax placed on specific items. These taxes are most commonly found on such items as gasoline, tires, and amusements. Why do you suppose the government taxes these things?

Estate, Inheritance, and Gift Taxes

When a person dies, the government may collect two types of taxes. An *estate tax* is assessed on the value of the dead person's wealth and property *before* it passes on to the heirs of the estate. In addition, an *inheritance tax* may be taken out of each person's share of the will. The federal government collects only an estate tax. Some state governments levy both inheritance and estate taxes.

You may wonder why people don't just turn over large sums while living so heirs can avoid these taxes. Gifts up to a certain amount are tax free. Beyond that figure, however, the person receiving the money must pay a *gift tax.*

THE FEDERAL INCOME TAX

In 1913, Congress passed the 16th Amendment to the Constitution, which gave the government the

FIGURE 26-5 The first income tax was imposed in 1862 to help pay the costs of the Civil War.

10. Gifts up to $10,000 per year ($20,000 if given by a couple) are free from federal gift tax. Several states also have gift taxes.

356 ■ SECTION 5 Managing Your Money

right to tax incomes. A few months later, an income tax on individuals and corporations was imposed. Since 1913, income tax laws have changed many times, and income tax rates have increased greatly.

In 1911, Wisconsin became the first state to tax income. The success of this tax led many states to pass similar laws. By the mid-1970s, almost all states had passed some form of income tax. After World War II, many cities also adopted income taxes. Added revenues were needed to catch up with needs neglected during the war.

Who Must Pay?

Unless excused by law, individuals, corporations, trusts, and estates must pay income tax. For example, the government doesn't tax certain individuals and families who have low incomes. Nonprofit organizations such as churches, charities, and hospitals are also tax exempt.

Aliens, who are citizens of other countries who live and work in the United States, must pay income taxes. All corporations pay income taxes. Small businesses don't pay corporate taxes (unless they have been incorporated). Instead, owners of such businesses pay individual income taxes on their shares of the business income.

The Graduated Income Tax

Most Americans recognize that paying taxes is a necessary part of being a good citizen. The income tax is seen by most of us as being the fairest type of tax. People who earn more money should be able to pay more taxes. A system in which taxes are tied to one's income is called a graduated tax. See Figure 26-7.

Each taxpayer is allowed a certain level of tax-free income. The amount of tax-free income is determined by marital status and number of dependents. Based on 1988 tax rates, a single person without

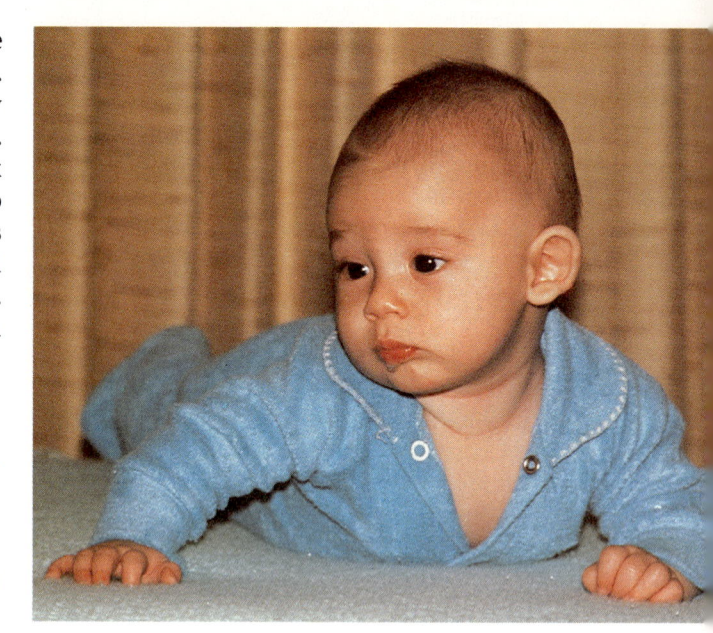

FIGURE 26-6 This baby must pay federal income tax. Her grandfather left her a large amount of money that earns interest. *Photo by Paul E. Meyers*

12. Another name for the graduated tax is *progressive* tax. A progressive tax rate increases as income increases.

SCHEDULE X—Single Taxpayers

If line 5 is: Over—	but not over—	The tax is:	of the amount over—
$0	$17,850	------ 15%	$0
17,850	-------	$2,677.50 + 28%	17,850*

SCHEDULE Z—Heads of Household

If line 5 is: Over—	but not over—	The tax is:	of the amount over—
$0	$23,900	------ 15%	$0
23,900	-------	$3,585 + 28%	23,900*

SCHEDULE Y—Married Taxpayers and Qualifying Widows and Widowers

Married Filing Joint Returns and Qualifying Widows and Widowers

If line 5 is: Over—	but not over—	The tax is:	of the amount over—
$0	$29,750	------ 15%	$0
29,750	-------	$4,462.50 + 28%	29,750*

Married Filing Separate Returns

If line 5 is: Over—	but not over—	The tax is:	of the amount over—
$0	$14,875	------ 15%	$0
14,875	-------	$2,231.25 + 28%	14,875*

FIGURE 26-7 The rate of tax that you pay is based upon the amount of taxable income and your filing status.

11. The Tax Reform Act of 1986 is regarded by some as the most sweeping tax reform since 1913. Fifteen tax brackets, ranging up to 50 percent were cut to two with a top bracket of 28 percent.

13. In Figure 26-7, the filing status "head of household" refers to someone who is unmarried and pays more than half the cost of keeping a home for themselves and a dependent.

14. A flat tax is also called a *proportional* tax.
15. Loopholes are things that were written into tax laws years ago for good reasons, but which may be less valid today.

additional dependents paid no tax on the first $4,950 of earned income ($3,000 standard deduction plus $1,950 personal exemption). Marie and Frank are a married couple with two children. The family paid no taxes on the first $12,800 of earned income ($5,000 standard deduction plus four personal exemptions). The standard deduction for most students who can be claimed as a dependent on another person's return is limited to not more than $3,000 earned income.

The income-tax rate, then, requires nothing from people with very low incomes. Large families pay less in taxes than small families. Married people pay less than single people.

FIGURE 26-8 The winner of this raffle will have to pay income tax based on the car's value. *Photo by Liane Enkelis*

Most state and local income taxes are also graduated. Some state and local governments, however, use a flat tax. This means that a flat percentage (usually one to six percent) is assessed on income regardless of its amount. If the flat rate were five percent, a $20,000 income would be assessed $1,000. Someone earning $30,000 would have to pay $1,500 in taxes.

Over the years, many kinds of exemptions and deductions have been written into the tax laws. Some of them are called *loopholes* because they permit certain individuals to reduce or avoid income taxes. Loopholes are criticized by some people because they are regarded as unfair. A so-called loophole, however, is a legal tax provision that any eligible person can take advantage of. For example, one loophole involves interest paid on a home mortgage. People buying homes can deduct

16. Congress has the power to tax total income, but it allows taxpayers to exclude certain items from taxation.

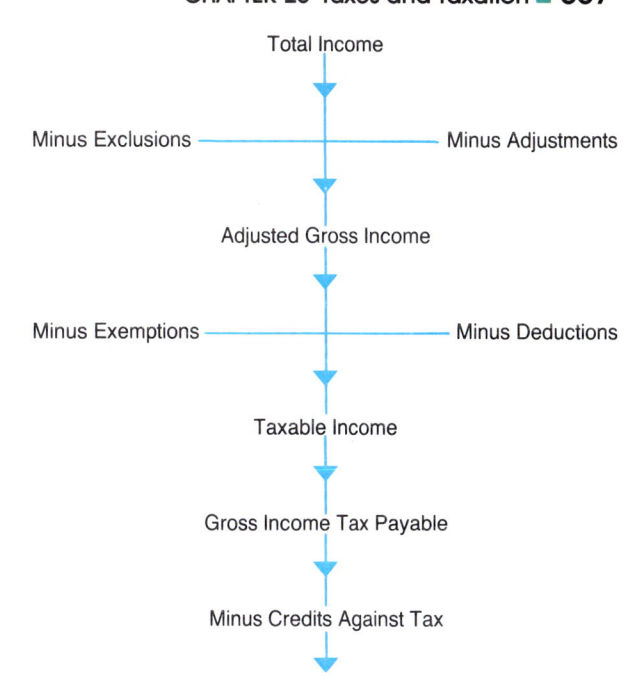

CHAPTER 26 Taxes and Taxation ■ 357

```
                 Total Income
                      ↓
Minus Exclusions ─────┼───── Minus Adjustments
                      ↓
              Adjusted Gross Income
                      ↓
Minus Exemptions ─────┼───── Minus Deductions
                      ↓
                 Taxable Income
                      ↓
            Gross Income Tax Payable
                      ↓
            Minus Credits Against Tax
                      ↓
     Income Tax Payable to the Federal Government
```

FIGURE 26-9 This is the general process used to determine the amount of federal income tax owed. The actual process varies among individuals.

the interest paid from their taxes. People paying rent have no such deductions.

How the Tax is Determined

Your total income for a given year consists of money you earned from your job plus income from savings, investments, and other sources. But you don't have to pay taxes on your total income, Figure 26-9.

To determine income subject to tax, you first subtract certain nontaxable items called exclusions and adjustments. *Exclusions* are nontaxable income items such as social security payments and veterans' benefits. *Adjustments* to income may include alimony paid and contributions to an Individual Retirement Account. After you subtract exclusions and adjustments, you are left with an *adjusted gross income*.

Next, you are allowed to subtract various *deductions*. For example, mortgage interest, property taxes, and other expenses can be deducted. The next thing you subtract is a set amount for each dependent. These are your *exemptions*. A married couple with one child, for example, would have three exemptions. Subtraction of amounts for deductions and exemptions leaves you with your *taxable income*.

17. The process shown in Figure 26-9 is an effort to illustrate the steps followed by an average taxpayer in completing a federal income tax form.

358 ■ SECTION 5 Managing Your Money

If line 37 (taxable income) is—		And you are—			
At least	But less than	Single	Married filing jointly *	Married filing separately	Head of a household
		Your tax is—			
23,000						
23,000	23,050	4,127	3,454	4,513	3,454
23,050	23,100	4,141	3,461	4,527	3,461
23,100	23,150	4,155	3,469	4,541	3,469
23,150	23,200	4,169	3,476	4,555	3,476
23,200	23,250	4,183	3,484	4,569	3,484
23,250	23,300	4,197	3,491	4,583	3,491
23,300	23,350	4,211	3,499	4,597	3,499
23,350	23,400	4,225	3,506	4,611	3,506
23,400	23,450	4,239	3,514	4,625	3,514
23,450	23,500	4,253	3,521	4,639	3,521
23,500	23,550	4,267	3,529	4,653	3,529
23,550	23,600	4,281	3,536	4,667	3,536
23,600	23,650	4,295	3,544	4,681	3,544
23,650	23,700	4,309	3,551	4,695	3,551
23,700	23,750	4,323	3,559	4,709	3,559
23,750	23,800	4,337	3,566	4,723	3,566
23,800	23,850	4,351	3,574	4,737	3,574
23,850	23,900	4,365	3,581	4,751	3,581
23,900	23,950	4,379	3,589	4,765	3,592
23,950	24,000	4,393	3,596	4,779	3,606

FIGURE 26-10 Sample from tax table

18. You determine the amount of tax owed by using the appropriate tax table, Figure 26-10. For example, suppose you are married and filing a joint return. If you made $23,430 in taxable income, the tax is $3,514. A single person earning the same amount would owe $4,239.

Your figure from the tax table may be reduced if you are eligible for any *tax credits*. These include child care and certain other expenses. The amount left after subtracting credits will be the amount of federal income tax you owe.

19. A final step in determining your tax is to compare the amount owed with the tax you have already paid. Because your employer withheld taxes from each paycheck, most or all of your tax obligation should be satisfied. If too much tax has been withheld, you can claim a refund. However, if too little has been withheld, you will have to pay an additional amount.

18. The IRS has found that the No. 1 numerical error made on tax returns is that the wrong numbers are copied from the tax tables. Refer to Figure 26-10 and solve several examples.

FIGURE 26-11 Don't wait until the last minute to file your income tax return. *Photo by Paul E. Meyers*

19. To avoid errors on a tax return, the IRS recommends that the "completed" return be set aside a day or two. Then, recheck the math and check for completeness (i.e., Social Security number,

You must sign and mail your return and any attachments by April 15. In signing your name, you signify that everything contained on the form is accurate and truthful. If you mail the form late, you will have to pay a late penalty. People who don't file their forms at all are practicing *tax evasion*. If they are found guilty of this charge, they will have to pay a heavy fine and perhaps serve a prison sentence.

FILING AN INCOME TAX RETURN

The term *filing* is used to refer to the process of completing and submitting an income tax return. Filing a tax return can be simple or complex, depending on your filing status, source(s) of income, number of deductions, and so on. The easiest form to file is Form 1040EZ. You can use this form if:

- Your filing status is single.
- You do not claim any dependents.
- You are not 65 or over, or blind.
- Your taxable income is less than $50,000.
- You had *only* wages, salaries, and tips, and your taxable interest income was $400 or less.

In calendar year 1988, John Nye worked afternoons during school and all day on Saturdays at Barden Ruddens ice cream parlor. During the summer months, he worked a full forty-hour week.

signature, supporting tax forms, a check). About 10 percent of all individual tax returns contain some sort of mistake.

F·E·A·T·U·R·E

Electronic Tax Filing

♦ ♦ ♦

In 1986, the Internal Revenue Service (IRS) began an experiment in which people could electronically file (by computer) their tax return directly with the IRS. The first year, 25,000 returns were filed. Two years later, the number had increased to 600,000.

One tax expert calls electronic filing the most significant advance in tax preparation since the tax code was invented. The process should cut down on the pile of paper at the ten IRS processing centers. Currently, IRS employees must open the envelopes, organize and read the information, and key the data into a computer. By filing direct, the first two steps are eliminated. The IRS hopes that by the early 1990s, all but the most complex returns can be filed electronically.

If electronic filing succeeds in eliminating paper forms, the next step may be a "returnless" system. In the future, IRS computers may keep wages, social security, and other data on taxpayers. Then each year, the IRS would send either a bill or a refund without a return ever being filed. It may even be possible for taxpayers with home computers to interact directly with the IRS. You might go to your computer some day and discover on your "bulletin board" that the IRS has deposited a tax refund in your account!

FIGURE 26-FEATURE Electronic tax filing is another illustration of how computers are influencing our lives. *Photo by Paul E. Meyers*

Electronic Tax Filing. In 1989, taxpayers in 39 states were able to file their 1988 tax returns electronically. Only returns showing a refund could be accepted, and they had to be filed through a qualified tax preparation firm. IRS Publication 910 (noted in Activity 5) contains additional information about electronic filing.

360 ■ SECTION 5 Managing Your Money

1 Control number			4 Employer's state I.D. number 0348-4321	Copy 2 To be filed with employee's State, City, or Local income tax return.
Barden Ruddens Inc. 1640 W. Main Street Carbondale, IL 72901			3 Employer's identification number 37-5732196	Employee's and employer's copy compared.
			5 Stat. emp. Deceased Pension box Legal rep. 942 emp. Def. comp.	
			6 Allocated tips	7 Advance EIC payment
2 Employer's name, address, and ZIP code				
8 Employee's social security number 315-20-4024	9 Federal income tax withheld 231.50		10 Wages, tips, other compensation 4,140.00	11 Social security tax withheld 310.14
12 Employee's name, address, and ZIP code			13 Social security wages 4,140.00	14 Social security tips
John R. Nye 1612 Fredrick St. Carbondale, IL 72901			16	16a Fringe benefits incl. in Box 10
			17 State income tax 79.25	18 State wages, tips, etc. 4,140.00	19 Name of state IL
Form W-2 Wage and Tax Statement OMB No. 1545-0008			20 Local income tax	21 Local wages, tips, etc.	22 Name of locality

FIGURE 26-12 A Form W-2, Wage and Tax Statement will be provided to you in late January by your employer.

John's W-2 Form for calendar year 1988 appears in Figure 26-12. Form W-2 Wage and Tax Statement is an IRS form that your employer prepares and sends to you by January 31 of the following year. The form summarizes the total earnings and tax withholding.

When John got his W-2, he went to the IRS office and picked up a copy of Form 1040EZ. A copy of John's completed return is shown in Figure 26-13.

What Would You Do?

You are in the process of filling out your income tax return. The next line on the form deals with "charitable contributions." You go over your canceled checks and discover several that qualify as deductions. You can remember several other cash contributions, but you don't have the receipts. Also, you had some out-of-pocket expenses for church activities. These are allowable deductions. But you don't have records for those either. You aren't sure how much you should claim for charitable contributions. What would you do?

As you can see, it wasn't difficult for John Nye to file an income tax return. Not all returns, however,

are as simple as this. Because John's older sister had dividend income from stock, she had to use Form 1040A. John's parents used a third type of common form, Form 1040, because they itemize deductions and also receive income from a property they rent.

As a result of completing his own Form 1040EZ, John discovered that he enjoyed that type of work. When he asked his sister and parents if he might help them with their forms, they quickly accepted his offer. By helping to fill out their forms, John

FIGURE 26-14 John's sister is happy to have help in completing her tax return. *Photo by Paul E. Meyers*

* WWYD Feature B. This situation only applies to individuals who are itemizing deductions. Take advantage of every legal deduction you are entitled to. The deductions for cash contributions and out-of-pocket expenses should be taken with the knowledge that the IRS might not allow them later if an audit is conducted. Point out the need to keep accurate records of deductions.

Form 1040EZ — Income Tax Return for Single filers with no dependents (1988)

Department of the Treasury - Internal Revenue Service

Name & address:
John R. Nye
1612 W. Main Street
Carbondale, IL 72901

Your social security number: 315 20 4024

Presidential Election Campaign Fund — Do you want $1 to go to this fund? ☒

Report your income

1. Total wages, salaries, and tips. This should be shown in Box 10 of your W-2 form(s). (Attach your W-2 form(s).) **4,140.00**
2. Taxable interest income of $400 or less. If the total is more than $400, you cannot use Form 1040EZ. **35.00**
3. Add line 1 and line 2. This is your **adjusted gross income**. **4,175.00**
4. Can your parents or someone else claim you on their return?
   ☒ Yes. Do worksheet on back; enter amount from line E here.
   ☐ No. Enter 3,000 as your standard deduction. **3,000.00**
5. Subtract line 4 from line 3. If line 4 is larger than line 3, enter 0. .... **1,175.00**
6. If you checked the "Yes" box on line 4, enter 0.
   If you checked the "No" box on line 4, enter 1,950.
   This is your **personal exemption**. **0.00**
7. Subtract line 6 from line 5. If line 6 is larger than line 5, enter 0. This is your **taxable income**. **1,175.00**

Figure your tax

8. Enter your Federal income tax withheld from Box 9 of your W-2 form(s). **232.00**
9. Use the **single** column in the tax table on pages 37–42 of the Form 1040A/1040EZ booklet to find the **tax** on the amount shown on line 7 above. Enter the amount of tax. **178.00**

Refund or amount you owe

10. If line 8 is larger than line 9, subtract line 9 from line 8. Enter the **amount of your refund**. **54.00**
11. If line 9 is larger than line 8, subtract line 8 from line 9. Enter the **amount you owe**. Attach check or money order for the full amount, payable to "Internal Revenue Service." ....

Sign your return

Your signature: John R. Nye   Date: Feb. 20, 1989

Form **1040EZ** (1988)

FIGURE 26-13 Most teenage workers use Form 1040EZ.

learned a great deal more about income tax returns. Why don't you offer to help a family member or friend with income tax preparation? You will probably learn a lot, too!

20. Form 1040EZ constitutes about 18 percent of all individual tax returns.
21. Have on hand copies of the three different forms to show students differences among them.

CHAPTER REVIEW

Chapter in Brief

- The process by which the expenses of government are paid is called taxation. A tax is a compulsory contribution of money people make to the government. Most taxes are revenue taxes.
- A direct tax is paid directly to the government. Examples include payroll deductions and property taxes. An indirect tax is one that is included in the cost of goods and services you buy. Excise taxes are one of the most common types of indirect taxes.
- Individuals and businesses pay a variety of direct and indirect taxes. The major types of taxes are: income; payroll; sales and excise; and estate, inheritance, and gift.
- Most individuals and corporations pay income taxes. Income from a small unincorporated business is taxed as individual income rather than as corporate income.
- The graduated income tax is one in which the amount of tax paid is tied to income. The more you earn, the more you pay. The federal government, and most state and local governments, levy a graduated income tax. Some state and local governments use a flat tax. This means that a flat percentage is assessed on income regardless of its amount.
- To determine income subject to tax, you first subtract certain nontaxable items called exclusions and adjustments. This leaves you with an adjusted gross income. Next, you are allowed to subtract various deductions and exemptions. This leaves you with your taxable income. You figure your tax based on this amount. This amount can sometimes be further reduced by subtracting tax credits. The resultant figure is the amount of federal income tax you owe.
- The easiest tax form to file is 1040EZ. Most teenage workers are eligible to use this form.

Words to Know

adjusted gross income the amount on an income tax form that results after you subtract exclusions and adjustments from total income.

adjustments items that can be subtracted from income when filing an income tax return.

deductions items on an income tax form that can be subtracted from the adjusted gross income.

exclusions items for which income taxes do not have to be paid.

exemptions a set amount based on the number of dependents that is subtracted from adjusted gross income when filing an income tax form.

filing the process of completing and submitting an income tax form.

loopholes a legal tax provision that allows some people to reduce or avoid income taxes.

revenue money that is raised through taxes to pay the cost of government.

tax a required contribution of money made to the government.

taxable income the amount on an income tax form left after all exclusions, adjustments, exemptions, and deductions have been subtracted; the amount of income on which tax is paid.

taxation the process by which the expenses of government are paid.

tax credits certain expenses that can be deducted from the amount of income tax owed.

tax evasion the illegal practice of avoiding payment of some or all of one's income tax obligation.

Questions to Answer
1. Why do all of us need to pay taxes?
2. What is a revenue tax?
3. Is an excise tax on tires a direct or an indirect tax?
4. Name and briefly describe the seven major types of taxes.
5. Do aliens working in the U.S. have to pay income taxes? Why?
6. What is a flat tax? How is a graduated tax different?
7. How are owners of small businesses taxed?
8. Based on Figure 26-10, how much tax does a married couple filing jointly owe on an income of $23,945? How much does a single person owe on the same amount?
9. If you are married, can you use Form 1040EZ to file your federal income tax?
10. What happens if you have earned income and fail to file an income tax?

Activities to Do
1. As a class, obtain a copy of the most recent federal budget. What is the total amount of the budget? How much has it increased from the one shown in Figure 26-2? What parts of the budget have gone up the most? The least? Discuss your answers in class.
2. Get a copy of and instructions for Form 1040EZ. Fill out the form using the following figures: wages of $12,648, tips of $943, and $183 in interest income. Federal income tax in the amount of $1,766 was withheld. What is the amount of tax? Your instructor may assign additional problems.
3. If your state has an income tax, obtain a copy of the income tax form and instructions. Using the amounts shown in Figure 26-13, see if you can complete the form by yourself. When finished, ask your instructor to check the figures.
4. Let's assume that you make $305 a week in salary for 52 weeks. You pay $2,070 a year in federal income tax, and $482 in state income tax. You also pay $218 in sales tax, $73 in property tax, and $990 in FICA tax. A variety of other taxes add an additional $132. What is the total amount in taxes paid during the year? How many weeks must you work just to pay taxes?
5. Obtain a copy of Publication 910, "Guide to Free Tax Services" at your nearest IRS Forms Distribution Center. Using the publication, find out what the IRS offers regarding:
   a. Toll-free telephone assistance.
   b. Recorded tax information (Tele-Tax).
   c. Tax publications and forms.
   d. Films and videocassettes.
   Your instructor may arrange to have you view a film or videocassette.

Topics to Discuss
1. Why do you think so many people dislike paying income taxes? How do you feel?
2. Which do you think is more fair, the graduated tax or the flat tax?
3. In what ways might the federal income tax system be improved? Give specific illustrations.
4. Have you ever heard of the "underground economy"? What does it refer to? Give examples.

---

1. Taxes pay for all of the government services that we expect and enjoy, including schools, roads, fire protection, national defense, and so on.
2. One that raises money (revenue).
3. Indirect tax.
4. (a) *Income*—taxes paid on money earned by individuals and corporations. (b) *Payroll*—taxes used to support social security insurance programs. (c) *Sales*—taxes paid on consumer products. (d) *Excise*—type of sales tax placed on specific products. (e) *Estate*—tax assessed on dead person's estate before it passes to heirs. (f) *Inheritance*—tax taken out of each person's share of the will. (g) *Gift*—tax paid on money received as a gift.
5. Yes, because they receive most of the same government services available to citizens.
6. (a) *Flat tax*—a straight percentage assessed on income regardless of the amount. (b) *Graduated tax*—one that is based on the amount of income. The higher the income, the higher the tax.
7. Owners of unincorporated businesses pay income tax on business income at the same rate as other income.
8. (a) $3,589. (b) $4,379.
9. No.
10. You are guilty of tax evasion and subject to a heavy fine and a possible jail term.

22. The President's annual budget is widely publicized in newspapers and magazines. It is typically reported in the form of a pie chart as shown in Figure 26-2. Clip and save future budgets for use here.
23. With a little advance preparation, you should be able to obtain multiple copies of both federal and state tax forms at your local IRS office, bank, post office, or library.
24. $3,965 paid in total taxes; 13 weeks to pay taxes.
25. The effort here is to make students aware of the wide variety of information and services provided by the IRS. This is a very useful publication.
26. This refers to financial transactions and bartering among individuals and companies, the income from which goes unreported to the IRS. Many of the transactions are made by cash, without any records being kept.

1. Recall from Chapter 10 that social security is called Federal Insurance Contributions Act (FICA) tax.

2. Ask if any students or members of their family receive social security. Note that welfare is one form of social security. Be sensitive about this subject.

CHAPTER TWENTY-SEVEN

Social Security

OUTLINE
Social Security
Major Social Insurance Programs
Eligibility and Financing
Individual Retirement Accounts
Chapter Review

OBJECTIVES
After reading this chapter, you should be able to:
- Identify the two forms of social security.
- Name and describe the six major federal and state social insurance programs.
- Explain how state workers' compensation is financed.
- Describe who is eligible for federal social security payments and how the program is financed.
- Explain the purpose of an Individual Retirement Account (IRA).
- Name two tax benefits of an IRA.

You know that your employer withholds money from your paycheck for federal, and perhaps state and local, income taxes. A sum is probably also withheld for *social security* taxes.

You may have little interest in social security now. After all, it will be a long time before you retire. However, you need to be aware that social security is more than just a retirement program. What is called social security is actually a broad state and federal effort consisting of various types of social insurance. These programs will be explained later in this chapter.

FIGURE 27-1 Sally's father died last year. The monthly payments she received from Social Security allowed her to remain in school. *Courtesy of SIUC Photocommunications*

SOCIAL SECURITY

At one time, most Americans lived in rural areas and were farmers. Rural families lived off of the land. They built their own homes; raised their own food; and traded or sold surplus food, crops, and livestock. Families and neighbors helped each other during difficult times.

Gradually, the country began to change from an agricultural economy to an industrial one. Increasing numbers of people moved to cities and took jobs in factories. Instead of living off of the land, families began to depend on wages paid by an employer. If the income stopped for some reason, such as a worker's illness or old age, the whole family suffered.

The Great Depression of 1929-1933 showed on a large scale how painful unemployment could be. To help deal with unemployment and the many other social problems brought on by the Depression, Congress, in 1935, passed the Social Security Act. This law provided for a system of old-age (retirement) pensions, unemployment insurance, aid for

3. Most people are not aware of the two forms of social security: *public assistance* and *social insurance*. Further, social insurance is divided into two types, Figure 27-3. It is okay to refer to

364

social insurance as "social security," since this is the more common term. However, make sure students know the difference.

CHAPTER 27 Social Security ■ 365

FIGURE 27-2 The food stamp program is one type of public assistance. It helps low income and temporarily unemployed people buy food. *Courtesy of USDA*

dependent children, and benefits for the blind. Over the years, Congress has made several changes in the act. Two examples are the extension of *benefits* to more groups and an increase in tax rates. Does anyone in your family receive social security?

Government programs that help people meet social and economic needs are called social security. There are two forms of social security. The first is known as public assistance (or welfare). This program aids the needy regardless of their work record. General taxes finance public assistance.

Social insurance, the second form of social security, pays benefits to people who have earned them by working and paying social security payroll taxes. In some cases, a worker's family can receive benefits. In many ways, social insurance is similar to other types of insurance. During your working years, you and your employer pay taxes that go into special funds. The risks and costs are thus spread among many people. When your earnings stop because of retirement or certain other situations, you receive benefits. If you die, payments are made to your survivors.

MAJOR SOCIAL INSURANCE PROGRAMS

National and state systems of social security have changed greatly from the way there were in 1935. The six major social insurance programs in the

4. Point out that social insurance works similar to other types of insurance discussed in Chapter 25.

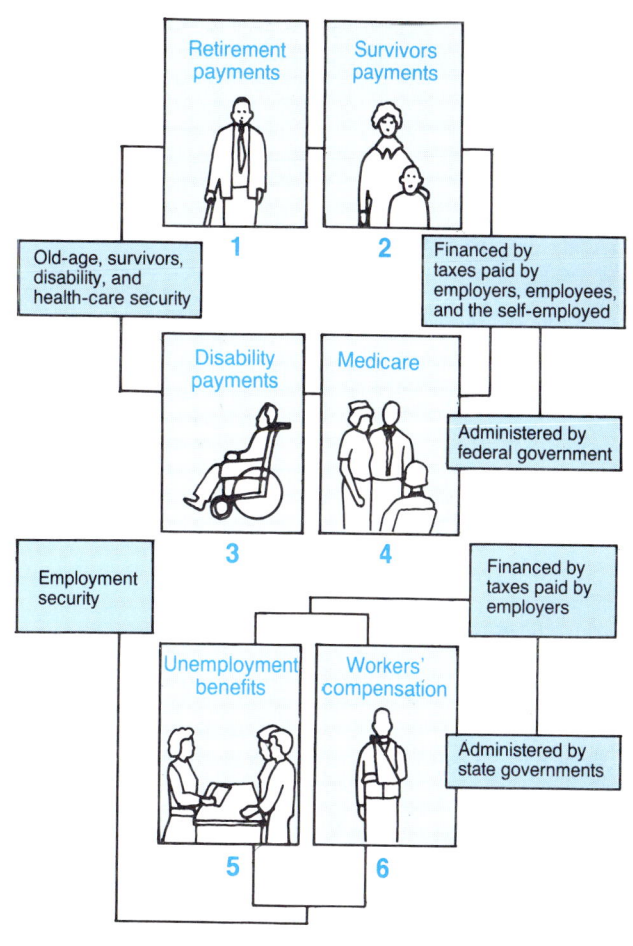

FIGURE 27-3 These are the six major types of social insurance programs in the United States. Most people call the first four "social security."

United States are shown in Figure 27-3. The general nature of each of these programs is described in this chapter. As some of the rules are quite technical, no effort is made to explain all details regarding eligibility and payments. More specific information can be obtained from your local Social Security Administration office. More than 1,300 such offices are located across the country.

Retirement Payments

This is the best known social security program. It provides a monthly *pension* to retired workers who reach age 65. If you wish, you may choose to retire at age 62. If you do, you will collect on 80 percent of the rate established for a person retiring at age 65.

5. Provide students with information on the location of the nearest SSA office. Pick up or request by phone a variety of information and display it on the bulletin board.

366 ■ SECTION 5 Managing Your Money

Retired worker age 65 or older	$514
Aged spouse of retired worker not having own coverage	$265
Widow or widower of deceased worker	$466
Child of deceased worker	$354
Disabled worker	$508
Spouse of disabled worker	$134
Child of disabled worker	$147

FIGURE 27-4 This illustrates average monthly benefits for different Social Security recipients. *Courtesy of Social Security Administration*

The amount of monthly benefits received is based on your average annual earnings. See Figure 27-4 for examples of various types of retirement and other benefits.

Benefits under the program are also payable to the spouse of the retired worker. A spouse's benefit equals about 50 percent of the worker's benefit. Under certain conditions, unmarried children of the retired worker may also be eligible for benefits.

Retirement-age rules will change in the future as a result of revisions made in 1983 to the Social Security Act. Between the years 2003 and 2027, the retirement age will gradually increase from 65 to 67. This means that if you are a high school student now, you will not be eligible to receive full retirement benefits until you reach age 67. Early retirement benefits (age 62) will be reduced to 75 percent by 2009 and to 70 percent by 2027.

FIGURE 27-5 Millions of senior citizens live more comfortably in retirement because of Social Security. *Courtesy of Sears, Roebuck and Co. 1987 Annual Report*

6. Note that these are only average benefits.
7. Be receptive to student's comments about their age group not being able to retire until 67.

8. In 1989, the lump-sum payment was $255.

Survivors Payments

If you are insured and you die (either before or after retirement), your dependents may be eligible for survivors payments. These benefits are of two types. First, a *lump-sum payment* is made to your spouse or child. Second, your dependents may be eligible for a monthly survivors benefit.

Monthly payments may be made to a surviving spouse age 60 or older. Under certain conditions, surviving unmarried children and dependent parents may also receive payments. The amount of monthly payments is based on the benefits the worker was getting at the time of death. Suppose the person had not yet retired. The survivor would then be entitled to the benefits the deceased worker would have received.

Disability Payments

If you are unable to work because of a severe physical or mental disability, you may be eligible for benefits. The disability must have lasted at least twelve months or be expected to last that long. Payments can start upon the sixth full month of disability.

FIGURE 27-6 State vocational rehabilitation agencies help restore many disabled workers to productive employment. Costs of rehabilitation services may be paid from Social Security trust funds. *Photo by David W. Tuttle*

9. Medicare and Medicaid are frequently confused. Explain the difference.

10. Many private companies sell insurance to cover the part not paid by Medicare.

Benefits are also paid to a disabled worker's spouse. A dependent spouse may collect full benefits at age 65 or reduced benefits at age 62. Unmarried children under 18 can also receive benefits. If a worker has a disabled child, special benefits may apply.

Medicare

In 1965, Congress added hospital and medical insurance benefits to the social security program. This coverage, known since as Medicare, is for people age 65 or older. (This is sometimes confused with Medicaid, which is a health service program for welfare recipients.) Disabled workers under 65 who have received disability benefits for two years are also eligible.

Medicare consists of both hospital insurance and supplementary medical insurance. Hospital coverage pays for nursing care as well as hospital expenses. The insured person must pay an initial amount (a deductible) for each hospital stay. Medicare then pays the rest of the hospital expenses for up to 60 days. Once a stay lasts over 60 days, additional limitations apply.

The hospital insurance part of medicare is automatically provided to eligible workers (and spouses). However, the medical coverage is an *optional* health insurance plan. It pays the cost of doctor's fees and other medical services not included in hospital insurance. If you want medical coverage, you must pay a monthly premium for the service. Under this plan, you must pay a deductible each year. The program then pays 80 percent of the remaining expenses.

Unemployment Benefits

Unemployment insurance, which was included as a part of the original 1935 Social Security Act, is not a federal program. The purpose of the law was to motivate states to pass their own laws. Each state finances and administers its own unemployment insurance program.

Unemployment insurance provides weekly cash payments to workers who have lost their jobs. Paul Miller, for instance, was laid off from his job at the Black Gold Coal Mine. He had to go to the local state employment service office to register for unemployment benefits. Paul has started receiving weekly checks amounting to half of his normal full-time pay at the time. He is eligible to receive payments for up to 26 weeks. However, during the time he is receiving unemployment benefits, Paul is required to accept any suitable job that the employment service has available.

The amount of the weekly payment and the number of weeks of eligibility varies from state to state. Otherwise, state programs of unemployment insurance operate in the same general manner.

Workers' Compensation

Every state in the United States has a workers' compensation law, which helps people who are injured or who develop a disease as a result of their job. The program pays the cost of medical care and helps replace lost income. Workers' compensation also pays death benefits and pensions to dependents of workers killed on the job.

FIGURE 27-7 Unemployment benefits are not provided to workers who are on strike, are fired for misconduct on the job, or quit their job without good cause. *Courtesy of George Meany Memorial Archives*

11. Ask students who pays for unemployment benefits and workers' compensation (taxes paid by employers, Figure 27-3).

12. Paul may also be eligible for food stamps or other forms of public assistance.

F·E·A·T·U·R·E

Job Stress and Workers' Compensation

In the early 1900s, a handful of states passed laws to provide benefits for workers injured on the job. Most early laws covered only workers in hazardous occupations like miners or steelworkers. Benefits were paid only for major accidents such as losing an arm or a leg. Over the years, the idea of workers' compensation expanded to include all states, most occupations, and most job-related accidents and illnesses.

In 1955, workers' compensation took a new turn. Two men had been working on a scaffold when a rope broke. One fell to his death. The other was caught by the rope and dangled in the air until he was rescued. His most serious injury was a rope burn. But the guy was a psychological wreck. He was afraid to get on the scaffold ever again. So he filed a claim for workers' compensation. After a lengthy legal battle, Texas courts upheld an award for the man.

Since then, state courts, to varying degrees, have allowed compensation for three new categories of workers: (1) those who suffer a physical injury that leaves a psychological aftereffect; (2) those who suffer mental trauma that leads to a physical ailment; and (3) those who suffer mental strain that leads to more serious mental problems. The last type is the most controversial. Here is an example.

The department in which an employee worked was eliminated. She transferred to another job. She developed chest pains and suffered an emotional breakdown. She quit working and filed a workers' compensation claim against the company. She argued that the job transfer caused her breakdown. Ultimately, the state supreme court awarded her payment of medical bills and two-thirds of her salary.

FIGURE 27-FEATURE Work-stress experts say that the computer age is taking its toll in the form of mental strain. *Courtesy of Knight-Ridder Inc.*

Job-stress cases such as this have mushroomed in the past few years. They are creating problems for employers and states all across the country. According to recent information, seven states recognize everyday mental stress as grounds for workers' compensation benefits. But courts in nine states have rejected all such claims. This is likely to remain a hot issue for a long time to come.

* *Job Stress and Workers' Compensation.* This describes a special type of workers' compensation available in a few states. Find out if your state is one that provides benefits for job stress, or is one that has rejected all such claims. Ask students what they think about this issue.

Benefits vary among states. How much workers receive depends on the type and duration of the disability and on the worker's weekly earnings. States have minimum and maximum benefit limits and benefit periods. But injured workers typically receive less than half of what they would have earned. In return for compensation, workers give up their right to sue an employee for damages arising from their disability.

In most states, employers are required to participate in a workers' compensation program. However, many states don't cover farmworkers, household workers, and employees of small firms. And some states refuse to extend protection to workers in dangerous jobs.

What Would You Do?

You injured your leg very badly in a warehouse accident. The leg was put into a cast. You have been confined to bed for several weeks. It will probably be months before you can go back to work. You are glad you have workers' compensation benefits.

Your co-workers stop by to see you every few days. During one visit, you remark that you can't wait to get the cast off and go back to work. Your buddy laughs and says that if he were you, he would lie about the leg hurting and stay home as long as possible. He says that a lot of people do it. What would you do?

This Card Furnished Through Courtesy of

Request for Earnings and Benefit Estimate Statement

To receive a free statement of your earnings covered by Social Security and your estimated future benefits, all you need to do is fill out this form. Please print or type your answers. When you have completed the form, fold it and mail it to us.

1. Name shown on your Social Security card:
   _____
   First   Middle Initial   Last

2. Your Social Security number as shown on your card:
   ☐☐☐-☐☐-☐☐☐☐

3. Your date of birth: ___ ___ ___
   Month Day Year

4. Other Social Security numbers you have used:
   ☐☐☐-☐☐-☐☐☐☐
   ☐☐☐-☐☐-☐☐☐☐

5. Your Sex: ☐ Male   ☐ Female

6. Other names you have used (including a maiden name):
   _____

7. Show your actual earnings for last year and your estimated earnings for this year. Include only wages and/or net self-employment income subject to Social Security tax.
   A. Last year's actual earnings:
      $☐☐☐,☐☐☐.00
      Dollars only
   B. This year's estimated earnings:
      $☐☐☐,☐☐☐.00
      Dollars only

8. Show the age at which you plan to retire: _____

9. Below, show an amount which you think best represents your future average yearly earnings between now and when you plan to retire. The amount should be a yearly average, not your total future lifetime earnings. Only show earnings subject to Social Security tax.

   Most people should enter the same amount as this year's estimated earnings (the amount shown in 7B). The reason for this is that we will show your retirement benefit estimate in today's dollars, but adjusted to account for average wage growth in the national economy.

   However, if you expect to earn significantly more or less in the future than what you currently earn because of promotions, a job change, part-time work, or an absence from the work force, enter the amount in today's dollars that will most closely reflect your future average yearly earnings. Do not add in cost-of-living, performance, or scheduled pay increases or bonuses.

   Your future average yearly earnings:
   $☐☐☐,☐☐☐.00
   Dollars only

10. Address where you want us to send the statement:
    _____
    Name
    _____
    Street Address (Include Apt. No., P.O. Box, or Rural Route)
    _____
    City   State   Zip Code

I am asking for information about my own Social Security record or the record of a person I am authorized to represent. I understand that if I deliberately request information under false pretenses I may be guilty of a federal crime and could be fined and/or imprisoned. I authorize you to send the statement of my earnings and benefit estimates to me or my representative through a contractor.

▶ _____
Please sign your name (Do not print)

_____ _____
Date   (Area Code) Daytime Telephone No.

ABOUT THE PRIVACY ACT
Social Security is allowed to collect the facts on this form under Section 205 of the Social Security Act. We need them to quickly identify your record and prepare the earnings statement you asked us for. Giving us these facts is voluntary. However, without them we may not be able to give you an earnings and benefit estimate statement. Neither the Social Security Administration nor its contractor will use the information for any other purpose.   SP

Specifications for this form were secured from the Social Security Administration

FIGURE 27-8 This form is submitted to receive a free statement of social security earnings record. It is a good idea to do this at least once every three years. *Courtesy of Social Security Administration*

---

13. Contact the local Department of Employment Security for information about your state's unemployment and workers' compensation benefits. Share the information with students.

* *WWYD Feature A.* Even though some people probably do lie about workers' compensation injuries, it is unethical (and perhaps illegal) to do so.

ELIGIBILITY AND FINANCING

In the previous section, you learned about four federally administered social security programs and two state administered ones (review Figure 27-3). This section explains how the federal program is financed, as well as how you become eligible for federal social security benefits. Eligibility and financing for state programs varies widely among states.

Who is Eligible

To be eligible for social security benefits, you must earn a certain amount of *work credit* in jobs covered by social security. Work credit is measured in *quarters of coverage*. A three-month period equals one quarter of coverage. In 1988, you would have received a quarter of coverage for each $474 of covered annual earnings. The amount of earnings needed for a quarter of coverage increases periodically. You are limited to four quarters of coverage per year no matter how much money you make.

There are two different eligibility statuses—fully insured and currently insured. A *fully insured* worker has earned forty quarters of coverage. Fully insured workers are eligible to receive complete retirement, survivors, disability, and health benefits. A *currently insured* worker has earned at least six quarters of credit during the thirteen quarters before death or retirement. Such a worker is only eligible for limited survivors benefits.

FIGURE 27-9 Visit your nearest Social Security office. You may be surprised at the amount of useful information they have available. *Photo by Paul E. Meyers*

14. You may wish to conduct Activity 1 at this time.
15. You may wish to assign Activity 2 at this time.

FIGURE 27-10 Don't wait until you get old to begin thinking about retirement. *Photo by Paul E. Meyers*

Financing the Program

You and your employer share equally the cost of financing federal social security. This tax is called the *Federal Insurance Contributions Act (FICA)* tax. Your employer deducts your share of FICA tax from your paycheck. Your employer then adds an equal contribution and sends the Treasury Department the total amount monthly or quarterly. That department then distributes the money among the various funds that will pay benefits.

Up to a certain limit, taxes are figured on your gross annual wages. The salary limit is called the *wage base*. In 1937, when the first FICA taxes were collected, both the worker and employer paid 1 percent tax on the first $3,000 (wage base) of earnings. In 1990, the tax rate was 7.65 percent on the first $54,000 of earnings. Earnings in excess of the wage base are not subject to FICA tax.

INDIVIDUAL RETIREMENT ACCOUNTS

The social security retirement program is designed to provide a minimum standard of living for retired workers. Social security was never designed to meet *all* of a retired person's financial needs. To live reasonably well in retirement, it will be necessary for you to supplement social security retirement income with other sources. These might include savings, investments, or private pension coverage.

About 90 percent of all employed workers are covered by social security. Approximately half of these are also covered by a private pension plan. To

16. You may wish to conduct Activity 3 at this time. Also work several additional problems.

17. Refer to Figure 27-4 for a listing of average monthly benefits.

372 ■ SECTION 5 Managing Your Money

encourage more people to establish private pension programs, Congress passed legislation in 1981 making almost every working person eligible for an *Individual Retirement Account (IRA)*.

Anyone who earns income from working and is under age 70½ can open an *IRA*. You are eligible to put up to $2,000 a year into an IRA. When your spouse also works, you can each invest up to $2,000 per year. If your spouse doesn't work outside the home, you can still both open an account. However, in this case, you are limited to a combined total of $2,250. This amount can be split in any combination, but no more than $2,000 can be in either account.

Tax Benefits

An IRA has *two* big tax benefits. First, people can deduct IRA contributions from their income tax. This depends, however, on whether you have a retirement plan at work and on how much you earn. A person who is not covered by a retirement plan at work is able to put up to $2,000 a year into an IRA and deduct the full amount. People who have retirement plans at work are able to get the full deduction only if their incomes are below a certain level.

Yearly Income	If You or Your Spouse are Covered by a Retirement Plan	If You or Your Spouse are not Covered by a Retirement Plan
Married $40,000 & under / Single $25,000 & under	Full Deduction	Full Deduction
Married $40,000–$50,000 / Single $25,000–$35,000	Partial Deduction	Full Deduction
Married $50,000 & above / Single $35,000 & above	No Deduction	Full Deduction

FIGURE 27-11 Based on your adjusted gross yearly income, this chart will help you determine if you can deduct your IRA contribution.

Let's say that a married couple had taxable income in 1987 of $35,000. By placing $2,000 into an IRA, they would only pay taxes on $33,000. This would result in a tax savings of $560. Its costs this couple, in effect, $1,440 to make a $2,000 investment. For people earning higher incomes (up to the $40,000 limit), the savings are even greater.

18. Refer to Figure 27-11 for a summary of IRA tax benefits. The amount of the "partial deduction" is determined by completing a worksheet in the 1040 tax instruction booklet.

The second tax benefit of an IRA is that interest and other earnings on the IRA investment are not taxed until they are withdrawn. This allows an investment to compound at a much greater rate than if taxes were deducted. Examples of how an IRA investment can multiply are shown in Figure 27-12. You can see that it is possible for a young person like you to accumulate a one million dollar nest egg by age 65. Remember that inflation will probably increase over the years, too.

Even if you can't put $2,000 into an IRA, try to put in what you can afford. The key to getting the most from an IRA is to start early, put in as much as you can, and make a contribution each and every year.

What Would You Do?

You work for a large company that employs hundreds of workers. Every several months, the personnel department conducts "brown-bag" lunches for interested employees on such topics as investing, tax planning, and the like. An announcement is included in your pay envelope indicating that a program on IRAs will be offered next week. You are supposed to mark and return the form if you are interested. You don't think you will go. You still have about forty years before retirement. What would you do?

Opening an IRA

Companies that offer IRAs include banks, savings and loan associations, insurance companies, stockbrokers, credit unions, and mutual funds. To open an account, you only have to complete a simple application form and make an initial deposit. In most cases, you can make contributions to the account anytime during the year and in any amount.

The type of investment you select is very flexible. You can use your contributions to purchase certificates of deposit, U.S. treasury securities, bonds, stocks, mutual funds, and many other types of investments. You may even purchase several different types of investments and build up a diversified account. Also, you are allowed to switch from one investment to the other as you wish.

19. You may wish to conduct Activity 4 at this time.
20. *Everyone* with an IRA is exempt from paying taxes on interest and other earnings.

DISCLOSURE OF FINANCIAL INFORMATION

Because the growth in value of your IRA funds will depend on your investment decisions, we can not make any guarantee or projection of growth in the value of your IRA. However, to show you how your IRA contributions can grow if they are invested in the fixed rate time deposits we are currently offering, we are including the three tables below. These tables show you the value of your IRA at the end of various years, based on your age when you open the IRA and on the following circumstances:

(a) *Contributions* of $1,000 annually (Tables A and C) and of $1,000 in a one-time rollover (Tables B and C), each made on the first day of the year.
(b) *Investment* in a 3-year, fixed rate time deposit, which will be renewed at maturity for the same term and interest rate.
(c) *Annual interest rate* of 6%, yielding 6.18% on daily compounding using a 365/365 factor.
(d) *Withdrawals* are made at the end of each of the first five years and at the end of the years in which ages 60, 65, and 70 would be attained.
(e) *No annual fees* or any other administrative fees are reflected in these tables. We will advise you in writing if we decide to impose such fees.

(f) *A penalty* for withdrawals before maturity may be imposed. The tables show the value of your IRA computed with and without a penalty for premature withdrawal. The "With Penalty" tables assume the penalty is equal to 91 days of interest on the deposit withdrawn at a rate of 6% per year compounded daily based on a 365-day year. Our policies governing penalties may change from time to time, and the terms of a time deposit agreement will govern the imposition of penalties for premature withdrawal. Although currently we do not impose premature withdrawal penalties for distributions due to death or disability, the terms of the time deposit will govern the imposition of premature withdrawal penalties, if any, for distributions due to other reasons.
(g) *Any commissions*, fees or charges imposed by a broker in connection with an investment of your IRA Trust Account are not included in the tables.

Of course, interest rates will probably change from time to time. There is no guarantee that the rate used in the tables will be available at maturity of your deposit. The terms of all time deposits require that payment of the deposit be made only at maturity. The growth in value of the portion of your IRA funds invested in variable rate time deposits or in non-deposit types of investments can be neither guaranteed nor projected.

TABLE A — $1,000 ANNUAL CONTRIBUTION

WITHOUT PENALTY					WITH PENALTY				
YEAR 1	YEAR 2	YEAR 3	YEAR 4	YEAR 5	YEAR 1	YEAR 2	YEAR 3	YEAR 4	YEAR 5
1,062	2,189	3,387	4,658	6,008	1,047	2,159	3,356	4,610	5,941

TABLE B — ONE TIME $1,000 ROLLOVER CONTRIBUTION

WITHOUT PENALTY					WITH PENALTY				
YEAR 1	YEAR 2	YEAR 3	YEAR 4	YEAR 5	YEAR 1	YEAR 2	YEAR 3	YEAR 4	YEAR 5
1,062	1,127	1,197	1,271	1,350	1,047	1,112	1,197	1,253	1,332

TABLE C

AGE OPEN IRA	ANNUAL $1,000 CONTRIBUTION						ONE TIME $1,000 CONTRIBUTION						AGE OPEN IRA
	WITHOUT PENALTY			WITH PENALTY			WITHOUT PENALTY			WITH PENALTY			
	AGE 60	AGE 65	AGE 70	AGE 60	AGE 65	AGE 70	AGE 60	AGE 65	AGE 70	AGE 60	AGE 65	AGE 70	
18	209,414	288,680	395,675	207,480	286,110	391,926	13,194	17,810	24,040	13,007	17,810	23,719	18
19	196,220	270,870	371,634	194,473	268,300	368,207	12,426	16,773	22,641	12,426	16,549	22,319	19
20	183,793	254,097	348,994	182,047	251,752	345,888	11,702	15,796	21,322	11,546	15,572	21,322	20
21	172,091	238,300	327,672	170,501	236,180	324,566	11,021	14,876	20,081	10,865	14,876	19,812	21
22	161,070	223,424	307,591	159,636	221,303	304,753	10,379	14,010	18,911	10,379	13,823	18,643	22
23	150,691	209,414	288,680	149,257	207,480	286,110	9,775	13,194	17,810	9,644	13,007	17,810	23
24	140,916	196,220	270,870	139,613	194,473	268,300	9,206	12,426	16,773	9,075	12,426	16,549	24
25	131,710	183,793	254,097	130,538	182,047	251,752	8,670	11,702	15,796	8,670	11,546	15,572	25
26	123,041	172,091	238,300	121,868	170,501	236,180	8,165	11,021	14,876	8,056	10,865	14,876	26
27	114,876	161,070	223,424	113,813	159,636	221,303	7,689	10,379	14,010	7,580	10,379	13,823	27
28	107,187	150,691	209,414	106,233	149,257	207,480	7,242	9,775	13,194	7,242	9,644	13,007	28
29	99,945	140,916	196,220	98,991	139,613	194,473	6,820	9,206	12,426	6,729	9,075	12,426	29
30	93,125	131,710	183,793	92,262	130,538	182,047	6,423	8,670	11,702	6,332	8,670	11,546	30
31	86,702	123,041	172,091	85,931	121,868	170,501	6,049	8,165	11,021	6,049	8,056	10,865	31
32	80,654	114,876	161,070	79,882	113,813	159,636	5,697	7,689	10,379	5,620	7,580	10,379	32
33	74,957	107,187	150,691	74,262	106,233	149,257	5,365	7,242	9,775	5,289	7,242	9,644	33
34	69,592	99,945	140,916	68,973	98,991	139,613	5,052	6,820	9,206	5,052	6,729	9,075	34
35	64,540	93,125	131,710	63,921	92,262	130,538	4,758	6,423	8,670	4,695	6,332	8,670	35
36	59,782	86,702	123,041	59,226	85,931	121,868	4,481	6,049	8,165	4,418	6,049	8,056	36
37	55,301	80,654	114,876	54,808	79,882	113,813	4,220	5,697	7,689	4,220	5,620	7,580	37
38	51,080	74,957	107,187	50,588	74,262	106,233	3,974	5,365	7,242	3,921	5,289	7,242	38
39	47,106	69,592	99,945	46,667	68,973	98,991	3,743	5,052	6,820	3,690	5,052	6,729	39
40	43,363	64,540	93,125	42,977	63,921	92,262	3,525	4,758	6,423	3,525	4,695	6,332	40
41	39,838	59,782	86,702	39,452	59,226	85,931	3,320	4,481	6,049	3,275	4,418	6,049	41
42	36,518	55,301	80,654	36,176	54,808	79,882	3,126	4,220	5,697	3,082	4,220	5,620	42
43	33,392	51,080	74,957	33,094	50,588	74,262	2,944	3,974	5,365	2,944	3,921	5,289	43
44	30,447	47,106	69,592	30,150	46,667	68,973	2,773	3,743	5,052	2,736	3,690	5,052	44
45	27,674	43,363	64,540	27,414	42,977	63,921	2,611	3,525	4,758	2,574	3,525	4,695	45
46	25,063	39,838	59,782	24,840	39,452	59,226	2,459	3,320	4,481	2,459	3,275	4,418	46
47	22,603	36,518	55,301	22,380	36,176	54,808	2,316	3,126	4,220	2,285	3,082	4,220	47
48	20,287	33,392	51,080	20,095	33,094	50,588	2,181	2,944	3,974	2,150	2,944	3,921	48
49	18,106	30,447	47,106	17,945	30,150	46,667	2,054	2,773	3,743	2,054	2,736	3,690	49
50	16,051	27,674	43,363	15,890	27,414	42,977	1,935	2,611	3,525	1,909	2,574	3,525	50
51	14,117	25,063	39,838	13,981	24,840	39,452	1,822	2,459	3,320	1,796	2,459	3,275	51
52	12,295	22,603	36,518	12,185	22,380	36,176	1,716	2,316	3,126	1,716	2,285	3,082	52
53	10,579	20,287	33,392	10,469	20,095	33,094	1,616	2,181	2,944	1,594	2,150	2,944	53
54	8,963	18,106	30,447	8,875	17,945	30,150	1,522	2,054	2,773	1,500	2,054	2,736	54
55	7,441	16,051	27,674	7,375	15,890	27,414	1,433	1,935	2,611	1,433	1,909	2,574	55
56	6,008	14,117	25,063	5,941	13,981	24,840	1,350	1,822	2,459	1,332	1,796	2,459	56
57	4,658	12,295	22,603	4,610	12,185	22,380	1,271	1,716	2,316	1,253	1,716	2,285	57
58	3,387	10,579	20,287	3,356	10,469	20,095	1,197	1,616	2,181	1,197	1,594	2,150	58
59	2,189	8,963	18,106	2,159	8,875	17,945	1,127	1,522	2,054	1,112	1,500	2,054	59
60	1,062	7,441	16,051	1,047	7,375	15,890	1,062	1,433	1,935	1,047	1,433	1,909	60
61	—	6,008	14,117	—	5,941	13,981	—	1,350	1,822	—	1,332	1,796	61
62	—	4,658	12,295	—	4,610	12,185	—	1,271	1,716	—	1,253	1,716	62
63	—	3,387	10,579	—	3,356	10,469	—	1,197	1,616	—	1,197	1,594	63
64	—	2,189	8,963	—	2,159	8,875	—	1,127	1,522	—	1,112	1,500	64
65	—	1,062	7,441	—	1,047	7,375	—	1,062	1,433	—	1,047	1,433	65
66	—	—	6,008	—	—	5,941	—	—	1,350	—	—	1,332	66
67	—	—	4,658	—	—	4,610	—	—	1,271	—	—	1,253	67
68	—	—	3,387	—	—	3,356	—	—	1,197	—	—	1,197	68
69	—	—	2,189	—	—	2,159	—	—	1,127	—	—	1,112	69
70	—	—	1,062	—	—	1,047	—	—	1,062	—	—	1,047	70

FIGURE 27-12 Here is what an IRA could earn. *Reprinted with permission. Copyright 1989 Banking Spectrum Inc. New York, NY*

21. The figures shown in Figure 27-12 are a good illustration of the power of compound interest discussed in Chapter 24.
22. You may wish to conduct Activity 5 at this time.

WWYD Feature B. Encourage students to participate in such activities. By starting young, they could amass sizable retirement savings.

374 ■ SECTION 5 Managing Your Money

APPLICANT: If applying by mail, type or print the information on the front portion of the Application. **KEEP THE IRA DISCLOSURE STATEMENT AND TRUST AGREEMENT** for your files. **RETURN TO US ALL COPIES** of the Application **WITH YOUR CHECK** for the contribution.

I106S

Application and Adoption Agreement
For Your Self-Directed Individual Retirement Account

SDIRA
Self-Directed Individual Retirement Account
(Terms and conditions on the reverse side.)

1. YOUR NAME AND ADDRESS (Print or Type)

First Name | Middle Name/Initial | Last Name
Street
City | State | Zip
Social Security No. | Date of Birth | Telephone No.
Employer's Name | Address | Business Telephone No.

2. TYPE OF ACCOUNT
☐ Regular ☐ Spousal ☐ Rollover ☐ SEP ☐ Transfer: _____
(Name and Address of previous Trustee/Custodian)

3. CONTRIBUTION AND INVESTMENT DIRECTIONS

Enclosed is a check for $_____ for deposit to my IRA, as a contribution for Tax Year 19___. (If I fail to enter a Tax Year, the Trustee will treat it as a contribution for the current year.)

This IRA account is a self-directed account, and I hereby direct that this contribution be invested as indicated below. In addition, from time to time I may direct the Trustee to invest and reinvest all or any part of the funds in the Account in other deposit accounts or in other permitted investments.

☐ _____ Month Time Deposit Account   ☐ Other Investment _____ (specify)

Subject to the Trustee's approval, I appoint _____ to act as the broker for purposes of executing my investment directions in securities and property under Article 11.3 of the Trust Agreement. If I do not appoint a broker, the Trustee may appoint a broker for me. In accordance with the Trust Agreement, the Trustee shall be authorized to execute my investment directions directly or through a broker, whether appointed by me or by the Trustee.

Funds invested pursuant to this agreement are not insured by the Federal Savings and Loan Insurance Corporation ("FSLIC") or the Federal _____ is an institution the accounts of which are covered by such insurance. _____ y the FSLIC or the FDIC, subject to their rules and regulations.

Contingent Beneficiary
If my Primary Beneficiary dies before me, I name as Contingent Beneficiary:

(Name & Relationship) | (% of Account)
(Social Security Number) | (Date of Birth)
(Address)

provided herein and in the IRA Trust Agreement. To name additional primary or

___ Individual Retirement Account Trust Agreement. I certify that I am eligible to ___ the Individual Retirement Account Trust Agreement, agreeing to its terms and ___ cial institution named above as Trustee of my IRA. My IRA shall become effective ___ stitution named above, as Trustee. By signing this Application and Adoption ___ er shown above is my correct taxpayer identification number.

___ king this IRA rollover within 60 days of my receipt of the funds contributed. I also ___ ied plan, it is eligible for rollover treatment and does not include any Voluntary ___ er as irrevocable, and (b) if this rollover is of a distribution from another IRA, I did ___ he 12 months prior to receipt of this distribution.

(Your Signature) | (Date)

6. TRUSTEE ACCEPTANCE (Internal Use Only)
We have received your executed IRA Application and Adoption Agreement and your contribution. We hereby accept the IRA and our designation as Trustee.

(Authorized Signature) | (Date) | (Plan Number)

APP/FRONT 12/88   **Mail Applications: Return All Copies of Application with Check to Us.**   © BANKING SPECTRUM INC

TRUSTEE COPY

FIGURE 27-13 Completing a form like this is all that is usually required to open an IRA. *Reprinted with permission.* Copyright 1989 Banking Spectrum Inc. New York, NY. Photo by Paul E. Meyers

CHAPTER REVIEW

Chapter in Brief

- Government programs that help people meet social and economic needs are called social security. One form of social security is known as public assistance (or welfare). General taxes finance public assistance. The second form of social security is social insurance. It is financed by taxes on earnings paid by workers and employers.
- The four social insurance programs (most people call them social security) administered by the federal government are: retirement payments, survivors payments, disability payments, and Medicare. The two types of state-administered social insurance programs are unemployment benefits and workers' compensation.
- To be eligible for federal social security benefits, you must earn a certain amount of work credit in jobs covered by social security. Work credit is measured in quarters of coverage. A fully insured worker has earned forty quarters of coverage. He or she is eligible to receive complete benefits. A currently insured worker has earned at least six quarters of credit during the thirteen quarters before death or retirement. Such a worker is only eligible for limited survivors benefits.
- The four federal social security programs are financed by payroll taxes on earnings. In 1990, the tax rate was 7.65 percent on a wage base of $54,000. Your employer contributes an amount equal to what you pay. State-administered employment security programs are financed through taxes paid by employers only.
- Anyone who earns income from working and is under age 70½ can open an Individual Retirement Account (IRA). You are eligible to put up to $2,000 a year into an IRA. An IRA can provide two big tax benefits. First, IRA contributions can be deducted from income taxes. (Restrictions apply to people earning more than a certain amount.) Second, interest and other earnings in an IRA are not taxed until they are withdrawn. An IRA started at an early age can compound to a large amount of money prior to retirement.

Words to Know

benefits financial help in time of sickness, old age, disability, or the like.

FICA an acronym for Federal Insurance Contributions Act; the federal law requiring employers to deduct an amount from workers' paychecks for Social Security.

IRA an acronym for Individual Retirement Account; voluntary private pension plans that allow employed individuals to save up to $2,000 annually toward retirement and receive certain tax benefits.

lump-sum payment a one-time payment of money to the surviving spouse or child of a deceased person covered by Social Security.

pension a regular payment of money to a retired person.

quarters of coverage a three-month period during which a certain amount of income is earned; used to determine eligibility for Social Security. *See* work credit.

social security government programs that help people meet social and economic needs; commonly used to refer to the federal system of retirement pensions, survivors payments, and hospital insurance for the elderly.

wage base the amount of gross salary or wages subject to Social Security tax.

work credit a guideline used to determine eligibility for Social Security benefits; measured in quarters of coverage.

Questions to Answer

1. There are two forms of social security. Name them.
2. List and briefly describe the six major types of social insurance programs.
3. How long must you be disabled in order to receive social security disability payments?
4. Name the two types of Medicare insurance. Which type is **not** automatically provided to eligible workers?
5. How many quarters of coverage are required to be a fully insured worker? A currently insured worker?
6. How is federal social security financed? How is state employment security financed?
7. What percentage of a worker's income is withheld for FICA tax in 1990? What is the wage base?
8. How much can a single worker contribute annually to an IRA? A married couple who both work? A married couple in which only one works?
9. What are the two tax benefits of having an IRA?
10. IRA contributions are tax deferred, not tax free. Explain what this means.

Activities to Do

1. Have you ever worked at a job in which FICA tax was withheld from your paycheck? If so, prepare a list of all such jobs and the length of time you were employed in each. Then, figure out how much work credit (quarters of coverage) you have accumulated to date. Compare your results with those of your classmates.
2. Go to your local social security office and pick up several "Request for Statement of Earnings" forms. This is the form shown in Figure 27-9. Complete and mail one of the forms. If you haven't worked at a job covered by social security, fill out copies of the form for one of your family members.
3. In 1990, Shirley Jefferson earned $26,700. The FICA tax rate was 7.65 percent. How much money was withheld for social security from Ms. Jefferson's income in 1990? What was the total amount paid by Ms. Jefferson **and** her employer in 1990?
4. Assume that three single workers had taxable incomes of $17,000, $21,000, and $25,000 respectively. Each is planning to make a $2,000 contribution to an IRA. Using a current federal tax table, figure out how much tax each person will save. Now, figure out how much each $2,000 contribution "actually" costs each person.
5. Invite a banker or stockbroker to class to discuss IRAs. Ask him or her to explain the various kinds of investments that can be purchased with an IRA contribution.

---

1. (a) Public assistance [welfare]. (b) Social insurance.
2. (a) *Retirement payments*—provides monthly pensions to workers upon retirement. (b) *Survivors payments*—provides benefits to dependents of a deceased worker. (c) *Disability payments*—provides benefits to a worker and dependents if employee is disabled for twelve months or longer. (d) *Medicare*—hospital insurance and optional medical insurance for retired or disabled workers. (e) *Unemployment benefits*—weekly cash payments to workers who have lost their jobs. (f) *Workers' compensation*—benefits to workers and dependents who are injured or become ill on the job.
3. The disability must last or be expected to last twelve months.
4. *Hospital insurance* and *supplementary medical insurance.* The medical coverage is optional.
5. *Fully insured*—forty; *currently insured*—six quarters during the thirteen quarters before death or retirement.
6. (a) Federal social security is paid for by payroll withholding taxes on the workers' earnings. The worker and the employer pay equal amounts. (b) State employment security programs are paid by the employer only.
7. 7.65 percent; $54,000.
8. (a) *Single worker*—$2,000. (b) *Married couple/both working*—$4,000. (c) *Married couple/one working*—$2,250.
9. (a) IRA contributions can be deducted from income tax [subject to certain restrictions]. (b) Interest and other IRA earnings are not taxed until they are withdrawn.
10. *Tax deferred* means that taxes do not have to be paid on the income until it is withdrawn from the IRA. *Tax free* means that no taxes are assessed at any time.

23. This can also be done by phone.
24. $2,042.55 was withheld; total was $4,085.10.
25. Let's assume that a taxable income of $17,000 owes $2,554 in tax; a taxable income of $15,000 owes $2,254. By making a $2,000 IRA deduction, $300 in taxes would be saved. In effect, the IRA contribution "costs" $1,700. Use a current tax table and figure the three problems in a like manner.

Topics to Discuss

1. Assuming they have no house or rent payment to make, about how much monthly income do you think a retired couple would need to live comfortably?
2. Why is inflation such a major concern for most retired people?
3. Some people would like to make federal social security optional. In other words, people could take the 7 percent or so withheld for FICA and invest it in their own retirement programs. Discuss the positive and negative aspects of such a change.

26. Living "comfortably" has different meanings for different individuals. The value of this is to cause students to think about how much is needed to live as a retired couple.
27. Because a higher cost of living eats into relatively fixed incomes.
28. A positive aspect is that an individual might be able to build through wise investments a larger retirement income than provided by social security. A negative aspect is that some people couldn't or wouldn't save on their own. Students should be able to provide additional positive and negative reasons.

High Five

FEELING GOOD ABOUT THE FUTURE

Jason Bosley became involved in cooperative education through a program in Schenectady, New York entitled *Introduction to Occupations*. He works as a bottle return clerk at Price Chopper supermarket. Jason remembers being "scared to go for the job interview." His prior experiences in getting along with people were often unpleasant.

Jason was raised in a single parent family. He admits to not getting along with his mother. He often skipped school and used to hang out with the "wrong people." Having a lot of free time on his hands increased the opportunity for involvement with alcohol and drugs.

Because of these circumstances, Jason was sent to a half-way home for "persons in need of support." He got into a fight at the home, however, and was arrested. He stayed in jail for about a week. "This was the low point in my life," he recalls.

Jason enrolled in the *Introduction to Occupations* program and soon began to feel better about himself. He started to treat others differently. The relationship with his mother improved. He helped her more with things around the house. He began to understand that "not everything was her fault." His attendance at school improved.

Having a job has made Jason more responsible. He likes earning money and being able to buy his own clothes. He also uses the added income to buy fishing tackle, Nintendo games, and go to the movies. Jason now looks to the future instead of dwelling on past mistakes.

Section Six

Independent Living

Chapter 28 The Legal System
Chapter 29 Where to Live
Chapter 30 Healthful Living
Chapter 31 Responsible Citizenship
Chapter 32 Education Beyond High School

The nature of law and the two main types of law, civil and public, are dealt with in Chapter 28. The general process by which laws are enforced and how a court works are summarized. Guidelines for choosing and working with a lawyer are also provided.

In Chapter 29, different housing alternatives are examined. You will learn how to locate and evaluate an apartment. Understanding a lease and landlord-tenant relationships are also covered.

Healthful living is related to your productivity and success in work and life. There are three aspects of healthful living: nutrition and diet, controlling stress, and physical fitness. These are explained in Chapter 30.

The responsibilities of citizenship and the importance of voting are discussed in Chapter 31. Registering to vote and casting a ballot are summarized. Distinguishing between rumor, opinion, prejudice, allegation, bias, propaganda, and fact when choosing a candidate or a position on an issue is discussed.

Will your education end upon graduation from high school? Additional education and training will be one of the best investments you can make in your future. Chapter 32 explains the six most common types of education and training: on-the-job training, apprenticeship, vocational and technical schools, community and junior colleges, colleges and universities, and military training. Sources of educational information and financial aid are included.

CHAPTER TWENTY-EIGHT

1. Ask students if they can name additional everyday matters that are concerned with law (nine are listed on pages 385-386).

The Legal System

OUTLINE
The Nature of Law
The Court System
Legal Services
Chapter Review

OBJECTIVES
After reading this chapter, you should be able to:
- Explain the difference between civil and public law.
- Describe the general process by which laws are enforced.
- Summarize how a court works.
- Identify situations that may require legal advice.
- Explain how to go about choosing a lawyer.
- Name the three types of legal fees.

FIGURE 28-1 No one is above the law. President Nixon resigned from office in 1974 rather than face trial for impeachment charges.

Hopefully, you will never become involved with the legal system because of law-breaking. Even if you never break the law, though, you might sometime be accused of a crime that you didn't commit. Or you may become an innocent victim of crime.

Not all law deals with crime. For example, Terry and Susan adopted a baby. To finalize the adoption, they had to hire a lawyer and appear before a judge in a law court.

1 Law, then, is concerned with many everyday matters, too. Understanding laws and the court system is an important part of informed citizenship. It is also necessary to know how to find legal help. It is good to learn this *before* needing such services.

THE NATURE OF LAW

Law is the body of enforced rules by which people live together. If all people did as they pleased, society could not function. For example, what would happen if everyone drove an auto as fast as they wanted? Or an employer decided to ignore the safety rules? The law defines and makes clear the relationships among individuals and between individuals and society. Law tries to give as much freedom to each person as possible, while protecting the freedom of others. Current laws are developed from the long-established customs (unwritten rules) of a people.

2. Even in primitive societies, people develop rules that govern social behavior.

380

F·E·A·T·U·R·E

Common Law

The system of law used in the United States is called *common law*. (Except in Louisiana where the Code Napoleon is followed.) It originated in England as a way of settling disputes. The law at first was based on customs. But in the twelfth century, the king's courts began to take over settling disputes from the local customary courts.

The decisions of the king's justices were supposed to be based on customs. On occasion, there were no customs. The courts then had to reach a decision based upon logic and reason. As a result, a body of common law grew up from the judges' decisions.

The early colonists who settled America brought with them the practices of common law. After the American Revolution, the tradition of English common law continued. Over the years, American judges gradually changed the common law to make it more suitable for our society.

As new conditions arose, common law often did not apply. A new source for law emerged. This type of law is called statute law, or legislation. Statute law is that type of law made by Congress and state legislatures. In present society, legislation and judge-made law are equally important.

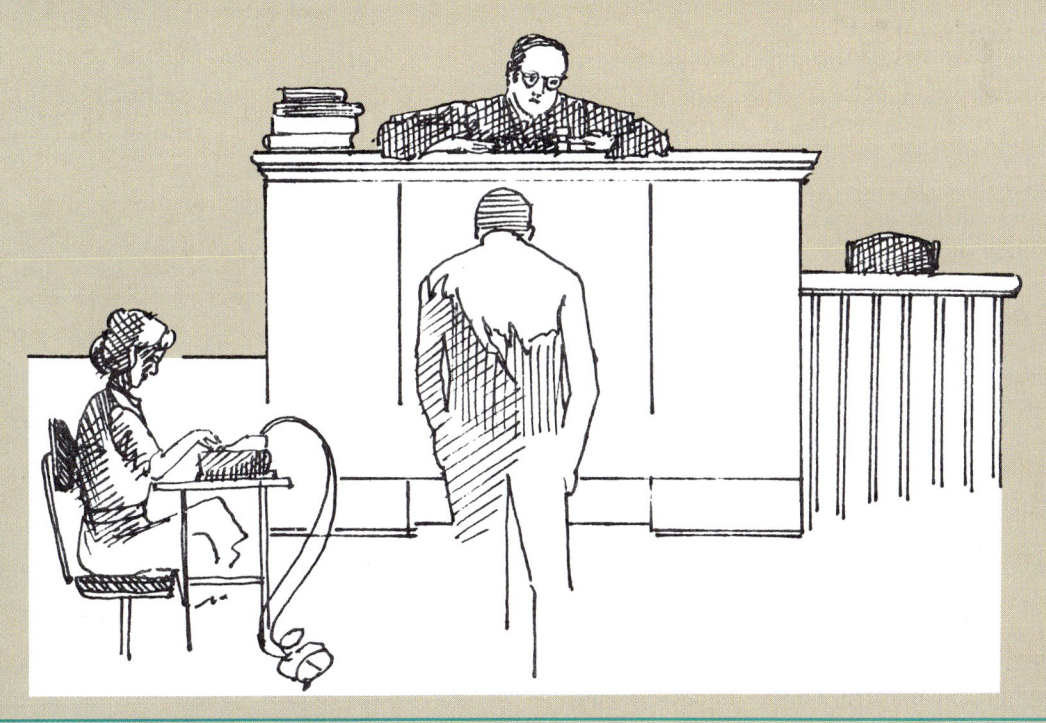

FIGURE 28-FEATURE Common law is judge-made law.

*Common Law. This is intended to be a brief and interesting history of the origin of law. Make sure students understand the difference between *common law* (judge-made) and *statute law* (legislation).

382 ■ SECTION 6 Independent Living

4. The major types of public law include: administrative, constitutional, criminal, and international law. See an encyclopedia for more information.

FIGURE 28-2 Drivers who get too many speeding tickets lose their right to drive. *Courtesy of Police Department, Town of Colonie, NY*

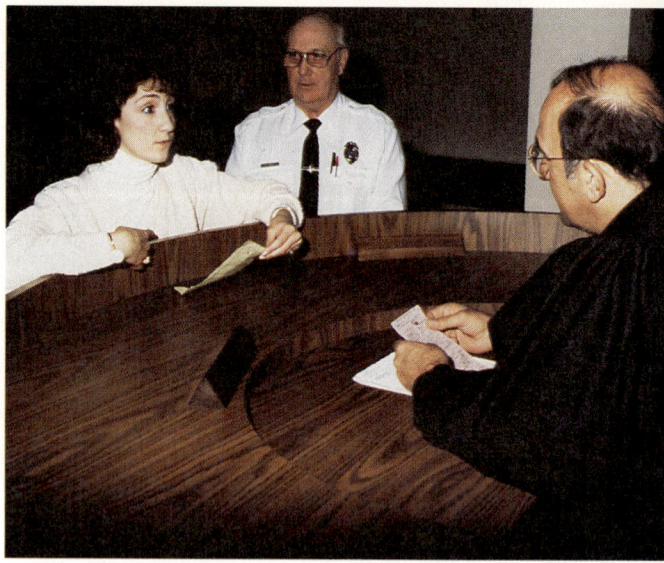

FIGURE 28-3 This motorist is challenging her speeding ticket. She lost, but the person before her won. *Courtesy of Police Department, Town of Colonie, NY*

Branches of the Law

The two main types of law are civil and public.

3   *Civil Law.* Sometimes called private law, civil law determines a person's legal rights and obligations in activities that involve other people. Examples include credit purchases, renting an apartment, and signing a job contract. Judges and lawyers spend most of their time on civil law matters. Most civil law cases are settled out of court. Even so, more than a million lawsuits are tried yearly in U.S. courts.

4   *Public Law.* The purpose of public law is to define citizens' rights and responsibilities under local, state, federal, and international laws. Criminal law is the most familiar kind of public law. Public law also deals with different divisions of government and their powers. An example of public law is the requirement that all cars have seat belts. Workers' wages and hours and public safety also come under public law.

Law Enforcement

Most of us obey laws. But what about people who don't? The police may arrest anyone they see violating the law. They may also arrest someone they reasonably believe has committed a crime. In some cases, a court order called a *warrant* is required before a police officer can make an arrest.

3. The major types of civil law include: contract and commercial, corporation, family, inheritance, property, and tort law. See an encyclopedia for more information.

FIGURE 28-4 We all have to pay for shoplifting.

FIGURE 28-5 Serving on a jury is an important civic duty.

After the suspect has been arrested, a charge is entered in the arrest book. The criminal evidence is then turned over to a government attorney or prosecutor. An *arraignment* (hearing) is then held before a judge. During the arraignment, charges are brought against the arrested person. This is called an *indictment*. The person being held can answer the charges. If the individual pleads guilty, the judge gives a sentence or sets a future date for sentencing.

If the accused pleads not guilty, a trial to determine guilt must be held. Rather than remain in jail until the trial, an individual is usually released on *bail*. This is a certain sum of money paid to the court to guarantee that the person will show up for trial. For certain serious crimes, someone may be held without bail. A person without bail money must remain in jail until the trial. If he or she can't afford an attorney, the judge provides one.

The purpose of a trial is to decide the case. Attorneys for both sides present their evidence. A decision of guilty or not guilty is then made. If the defendant is found guilty, the judge imposes a sentence.

Criminal laws generally specify the minimum and maximum prison terms for which a criminal can be sentenced. Not everyone goes to jail, however. In certain cases, the judge may decide to release a person on *probation* instead. In such instances, the person must report regularly to a parole officer. For some crimes, the judge may impose a fine as part of the sentencing.

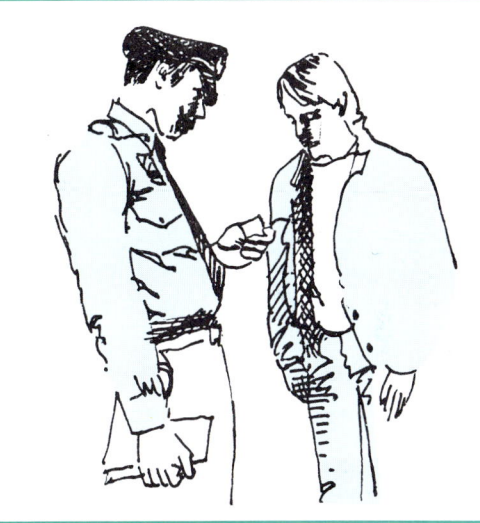

FIGURE 28-6 How might one's future job prospects be influenced by a criminal record?

FIGURE 28-7 One purpose of a jail term is to show potential lawbreakers what could happen to them.

5. For some types of crime, a *grand jury* receives the criminal evidence. Based on study of the evidence, the grand jury decides whether the accused should be put on trial.

6. The attorney that presents that state's case is called the *prosecuting attorney*. The accused person's attorney is the *defense attorney*.

What to Do if Arrested

Any law enforcement person, such as a police officer, sheriff, state trooper, or game warden can make an arrest. What if a law enforcement officer wants to arrest or search you? Don't resist. Your guilt or innocence can be determined later. If the arrest is legal and you resist, you may be guilty of the crime of resisting arrest. If the arrest is illegal, you can bring an action for false arrest against the arresting officer.

Even if you aren't arrested, an officer may stop you if he or she has reason to believe that you have committed or are about to commit a crime. The officer may ask your name and address and an explanation for your actions. You may be searched for weapons if the officer suspects you might attack.

What Would You Do?

You go to answer the door. You open it and are surprised to find a police officer. It seems that a car like yours was seen last night leaving the scene of a gas station holdup. The officer wants you to come to the station to answer some questions. What would you do?

WWYD Feature A. The person should cooperate and do as the officer asks.

FIGURE 28-8 A typical courtroom setting *Reprinted by permission of the Times Union, Albany, NY*

7. The law also permits a private citizen to detain, or place under arrest (i.e., *citizen's arrest*) a person who commits or attempts to commit a criminal offense other than an ordinance violation.

8. The bar association publishes public service materials.
9. A case may start at the general trial level. Or a trial court may retry a case that was heard in a magistrate court.

THE COURT SYSTEM

A court is the branch of government having the power to settle disputes. Figure 28-8 shows the various people present in a typical courtroom.

Courts are an essential part of government. Without courts to interpret them, laws would be meaningless. Although they differ in some ways, all courts decide civil disputes between individuals or other parties, determine the guilt or innocence of accused persons, and impose punishment on the guilty.

Types of Courts

The two types of U.S. court systems are state and federal.

State Courts. Each state has its own court system. The lowest or first courts are the magistrates' courts in cities and the justices of the peace in villages and rural communities. There may also be various special and municipal courts. No jury is used in these local courts.

Above the magistrates' courts are general trial courts. These courts, also known as county or circuit courts, deal with civil and public matters.

Many states have appellate courts, which are between the general trial courts and the state supreme court. Appellate courts hear appeals from the trial courts. The highest appellate court in a state is usually called a supreme court. Several judges (usually five to seven) sit on a state supreme court.

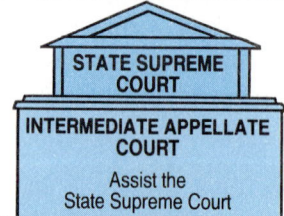

STATE COURT STRUCTURE

- **STATE SUPREME COURT**
- **INTERMEDIATE APPELLATE COURT** — Assist the State Supreme Court
- **GENERAL TRIAL COURTS** (County, District, Circuit, Superior, Common Pleas) Handle felonies and major civil cases.
- **LOCAL COURTS OF LIMITED JURISDICTION**
  - **Municipal Courts:** Handle particular kinds of cases.
  - **Special Courts:** Traffic, Domestic Relations, Juvenile, Small Claims, Probate, Others
  - **Justices of the Peace** (rural)
  - **Police or Magistrate Courts** (urban)

FIGURE 28-9 Although court systems vary from state to state, this pattern is typical.

10. Appellate courts do not actually rehear witnesses. An appellate court tries to determine whether any errors were committed during the lower court trial.

11. The U.S. is divided into eleven judicial circuits. The circuits are further divided into smaller divisions called districts. There are ninety-one of these federal district courts.

13. As noted earlier, most civil cases are settled out of court.

CHAPTER 28 The Legal System ■ 385

The defendant must then submit a written report that tells his or her side of the story. By comparing the two sides, the court can see where the difference of opinion lies. If grounds for a suit are present, the judge sets a trial date.

What Would You Do?

In sorting through the day's mail, you find a postcard addressed to you. It says that you have been chosen for jury duty. You are instructed to appear at the courthouse next Wednesday at 9:00 A.M. for possible jury selection. "I can't go," you think to yourself. "I have to work." What would you do?

FIGURE 28-10 Sandra Day O'Connor is the first woman to be a Justice of the Supreme Court. *Courtesy of The Supreme Court*

Federal Courts. The United States Constitution provides for a federal court system. Federal courts handle cases involving the Constitution, violations of federal laws, and cases in which the U.S. government is a party.

The lowest courts of the federal system are the U.S. district courts. The trial of both civil and public cases begins in the district courts. The manner of arrest, indictment, trial, and appeal is very similar to that of state courts.

Above the trial level are the circuit courts of appeal. These courts operate about the same way as state appellate courts. A court of appeal is made up of three judges.

The highest federal court is the Supreme Court of the United States. This court is made up of nine justices (judges). It is presided over by one of them who is called the Chief Justice of the United States. Most cases the Supreme Court hears are appeals from the circuit courts and appeals from state supreme courts if they present federal questions.

How a Court Works

Disputes may arise between two or more persons over money, personal injury, property, or many other issues. To better understand how a court works, let's outline a typical civil case. One person (the *plaintiff*) files a complaint against the other (the *defendant*) in a court. The court clerk then issues a *summons,* which commands the defendant to appear in court on a certain day.

12. The Supreme Court accepts less than ten percent of the petitions it receives for review. You may wish to assign Activity 1 at this time.

When the trial is held, attorneys for the plaintiff and defendant produce evidence to try and show the truth in the case. Part of the evidence may be supplied by other persons called witnesses. The judge, or the jury if there is one, decides questions of fact and reaches a verdict.

When the case is decided, the judge will make a *judgment* in favor of either the plaintiff or the defendant. ("Guilty" and "not guilty" aren't used in civil cases.) If the case is decided in favor of the plaintiff, the judgment will depend on the nature of the original complaint. One type of judgment is the award of a sum of money to the plaintiff. Another is a solution for the dispute, such as cancellation of a contract. A third type of judgment is for the court to *decree* (order) the defendant to stop doing whatever he or she was doing that harmed the plaintiff.

LEGAL SERVICES

During your lifetime, you will probably face many legal problems. You may be able to resolve some of them yourself. If you can't, you will need an attorney.

Deciding If You Need A Lawyer

Whether or not you need a lawyer depends on your situation. Following are some types of situations that may require legal advice:

1. Being charged with a crime.
2. Buying a house.
3. Starting a business.
4. Suffering accident or injury.

* *WWYD Feature B.* This is one of the responsibilities of citizenship. The person should show the notice to her/his supervisor and report to the courthouse as directed.

386 ■ SECTION 6 Independent Living

5. Buying a faulty consumer product or service.
6. Being discriminated against in employment.
7. Preparing a will.
8. Declaring bankruptcy.
9. Getting a divorce.

A lawyer is not absolutely necessary in all these cases. The more you learn about the law and legal services, the better able you will be to decide when you need a lawyer.

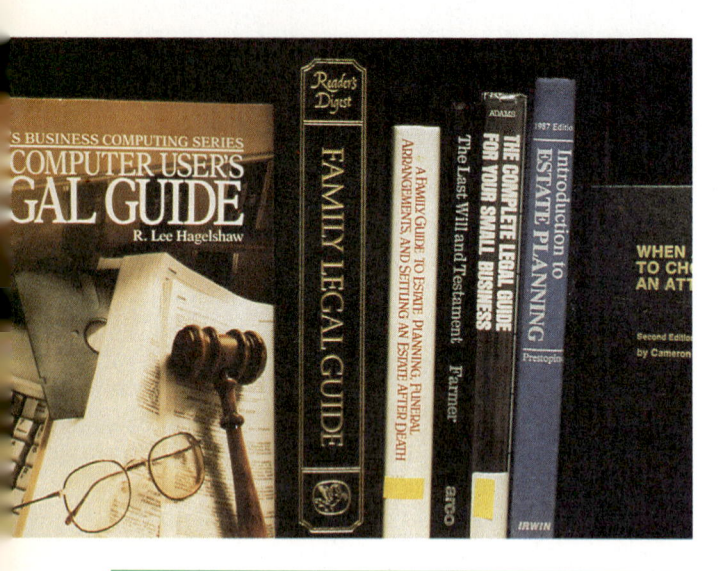

FIGURE 28-11 Many how-to books have been written to help people solve their own legal problems. Know when to seek a lawyer's help, though. *Photo by Paul E. Meyers*

Choosing A Lawyer

Lawyers, like doctors, are in either a general or specialized practice. Most lawyers are general practitioners who handle a variety of legal work. For most situations, a general attorney will be adequate. General lawyers who can't handle a particular problem will usually refer clients to a specialist.

Choosing a lawyer is similar to selecting a doctor, banker, or other professional. Ask enough people and the same name may come up repeatedly. This is a good sign that you are on the right track.

In 1937, the American Bar Association established the Lawyer Referral Service or LRS. Its purpose is to help people obtain legal assistance at moderate costs.

In over 250 U.S. cities, the LRS is administered through the local bar association. You can contact the LRS by looking in your phone book's Yellow Pages under "Lawyer (or Attorney) Referral Service."

14. Previous chapters described sources of assistance for consumer and employment problems. Review as appropriate.
15. Investigate the origin of the term *bar association*.
16. Ask students to be alert to advertising on radio, TV, and in newspapers. Discuss in class the ethics of advertising by attorneys. Recall from Chapter 22 that one of the purposes of

FIGURE 28-12 Most lawyers donate some of their time to helping clients who can't afford to pay. *Photo by Paul E. Meyers*

Another way to choose a lawyer is through advertising. In recent years, lawyers have been able to advertise their services, although few do so. If you read or hear an ad that you like, give the attorney a try. Many attorneys provide a free initial consultation. Before deciding on an attorney, it may be wise to meet with several different ones.

If you can't afford a lawyer, you have several options. In a criminal case, the court will provide a lawyer for you. For civil cases, there are more than 800 free legal services and defender programs in the United States. You can find such agencies by looking up "Legal Aid" or "Legal Assistance" in the phone book. Another source is the *Directory of Legal Aid and Defender Services,* which is available in many libraries.

Legal Fees

The fees lawyers charge vary depending on the type of situation you have. Don't be afraid to ask about fees at your first meeting. You are entitled to know in advance the approximate cost of legal services.

Lawyers may charge a flat fee, an hourly fee, or a contingency fee. A *flat fee* often covers routine services that take about the same amount of time in all instances. Examples might be a real estate closing or an uncontested divorce. An *hourly fee* is a specific amount paid for each hour the lawyer

advertising is to provide information about goods and services for sale.

17. Attorneys are often criticized for the amounts they receive in multimillion dollar settlements. Ask students for their opinions.
18. You may wish to assign Activity 4 at this time.

CHAPTER 28 The Legal System ■ 387

spends on your case. Rates per hour may range from $50 to several hundred dollars.

The *contingency fee* is used for certain kinds of cases, such as personal injury or medical malpractice. It is called a contingency fee because you don't pay unless the case is won. If the attorney does win, you must pay a certain percentage of the amount awarded. A one-third contingency fee is common. For example, if you receive $15,000 in a legal judgment, the attorney will receive $5,000.

Small Claims Courts

There may be times when you don't need a lawyer. Small claims courts, sometimes called people's courts, have been around since 1913. They allow you to sue someone without using an attorney. For example, let's say that you worked two days for Ms. Adams, a local businessperson, and she refuses to pay you. To get your money, you could file a claim in small claims court.

The amount of money that can be recovered in small claims court varies among states. Usually though, the amount is limited to several thousand dollars. You can't sue for lost time or hurt pride and you can't collect damage beyond your loss.

A small claims court is usually part of the general trial court in a county or city. To learn more about the court in your area, call the office of the county or city government.

ON THE JOB ACCIDENTS
CONSTRUCTION ACCIDENTS
JAMES T. RONAN
NO CHARGE FOR CONSULTATION
463-1107
732 MADISON AVE., ALBANY

MOTORCYCLE INJURIES
FREE CONSULTATION
463-1107
GEORGE L. SARACHAN
732 Madison Ave
Albany NY

FIGURE 28-13 Advertising by lawyers is becoming more common. *Courtesy of George L. Sarachan and James T. Ronan*

CHAPTER REVIEW

Chapter in Brief

■ Law is the body of enforced rules by which people live together. The law defines and makes clear the relationships among individuals and between individuals and society. The two main types of law are civil law and public law.

■ The police may arrest anyone they see violating the law or they reasonably believe has committed a crime. A charge is then entered in the arrest book. An arraignment is held and the arrested person is indicted. If the accused pleads not guilty, a trial is held. Evidence is presented at the trial and a decision is made regarding guilt. If the defendant is found guilty, the judge imposes a sentence.

■ If a law enforcement officer wants to arrest or search you, don't resist. Your guilt or innocence can be determined later.

■ A court is the branch of government having the power to settle disputes. All courts basically do the same three things: decide

- civil disputes between individuals or other parties, determine the guilt or innocence of accused persons, and impose punishment on the guilty. The two types of court systems are state and federal.
- In a typical civil case, the plaintiff files a complaint against the defendant in a court. A summons is issued for the defendant to appear in court. The defendant must then submit a written report of his or her story. If grounds for a suit are present, the judge sets a trial date. Attorneys for both sides present evidence at the trial. The judge (or jury) reaches a verdict. When the case is decided, the judge will make a judgment in favor of the plaintiff or the defendant.
- Someday, you will probably face a situation in which you will need an attorney. Choosing a lawyer is similar to selecting a doctor, banker, or other professional. The Lawyer Referral Service is available in over 250 cities to help people obtain legal assistance at moderate cost.
- The fees lawyers charge vary depending on the type of situation. They may charge a flat fee, an hourly fee, or a contingency fee. Don't be afraid to ask about fees at your first meeting.
- There may be times when you don't need a lawyer. Small claims courts are available to allow an individual to sue someone without using an attorney. A small claims court is usually part of the general trial court in a county or city.

Words to Know

arraignment a hearing before a judge during which formal charges are brought against an arrested person.

bail a sum of money paid to the court guaranteeing that an accused person will show up for trial.

common law the system of law used in the United States; judge-made law.

decree an order by the court to the defendant to stop doing whatever is harming the plaintiff.

defendant a person required to answer charges in a lawsuit.

indictment the formal statement charging a person with an offense.

judgment the judge's decision in a civil suit in favor of either the plaintiff or the defendant.

law the body of enforced rules by which people live together.

plaintiff the complaining party in a lawsuit.

probation releasing a convicted person on a suspended sentence under supervision and upon specified conditions.

summons an order commanding the defendant in a lawsuit to appear in court on a certain day.

warrant a court order authorizing a police officer to make a search, seizure, or arrest.

Questions to Answer

1. Why do we have laws?
2. Name the two main branches of law. Give an example of each.
3. What happens if a person is arrested and cannot afford to hire an attorney?
4. If you are stopped by a police officer and arrested for a crime that you didn't commit, how should you act?

1. To define and make clear the relationships among individuals and between individuals and society. If everyone did as they pleased, society would break down.
2. (a) *Civil law*—examples include credit purchases, renting an apartment, and signing a job contract. (b) *Public law*—criminal law is the most familiar kind.
3. The judge appoints one.
4. Cooperate; do not resist. Your guilt or innocence can be determined later.

5. What are the three basic things that courts do?
6. What is the name of the highest federal court in the United States? Who presides over this court?
7. In a court case, who does the prosecuting attorney represent? Who does the defense attorney represent?
8. Explain the purpose of the Lawyer Referral Service.
9. Name three methods of paying for legal services.
10. What is the purpose of a small claims court?

Activities to Do
1. The United States Supreme Court has a very important role in our society. With the help of your teacher, identify a recent Supreme Court decision. Investigate this decision and then give a short oral report to the class.
2. As a class, invite a department store manager to talk about the problem of shoplifting and how a shoplifter is dealt with.
3. Invite a member of SADD (Students Against Drunk Driving) to class. Talk with him or her about the legal issues surrounding drunken driving.
4. Find out the location of your nearest Small Claims Court. Contact the clerk's office and obtain a copy of any written guidelines and forms for how to file a complaint. Discuss in class the types of situations that might be taken to Small Claims Court.

Topics to Discuss
1. How might you be influenced in the future by having a criminal record?
2. What is meant by the term *white collar crime*? Do you think white collar criminals should be treated differently than other criminals?
3. In what types of legal situations would you probably need a specialized lawyer (as opposed to a general lawyer)?
4. A great deal has been said and written about the United States being a "litigious-intensive society." This means that we have a tendency as a people to file too many lawsuits. Do you thing that this is true?

---

5. (a) Decide civil disputes between individuals or other parties. (b) Determine the guilt or innocence of accused persons. (c) Impose punishment on the guilty.
6. (a) Supreme Court of the United States. (b) Chief Justice of the United States.
7. (a) Plaintiff. (b) Defendant.
8. To help people obtain legal assistance at a moderate cost.
9. (a) Flat fee. (b) Hourly fee. (c) Contingency fee.
10. To allow an individual to sue someone without using an attorney.

19. You may wish to compile and duplicate a list of famous Supreme Court cases. Check encyclopedias beforehand to make sure information is readily available.
20. A criminal record can automatically eliminate one from consideration for certain types of jobs and be a negative factor for most others.
21. This refers to crimes such as fraud and embezzlement that are committed by people in business and professional fields. These cases are often treated differently by the courts under the rationale that the guilty party poses no physical threat to society.
22. As in medicine, the more serious or unusual the case, the more likely a specialized attorney is needed.
23. This is a matter of opinion, but there is evidence of an excessive number of cases and a lot of frivolous suits filed.

1. Ask students if they have given any thought to finding a place of their own. Allow them to discuss plans, hopes, concerns, and so on. Not all students, of course, are currently living with parents. Be sensitive to alternative living arrangements.

CHAPTER TWENTY-NINE

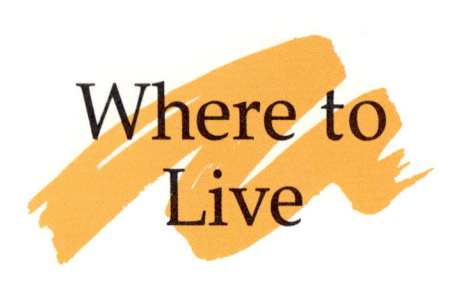

Where to Live

OUTLINE
Choosing a Type of Housing
Rent or Buy?
Apartment Hunting
The Rental Agreement
Landlord-Tenant Relationships
Chapter Review

OBJECTIVES
After reading this chapter, you should be able to:
- Identify types of housing alternatives.
- Discuss advantages and disadvantages of renting and buying.
- Name and describe factors to consider in apartment hunting.
- Summarize items included in an apartment lease.
- Explain rights and responsibilities of a tenant.

FIGURE 29-1 Buying a home is the largest single purchase that most people will make. *Courtesy of Wes Coulter*

Jack's life is changing very rapidly. In a few weeks, he will graduate from high school. He has accepted a job as a mechanic at Porter Tire and Auto. Although he doesn't mind living at home, he would like a place of his own.

At some point in your life, you will probably leave your parents' home. When that time comes, deciding where to live will become important to you. The choice is a difficult one that involves both personal and financial considerations. Young people who have never before lived away from home may not know what is involved in renting or buying their own place. They may also underestimate the total cost of a house or an apartment.

CHOOSING A TYPE OF HOUSING

If you decide to get a place of your own, housing will probably be the largest single expense in your budget. In many areas, rents and home prices are high and the costs continue to soar. But cost isn't the only problem. Many desirable communities have housing shortages.

Since housing is such a major expense, plan carefully. Begin by analyzing your needs and wants. Based on what you learn, you can then decide whether buying or renting is best for you.

Housing Needs and Wants

The "perfect" place to live may not be available or affordable. So it may be necessary to make some compromises that suit you and your budget. Nonetheless, it will be important to consider need and want in a place to live. Identify your needs and wants *before* you start looking.

It is a good idea to make a list of the features you think are essential or important in a place to live. That way you won't be attracted by some eye-catching feature that you don't really need or want. Know the difference between *essential* and *important*.

Rosanna is looking for an apartment. She doesn't

2. The "perfect" place to live is somewhat of an ideal for everyone, but especially so for one just starting out.

390

3. Place on the board two column headings labeled "essential" and "important." Ask students to provide examples.

CHAPTER 29 Where to Live ■ 391

FIGURE 29-2 Places to live differ a great deal in size, style, and price. Why? The needs and wants of people also vary greatly. *Courtesy of University of Massachusetts Photo Services and Jay Whitney*

want a long commute to work. For Rosanna, being near her office is essential. She also thinks having a garage is important. But if she found a place near the office that didn't have a garage, Rosanna would probably rent it anyway.

Individuals and families differ greatly in how they feel about housing. For some people, a house or apartment is simply a place to stay. For others, their lifestyles, hobbies, and goals revolve around their home.

Housing Alternatives

Different types of housing are available. One alternative is the single-family detached house. This kind of house usually offers more space, a larger yard, and more privacy than other types of housing. Also, many people consider a house the

4. You may wish to assign Activity 1 at this time.

FIGURE 29-3 A home with a fenced-in backyard was very important to this family. *Photo by Paul E. Meyers* most convenient and desirable place to raise children. A detached house is often the most expensive type of housing.

Attached houses, also called *townhouses,* are common in some communities. This kind of housing often includes a small yard. The houses may also share common properties such as a pool, tennis courts, and other extras.

Housing is also available in apartments. These may range in size from one room to many rooms. An apartment usually does not include a yard. A townhouse or apartment may also be called a *cooperative* (a share of an apartment building complex) or *condominium* (ownership of a specific unit).

Still another housing alternative is a mobile home. Mobile homes may have several rooms. They are usually located on small lots in mobile home parks in or near a city or a town.

RENT OR BUY?

To get the type of housing that you or your family needs and wants, should you rent or buy? Now that you have analyzed your needs and wants and considered the types of housing available, give some serious thought to this question.

Buying and renting have advantages and disadvantages. In deciding which is best for you, you will want to consider various factors. These include the number and ages of the people in your family, your financial situation, your lifestyle, and the housing alternatives available in your community. Remember that buying generally means making a down payment and then paying a mortgage every month for fifteen to thirty years.

Renting

Some advantages of renting are:

- Rent is usually a fixed amount for the term of the lease. Renters face no unexpected costs.
- Renting only obligates you for the length of the lease. If you want to move, you can make other arrangements when the lease expires.
- Renters have limited responsibility. You aren't responsible for taxes and repairs.
- Overall expenditures for renters are usually lower than those for buyers.
- If a job opportunity in another city comes along, it is easier to move if you are renting.
- When you are new to an area, renting gives you an opportunity to learn about the community. After you have been there for while, you may decide to move somewhere else.
- When future housing needs are uncertain, you can postpone a decision by renting.

Renting may involve different costs and responsibilities depending on what you rent. If you rent a detached house, you will probably have to pay not only the rent, but also all the normal expenses for running a home. You will probably also be responsible for all maintenance tasks and repairs. Likewise, if you rent a townhouse, you will probably have some maintenance and repair responsibilities.

If you rent an apartment, you will generally not be responsible for maintenance or repairs. These will be provided by the landlord. Also, if you don't want to buy furniture, you can find apartments where the major pieces are provided. For all these reasons, renting an apartment is probably the most common choice of young people who are living away from home for the first time.

Buying

Some of the advantages of buying a home are:

- Spending money to buy a home is a fairly safe form of investment. Unlike most investments, a home can be used.
- During inflationary times, property values rise. If you have a mortgage loan, you will be paying it off with cheaper dollars.
- Owning your home saves money on income taxes through deductions for mortgage interest and real estate taxes.

FIGURE 29-4 Many apartment owners try to attract young renters by providing swimming pools and other recreational facilities.

9. Provide an example to illustrate the meaning of home *equity*.
10. A homeowners' association often has a detailed booklet of specific rules and regulations.

CHAPTER 29 Where to Live ■ 393

FIGURE 29-5 If you rent, you still may have to buy furniture. And you will certainly need to purchase linen, cooking utensils, and other household items. *Photo by Paul E. Meyers*

- The *equity*, or money invested in a home, can be used as security for a loan.
- Home ownership can improve your credit rating.
- When you own your own home, you can decorate the way you wish. You may also make structural or landscaping alterations. These alterations sometimes increase the value of the property.

Buying involves different costs and levels of responsibility depending on what you buy. When you buy a house, you pay not only the mortgage, but also all expenses for home operation, upkeep, and repairs. Maintenance and repair work are also your responsibility.

When you buy a cooperative or a condominium, you are sharing with others the responsibilities, obligations, and maintenance costs. Very often, cooperative and condominium owners form a homeowners' association or a maintenance association. Monthly fees are paid to the association. The money is then used to provide for maintenance and improvements to common properties such as grounds, tennis courts, and other areas. A maintenance fee may add considerably to the cost of owning a cooperative or condominium.

Mobile homes are much less expensive to buy than houses. Mobile homes allow more people to enjoy the benefits of homeownership. However, mobile homes don't increase in value as much over time as houses and apartments generally do. Mobile homes may also be unsafe in storms and high winds.

APARTMENT HUNTING

Let's assume you have decided to rent an apartment. Available rental housing is often listed with a real estate agency or an apartment-finding business that charges fees for their services. More often, people find an apartment by checking the newspaper classified ads, by following through on tips from friends or co-workers, or by just walking or driving through a particular neighborhood. College students can often find an apartment through the school's housing office.

FIGURE 29-6 A condominium combines the advantages of an apartment with those of buying a home.

11. Bring to class a weekend newspaper to use as a resource for this section. You may wish to assign Activity 3 at this time.

What Would You Do?

You want to get an apartment closer to work, but haven't located anything you can afford. You get a call one evening from a person who works at an office near yours. She heard from a mutual acquaintance that you were looking for an apartment. The caller's roommate has left and she is looking for someone to move in and share expenses. You write down the information and indicate that you will think it over. You are uneasy about the idea of sharing an apartment with someone you don't know. What would you do?

*WWYD Feature A. Meet the potential roommate and inspect the apartment. The roommate who is leaving might be a good source of information about what to expect.

394 ■ **SECTION 6** Independent Living

FIGURE 29-7 A college dorm is often a person's first real experience in living away from home. *Courtesy of SIUC Photocommunications*

FIGURE 29-8 Don't rent an apartment unless you can inspect the actual unit you will be renting. *Photo by David W. Tuttle*

Things to Consider

Suppose you and a friend are looking for separate places at the same time. What you consider important in a rental may not be important to your friend. But both of you will need to be concerned about certain things.

Location. The neighborhood in which an apartment is located is important. However, the location is usually not as critical to a renter as it is to a home buyer. Renters have no financial investment in the property. So their interest is limited more to convenience factors. Depending on the person, finding an apartment that is near work or school, has nearby shopping, and is accessible to public transportation may be important.

Safety. Because of the nature of apartment living, you should pay careful attention to several things. The first one is safety. Well-lighted and uncluttered entrances, hallways, and stairways contribute to security. A locked outside entrance is another good feature. Apartment doors should be securely constructed and contain deadbolt or other types of strong locks. Basement or first-floor apartments should have special window grills or locking features in addition to the regular window latches.

Another aspect of safety is fire protection. Each apartment should have one or more fire alarms in good working order. The kitchen area ought to have a fire extinguisher available. *(Buy one yourself if it doesn't.)* Check to see if the apartment has an external fire-escape exit. If not, is there an evacuation plan to follow in case of fire?

Privacy and Noise. Find out what type of people currently live in the building. If possible, meet and talk with some of the tenants. Remember that you may be sharing a relatively small area with dozens or even hundreds of other people.

Since apartment residents live closely together, noise can be a real problem. Noise can come either from outside streets and parking lots, or from within other apartments. Buildings should be soundproofed to dampen the sounds of talking, plumbing, and music between apartments and between hallways and apartments. Noises from apartments above are usually more noticeable than sounds from apartments below.

Scott and Sandy Foster, for instance, have an upstairs neighbor who works from 3:30 to midnight. He usually wakes them up about 12:20 A.M. when he gets home and opens the apartment door. A few minutes later, he is heard taking a shower. Off and on throughout the night, Scott and Sandy are awakened by sounds of footsteps, closing doors, music, and so on. Their neighbor isn't unusually loud or inconsiderate. He just happens to live a different lifestyle than they do. This is not an unusual situation for apartment dwellers.

Ventilation. Can air enter easily? Most apartments that have air conditioning are well ventilated.

12. As these considerations are discussed, encourage students to share their own experiences, suggestions, and points of view.

13. Perhaps students can suggest additional considerations involved in selecting an apartment.

FIGURE 29-9 When living in an apartment, be considerate of the rights of other residents. *Photo by Paul E. Meyers*

FIGURE 29-10 If something is not in good working order, agree upon repairs before you move in. *Photo by Paul E. Meyers*

In places without this feature, cooking odors and stagnant air may be problems. Does the stove have an exhaust fan for ventilating the kitchen? Is the number of windows adequate, and do they all open easily? Besides permitting good air circulation, windows provide natural light that adds to a place's cheerfulness.

Other Considerations. Check appliances such as refrigerators, stoves, and dishwashers. Do they work well? Be sure you know who pays for utilities. Is the electricity your responsibility? How about heat? Can you give other examples? Ask for an estimate of typical costs for utilities and other services that you will be responsible for.

You probably have friends or relatives who live in apartments. If so, ask them to describe how they found their living quarters. Also, find out if they have any advice to share about what to look for.

14. Guidelines for grooming and dress described in Chapter 11 are also good ones to follow in looking for an apartment.

How to Approach a Landlord

Looking for a place to live is a great deal like getting a job. As with a potential employer, it is important to make a good impression on the *landlord* or apartment manager. Apply for an apartment in person and be courteous and friendly.

Most landlords will ask you to fill out an application. The landlord is interested in checking your past rental record and credit references. Fill out the application form completely and honestly without blank spaces.

Some landlords will charge an application fee. Before you pay such a fee, ask if you will get it back. Also find out if you must rent the unit if your application is accepted. Be sure you know when you will be notified of the landlord's decision.

15. Obtain several examples of apartment applications to use here for illustration. You may wish to duplicate an example and have students practice filling it out.

F·E·A·T·U·R·E

Dealing With a Roommate

When young people leave home, they often move into an apartment which they share with a roommate. The major reason for having a roommate is economic necessity. Someone is needed with whom to share expenses.

Living with one or more roommates is a unique relationship. It is a business relationship because money is exchanged. But it is also an emotional relationship.

Roommates can grow to become good friends. Or they can grow to dislike each other. Before choosing or becoming a roommate, you should have a serious discussion with the other person. Professionals involved in roommate referral recommend having all agreements in writing. Items you will need to agree on in advance include: housework and laundry; food and beverage supplies; overnight guests; the security deposit and how it will be refunded; pets (and who takes care of them); smoking; boy or girl friends; and stereos and musical instruments. Particularly important are the terms for moving out. It is a good idea to have an agreement to give each other a thirty- or sixty-day notice. Without any prearranged agreements, a nonleaseholding roommate doesn't have much in the way of rights.

Here is how one group of four roommates have been able to get along. Each person signs a separate form outlining all the financial responsibilities involved and what will be shared. Each person contributes a fixed amount each week for household staples such as milk, toothpaste, garbage bags, and newspaper. Each person takes turn going out to buy what is needed. Apart from this, they buy their own food and do their own dishes. They occasionally cook a meal together for a holiday dinner or other special event.

Utility bills are divided equally. Each roommate has a separate phone and no one answers anyone else's phone. (Some of the worst disagreements between roommates are over phone use and phone bills.) Every two weeks, the group meets to discuss any problems.

Sharing living space can be difficult. But many roommate crises can be easily prevented or resolved. Set ground rules from the start. Discuss your feelings and expectations with your roommate. And always be willing to negotiate and compromise.

FIGURE 29-FEATURE Be prepared for give-and-take when living with a roommate. *Photo by Paul E. Meyers*

*Dealing With a Roommate. This is a good overview of the advantages and considerations involved in sharing housing with another person. As a class, compile a list of additional suggestions for maintaining a good relationship with a roommate.

printed form that contains most or all of the following parts and rules:

- The names of the landlord and *tenant* (renter).
- The address of the property.
- The beginning and ending dates of occupancy.
- The amount of rent and when and where it is to be paid for the term of the lease.
- The amount of the security deposit. If the renter obeys the lease, the money is to be refunded after the lease ends.
- Limits on the number of renters. Any rules against pets should be made clear also.
- Responsibilities for normal maintenance and repairs. The renter must repair any damage caused by carelessness.
- Responsibilities for electricity, trash pickup, and the like.
- (For furnished places) An attachment that shows an inventory of the items and their condition.
- Sublease permission. Suppose a renter needs to move before the lease is up. Can he or she rent it out *(sublet)*? **17**
- When the landlord can enter the apartment. The lease should explain such conditions.
- The procedures to be followed when the tenant wishes to end the lease. An automatic renewal clause may also be a part of the lease.

Any special arrangements between you and the landlord should be written into the lease. Read the lease very carefully before signing it. When you put

FIGURE 29-11 Sample apartment lease *Courtesy of National Legal Supply, Inc.*

THE RENTAL AGREEMENT

Most apartments are rented according to an agreement called a *lease*. This is a written legal contract between you and the landlord. For agreeing to pay rent and following the lease's rules, you are allowed to rent the apartment. The lease is often a pre-

16. Duplicate and distribute to the class a sample of a typical apartment lease. Relate the parts of the lease listed here to the sample provided.

FIGURE 29-12 A landlord's right of entry doesn't mean that your privacy can be invaded. *Photo by Paul E. Meyers*

17. Provide a specific example of what it means to *sublet*.

your name on a lease, you say that you understand and accept all conditions contained in it. Make sure you are provided with a signed copy of the agreement.

LANDLORD-TENANT RELATIONSHIPS

The relationship between you and a landlord is a legal one. Both of you have certain rights and responsibilities.

Rights and Responsibilities of Landlords

The landlord has the right to set reasonable rules and regulations for the management of the rental units. Unless you have agreed to repair or maintain the property, the landlord must keep the place in reasonable repair. This means the landlord must keep the premises in a clean, safe condition.

Rights and Responsibilities of Tenants

Your rights as a tenant are essentially the reverse of the landlord's responsibilities. You pay rent for housing and you expect to receive a safe and livable apartment. If something goes wrong, it should be repaired in a reasonable time. You are entitled to peace, quiet, and privacy. You shouldn't be cheated, or overcharged.

FIGURE 29-13 It is a good idea to tell your landlord or building manager when you will be away for a vacation or holiday. *Photo by Paul E. Meyers*

On the other hand, you have the responsibility to follow the rules in the lease. These basically deal with paying the rent on time, keeping your area clean and safe, and not abusing the landlord's property or the rights of other tenants.

Beyond your responsibilities as a tenant, try to maintain a proper business relationship with the landlord. Report all problems as they occur. The landlord will appreciate knowing this information as soon as possible. In addition, have in writing all communication with the landlord and make copies of everything. The landlord is used to dealing with people on a businesslike basis, and will appreciate this behavior.

A landlord-tenant relationship is like any other personal or business association. For the relationship to work, both parties must fulfill their obligations. Do your part by understanding your obligations and then carrying them out.

What Would You Do?

You come home from work to discover the landlord leaving your apartment. He seems surprised and says that he was checking on the furnace. Several times over the next month, you notice little things that suggest someone has been in the apartment. You are aware that the landlord has the right to enter your apartment for emergencies, maintenance, and the like. But you are upset by the thought that he may be in the apartment for other reasons. What would you do?

* *WWYD Feature B.* A lease will give the landlord a right to enter an apartment for inspection and maintenance. However, the tenant has a right to privacy and respect. The tenant should approach the landlord and request that prior notification be provided (except for emergencies) for future inspections of the apartment. Hopefully, this will remedy the situation.

18. You may wish to conduct Activity 2 at this time.
19. You may wish to assign Activity 4 at this time.
20. The guidelines in Chapter 9 regarding human relations are equally relevant here. Review as appropriate.

CHAPTER REVIEW

Chapter in Brief

- At some point in your life, you will probably leave your parents' home. When that time comes, deciding where to live will become important to you. The choice is a difficult one that involves both personal and financial considerations.
- Since housing is such a major expense, plan carefully. Begin by analyzing your needs and wants. It will probably be necessary to make compromises that suit you and your budget. Your housing alternatives may include a detached house, townhouse, apartment, or mobile home.
- Buying and renting have advantages and disadvantages. Become familiar with these. Renting an apartment is probably the most common choice of young people who are living away from home for the first time.
- When hunting for an apartment, you need to be concerned with certain things such as type and location of neighborhood, personal safety and fire protection, privacy and noise, ventilation, furnishings available, and so on. Looking for a place to live is a great deal like getting a job. It is important to make a good impression on the landlord or apartment manager.
- Most apartments are rented according to an agreement called a lease. It is a written legal contract between you and the landlord. Know what to expect in a lease. Read it carefully before signing.
- You and the landlord have certain legal rights and responsibilities. Your rights as a tenant are to receive a safe and livable apartment. You are entitled to peace, quiet, privacy, and fair treatment. You also have the responsibility to follow the rules in the lease. Deal with the landlord in a businesslike manner.

Words to Know

condominium ownership of a specific unit in a townhouse or apartment.

cooperative a share of an apartment building complex.

equity the value of a home above the amount owned on a mortgage.

landlord the owner or manager of a rental apartment.

lease a rental agreement between a tenant and a landlord.

sublet a lease by a tenant to another person.

tenant renter; the person who rents an apartment.

townhouse an individually-owned house that is attached to another house on one or both sides.

Questions to Answer

1. What is the first step in deciding where to live? Why is this important?
2. What are the four major types of housing alternatives?
3. There are reasons for renting and buying housing. Name three of each.
4. In what three ways do most people locate an apartment?
5. What two types of fire protection devices should you look for in an apartment?
6. Explain how renting an apartment is similar to getting a job.
7. What is the purpose of a security deposit? Do you think it is fair to require one?
8. If a furnished apartment is rented, what should be attached to the lease?
9. What is the landlord's basic responsibility? The tenant's basic responsibility?
10. In what way is the landlord-tenant relationship like any other association?

Activities to Do

1. Assume that you are going to move to a nearby town in a few months to begin a new job. A friend who works for the same company is also moving. The two of you decide to share a place to live. Prepare a list of what you need and want in housing. Turn the list in to your instructor. Then discuss this subject in class.
2. As a class, invite a landlord or apartment manager to visit and discuss landlord-tenant relationships. Prepare well. You may want to begin by asking the person what he or she looks for in a person who comes to rent an apartment.
3. Check local classified ads to find out the cost of renting in your area.
4. Find out if your state or city has a tenancy law, tenant ordinance, or housing code (not building code). What is the warranty of habitability? Can a tenant be evicted from an apartment? How may a tenant resolve complaints with a landlord?

Topics to Discuss

1. Sharing an apartment with others is a good way to economize on housing. However, living with roommates can be difficult at times. What do you think might be the most common problems with roommates? How can they be avoided?
2. Does your community have a neighborhood watch, neighborhood patrol, or other type of citizen-oriented crime prevention program? Discuss how such programs operate.
3. The price and availability of housing is often an important factor in the decision to accept a first job or to relocate in another job. Discuss and provide illustrations of this.

---

1. Identify your needs and wants. This may prevent being swept off your feet by some eye-catching feature that isn't needed or wanted.
2. (a) Detached houses. (b) Townhouses. (c) Apartments. (d) Mobile homes.
3. There are many reasons. See lists on pages 392-393.
4. (a) By checking the newspaper classified ads. (b) By following through on tips from friends or co-workers. (c) By walking or driving through a particular neighborhood.
5. (a) Fire alarm. (b) Fire extinguisher.
6. As with a potential employer, it is important to make a good impression on the landlord or apartment manager.
7. The security deposit is a sort of deterrent. In the event of damage or loss caused by the tenant, it pays for repairs or replacement. The question of fairness is a matter of opinion. It seems to be a reasonable requirement to protect the landlord's interests.
8. An inventory of furnishings and their condition.
9. (a) *Landlord*—to keep the premises in a clean, safe condition. (b) *Tenant*—to follow the conditions of the lease.
10. For the relationship to work, both parties must fulfill their obligations.

21. The intent here is to help students understand their legal rights as a tenant. A warranty of habitability means that in return for rent the landlord must supply a safe and decent unit. If this condition is not met, the tenant may not be obligated to pay some or all of the rent. Only a court can decide for sure.
22. Contact (or assign students to do so) your local police or sheriffs department for more information.
23. Newspapers and magazines often publish lists comparing housing costs in various geographic regions. A librarian can help find such information. Be alert to future information of this type.

1. In 1990, an estimated 1,500 companies had some kind of health and fitness program (see Feature). Discuss this with students before beginning the chapter.

2. Emphasize that being in good health is more than just an absence of illness or disease.

CHAPTER THIRTY

Healthful Living

OUTLINE
Nutrition and Diet
Stress and Its Control
Physical Fitness
Chapter Review

OBJECTIVES
After reading this chapter, you should be able to:
- Describe how each of the four broad food groups contributes to a balanced diet.
- Identify own recommended weight and daily calorie needs.
- Name and illustrate the three major ways to reduce or eliminate stress.
- Discuss benefits of physical exercise.
- Name and describe the three types of exercises that should be included in a workout.

FIGURE 30-1 Looking great doesn't always mean that you are in good health. *Courtesy of Johnson & Wales College*

1 Sherri had not been feeling well for a long time. Her appetite was poor and she always seemed tired. She spent much time in her room and had little interest in going out with her friends. She had frequent headaches. Sherri's parents became very concerned and took her to the doctor for a checkup.

After a complete exam and several tests, Dr. Williams sat down with Sherri to explain the results. "Well, Sherri," said the doctor, "I don't find any major problems. But I don't think you're in very good health."

2 The doctor's statement confused Sherri. Dr. Williams then explained to Sherri that being healthy means more than just being free from illness or disease. Good health involves a person's overall physical and mental well-being.

Dr. Williams told Sherri that achieving and maintaining good health depends on nutrition and diet, stress control, and exercise. In this chapter, you will read about what Sherri learned from her doctor. Good health is related to your success and productivity at school and on the job.

NUTRITION AND DIET

Nutrition is the process by which plants and animals take in and use food. What we eat provides certain chemical substances needed for good health. These substances, called *nutrients,* serve as fuel to provide energy, help regulate body processes, and furnish basic materials for building, repairing, or maintaining body tissues.

Daily Food Guide
Nutrients are supplied by foods that people eat. Foods vary in the kinds and amount of nutrients they contain. No one food provides all the nutrients in the amounts required for growth and health. To make sure you get the required nutrients, you need to eat a variety of foods each day.

401

THE BASIC FOUR FOOD GROUPS

Meat, Poultry, Fish and Beans. Two servings daily. One serving equals 2 to 3 ounces of lean cooked meat, poultry or fish. Or substitute for 1 ounce of meat: 1 egg; ½ to ¾ cup cooked dry beans or peas; 2 T. peanut butter; ¼ to ½ cup nuts, sesame or sunflower seeds.

Fruits and Vegetables. Four servings daily, including one good vitamin C source and one deep-yellow or dark-green vegetable. One serving equals ½ cup or a typical portion such as 1 orange, 1 medium potato, or 1 bowl of salad.

Milk and Cheese. At least two servings daily. One serving equals 8 ounces of milk, 1 cup yogurt, 2-inch cube hard cheese, or 2 cups of cottage cheese.

Bread and Cereal. Four servings daily, including at least 1 of whole grain. One serving equals 1 small roll, pancake, slice of bread; ½ English muffin, bagel, hamburger bun; ½ to ¾ cup cooked cereal, pasta, rice; or 1 ounce dry cereal.

FIGURE 30-2 Study and follow this daily food guide.

Nutrition scientists have developed the easy-to-use, daily food guide shown in Figure 30-2. The guide is based on an understanding of the nutrient needs of people and the nutritive values of food. Using this guide will help you choose the proper foods to eat daily. Each of the four food groups contributes to a balanced diet.

Fats, oils, sugars, and sweets are not included in the guide because they are common in most diets. The main contribution of these foods is their energy value.

Energy Requirements

Calories are units of food energy needed for continuous body functions such as breathing and heart rate. To carry out work and leisure activities, we all need calories. In addition, children and young people require calories for growth.

When the foods you eat provide more energy than you need to meet the demands of the body, your body stores the extra energy as fat. If you regularly eat too much food, you gain weight. On the other hand, if your energy level requires more calories than you take in, the body uses stored fat. You then lose weight.

Ideal weight varies among individuals. You can get an idea of your desirable weight from the table shown in Figure 30-3. For example, if you are a six-foot tall male, your ideal weight should be between 145 and 182 pounds. The range takes into account that there are small, average and large body frames.

3. There is a general consensus among nutrition experts that the best diet is one that samples from among the four food groups shown in Figure 30-2.

4. You may wish to assign Activity 1 at this time.
5. People whose weight approximates the "ideal" weight live longer than people who are heavier. Use the weights shown in

DESIRABLE BODY WEIGHT RANGES

Height without shoes	Weight without clothes	
	Men (pounds)	Women (pounds)
4'10"		92-121
4'11"		95-124
5'0"		98-127
5'1"	105-134	101-130
5'2"	108-137	104-134
5'3"	111-141	107-138
5'4"	114-145	110-142
5'5"	117-149	114-146
5'6"	121-154	118-150
5'7"	125-159	122-154
5'8"	129-163	126-159
5'9"	133-167	130-164
5'10"	137-172	134-169
5'11"	141-177	
6'0"	145-182	
6'1"	149-187	
6'2"	153-192	
6'3"	157-197	

Note: For women 18-25 years, subtract one pound for each year under 25.

Source: Adapted from the 1959 Metropolitan Desirable Weight Table.

FIGURE 30-3 Recommended weights for young adults
Courtesy of USDA

The number of calories used by the body each day to maintain weight is called the daily calorie need. Part of this is for continuous body functioning called *basal metabolism*. The remainder is used by the body as it carries out various work and leisure activities.

For a general idea of the number of calories you need daily, use this simple method. First, from Figure 30-3, find your recommended weight. Then multiply that figure by 18 for a man, and by 16 for a woman. To illustrate, a woman who is 5 feet 4 inches tall with a small frame, will use about 1,760 calories (110 × 16) per day if her activities are "average."

Controlling Weight

For good health, it is wise to maintain your recommended weight. Do this by controlling the amount of food intake (calories) or level of activity, or both. To maintain the same body weight, the amount of calories eaten must balance the amount of calories used. To lose weight, you need to take in (or use up through exercise) fewer calories than your body needs. To gain weight, extra calories must be

Figure 30-3 only as guidelines and avoid overemphasizing the terms *ideal* or *desirable*.

6. The best indicator of body frame size is elbow width. People with large bony elbows can weigh more; people with slender elbows should weigh less.

	Calories
Boiled, diced, no fat added	55
Mashed, milk and fat added	100
Hash-browned	175
French-fried, 10 pieces	215
Pan-fried, beginning with raw potatoes	230

FIGURE 30-4 Calories vary according to how food is prepared. Here are the calories contained in a half-cup serving of potatoes.

consumed. For each pound you want to gain or lose, you must take in about 3,500 calories more or less than the body uses.

If you are interested in gaining or losing weight, the first step is to learn about the number of calories that various foods contain. Charts showing the calorie values of common foods appear in most cookbooks. If you can't find a calorie chart on your own, your public librarian can help you.

What Would You Do?

It seems like you are always on a diet. You don't eat much, but still can't lose weight. For instance, all that you have had today is a couple of donuts for breakfast and an order of french fries and a soft drink for lunch. You guess that you will just have to get used to dieting continually. What would you do?

*WWYD Feature A. The individual purports to be on a diet, but in reality is eating a low-nutrition, high-calorie diet. Many people know little about nutrition or calorie counting. The person needs to follow a doctor-recommended diet program if he/she is serious about losing weight.

FIGURE 30-5 Food can be both nutritious and low in calories. *Photo by Paul E. Meyers*

7. Have students calculate their average daily calorie needs.
8. Charts are available that show the number of calories used up in various types of activity.
9. You may wish to assign Activity 2 at this time.

CHAPTER 30 Healthful Living ■ 403

If you are trying to gain or lose weight, remember that you still need proper nutrients. Even though the number of calories may vary, you need daily servings from the basic four food groups. It is a good idea never to go below 1,200 calories a day. By taking in less than that, you probably won't get the vitamins and minerals you need.

FIGURE 30-6 Stress is a normal part of life. You must learn to recognize and deal with it. *Reproduced with permission of AT&T*

STRESS AND ITS CONTROL

Stress, an unavoidable part of life, is a response the body makes to any demand made upon it. Causes of stress, called *stressors,* may be physical, biological, or emotional; they may be good or bad; and they may range from mild to severe. Following are the most common causes of stress:

- Daily activities, events, frustrations, and challenges cause stress. Examples might include missing a bus to school, giving a speech, taking a test, overcooking dinner, or going out on a blind date.
- Illness adds to stress because it forces the body to use its defenses. Stress also results when the body must heal an injury or adjust to conditions such as extreme heat, noise, air pollution, or the like.

10. Begin this section by discussing with students what the term *stress* means to them.
11. Point out that causes of stress may be *positive* or *negative*.

12. Emphasize how stress affects people differently.
14. Encourage students to experiment with these three main approaches to reducing stress.
15. Ask students to provide personal illustrations of the merits of planning and organizing.

404 ■ SECTION 6 Independent Living

- A life change is often stressful. Examples might include moving into a new house, getting married, or changing schools. Such changes require many adaptations to new surroundings and situations.
- Life crises produce the greatest stress. These events might include the death of a parent, the loss of a job, or a divorce. The more serious the crisis, the greater the stress.

An event that causes great stress for one person may only be a minor problem for another. Your existing physical or mental condition influences your ability to handle a new stress. Your response may also depend on whether you feel in control of the situation. A difficulty may cause little stress if you can predict it, overcome it, or at least understand it.

Most people are able to cope with life's everyday stresses. However, when stressors build up faster than you can solve them, your capacity may be overloaded. Continual stress exhausts the body's resources that maintain energy and resist disease. The result may be anxiety, depression, or serious illness.

Coping With Stress

A well-balanced life can help you prevent and reduce stress. Managing stress may include alternating mental activity with physical activity, sharing emotional feelings with others, reading inspirational books, and having interests outside of school or work. In addition, developing positive emotions such as hope, confidence, and love can enable you to develop a lifestyle that will help you resist daily life stresses. Worrying less and having a sense of humor also helps a great deal. The three major ways to reduce or eliminate stress are plan how to deal with stress, learn how to relax, and change your life.

Plan How to Deal With Stress. Some crises and other types of stressors cannot be predicted. For instance, a loved one may die suddenly. Other stressors, though, such as taking a test, leaving home to go to school, or giving a speech are known in advance. For those kinds of stressors, you don't have to wait for them to happen. Plan and prepare for them. For example, reduce stress associated with test-taking by thoroughly studying the test material until you are confident that you know it well.

13. Most everyone experiences daily stress. Problems come when a high level of stress persists for a long time.

FIGURE 30-7 Have you ever felt wiped out after taking a test? This feeling is the result of stress. *Photo by David W. Tuttle*

If possible, do not schedule several stressful activities during the same time period. When you know a stressful activity or event is coming up, learn to pace yourself. During stressful times, eat well, get plenty of rest, and exercise at an enjoyable pace.

Learn How to Relax. Because stress is unavoidable, it is very useful to learn a method that reduces or eliminates stress. Some common methods include transcendental meditation (TM), yoga, and various forms of relaxation exercises. You can find books on these subjects at most libraries and bookstores.

One doctor suggests this very simple relaxation method. Sit or lie in a comfortable position in a quiet place where you won't be disturbed. Close your eyes, and silently repeat the word *one* over and over for ten to twenty minutes. This activity seems to produce bodily changes that are the reverse of the ones stress causes. Muscle tension is reduced and a variety of other changes occur in the heart, blood, and respiratory systems. In order to learn and use a meditation technique, it should be practiced once or twice a day.

If meditation doesn't appeal to you, learn some other method that will help you relax and will have a calming effect. The activity may be jogging, listening to music, walking in the park, riding a horse, or sitting in a sauna. Use whatever works for you. Bear in mind that the bodily changes associated with stress can be reversed if you take steps to do so.

16. Teach this relaxation method to the class and try it out for several minutes. Assign Activity 3 at this time.
17. Perhaps students can suggest activities that work for them.

18. Changing one's life is often very difficult to accomplish, especially for a young person who has less independence than an adult.

FIGURE 30-8 Which relaxation method works best for you? *Courtesy of Outboard Marine Corporation*

What Would You Do?

You have been studying all weekend for a test on Monday. You feel tense and your neck and shoulders ache from leaning over a desk. One of your friends calls asking you to go to the recreation center for a workout. You would like to go, but don't feel that you can take time away from studying. What would you do?

Change Your Life. The methods previously mentioned are some important ways of managing stress. However, if the same stressor is always present, stress-release techniques may not be very beneficial. You may have a situation in your life that simply makes you miserable. This may be a class at school, a job, a roommate, or some other situation or relationship. If these situations can't be relieved through other means, your last resort may be to drop the class, quit the job, or find a new roommate.

18

Of course, turning away from all stressful situations would be bad. But some situations and relationships are so stress-producing, that it is often better to change them than to continue.

PHYSICAL FITNESS

No matter how good your diet or how well you control stress, you cannot be healthy without

* *WWYD Feature B.* A person who has been studying all weekend is due for a break. Going to the rec center to exercise would seem to be a wise choice.

CHAPTER 30 Healthful Living ■ 405

physical fitness. People have different ideas about what fitness means. For some, it is not being ill, while for others, it is having a trim body.

Physical fitness refers to how well your heart and other organs function. Your physical fitness is determined by such factors as age, heredity, and behavior. Although you cannot control your age or heredity, your behavior can help you become physically fit. People vary greatly in their capacity for physical fitness, but almost anyone can improve by exercising regularly.

19

FIGURE 30-9 Exercising is a wonderful activity to do with family or friends. *Photo by Paul E. Meyers*

All of us need physical exercise. The years between adolescence and middle age are generally the peak period for physical fitness. However, people of all ages can stay fit if they maintain good health habits and get regular exercise. According to the American Medical Association, exercise:

1. Improves strength, endurance, and coordination, thus increasing the ease with which daily tasks are accomplished.
2. Aids weight control, thus helping to ward off heart disease, arthritis, diabetes, and other ailments often associated with being overweight.
3. Helps ensure the proper growth and development of young bones and muscles.
4. Improves the ability to avoid and recover from illnesses and accidents.
5. Strengthens muscles that support the body. Posture and appearance then improve.
6. Increases poise by developing grace and ease of movement.
7. Reduces stress, thus acting as a natural tranquilizer.

19. Doctors refer to this as *cardiopulmonary fitness*—how efficiently the heart *(cardio)* and lungs *(pulmonary)* work to supply the body's need for oxygen and removal of chemical wastes.

F•E•A•T•U•R•E

Corporate Fitness Programs

Faced with spiraling medical costs and insurance premiums, more and more companies are promoting preventive health care. This may include health screening for employees, educational seminars and workshops, and opportunities for physical activity.

Here is how the program operates at one large corporation. The program, called "Live for Life," offers classes on stress management and how to quit smoking. It teaches employees the importance of blood pressure testing, weight control, and exercise. The company has a fitness center on site.

In the center, an aerobics instructor leads exercise classes before and after work and at lunch time. Free laundry service is provided. The company distributes a monthly newsletter on fitness and sponsors regular seminars on good nutrition and other topics.

The program is voluntary, but incentives to participate are provided. For every twenty minutes of exercise, employees get $1 of "play money." They can use it to purchase jogging suits, ankle weights, and other health-related items. About sixty percent of the company's 30,000 employees participate.

Research has shown that fitness programs such as this pay off. There are fewer illnesses and accidents, reduced absenteeism, and a more vigorous, creative, positive workforce. In one company, it was found that the average yearly medical cost for exercisers was less than fifty percent of that for nonexercisers. Some companies even share the reduced medical costs with employees.

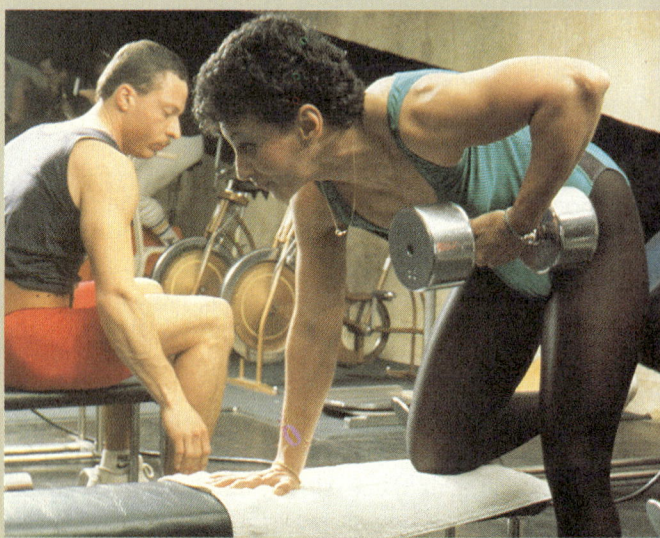

FIGURE 30-FEATURE Fitness programs benefit businesses and employees. *Photo courtesy of Health & Tennis Corporation of America and by David W. Tuttle*

* *Corporate Fitness Programs.* These types of programs (sometimes called wellness programs) were originated to reduce company absenteeism and spiraling health-care costs. They have generally proven to be good investments for companies and workers.

20. Cardiopulmonary fitness is achieved by raising the pulse rate to a level about 75 percent of the maximum rate. A healthy person's maximum pulse rate should be no higher than 220

CHAPTER 30 Healthful Living ■ 407

Types of Exercise

Your level of physical fitness depends largely on how often and how hard you exercise. Experts say that you should exercise at least three times weekly for at least thirty minutes at a stretch. Improvement in fitness may occur faster with even more frequent workouts.

The President's Council on Physical Fitness and Sports recommends a thirty-minute workout of continuous exercise. To be beneficial, the exercise doesn't have to be difficult or strenuous. But, as your condition improves, you should increase the number of times you do each activity. Every workout should include exercises for flexibility, endurance, and strength.

FIGURE 30-10 Jogging is good exercise, but so are many other activities. Choose what is most enjoyable for you. *Courtesy of U.S. Army Recruiting Command*

Flexibility Exercises. These stretch the connective tissues and move the joints through a wide range of motions. Such exercises include touching the toes, swinging the arms in circles, rotating the upper body from the waist, and jogging slowly. These should be performed before and after each workout.

Endurance Exercises. Running, cycling, skipping rope, swimming, and brisk walking speed up action of the heart and lungs. These are called *aerobic exercises.* Such exercises strengthen the heart, blood vessels, and lungs.

Strength Exercises. Pullups, pushups, situps, lifting weights, and other exercises increase the strength and endurance of the body's major muscle groups. For example, lifting weights increases the strength of arms, shoulders, and back muscles.

beats per minute, minus her/his age. Therefore a 17-year-old person should do regular exercise that maintains the pulse at about 150 beats per minute.

FIGURE 30-11 In the last couple of decades, more women have begun to exercise and to participate in sports. *Photos by David W. Tuttle and Kenneth Deitcher*

Guidelines for Physical Fitness

Exercise is basic to healthful living. Beginning or maintaining an exercise program should be done with the following guidelines in mind:

1. Don't keep finding excuses not to exercise.
2. Don't think of fitness as a crash program. To avoid injury and fatigue, start slowly and build yourself up.
3. Enjoy yourself. Exercise can be fun.

21. These are also called "warm-up" and "cool-down" exercises.
22. *Endurance* and *strength* exercises may be done separately or simultaneously.

4. Don't set unrealistic expectations. Remember, you are not training for the Olympics.
5. To avoid boredom, vary your exercise routine.
6. Once you get in shape, keep up your exercise program. If you get lazy and quit, your fitness level can deteriorate rather rapidly. The longer you allow yourself to be inactive, the harder it is to get back in shape.
7. Harmful health habits such as drugs, smoking, alcohol, and lack of sleep can undo the results of regular exercise.

As a young person, you have most of your life ahead of you. The quality of that life will depend a great deal on your physical and mental health. Begin now to follow the guidelines in this chapter regarding nutrition and diet, reducing stress, and physical fitness. This will better allow you to live and enjoy your life to its fullest.

FIGURE 30-12 Some American companies with Japanese roots, begin the workday with a few minutes of stretching exercises. *Courtesy of Toyota Motor Manufacturing, U.S.A., Inc.*

23. It's a real bonus when something that is good for your health (i.e., exercise) can be enjoyable and make you feel better!

CHAPTER REVIEW

Chapter in Brief

- What we eat provides nutrients needed for good health. These chemical substances serve as fuel to provide energy, regulate body processes, and furnish basic structural material for building, repairing, and maintaining body tissues. To make sure you get the required nutrients, you need to eat a variety of foods each day.
- Calories are units of food energy needed for basal metabolism and for energy. The number of calories used by the body each day to maintain weight is called the daily calorie need.
- For good health, it is wise to maintain your recommended weight. Do this by controlling your calories or your level of activity, or both.
- Stress is a response the body makes to any demand made upon it. The most common causes of stress are daily activities, frustrations and challenges, illness or injury, life changes, and life crises. Continual stress exhausts the body's resources that maintain energy and resist disease. The result may be anxiety, depression, or serious illness.
- A well-balanced life can help you avoid or reduce stress. Three major ways to reduce or eliminate stress are: plan how to deal with stress, learn how to relax, and change your life.
- No matter how good your diet or how well you control stress, you cannot be healthy without physical fitness. This refers to how well your heart and other organs function. Physical fitness is determined by your age, heredity, and behavior.
- Your level of physical fitness depends largely on how often and how hard you exercise. You should exercise at least three times weekly for at least thirty minutes at a stretch. Every workout should include exercises for flexibility, endurance, and strength.

CHAPTER 30 Healthful Living ■ 409

■ Harmful health habits such as drugs, alcohol, smoking, and lack of sleep, can undo the results of regular exercise. You have most of your life ahead of you. The quality of that life will depend a great deal on your physical and mental health.

Words to Know

aerobic exercise exercise that conditions the heart and lungs by increasing the body's ability to take in oxygen.

basal metabolism the sum of all chemical changes taking place in the cells of the body.

calories units of food energy produced by food when it is used by the body.

nutrients chemical substances contained in food that are needed for good health.

nutrition the process by which plants and animals take in and use food.

physical fitness how well your heart and other organs function.

stress a response the body makes to any demand made upon it.

stressors physical, biological, or emotional causes of stress.

Questions to Answer

1. Name the three functions that nutrients perform.
2. In order to eat a balanced diet, you should select foods daily from the four food groups. Name the groups.
3. Based on the table shown in Figure 30-3, what is your ideal weight? About how many calories should you eat each day?
4. Why is it important to not go below 1,200 calories a day?
5. Stress sometimes comes from a positive event. Give an example.
6. Do people respond the same to stress? Answer and explain your answer.
7. Name three possible ways to cope with stress.
8. Name four benefits of exercise.
9. Briefly explain the three basic types of exercise.
10. Harmful health habits can undo the results of exercise. Name four bad health habits.

Activities to Do

1. For one full day, keep track of everything you eat and the approximate amount of each. After you have done this, compare what you have eaten with the daily food guide shown in Figure 30-2. How well does your diet compare with the recommendations? What foods, if any, are missing from your diet?
2. Using the daily food guide as a reference, plan a sample menu for one day. Be sure to include snacks, too. The total calories of all menu items should be enough to maintain your weight. Turn the menu in to your teacher.
3. Learning a relaxation method can be very helpful. For several days, practice the method described on page 404. Discuss in class whether you notice any difference in how you felt as a result of the meditation.
4. As a class, survey various businesses and industries in your area (or search for information at a library) to find out what things employers do to encourage workers to be more physically fit. How do employers benefit from having exercise breaks, exercise rooms, and related activities and facilities?

1. (a) Serve as fuel to provide energy. (b) Regulate body processes. (c) Furnish basic structural material for building.
2. (a) Meat group. (b) Vegetable-fruit group. (c) Milk group. (d) Bread-cereal group.
3. Each student will need to identify her/his recommended weight. Then, multiply this figure by 18 (man) or 16 (woman).
4. By taking in less than that amount, you probably will not get the necessary vitamins and minerals.
5. Two examples are getting married and moving into a new house. Other examples could be cited.
6. No. The response to stress varies from person to person. It seems to depend on physical and mental condition and the degree to which one feels in control of the situation.
7. (a) Plan how to deal with stress. (b) Learn how to relax. (c) Change your life.
8. Any of the seven benefits listed in the chapter.
9. (a) *Flexibility exercises*—these stretch the connective tissues and move the joints through a wide range of motion. (b) *Endurance exercises*—these strengthen the heart, blood vessels, and lungs. (c) *Strength exercises*—these increase the strength and endurance of the body's major muscle groups.
10. (a) Smoking. (b) Using drugs. (c) Excess alcohol consumption. (d) Lack of sleep.

24. Begin this activity by finding out if any students work at companies that have health and fitness programs. Provide students direction as needed in collecting information. This can be an interesting and informative activity.

Topics to Discuss

1. It has been said that Americans are the most "overfed and undernourished" people in the world. Why might this be true?
2. Eating disorders such as anorexia and bulimia have become serious health problems. What are some of the possible causes of these?
3. In what ways may short-term stress be beneficial?
4. How does physical fitness differ from body building?
5. A good diet, control of stress, and physical exercise are all interrelated. Discuss how one may benefit others.

25. The meaning is that Americans eat too much of the wrong types of foods (red meat, junk foods, foods high in fat and sugar content) and not enough fruits and vegetables.
26. These eating disorders may have emotional causes. Consult an encyclopedia for more information.
27. Stress can help you prepare for everyday demands such as taking a test or engaging in sports. It can help you deal with sudden dangers, emergencies, and increasing responsibilities.
28. Physical fitness refers to cardiopulmonary fitness, whereas body building refers to increasing muscle size.

1. The word *citizenship* comes from the Latin word *civitas*, which means "citizen united in a community."
2. Citizenship involves participation in several interrelated roles. While the primary responsibility for citizenship education falls on social studies teachers, work experience teacher/coordinators can and should encourage and reinforce the rights and obligations of citizenship.

* WWYD Feature A. This is an instance in which concerned citizens (students) have a *right* and a *duty* to make their views known to the school board.

CHAPTER THIRTY-ONE

Responsible Citizenship

OUTLINE
Responsibilities of Citizenship
Voting and Self-government
Thinking Clearly
Chapter Review

OBJECTIVES
After reading this chapter, you should be able to:
- Explain the four responsibilities of citizenship.
- Summarize the process of registering to vote and casting a ballot.
- Discuss the importance of voting in local, state, and national elections.
- Identify and describe those things that get in the way of clear thinking.

1 One of your most important roles in life is that of a citizen. *Citizenship* is a part of daily living. It involves participation in home, school, community, and work life. In this chapter, you will learn more about citizenship and how to be a more effective citizen.

RESPONSIBILITIES OF CITIZENSHIP

2 The responsibilities of citizenship involve *personal, economic, political,* and *national-defense* activities. On the personal level, good citizens are considerate of the needs of others. They help develop and preserve basic institutions such as home, family, and community. They adhere to the customs and laws of society. Good citizens stand up for what they believe is right and take action against what they know is wrong.

3. Ask students what it means "...to protect the rights of others to work."

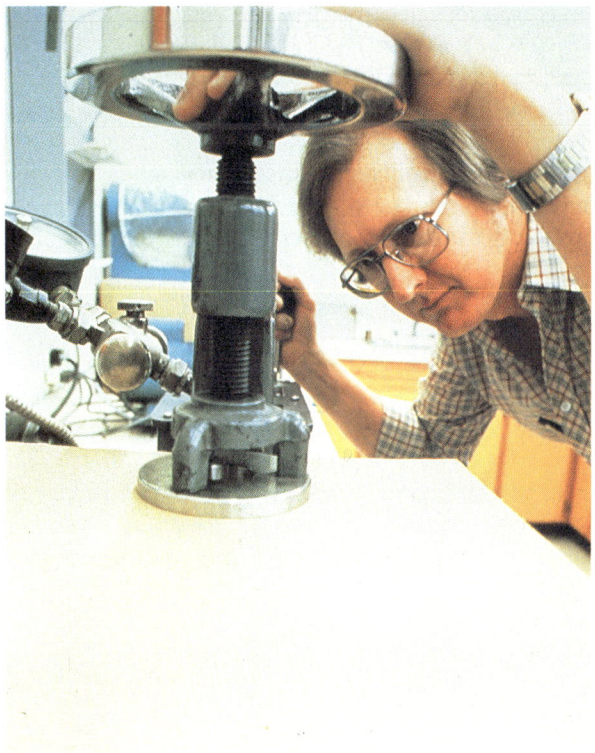

FIGURE 31-1 Economic citizenship means being a productive worker. *Courtesy of Boise Cascade Corporation*

What Would You Do?

The school board has voted to make drastic cuts in the district's vocational education program. The board says that it is too expensive to operate. Many students are very upset. A group of them are meeting after school to discuss what they might do. You have been asked to come to the meeting. You are concerned about the cuts, but aren't sure you want to get involved. What would you do?

3 Economically, being a good citizen means producing efficiently and consuming wisely. It also means helping to protect the rights of others to work. Good citizens use their talents and abilities to further the economic welfare of the society.

411

412 ■ SECTION 6 Independent Living

In the political area, every citizen of age should be a registered voter and participate in all elections. A good citizen keeps up with politics and informs politicians of his or her opinions. People can serve the government directly in such ways as doing jury duty when asked. They also can contribute to the national defense.

Some full-time workers belong to the military reserve. Dan Hartley, for instance, is a member of the Air National Guard. His regular job is working as a cabinetmaker at Blue Ridge Woodworks. Dan also attends monthly reserve meetings and spends two weeks at reserve summer camp. In a national emergency, Dan would be called into active duty.

VOTING AND SELF-GOVERNMENT

Voting is both a privilege and a right. You have the responsibility to vote in local, state, and national elections. If everyone refused to vote, self-government would come to a standstill. "What difference will my vote make?" you ask. Election outcomes often hinge on a few votes. Yours might make the difference!

Voting Qualifications and Procedures

In all states, voters must be U.S. citizens at least eighteen years of age and meet state residency requirements. For state and local elections, residency requirements vary among states. For national elections, it is thirty days.

FIGURE 31-2 Citizens coming to the defense of their country have allowed the United States to remain free. *Courtesy of Department of Defense*

4. Do you have any eighteen-year-olds in class? If so, ask how many have registered and voted.
5. You may wish to assign Activity 2 at this time.

FIGURE 31-3 This person didn't forget to go for her driver's license the day she was eligible. Will she remember to vote when she is eighteen? *Photo by David W. Tuttle*

Once you are eighteen and meet residency requirements, you should register to vote. In the registration process, a person's name is added to the list of eligible voters. In many areas, voters may register in person or by mail. To be eligible to vote in an election, it is usually necessary to register at least thirty days beforehand. In most states, registration is permanent unless the voter moves to another town or fails to vote for several years. If you ever move to a different place in the same town, notify the appropriate county office. They will need to update their records.

Casting a Ballot

In the United States, each county or ward of a state is divided into voting districts called *precincts*. A person must vote at the polling place for the precinct in which he or she lives. The polling place may be a public building such as a school, in a place of business, or even in a private home. At the polling place, election officials check eligibility for voting, distribute ballots, and count the votes after the polls close.

Basic to our system of voting is the right to cast a secret ballot. At every polling place, some type of private booth is provided. Only one voter at a time is permitted to be in the voting booth. The voting itself is made as easy as possible. Voters either mark a printed ballot or use some type of voting machine.

6. Ask students if they know what ward or precinct they are in and where the polling place is. If the answer is no, assign them to find out.

F•E•A•T•U•R•E

Citizen Lawmakers

◆ ◆ ◆

Most laws are passed by national, state, and local legislative bodies. However, through a method called an *initiative,* citizens can introduce a law. The initiative is used primarily at the state and local levels. Twenty states in the U.S. provide for the initiative in their constitutions.

In states or cities that use the initiative, anyone can draw up a proposed law. The next step is to collect a specific number of signatures on a petition favoring it. Once the initiative petition has qualified, it is voted on.

An initiative may be direct or indirect. In the first case, the proposed law is placed on a ballot and goes directly to the voters. In an indirect initiative, the proposed law goes first to the legislature. Should the legislative body approve the initiative, it goes into law. In some states, the question is ended if the legislature votes the bill down. In other states, a rejected bill is submitted to the people. If they vote for it, the bill becomes law. The governor cannot veto a bill passed in this way.

In recent years, the following initiatives have appeared on ballots in various states:

- Create overnight shelters for the homeless.
- Remove sales tax from food products.
- Roll back tax hikes.
- Establish a state lottery.
- Regulate pornography on cable TV.
- Limit medical malpractice damages.

FIGURE 31-FEATURE A number of important state laws have been achieved through the process of an initiative. *Photo by David W. Tuttle*

The initiative works in much the same way in a city as it does in a state. Whether at the state or local level, an initiative is a device that enables people to take direct political action if their elected representatives ignore their wishes.

*

Citizen Lawmakers. This piece illustrates the power of individual citizens to affect government policy. Does your state constitution allow for use of an initiative? Even in those states without initiatives, a similar process of collecting signatures on a petition is often successfully used to influence a legislature. If possible, share examples of initiatives or initiative-type political actions in your state or region.

414 ■ SECTION 6 Independent Living

8. What are the rules for class elections in your school?
9. For those students who have voted, ask them to describe the experience and how they felt.

FIGURE 31-4 Casting a ballot is a private matter.

FIGURE 31-5 Voters approved a bond referendum to build this new school. *Photo by Paul E. Meyers*

7   When voting for various offices, people may vote a "straight ticket" or "split" their ballots. Voting a straight ticket is when someone simply votes for all candidates of a particular party. Splitting a ticket is voting for some candidates of one party and some of another. For example, someone might vote for a Democratic candidate for President and a Republican candidate for governor. And if they desire, people may also write in the name of someone whose name isn't on the ballot. Any issues and questions on the ballot require only a "yes" or "no" vote.

The Election of Candidates

8   In most elections, the candidate with the most votes is the winner. This is probably what happens in your school elections. Suppose that in a class election Leroy Johnson receives 98 votes, Tiffany Anderson 95 votes, and Eric Washington 80 votes. Leroy Johnson would be the winner.

In some elections, though, a candidate must have a majority of the votes cast. If that were the case in the class election, Leroy Johnson would not be the

7. Ask students to provide specific examples of voting a "straight ticket" and "splitting" a ballot.

winner. He failed to receive at least half of the 273 votes. When a candidate like Johnson does not receive a majority, a "run-off" election is usually held between the top two candidates. Johnson runs against Anderson. The one with the most votes is the winner.

Voting Behavior

Our ancestors struggled to earn the right to vote. Unfortunately, too many people now take this privilege for granted. Middle-aged and older citizens are much more likely to vote than are young adults. Less than half of the people under twenty-five vote. In the last three Presidential elections, an average of about 37 percent of the eighteen-to-twenty age group voted. In "off-year" Congressional elections, only about 20 percent of eighteen-to-twenty year olds vote.

Too many people are like Roger's friend, Ted. On election day, Roger awoke before the alarm sounded. He got up and dressed quickly. This was the first election in which he was old enough to vote. After breakfast, he headed off to the polling place.

On the way, Roger saw Ted jogging on the sidewalk. "Hey Ted," said Roger, "Do you want to go with me to vote?" "Are you nuts, man," exclaimed Ted. "It doesn't do any good to vote. Those politicians don't care about anyone except themselves." Roger was very disappointed in Ted's reaction.

CHAPTER 31 ■ Responsible Citizenship ■ 415

finished, Roger gave the ballot to a clerk and watched her put it into a box. He left the polling place with a feeling of satisfaction. He was glad he had voted, but couldn't help but think about Ted. I wonder what I could do to change Ted's mind, he thought. Do you have any suggestions about what Roger might do?

Because of the publicity of a national campaign, more people vote in a presidential election than in any other. On the average, fewer voters participate in elections for state and local officials. This is interesting because our lives are influenced directly by the actions of our state and local officials. What reasons might people give for not voting in these elections?

THINKING CLEARLY

It is not always easy to choose between two political candidates or to decide which position on an issue is the correct one for you. Many issues such as nuclear power, federal spending, and the role of labor unions are not clearcut. To clarify your thinking about a candidate or an issue, gather all the *facts* you can. Remember that facts can be proven. It is fact, for example, that the earth is round and not flat. Following are a number of things that are frequently confused with facts.

FIGURE 31-6 Some people let others vote for them. How many people do you know who let others vote for them? *Photo by David W. Tuttle*

Roger went on to the polling place. There was a short line in front of the building, but no one seemed to mind. They quietly chatted among themselves until their turns came. Roger signed the register and got in line.

Several minutes later, a booth became available. Roger entered and marked his ballot. After he

Highway death toll

A report by the National Highway Traffic Safety Administration reveals that states that raised the speed limit on rural highways to 65 miles per hour recorded a substantial increase in the number of highway deaths, while death tolls on other roads slightly decreased.

Highway deaths in states whose urban interstates and other roads retained the 55-mph limit were almost precisely the same in 1987 as in 1986. By contrast, fatalities in states that raised the speed limit increased by an average of 19 percent. Critics of the higher speed limit were quick to respond. Sen. Frank Lautenberg of New Jersey said, "This report can be summed up on two words: speed kills."

Well, it turns out not to be a simple and straightforward as all that. The increased speed limit did result in many more deaths on some roads. But for some states, including Colorado, Indiana, Maine, New Hampshire, Montana and a couple others, the rate of highway deaths actually declined following the raised speed limits. Some other states that raised their limits, such as Arizona and New Mexico, experienced large increases in highway fatalities. To complicate matters, still other states, like Connecticut and Georgia, experienced large increases in highway deaths even though they didn't change their speed limit from 55.

What is one to make of this? Even the NHTSA doesn't know. It said there simply wasn't enough evidence to determine the speed limits' "long-term" impact on highway safety. But it would seem that NHTSA doesn't know what the short-term effect is either. At any rate, it continues to believe that "setting speed limits is a matter for state legislatures to decide based on their review of available fatality and injury data, actual experience and local conditions."

The problem, of course, is that it is difficult, in a non-laboratory experiment, to isolate the effect of a single causal variable, in this case, speed, on highway deaths. Too many other variables can intervene to make any simple cause-effect statement, if not impossible, difficult.

Still, though there is no clear pattern among the states looked at separately, it can hardly be ignored that taken together, highway fatalities increased markedly where the speed limit went to 65. That, by itself, should be give legislatures pause before rush to join the 65-mph craze.

FIGURE 31-7 Your political participation can make a difference. *Photo by Edith Raviola*

FIGURE 31-8 Editorials, which are a type of opinion, are a popular feature of many newspapers and magazines. *Reprinted by permission of the Times Union, Albany, NY*

10. Two of the most common reasons given for not voting are "too busy" and "wouldn't make any difference." Perhaps students can provide other reasons.

11. As the following impediments to clear thinking are discussed, ask students to provide examples and illustrations of each.

Rumor

A *rumor* is a popular report or story that has not been proven. Most rumors are spread by word of mouth. People often treat rumors as if they are fact.

Opinion

An *opinion* is one person's views about something. We reveal our opinions when we show preference for a certain candidate or take a particular side in an issue. Although opinions may be based on fact, they are not fact in themselves.

Prejudice

A *prejudice* is an opinion that is based on insufficient information (a prejudgment). People might express prejudice toward a person's sex, race, religion, or some other factor. Prejudice frequently causes great harm to innocent people and is the opposite of clear thinking.

What Would You Do?

An election will be held in a couple of weeks for class officers. Small groups of students have organized to push for certain candidates. Campaign workers are putting up posters and passing out literature. The campaign is starting to get dirty. A representative of one group has come to you asking that you not vote for Christine because "we don't want a girl for president." What would you do?

Allegation

An *alllegation* is an unproved statement about someone or something. For example, you might state that Elliot Chemical Company dumps hazardous waste into the river. An allegation is a very serious charge. Because you can be sued, you should never make an allegation unless you have the supporting facts.

Bias

When you have a tendency to lean toward something because of familiarity or preference, you have a *bias*. You might then make overexaggerated claims. For example, even though running is good exercise, joggers often exaggerate its benefits. Biases are not necessarily harmful. We all have them. But, when making choices and decisions, carefully keep in mind who is saying what.

Propaganda

Propaganda involves any organized effort or movement to spread certain information. The information may be true or false. Like biases, *propaganda* isn't always negative. For example, the American Heart Association uses propaganda to convince people of the hazards of smoking.

FIGURE 31-9 Is this message considered propaganda? Why? *Photo by David W. Tuttle*

---

* **WWYD Feature B.** This has the appearance of narrow-minded prejudice. The "representative" should be told that this action is offensive. People should vote for or against Christine based on her ability and potential, not on her gender.

12. Two common types of rumors are "fear rumors" (something bad is going to happen) and "hope rumors" (something good is going to happen).
13. You may wish to assign Activity 3 at this time.
14. Ask students if they have ever thought someone was "stuck-up" only to later find out that the person was just shy. Ask for other examples of prejudice.
15. Some allegations that suggest fact are very cleverly worded to sidestep legal liability. To illustrate, bring to class an example of a supermarket tabloid.
16. Ask students to name some of their "harmless" biases.
17. You may wish to assign Activity 4 at this time.

CHAPTER 31 Responsible Citizenship ■ 417

CHAPTER REVIEW

Chapter in Brief

- Citizenship is a part of daily living. The responsibilities of citizenship involve personal, economic, political, and national-defense activities.
- You have the responsibility to vote in local, state, and national elections. In all states, voters must be U.S. citizens at least eighteen years of age and meet state residency requirements. To be eligible to vote, you must register beforehand.
- A person must vote at the polling place for the precinct in which he or she lives. At every polling place, some type of private booth is provided. People may vote a straight ticket or split their ballots.
- Too many people take the privilege of voting for granted. Less than half of the people under twenty-five vote. On the average, fewer voters participate in state and local elections than in presidential elections.
- It is not easy to choose between two political candidates or to decide which position on an issue is the correct one. Many issues are not clearcut. To clarify your thinking, gather all the facts you can.
- Facts are things that exist and can be proven. A number of things are confused with facts. These include rumor, opinion, prejudice, allegation, bias, and propaganda.

Words to Know

allegation an unproven statement about someone or something.

bias a tendency to favor something because of preference or familiarity.

citizenship membership in a state or country; carrying out the duties and responsibilities of a citizen.

initiative the process by which legislation may be introduced or enacted directly by the people.

naturalization the process by which a foreign-born person becomes a citizen of the United States.

opinion one person's views about something.

precincts a division of a city, ward, or county for election purposes.

prejudice a prejudgment; an opinion that is based on insufficient information.

propaganda any organized effort or movement to spread certain information.

rumor a popular report or story that has not been proven.

Questions to Answer

1. Name the four types of citizenship responsibilities.
2. Give three examples of how citizens might exercise economic responsibilities.
3. What would happen if all but a very few people failed to vote?
4. In order to vote in an election, what must you do beforehand?
5. What is it called when a person votes for candidates of different political parties?
6. Why do more people tend to vote in a national than in a local election?

1. (a) Personal. (b) Economic. (c) Political. (d) National defense.
2. Any three of the following: producing efficiently, consuming widely, helping to protect the rights of others to work, using one's talents and abilities to further the economic welfare of the society.
3. Our system of self-government would come to a standstill.
4. Register to vote.
5. Splitting a ballot (or ticket).
6. The publicity of a national campaign seems to create more of an interest in voting.

7. A prejudice can be thought of as a prejudgment. Give an example.
8. Why should you be careful in making an allegation?

7. One example is that tall people are clumsy. Other examples could be cited.
8. You could be sued for making a false allegation.

Activities to Do

1. Identify someone (perhaps a friend or relative) in your community who is a *naturalized* citizen. Invite the person to class to talk about why he or she chose to become a U.S. citizen. Make a list of questions to ask.
2. Find out the residency requirements for voting in your community or city. Also, find out how you go about registering to vote where you live.
3. Newspaper and magazine editorials are a special type of opinion. Bring copies of editorials of interest to class. Discuss them. Are there any about which the class disagrees? If so, compose your own class opinion and send it to the proper source.
4. Bring to class a brochure or other statement that can be considered propaganda. Identify the main idea that the propaganda is attempting to communicate. Then, discuss the following questions: (a) Who wants you to believe this? (b) Why does the person or group want you to believe it? (c) Are there arguments on the other side?

18. Explain that naturalization refers to the process whereby foreign-born individuals can gain American citizenship.
19. It might also be interesting to conduct a debate on some relevant national or local issue.

Topics to Discuss

1. If you were an employer, how might you feel if several of your employees were called away for emergency military reserve duty?
2. Citizens may be of three types. One type is like a *stone* that stays where it is, neither hearing nor responding. A second type is like a *sponge* that absorbs and retains, but doesn't respond. The third type is like a *generator* that converts energy into power. Generators are the people who get things done.
    What percentages of students in your school, do you think, fall into each of these three groups? In which group do you belong? Discuss your answers in class.
3. Why do you think so few young adults vote? What can be done to increase the number of young voters?
4. On federal income tax forms, there is a place to mark if you want $1 of your tax to go to the Presidential Election Fund. How is this money used? Do you support this approach?

1. Recall the feature in Chapter 1 on "The Changing Workplace" and the section in Chapter 14 on "Tomorrow's Jobs." Future jobs are going to demand more education and training.

2. Ask students to describe the types of OJT they have received.

CHAPTER THIRTY-TWO

Education Beyond High School

OUTLINE
Education and Training
Types of Education and Training
Educational Information
Chapter Review

OBJECTIVES
After reading this chapter, you should be able to:
- Discuss why additional education or training beyond high school may be needed.
- Illustrate how the amount of required preparation varies among occupations.
- Name and describe the six common types of education and training.
- Explain how education or training requirements may vary for a given occupation.
- Know sources of information regarding education and training and financial aid.

FIGURE 32-1 What are *your* future educational plans? Photo by David W. Tuttle

One day Lionel and several of his friends were discussing what they were going to do after high school. "I can't wait to get my diploma," said Lionel. "I'm sick of school."

"I'm going to get a job in a factory," remarked Marty. "That way, I don't have to go on to school."

"Yea," said Henry, "who wants to get more education? I have a cousin who graduated from college and she can't get a job."

"I think you people are wrong," said Samantha. "*Most jobs require some type of education or training.* And there is a lot of competition for jobs, even among people who have degrees or training."

The conversation among these students shows some truths and some misunderstandings about the relationship between education and employment. It is true that not all jobs require additional schooling. But such jobs tend to be low-paying and have little security.

It is also true that getting a college degree will not automatically guarantee you a job. Some types of degrees do not lead directly to employment. For instance, to get a job in psychology, most students will need at least one graduate degree. And, with some programs, there are more graduates with degrees than there are available jobs. So people take jobs requiring less education. These are often jobs that high school graduates usually fill. So competition for those jobs increases.

On the other hand, it is a mistake to think that you won't need more education or training after high school. Most entry-level (beginning) jobs in factories, businesses, mines, and other workplaces require some on-the-job training. If you want to advance in a company, you will probably have to continue education throughout your lifetime. Your attitude toward future schooling is one of the things your employer will probably consider in judging you for a promotion or raise.

Linda and Vicki were in the same high school graduation class. After graduating, they were both

419

420 ■ SECTION 6 Independent Living

hired as assemblers at General Electronics. Their work involved putting together electrical components for radio receivers.

General Electronics has an agreement with Northwest Community College to offer courses at the plant. Classes start at 4:00 P.M. after employees get off work. The company pays for tuition. Linda enrolled in the program because she wanted a more challenging, better-paying job. Vicki ignored the program, saying that the courses were a waste of time.

New jobs at General Electronics frequently open up at all levels from assemblers to supervisors. Employees with two years of experience may apply for higher level jobs. As soon as they were eligible, both Linda and Vicki applied for the first available job in the records department. Linda got the job. The personnel manager was impressed by the fact that she had the initiative to continue her education. Vicki has since been passed over for several other jobs. Could it be due to her feelings about further training?

Career ladders exist in most industries. A *career ladder* is a series of occupations divided into ranks like steps on a ladder. Two examples of career ladders in the food service industry are shown in Figure 32-2. It is possible for one to start at the bottom of a career ladder and "climb" to the top. To do so, however, on-the-job experience and additional training are required.

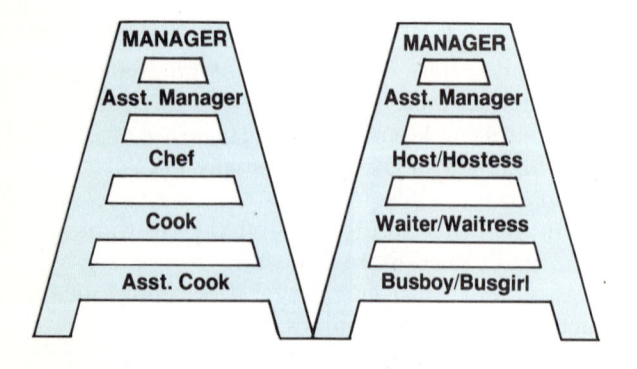

FIGURE 32-2 Two possible food service career ladders are shown here. Opportunities also exist for management positions above the manager level—particularly in chain restaurants and hotels. *Courtesy of Educational Foundation of the National Restaurant Association*

3. Ask students if opportunities for education and training during off-duty hours are provided by companies where they work.

* WWYD Feature A. Many vocational/technical schools and community/junior colleges have programs and services to assist weaker students.

Even though you are looking forward now to completing high school, don't turn your back on education at a later time. Some type of education or training program will probably be suited to your interests and abilities. Think it over carefully. Education and training will be one of the best investments you can make in your future.

What Would You Do?

After several years in your present job, you have reached a dead-end. You can't advance without additional training. But you never were a very good student. You are a poor reader, have difficulty memorizing, and nearly panic whenever you have to take a test. You don't want to admit it, but you are scared by the thought of taking a course. What would you do?

EDUCATION AND TRAINING

Do you have any idea of how you might go about becoming a hotel manager? A toolmaker? A computer programmer? A pilot? The first thing you would have to do for each of these occupations is learn a set of skills. To work as a hotel manager, you would have to learn about accounting, hiring, employee relations, and food service management. Toolmakers need to know machining operations, math, and blueprint reading and be able to use machine tools and special measuring instruments. To work as a computer programmer, you would have to learn how to translate ideas into computer language the computer could understand and write instructions it could follow. To become a pilot, of course, you would have to learn how to fly a plane.

Like a hobby or a sport, every occupation involves knowledge and skills that must be learned. But the amount of preparation needed varies among occupations. Deciding how much time and effort you are willing to put into education or training is important to career planning. It doesn't make sense to aim for a career as a veterinarian, for instance, unless you do well in school, are interested in science, and are willing to put in at least six years of hard work and study after high school.

The best way to begin a career is to complete high school. High school courses teach basic skills that

4. You may wish to assign Activity 1 at this time. Point out that individual occupations may also have different levels. For example, civil service secretarial positions are often denoted

as Level I, II, III, and so on, depending on the knowledge and skill required. Military ranks also represent a kind of career ladder.

CHAPTER 32 Education Beyond High School ■ 421

will help you be a better worker, consumer, and citizen. A high school diploma is necessary if you want to go to college, too. And you will usually need one to get into trade schools, technical institutes, apprenticeship programs, or the military. Moreover, most employers prefer to hire people who are at least high school graduates.

The choices that are open to you after high school are shown in Figure 32-4. As you can see, many ways are available to get necessary education and training. The path you choose depends on the kind of occupation you have in mind—and the time and effort you are willing to put into your training.

TYPES OF EDUCATION AND TRAINING

From hearing people talk, you may sometimes get the feeling that almost everyone gets a college education. That is not so. About half of all high school graduates *do* continue their school, though not necessarily in college.

On-the-Job Training

Almost all occupations involve some sort of learning by doing, also known as on-the-job training (OJT). A skilled worker teaches you as you watch. You then do the task under that worker's supervision. An advantage of OJT is that you are paid while you learn. Some jobs are almost always learned through OJT. Examples include postal clerk, machine-tool setter, shoe repairer, and furniture upholsterer. Generally, OJT is given for jobs that take more than a few days to learn, but less than formal apprenticeship would require.

FIGURE 32-3 Do you know what type of training it takes to become a television producer? *Courtesy SIUC Photocommunications*

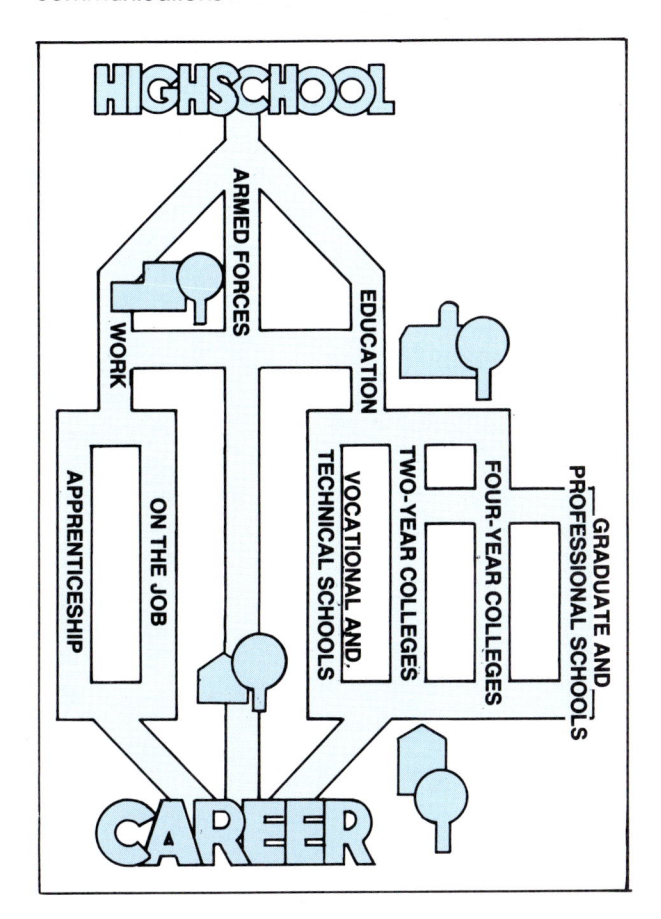

FIGURE 32-4 Several different paths may lead to your career goal.

5. More than 95 percent of military enlistees are high school graduates.

FIGURE 32-5 Most occupations require some on-the-job training. *Courtesy Ametek, Inc.*

6. For clarity, the six types of education and training that follow are described separately. However, different alternatives can be pursued at the same time.

F•E•A•T•U•R•E

Training and More Training

◆ ◆ ◆

In the last decade or so, the automobile industry has undergone dramatic change. Competition has forced companies to modernize plants and alter manufacturing methods to improve quality and productivity. A different type of worker is also being recruited and trained.

An illustration of such change is the new Mazda Motor Manufacturing plant opened in 1988 at Flat Rock, Michigan. Employees are hired ten to twelve weeks before they are placed on the assembly line.

New hires receive three weeks of "soft training" in which they learn the basics of teamwork and company philosophy. They are then assigned to an area such as the body shop where they get seven weeks of classroom and hands-on training. During this time, they are screened according to job capabilities. Individuals are assigned to a job for which they are best suited.

Next, they are assigned to a unit leader (similar to a foreman). The unit leader further screens the workers and decides at which point on the assembly line they will work best. Three or four more weeks of off-line training is then given.

The cost of recruiting and training a single employee averages about $13,000. Mazda spent about $40 million to staff its Flat Rock plant. The company believes that the key to success is picking the best employees and training them well. Similar recruitment and training efforts are becoming standard throughout the automobile manufacturing industry. The emphasis on quality employees and training is shared by hundreds of other businesses and industries.

Training and More Training. This piece describes the new reality in increasing numbers of companies throughout the U.S. In order to compete in a worldwide economy, companies have been forced to pay more attention to employee selection and training. Emphasize to students that there are fewer and fewer well-paying jobs where you can be "hired on Friday and start working on Monday."

Very often, OJT is combined with short-term classroom training. A power truck operator, for example, may take a safe driving course lasting several days. In some cases, OJT goes on for a few years. Air traffic controllers, for example, need two or three years of training and work experience before they are considered fully qualified to handle their jobs.

Apprenticeship

Apprenticeship is a formal on-the-job program during which a worker (called an *apprentice*) learns a trade. Extensive OJT and related instruction are involved. Apprenticeships usually last about four years, but may range from one to six years. During this time, apprentices work under *journey workers*. Under the journey worker's guidance, the apprentice gradually learns the trade and performs the work under less and less supervision. Apprentices are full-time employees. An apprentice's pay generally starts out at about half that of an experienced worker and gradually increases throughout the apprenticeship. Many programs are co-sponsored by trade unions that offer apprentices union membership.

The main drawback to apprenticeship is the stiff competition to get into a program. Generally, program sponsors seek people who seem to have the greatest chances of completing the program. To get your name placed on the *apprenticeship register* (waiting list) you usually have to take an aptitude test, have an interview, and meet the necessary physical requirements. Once on the register, the wait can last months or even years. In the construction trades alone, an estimated eight applicants are qualified for every opening.

Vocational and Technical Schools

Many types of schools offer vocational training to teach skills used on the job. Vocational programs are offered by high schools, vocational high schools, and area vocational centers. Common areas of study include business and office, consumer and homemaking, trade and industrial, health occupations, and agriculture.

Other sources of training include trade schools, technical institutes, business schools, and correspondence or home-study schools. Privately run schools such as these are often called *proprietary schools*. In classes lasting from several weeks to several years, these schools will teach you cosmetology, barbering, flying, office procedures, computer operations, fashion design, locksmithing, and many other skills. The cost of training at a proprie-

Apprenticeable Occupations

aircraft mechanic, electrical and radio	carpenter	foundry metallurgist	optician	roofer
airframe and power plant mechanic	cement mason	furrier	optomechanical technician	rotogravure-press operator
airplane mechanic, armament	chemical laboratory technician	glazier	ornamental ironworker	sheet-metal worker
assembler, electro-mechanical	computer peripheral equipment operator	instrumentation technician	orthotist	shipwright
automobile body repairer	cook	jeweler	painter	sign writer
automobile mechanic	cosmetologist	laboratory technician	patternmaker	silversmith
baker	custom tailor	landscape gardener	photoengraver	stationary engineer
biomedical equipment technician	dairy equipment repairer	lead burner	plasterer	stereotyper
blacksmith	dental laboratory technician	leather stamper	plater	stonemason
bookbinder	drafter, mechanical	lithographic plate maker	plate finisher	stone setter
bricklayer	dry cleaner	locksmith	plumber	television and radio repairer
butcher, all-round	electrical repairer	machinist	pottery machine operator	terrazzo worker
cabinetmaker	electronics mechanic	maintenance mechanic	printer-slotter operator	tile setter
calibration laboratory technician	engraver	metal fabricator	private branch exchange installer	tool-and-die maker
car repairer	environmental control system installer-servicer	millwright	programmer, business	truck-body builder
	farm equipment mechanic	model maker	prosthetics technician	upholsterer, inside
	firefighter	monotype keyboard operator	pumper-gager	wallpaper printer
	floor layer	numerical control machine operator	quality control inspector	wastewater treatment plant operator
		operating engineer	radiographer	welding technician
			rigger	X-ray equipment tester

Source: Occupational Outlook Quarterly, Winter 1983, p. 21

FIGURE 32-6 These are among the more than 700 occupations that can be learned through apprenticeship.

424 ■ SECTION 6 Independent Living

tary school is often more expensive than at a public institution such as a community college.

What Would You Do?

You notice an advertisement in the paper for Whitney Business College. The ad states, "Flexible hours, credit for life experiences, tuition financing arranged, guaranteed job upon graduation." The school isn't too far from your home.

"This could be just what I'm looking for," you say to yourself. "I think I'll give them a call." What would you do?

In a vocational or technical school, you will practice in the classroom those skills you will need on the job. In business school, you might do word processing, file, use a dictaphone, or keep books. In programs for health occupations, you might operate medical equipment. People learning to be mechanics and repairers would take classes in blueprint reading and shop math.

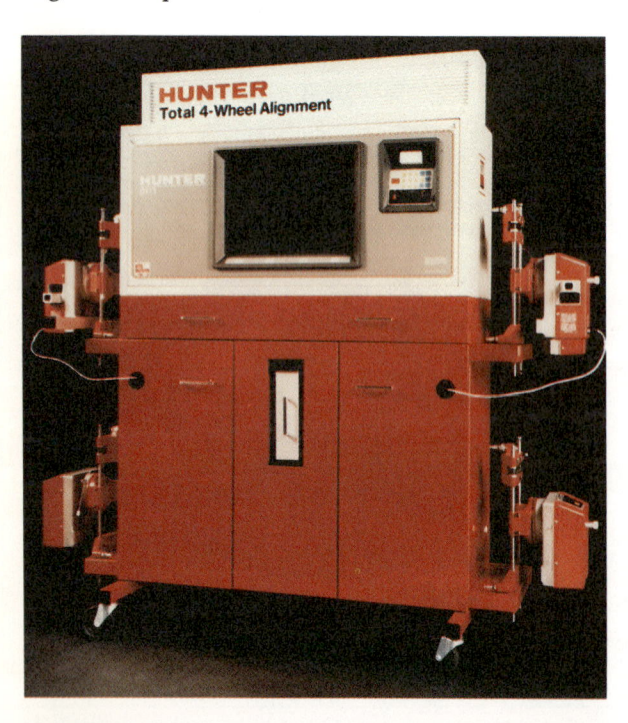

FIGURE 32-7 Many vocational schools provide first-class training on modern tools and equipment. *Courtesy of Hunter Engineering Co.*

* *WWYD Feature B.* The individual should refer to the section on private trade and technical schools in the *OOH* and write the NATTS for more information.

10. Community/Junior Colleges provide wonderful opportunities for many students who seek additional training, but who don't want to go to college full-time. Obtain catalogs and other

When you complete your program, you will receive a certificate. You will then be ready to begin work, though your employer may also want to give you some on-the-job training.

Community and Junior Colleges

These two-year colleges provide two types of education. One is the college transfer program, a two-year general education program for students who plan to transfer later to a four-year college. General education courses include English, history, science, art, and music. The other type of program is the occupational or career program, which offers specialized skill training leading directly to employment. Though a typical occupational program lasts two years, some such as licensed practical nurse, can be learned within one year.

A typical community or junior college offers training in many occupational areas. Examples include computer service technician, dental hygienist, forestry technician, emergency medical technician, recreation leader, auto mechanic, and welder.

Community and junior colleges offer two main advantages. First, they have close ties with local business and industry and try to tailor their training programs to the needs of the local area. This makes it easier for students to find jobs after training. Another advantage is that these colleges are usually less expensive to attend. Since they are supported by local property taxes, many colleges charge low tuition.

FIGURE 32-8 Community and junior colleges are popular with working adults who can only attend school part-time. *Photo by David W. Tuttle*

descriptive information for those colleges in your area and make it available for student use. You may also wish to invite a college representative/recruiter to talk to the class.

11. Obtain information and share with students the average cost for tuition and fees at a community/junior college compared to a four-year state university.

13. You may wish to assign Activity 4 at this time.

CHAPTER 32 Education Beyond High School ■ 425

Colleges and Universities

Colleges and universities are four-year institutions that vary widely in their concern for training students in specific occupations. Some are primarily liberal arts schools that offer a broad, general education. Others are very specialized and are oriented toward engineering and technology. Still others, such as large state universities, offer a combination of general and specialized education.

A typical state college or university offers 100 or more areas of study called *majors*. Common majors include Business and Administration, Journalism, Education, Engineering, Political Science, Chemistry, Economics, Plant and Soil Science, Art, Theatre, and Psychology.

By and large, college doesn't prepare you for one particular occupation. Instead, most undergraduate programs give you a foundation upon which many careers can be built. In four years of college, you can expect to gain a basic education in your chosen field of study. In addition, you will be expected to broaden your knowledge of literature, mathematics, science, history, the fine arts, and many other areas. An advantage of college, however, is that you usually have a lot of freedom in choosing courses that interest you.

Kurt is attending a state university. His major is Administration of Justice. Within his major, he takes courses in law enforcement, correctional management, juvenile justice, and delinquency prevention. Administration of Justice graduates get jobs as police officers, corrections counselors, parole officers, and so on. Kurt plans to get additional training and hopes to become an FBI agent.

Military Training

Another way to get education and training is to join a branch of the military service—Army, Navy, Air Force, Marines, or Coast Guard. The military prepares people for a variety of occupations in which civilians also work. These include cook, nurse, computer operator, mechanic, firefighter, and hundreds of others. While in the service, you can learn occupational skills and gain work experience. Then, when you get out, you can use your skills to get a civilian job. Or you may decide to make a career of military service.

EDUCATIONAL INFORMATION

To make a good educational decision, you will need information on various schools—their courses of study, admissions requirements, costs, and so on.

14. Over 75 percent of all military occupations have counterparts in the civilian work force.

FIGURE 32-9 Colleges and universities provide more than training for an occupation. *Courtesy SIUC Photocommunications*

12. An important difference between colleges and junior colleges is that the former usually have specific entrance requirements while the latter usually have "open entry."

FIGURE 32-10 If these individuals were not in uniform, you wouldn't know that they were receiving training in the military. *Courtesy of Ed Masterson, San Diego, CA*

15. You may wish to conduct Activity 5 at this time. The recruiter should be able to provide a copy of the *Military Career Guide* and related materials for student use.

426 ■ SECTION 6 Independent Living

Sources of Additional Information

General information on a career as a legal assistant and a list of legal assistant schools approved by the American Bar Association are available from:

Standing Committee on Legal Assistants, American Bar Association, 750 North Lake Shore Dr., Chicago, IL 60611.

For information on certification of legal assistants, schools that offer training programs in a specific State, and standards and guidelines for legal assistants, contact:

National Association of Legal Assistants, Inc., 1420 South Utica, Tulsa, OK 74104.

Information on a career as a legal assistant, training programs, and local legal assistant associations can be obtained from:

National Federation of Paralegal Associations, Suite 201, 104 Wilmot Rd., Deerfield, IL 60015-5195.

General information about job opportunities for legal assistants is available from:

Legal Assistant Management Association, P.O. Box 40129, Overland Park, KS 66204.

For information on legal assistant careers, training programs, and job opportunities, contact:

National Paralegal Association, P.O. Box 629, Doylestown, PA 18901.

Source: Occupational Outlook Handbook: 1988-89 edition, p. 209

FIGURE 32-11 Many trade and professional associations provide information about education and training opportunities.

Sources of Information

In Chapter 14, you learned how to use the *Occupational Outlook Handbook (OOH)* in an occupational search. For each occupation described in the OOH, a section titled "Sources of Additional Information" appears at the end, Figure 32-11. For each occupation in which you are interested, write to the sources listed. The information you receive frequently lists places where education and training are available.

Both private and government publishers put out guides to education and training programs. A listing of guides to vocational and technical schools as well as two-year and four-year colleges is shown in Figure 32-12. Your school guidance office or career center should have a collection of such guides. So, too, should your local public library.

16. Refer students to Figure 32-11 and illustrate additional examples in an actual *OOH*.
17. You may wish to assign Activity 2 at this time.

VOCATIONAL AND TECHNICAL TRAINING

Title	Publisher
Postsecondary Schools with Occupational Programs	Superintendent of Documents U.S. Government Printing Office USGPO Stop SSMR Washington, DC 20402-9325
Handbook of Trade and Technical Careers and Training	National Association of Trade and Technical Schools 2251 Wisconsin Avenue, NW Suite 200 Washington, DC 20007
Occupational Education	Macmillan Publishing Company, Inc. 866 Third Avenue New York, NY 10022

TWO-YEAR AND FOUR-YEAR COLLEGES

Director of Educational Institutions	Association of Independent Colleges and Schools 1 Dupont Circle, NW Suite 350 Washington, DC 20036
Barron's Guide to the Two-Year Colleges	Barron's Educational Series, Inc. 20 Wireless Boulevard Hauppauge, NY 11788
Barron's Profiles of American Colleges	Barron's Educational Series, Inc. 20 Wireless Boulevard Hauppauge, NY 11788
College Planning/Search Book	The American College Testing Program 2201 North Dodge Street P.O. Box 168 Iowa City, IA 52243
The College Handbook	The College Board 45 Columbus Avenue New York, NY 10023-6992
The College Blue Book	Macmillan Publishing Company, Inc. 866 Third Avenue New York, NY 10022
Comparative Guide to American Colleges	Harper & Row Publishers, Inc. 10 East 53rd Street New York, NY 10022
Lovejoy's College Guide	Monarch Press Division of Simon & Schuster, Inc. 1 Gulf & Western Building Gulf & Western Plaza, 16th Floor New York, NY 10023
Guide to Two-Year Colleges	Peterson's Guides P.O. Box 2123 Princeton, NJ 08543-2123
Guide to Four-Year Colleges	Peterson's Guides P.O. Box 2123 Princeton, NJ 08543-2123

FIGURE 32-12 Here are some resources for information about education and training institutions.

Many of these guides are updated annually, so be sure to use the most recent edition.

To learn more about apprenticeship, your local Job Service is probably the best source of information. In some cities, Apprenticeship Information Centers (AICs) furnish information, counseling, and aptitude testing. They also direct people needing more specific help to union hiring halls, Joint Apprenticeship Committees, and employer sponsors. Ask a Job Service counselor if there is an AIC in your community.

For information about education and training in the Armed Forces, contact the local recruiting office of the branch you are interested in. Each branch of the service has information available describing its specific program.

Financial Aid

The cost of education or training is an important consideration in making educational decisions. You will have to think about how much training you or your family can afford as well as how much you would like to get. The cost of schooling needed to become a doctor is much greater than the cost of training to become a lab technician.

In some cases, the training requirements for a specific occupation will vary greatly. For example, to become a registered nurse, you could attend one of three different types of programs:

- A two-year associate degree program at a junior or community college.
- A three-year diploma program operated in conjunction with a hospital.
- A four-year degree program at a college or university.

The costs per year of training will also be quite different.

Don't be discouraged if you want to pursue education beyond high school, but you or your family cannot afford the cost. Begin by talking to your school guidance counselor. *Financial aid* may be available. *Scholarships,* loans, *grants,* and the like are available from schools, educational foundations, business firms, religious groups, community organizations, and the government. A good section on "Sources of Financial Aid Information" is contained in the *OOH.* Make sure you use the most recent edition.

Take advantage of educational opportunities. Education is never wasted. Whether you take formal coursework, learn on the job, or study on your own, you will benefit as a worker and human being by continuing to learn and grow.

FIGURE 32-13 The number of women enrolled nationwide in colleges and universities now exceeds the number of men. *Courtesy of Bay Path Junior College, Longmeadow, MA*

18. Because of the increasing cost of higher education, a number of states have initiated "tuition savings programs" in which the interest from state bonds or bank accounts used to finance a college education are tax exempt. Sentiment is growing in Congress for some type of national program. Also, beginning in 1990, the interest on U.S. savings bonds is tax free if used to finance a child's college education (certain restrictions apply).
19. Duplicate the section on "Sources of Financial Aid Information" from the current *OOH* and disseminate it to students. Assist individual students as required to obtain additional information.

CHAPTER REVIEW

Chapter in Brief

- Not all jobs require additional schooling. Such jobs, however, tend to be low paying and have little job security. Getting a college degree will not automatically guarantee you a job. On the other hand, it is a mistake to think that you won't need more education or training after high school. Additional education and training will be one of the best investments you can make in your future.

- Every occupation involves knowledge and skills that must be learned. But the amount of preparation needed varies among occupations. Deciding how much time and effort you are willing to put into education or training is important to career planning.

- The most common education and training options are: (a) *On-the-job training*—short-term training provided while you work. (b) *Apprenticeship*—formal on-the-job training ranging from one to six years. (c) *Vocational and technical schools*—skill training for a specific occupation conducted in classrooms, labs, shops, and workplaces. (d) *Community and junior colleges*—two-year programs for college transfer or skill training in a specific occupation. (e) *Colleges and universities*—four-year schools offering a variety of programs ranging from general to specialized education in hundreds of majors. (f) *Military training*—training and employment in hundreds of different occupations while serving in the Armed Forces.

- To make a good educational decision, you will need information on various schools (course of study, admissions requirements, costs, and so on). Both commercial and government publishers put out a variety of educational information and guides.

- The cost of education or training is an important consideration in making educational decisions. There are many sources of financial aid to help pay for education or training. A good section on "Sources of Financial Aid Information" is contained in the *Occupational Outlook Handbook*.

- Education is never wasted. You will benefit as a worker and human being by continuing to learn and grow.

Words to Know

apprentice a trainee engaged in learning an occupation under the guidance and direction of a skilled worker. *See* apprenticeship.

apprenticeship a formal program of on-the-job training and related instruction by which a young worker learns an occupation under the direction of a journey worker.

apprenticeship register a waiting list for individuals who have met the preliminary requirements for entrance into an apprenticeship program.

career ladder a group of related occupations that have different skill requirements that can be arranged in a ladder-type fashion from low to high.

financial aid a broad term that includes all forms of financial assistance (scholarships, loans, grants, and so on) to individuals pursuing postsecondary education.

grants grants-in-aid; funds provided to qualified persons to assist them in attending college or other postsecondary education.

CHAPTER 32 Education Beyond High School ■ 429

journey workers skilled, experienced workers; the status achieved by apprentices upon completion of an apprenticeship program.
major the primary area of study chosen by a student for a college or other degree.
proprietary schools a privately operated postsecondary vocational, technical, or business school.
scholarships financial aid awarded to a student on the basis of outstanding academic achievement.

Questions to Answer

1. Give three reasons why you should consider taking additional education or training beyond high school.
2. What is the best way to begin a career?
3. Identify the six most common types of education and training.
4. What is the difference between OJT and apprenticeship?
5. Which is more expensive to attend, a public vocational/technical school or a proprietary school? Why?
6. Community and junior colleges provide two main types of programs. Name them.
7. Name three types of information that you will need to make a good educational decision.
8. Name two sources of information about apprenticeships.
9. Provide an example to illustrate how education or training requirements may vary for a given occupation.
10. What publication contains information about types of financial aid?

Activities to Do

1. Select an entry-level occupation of interest. Develop a career ladder for the occupation similar to those in Figure 32-2. You will probably need to ask people in related occupations for assistance.
2. Go to your school or public library. What sources of education and training information do you find there? Are there information sources about financial aid? Your instructor may assign you a specific task. List the information your teacher requests and duplicate a copy for each class member.
3. Contact your local Job Service to find out what types of information it has about apprenticeship. Also check with them to find out the location of the nearest Apprenticeship Information Center.
4. Identify a school or college in which you may be interested. Use one of the resources listed in this chapter and find out the following information: (a) What are the entrance requirements? (b) How long does it take to complete the program you are interested in? (c) How much does it cost to attend? (d) Is any financial aid available? (e) Does the institution provide job-placement services? Summarize your findings on paper and submit your report to your instructor.
5. Invite to class a recruiter from the military services and have him or her discuss types of training programs and educational benefits provided by the military.

---

1. (a) Most entry-level jobs require some OJT. (b) If you want to advance in a company, continuing education will probably be required. (c) Your attitude toward further schooling will probably be of interest to an employer.
2. To graduate from high school.
3. (a) On-the-job training. (b) Apprenticeship. (c) Vocational and technical schools. (d) Community and junior colleges. (e) Colleges and universities. (f) Military training.
4. *OJT* is informal, short-term training. *Apprenticeship* is OJT, but a formal, lengthy program of study is required.
5. A proprietary school. Because public schools are supported by taxes. Proprietary schools are private, profit-making businesses.
6. (a) College transfer general education program. (b) Occupational skill training program leading directly into employment.
7. (a) Courses of study offered. (b) Admissions requirements. (c) Costs.
8. (a) Job Service office. (b) Apprenticeship Information Center.
9. Registered nursing is a good example. A nurse can be trained in a two-year associate degree program, a three-year diploma program, or a four-year baccalaurate degree program. Other examples could be cited.
10. The *Occupational Outlook Handbook*.

20. You may wish to develop one example of a career ladder in class (e.g., illustrate the progression from beginning teacher, master teacher, department head, principal, assistant superintendent, and so on). Assist students as required in developing their own.
21. An alternative to this would be to invite a librarian or counselor to class to share such information.
22. Some schools have access to computerized data banks that students can use to obtain such information.

Topics to Discuss

1. Most of you are probably employed as part of a work experience education program. Discuss how learning on the job is different from learning at school.
2. Has working made you more aware of the need for education or training? If so, how?
3. Many companies encourage their employees to pursue additional education (beyond that received on the job). How does this benefit the employer?
4. More and more adults are returning to college and other types of education. What is behind this trend?
5. If you are working now, find out what type of education or training you would need to move ahead in your job. Discuss this in class.

23. A better educated employee is often a more skilled, productive, and satisfied worker.
24. Common reasons behind the trend are (a) more adults seeking career changes and/or advancement, (b) more employers providing educational benefits, and (c) more colleges actively recruiting adults and modifying programs to meet adult needs. Perhaps students can name additional reasons.

GLOSSARY

Accident: an unplanned event often resulting in personal injury, property damage, or both (17).

Adjusted gross income: the amount on an income tax form that results after you subtract exclusions and adjustments from total income (26).

Adjustments: items that can be subtracted from income when filing an income tax return (26).

Advertising: a public notice or message intended to aid in the sale of a product or service (22).

Aerobic exercise: exercise that conditions the heart and lungs by increasing the body's ability to take in oxygen (30).

Affirmative action: government policies and programs designed to correct past discrimination (8).

Agenda: the list of items to be followed in an actual business meeting (18).

Allegation: an unproven statement about someone or something (31).

Allocation: the process of distributing income to the various items in a budget (24).

Allowances: the number of tax exemptions one is entitled to (6).

Alternatives: the choices or options available in making a decision (12).

Annual percentage rate (APR): the percentage cost of credit on a yearly basis (23).

Anxiety: a feeling of concern, worry, or unease, such as concern about a forthcoming job interview (6).

Appraise: to evaluate someone or something, such as a potential employer (5).

Apprentice: a trainee engaged in learning an occupation under the guidance and direction of a skilled worker. See apprenticeship (32).

Apprenticeship: a formal program of on-the-job training and related instruction by which a young worker learns an occupation under the direction of a journey worker (32).

Apprenticeship register: a waiting list for individuals who have met the preliminary requirements for entrance into an apprenticeship program (32).

Aptitudes: developed abilities; those things that one is good at doing (13).

Area: the number of square units of space on the surface of a figure enclosed by the perimeter (16).

Arraignment: a hearing before a judge during which formal charges are brought against an arrested person (28).

Assertive: firmly and positively stating one's position or point of view (22).

Authority: the power or rank to give orders or make assignments to others (6).

Automated teller machine (ATM): one type of electronic banking in which a plastic card is used in an electronic terminal to withdraw cash, make deposits, or transfer funds to another account (23).

Automatic raise: a regular pay raise received by all employees (10).

Bail: a sum of money paid to the court guaranteeing that an accused person will show up for trial (28).

Basal metabolism: the sum of all chemical changes taking place in the cells of the body (30).

Beneficiary: the person to whom the death benefits from a life insurance policy are to be paid (25).

Benefits: Financial help in time of sickness, old age, disability, or the like (27).

Bias: a tendency to favor something because of preference or familiarity (31).

Board of directors: individuals elected by the shareholders to assume responsibility for the management of their company (20).

Body language: nonspoken communication through physical movements, expressions, and gestures (5).

Bonds: interest-bearing certificates issued by a government or corporation (24).

Brand name: nationally known brand; a product made or sold by a well-known company (22).

Brokers: individuals who specialize in selling stock and other financial investments (24).

Budget: a plan for managing income and expenditures (24).

Bylaws: printed information that defines the basic characteristics of an organization and describes how it will operate (18).

Calories: units of food energy produced by food when it is used by the body (30).

431

Capital gain: an increase in the selling price of a stock (24).
Career guidance: assisting students in career planning and decision-making (1).
Career ladder: a group of related occupations that have different skill requirements and can be arranged in a ladder-type fashion from low to high (32).
Cash discount: a discount of several percent offered to the buyer to encourage early payment on an account (16).
Catastrophe: a sudden disaster or misfortune (25).
Charter: a legal document giving a corporation permission to conduct certain business activities (20).
Check register: a ruled form used to record all of the transactions that occur in a checking account (23).
Circumference: the perimeter of a circle (16).
Citizenship: membership in a state or country; carrying out the duties and responsibilities of a citizen (31).
Civil service test: a pre-employment test that is administered to a job applicant seeking a government job (4).
Clients: the business customers of a professional worker (9).
Code of ethics: rules for professional practice and behavior (18).
Co-insurance: a provision of health insurance in which the insured person is required to share in the expenses (typically 20 percent) beyond the deductible amount (25).
Commission: a fee paid to a broker upon purchase of a stock (24).
Common law: the system of law used in the United States; judge-made law (28).
Communication: sending information, ideas, or feelings from one person to another (15).
Comparison shopping: the process of finding out the cost of a product or service at several different places before making a decision to buy (22).
Compatible: something that is pleasant or agreeable, such as a relationship with a job interviewer (5).
Compensation: the total amount of income and benefits received from a job (10).
Competition: the efforts of sellers to win potential customers (21).
Complaint: an expression of dissatisfaction with a product or service (22).
Compounding: compound interest; a process in which interest is periodically added to the account balance, causing savings to steadily grow (24).
Computer: an electronic tool that can store and process data, and can direct the work of other tools (19).
Computer literacy: a general knowledge of what computers are, how they work, and what they can be used for (19).
Conditions of employment: the specific details of a job offer such as working hours, salary or wages, fringe benefits, and so on (5).
Condominium: ownership of a specific unit in a townhouse or apartment (29).
Confirm: to verify or make firm, such as calling to confirm (check on) an appointment (5).

Consumer: someone who buys or uses goods and services (22).
Consumption: the process of using goods and services that have been produced (21).
Cooperation: getting along with and working well with others (7).
Cooperative: a share of an apartment building complex (29).
Corporation: a form of business organization in which shareholders own the business and elect a board of directors to manage the company (20).
Cover letter: a letter of application accompanied by a job resume that is sent to a potential employer (4).
Credit: the receipt of money, goods, or services in exchange for a promise to pay at a later time (23).
Creditors: persons or companies to whom money is due (20).

Decision-making: the process of choosing between two or more alternatives or options (12).
Decision-making styles: the typical manner in which a person makes a decision (12).
Decree: an order by the court to the defendant to stop doing whatever is harming the plaintiff (28).
Deductible: a provision of insurance in which the insured person is required to pay a certain initial amount before the insurance company pays the balance (25).
Deductions: 1. Certain amounts that are withheld from the paycheck of an employee (10). 2. Items on an income tax form that can be subtracted from the adjusted gross income (26).
Defendant: a person required to answer charges in a lawsuit (28).
Deficits: when the government spends more than it takes in (21).
Demand: the willingness of consumers to spend money for goods and services (when demand increases, the price generally goes up) (21).
Deposit ticket: a preprinted form used to make a deposit in a checking account (23).
Depression: a severe recession marked by stagnant business activity, scarcity of goods and money, and high unemployment (21).
Direct-mail advertising: advertising that is sent to potential customers through the mail (22).
Disabling injury: one causing death, permanent disability, or any degree of temporary total disability beyond the day of the accident (17).
Discrimination: treating or favoring one person as compared to another (8).
Distractions: things that draw attention away from what one is doing (15).
Diversify: to spread out money over several different types of investment options (24).
Dividends: company profits that are divided among the stockholders (24).
Due process: the legal right to state one's case or point of view before a decision is made (6).

GLOSSARY 433

Economics: the study of how goods and services are produced, distributed, and used (21).
Electrocute: to cause death by an electric shock (17).
Electronic banking: a broad term used to describe various types of electronic fund transfers (23).
Employability skills: the general work habits and attitudes required in all jobs (1).
Endorsement: a signature on the back of a check used to cash or transfer ownership of the check (23).
Enthusiasm: eagerness; a strong interest in something (7).
Entrepreneur: one who runs her/his own business; a self-employed person (20).
Entry-level job: a beginning job that does not require any previous knowledge or experience (3).
Enunciation: speaking and pronouncing words clearly (15).
Environment: the sum total of one's surroundings (12).
Equal employment opportunity: the idea that a person cannot be discriminated against in hiring or employment because of age, race, color, religion, sex, national origin, or handicapping condition (8).
Equal Employment Opportunity Commission (EEOC): the government agency that administers the Civil Rights Act of 1964 (8).
Equity: the value of a home above the amount owed on a mortgage (29).
Exclusions: items for which income taxes do not have to be paid (26).
Exempt: to be free of something, such as not having to pay taxes (6).
Exemptions: a set amount based on the number of dependents that is subtracted from adjusted gross income when filing an income tax form (26).
Expenditures: money that is spent (24).
Experiences: the sum total of events that compose an individual's life (12).

Face value: regarding life insurance, the amount of money that is paid in the event of the insured's death (25).
Federal Insurance Contributions Act (FICA): the federal law requiring employers to deduct an amount from worker's paychecks for Social Security (27).
Fee: a sum of money charged by a private employment agency for helping someone to find a job (3).
Filing: the process of completing and submitting an income tax form (26).
Finance charge: the total dollar amount paid for the use of credit (23).
Financial aid: a broad term that includes all forms of financial assistance (scholarships, loans, grants, and so on) to individuals pursuing postsecondary education (32).
Follow-up letter: a thank-you letter sent to an interviewer following a job interview (5).
Franchise: a contract with a parent company to use its name and sell goods or services within a certain area (20).

Full-service bank: one that offers customers a full range of financial conveniences and services (23).

Generic products: goods that state only the common name of the product on the label (22).
Goods-producing industries: those companies and businesses such as manufacturing, construction, mining, and agriculture that produce some type of a product (14).
Goodwill: acts of kindness, consideration, or assistance (9).
Grammar: a set of rules about correct speaking and writing (15).
Grants: grants-in-aid; funds provided to qualified persons to assist in attending college or other postsecondary education (32).
Grooming: maintaining a neat, attractive appearance (11).
Gross pay: the amount of salary or wages earned for a certain period before deductions are withheld (10).
Guarantee: a pledge that something is exactly as stated or advertised. *See* warranty (22).

Health maintenance organization (HMO): a type of insurance in which unlimited group health care is provided for a fixed monthly or yearly fee (25).
Honesty: a refusal to lie, steal, or mislead in any way (7).
Human relations: interactions among people (9).
Hypothetical: something imagined or pretended, such as a potential job (5).

Incentive: something to work toward; a potential reward (10).
Income: money coming in (24).
Indictment: the formal statement charging a person with an offense. *See* arraignment (28).
Individual Retirement Account (IRA): voluntary private pension plan that allow employed individuals to save up to $2,000 annually toward retirement and receive certain tax benefits (27).
Industries: places of employment, such as factories, hospitals, restaurants, banks, and so on (14).
Inflation: a sharp increase in the cost of goods and services (21).
Initiative: the process by which legislation may be introduced or enacted directly by the people (31).
Interest: feeling of excitement and involvement (7).
Interests: things that you like to do; preferences for certain kinds of work activities (13).
Interpersonal attraction: a tendency to be drawn to another person because of similar characteristics and preferences (9).
Intuition: a feeling or hunch (12).
Investing: using money not required for personal and family needs to increase overall financial worth (24).
Invoice: a bill for goods; an itemized statement of merchandise sent to a purchaser (16).

Job: a paid position at a specific place or setting (1).

Job application form: a form used by employers to collect personal, educational, and occupational information from a job applicant (4).

Job interview: a face-to-face meeting between a job seeker and a potential employer (5).

Job-lead card: a card on which information and notes about job leads are recorded (3).

Job Service: local branches of the state employment service that help unemployed people find jobs (3).

Journey workers: skilled, experienced workers; the status achieved by apprentices upon completion of an apprenticeship program (32).

Judgment: 1. Thinking about a problem and making the right decision (7). 2. The judge's decision in a civil suit in favor of either the plaintiff or the defendant (28).

Keyboarding skills: the ability to operate a computer by use of the typewriter-like keyboard terminal (19).

Landlord: the owner or manager of a rental apartment (29).

Law: the body of enforced rules by which people live together (28).

Leadership: the process of influencing people so as to accomplish the goals of the organization (18).

Lease: a rental agreement between a tenant and a landlord (29).

Letter of application: a letter written by a job applicant to a potential employer applying for a job (4).

Letter of resignation: a letter by an employee notifying an employer of the intent to quit a job (10).

Liability: that for which one is responsible, such as an accident occurring in your home (25).

Life roles: the various parts of one's life, such as citizen, parent, spouse, worker, and so on (13).

Lifestyle: the way in which a person lives (13).

Line item: a single entry in a budget; a budgeted item (24).

Liquidity: easily converted into cash (24).

Loopholes: a legal tax provision that allows some people to reduce or avoid income taxes (26).

Loyalty: faithfulness; believing in and being devoted to something (7).

Lump-sum payment: a one-time payment of money to the surviving spouse or child of a deceased person covered by Social Security (27).

Major: the primary area of study chosen by a student for a college or other degree (32).

Majority: a vote of at least one more than half of the people who vote (18).

Markdown: a reduction in the selling price of a product (16).

Market: marketplace; the place where buyers and sellers meet to conduct business (21).

Markup: an amount added by a retailer to the cost price of goods that allows it to cover expenses and make a fair profit (16).

Measurement: the act of determining the dimension, quantity, or degree of something (16).

Merit raise: a pay raise that is based on job performance (10).

Minimum wage: by law, the lowest hourly wage that can be paid to an employee (8).

Minor: a person who has not reached the full legal age (3).

Modem: an electronic device that allows computers to be linked through standard telephone lines (19).

Money market fund: a type of mutual fund in which the pooled funds are used to buy interest-bearing notes and certificates of deposit (24).

Monopoly: exclusive control of the supply of any good or service in a given market (21).

Motion: a statement of proposed action by a participant in a business meeting (18).

Mutual fund: an investment company that pools the money of many investors and buys a collection of stocks or bonds (24).

Natural disaster: destruction of life or property resulting from an uncontrollable event in nature (17).

Naturalization: the process by which a foreign-born person becomes a citizen of the United States (31).

Negotiable order of withdrawal (NOW): a type of interest-bearing checking account in which a withdrawal order (check) is written against a savings account rather than a checking account (23).

Net pay: the amount on a paycheck; the take-home pay of an employee after deductions are subtracted from gross pay (10).

Nutrients: chemical substances that are contained in food and are needed for good health (30).

Nutrition: the process by which plants and animals take in and use food (30).

Obsolete: outdated; no longer in use (2).

Occupation: name given to a group of similar tasks that a person performs for pay (1).

Occupational description: information about a specific occupation that explains what the work is like (14).

Occupational Outlook Handbook (OOH): a printed resource that is produced by the government to provide occupational information (14).

Occupational Safety and Health Administration (OSHA): the government agency that sets and enforces standards for safe and healthful working conditions (8).

Occupational search: collecting information about an occupation of interest using some type of printed resource or data base (14).

Occupational skills: learned abilities to perform tasks or duties of a specific occupation (1).

Opinion: one person's views about something (31).

Order of business: a standard series of steps followed in a business meeting (18).

Overdraft: a check written for an amount greater than is available in the account (23).

Overtime: time worked beyond the standard forty-hour workweek (8).

Overtime pay: the wage received for working overtime, usually 1½ times the normal hourly wage (10).

Parliamentarian: the individual in an organization who advises the chair on matters regarding correct parliamentary procedure (18).

Parliamentary procedure: the formal rules used to conduct a meeting in a fair and orderly manner (18).

Partnership: a form of business organization in which two or more persons co-own the business (20).

Patients: persons under treatment or care by a medical practitioner (9).

Patronize: to trade with, or give one's business to, a certain individual or company (9).

Patrons: customers of certain service-producing businesses or institutions (9).

Payee: the person or agency to whom a check is written (23).

Pension: a regular payment of money to a retired person (27).

Performance evaluation: the process of judging how well an employee is doing on the job (7).

Perils: the possible damages from which one seeks protection through the purchase of home insurance (25).

Perimeter: the distance around the outside of an object (16).

Personal data sheet: a summary of personal, educational, and occupational information that is used to help fill out a job application form and to prepare a job resume (4).

Personal hygiene: keeping one's body clean and healthy (11).

Physical fitness: how well your heart and other organs function (30).

Plaintiff: the complaining party in a lawsuit (28).

Portfolio: a collection of stocks or bonds (24).

Postdating: placing a date on a check that is ahead of the current date (23).

Posture: the position of a person's body while standing, walking, or sitting (11).

Precedence: the order of priority among the four types of motions used in a business meeting (18).

Precincts: a division of a city, ward, or county for election purposes (31).

Pre-employment test: a paper-and-pencil test or performance exercise administered by an employer as part of the job application process (4).

Prejudice: a prejudgment; an opinion that is based on insufficient information (31).

Premium: the cost of an insurance policy (25).

Pride: feeling satisfied with what one has accomplished (7).

Probation: 1. A trial period during which one's performance is being observed and evaluated (6). 2. Releasing a convicted person on a suspended sentence under supervision and upon specified conditions (28).

Problem: a question in need of a solution or answer (12).

Production: the making of goods available for human needs and wants (21).

Productivity: the output of a worker; how much a worker produces on the job (7).

Program: coded instructions that cause a computer to perform a certain task. *See* software (19).

Promotion: advancement to a higher level job or position within a company (2).

Pronunciation: the way in which words are spoken (15).

Propaganda: any organized effort or movement to spread certain information (31).

Proprietary school: a privately operated postsecondary vocational, technical, or business school (32).

Proprietorship: a form of business organization in which one person owns the business (20).

Prosperity: a period of expanding economic growth (21).

Public safety: all efforts by federal, state, and local governments to protect persons and property (17).

Punctuality: being on time (7).

Qualify: to meet the preliminary requirements for another job or position (2).

Quarters of coverage: a three-month period during which a certain amount of income is earned; used to determine eligibility for Social Security. *See* work credit (27).

Quorum: a majority of the total membership of an organization (18).

Random-access memory (RAM): the working memory in a computer (19).

Read-only memory (ROM): the permanent memory in a computer (19).

Reality factors: those persons, events, or situations that are real and present, such as the high cost of going to an Ivy League college (12).

Recall: to call back; a request to return something (22).

Recession: a period of declining economic growth (21).

References: names of individuals listed on a job application form or resume who are qualified to provide information about the applicant (4).

Referrals: directing a student to a potential employer for a job interview (3).

Regular (fixed) expenditures: in budgeting, those essential payments that are about the same amount each month (24).

Reimburse: to pay back money already spent (6).

Responsibility: the duty to follow an order or carry out a work assignment (6).

Resume: a one-page description of a job seeker's history and qualifications for employment (4).

Retailers: businesses that sell directly to the consumer (20).

Revenue: money that is raised through taxes to pay the cost of government (26).

Risk: the chance of an accident or loss (25).

Rumor: a popular report or story that has not been proven (31).

Safety: freedom from harm or the danger of harm (17).

Savings: cash set aside in a bank account to be used for financial emergencies and goals (24).

Scholarships: financial aid awarded to a student on the basis of outstanding academic achievement (32).

Self: what you are; your personal characteristics or traits (13).

Self-direction: setting goals and working toward them (2).

Self-employed: an individual who owns and operates a business; an entrepreneur (20).

Seniority: the length of time someone has worked for a company (9).

Service-producing industries: those companies and businesses that produce (provide) some type of personal or business service, such as transportation, finance, insurance, trade, and so on (14).

Share-draft account: a type of checking account in which a draft (check) is written against a credit union savings account (23).

Signature card: a form that is completed to open a checking account (23).

Social Security: government programs that help people meet social and economic needs; commonly used to refer to the federal system of retirement pensions, survivors payments, and hospital insurance for the elderly (27).

Software: the electronic instructions and programs that direct a computer to perform certain applications (19).

Stable job: a job considered to be permanent and which may last several years (2).

Standard English: the usual form of language used by the majority of Americans (15).

Standard Industrial Classification (SIC): a system of grouping industries according to the type of product or service produced (14).

Standard Occupational Classification (SOC): a system of grouping occupations based on the type of work performed (14).

Standard workweek: by law, the completion of forty hours of work during a seven-day period (8).

Statement of account: a summary of all of the transactions completed in a checking account for a given time period (23).

Statement of earnings: a pay statement; the attachment to a paycheck that shows gross pay, deductions, and net pay (10).

Stockholders: individuals who purchase stock, or shares of ownership in a company (20).

Stocks: shares of ownership in a company (24).

Stop-loss provision: a condition of health insurance which limits the amount of the bill for which the insured person is responsible (25).

Stress: a response the body makes to any demand made upon it (30).

Stressors: physical, biological, or emotional causes of stress (30).

Sublet: a lease by a tenant to another person (29).

Summons: an order commanding the defendant in a lawsuit to appear in court on a certain day (28).

Sunscreen: a special lotion used to protect the skin from the sun's ultraviolet rays (11).

Supervisor: a boss; one who gives directions and orders and oversees the work of others (6).

Supplier: a person or agency that distributes goods to retailers (20).

Supply: the amount of goods available for sale (when the supply is plentiful, the price generally decreases) (21).

Task group: a work group formed to accomplish a particular objective (9).

Tax: a required contribution of money made to the government (26).

Taxable income: the amount on an income tax form left after all exclusions, adjustments, exemptions, and deductions have been subtracted; the amount of income on which tax is paid (26).

Taxation: the process by which the expenses of government are paid (26).

Tax credits: certain expenses that can be deducted from the amount of income tax owed (26).

Tax evasion: the illegal practice of avoiding payment of some or all of one's income tax obligation (26).

Technology: application of scientific knowledge to practical uses (2).

Telecommuting: an application of computers in which an employee based at home (or other location) receives assignments and returns completed work via a phone modem (19).

Tenant: renter; the person who rents an apartment (29).

Terms: terms of sale; the time limit within which the buyer must pay for merchandise received from the seller (16).

Territorial rights: unwritten rules concerning respect for the property and territory of others (9).

Townhouse: an individually owned house that is attached to another house on one or both sides (29).

Trade discount: a deduction from the catalog (list) price of an item (16).

Training agreement: a signed agreement outlining the relationships and responsibilities of the parties involved in a work experience education program (1).

Training plan: a listing of knowledges, attitudes, and skills to be developed by the student participating in a work experience education program (1).

Training station: a work experience student's place of employment (1).

Variable expenditures: in budgeting, day-to-day living expenses (24).

Vocabulary: the total of words known by an individual (15).

Vocational student organization (VSO): nonprofit, national organizations with state and local chapters that exist to develop leadership skills and good citizenship among members. Each organization is composed of vocational students interested in a specific occupational area (18).

Wage base: the amount of gross salary or wages subject to Social Security tax (27).

Wardrobe: wearing apparel; one's clothing (11).
Warrant: a court order authorizing a police officer to make a search, seizure, or arrest (28).
Warranty: a guarantee; a promise that the product is free from defects (22).
Wholesale houses: businesses that sell to retailers rather than to consumers. *See* supplier (20).
Work: activity directed toward a purpose or goal that produces something of value to oneself and/or to society (1).
Work credit: a guideline used to determine eligibility for Social Security benefits; measured in quarters of coverage (27).
Work experience education: education programs designed to provide opportunities for students to explore or participate in work as an extension of the regular school environment (1).
Work history: all of the jobs that one holds during the course of a working lifetime (2).
Work permit: a form issued by school officials that gives a student permission to work during school hours as part of a work experience education program (3).
Work values: attitudes and beliefs about the importance of various work activities (13).
World of work: an informal phrase used to describe the network of industries and occupations (14).

INDEX

Accidents
    class of, 212
    defined, 211
    types of, *211*
Advertising
    consumers and, 285–292
    defined, 285
    techniques, 289–290
        association, 289
        conformity, 290
        economic appeal, 290
        emotional appeal, 289
        endorsements, 289
        familiarity, 289
        goodwill, 289
        health and comfort, 290
        intellectual appeal, 290
        scare tactics, 290
        successful living, 289
    traps, 290–292
        bait and switch, 291
        false claims, 291–292
        false pricing, 291
        referral sales plans, 291
Affirmative action, 96
Age Discrimination Act of 1967, 96
Annual interest rate, 331
Antiperspirants, personal hygiene and, 130
Anxiety, pre-employment, 64
Apartments
    landlords and, 395
    location of, 394
    privacy and, 394
    rental agreements and, 397–398
    roommates and, 396
    safety and, 394
    searching for, 393–398
        considerations about, 394–395
    ventilation of, 394–395
Appearance, 129–132
    job interviewing and, 51–52

Apprenticeships, 423
Aptitudes, 155–156
Area
    conversion chart, 207
    defined, 203–204
Arithmetic, computers and, 240
Attendance, 70
    employer expectations and, 82
Automobiles
    budgeting and, 324
    insurance, 347–349
        cost of, 348
        no-fault, 349
    purchasing, 286–287

Bank statements, *308*, *309*
Banks
    commercial, 299
    mutual savings, 300
Benefits, 70
Bonds, investing in, 333–334
Bonuses, 118
Bosses, getting along with, 105
Budgets, 320–324, 326–327
    estimating income and expenditures, 321–322
    following, 326–327
    goals establishment, 320–321
    revising, 326–327
    setting up, 322–327
        regular expenditures, 323–324
        variable expenditures, 324, 326
Business forms, writing skills and, 189–190
Business letters, writing skills and, 192–193
Business math, 196–200
    cash discount, 198–199
    markdown, 200
    markup, 199
    sales tax, 199–200

    total purchase amount, 197
    trade discount, 198
Business Professionals of America (BPA), 228
Business, small. *See* Small business

Calculators, 201
Capital, economics and, 270
Career information, 164–179
    classifying industries, 166–167
    classifying occupations, 165–166
Career planning
    decision making process, 140–143
        evaluating information, 141–142
        gathering information, 141
        influences on, 148–149
        problem definition, 141
    decision making styles, 145
Careers
    changing employment in, 170–173
    decision making styles, 145
    fastest growing, *171*
    future, 168, 170–173
    information concerning, 164–179
        classifying industries, 166–167
        classifying occupations, 165–166
    largest increase in, *172*
    military, 169
    search form, 174–175
Cash. *See* Money
Cash discount, 198–199
Cash-value life insurance, 345
Change, work world and, 19–20
Changing employment in, careers, 170–173
Charity, 121

INDEX ■ 439

Checking accounts, 301–310
  bank statements, *308*, 309
  managing, 304–310
    check registers, 305–306
    check writing, 304
    deposits and, 307, 309
  opening, 304
  types of, 302–304
Checks
  endorsing, 306–307
  writing, 304
Child labor, fair employment practices and, 93–94
Child-care assistance, 119
Circumference, defined, 202–203
Citizenship
  keeping informed, 415–416
  responsibilities of, 411–412
  self-government and, 412, 414–415
  voting and, 412, 414–415
Civil law, 382
Civil Rights Act of, 1964, 96
Clothing, 132–135
  budgeting and, 324
Co-workers, getting along with, 105–107, 109
Collective bargaining, 100
Commercial banks, 299
Commissions, 117–118
Common law, 381
Communication
  asking questions, 56
  effective, 55
  nonverbal, 56
  skills, 182–195
    guidelines for good, 185
    listening, 183–185
    pronunciation, 185
    reading, 188
    speaking, 185–188
    standard English, 187
    telephone skills, 187
    writing, 189–193
Communications, computers and, 242–243
Community colleges, 424
Compensation, 116–118
Competition, free enterprise and, 273, 275
Compounding interest, 331
Computers, 236–249
  described, 236–237
  education
    engineering, 244–245
    medicine, 245

    science, 244–245
  future of, 245, 247
  keyboard skills, 236–237
  operation of, 238–241
    arithmetic and logic, 240
    control, 240
    input, 239
    memory, 240
    output, 240–241
  workplace and, 241–245
    communications, 242–243
    education, 244
    government, 242
    transportation, 243
Consumers
  advertising and, 285–292
    techniques, 289–290
  automobile purchases and, 286–287
  complaints, 293–295
  defined, 283
  goods and services
    defined, 283
    using wisely, 284–285
  making choices, 283
  rainchecks and, *291*
  responsibilities of, 293
  rights of, 292–293
  wise buying by, 283–284
Consumption, economics and, 270–271
Contributions, budgeting and, 326
Cooperation, employer expectations and, 82–83
Cooperative vocational education, 6–9
Corporation, definition of, 253
Cosmetics, 130, 132
Cost-per-check account, 302
Court system, 384–385
Courts
  small claims, 387
  types of, 384–385
Credit, 310–314
  budgeting and, 324, 325
  cost of, 313–314
  history, 311
  loan, 310, 312
  sales, 312–313
Credit unions, 300
Customers, getting along with, 109–111

Decision making
  influences on, 148–149
  occupational, 143–145

  process, 140–143
    evaluating information, 141–142
    gathering information, 141
    problem definition, 141
  styles, 145
Deductions, paycheck, 120–121
Deodorants, personal hygiene and, 130
Diet, 401–403
Direct-mail advertising, 285
Disability payments, 366–367
Disabling injury, 213–214
Disasters, largest U. S., *217*
Discounts
  cash, 198–199
  trade, 198
Discrimination
  protection from, 96
  affirmative action, 96
Distributive Education Clubs of America (DECA), 228
Dress, jobs and, 132–135
Due process, defined, 70

Earnings, 116–118
Economic growth, 275–278
  inflation and, 277–278
  patterns of, 277
Economic systems, 272–273
  free enterprise, 273, 275
Economics
  principles of, 269–272
    consumption and, 270–271
    market, 273–274
    production factors, 269–270
    supply and demand and, 273
Education
  computers and, 244
  financial help for, 427
  information about, 425–426
  sources of, 426
  post high school, 419–429
    apprenticeship, 423
    colleges, 425
    community colleges, 424
    junior colleges, 424
    military training, 425
    on-the-job training and, 421, 423
    training and, 420–421
    universities, 425
    vocational and training schools, 423–424
  work experience, 6–12
    benefits of, 11–12

440 ■ INDEX

cooperative vocational
education, 6–9
exploratory work experience,
9, 11
Elections, 414
Electronic banking, 309–310
Employees
discrimination, protection from,
96
fair employment practices,
93–95
child labor and, 93–94
equal pay, 95
wages and hours, 94–95
performance evaluations, 86–88
rights of, 92–103
discrimination protection, 96
fair employment practices,
93–95
safety and health, 97–99
See also Employers
Employers
child-care assistance, 119
contacting, 40–42
letter of application, 42
in person, 40–41
telephone, 41
expectations of, 78–91
attendance, 82
cooperation, 82–83
equipment care, 81–82
good judgment, 80
honesty, 84
interest and enthusiasm, 83
loyalty, 84
productivity, 78
punctuality, 82
quality of work, 79
safety consciousness, 81
work habits, 82–84
getting along with, 105
See also Employees
Employment
accepting or rejecting, 59
agencies, 31
anxiety prior to, 64
changing, 125–126
compensation for, 116–118
decision making about, 143–145
fired from, 126
Engineering, computers and,
244–245
Entertainment, budgeting and, 326
Entrepreneur
defined, 250
rating scale, *260*

Entrepreneurial skills, 250–265
Envy, 147
Equal pay, 95
Equipment, care of, 81–82
Estate taxes, 355
Excise taxes, 355
Exercise
benefits of, 405
guidelines for, 407–408
types of, 407
Expenditures
estimating, 321–322
regular, 323–324
variable, 324, 326
Exploratory work experience,
9, 11

Fair employment practices, 93–95
child labor and, 93–94
Feature
Calculator Review, 201
Citizen Lawmakers, 413
Collective Bargaining, 100
Common Law, 381
Corporate Fitness Programs, 406
Counterfeit Goods Undercut the
Economy, 274
Credit Billing Blues, *325*
Dealing With a Roommate, 396
Drug Testing, 72
Electronic Tax Filing, 359
Eliminating Gobbledygook, 186
Employer-sponsored Child-care
Assistance, 119
Envy in the Workplace, 147
Growth of Small Business, 251
Job Stress and Workers'
Compensation, 368
Labor Unions, 85
Lie Detector and Honesty Tests,
43
Mid-career Change, 160
Military Occupations, 169
Safety-belt Laws Start to Click,
216
Shift Work, 21–22
Sun Protection, 131
Teleconferencing, 54
Temporary Work, 30–32
Trade and Professional
Associations, 226
Training and More Training,
422
Walk-in Medical Clinics, 343
Workerless Factory, 246

Your Credit History, 311
Federal courts, 385
Federal income taxes, 355–361
determining, 357–358
electronic filing, 359
filing returns, 358–361
graduated, 356–357
FICA taxes, 121
Financial help for education, 427
Financial institutions
changes in, 300–301
checking accounts
managing, 304–310
opening, 304
commercial banks, 299
credit unions, 300
mutual savings banks, 300
savings and loan associations,
300
Financial services
checking accounts, 301–310
types of, 302–304
Food
budgeting and, 324
daily guide, 401–402
energy requirements, 402
weight control and, 402–403
Forms
job application, 37–39
personal data sheet, 36
W-4, 74
writing skills and, 189–190
Free checking accounts, 302
Free enterprise economic system,
273, 275
competition and, 273, 275
freedom of choice and, 275
private ownership and, 273
profit motive and, 273
Fringe benefits, 118
Future Business Leaders of
America (FBLA), 228
Future Farmers of America (FFA),
228
Future Homemakers of America
(FHA), 228

General ability tests, 44
Gift taxes, 355
Gifts, budgeting and, 326
Goals, job, 25–26
Goods, defined, 283
Government, computers and, 242
Grooming, 129–132
Groups, participation in, 111–113

INDEX ■ 441

Hairstyling, 130
Health
    diet and, 401–403
    employee rights and, 97–99
    insurance, 340–342
    nutrition and, 401–403
    physical fitness and, 405–408
    stress and, 403–405
    weight control, 402–403
Health Occupations Students of America (HOSA), 228
Home
    insurance, 346–347
    safety, 212–213
Home Economics Related Occupations (HERO), 228
Honesty tests, employment and, 43
Hours, fair employment practices and, 94–95
Household expenses, budgeting and, 324
Housing
    alternatives, 391–392
    apartments, searching for, 393–398
    buying, 392–393
    needs, 390–391
    renting, 392
    wants, 390–391
Human relations, 104–115
    bosses and, 105
    co-workers and, 105–107, 109
    customers and, 109–111
    groups, 111–113
    workaholics and, 100

Income
    estimating, 321–322
    spending and, 318–320
Income taxes, 120–121, 355
    federal, 355–361
    determining, 357–358
    electronic filing, 359
    filing returns, 358–361
    graduated, 356–357
Individual retirement accounts (IRAs), 371–374
Industries
    classifying, 166–167
    future, 168, 170–173
Information
    about self
        aptitudes, 155–156
        interests, 152–154
        work values, 157–159
        career, 164–179

    classifying industries, 166–167
    classifying occupations, 165–166
    evaluating, 141–142
    gathering, 141
Inheritance taxes, 355
Injuries, disabling, 213–214
Input, computers, 239
Insurance, 121
    budgeting and, 324
    description of, 339–340
    health, 340–342
    home, 346–347
    life, 244–246, 342
Interest
    annual percentage yield, 331
    frequency of compounding, 331
    pay periods, 331
    rates, figuring, 331–332
Interests, 152–154
Interviewing
    job, 48–62
        appearance during, 51–52
        conduct during, 53, 55–57
        materials needed, 51
        skills for, 49–50
IRAs. *See* Individual retirement accounts

Job
    application form, 37–39
    interview, defined, 48
    performance, 78–84
    safety, 214–215
    searching, self-direction, 18
    services, 29–30
    stress, workers' compensation and, 368
Jobs
    accepting or rejecting, 59
    appearance and, 129–132
    applying for, 35–47
        contacting employers, 40–42
        form, 37–39
        letters, 42
        personal data sheet, 36
        resume writing and, 39–40
    changing, 125–126
    defined, 6
    dress and, 132–135
    employment agencies and, 31
    fired from, 126
    getting ready for, 26–27
    goals, 25–26
    grooming and, 129–132

    interviewing for, 48–62
        appearance during, 51–52
        conduct during, 53, 55–57
        materials needed, 51
        skills, 49–50
    leads, 27–30
        classified ads, 29
        family and friends, 28
        in-school sources, 28
        job services, 29–30
        keeping track of, 31–32
    reporting to, 65–68
    searching for, 18–20, 25–33
    See also Work
Junior colleges, 424
Jury duty, 70

Keyboard skills, 236–237

Labor, economics and, 270
Labor unions, 85
Landlords, 395
    tenant relationships, 398
Law
    branches of, 382
    common, 383
    court system, 384–385
    enforcement, 382–384
    legal services, 385–387
    nature of, 380
Lawyers
    choosing, 386
    determining need of, 385
    fees, 386–387
Leadership, 223–235
    characteristics of, 224–225
    defined, 223
    organizational, 223–225
Legal services, 385–387
Length, conversion chart, 207
Letter of application, 42
Letters, writing skills and, 192–193
Lie detectors, employment and, 43
Life insurance, 244–246, 342
Life roles, 161
Listening skills, 183–185
    guidelines for good, 185
Loan credit, 310, 312
Logic, computers and, 240

Management, economics and, 270
Markdown, 200
Markup, 199
Mass, conversion chart, 207
Math skills. *See* Business math

442 ■ INDEX

Measurement, 200, 202–205
  surface, 202–204
  systems of, 205–207
    conventional, 205
    conversion charts, 207
    metric, 206
  volume, 204–205
Medical care, budgeting and, 324, 326
Memorandums, writing skills and, 191–192
Memory, computers and, 240
Merit raises, 123
Metric system of measurement, 206
  conversion from conventional, 207
  conversion to conventional, 207
Mid-career change, 160
Military
  occupations, 169
  training, 425
Money
  budget, developing and using, 320–324, 326–327
  income and spending, 318–320
  interest rates and, 331–332
  investing, 332–334
  saving, 327–329
  working and, 2
Money market funds, 334
Mortgages, budgeting and, 323
Motions
  defined, 231
  types of, 232
Mutual savings banks, 300

Natural resources, economics and, 269–270
Negotiable Order of Withdrawal (NOW), 302–303
No-fault automobile insurance, 349
Notes, writing skills and, 189–190
Nutrition, 401–403

Occupation, defined, 5–6
Occupational Outlook Handbook (OOH), 166
  using, 173, 175–178
Occupational Safety and Health Administration (OSHA), 97
Occupations
  changing employment in, 170–173
  classifying, 165–166
  fastest growing, 171

largest increase in, 172
military, 169
search form, 174–175
On-the-job training (OJT), 421, 423
Organizational leadership, 223–225
Organizations
  policies and rules, 69–71, 73
  structure of, 68–71, 73–74
  student vocational, 225, 227–228
    bylaws, 229
    holding meetings of, 230, 231
    officers and committees, 229
Output, computers and, 240
Overtime pay, 117

Parliamentary procedure, 228–233
Partnership, definition of, 253
Passbook accounts, 329–330
Pay
  raises, 122–123
  withholding and, 74
Paychecks, 120–121
Payroll taxes, 355
Performance evaluations, 86–88
Performance tests, 44
Perimeter, defined, 202
Personal data sheet, job applications and, 36
Personal safety, 212–218
Phi Beta Lambda, Inc. (PBL), 228
Physical fitness, 405–408
  guidelines for, 407–408
Piece-rate, 117
Policies and rules of organizations, 69–71, 73
Posture, 132
Pre-employment tests, 44
Private ownership, free enterprise and, 273
Probation, 71
Production
  factors of, 269–270
    capital, 270
    labor, 270
    management, 270
    natural resources, 269–270
Productivity, 78
Promotions, 124–125
Pronunciation, speaking and, 185
Proprietorship, definition of, 253
Public law, 382
Public safety, 218–219
Punctuality, 70, 82

Quorum, defined, 230

Raises, pay, 122–123
Random access memory (RAM), 240
Read only memory (ROM), 240
Reading skills, 188
Recreation safety, 215, 217
Rectangle, defined, 202
Rehabilitation Act of, 1973, 96
Rental agreements, 397–398
Renting
  apartments, 393–398
  budgeting and, 323
  houses, 392
  rental agreements, 397–398
Resume, writing, 39–40
Retirement, social security and, 365–366
Road safety, 217
ROM. *See* Read only memory
Roommates, 396

Safety
  accidents and, 211, 212
    class of, 212
    types of, 212
  conditions concerning, 211
  consciousness, 81
  emergency situations and, 218
  employee rights and, 97–99
  E's of, 219
  home, 212–213
  job, 214–215
  personal, 212–218
  public, 218–219
  recreation, 215, 217
  road, 217
  school, 213–214
  skills, 211–222
  U. S. disasters and, 217
Salaries, 70, 117
Sales
  credit, 312–313
  tax, 199–200, 355
  traps, 290–292
Saving money, 327–329
Savings, 121
  individual retirement accounts, 371–374
Savings accounts, types of, 329–330
Savings and loan associations, 300
School safety, 213–214
Science, computers and, 244–245
Self-direction in job searching, 18
Self-employment
  advantages and disadvantages of, 254–258

INDEX 443

case study, 255–258
    requirements for success, 258–260
Self-information
    life roles and, 161
    types of, 152–159
        aptitudes, 155–156
        interests, 152–154
        relationships among, 159
        work values, 157–159
Seniority, 106
Services, defined, 283
Share-draft account, 303–304
Shaving, personal hygiene and, 130
Shop math, 196
SIC. *See* Standard Industrial Classification
Sick leave, 70
Skin care, 130, 132
Skin protection, sun protection, 131
Small business, 252–253
    advantages and disadvantages of, 254–258
    case study, 255–258
    growth of, 251
    importance of, 252–253
    requirements for success, 258–260
    types of, 253
Small claim courts, 387
SOC. *See* Standard Occupational Classification
Social satisfaction, work and, 2, 4
Social security, 364–377
    disability payments, 366–367
    eligibility, 370
    financing, 371
    individual retirement accounts and, 371–374
    number, obtaining, 26–27
    retirement payments, 365–366
    survivors payments, 366
    unemployment benefits, 367
    workers' compensation, 367, 369
Speaking skills, 185–188
    enunciation, 185
    good grammar rules, 187
    pronunciation, 185
    standard English, 187
    telephone skills, 187–188
Standard Industrial Classification (SIC), 166–167
Standard Occupational Classification, (SOC), 165–166
State courts, 384
Stocks, investing in, 332–333

Stress, 403–405
    job, workers compensation and, 368
Student organizations, 225, 227–228
    bylaws, 229
    holding meetings of, 230, *231*
    officers and committees, 229
Sun protection, 131
Supervision, working under, 73–74
Supply and demand, economics and, 273
Surface measurement, 202–204
Survivors payments, 366

Taxes
    budgeting and, 326
    direct, 354
    federal income, 355–361
        determining, 357–358
        electronic filing, 359
        filing returns, 358–361
        graduated, 356–357
    indirect, 354
    individual retirement accounts and, 371–374
    purpose of, 354
    sales, 199–200
    social security, 364–377
        disability payments, 366–367
        eligibility, 370
        financing, 371
        individual retirement accounts and, 371–374
        retirement payments, 365–366
        survivors payments, 366
        unemployment benefits, 367
        workers' compensation, 367, 369
    types of, 354–355
Technology Student Association (TSA), 228
Telecommuting, 241
Teleconferencing, 54
Telephone, job application with, 41
Temperature, conversion chart, 207
Temporary work, 30–32
Term life insurance, 344–345
Tests
    drug, 72
    general ability, 44
    honesty, 43
    lie detectors, 43

    performance, 44
    pre-employment, 44
    taking, 44
Time deposits, 330
Tips, 118
Total purchase amount, 197
Trade discount, 198
Training. *See* Education
Training agreement, *8*
Training schools, 423–424
Transportation
    budgeting and, 324
    computers and, 243

Unemployment benefits, 367
Union dues, 121
Utilities, budgeting and, 323–324

Vacation, 70
Value scale of work values, 158
Vocabulary, communication skills and, 188
Vocational
    math, 196
    schools, 423–424
    student organizations, 225, 227–228
Vocational Industrial Clubs of America (VICA), 228
Volume, conversion chart, 207
Volume measurement, 204–205
Voting, 412, 414–415

Wages, 70, 116
    fair employment practices and, 94–95
Weight
    control, 402–403
    conversion chart, 207
Work
    attendance, 82
    defined, 5
    experience education, 6–12
    finding stable, 18–20
    histories, 16–18
    quality of, 79
    rating employees, 86–88
    reporting to, 65–68
    safety, 214–215
    schedule, 70
    shift, 21–22
    temporary, 30–32
    See also Job
Work experience
    educational
        benefits of, 11–12

cooperative vocational education, 6–9
exploratory work experience, 9, 11
Work permit, obtaining, 27
Work values, 157–159
Workaholics, 100
Workers. *See* Employees
Workers' compensation, 367, 369
   job stress and, 368
Working
   reasons for, 2, 4–5
   supervision and, 73–74
Workplace
   changing, 3–4
   computers and, 241–245
      communications, 242–243
      education, 244
      engineering, 244–245
      government, 242
      medicine, 245
      science, 244–245
      transportation, 243
   drug testing in, 72
   envy in, 147
   orientation to the, 68
   policies and rules, 69–71, 73
   structure of, 68–71, 73–74
Writing skills, 189–193
   business forms and, 189–190
   business letters and, 192–193
   memorandums and, 191–192
   notes and, 189–190

TEACHER'S GUIDE

CHAPTER ONE
LEARNING ABOUT WORK

OVERVIEW

The purpose of this chapter is for students to learn concepts and definitions about work and to become familiar with the nature and organization of work experience education programs.

TEXTBOOK CHAPTER OUTLINE	TEXTBOOK PAGE
1. Why People Work	2
Earn Money	
Social Satisfaction	
Feature: The Changing Workplace	
Positive Feelings	
Prestige	
Personal Development	
Contributions to Health	
Self-expression	
2. Work, Occupation, and Job	5
Feature: What Would You Do?	
Work	
Occupation	
Job	
3. Work Experience Education	6
Types of Work Experience Programs	
Feature: What Would You Do?	
Benefits of Work Experience	
Chapter Review	13
Chapter in Brief	
Words to Know	
Questions to Answer	
Activities to Do	
Topics to Discuss	

CHAPTER OBJECTIVES

A student should be able to:
- Discuss reasons why people work.
- Define what is meant by the terms *work, occupation,* and *job.*
- Name three types of work experience education.
- Explain the role of a related class as part of a cooperative vocational or work-study program.
- Identify the benefits of work experience education.

STUDENT ACTIVITY WORKBOOK

Activity Objectives. The following activities provide additional opportunities for students to apply chapter objectives.

Activity 1.1 Why People Work: For students to become aware of the different reasons why people work.

Activity 1.2 Occupations and Jobs: For students to recognize that a person having an occupation can work at many different jobs.

Activity 1.3 Training Agreement Responsibilities: For students to understand the responsibilities of the three parties involved in a training agreement.

Activity 1.4 Benefits of Work Experience Education: For students to explain how selected individuals might benefit from work experience education.

Answer Key. Answers to activities in the student workbook are provided below.

Activity 1.1. Individual rankings will vary. Emphasize the fact that individuals work for a variety of reasons.

Activity 1.2. Each occupation can be found in a variety of work settings. For example, an auto mechanic can work at an auto dealership, department store auto service shop, service station, franchise repair shop, self-owned shop, and so on. Encourage students to identify jobs in their city or community.

Activity 1.3. The training agreement shown in Chapter One or the one used in your work experience program should be used as a point of reference.

Activity 1.4. Answers should include the following:

Frank - he could be placed in a training station where he might use more sophisticated equipment and learn to weld different metals and types of joints not usually found in schools.

Amy - by working part-time, she could earn money and learn employability skills while still participating in sports and related school activities.

Seymour - a job might give him a new outlook toward school and provide him with permanent employment upon graduation from high school.

REFERENCE AND RESOURCE MATERIALS

Gooch, Bill G. *Cooperative Vocational Education Handbook, Second Edition.* Carbondale, IL: Southern Illinois University, June 1988.

Naisbitt, John. *Megatrends: Ten New Directions Transforming Our Lives.* New York, NY: Warner Books, 1982.

Parsons, Cynthia. *The Bridge: Cooperative Education for All High School Students.* Washington, DC: William T. Grant Foundation on Youth and America's Future, 1987.

RELATED INSTRUCTIONAL MATERIALS

1. The introductory video should be used to familiarize the class with the nature and characteristics of work experience education.
2. Refer to the Teacher's Resource Package for additional activities related to Chapter 1 objectives.
3. Refer to the Teacher's Resource Package for test items and answers related to Chapter 1.
4. Refer to the Microtest, the computerized test bank, for items related to Chapter 1 content and objectives.

CHAPTER TWO
THE JOB AHEAD

OVERVIEW

The purpose of this chapter is for students to become aware of the nature of a work history and how this information can help them think about and plan for their own careers.

TEXTBOOK CHAPTER OUTLINE	TEXTBOOK PAGE
1. Sample Work Histories	16
2. Moving Toward a Stable Job	18
Self-direction	
Feature: What Would You Do?	
Effort Pays Off	
Change is Certain	
Feature: What Would You Do?	
Feature: Coping With Shift Work	
3. The Future Begins Now	22
Chapter Review	23
Chapter in Brief	
Words to Know	
Questions to Answer	
Activities to Do	
Topics to Discuss	

CHAPTER OBJECTIVES

A student should be able to:
- Explain what is meant by a work history
- Discuss how different work histories can lead to a stable job.
- List characteristics of stable jobs.
- Identify what you can do to shape your own career.

STUDENT ACTIVITY WORKBOOK

Activity Objectives. The following activities provide additional opportunities for students to apply chapter objectives.

Activity 2.1 About Work Histories: For students to review what they have learned about work histories.

Activity 2.2 Different Routes to a Stable Job: For students to recognize that individuals having different work histories can end up having the same or similiar jobs.

Activity 2.3 Controlling Your Career: For students to explain how various decisions, actions, and sacrifices might pay off later in a career.

Answer Key. Answers to activities in the student workbook are provided below.

Activity 2.1. For the first part, one fact for each work history follows.

Terry - It is usually necessary to work for someone else for a period of time before going into business for one's self.

Marie - People can interrupt and successfully re-enter employment at various times in a career.

Cindy - People can successfully change occupations and jobs during a career.

Rick - His seemingly negative attitude and lack of direction are hampering his educational and career progress.

Answers for the second part are: 1-T, 2-F, 3-T, 4-F, 5-T, 6-T, 7-T, 8-F, 9-T, 10-F.

Activity 2.2. Students should consult an encyclopedia and list the various jobs and positions held by each individual before becoming President.

Activity 2.3. A sample answer for each item follows.
1. The option of transferring to a university after completing a two-year degree will still be open.
2. The important thing is to begin a job and acquire some work experience. Also, a temporary or part-time position may evolve into a full-time job.
3. Such behavior demonstrates commitment and may be recognized and rewarded later.
4. Doing your best can be personally rewarding and will probably be recognized by an employer or customer.
5. Learning a new skill can enhance job performance and lead to a raise or promotion.
6. Saving money for college is a sound investment in the future.

REFERENCE AND RESOURCE MATERIALS

High Schools and the Changing Workplace. Report on Secondary School Education for the Changing Workplace, Washington, DC: National Academy Press, 1984.

RELATED INSTRUCTIONAL MATERIALS

1. Refer to the Teacher's Resource Package for additional activities related to Chapter 2 objectives.
2. Refer to the Teacher's Resource Package for test items and answers related to Chapter 2.
3. Refer to the Microtest, the computerized test bank, for items related to Chapter 2 content and objectives.

CHAPTER THREE
LOOKING FOR A JOB

OVERVIEW

The purpose of this chapter is for students to learn how to find a job.

TEXTBOOK CHAPTER OUTLINE	TEXTBOOK PAGE
1. Thinking About Your Job Goals	25
2. Getting Ready	26
Social Security Number	
Work Permit	
3. Finding Job Leads	27
Feature: What Would You Do?	
Family and Friends	
In-school Sources	
Newspaper Classified Ads	
Job Service	
Feature: Temporary Work	

TEXTBOOK CHAPTER OUTLINE	TEXTBOOK PAGE
Private Employment Agencies	
Direct Employer Contact	
4. Keeping Track of Job Leads	31
Feature: What Would You Do?	
Job-lead Card	
Following Through	
Chapter Review	33
Chapter in Brief	
Words to Know	
Questions to Answer	
Activities to Do	
Topics to Discuss	

CHAPTER OBJECTIVES

A student should be able to:
- Describe the importance of clarifying job goals before looking for employment.
- Explain how to get a social security number and work permit.
- Identify different sources of job leads.
- Illustrate how to prepare a job-lead card.
- Summarize the benefits of using job-lead cards.

STUDENT ACTIVITY WORKBOOK

Activity Objectives. The following activities provide additional opportunities for students to apply chapter objectives.

Activity 3.1 Clarifying Job Goals: For students to think about and clarify their job goals.

Activity 3.2 Application for a Social Security Number: For students to practice filling out an application form.

Activity 3.3 Sources of Job Leads: For students to identify specific job leads associated with various sources.

Activity 3.4 Help-wanted Ads: For students to identify and describe examples of four types of help-wanted ads.

Activity 3.5 Reading Help-wanted Ads: For students to learn common abbreviations found in help-wanted ads.

Answer Key. Answers to activities in the student workbook are provided below.

Activity 3.1. Point out to students that answers to the question "Why do you want a job?" should be phrased in terms of their job goals which were ranked above.

Activity 3.2. Encourage students to accurately record all information and to note the required evidence of age, citizenship, and identity.

Activity 3.3. Students should try to identify at least one specific lead for each source.

Activity 3.4. An *open ad* tells about the job requirements, identifies the employer, and tells how to apply. A *blind ad* omits the name, address, and phone number of the employer to prevent the employer from being bombarded with phone calls. A *catch-type ad* promises a good salary and downplays the necessary qualifications. An *agency spot ad* is used by private employment agencies to advertise jobs available through the agency.

Activity 3.5. The abbreviations are as follows.

appointment	hourly
assistant	heavy equipment
available	information
as soon as possible	licensed
cathode ray tube (computer monitor)	manager
degree	manufacturing
experience preferred	over-the-road driver
experience required	part-time
evenings and weekends	personal computer operator
electronic data processing	sales representative
equal opportunity employer/ male-female-handicapped-veteran	salary negotiable
flexible hours	temporary
fringe benefits	training
full-time	workers
gal/guy Friday (someone to run errands)	words per minute

REFERENCE AND RESOURCE MATERIALS

Bolles, Richard. *What Color Is Your Parachute?* Berkely, CA: Ten Speed Press, 1988.

RELATED INSTRUCTIONAL MATERIALS

1. Refer to the Teacher's Resource Package for additional activities related to Chapter 3 objectives.
2. Refer to the Teacher's Resource Package for test items and answers related to Chapter 3.
3. Refer to the Microtest, the computerized test bank, for items related to Chapter 3 content and objectives.

CHAPTER FOUR
APPLYING FOR A JOB

OVERVIEW

The purpose of this chapter is for students to learn how to apply for a job, develop a job resume, and prepare for an employment interview.

TEXTBOOK CHAPTER OUTLINE	TEXTBOOK PAGE
1. Personal Data Sheet	36
2. Job Application Form	37
Feature: What Would You Do?	
3. Writing a Resume	39
4. Contacting Employers	40
Applying in Person	
Applying by Telephone	
Feature: What Would You Do?	
Letter of Application	

TEXTBOOK CHAPTER OUTLINE	TEXTBOOK PAGE
Feature: Lie Detector and Honesty Tests	
5. Pre-employment Tests	44
General Ability Tests	
Performance Tests	
Taking a Test	
Chapter Review	46
Chapter in Brief	
Words to Know	
Questions to Answer	
Activities to Do	
Topics to Discuss	

CHAPTER OBJECTIVES

A student should be able to:
- Prepare a personal data sheet.
- Complete a job application form.
- Prepare a job resume.
- Explain the three methods of contacting employers about a job.
- Describe the two most common types of pre-employment tests.

STUDENT ACTIVITY WORKBOOK

Activity Objectives. The following activities provide additional opportunities for students to apply chapter objectives.

Activity 4.1 Personal Data Sheet: For students to prepare a personal data sheet.
Activity 4.2 Job Application Form: For students to practice filling out a job application form.
Activity 4.3 Letter of Application: For students to write a sample letter of application.
Activity 4.4 Developing a Resume: For students to prepare a job resume.
Activity 4.5 Pre-employment Tests: For students to become familiar with the nature of a general ability test.

Answer Key. Answers to activities in the student workbook are provided below.
Activity 4.1. Students should review the section in Chapter 4 on personal data sheets and complete this activity.
Activity 4.2. Students should use their personal data sheets to aid them in filling out the sample job application form.
Activity 4.3. Students should follow the four guidelines provided in Chapter 4 to write a sample letter of application.
Activity 4.4. Students should use their personal data sheets to aid them in preparing a draft of a job resume.
Activity 4.5. 1-B, 2-D, 3-C, 4-D, 5-D, 6-B, 7-D, 8-B, 9-C, 10-A, 11-A.

REFERENCE AND RESOURCE MATERIALS

Lee, Chris. "Testing Makes a Comeback." *Training*, December 1988, 49-59.
Hampton, William J. "How Does Japan Inc. Pick Its American Workers?" *Business Week*, October 3, 1988, 84-88.

RELATED INSTRUCTIONAL MATERIALS

1. Refer to the Teacher's Resource Package for additional activities related to Chapter 4 objectives.

2. Refer to the Teacher's Resource Package for test items and answers related to Chapter 4.
3. Refer to the Microtest, the computerized test bank, for items related to Chapter 4 content and objectives.

CHAPTER FIVE
INTERVIEWING FOR A JOB

OVERVIEW

The purpose of this chapter is for students to learn how to prepare for, participate in, and follow-up on a job interview.

TEXTBOOK CHAPTER OUTLINE	TEXTBOOK PAGE
1. Before the Interview	48
Practice Your Interview Skills	
Learn About the Company	
Assemble Needed Materials	
Attend to Appearance	
Feature: What Would You Do?	
Check Last-minute Details	
2. During the Interview	53
Feature: Teleconferencing	
Effective Communication	
Nonverbal Communication	
Asking Questions	
Concluding the Interview	
3. After the Interview	57
4. Accepting or Rejecting a Job	59
Feature: What Would You Do?	
Chapter Review	60
Chapter in Brief	
Words to Know	
Questions to Answer	
Activities to Do	
Topics to Discuss	

CHAPTER OBJECTIVES

A student should be able to:
- Name and describe the five things to do in preparation for a job interview.
- List and discuss types of questions asked by interviewers.
- Summarize how one should act during a job interview.
- Name and describe the two things to do after an interview.
- Discuss how to respond to a job offer.

STUDENT ACTIVITY WORKBOOK

Activity Objectives. The following activities provide additional opportunities for students to apply chapter objectives.

Activity 5.1   Interviewer's Questions, I: For students to prepare responses to standard questions asked at a job interview.

Activity 5.2   Interviewer's Questions, II: For students to prepare responses to potential interview questions related to a specific company and job.

Activity 5.3   Background Research: For students to learn about the work performed in various types of companies.

Activity 5.4   Follow-up Letter: For students to practice writing a sample follow-up letter.

Answer Key. Answers to activities in the student workbook are provided below.

Activity 5.1.   Individual responses will vary. Encourage students to answer the questions thoughtfully and honestly.

Activity 5.2.   Individual responses will vary in relation to the company and job title named.

Activity 5.3.   Have students share in class current knowledge about any of the types of companies. Have them use the *Standard Industrial Classification Manual*, encyclopedia, or other reference source to locate information about the remaining companies.

Activity 5.4.   Students should follow the guidelines provided in Chapter 5 to write a sample follow-up letter.

REFERENCE AND RESOURCE MATERIALS

Standard & Poor's Register of Corporations, Directors, and Executives.   Volume 1 is an alphabetical listing of over 45,000 U.S. and Canadian companies. (Published annually)

"Moody's manuals."   Seven volumes. Contains financial information about companies listed on U.S. stock exchanges. Includes a brief corporate history and a description of the products or services produced. (Published annually)

Standard Industrial Classification Manual, 1987. Office of Management and Budget, Washington, DC: U.S. Government Printing Office. Contains hundreds of short descriptions of the primary activity of various industries (places of employment).

RELATED INSTRUCTIONAL MATERIALS

1. Refer to the Teacher's Resource Package for additional activities related to Chapter 5 objectives.
2. Refer to the Teacher's Resource Package for test items and answers related to Chapter 5.
3. Refer to the Microtest, the computerized test bank, for items related to Chapter 5 content and objectives.

CHAPTER SIX
BEGINNING A NEW JOB

OVERVIEW

The purpose of this chapter is for students to become aware of what to expect in beginning a new job and to learn facts and information that will help them get off to a good start.

TEXTBOOK CHAPTER OUTLINE	TEXTBOOK PAGE
1. Pre-employment Anxiety	64
2. Reporting for Work	65
Feature: What Would You Do?	
Feature: What Would You Do?	
3. Orientation to the Workplace	68
4. Organizational Structure	68
Policies and Rules	
Feature: Drug Testing in the Workplace	
Unwritten Rules	
5. Working Under Supervision	73
6. Payroll Withholding	74
Chapter Review	75
Chapter in Brief	
Words to Know	
Questions to Answer	
Activities to Do	
Topics to Discuss	

CHAPTER OBJECTIVES

A student should be able to:
- Recognize that anxiety toward beginning a new job is normal.
- Explain what to expect from an employer when beginning a new job.
- Describe how an organization chart shows the flow of authority and responsibility within an organization.
- List areas for which employers have policies and rules.
- Identify ways to work effectively with a supervisor.
- Illustrate how to fill out a Form W-4.

STUDENT ACTIVITY WORKBOOK

Activity Objectives. The following activities provide additional opportunities for students to apply chapter objectives.

Activity 6.1 Payroll Withholding: For students to recognize the basis by which an employer deducts an amount for federal income tax.

Activity 6.2 Organizational Structure: For students to develop a relevant organization chart and to explain their role within the organization.

Activity 6.3 Policies and Rules: For students to explain the underlying rationale for various workplace policies and rules.

Answer Key. Answers to activities in the student workbook are provided below.
Activity 6.1.
1. $25.00, $21.00, $44.00
2. If the individual has dependents for whom support is provided.
3. If the individual anticipates receiving additional income for which taxes are not withheld.
4. If you can be claimed as a dependent on another person's tax return.
5. Students may disagree about this. The rationale is that married persons have greater expenses than single persons.

Activity 6.2. Individual charts will vary. Or, you may decide to develop a chart in class as a group activity. Either way, you might wish to have students develop a draft chart on paper before copying the final version in their workbooks.

Activity 6.3.
1. Employers want an accurate, honest record of the actual time worked by each employee in order to figure the payroll.
2. This is designed to penalize people who are late and to serve as an incentive to be at work on time.
3. This will give the employer some lead time to hire a replacement or to revise the work schedule as needed.
4. For public employees, it may be a violation of law. Irrespective of the law, employers don't want tools and equipment lost, abused, or worn-out as a result of non-job use.
5. The employer is paying for time on the job and has a right to expect employees to be working. Prohibition of personal, long-distance phone calls is self-evident.
6. So the employer can schedule vacations in a way that provides minimal disruptions to the work flow.
7. To allow the employer time to hire and perhaps train a replacement.

REFERENCE AND RESOURCE MATERIALS

Baxter, Neale. "First Jobs: School Was Never Like This -- or Was It?" *Occupational Outlook Quarterly*, Winter 1988, 3-7.

Gordon, Jack. "Drug Testing As a Productivity Booster?" *Training*, March 1987, 22-34.

RELATED INSTRUCTIONAL MATERIALS

1. Refer to the Teacher's Resource Package for additional activities related to Chapter 6 objectives.
2. Refer to the Teacher's Resource Package for test items and answers related to Chapter 6.
3. Refer to the Microtest, the computerized test bank, for items related to Chapter 6 content and objectives.

CHAPTER SEVEN
EXPECTATIONS OF EMPLOYERS

OVERVIEW

The purpose of this chapter is for students to learn what employers expect regarding job performance, why it is expected, and how performance is evaluated on the job.

TEXTBOOK CHAPTER OUTLINE	TEXTBOOK PAGE
1. Job Performance	78
Productivity	
Quality of Work	
Good Judgment	
Feature: What Would You Do?	
Safety Consciousness	
Care of Equipment	
2. Work Habits and Attitudes	82
Attendance and Punctuality	
Cooperation	
Interest and Enthusiasm	
Honesty	
Feature: What Would You Do?	
Loyalty	
Feature: Labor Unions	
3. Rating Work Behavior	86
Purposes of Evaluation	
How You Are Evaluated	
After the Evaluation	
Chapter Review	89
Chapter in Brief	
Words to Know	
Questions to Answer	
Activities to Do	
Topics to Discuss	

CHAPTER OBJECTIVES

A student should be able to:
- Name and describe the five things that employers expect regarding job performance.
- Name and describe the six things that employers expect regarding work habits and attitudes.
- Describe the purposes of performance evaluation.
- Explain the two-step process of performance evaluation that is used by most large companies.

STUDENT ACTIVITY WORKBOOK

Activity Objectives. The following activities provide additional opportunities for students to apply chapter objectives.

Activity 7.1 Expectations of Employers: For students to identify the term or concept associated with various employer expectations regarding job performance, work habits, and attitudes.

Activity 7.2 Cost of Lost Production: For students to recognize the financial losses incurred by employers when workers waste time on the job.

Activity 7.3 Rating Work Behavior: For students to rate and analyze their own performance on the job.

Answer Key. Answers to activities in the student workbook are provided below.

Activity 7.1.
1. cooperation
2. honesty
3. quality
4. punctuality
5. accident
6. productivity
7. judgment
8. attendance
9. maturity
10. pride
11. interest
12. loyalty
13. equipment
14. enthusiasm
15. contract

Activity 7.2.
1. $475.00
2. $9,500.00
3. $22.80
4. It appears that no bonus was received because Richard and his buddies waste so much production time.
5. The idea is that employers should not have to pay employees who are late to work. Help students to understand the employers point of view.

Activity 7.3. This is a good opportunity for students to rate themselves and then get feedback regarding their job performance. Encourage students to judge themselves accurately and honestly.

REFERENCE AND RESOURCE MATERIALS

"America's Blue Collars Get Down to Business." *U.S. News & World Report*, February 29, 1988, 52-53.

"Grading 'Merit Pay'." *Newsweek*, November 14, 1988, 45-46.

A variety of supplemental materials on organized labor may be obtained by writing to: AFL-CIO Department of Education, 815 16th Street, N.W., Room 407, Washington, DC 20006.

RELATED INSTRUCTIONAL MATERIALS

1. Refer to the Teacher's Resource Package for additional activities related to Chapter 7 objectives.
2. Refer to the Teacher's Resource Package for test items and answers related to Chapter 7.
3. Refer to the Microtest, the computerized test bank, for items related to Chapter 7 content and objectives.

CHAPTER EIGHT
WORKER RIGHTS AND PROTECTIONS

OVERVIEW

The purpose of this chapter is for students to recognize what an employer's responsibilities are to its employees and to learn what rights and protections they have as workers.

TEXTBOOK CHAPTER OUTLINE	TEXTBOOK PAGE
1. Honesty and Respect	93
2. Fair Employment Practices	93
Child Labor	
Wages and Hours	
Feature: What Would You Do?	
Equal Pay	
3. Protection from Discrimination	96
Equal Employment Opportunity	
Affirmative Action	
4. Worker Safety and Health	97
Protecting New Workers	
Feature: What Would You Do?	
What Workers Can Do	
5. Agencies Providing Services to Workers	99
Feature: Collective Bargaining	
Chapter Review	102
Chapter in Brief	
Words to Know	
Questions to Answer	
Activities to Do	
Topics to Discuss	

CHAPTER OBJECTIVES

A student should be able to:
- Name and describe the six things that employers owe their workers.
- Discuss the importance of employers treating workers with honesty and respect.
- Name and describe the three types of fair employment practices.
- Explain worker's rights regarding protection from discrimination.
- Explain the roles of employers and workers regarding safety and health in the workplace.
- Identify agencies that deal with workers' complaints.

STUDENT ACTIVITY WORKBOOK

Activity Objectives. The following activities provide additional opportunities for students to apply chapter objectives.

Activity 8.1 Fair Employment Practices: For students to summarize the requirements regarding fair employment practices for the state in which they live.

Activity 8.2 Equal Employment Opportunity: For students to name the term or concept associated with various equal opportunity principles and practices.

Activity 8.3 Labor-Management Relations: For students to recognize the position of each party on a representative labor-management issue.

Answer Key. Answers to activities in the student workbook are provided below.

Activity 8.1. Answers will vary according to state. You will probably need to provide or help students locate relevant reference materials.

Activity 8.2.

1. federal
2. affirmative
3. legislation
4. protection
5. minorities
6. fair
7. women
8. victims
9. Congress
10. veterans
11. opportunity
12. handicapped
13. EEOC
14. Johnson

Activity 8.3. Answers will vary according to the issue selected. Choose an issue or have students select one for which information is readily available. Student can collect information from printed materials or from individuals familiar with the issue.

REFERENCE AND RESOURCE MATERIALS

A variety of posters, pamphlets and other materials related to this chapter may be obtained by writing to the three government agencies listed in Figure 8-13.

"Hands Off at the Office." *U.S. News & World Report,* August 1, 1988, 56-58.

RELATED INSTRUCTIONAL MATERIALS

1. Refer to the Teacher's Resource Package for additional activities related to Chapter 8 objectives.
2. Refer to the Teacher's Resource Package for test items and answers related to Chapter 8.
3. Refer to the Microtest, the computerized test bank, for items related to Chapter 8 content and objectives.

CHAPTER NINE
HUMAN RELATIONS AT WORK

OVERVIEW

The purpose of this chapter is for students to become aware of the nature of human relations and to learn human relations skills required for success on the job.

TEXTBOOK CHAPTER OUTLINE	TEXTBOOK PAGE

1. Bosses, Co-workers, and Customers
    Getting Along with Bosses
    Getting Along with Co-workers
    Feature: Relating to Workaholics
    Getting Along with Customers
    Feature: What Would You Do?
	104

TEXTBOOK CHAPTER OUTLINE	TEXTBOOK PAGE
2. Group Participation	111
Feature: What Would You Do?	
Chapter Review	114
Chapter in Brief	
Words to Know	
Questions to Answer	
Activities to Do	
Topics to Discuss	

CHAPTER OBJECTIVES

A student should be able to:
- Explain the importance of good human relations to success on the job.
- Discuss ways to get along with co-workers.
- Identify three reasons why customers patronize a particular business.
- Discuss ways to participate effectively in a task group.

STUDENT ACTIVITY WORKBOOK

Activity Objectives. The following activities provide additional opportunities for students to apply chapter objectives.

Activity 9.1 Interpersonal Relations: For students to analyze a personal relations problem that they have had with a family member, employer (or teacher), and co-worker (or fellow student).

Activity 9.2 Customer Relations: For students to describe an appropriate response to various types of customer relations situations.

Activity 9.3 Productivity of Groups: For students to name the term or concept associated with participation in group activities.

Answer Key. Answers to activities in the student workbook are provided below.

Activity 9.1. Answers will vary according to each student's choice of problems. Each problem may also have several possible solutions. Help students to understand how their behavior may have caused or exacerbated the problem.

Activity 9.2. A sample answer for each item follows.
1. Approach the customer in a friendly manner and ask if you can help her or him. If it is a small store or one engaged in personal services, it would be appropriate to introduce oneself.
2. Greet the customer by name and ask how you may help her or him.
3. Tell the customer to "feel free to look around" and to call on you if he/she needs any help.
4. Express sincere regrets that the product is unsatisfactory. Follow company policy on such matters, which is probably to offer an exchange or refund.
5. Apologize for the fact that the product doesn't work. Follow company policy, which is probably to offer an exchange or refund.
6. Explain why you think the product doesn't fit. If you are asked to give your opinion regarding the appearance, do so in a sensitive way that focuses on the garment and not the person. If you are not asked, don't offer your opinion. People have varying tastes in clothing.
7. Carefully review the sales receipt and explain how the amount was figured. Apologize if a mistake was made.
8. Find out as much as you can about the person for whom the gift is intended. Then, do your professional best in offering *several* possible suggestions.

9. Follow company policy, which is probably to notify your supervisor or company security personnel.
10. Thank them for shopping and invite them to come again.

Activity 9.3.

1. participative	5. structure	9. cohesiveness
2. leadership	6. democratic	10. communications
3. purpose	7. status	11. authoritarian
4. standard	8. size	12. style

REFERENCE AND RESOURCE MATERIALS

Machlowitz, Marilyn. *Workaholics: Living With Them, Working With Them.* Reading, MA: Addison-Wesley Publishing Company, 1980.

Geber, Beverly. "Quality Circles: The Second Generation." *Training*, December 1986, 54-61.

RELATED INSTRUCTIONAL MATERIALS

1. Refer to the Teacher's Resource Package for additional activities related to Chapter 9 objectives.
2. Refer to the Teacher's Resource Package for test items and answers related to Chapter 9.
3. Refer to the Microtest, the computerized test bank, for items related to Chapter 9 content and objectives.

CHAPTER TEN
EARNINGS AND JOB ADVANCEMENT

OVERVIEW

The purpose of this chapter is for students to learn about different forms of compensation, how a paycheck is figured, and how to advance in and change jobs.

TEXTBOOK CHAPTER OUTLINE	TEXTBOOK PAGE
1. Your Job Earnings	116
Forms of Compensation	
Feature: Employer Sponsored Child-Care Assistance	
2. Your Paycheck	120
Feature: What Would You Do?	
3. Pay Raises	122
Getting a Pay Raise	
4. Job Advancement	124
Job Promotion	
Changing Jobs	
Feature: What Would You Do?	
Being Fired	

TEXTBOOK CHAPTER OUTLINE	TEXTBOOK PAGE
Chapter Review	127

    Chapter in Brief
    Words to Know
    Questions to Answer
    Activities to Do
    Topics to Discuss

CHAPTER OBJECTIVES

A student should be able to:
- Identify and describe different forms of compensation.
- Describe how a paycheck is figured.
- State three guidelines regarding working for a pay raise.
- Identify the most common reasons for changing jobs.
- Explain what to do when voluntarily leaving a job.

STUDENT ACTIVITY WORKBOOK

Activity Objectives. The following activities provide additional opportunities for students to apply chapter objectives.

Activity 10.1 Your Paycheck: For students to figure earnings and deductions for a sample paycheck.

Activity 10.2 Figuring Compensation: For students to calculate various types of compensation.

Activity 10.3 Letter of Resignation: For students to write a sample letter of resignation.

Answer Key. Answers to activities in the student workbook are provided below.

Activity 10.1.
1. 45
2. $208.00, $39.00
3. $247.00
4. $29.00, $4.94
5. $16.55
6. $8.75
7. $59.24
8. 24%
9. $988.00
10. To verify that your deductions are correct and that you were paid the correct amount.

Activity 10.2.
1. $200.63, $802.52
2. $16,380.00
3. $289.75
4. $295.00, $1180.00
5. $1480.00
6. $1,410.00
7. $89.45, $8.95
8. $1,916.67
9. $33.60
10. $29,900.00

Activity 10.3. Have students review in Chapter 10 the four points to include in a cover letter and peruse Figure 10-14 before completing this activity.

REFERENCE AND RESOURCE MATERIALS

"When Companies Play Nanny." *U.S. News & World Report*, September 19, 1988, 43-45.
"You're Fired." *U.S. News & World Report*, March 23, 1987, 50-57.

RELATED INSTRUCTIONAL MATERIALS

1. Refer to the Teacher's Resource Package for additional activities related to Chapter 10 objectives.
2. Refer to the Teacher's Resource Package for test items and answers related to Chapter 10.
3. Refer to the Microtest, the computerized test bank, for items related to Chapter 10 content and objectives.

CHAPTER ELEVEN
APPEARANCE ON THE JOB

OVERVIEW

The purpose of this chapter is for students to learn rules and guidelines for good grooming and proper dress on the job.

TEXTBOOK CHAPTER OUTLINE	TEXTBOOK PAGE
1. Grooming and Appearance	129
Feature: What Would You Do?	
Hair Styling	
Shaving	
Deodorants and Antiperspirants	
Skin Care and Cosmetics	
Feature: Sun Protection	
Posture	
2. Dressing for the Job	132
Feature: What Would You Do?	
Chapter Review	136
Chapter in Brief	
Words to Know	
Questions to Answer	
Activities to Do	
Topics to Discuss	

CHAPTER OBJECTIVES

A student should be able to:
- Explain why good hygiene, grooming, and proper dress are important on the job.
- List five rules for good grooming and appearance.
- Describe the benefits of good posture.
- Summarize guidelines on dressing for the job.

STUDENT ACTIVITY WORKBOOK

Activity Objectives. The following activities provide additional opportunities for students to apply chapter objectives.

Activity 11.1 Personal Hygiene: For students to name terms and concepts associated with personal hygiene.

Activity 11.2 Hair Styling and Care: For students to recognize that choice of a hair style may be based on one's facial features and hair characteristics.

Activity 11.3 Dressing for the Job: For students to recognize that jobs have different dress needs and requirements.

Answer Key. Answers to activities in the student workbook are provided below.

Activity 11.1. 1-F, 2-H, 3-J, 4-B, 5-D, 6-K, 7-N, 8-A, 9-L, 10-M, 11-G, 12-O, 13-C, 14-I, 15-E. Answers to the last part of the activity will vary according to the occupation named.

Activity 11.2. Many hair styling articles and books contain charts which provide suggested hair styles based on different facial shapes and hair characteristics. Students will need to use such materials for this activity or consult the advice of a hair stylist. If your vocational program has a cosmetology program, invite several student hair stylists to class to assist with this activity.

Activity 11.3. Answers to the first part of the activity will vary according to the type of job named. Answers to the last part of the activity might include the following.

Appearance: most professional level jobs, marketing and sales jobs, managers, office workers.
Comfort: most technicians, production workers, material handlers.
Protection: firefighters, welders, several kinds of medical technicians.
Sanitation: food preparation and handling jobs, most health service jobs, barbers and cosmetologists.
Durability: construction workers, farmers, timber cutters.

REFERENCE AND RESOURCE MATERIALS

"The Dark Side of the Sun." *Newsweek*, June 9, 1986, 60-62+.

RELATED INSTRUCTIONAL MATERIALS

1. Refer to the Teacher's Resource Package for additional activities related to Chapter 11 objectives.
2. Refer to the Teacher's Resource Package for test items and answers related to Chapter 11.
3. Refer to the Microtest, the computerized test bank, for items related to Chapter 11 content and objectives.

CHAPTER TWELVE
CAREER DECISION-MAKING

OVERVIEW

The purpose of this chapter is for students to recognize the nature of decision-making and to learn a systematic five-step process of decision-making.

TEXTBOOK CHAPTER OUTLINE	TEXTBOOK PAGE

1. The Decision-making Process
   Defining the Problem
   Gathering Information
   Evaluating the Information
   Making a Choice
   Feature: What Would You Do?
	140

TEXTBOOK CHAPTER OUTLINE	TEXTBOOK PAGE
Taking Action	
Occupational Decision-making	
Feature: What Would You Do?	
2. Individuals and Decision-making	145
Decision-making Styles	
Benefits of Good Planning	
Taking Charge of Your Life	
Feature: Envy in the Workplace	
3. Other Influences on Decision-making	148
Previous Decisions	
Environment and Experience	
Real-world Restrictions	
Chapter Review	150
Chapter in Brief	
Words to Know	
Questions to Answer	
Activities to Do	
Topics to Discuss	

CHAPTER OBJECTIVES

A student should be able to:
- Discuss instances in which an organized decision-making process is needed.
- List and summarize each step in the decision-making process.
- Identify and describe different decision-making styles.
- Discuss the need to accept responsibility for career planning.
- Explain how previous decisions, environment and experience, and real-world restrictions influence decision-making.

STUDENT ACTIVITY WORKBOOK

Activity Objectives. The following activities provide additional opportunities for students to apply chapter objectives.

Activity 12.1 The Decision-making Process: For students to use the decision-making process to make and implement a decision.

Activity 12.2 Decision-making Styles: For students to recognize the characteristic approach used in various styles of decision-making.

Activity 12.3 Influences on Decision-making. For students to describe and illustrate how various factors influence decision-making.

Answer Key. Answers to activities in the student workbook are provided below.

Activity 12.1. Students should work in small groups to complete this activity. The focus, selecting a movie, can be changed to another activity if you wish. The five-step process should be reviewed before and during the activity as required. Note that the last step cannot be completed until after the decision has been implemented.

Activity 12.2.
1. The agonizer: This person has collected so much information and spent so much time evaluating it that he/she is overwhelmed by all the data.
2. The mystic: This person makes the decision based on hunch or "gut feeling."
3. The fatalist: This person spends little time gathering information because of the belief that he/she has no control over the choice.

4. The evader: This person hasn't decided yet, but may get around to it one of these days.
5. The plunger: This person chooses the first alternative to present itself.
6. The submissive: This person is waiting for her/his parents (or someone else) to make the choice.
7. The planner: This person uses a systematic decison-making process to arrive at a choice.
8. Answers will vary. The intent here is not to be judgemental. If students aren't already doing so, encourage them to become more planful.

Activity 12.3. A sample answer for each question follows.
1. To accept a full-time position at your cooperative education training station after graduation.
2. To take a computer science course at school because you enjoy working on your parents' personal computer at home.
3. To continue working at your present job because you don't have the money or experience yet to go into business for yourself.
4. Money, location, age, experience, qualifications, abilities, physical limitations.
5. Despite having only one arm, Kelly McCormack (see Section Two success story) became the fastest typist in her class. Refer to other student success stories as appropriate.

REFERENCE AND RESOURCE MATERIALS

Cohen, Betsy. *The Snow White Syndrome.* New York, NY: Macmillian, 1987.

RELATED INSTRUCTIONAL MATERIALS

1. Refer to the Teacher's Resource Package for additional activities related to Chapter 12 objectives.
2. Refer to the Teacher's Resource Package for test items and answers related to Chapter 12.
3. Refer to the Microtest, the computerized test bank, for items related to Chapter 12 content and objectives.
4. Refer to Transparencies 1 and 2 for the transparencies related to Chapter 12.

CHAPTER THIRTEEN
INFORMATION ABOUT YOUR SELF

OVERVIEW

The purpose of this chapter is for students to learn about the nature of self and how self-information can be used in making more informed career decisions.

TEXTBOOK CHAPTER OUTLINE	TEXTBOOK PAGE

1. Types of Self-information
   Interests
   Feature: What Would You Do?
   Aptitudes
   Work Values
	152

TEXTBOOK CHAPTER OUTLINE	TEXTBOOK PAGE
Feature: What Would You Do?	
2. Relationships Among Self-information Factors	159
Feature: Mid-career Change	
3. Self and Other Life Roles	161
Chapter Review	162
Chapter in Brief	
Words to Know	
Questions to Answer	
Activities to Do	
Topics to Discuss	

CHAPTER OBJECTIVES

A student should be able to:
- Discuss how self-information can help you make more satisfying occupational decisions.
- Name and describe the three types of self-information.
- Describe how interests, aptitudes, and work values are measured.
- Explain how interests, aptitudes, and work values may be similiar or different.
- Illustrate how interests, aptitudes, and work values may be expressed outside of one's job.

STUDENT ACTIVITY WORKBOOK

Activity Objectives. The following activities provide additional opportunities for students to apply chapter objectives.

Activity 13.1   Learning About Your Self: For students to explain the meaning and implication of self-information concepts.

Activity 13.2   Rating Interests: For students to identify their interests and relate them to occupations.

Activity 13.3   Rating Aptitudes: For students to identify their aptitudes and relate them to occupations.

Activity 13.4   Rating Work Values: For students to identify their work values and relate them to occupations.

Answer Key. Answers to activities in the student workbook are provided below.

Activity 13.1.
1. This means that information about your self (interests, aptitudes, and work values) can help you in choosing an occupation.
2. *Interests* - these are indications of things that you like to do. *Aptitudes* - these represent things that you are good at doing. *Work values* - these are feelings about the importance or worth of an activity or occupation.
3. Individual answers will vary. Have students rate their job first in terms of each of the three factors. Then they should add the numbers and divide by three to get an average rating.
4. Before students complete this, review in the text how Gregorio, Marcy, Bill, and Yvonne expressed themselves outside of their jobs.

Activity 13.2.   Read instructions to the class and show an example on the board before students begin to rate their interests. Have students stop after they have finished Group 11. Now explain how to sum the number of "L's" for each group and where to record the totals.

If possible, have available the *Guide to Occupational Exploration* (GOE), which groups occupations according to the eleven interest areas listed. This resource can be used by students to translate their preferred interests into occupations to explore. If the GOE isn't available, have students as a group name as many occupations as possible for each of the eleven interest areas. Then have students complete the last step of the activity.

Activity 13.3. Read instructions to the class and show an example on the board before students begin to rate their aptitudes. To interpret, it should be apparent from inspection which two types of aptitudes are rated the highest. Unlike some formal aptitude tests, there is no way to directly relate these six types of aptitudes to occupations. Have students as a group name as many occupations as possible for each of the six types of aptitudes. Then have them complete the last step of this activity.

Activity 13.4. Read instructions to the class and show an example on the board before students begin to rate their work values. Have them stop at the end of item 27. Then explain how to interpret the ratings and complete the table shown. Unlike some formal measures of work values, there is no way to directly relate these nine types of work values to occupations. Have students as a group name as many occupations as possible for each of the nine types of work values. Then have students complete the last step of the activity.

REFERENCE AND RESOURCE MATERIALS

Harrington, Thomas and O'Shea, Arthur (Eds). *Guide for Occupational Exploration: Second Edition*. Circle Pines, MN: American Guidance Service, 1984.

Kapes, Jerome and Mastie, Marilyn (Eds). *A Counselor's Guide to Career Assessment Instruments: 2nd Edition*. Alexandria, VA: The National Career Development Association, 1988. (This contains a description of all available instruments for assessing interests, aptitudes, and work values.)

Contact a local military recruiter (any branch) for information about administering, free of charge, the *Armed Services Vocational Aptitude Battery (ASVAB)*. The ASVAB is an excellent aptitude test that is accompanied by a student workbook entitled *Exploring Careers*. Students who take the test are under no pressure or obligation to join the military. Recruiters only contact those students who have indicated an interest in the military.

RELATED INSTRUCTIONAL MATERIALS

1. Refer to the Teacher's Resource Package for additional activities related to Chapter 13 objectives.
2. Refer to the Teacher's Resource Package for test items and answers related to Chapter 13.
3. Refer to the Microtest, the computerized test bank, for items related to Chapter 13 content and objectives.
4. Refer to Transparencies 3 and 4 for the transparencies related to Chatper 13.

CHAPTER FOURTEEN
CAREER INFORMATION

OVERVIEW

The purpose of this chapter is for students to learn about systems for classifying industries and occupations, future trends in the world of work, and how to use the *Occupational Outlook Handbook*.

TEXTBOOK CHAPTER OUTLINE	TEXTBOOK PAGE
1. The World of Work	164
Classifying Occupations	
Classifying Industries	
2. Tomorrow's Jobs	168
Changing Employment in Industries	
Feature: Military Occupations	
Changing Employment in Occupations	
Feature: What Would You Do?	
3. Exploring Occupations	173
Using the Occupational Outlook Handbook	
Doing a Search	
Feature: What Would You Do?	
Other Sources of Career Information	
Chapter Review	177
Chapter in Brief	
Words to Know	
Questions to Answer	
Activities to Do	
Topics to Discuss	

CHAPTER OBJECTIVES

A student should be able to:
- Explain how occupations and industries are grouped.
- Describe trends in the growth of goods and service industries.
- Discuss reasons for the rapid growth of service industries.
- Identify occupations having the fastest rate of growth and those having the greatest numerical increase during 1986-2000.
- Use the *Occupational Outlook Handbook (OOH)* to conduct an occupational search.

STUDENT ACTIVITY WORKBOOK

Activity Objectives. The following activities provide additional opportunities for students to apply chapter objectives.

Activity 14.1 Reading Tables and Charts: For students to interpret labor market information contained in tables and charts.

Activity 14.2 Exploring Occupational Groups: For students to explore one of the 20 SOC groups contained in the *OOH*.

Activity 14.3 Conducting an Occupational Search: For students to explore one specific occupation using the *OOH*.

Answer Key. Answers to activities in the student workbook are provided below.
Activity 14.1.
1. 51.5, 95.7, 44.2.
2. 27.2, 27.6, .4.
3. Virtually all employment growth through the year 2000 will be in service industries.
4. 7, Services.
5. 3, Agriculture.
6. 27%, 10%, - 4%.
7. 12, 6.
8. 111,000, 80%.
9. Most require some type of technical training, but not necessarily a college degree.
10. 575,000, 27%.
11. Computer programmers, computer systems analysts.
12. Most require some type of vocational education or on-the-job training.

Activity 14.2. This activity requires use of the *Occupational Outlook Handbook*. Students should select a group of interest from Figure 14-3 and answer the five questions as indicated.
Activity 14.3. This activity also requires the *Occupational Outlook Handbook*. Students should select an occupation to explore, locate the occupation in the OOH, and complete the activity as required. Be aware that the OOH does not contain information on every possible occupation. Note that the eight parts of this activity parallel the eight parts of each occupational brief in the OOH.

REFERENCE AND RESOURCE MATERIALS

Kutscher, Ronald. "An Overview of the Year 2000," *Occupational Outlook Quarterly*. Spring 1988, 2-9.

Military Career Guide. Washington, DC: Department of Defense. (Published periodically. Available free of charge from a local military recruiter.)

Occupational Outlook Handbook. Washington, DC: U.S. Government Printing Office. (Published semi-annually.)

Note: The introductory section of the OOH is entitled "Tomorrow's Jobs." It contains an excellent overview of trends and projection for various industries and occupations. As new editions of the OOH become available, use the data in Tomorrow's Jobs to update this chapter. Further note that Appendix C of the OOH contains a listing of sources of state and local job outlook information. Contact the State Occupational Information Coordinating Committee where you live to find out what types of information and services they provide.

RELATED INSTRUCTIONAL MATERIALS

1. Refer to the Teacher's Resource Package for additional activities related to Chapter 14 objectives.
2. Refer to the Teacher's Resource Package for test items and answers related to Chapter 14.
3. Refer to the Microtest, the computerized test bank, for items related to Chapter 14 content and objectives.
4. Refer to Transparencies 5–10 for the transparencies related to Chapter 14.

CHAPTER FIFTEEN
COMMUNICATION SKILLS

OVERVIEW

The purpose of this chapter is for students to review communication skills and learn why such skills are important on the job.

TEXTBOOK CHAPTER OUTLINE	TEXTBOOK PAGE
1. Listening	183
Distractions	
Prejudging and Overstimulation	
Partial Listening	
2. Speaking	185
Correct Pronunciation	
Clear Enunciation	
Feature: Eliminating Gobbledygook	
Use of Standard English	
Rules of Good Grammar	
Telephone Skills	
3. Reading	188
Improve Your Vocabulary	
Practice Reading	
Feature: What Would You Do?	
4. Writing	189
Notes and Business Forms	
Feature: What Would You Do?	
Memorandums	
Business Letters	
Chapter Review	194
Chapter in Brief	
Words to Know	
Questions to Answer	
Activities to Do	
Topics to Discuss	

CHAPTER OBJECTIVES

A student should be able to:
- State guidelines for good listening.
- Discuss rules for effective speaking.
- Identify ways to improve reading skills.
- Explain why writing is the most important form of business communication.
- Illustrate different forms of business communication.

STUDENT ACTIVITY WORKBOOK

Activity Objectives. The following activities provide additional opportunities for students to apply chapter objectives.

Activity 15.1 Communication Skills: For students to name terms and concepts associated with communication.
Activity 15.2 Effective Listening: For students to provide examples of different barriers to effective listening.
Activity 15.3 Spelling and Grammar: For students to identify and correct various spelling and grammar errors.
Activity 15.4. Writing a Memo: For students to practice writing a hypothetical memo.
Answer Key. Answers to activities in the student workbook are provided below.
Activity 15.1.

1. vocabulary	6. pronunciation	11. enunciation
2. overstimulation	7. communication	12. writing
3. speaking	8. noise	13. reading
4. prejudging	9. grammar	14. English
5. distractions	10. listening	15. language

Activity 15.2. Examples for each type of barrier should illustrate the following characteristics.
Distraction: A telephone call, loud noise, flickering light, change in temperature, strange smell, and the like.
Prejudging: Trying to outguess the speaker or assume that you know what the speaker is going to say.
Overstimulation: Becoming overeager to ask a question or make a comment.
Partial listening: Listening only for certain things (fragmented listening) or not caring about what is being said (pretend listening).
Answers to the last item will vary according to the incident that each student provides.
Activity 15.3. Misspelled words are as follows.

accesible (accessible)
apparant (apparent)
changable (changeable)
committ (commit)
desparete (desperate)
excillent (excellent)
fourty (forty)
greevance (grievance)
hoping (hopping)
imediately (immediately)
medacine (medicine)
ninty (ninety)
originel (original)
refering (referring)
usefull (useful)

Grammatical errors are as follows.

1. ... it ain't here.   (isn't)
2. I ain't had ...   (haven't)
3. It don't seem ...   (doesn't)
4. ... he don't work ...   (doesn't)
5. I done that ...   (did)
6. ... already did it ...   (done)
7. I seen them ...   (saw)
8. ... I have saw ...   (seen)
9. ... have nothing ...   (anything)
10. ... couldn't scarcely ... (hardly)
11. ... robots are ...   (is)
12. ... calculator is ...   (are)

Activity 15.4. Students should review guidelines for writing a memo in the chapter before starting the activity. You may wish to have students write a draft on another sheet of paper before copying a final version in the workbook. The memo could be written as follows.

MEMORANDUM
TO: Terry Foster, Accounting Department
FROM: Jill Yount, Shipping Department
DATE: April 21, 19__
SUBJECT: "Invoice Error"

I had just finished packing the order for Bradley and Company when I noticed a possible error on the invoice. The invoice lists the unit price for our Model D-47 bearings as "$3.67" each. I believe the price should be $2.67. You may wish to check the amount. I will hold the order until I hear from you.

REFERENCE AND RESOURCE MATERIALS

The Bottom Line: Basic Skills in the Workplace. Washington, DC: U.S. Government Printing Office, 1988.

Carnevale, Anthony, Gainer, Leila and Meltzer, Ann. *Workplace Basics: The Skills Employers Want.* Washington, DC: U.S. Government Printing Office, 1988.

Skagen, Anne (Ed.). *Workplace Literacy.* New York: NY: American Management Association. 1986.

RELATED INSTRUCTIONAL MATERIALS

1. Refer to the Teacher's Resource Package for additional activities related to Chapter 15 objectives.
2. Refer to the Teacher's Resource Package for test items and answers related to Chapter 15.
3. Refer to the Microtest, the computerized test bank, for items related to Chapter 15 content and objectives.
4. Refer to Transparency 11 for the transparency related to Chapter 15.

CHAPTER SIXTEEN
MATH AND MEASUREMENT SKILLS

OVERVIEW

The purpose of this chapter is for students to review math and measurement skills and learn why such skills are important on the job.

TEXTBOOK CHAPTER OUTLINE	TEXTBOOK PAGE
1. Basic Math	196
Feature: What Would You Do?	
Total Purchase Amount	
Trade Discount	
Cash Discount	
Markup	
Sales Tax	
Markdown	
2. Basic Measurement	200
Feature: Calculator Review	
Surface Measurement	

TEXTBOOK CHAPTER OUTLINE   TEXTBOOK PAGE
    Volume Measurement
    Feature: What Would You Do?
3. Systems of Measure   205
Chapter Review   208
    Chapter in Brief
    Words to Know
    Questions to Answer
    Activities to Do
    Topics to Discuss

CHAPTER OBJECTIVES

A student should be able to:
- Identify occupations requiring math and measurement skills.
- Apply math skills to computation of: total purchase amount, trade discount, cash discount, markup, sales tax, and markdown.
- Calculate surface measures and volume measures.
- Convert measures from one unit to another.

STUDENT ACTIVITY WORKBOOK

Activity Objectives. The following activities provide additional opportunities for students to apply chapter objectives.

Activity 16.1 Math and Measurement Terminology: For students to name terms and concepts associated with math and measurement.

Activity 16.2 Basic Math: For students to compute the answer to various business math problems.

Activity 16.3 Basic Measurement: For students to compute the answer to various measurement problems.

Answer Key. Answers to activities in the student workbook are provided below.

Activity 16.1.

1.	invoice	8.	markdown	15.	volume
2.	trade discount	9.	measurement	16.	cubic
3.	terms	10.	perimeter	17.	3.14
4.	cash	11.	radius	18.	English
5.	cost	12.	circumference	19.	metric
6.	markup	13.	area	20.	conversion
7.	sales	14.	length X width		

Activity 16.2.

1.	$17.90	8.	$36.00, 60%	15.	$1.88, $95.88
2.	$111.61	9.	$50.00, 25%	16.	$15.00, $45.00
3.	$1,414.67	10.	$15.00, $65.00	17.	$82.50, $82.50
4.	$43.75, $131.25	11.	$28.75, $143.75	18.	$26.85, $62.65
5.	$588.00, $882.00	12.	$2.40, $50.40	19.	$129.60, $194.40
6.	$270.60, $549.40	13.	$5.40, $140.40		
7.	$15.80, $63.20	14.	$9.10, $269.10		

Activity 16.3.
1. 22.5 feet
2. 35 feet
3. 6' X 18'
4. 10.205 feet
5. 2 feet
6. 267 square feet
7. 14 feet
8. $334.60
9. 615.44 square inches
10. 5 feet
11. 48,384 cubic inches
12. 2,090.3 bushels
13. 32 cubic yards
14. 91.4 meters
15. approximately 11 inches
16. 91.44 centimeters
17. 59.02 kilograms
18. 44,400 pounds
19. 48.96 cubic meters
20. 10.04 liters

REFERENCE AND RESOURCE MATERIALS

References cited for the previous chapter on workplace literacy deal also with math and measurement skills.

Dillon, William M. *Business Mathematics*, 2E, Albany, N.Y.: Delmar Publishers Inc., 1989.

RELATED INSTRUCTIONAL MATERIALS

1. Refer to the Teacher's Resource Package for additional activities related to Chapter 16 objectives.
2. Refer to the Teacher's Resource Package for test items and answers related to Chapter 16.
3. Refer to the Microtest, the computerized test bank, for items related to Chapter 16 content and objectives.
4. Refer to Transparencies 12–41 for the transparencies related to Chapter 16.

CHAPTER SEVENTEEN
SAFETY SKILLS

OVERVIEW

The purpose of this chapter is for students to become aware of the nature of accidents and to learn safety rules in the home, at school, on the job, in recreation, and on the road.

TEXTBOOK CHAPTER OUTLINE	TEXTBOOK PAGE
1. Accidents	212
2. Personal Safety	212
In the Home	
At School	
On the Job	
Feature: What Would You Do?	
In Recreation	
Feature: Safety Belt Laws Start to Click	
On the Road	
Feature: What Would You Do?	
Emergency Situations	

TEXTBOOK CHAPTER OUTLINE	TEXTBOOK PAGE
3. Public Safety	218
Government Agencies	
Private Organizations	
The Three E's of Safety	
Chapter Review	220
Chapter in Brief	
Words to Know	
Questions to Answer	
Activities to Do	
Topics to Discuss	

CHAPTER OBJECTIVES

A student should be able to:
- Describe the nature of accidents according to type and class.
- Discuss rules for personal safety in the home, at school, on the job, in recreation, and on the road.
- Explain what to do in a flood, tornado, hurricane, and earthquake.
- Name examples of government agencies and private organizations that promote public safety.
- State the three E's of safety.

STUDENT ACTIVITY WORKBOOK

Activity Objectives. The following activities provide opportunities for students to apply chapter objectives.

Activity 17.1 Safety Practices Self-rating: For students to judge themselves in relation to the extent to which they follow various safety practices.

Activity 17.2 Preventing Accidents: For students to identify common accidents for a given occupation and how they can be avoided.

Activity 17.3 Auto Safety Check Sheet: For students to conduct a safety inspection of an automobile.

Activity 17.4 Safety Organizations: For students to investigate and prepare a short, written report about a specific safety prevention organization.

Answer Key. Answers to activities in the student workbook are provided below.

Activity 17.1. Answers will vary according to individuals. Encourage students to change their behavior regarding items rated "seldom" and "never."

Activity 17.2. Answers will vary according to the occupation selected. You might have students who name the same occupation compare responses after they have finished. Or, you might wish to discuss as a class each person's occupation and responses.

Activity 17.3. Answers will vary according to the auto that is inspected. Students can be assigned to do this on their own, or you could take the class out to the school parking lot and do several inspections. Encourage students to correct or repair any problems identified during the inspection.

Activity 17.4. You might wish to assign an organization to each student rather than have them select one. Each report should include at least the following points: (a) when the organization was founded, (b) the purpose of the organization, (c) types of activities in which it engages, and (d) how it is supported.

REFERENCE AND RESOURCE MATERIALS

Accident Facts. Chicago, IL: National Safety Council. (Published annually.)

RELATED INSTRUCTIONAL MATERIALS

1. Refer to the Teacher's Resource Package for additional activities related to Chapter 17 objectives.
2. Refer to the Teacher's Resource Package for test items and answers related to Chapter 17.
3. Refer to the Microtest, the computerized test bank, for items related to Chapter 17 content and objectives.
4. Refer to Transparencies 42–44 for the transparencies related to Chapter 17.

CHAPTER EIGHTEEN
LEADERSHIP SKILLS

OVERVIEW

The purpose of this chapter is for students to recognize the nature of leadership, become aware of vocational student organizations, and to learn the principles of parliamentary procedure.

TEXTBOOK CHAPTER OUTLINE	TEXTBOOK PAGE
1. Organizational Leadership	223
Leaders are Good Communicators	
Leaders Develop Committed Followers	
Leaders Inspire High Accomplishments	
Leaders are Role Models	
Leaders Search Out Key Issues and Problems	
Leaders are Involved in External Relations	
Summary	
2. Vocational Student Organizations	225
Feature: Trade and Professional Associations	
Technology Student Association (TSA)	
Business Professionals of America (BPA)	
Distributive Education Clubs of America (DECA)	
Future Business Leaders of America -- Phi Beta Lambda Inc. (FBLA -- PBL)	
National FFA Organization	
Future Homemakers of America/Home Economics Related Occupations (FHA/HERO)	
Health Occupations Students of America (HOSA)	
Vocational Industrial Clubs of America (VICA)	
3. Parliamentary Procedure	228
Bylaws	
Officers and Committees	
Feature: What Would You Do?	
Holding a Meeting	
Feature: What Would You Do?	

TEXTBOOK CHAPTER OUTLINE — TEXTBOOK PAGE 233
Chapter Review
    Chapter in Brief
    Words to Know
    Questions to Answer
    Activities to Do
    Topics to Discuss

CHAPTER OBJECTIVES

A student should be able to:
- Define what is meant by leadership.
- Name and illustrate six types of leadership behaviors.
- Explain the purpose of a vocational student organization.
- Identify types of vocational student organizations.
- Demonstrate knowledge of parliamentary procedure.

STUDENT ACTIVITY WORKBOOK

Activity Objectives. The following activities provide additional opportunities for students to apply chapter objectives.

Activity 18.1 Leadership Characteristics: For students to recall characteristics associated with leadership.

Activity 18.2 Vocational Student Organizations: For students to describe the purposes, activities, and benefits of a specific vocational student organization.

Activity 18.3 Parliamentary Terms and Procedures: For students to identify terms, concepts, and procedures associated with parliamentary procedure.

Answer Key. Answers to activities in the student workbook are provided below.

Activity 18.1. 1-F, 2-T, 3-F, 4-F, 5-T, 6-F, 7-T, 8-F, 9-T, 10-T, 11-T, 12-F, 13-F, 14-T, 15-F, 16-T, 17-F, 18-F, 19-F, 20-T, 21-T, 22-F, 23-T, 24-T, 25-F.

Activity 18-2. Answers will vary according to the VSOs available in your school and in relation to the ones in which students are interested.

Activity 18-3. Matching, 1-E, 2-C, 3-J, 4-F, 5-A, 6-I, 7-D, 8-G, 9-B, 10-H. Ranking, 1-6, 2-3, 3-8, 4-1, 5-10, 6-2, 7-9, 8-4, 9-7, 10-5.

REFERENCE AND RESOURCE MATERIALS

Bennis, Warren and Nanus, Burt. *Leaders: The Strategies for Taking Charge.* New York, NY: Harper & Row, 1985.

Robert's Rules of Order. (Available from several different publishers.)

Zenger, John. "Leadership: Management's Better Half," *Training.* December 1985, 44-53.

RELATED INSTRUCTIONAL MATERIALS

1. Refer to the Teacher's Resource Package for additional activities related to Chapter 18 objectives.
2. Refer to the Teacher's Resource Package for test items and answers related to Chapter 18.
3. Refer to the Microtest, the computerized test bank, for items related to Chapter 18 content and objectives.
4. Refer to Transparency 45 for the transparency related to Chapter 18.

CHAPTER NINETEEN
COMPUTER SKILLS

OVERVIEW

The purpose of this chapter is for students to learn how a computer works and to show awareness of the role of computers in the workplace.

TEXTBOOK CHAPTER OUTLINE	TEXTBOOK PAGE
1. Keyboarding Skills	236
Feature: What Would You Do?	
2. How Computers Work	238
Input	
Memory	
Arithmetic and Logic	
Control	
Output	
3. Computers in the Workplace	241
Business and Industry	
Feature: What Would You Do?	
Government	
Communications	
Transportation	
Education	
Science and Engineering	
Medicine	
4. The Future of Computers	245
Feature: The Workerless Factory	
Chapter Review	248
Chapter in Brief	
Words to Know	
Questions to Answer	
Activities to Do	
Topics to Discuss	

CHAPTER OBJECTIVES

A student should be able to:
- Explain the importance of keyboarding skills.
- Name and describe the five sections of a computer.
- Summarize how a computer works.
- Show awareness of the role computers play in the workplace.
- Discuss the possible future impact of computers.

STUDENT ACTIVITY WORKBOOK

Activity Objectives. The following activities provide additional opportunities for students to apply chapter objectives.

Activity 19.1 Computer Literacy: For students to name terms and concepts associated with computer operation.

Activity 19.2 Occupations and Computers: For students to describe how computers are used in relation to a specific occupation of interest.

Activity 19.3 Robots: For students to investigate and prepare a short, written report on the subject of robots.

Answer Key. Answers to activities in the student workbook are provided below.

Activity 19.1. 1-H, 2-J, 3-E, 4-L, 5-B, 6-N, 7-A, 8-C, 9-O, 10-F, 11-D, 12-I, 13-G, 14-K, 15-M.

The input-processing-output sequence is as follows. The computer receives information in the form of electronic signals. Bringing the data from input and the instructions from memory, the computer processes the data. The data is then changed from electronic language to human language. The output is presented in print, sound, or other form.

Activity 19-2. Answers will vary depending on the occupation selected. You might wish to have students who select the same occupation work together on the activity.

Activity 19-3. This can be conducted as an individual or group activity. If done as a group activity, assign individuals or teams different sub-topics to investigate such as history, types, operation, and so on. Have the individuals or teams report in class on their findings.

Rather than have all students investigate robotics, you might wish to provide additional "high-tech" topics such as artificial intelligence, cybernetics, communication satellites, information sciences, and lasers. Perhaps you can add other topics.

REFERENCE AND RESOURCE MATERIALS

Computers in the Workplace: Selected Issues. Report No. 19, Washington, DC: National Commission for Employment Policy, March 1986.

"Robots Find Their Place." *Newsweek*. March 28, 1988, 58-59.

RELATED INSTRUCTIONAL MATERIALS

1. Refer to the Teacher's Resource Package for additional activities related to Chapter 19 objectives.
2. Refer to the Teacher's Resource Package for test items and answers related to Chapter 19.
3. Refer to the Microtest, the computerized test bank, for items related to Chapter 19 content and objectives.
4. Refer to Transparencies 46 and 47 for the transparencies related to Chapter 19.

CHAPTER TWENTY
ENTREPRENEURIAL SKILLS

OVERVIEW

The purpose of this chapter is for students to become aware of the nature of entrepreneurship and to learn what it is like to own and operate a small business.

TEXTBOOK CHAPTER OUTLINE	TEXTBOOK PAGE
Feature: The Growth of Small Business	
1. Nature of Small Business	252
Importance of Small Business	
Form of Organization	
Feature: What Would You Do?	
2. Advantages and Disadvantages of Self-employment	254

TEXTBOOK CHAPTER OUTLINE	TEXTBOOK PAGE
Self-employment Case Study	
3. Ingredients for Success	258
Personality	
Know-how	
Money	
4. Are You the Type?	260
5. Choosing a Business	260
Feature: What Would You Do?	
Chapter Review	263
Chapter in Brief	
Words to Know	
Questions to Answer	
Activities to Do	
Topics to Discuss	

CHAPTER OBJECTIVES

A student should be able to:
- Name contributions that small business makes to our society.
- Discuss advantages and disadvantages of self-employment.
- Outline what it is like to own and operate a small business.
- Identify ingredients necessary for a successful business.
- Evaluate own self-employment traits.
- Describe factors to consider in choosing a business.

STUDENT ACTIVITY WORKBOOK

Activity Objectives. The following activities provide additional opportunities for students to apply chapter objectives.

Activity 20.1 Advantages and Disadvantages of a Small Business: For students to identify and explain the advantages and disadvantages of being a small business owner.

Activity 20.2 Entrepreneur Rating Scale: For student to judge themselves in relation to traits considered important for success in business.

Activity 20.3 Interviewing an Entrepreneur: For students to interview a small business owner.

Answer Key. Answers to activities in the student workbook are provided below.

Activity 20.1. Among the advantages are:
1. Can make own decisions.
2. Can make decisions quickly.
3. Can pursue new ideas.
4. Have a flexible schedule.
5. Have control over the hours worked.
6. Do a variety of tasks.
7. Can work from beginning to end on a project.
8. Take pride in ownership.
9. Cannot be fired.
10. Be one's own boss.

Among the disadvantages are:
1. Takes a while to become established.
2. Income may vary.
3. Expenses continue regardless of income.

4. Personal accident or illness may jeopardize business.
5. Business effected by external factors such as the economy or competition.
6. Risk of losing money or going out of business.
7. Often long work hours.
8. Demanding responsibilities.
9. Have obligations to creditors, customers, and employees.
10. Must follow health/safety standards and other laws.

Activity 20.2. Answers will vary according to the individual. Encourage students to rate themselves honestly and accurately. Emphasize that not everyone is suited to being an entrepreneur.

Activity 20.3. Answers will vary according to the type of business chosen. Encourage students to select a type of business that holds an interest for them.

REFERENCE AND RESOURCE MATERIALS

A wide variety of free and inexpensive materials on small business may be obtained by writing to the Small Business Administration, 1441 L Street, N.W., Washington, DC 20416.

Bond, Robert. *The Source Book of Franchise Opportunities.* Homewood, IL: Dow Jones-Irwin. (Published annually.)

Franchise Opportunities Handbook. Washington, DC: U.S. Government Printing Office. (Published annually.)

Silver, David. *Entrepreneurial Megabucks.* New York, NY: John Wiley & Sons, 1986.

RELATED INSTRUCTIONAL MATERIALS

1. Refer to the Teacher's Resource Package for additional activities related to Chapter 20 objectives.
2. Refer to the Teacher's Resource Package for test items and answers related to Chapter 20.
3. Refer to the Microtest, the computerized test bank, for items related to Chapter 20 content and objectives.
4. Refer to Transparency 48 for the transparency related to Chapter 20.

CHAPTER TWENTY-ONE
OUR ECONOMIC WORLD

OVERVIEW

The purpose of this chapter is for students to learn basic concepts and principles of the American free enterprise system.

TEXTBOOK CHAPTER OUTLINE	TEXTBOOK PAGE
1. Principles of Economics	269
Factors of Production	
Consumption	
The Market	
Feature: What Would You Do?	
2. Economic Systems	272
3. The American Free Enterprise System	273
Private Ownership	

TEXTBOOK CHAPTER OUTLINE	TEXTBOOK PAGE
Profit Motive	
Competition	
Feature: Counterfeit Goods Undercut the Economy	
Freedom of Choice	
4. Economic Growth	275
Patterns of Economic Growth	
Feature: What Would You Do?	
Inflation	
5. Economic Freedom	278
Chapter Review	279
Chapter in Brief	
Words to Know	
Questions to Answer	
Activities to Do	
Topics to Discuss	

CHAPTER OBJECTIVES

A student should be able to:
- List the four factors of production.
- Explain the circular flow of economic activity.
- Illustrate how supply and demand influence market prices.
- Name and describe the two basic types of economic systems.
- Summarize characteristics of the American free enterprise system.
- Name the three things required for economic growth.
- Discuss types of economic freedom that you enjoy.

STUDENT ACTIVITY WORKBOOK

Activity Objectives. The following activities provide additional opportunities for students to apply chapter objectives.

Activity 21.1 Economics Terminology: For students to name terms and concepts associated with economics.

Activity 21.2 Circular Flow of Economic Activity: For students to explain and illustrate the circular flow of economic activity.

Activity 21.3 You and Inflation: For students to explain how the actions of various individuals contribute to inflation.

Answer Key. Answers to activities in the student workbook are provided below.

Activity 21.1.
1. economics
2. capital
3. production
4. consumption
5. supply
6. demand
7. market
8. competition
9. free enterprise
10. profit
11. monopoly
12. self-regulated
13. standard of living
14. GNP
15. prosperity
16. recession
17. depression
18. inflation
19. deficit
20. economic freedom

Activity 21.2. First part. One example would be the following. You agree to work for Wilson Manufacturing (producer), who in return pays you wages for your labor. This is one circular flow. With your wages, you (consumer) purchase goods and services. This is another circular flow.

Second part. There are four possibilities here. (a) If "consumer spending" is interrupted, producers cut back on production, lay off workers, and workers have less income. (b) If "goods & services" are interrupted, consumers have less to buy; income to producers drops causing them to curtail production and reduce salary and wages to workers. (c) If "labor & skills" are interrupted, workers have less income, they buy less as consumers which results in producers making less money. (d) If "salaries & wages" are interrupted, consumers buy less, producers reduce production and cut back on the number of employees.

Activity 21.3.
1. A union leader negotiates a ten percent annual raise for workers. The employer has to charge more for goods or services to cover the increased cost of production.
2. A merchant increases the price of a product by five percent. Consumers who want the product, must pay the additional cost.
3. A factory worker wastes time on the job, resulting in added labor costs to produce an auto. To cover overhead, the manufacturer has to charge more for the auto.
4. A consumer wants to buy a popular VCR that is already in short supply. Because of heavy demand for the product, the merchant may raise the cost of the VCR.
5. An elected official proposes a budget calling for greater spending than is available in revenue. To pay for the deficit, taxes must be raised.
6. A voter casts a ballot for a candidate who pledges to raise taxes and increase spending.

RELATED INSTRUCTIONAL MATERIALS

1. Refer to the Teacher's Resource Package for additional activities related to Chapter 21 objectives.
2. Refer to the Teacher's Resource Package for test items and answers related to Chapter 21.
3. Refer to the Microtest, the computerized test bank, for items related to Chapter 21 content and objectives.

CHAPTER TWENTY-TWO
THE CONSUMER IN THE MARKETPLACE

OVERVIEW

The purpose of this chapter is for students to recognize their roles and responsibilities as consumers and to learn how to chose, buy, and properly use goods and services.

TEXTBOOK CHAPTER OUTLINE	TEXTBOOK PAGE
1. You as a Consumer	283

2. What is Consuming?
    Making Choices
    Buying Wisely
    Feature: What Would You Do?
    Using Goods and Services Properly
	283

3. Advertising and the Consumer
    Feature: Buying a Used Car
    Advertising Techniques
    Sales Traps to Avoid
	285

TEXTBOOK CHAPTER OUTLINE   **TEXTBOOK PAGE**
      Feature: What Would You Do?
  4. Consumer Rights   292
  5. Consumer Responsibilities   293
      Assertiveness
      Honesty
  6. Consumer Complaints   293
      Before Complaining
      Making a Formal Complaint
Chapter Review   296
      Chapter in Brief
      Words to Know
      Questions to Answer
      Activities to Do
      Topics to Discuss

CHAPTER OBJECTIVES

A student should be able to:
- Give examples of goods and services that are consumed.
- Name and describe the three stages involved in consuming goods and services.
- Identify different advertising techniques.
- Discuss types of consumer rights.
- Describe responsibilities of consumers.
- Summarize steps to take in dealing with consumer problems.

STUDENT ACTIVITY WORKBOOK

Activity Objectives. The following activities provide additional opportunities for students to apply chapter objectives.

Activity 22.1 Comparison Shopping: For students to compare the costs of selected products at three different types of retail stores.

Activity 22.2 Advertising Techniques: For students to explain how a specific piece of advertising accomplishes the four steps involved in selling.

Activity 22.3 Sales Come-ons: For students to explain the message contained in various examples of advertising.

Activity 22.4 Used Car Prices: For students to obtain information about a used car from the *NADA Used Car Guide*.

Activity 22.5 Letter of Complaint: For students to practice writing a hypothetical letter of complaint about a consumer product.

Answer Key. Answers to activities in the student workbook are provided below.

Activity 22.1. Answers will vary according to the stores selected. This activity can be conducted by individual students, by small teams of students, or by the class as a whole. You might assign small teams to obtain the price for several products only at the three stores. Or, you might have teams obtain prices for all products at only one store. Many alternatives are possible. Price information can be pooled in class.

Activity 22.2. Answers will vary according to the piece of advertising selected. All ads don't necessarily accomplish each of the four steps. Indeed, some ads may focus primarily on one or two steps.

Activity 22.3.
    1. "Up to 50 percent off" generally means that only selected items are priced half-off.

2. "Lowest prices ever" doesn't provide you with any information about the actual prices of products.
3. "Sale on selected items" usually means that only a few of the items are on sale.
4. "While quantity lasts" suggests that only a few items are available to begin with.
5. "Sold elsewhere for . . . " doesn't mean anything because the advertiser is probably using the highest available price for reference.
6. "Ridiculous, giveaway prices" doesn't provide any information about the actual price. Merchants generally do not give products away.
7. "Item shown typical . . . " usually means that the actual product for sale is different from the one shown in the ad.
8. "Huge truckload sale" is intended to suggest that lower prices are available because of greater volume. But, the ad makes no mention of actual price.

Activity 22.4. Answers will vary according to the auto selected and the issue of the price guide that is used. Students can probably obtain the NADA guide at a public library. Or, perhaps you can obtain a number of outdated copies from an auto dealer, credit union, or public library. The primary objective is for students to know how to use the guide.

Activity 22.5. Have students review in the chapter those things to include in a complaint letter before beginning. You might have students write a draft letter on a separate sheet, before revising and copying it in their workbooks. The body of the letter could be written as follows.

"On May 14, 1988, I purchased a Soundblaster car radio (Serial No. 87492) made by your company from Hank's Stereo in Highland, Arizona. A copy of the sales receipt is attached.

The radio quit working on May 21, 1989. I took the radio back to Hank's, but he refused to fix it since the warranty had expired a week earlier.

I fully realize that the radio is out of warranty. However, I am sure you can understand my frustration regarding this matter. This is to request that you authorize the dealer to fix the radio under terms of the original warranty.

Your review and consideration will be appreciated."

REFERENCE AND RESOURCE MATERIALS

A number of free and low-cost consumer materials may be obtained from the Consumer Information Center, Pueblo, CO 81009. Write and request two free items: *Consumer Information Catalog* and *Consumer's Resource Handbook*.

RELATED INSTRUCTIONAL MATERIAL

1. Refer to the Teacher's Resource Package for additional activities related to Chapter 22 objectives.
2. Refer to the Teacher's Resource Package for test items and answers related to Chapter 22.
3. Refer to the Microtest, the computerized test bank, for items related to Chapter 22 content and objectives.

CHAPTER TWENTY-THREE
BANKING AND CREDIT

OVERVIEW

The purpose of this chapter is for students to learn about managing a checking account and the wise use of credit.

TEXTBOOK CHAPTER OUTLINE	TEXTBOOK PAGE
1. Financial Institutions and Services	299
Commercial Banks	
Mutual Savings Banks	
Savings and Loan Associations	
Credit Unions	
Changes in Financial Institutions	
2. Checking Accounts	301
Types of Checking Accounts	
Opening a Checking Account	
3. Managing a Checking Account	304
Writing a Check	
Feature: What Would You Do?	
Keeping a Check Register	
Endorsing a Check	
Making a Deposit	
Balancing a Statement	
Electronic Banking	
4. Credit and Its Use	310
Loan Credit	
Feature: Your Credit History	
Sales Credit	
The Cost of Credit	
Feature: What Would You Do?	
Chapter Review	314
Chapter in Brief	
Words to Know	
Questions to Answer	
Activities to Do	
Topics to Discuss	

CHAPTER OBJECTIVES

A student should be able to:
- Name and describe the four major types of financial institutions.
- Describe how to open a checking account.
- Illustrate how to write and endorse a check.
- Illustrate how to maintain a check register and reconcile a bank statement.
- Illustrate how to make a bank deposit.
- Discuss how electronic banking may change money management.
- Name and describe the two basic types of credit.
- Calculate the cost of credit.

STUDENT ACTIVITY WORKBOOK

Activity Objectives. The following activities provide additional opportunities for students to apply chapter objectives.

Activity 23.1 Managing a Checking Account: For students to write and endorse a check, complete a deposit ticket, and record information on a check register.

Activity 23.2 Balancing a Bank Statement: For students to balance an account statement.

Activity 23.3 Cost of Credit: For students to complete various questions and problems regarding the cost of credit.

Activity 23.4 Credit Application: For students to practice filling out a credit application.

Answer Key. Answers to activities in the student workbook are provided below.

Activity 23.1.

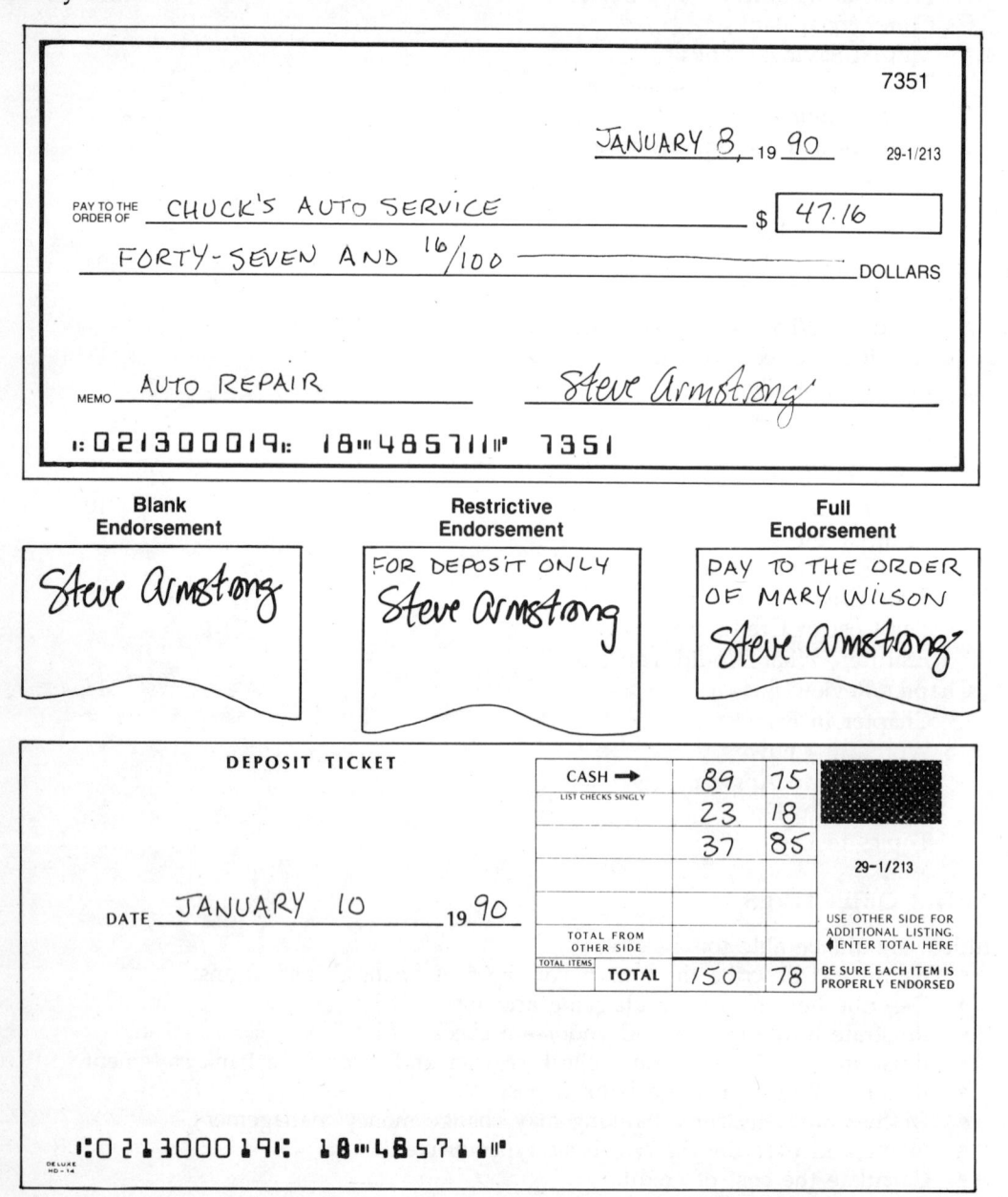

Check #7351

Date: January 8, 1990
Pay to the order of: Chuck's Auto Service — $47.16
Forty-seven and 16/100 Dollars
Memo: Auto Repair
Signed: Steve Armstrong

Blank Endorsement: Steve Armstrong

Restrictive Endorsement: For Deposit Only / Steve Armstrong

Full Endorsement: Pay to the Order of Mary Wilson / Steve Armstrong

---

Deposit Ticket

Date: January 10, 1990

Cash	89	75
	23	18
	37	85
Total	150	78

TG-44

RECORD ALL CHARGES OR CREDITS THAT AFFECT YOUR ACCOUNT

NUMBER	DATE	DESCRIPTION OF TRANSACTION	PAYMENT/DEBIT (-)	√T	FEE (IF ANY) (-)	DEPOSIT/CREDIT (+)	BALANCE $235 46
237	1/8	CHUCK'S AUTO SERVICE	$47 16		$	$	188 30
	1/10	DEPOSIT				150 78	339 08
238	1/15	RECORD MART	12 37				326 71
239	1/18	FOODLAND GROCERY	31 53				295 18

Activity 23.2.

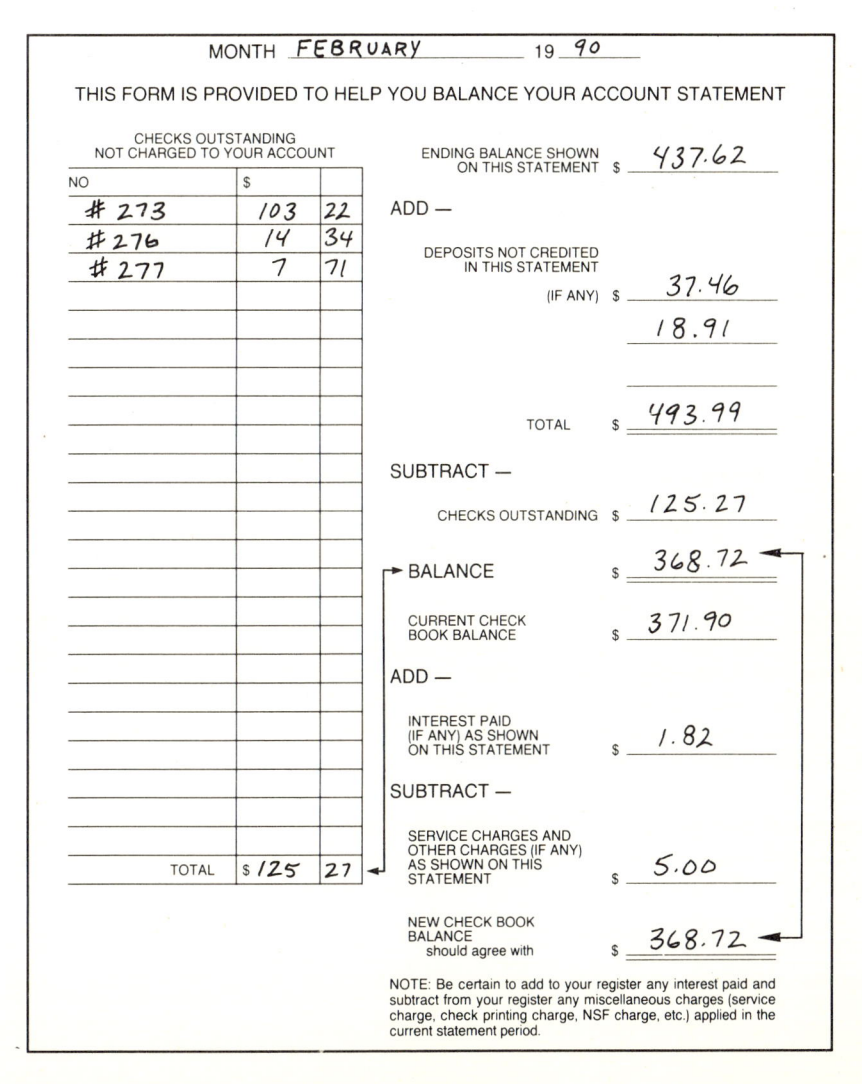

MONTH **FEBRUARY** 19 **90**

THIS FORM IS PROVIDED TO HELP YOU BALANCE YOUR ACCOUNT STATEMENT

CHECKS OUTSTANDING NOT CHARGED TO YOUR ACCOUNT

NO	$
#273	103 22
#276	14 34
#277	7 71

TOTAL $ **125 27**

ENDING BALANCE SHOWN ON THIS STATEMENT $ **437.62**

ADD —
DEPOSITS NOT CREDITED IN THIS STATEMENT
(IF ANY) $ **37.46**
$ **18.91**

TOTAL $ **493.99**

SUBTRACT —
CHECKS OUTSTANDING $ **125.27**

BALANCE $ **368.72**

CURRENT CHECK BOOK BALANCE $ **371.90**

ADD —
INTEREST PAID (IF ANY) AS SHOWN ON THIS STATEMENT $ **1.82**

SUBTRACT —
SERVICE CHARGES AND OTHER CHARGES (IF ANY) AS SHOWN ON THIS STATEMENT $ **5.00**

NEW CHECK BOOK BALANCE
 should agree with $ **368.72**

NOTE: Be certain to add to your register any interest paid and subtract from your register any miscellaneous charges (service charge, check printing charge, NSF charge, etc.) applied in the current statement period.

Activity 23.3.
1. finance charge
2. Interest, service charges, insurance premiums, other fees.
3. $413.00, $100/54
4. $1706.00, $142.17, $8.83
5. annual percentage rate (APR)
6. You are repaying a portion of the loan back each month, which means that you have use of less and less of the loan amount each month.
7. $129.00
8. $310.00
9. No. The total cost of the loan is $117.00 more ($67.00 after deducting the $50.00 gift certificate).
10. (a) Do I really need to purchase this item? (b) Can I afford to make the monthly payments? (c) Can I get cheaper credit elsewhere?

Activity 23.4. Students should provide information on the credit application form as requested.

REFERENCE AND RESOURCE MATERIALS

"Fixing your credit file." *U.S. News & World Report*, June 29, 1987, 49.

RELATED INSTRUCTIONAL MATERIAL

1. Refer to the Teacher's Resource Package for additional activities related to Chapter 23 objectives.
2. Refer to the Teacher's Resource Package for test items and answers related to Chapter 23.
3. Refer to the Microtest, the computerized test bank, for items related to Chapter 23 content and objectives.

CHAPTER TWENTY-FOUR
BUDGETING, SAVING and INVESTING MONEY

OVERVIEW

The purpose of this chapter is for students to learn about budgets, savings accounts, and different forms of investments.

TEXTBOOK CHAPTER OUTLINE	TEXTBOOK PAGE
1. Income and Spending Patterns	318
Feature: What Would You Do?	
2. Developing and Using a Budget	320
Establishing Goals	
Estimating Income and Expenditures	
Setting Up the Budget	
Regular Expenditures	
Variable Expenditures	
Feature: Credit Billing Blues	

TEXTBOOK CHAPTER OUTLINE	TEXTBOOK PAGE
Following and Revising the Budget	
Feature: What Would You Do?	
3. Saving Money	327
Where to Save	
Feature: What Would You Do?	
4. Types of Savings Accounts	329
Regular Savings Accounts	
Time Deposits	
5. Figuring Interest Rates	331
Annual Interest Rate	
Frequency of Interest Compounding	
Interest Pay Periods	
Annual Percentage Yield	
Other Information	
6. Investing Money	332
Feature: What Would You Do?	
Stocks	
Bonds	
Money Market Funds	
Chapter Review	335
Chapter in Brief	
Words to Know	
Questions to Answer	
Activities to Do	
Topics to Discuss	

CHAPTER OBJECTIVES

A student should be able to:
- Identify personal income and spending patterns.
- Name and describe the four steps involved in developing and using a budget.
- Discuss the importance of setting aside a portion of income for savings.
- Name and describe the two basic types of savings accounts.
- Compute interest rate returns on savings.
- Explain the following types of investments: stocks, bonds, and money market funds.

STUDENT ACTIVITY WORKBOOK

Activity Objectives. The following activities provide additional opportunities for students to apply chapter objectives.

Activity 24.1 Setting Financial Goals: For students to identify and evaluate their future financial goals.
Activity 24.2 Record of Income and Expenditures: For students to maintain a record of their income and expenditures.
Activity 24.3 Preparing a Budget: For students to develop a sample budget.
Activity 24.4 Selecting a Savings Account: For students to collect and evaluate information regarding savings account options.
Activity 24.5 Managing a Savings Account: For students to fill out savings account deposit and withdrawal tickets.
Activity 24.6 Return on Savings and Investments: For students to calculate the return on various forms of savings and investments.

Answer Key. Answers to activities in the student workbook are provided below.
Activity 24.1. Answers will vary. Encourage students to think seriously about their future plans and goals.
Activity 24.2. Answers will vary. Remind students to record information on the form daily. Discuss the last question in class after students have completed the activity.
Activity 24.3. This activity could be done by individuals, small teams, or the class as a whole. It might be a good idea to have small teams develop budgets and then compare and discuss them in class.
Activity 24.4. This activity could be conducted in several ways. You might have small teams obtain information at only one institution. Then, the information can be pooled and discussed in class.
Activity 24.5.

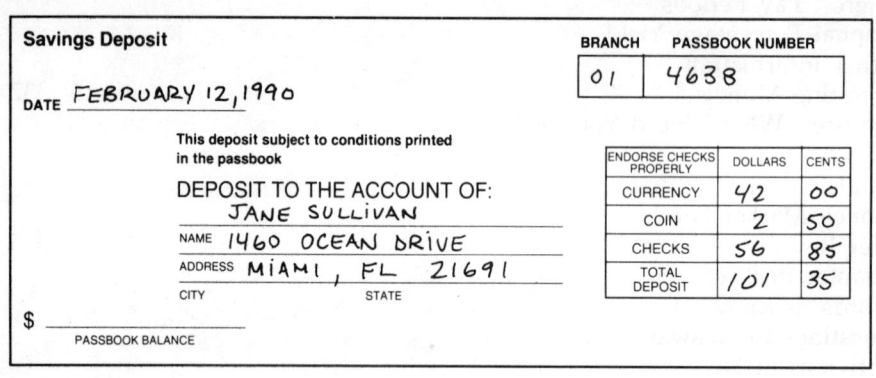

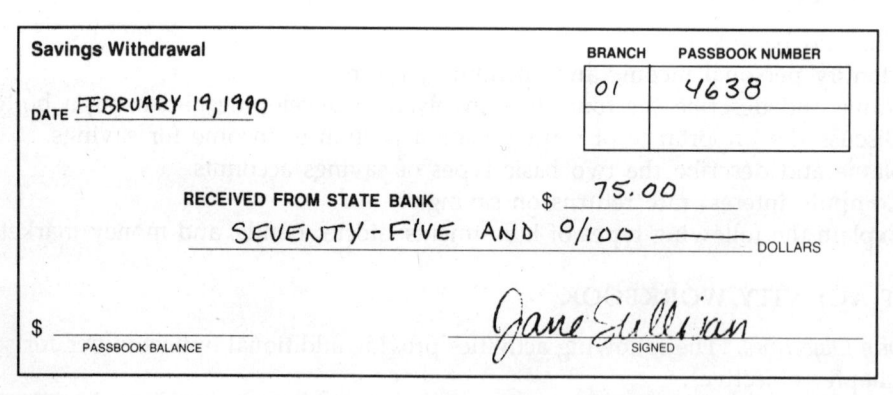

Savings Deposit

DATE FEBRUARY 12, 1990

BRANCH 01   PASSBOOK NUMBER 4638

This deposit subject to conditions printed in the passbook

DEPOSIT TO THE ACCOUNT OF: JANE SULLIVAN
NAME 1460 OCEAN DRIVE
ADDRESS MIAMI, FL 21691

ENDORSE CHECKS PROPERLY	DOLLARS	CENTS
CURRENCY	42	00
COIN	2	50
CHECKS	56	85
TOTAL DEPOSIT	101	35

$ _____ PASSBOOK BALANCE

A

Savings Withdrawal

DATE FEBRUARY 19, 1990

BRANCH 01   PASSBOOK NUMBER 4638

RECEIVED FROM STATE BANK $ 75.00
SEVENTY-FIVE AND 0/100 _____ DOLLARS

$ _____ PASSBOOK BALANCE

SIGNED Jane Sullivan

B

Activity 24.6.
1. $10.20
2. $2376.20
3. $30.68, 6.14%
4. $229.22, 7.64%
5. $1885.00
6. $192.00, 6%
7. $15.00 a share
8. $1,320.00, 13.2%
9. $17.50
10. 6.84%

REFERENCE AND RESOURCE MATERIALS

Write the New York Stock Exchange, 11 Wall Street, New York, NY 10005 for information about its educational materials on the stock market.

RELATED INSTRUCTIONAL MATERIALS

1. Refer to the Teacher's Resource Package for additional activities related to Chapter 24 objectives.
2. Refer to the Teacher's Resource Package for test items and answers related to Chapter 24.
3. Refer to the Microtest, the computerized test bank, for items related to Chapter 24 content and objectives.

CHAPTER TWENTY-FIVE
INSURING AGAINST LOSS

OVERVIEW

The purpose of this chapter is for students to learn the nature and characteristics of health, life, home, and auto insurance.

TEXTBOOK CHAPTER OUTLINE	TEXTBOOK PAGE
1. Nature of Insurance	339
2. Health Insurance	340
Feature: What Would You Do?	
Hospital Expense	
Surgical Expense	
Medical Expense	
Major Medical Expense	
Disability Coverage	
3. Life Insurance	342
Feature: Walk-in Medical Clinics	
Term Insurance	
Cash-value Insurance	
Which Type to Buy?	
How Much Insurance Will You Need?	
4. Home Insurance	346
Feature: What Would You Do?	
5. Auto Insurance	347
Types of Auto Insurance Coverage	
The Cost of Auto Insurance	
No-fault Insurance	
Chapter Review	350
Chapter in Brief	
Words to Know	
Questions to Answer	
Activities to Do	
Topics to Discuss	

CHAPTER OBJECTIVES

A student should be able to:
- Explain the basic idea of insurance.

- Name and describe the five types of health insurance.
- Summarize the advantages and disadvantages of term and cash-value life insurance.
- Outline different characteristics of home insurance.
- Name and describe the six types of auto insurance coverage.
- Identify factors that influence the cost of auto insurance.

STUDENT ACTIVITY WORKBOOK

Activity Objectives. The following activities provide additional opportunities for students to apply chapter objectives.

Activity 25.1 Insurance Protection: For students to name the term or concept associated with various types and characteristics of insurance.

Activity 25.2 Which Type of Insurance?: For students to identify the specific type of insurance coverage applicable in various situations.

Activity 25.3 Renter's Insurance: For students to identify the nature of and need for renter's insurance.

Activity 25.4 Automobile Insurance: For students to investigate and describe auto insurance laws in their states.

Answer Key. Answers to activities in the student workbook are provided below.

Activity 25.1.
1. risk
2. co-insurance
3. personal
4. deductible
5. group
6. disability
7. expenses
8. beneficiary
9. term
10. compare
11. perils
12. HMO
13. catastrophe
14. premium
15. policy
16. protection
17. liability
18. property
19. permanent

Activity 25.2.
1. surgical expense
2. hospital expense
3. major medical expense
4. disability coverage
5. medical expense
6. term insurance
7. cash-value insurance
8. credit life (term)
9. "life paid-up at 55" (cash-value)
10. homeowner's insurance
11. renter's insurance
12. uninsured motorist
13. comprehensive
14. bodily injury liability
15. property damage liability
16. no-fault
17. Estelle - medical payment, passenger - bodily injury liability
18. auto collison

Activity 25.3. Renter's insurance is intended for individuals living in apartments or other types of rental housing who want to have insurance protection on their furniture, clothing, and other personal property.
Answers to the remainder of this activity will vary.

Activity 25.4. Answers to the first four questions will vary according to state.
5A. No, Yes
5B. No, Yes
5C. Yes, Yes
5D. Yes, Yes
5E. Yes, No
5F. Yes, No
6. E and F

REFERENCE AND RESOURCE MATERIALS

"The Surge in Self-Insurance." *Newsweek*, March 7, 1988, 74-75.

RELATED INSTRUCTIONAL MATERIALS

1. Refer to the Teacher's Resource Package for additional activities related to Chapter 25 objectives.
2. Refer to the Teacher's Resource Package for test items and answers related to Chapter 25.
3. Refer to the Microtest, the computerized test bank, for items related to Chapter 25 content and objectives.

CHAPTER TWENTY-SIX
TAXES AND TAXATION

OVERVIEW

The purpose of this chapter is for students to learn about the types and purposes of taxes and how to complete an income tax form.

TEXTBOOK CHAPTER OUTLINE	TEXTBOOK PAGE
Feature: What Would You Do?	
1. Taxation	353
Purpose of Taxes	
Direct and Indirect Taxes	
2. Types of Taxes	354
Income Taxes	
Payroll	
Sales and Excise Taxes	
Estate, Inheritance, and Gift Taxes	
3. The Federal Income Tax	355
Who Must Pay?	
The Graduated Income Tax	
How the Tax is Determined	
4. Filing an Income Tax Return	358
Feature: Electronic Tax Filing	
Feature: What Would You Do?	
Chapter Review	362
Chapter in Brief	
Words to Know	
Questions to Answer	
Activities to Do	
Topics to Discuss	

CHAPTER OBJECTIVES

A student should be able to:
- Explain the purpose of taxes.
- Identify and explain the major types of taxes.
- Illustrate the difference between a graduated tax and a flat tax.
- Summarize the general process by which the amount of income tax is determined.
- Complete a Form 1040EZ.

STUDENT ACTIVITY WORKBOOK

Activity Objectives. The following activities provide additional opportunities for students to apply chapter objectives.

Activity 26.1 Tax Terminology: For students to name the term or concept associated with taxes and taxation.

Activity 26.2 Tax Rules: For students to explain the purpose served by various income tax rules.

Activity 26.3 Tax Rates: For students to illustrate differences between a graduated tax and a flat tax.

Activity 26.4 Filing a Tax Return: For students to complete a sample Form 1040EZ tax return.

Answer Key. Answers to activities in the student workbook are provided below.

Activity 26.1.

1. taxation	9. estate	16. adjustments
2. tax	10. inheritance	17. adjusted gross income
3. revenue	11. gift	18. deductions
4. direct	12. graduated	19. exemption
5. income	13. flat	20. taxable income
6. payroll	14. loopholes	21. credit
7. sales	15. exclusions	22. tax evasion
8. excise		

Activity 26.2.
1. To provide a tax break for parents or guardians, in recognition of the costs of child-rearing.
2. Essentially the same as item one.
3. Originally designed to encourage home ownership; provides a tax break for people who pay interest on a home mortgage.
4. To encourage people to contribute to charity; to provide a tax break for those who do so.
5. To encourage people not covered by a retirement plan at work to set up a plan of their own; to provide a tax break for those who do so.
6. To provide a tax break for parents or guardians who must pay child-care, in recognition of the costs involved.
7. A loophole is a legal tax provision that allows people who take advantage of the provision to pay less taxes than others.
8. Opinions vary. Even though they may be legal, many people feel that such loopholes are unfair.

Activity 26.3.
1. 0, 8.5%, $3,131.00, 5.63 times
2. $40.00, 2%, $400.00, 3 times
3. That people with higher incomes have a greater ability to pay more taxes.
4. That everyone should pay taxes at the same rate.
5. Opinions vary. A majority of people favor the graduated tax.

Activity 26.4.

Form 1040EZ
Department of the Treasury - Internal Revenue Service
Income Tax Return for Single filers with no dependents (L) **1988**

Please print your numbers like this:
0 1 2 3 4 5 6 7 8 9

Name & address
Use the IRS mailing label. If you don't have one, please print.

Print your name above (first, initial, last)
Present home address (number, street, and apt. no.) (If you have a P.O. box, see back.)
City, town, or post office, state, and ZIP code

Your social security number

Please read the instructions on the back of this form. Also, see page 13 of the booklet for a helpful checklist.

Presidential Election Campaign Fund
Do you want $1 to go to this fund?
Note: Checking "Yes" will not change your tax or reduce your refund.
Yes No

Dollars | Cents

Report your income

Attach Copy B of Form(s) W-2 here

1 Total wages, salaries, and tips. This should be shown in Box 10 of your W-2 form(s). (Attach your W-2 form(s).) **1**   12,648.00

2 Taxable interest income of $400 or less. If the total is more than $400, you cannot use Form 1040EZ. **2**   83.00

3 Add line 1 and line 2. This is your **adjusted gross income.** **3**   12,731.00

Note: You must check Yes or No.

4 Can your parents or someone else claim you on their return?
☐ **Yes.** Do worksheet on back; enter amount from line E here.
☒ **No.** Enter 3,000 as your standard deduction. **4**   3,000.00

5 Subtract line 4 from line 3. If line 4 is larger than line 3, enter 0. **5**   9,731.00

6 If you checked the "Yes" box on line 4, enter **0.**
If you checked the "No" box on line 4, enter **1,950.**
This is your **personal exemption.** **6**   1,950.00

7 Subtract line 6 from line 5. If line 6 is larger than line 5, enter 0. This is your **taxable income.** **7**   7,781.00

Figure your tax

8 Enter your Federal income tax withheld from Box 9 of your W-2 form(s). **8**   1,766.00

9 Use the **single** column in the tax table on pages 37–42 of the Form 1040A/1040EZ booklet to find the **tax** on the amount shown on **line 7** above. Enter the amount of tax. **9**

Refund or amount you owe

Attach tax payment here

10 If line 8 is larger than line 9, subtract line 9 from line 8. Enter the **amount of your refund.** **10**

11 If line 9 is larger than line 8, subtract line 8 from line 9. Enter the **amount you owe.** Attach check or money order for the full amount, payable to "Internal Revenue Service." **11**

Sign your return
I have read this return. Under penalties of perjury, I declare that to the best of my knowledge and belief, the return is true, correct, and complete.
Your signature   Date

For Privacy Act and Paperwork Reduction Act Notice, see page 3.

Form **1040EZ** (1988)

TG-53

REFERENCE AND RESOURCE MATERIALS

The Internal Revenue Service publishes two useful general tax guides: *Your Federal Income Tax* (Publication 17) and *Guide to Free Tax Services* (Publication 910). You can pick up these publications at a local IRS office or write to the Forms Distribution Center, P.O. Box 25866, Richmond, VA 23289.

RELATED INSTRUCTIONAL MATERIALS

1. Refer to the Teacher's Resource Package for additional activities related to Chapter 26 objectives.
2. Refer to the Teacher's Resource Package for test items and answers related to Chapter 26.
3. Refer to the Microtest, the computerized test bank, for items related to Chapter 26 content and objectives.

CHAPTER TWENTY-SEVEN
SOCIAL SECURITY

OVERVIEW

The purpose of this chapter is for students to learn about the nature of social security and individual retirement accounts.

TEXTBOOK CHAPTER OUTLINE	TEXTBOOK PAGE
1. Social Security	364
2. Major Social Insurance Programs	365
Retirement Payments	
Survivor's Payments	
Disability Payments	
Medicare	
Unemployment Benefits	
Workers' Compensation	
Feature: Job Stress and Workers' Compensation	
Feature: What Would You Do?	
3. Eligibility and Financing	370
Who is Eligible	
Financing the Program	
4. Individual Retirement Accounts	371
Tax Benefits	
Feature: What Would You Do?	
Opening an IRA	
Chapter Review	375
Chapter in Brief	
Words to Know	
Questions to Answer	
Activities to Do	
Topics to Discuss	

CHAPTER OBJECTIVES

A student should be able to:
- Identify the two forms of social security.
- Name and describe the six major federal and state social insurance programs.
- Explain how state workers' compensation is financed.
- Describe who is eligible for federal social security payments and how the program is financed.
- Explain the purpose of an Individual Retirement Account (IRA).
- Name two tax benefits of an IRA.

STUDENT ACTIVITY WORKBOOK

Activity Objectives. The following activities provide additional opportunities for students to apply chapter objectives.

Activity 27.1   Social Security Coverage: For students to recall facts and characteristics regarding social security.

Activity 27.2   Administration and Financing of Social Security: For students to answer various questions and problems regarding the two types of social security programs.

Activity 27.3   Individual Retirement Accounts: For students to calculate the tax savings resulting from an IRA.

Answer Key. Answers to activities in the student workbook are provided below.

Activity 27.1.   1-F, 2-T, 3-F, 4-T, 5-T, 6-T, 7-F, 8-T, 9-F, 10-F, 11-T, 12-F, 13-F, 14-T, 15-T, 16-T, 17-F, 18-T, 19-F, 20-F.

Activity 27.2.
1. Public assistance (welfare) is financed by general taxes. Social insurance is financed by taxes paid by workers and employers.
2. The first four types of social insurance are administered by the federal government. The last two are administered by state governments.
3. Because if workers become ill, injured, or lose their jobs, these two programs provide some measure of income and support.

To complete questions 4 and 5, obtain current information from any social security office.

Activity 27.3.   Answers will vary according to which year's income tax table is used. Duplicate the relevant section of the tax table for students to use. Show students how to complete a sample problem on the board before they begin.

The exercise shows that the higher the taxable income, the greater the tax savings and the lower the "actual" cost of having an IRA.

Our economy and society benefits because IRA deposits are used to purchase stocks, bonds, CDs, and other investments and provide funds for individual and business loans.

REFERENCE AND RESOURCE MATERIALS

A variety of free information about social security is available from any Social Security Administration office.

"A Cure for Job Stress: Employees are Rushing to Workers 'Comp' for Emotional 'Injuries'." *Newsweek*, June 2, 1986, 46-47.

RELATED INSTRUCTIONAL MATERIALS

1. Refer to the Teacher's Resource Package for additional activities related to Chapter 27 objectives.

2. Refer to the Teacher's Resource Package for test items and answers related to Chapter 27.
3. Refer to the Microtest, the computerized test bank, for items related to Chapter 27 content and objectives.

CHAPTER TWENTY-EIGHT
THE LEGAL SYSTEM

OVERVIEW

The purpose of this chapter is for students to learn about the nature of law, how laws are enforced, and how to choose legal services.

CHAPTER OUTLINE	PAGE
1. The Nature of Law	380
Feature: Common Law	
Branches of the Law	
Law Enforcement	
What to Do if Arrested	
Feature: What Would You Do?	
2. The Court System	384
Types of Courts	
How a Court Works	
Feature: What Would You Do?	
3. Legal Services	385
Deciding If You Need a Lawyer	
Choosing a Lawyer	
Legal Fees	
Small Claims Courts	
Chapter Review	387
Chapter in Brief	
Words to Know	
Questions to Answer	
Activities to Do	
Topics to Discuss	

CHAPTER OBJECTIVES

A student should be able to:
- Explain the difference between civil and public law.
- Describe the general process by which laws are enforced.
- Summarize how a court works.
- Identify situations that may require legal advice.
- Explain how to go about choosing a lawyer.
- Name the three types of legal fees.

STUDENT ACTIVITY WORKBOOK

Activity Objectives. The following activities provide additional opportunities for students to apply chapter objectives.

Activity 28.1 The Nature of Law: For students to identify the term or concept associated with law and law enforcement.

Activity 28.2 Types of Courts: For students to identify and explain the types and roles of courts located in their regions.

Activity 28.3 Small Claims Court: For students to describe the nature and role of small claims court.

Answer Key. Answers to activities in the student workbook are provided below.

Activity 28.1.
1. decree
2. defendant
3. defense
4. plaintiff
5. judge
6. prosecution
7. indictment
8. arraignment
9. judgment
10. pardon
11. jury
12. witness
13. summons
14. bail
15. bailiff
16. law
17. warrant
18. probation

Activity 28.2. With the exception of Question 4. (answered below), answers will vary based on the geographic area in which you live.
4. A *citation* is an official summons to appear before a court. It is usually issued for violation of a minor ordinance or traffic law. Being *arrested* is when you are taken into custody by a law enforcement official.

Activity 28.3. Answers to Questions 1, 2, 4, and 5 will vary depending upon the nature of your local small claims court.
3. Examples of complaints for which a small claims suit might be filed include:
   a. You dropped your car off at a service station for an oil change. When you returned to pick it up, you discovered a rip in the driver's seat. The station owner denies any responsibility.
   b. You bought a new amplifier for your guitar. It quit working after a week. The music store owner refuses to repair it or refund your money.
   c. You paid a $50.00 deposit to a photographer for him to video-tape your high school graduation party. He never showed up for the event. He keeps making excuses about failing to return the deposit.

REFERENCE AND RESOURCE MATERIALS

The bar association in many states disseminates a variety of consumer information about the law and legal services. Contact the association for more information.

RELATED INSTRUCTIONAL MATERIALS

1. Refer to the Teacher's Resource Package for additional activities related to Chapter 28 objectives.
2. Refer to the Teacher's Resource Package for test items and answers related to Chapter 28.
3. Refer to the Microtest, the computerized test bank, for items related to Chapter 28 content and objectives.

CHAPTER TWENTY-NINE
WHERE TO LIVE

OVERVIEW

The purpose of this chapter is for students to recognize the factors involved in choosing housing and to learn about renting an apartment.

TEXTBOOK CHAPTER OUTLINE	TEXTBOOK PAGE
1. Choosing a Type of Housing	390
Housing Needs and Wants	
Housing Alternatives	
2. Rent or Buy?	392
Renting	
Buying	
3. Apartment Hunting	393
Feature: What Would You Do?	
Things to Consider	
How to Approach a Landlord	
Feature: Dealing With a Roommate	
4. The Rental Agreement	397
5. Landlord-Tenant Relationships	398
Rights and Responsibilities of Landlords	
Rights and Responsibilities of Tenants	
Feature: What Would You Do?	
Chapter Review	399
Chapter in Brief	
Words to Know	
Questions to Answer	
Activities to Do	
Topics to Discuss	

CHAPTER OBJECTIVES

A student should be able to:
- Identify types of housing alternatives.
- Discuss advantages and disadvantages of renting and buying.
- Name and describe factors to consider in apartment hunting.
- Summarize items included in an apartment lease.
- Explain rights and responsibilities of a tenant.

STUDENT ACTIVITY WORKBOOK

Activity Objectives. The following activities provide additional opportunities for students to apply chapter objectives.

Activity 29.1 Housing Needs and Wants: For students to consider their own housing needs and wants.

Activity 29.2 Lease Agreement: For students to explain the meaning of various statements often contained in an apartment lease.

Activity 29.3 Tenant Relationships: For students to explain how to deal with various tenant relationship problems and situations.

Answer Key. Answers to activities in the student workbook are provided below.

Activity 29.1. Answers will vary. The most common "extras" designed to attract young tenants are recreational facilities such as a swimming pool, tennis court, excercise/weight room, jacuzzi, and the like.

Activity 29.2.
1. The tenant has to take good care of the apartment and return it at the end of the lease in clean and satisfactory condition.
2. The tenant cannot paint, alter, or remodel the apartment without written permission.
3. The tenant must pay a security deposit in the amount specified at the time the lease is signed.
4. The landlord can enter the apartment to look around or to make repairs.
5. The tenant cannot rent the apartment to anyone else (sublet) or allow them to live there without approval of the landlord.
6. The landlord does not have to pay for any theft or accidental damage to the tenants' clothes, furniture, or other property.
7. If the tenant fails to follow what was agreed to in the lease, he/she may be asked to move.
8. Due to circumstances beyond control, the landlord can direct the tenant to move at any time (subject to a reasonable time period such as 30 days).

Activity 29.3. A sample answer for each situation follows. Several alternatives are possible. Discuss different points of view in class.
1. The landlord should be asked to deal with it, since it seems to be a recurring problem involving different individuals.
2. Politely say that you would like to be alone to relax.
3. People have a right to cook whatever they wish. Ask the landlord about improving the ventilation.
4. The next time he asks, indicate that you are out of the item yourself.
5. Unless it becomes a nuisance, it is probably better to ignore the barking and let the landlord enforce the rules.
6. Perhaps you should be more assertive; introduce yourself to others, initiate conversations, or invite a neighbor over for a drink or dessert.
7. The dilemma is whether the person is actually watching the apartment. Discuss the matter with the landlord.
8. Many things can happen to an unsupervised child. Politely tell the neighbor that you don't want to be responsible.

RELATED INSTRUCTIONAL MATERIALS

1. Refer to the Teacher's Resource Package for additional activities related to Chapter 29 objectives.
2. Refer to the Teacher's Resource Package for test items and answers related to Chapter 29.
3. Refer to the Microtest, the computerized test bank, for items related to Chapter 29 content and objectives.

CHAPTER THIRTY
HEALTHFUL LIVING

OVERVIEW

The purpose of this chapter is for students to recognize how good health is related to success and productivity at school and on the job.

TEXTBOOK CHAPTER OUTLINE	TEXTBOOK PAGE

1. Nurtrition and Diet
    Daily Food Guide
    Energy Requirements
    Controlling Weight
    Feature: What Would You Do?
	401

2. Stress and Its Control
    Coping With Stress
    Feature: What Would You Do?
	403

3. Physical Fitness
    Feature: Corporate Fitness Programs
    Types of Exercise
    Guidelines for Physical Fitness
	405

Chapter Review
    Chapter in Brief
    Words to Know
    Questions to Answer
    Activities to Do
    Topics to Discuss
	408

CHAPTER OBJECTIVES

A student should be able to:
- Describe how each of the four broad food groups contributes to a balanced diet.
- Identify own recommended weight and daily calorie needs.
- Name and illustrate the three major ways to reduce or eliminate stress.
- Discuss benefits of physical exercise.
- Name and describe the three types of exercise that should be included in a workout.

STUDENT ACTIVITY WORKBOOK

Activity Objectives. The following activities provide additional opportunities for students to apply chapter objectives.

Activity 30.1 Calorie Counting: For students to record and analyze their calorie intake for a day.
Activity 30.2 Calorie Expenditure: For students to complete questions and problems related to calorie consumption.
Activity 30.3 Healthstyle Self-rating: For students to judge their own health habits.
Activity 30.4 Learning to Relax: For students to practice a simple relaxation method for reducing stress.
Activity 30.5 Fitness Test: For students to evaluate their performance on five simple fitness tests.

Answer Key. Answers to activities in the student workbook are provided below.
Activity 30.1. A calorie chart will be needed for this activity. Answers will vary. Be sensitive to the feelings of students with weight problems and low-income students who may be less able to eat a balanced diet.
Activity 30.2.
    1. 270
    2. 410
    3. 165 more
    4. About 23 days. About 8 pounds.
    5. About 7 days. About 26 pounds.
    6. 3.5 days
    7. Reduce your calorie intake and increase your calorie consumption.
    8. 1,200. To insure that you still get the required vitamins and minerals.
Activity 30.3. Answers will vary. Discuss the last three questions in class.
Activity 30.4.
1. People react to stress differently. Common reactions to stress are fatigue, anxiety, and depression.
2. Meditation refers to a wide variety of relaxation techniques that consist primarily of quiet, concerted thought.
3. Meditation seems to produce bodily changes that are the reverse of what stress causes. Muscle tension is reduced and a variety of other changes occur in the heart, blood, and respiratory systems.
4. Encourage students to try this technique for several days. Have them describe any feelings that they notice.
5. Because stress lowers the quality of daily life and can eventually lead to serious illness.
Activity 30.5. This could be an optional activity for some students. The activity requires a fixed, horizontal bar about 7-8 foot high, padded mat, and a 12-inch high box. The best way to conduct it might be for teams of students to meet during after-school hours and record each other's times and performances.

REFERENCE AND RESOURCE MATERIALS

    Harris, George. "Does Your Company Help You Be . . . At Your Best On the Job?" *American Health.* June 1986, 48-53.
    "Stress on the Job." *Newsweek,* April 25, 1988, 40-45.

RELATED INSTRUCTIONAL MATERIALS

1. Refer to the Teacher's Resource Package for additional activities related to Chapter 30 objectives.
2. Refer to the Teacher's Resource Package for test items and answers related to Chapter 30.
3. Refer to the Microtest, the computerized test bank, for items related to Chapter 30 content and objectives.

CHAPTER THIRTY-ONE
RESPONSIBLE CITIZENSHIP

OVERVIEW

The purpose of this chapter is for students to review the nature and responsibilities of citizenship and how to be a more effective citizen and worker.

TEXTBOOK CHAPTER OUTLINE	TEXTBOOK PAGE
1. Responsibilities of Citizenship	411
Feature: What Would You Do?	
2. Voting and Self-government	412
Voting Qualifications and Procedures	
Casting a Ballot	
Feature: Citizen Lawmakers	
The Election of Candidates	
Voting Behavior	
3. Thinking Clearly	415
Rumor	
Opinion	
Prejudice	
Feature: What Would You Do?	
Allegation	
Bias	
Propaganda	
Chapter Review	417
Chapter in Brief	
Words to Know	
Questions to Answer	
Activities to Do	
Topics to Discuss	

CHAPTER OBJECTIVES

A student should be able to:
- Explain the four responsibilities of citizenship.
- Summarize the process of registering to vote and casting a ballot.
- Discuss the importance of voting in local, state, and national elections.
- Identify and describe those things that get in the way of clear thinking.

STUDENT ACTIVITY WORKBOOK

Activity Objectives. The following activities provide additional opportunities for students to apply chapter objectives.

Activity 31.1 The Nature of Citizenship: For students to name the term or concept associated with citizenship.

Activity 31.2 Elections and Voting: For students to complete questions regarding election and voting procedures and requirements.

Activity 31.3 Evaluating Propaganda: For students to critique a representative piece of propaganda.

Answer Key. Answers to activities in the student workbook are provided below.
Activity 31.1.

1. democracy	5. citizen	9. oath
2. birth	6. defense	10. political
3. Constitution	7. economic	11. participate
4. naturalization	8. personal	

Activity 31.2. Answers will vary according to the state and city in which you live.
Activity 31.3. Answers will vary according to the piece of propaganda selected. Students will probably need a day or so to identify a suitable example.

Be alert to propaganda yourself. Collect such material and file it away for future use during this activity. Try to obtain examples of both "positive" and "negative" propaganda.

RELATED INSTRUCTIONAL MATERIAL

1. Refer to the Teacher's Resource Package for additional activities related to Chapter 31 objectives.
2. Refer to the Teacher's Resource Package for test items and answers related to Chapter 31.
3. Refer to the Microtest, the computerized test bank, for items related to Chapter 31 content and objectives.

CHAPTER THIRTY-TWO
EDUCATION BEYOND HIGH SCHOOL

OVERVIEW

The purpose of this chapter is for students to recognize the importance of further education or training and learn about the types of education and training options.

TEXTBOOK CHAPTER OUTLINE	TEXTBOOK PAGE
Feature: What Would You Do?	
1. Education and Training	420
2. Types of Education and Training	421
On-the-Job Training	
Feature: Training and More Training	
Apprenticeship	
Vocational and Technical Schools	
Feature: What Would You Do?	
Community and Junior Colleges	
Colleges and Universities	
Military Training	
3. Educational Information	425
Sources of Information	
Financial Aid	

TEXTBOOK CHAPTER OUTLINE   TEXTBOOK PAGE
Chapter Review   428
   Chapter in Brief
   Words to Know
   Questions to Answer
   Activities to Do
   Topics to Discuss

CHAPTER OBJECTIVES

A student should be able to:
- Discuss why additional education or training beyond high school may be needed.
- Illustrate how the amount of required preparation varies among occupations.
- Name and describe the six common types of education and training.
- Explain how education or training requirements may vary for a given occupation.
- Know sources of information regarding education and training and financial aid.

STUDENT ACTIVITY WORKBOOK

Activity Objectives. The following activities provide additional opportunities for students to apply chapter objectives.

Activity 32.1 Evaluating Educational Alternatives: For students to obtain descriptive information regarding an education or training alternative of interest.

Activity 32.2 Seeking Educational Information: For students to practice writing a letter requesting information about education or training requirements and opportunities.

Activity 32.3 Apprenticeship Interview: For students to rate own self in relation to apprenticeship interview criteria.

Answer Key. Answers to activities in the student workbook are provided below.

Activity 32.1. Answers will vary. Perhaps the school guidance counselor or librarian can assist in assembling resources for students to use. Refer to Figure 32-12 in the text for sources of information.

Activity 32.2. Answers will vary. You might wish to have students write a draft copy on a seperate sheet of paper before copying it in the workbook. Encourage students to go ahead and type a final copy and mail it.

Activity 32.3. Answers will vary. Few students will probably actually enter an apprenticeship program. However, this is a relevant self-assessment for all students. The criteria are similiar to what employers look for in a job applicant.

REFERENCE AND RESOURCE MATERIALS

The *Occupational Outlook Handbook* contains an introductory section that includes "Sources of Education and Training Information" and "Sources of Financial Aid Information." Duplicate and disseminate this information to students.

RELATED INSTRUCTIONAL MATERIALS

1. Refer to the Teacher's Resource Package for additional activities related to Chapter 32 objectives.
2. Refer to the Teacher's Resource Package for test items and answers related to Chapter 32.
3. Refer to the Microtest, the computerized test bank, for items related to Chapter 32 content and objectives.